American Map® Corporation

S0-BMG-906

Road Atlas

United States • Canada • Mexico

Contents

Time Zone and Area Code Map
. . . . Facing Page
Mileage Chart 2-3
U.S. Interstate Highway Map 4-5
National Parks and Landmarks Map 6-7

Canada 8-9
Mexico 10-11
State Maps 12-89
City Maps 90-150
Index to Cities and Towns 151-176

State Maps

Alabama 13
Alaska 14
Arizona 16-17
Arkansas 15
California 18-21
Colorado 22-23
Connecticut 24-25
Delaware 43
Florida 26-27
Georgia 28-29
Hawaii 30
Idaho 31
Illinois 32-33
Indiana 34-35
Iowa 36
Kansas 37
Kentucky 38-39
Louisiana 40
Maine 41
Maryland 42-43
Massachusetts 24-25
Michigan 44-45
Minnesota 46-47
Mississippi 50
Missouri 48-49
Montana 51

Nebraska 52-53
Nevada 54
New Hampshire 55
New Jersey 56-57
New Mexico 62
New York 58-61
North Carolina 64-65
North Dakota 63
Ohio 66-67
Oklahoma 68-69
Oregon 70-71
Pennsylvania 72-73
Rhode Island 24-25
South Carolina 64-65
South Dakota 74
Tennessee 38-39
Texas 75-79
Utah 80-81
Vermont 55
Virginia 82-83
Washington 84-85
West Virginia 82-83
Wisconsin 86-87
Wyoming 88-89

City Maps

Atlanta, GA 90
Baltimore, MD 91
Birmingham, AL 92
Boston, MA 93
Buffalo, NY 94
Charlotte, NC 95
Chicago, IL 96-99
Cincinnati, OH 100
Cleveland, OH 101
Columbus, OH 102
Denver, CO 103
Dallas, TX 104-105
Detroit, MI 106-107
Fort Lauderdale, FL 120
Fort Myers, FL 108
Fort Worth, TX 104-105
Houston, TX 109
Indianapolis, IN 110
Jacksonville, FL 111
Kansas City, MO 112
Las Vegas, NV 113
Los Angeles, CA 114-117
Louisville, KY 118
Memphis, TN 119
Miami, FL 120
Milwaukee, WI 121
Minneapolis, MN 122-123
Nashville, TN 124

New Orleans, LA 125
New York, NY 126-129
Norfolk, VA 130
Oakland, CA 144-145
Oklahoma City, OK 131
Omaha, NE 132
Orlando, FL 133
Philadelphia, PA 134
Phoenix, AZ 135
Pittsburgh, PA 136
Portland, OR 137
Raleigh, NC 138
Richmond, VA 139
Rochester, NY 138
Sacramento, CA 141
Saint Louis, MO 140
Saint Paul, MN 122-123
Saint Petersburg, FL 148
Salt Lake City, UT 141
San Antonio, TX 142
San Diego, CA 143
San Francisco, CA 144-145
San Jose, CA 146
Seattle, WA 147
Tampa, FL 148
Tucson, AZ 149
Washington, DC 150
West Palm Beach, FL 120

2 Mileage Chart

	Albany, NY	Albuquerque, NM	Amarillo, TX	Atlanta, GA	Austin, TX	Baltimore, MD	Billings, MT	Birmingham, AL	Boise, ID	Boston, MA	Brownsville, TX	Buffalo, NY	Charleston, SC	Charleston, WV	Charlotte, NC	Chicago, IL	Cincinnati, OH	Cleveland, OH	Columbia, SC	Columbus, OH	Dallas, TX
Albany, NY	0	2125	1825	1007	1882	332	2073	1112	2601	170	2007	292	932	639	795	795	729	496	823	657	1679
Albuquerque, NM	2125	0	300	1387	716	1881	1022	1260	970	2214	988	1801	1695	1583	1628	1346	1394	1606	1598	1468	673
Amarillo, TX	1825	300	0	1087	485	1581	1037	965	1235	1914	784	1501	1517	1304	1338	1046	1094	1306	1298	1168	363
Atlanta, GA	1007	1387	1087	0	884	669	1804	160	2252	1068	1175	912	300	495	251	695	438	692	211	543	805
Austin, TX	1882	716	485	884	0	1550	1449	793	1716	1930	331	1566	1247	1251	1237	1100	1127	1371	1095	1233	203
Baltimore, MD	332	1881	1581	669	1550	0	1875	804	2416	409	1825	352	567	339	430	697	510	355	513	405	1347
Billings, MT	2073	1022	1037	1804	1449	1875	0	1759	586	2232	1771	1857	2222	1762	2027	1214	1479	1662	2075	1654	1395
Birmingham, AL	1112	1260	965	160	793	804	1759	0	2101	1267	1065	941	460	539	411	669	468	722	359	584	637
Boise, ID	2601	970	1235	2252	1716	2416	586	2101	0	2794	1921	2271	2503	2246	2408	1777	1983	2058	2289	2069	1610
Boston, MA	170	2214	1914	1068	1930	409	2232	1267	2794	0	2255	454	989	728	828	965	875	632	928	738	1727
Brownsville, TX	2007	988	784	1175	331	1825	1909	1065	1921	2255	0	1865	1500	1479	1426	1430	1426	1670	1360	1533	526
Buffalo, NY	292	1801	1501	912	1566	352	1857	941	2271	454	1865	0	947	430	666	543	438	195	822	333	1363
Charleston, SC	932	1695	1517	300	1247	567	2222	460	2503	989	1500	947	0	479	203	912	628	750	113	670	1164
Charleston, WV	639	1583	1304	495	1251	339	1762	539	2246	728	1479	430	479	0	276	469	178	284	376	156	1134
Charlotte, NC	795	1628	1338	251	1237	430	2027	411	2408	828	1426	666	203	276	0	738	446	543	100	453	1054
Chicago, IL	795	1346	1046	695	1100	697	1214	669	1777	965	1430	543	912	469	738	0	291	348	794	340	932
Cincinnati, OH	729	1394	1094	438	1127	510	1479	468	1983	875	1426	438	628	178	446	291	0	249	502	105	924
Cleveland, OH	496	1606	1306	692	1371	355	1662	722	2058	632	1670	195	750	284	543	348	249	0	627	138	1168
Columbia, SC	823	1598	1298	211	1095	513	2075	359	2289	928	1360	822	113	376	100	794	502	627	0	513	1032
Columbus, OH	657	1469	1168	543	1233	405	1654	584	2069	738	1533	333	670	156	453	340	105	138	513	0	1030
Dallas, TX	1679	673	363	805	203	1347	1395	637	1610	1727	526	1363	1164	1134	1054	932	924	1168	1032	1030	0
Daytona Beach, FL	1209	1716	1467	446	1158	876	2173	505	2576	1257	1353	1069	351	726	469	1096	883	952	381	901	1123
Denver, CO	1853	446	454	1401	1009	1692	579	1370	870	1953	1251	1602	1743	1377	1548	1037	1199	1407	1616	1270	806
Des Moines, IA	1193	1013	806	924	897	997	959	838	1402	1305	1184	867	1185	761	1029	357	583	672	1126	657	714
Detroit, MI	690	1537	1289	726	1330	511	1579	721	2020	795	1694	366	874	371	607	284	260	171	745	195	1203
El Paso, TX	2327	267	508	1453	583	1997	1274	1304	1241	2376	806	2011	1729	1672	1710	1435	1372	1716	1668	1540	648
Fargo, ND	1463	1314	999	1364	1333	1339	625	1311	1245	1625	1601	1185	1557	1126	1414	649	940	997	1446	989	1131
Fort Lauderdale, FL	1435	1953	1670	681	1326	1036	2466	764	2820	1492	1542	1400	586	1004	721	1348	1086	1232	622	1126	1097
Fort Wayne, IN	705	1410	1109	612	1200	550	1405	610	1871	847	1455	381	740	284	602	159	184	219	671	150	1030
Fort Worth, TX	1682	632	344	837	192	1379	1406	702	1598	1761	518	1395	1116	1056	1061	945	956	1200	1057	1062	33
Grand Rapids, MI	710	1491	1191	749	1288	624	1396	739	1917	908	1585	419	959	457	791	178	357	284	858	311	1110
Greensboro, NC	661	1677	1377	348	1281	346	1958	493	2408	739	1480	641	271	227	89	729	458	486	188	381	1122
Hartford	106	2084	1822	969	1867	308	2169	1058	2652	105	2094	397	867	662	763	875	746	539	836	641	1664
Houston, TX	1825	870	608	816	162	1409	1639	676	1854	1878	357	1492	1027	1246	1053	1160	1053	1297	1066	1159	243
Indianapolis, IN	836	1289	989	543	1111	584	1400	497	1890	933	1427	512	743	328	551	186	105	317	625	179	908
Jackson, MS	1320	1087	787	397	519	1006	1743	251	2091	1395	991	1119	702	790	640	762	680	924	610	786	422
Jacksonville, FL	1111	1678	1378	329	1057	770	2227	472	2579	1167	1264	1068	248	676	413	999	786	908	290	850	1005
Kansas City, MO	1279	811	552	810	680	1078	1078	724	1476	1435	1008	1007	1135	777	940	543	591	803	1025	665	511
Knoxville, TN	836	1407	1107	204	1051	503	1723	255	2022	871	1320	671	368	284	219	537	246	489	267	351	820
Las Vegas, NV	2609	576	876	1947	1297	2408	1060	1822	662	2765	1573	2254	2247	2119	2173	1749	1921	2059	2162	1995	1249
Lincoln, NE	1386	837	596	1013	851	1192	836	953	1205	1500	1216	1057	1287	960	1151	527	802	867	1199	776	648
Little Rock, AK	1370	883	607	540	520	1037	1439	394	1781	1472	819	1046	814	707	743	675	608	851	759	713	317
Los Angeles, CA	2911	823	1095	2197	1410	2676	1254	2067	837	2993	1678	2587	2521	2394	2617	1989	2164	2392	2426	2254	1401
Louisville, KY	868	1332	1041	421	1022	608	1550	373	1908	976	1321	543	608	258	438	300	105	349	494	211	819
Memphis, TN	1232	1021	721	397	658	900	1557	239	1833	1379	957	908	689	653	604	551	469	713	612	575	455
Miami, FL	1439	1994	1694	665	1338	1095	2580	788	2860	1516	1580	1524	630	1046	745	1338	1086	1264	658	1210	1321
Milwaukee, WI	933	1443	1143	784	1203	794	1143	766	1777	1078	1530	640	1032	566	835	92	388	445	891	448	1013
Minneapolis, MN	1215	1256	1062	1105	1120	1105	812	1088	1488	1362	1456	948	1316	874	1143	405	696	753	1276	753	1013
Mobile, AL	1322	1265	965	340	656	990	1854	269	2343	1379	851	1184	607	825	575	908	745	989	555	834	592
Montgomery, AL	1178	1345	1042	164	804	833	1836	93	2346	1232	1041	1076	464	632	405	762	561	815	379	707	677
Nashville, TN	993	1232	932	243	869	688	1640	195	2059	1062	1168	722	576	458	399	474	283	527	458	389	666
New Orleans, LA	1453	1187	875	493	535	1136	1820	352	2191	1526	730	1273	727	891	721	925	820	1078	701	940	530
New York City, NY	146	1995	1695	855	1728	201	1926	1019	2571	203	2002	390	786	524	625	794	628	446	715	551	1525
Norfolk, VA	505	1905	1632	551	1403	237	2098	711	2551	660	1735	569	454	369	341	851	681	493	412	559	1359
Oakland, CA	2982	1134	1430	2488	1786	2864	1218	2321	671	3124	2034	2745	2788	2600	2755	2098	2317	2498	2703	2391	1803
Oklahoma City, OK	1523	559	267	863	414	1322	1168	701	1451	1659	680	1242	1176	1031	1069	804	835	1047	1091	909	211
Omaha, NE	1308	905	754	989	847	1143	904	904	1274	1443	1249	1005	1303	899	1135	464	721	824	1283	795	693
Orlando, FL	1249	1751	1451	446	1142	917	2277	545	2695	1297	2034	1306	401	814	559	1127	892	1046	440	997	1078
Philadelphia, PA	251	1922	1622	766	1630	97	2051	880	2488	327	1954	397	688	517	522	757	559	430	627	460	1427
Phoenix, AZ	2512	446	746	1810	1030	2311	1220	1700	1022	2644	1289	2269	2222	2045	2061	1776	1808	2045	2025	1907	1013
Pittsburgh, PA	471	1654	1354	712	1412	245	1681	778	2203	584	1713	219	778	211	504	470	291	128	572	186	1209
Portland, Or	2869	1378	1636	2763	2059	2765	867	2571	439	3149	2468	2677	2952	2615	2757	2140	2474	2416	2972	2478	2051
Providence, RI	178	2156	1856	1027	1898	356	2238	1189	2701	41	2222	454	956	699	785	924	790	600	888	713	1695
Raleigh, NC	656	1759	1459	397	1355	324	2273	557	2560	713	1506	721	300	297	162	802	540	559	215	453	1152
Reno, NV	2763	1056	1345	2411	1775	2562	1021	2363	404	2871	2068	2433	2765	2407	2570	1897	2221	2238	2626	2295	1731
Richmond, VA	482	1833	1533	527	1463	155	1655	699	2594	544	1646	552	462	251	280	788	356	583	390	498	1313
Rochester, NY	219	1857	1557	1015	1623	300	1922	965	2352	381	1891	81	871	495	689	608	502	268	789	397	1420
Saint Louis, MO	1028	1054	754	588	806	827	1381	539	1727	1184	1216	747	884	544	689	292	340	552	737	414	641
Saint Paul, MN	1215	1362	1062	1105	1120	1095	812	1118	1398	892	1565	948	1316	870	1143	405	696	753	1320	745	1013
Salt Lake City, UT	2290	621	1324	1900	1341	2051	579	1825	349	2417	1775	1922	2254	1896	2059	1386	1710	1727	2115	1711	1287
San Antonio, TX	1986	684	530	965	81	1646	1600	895	1709	2052	300	1638	1371	1419	1272	1208	1208	1443	1180	1305	284
San Diego, CA	2855	787	1078	2174	1313	2714	1309	2034	1010	2992	1574	2613	2505	2402	2423	2335	2193	2334	2389	2277	1369
San Francisco, CA	2966	1135	1396	2511	1776	2765	1239	2371	595	3133	2044	2403	2923	2616	2756	2108	2329	2408	2738	2461	1865
Seattle, WA	2855	1500	1805	2656	2157	2685	815	2475	524	2961	2521	2531	2960	2748	2765	2043	2334	2336	2971	2408	2203
Shreveport, LA	1599	868	568	624	340	1229	1691	474	1912	1618	644	1265	945	899	885	916	826	1070	833	592	196
Spokane, WA	2652	1346	1563	2367	1981	2417	541	2469	369	2693	2359	2263	2700	2503	2505	1775	2066	2068	2572	2115	1978
Tallahassee, FL	1249	1508	1208	268	899	932	2306	302	2512	1312	1094	1155	364	868	559	957	706	949	408	828	835
Tampa, FL	1281	1759	1459	476	1150	949	2143	553	2763	1329	1345	1346	479	903	584	1143	908	1091	497	1013	1086
Toledo, OH	633	1526	1220	641	1315	454	1557	673	2020	742	1622	309	973	284	533	243	203	114	683	138	1112
Tuscon, AZ	2442	486	656	1785	908	2246	1342	1621	1144	2571	1176	2166	2100	2039	1913	1711	1750	1971	2080	1833	964
Tulsa, OK	1409	674	336	803	462	1208	1293	636	2020	1532	835	1128	1103	941	989	673	721	933	1018	795	259
Washington, DC	378	1864	1564	630	1509	41	2006	781	2441	430	1787	429	559	299	334	697	478	341	498	418	1306
West Palm Beach, FL	1396	1938	1638	632	1329	1046	2736	702	2942	1426	1524	1443	568	982	673	1289	1063	1192	586	1146	1265
Youngstown, OH	462	1632	1346	719	1368	298	1632	738	2090	568	1695	190	709	251	502	413	275	74	561	170	1193

	Daytona Beach, FL	Denver, CO	Des Moines, IA	Detroit, MI	El Paso, TX	Fargo, ND	Fort Lauderdale, FL	Fort Wayne, IN	Fort Worth, TX	Grand Rapids, MI	Greensboro, NC	Hartford, CT	Houston, TX	Indianapolis, IN	Jackson, MS	Jacksonville, FL	Kansas City, MO	Knoxville, TN	Las Vegas, NV	Lincoln, NE	Little Rock, AK
Albany, NY	1209	1853	1193	690	2327	1463	1403	705	1682	710	661	106	1825	836	1320	1111	1279	836	2609	1336	1370
Albuquerque, NM	1716	446	1013	1537	267	1314	1953	1410	632	1491	1677	2084	870	1289	1087	1678	811	1407	576	837	883
Amarillo, TX	1467	454	806	1289	508	999	1670	1109	344	1191	1377	1822	608	989	787	1378	552	1107	876	596	607
Atlanta, GA	446	1401	924	726	1453	1364	681	612	837	749	348	969	816	543	397	329	810	204	1947	1013	540
Austin, TX	1158	1009	897	1330	583	1333	1326	1200	192	1288	1281	1867	162	1111	519	1057	680	1051	1297	851	520
Baltimore, MD	876	1692	997	511	1997	1339	1036	550	1379	624	346	308	1409	584	1006	770	1078	503	2408	1192	1037
Billings, MT	2173	579	959	1579	1284	625	2466	1405	1406	1396	1958	2169	1739	1400	1743	2227	1078	1723	1060	836	1439
Birmingham, AL	505	1370	838	721	1304	1311	764	610	702	739	493	1058	676	497	251	472	724	255	1822	953	394
Boise, ID	2576	870	1402	2020	1241	1245	2820	1871	1598	1917	2408	2652	1854	1890	2091	2579	1476	2022	662	1205	1781
Boston, MA	1257	1953	1305	795	2376	1623	1492	847	1761	908	739	105	1878	933	1395	1167	1435	871	2765	1500	1472
Brownsville, TX	1353	1251	1184	1694	806	1601	1542	1455	518	1585	1480	2094	357	1427	791	1264	1008	1320	1573	1216	819
Buffalo, NY	1069	1602	867	366	2011	1185	1400	381	1395	419	641	397	1492	512	1119	1068	1007	671	2254	1057	1046
Charleston, SC	351	1743	1185	874	1729	1557	586	740	1116	959	271	867	1027	743	702	248	1135	368	2247	1287	814
Charleston, WV	726	1377	761	371	1672	1126	1004	284	1056	457	227	662	1246	328	790	676	777	284	2119	960	707
Charlotte, NC	469	1548	1029	607	1710	1414	721	602	1061	791	89	763	1053	551	640	413	940	219	2173	1151	743
Chicago, IL	1096	1037	357	284	1435	649	1348	159	945	178	729	875	1160	186	762	999	543	537	1749	527	675
Cincinnati, OH	861	1199	583	260	1472	940	1086	184	956	357	458	746	1053	105	680	786	591	246	1921	715	608
Cleveland, OH	952	1407	672	171	1716	997	1232	211	1200	284	486	539	1297	317	924	908	803	489	2059	867	851
Columbia, SC	381	1616	1126	745	1668	1446	622	671	1057	858	188	836	1066	625	610	290	1025	267	2162	1199	759
Columbus, OH	901	1270	657	195	1540	989	1126	150	1062	311	381	641	1159	179	786	850	665	351	1995	776	713
Dallas, TX	1123	806	714	1203	648	1131	1097	1030	33	1110	1122	1664	243	908	422	1005	511	820	1249	648	317
Daytona Beach, FL	0	1823	1329	1103	1728	1714	227	1006	1126	1143	551	1138	952	880	688	97	1209	603	2316	1401	904
Denver, CO	1823	0	695	1321	705	915	2067	1186	773	1201	1621	1988	1060	1091	1246	1779	608	1341	743	507	992
Des Moines, IA	1329	695	0	600	1114	475	1581	516	747	502	1028	1283	930	478	846	1270	203	821	1399	203	562
Detroit, MI	1103	1321	600	0	1701	922	1346	170	1240	162	567	701	1304	293	923	1046	791	506	2011	819	850
El Paso, TX	1728	705	1114	1701	0	1460	1869	1573	609	1554	1783	2263	743	1460	1070	1626	915	1488	722	946	960
Fargo, ND	1714	915	475	922	1460	0	2007	808	1072	827	1412	1531	1334	835	1335	1704	609	1195	1535	451	1091
Fort Lauderdale, FL	227	2067	1581	1346	1869	2007	0	1271	1129	1342	786	1403	1191	1232	883	332	1459	860	2530	1670	1184
Fort Wayne, IN	1006	1186	516	170	1573	808	1271	0	1053	172	551	768	1176	122	784	929	648	430	1878	686	711
Fort Worth, TX	1126	773	747	1236	609	1072	1129	1053	0	1121	1154	1696	264	912	446	1037	513	853	1203	648	349
Grand Rapids, MI	1143	1201	502	162	1554	827	1342	172	1121	0	707	794	1196	263	957	1071	638	573	1889	699	799
Greensboro, NC	551	1621	1028	567	1783	1412	786	551	1154	707	0	650	1167	563	770	483	1013	283	2237	1202	778
Hartford	1138	1988	1283	701	2263	1531	1403	768	1696	794	650	0	1773	805	1306	1071	1297	841	2675	1378	1344
Houston, TX	952	1060	930	1304	743	1334	1191	1176	264	1196	1167	1773	0	1041	406	891	754	922	1468	892	446
Indianapolis, IN	980	1091	478	293	1460	835	1232	122	912	263	563	805	1041	0	681	867	486	351	1816	673	608
Jackson, MS	688	1246	846	923	1070	1335	883	784	446	957	770	1306	406	681	0	591	716	506	1650	874	251
Jacksonville, FL	97	1779	1270	1046	1626	1704	332	929	1037	1071	483	1071	891	867	591	0	1110	555	2238	1321	843
Kansas City, MO	1209	608	203	791	916	609	1459	648	513	638	1013	1297	754	486	716	1110	0	752	1345	211	409
Knoxville, TN	603	1341	821	506	1488	1195	860	430	872	573	283	841	922	351	506	555	752	0	1983	944	523
Las Vegas, NV	2316	743	1399	2011	722	1535	2530	1878	1203	1889	2237	2675	1468	1816	1650	2238	1345	1983	0	1224	1483
Lincoln, NE	1401	507	203	819	946	451	1670	686	648	699	1202	1378	892	673	874	1321	211	944	1224	0	616
Little Rock, AK	904	992	562	850	960	1091	1184	711	349	799	778	1344	446	608	251	843	409	523	1483	616	0
Los Angeles, CA	2407	1009	1654	2270	818	1844	2704	2137	1361	2148	2478	2829	1581	2075	1880	2402	1589	2201	275	1476	1678
Louisville, KY	801	1127	591	365	1467	949	1078	222	851	373	462	867	948	129	575	729	519	246	1861	730	502
Memphis, TN	749	1151	599	712	1103	1224	989	592	487	690	640	1209	584	470	211	697	470	385	1581	647	138
Miami, FL	259	2131	1582	1386	1958	1986	24	1326	1353	1356	810	1427	1207	1208	907	356	1475	859	2570	1673	1208
Milwaukee, WI	1180	1070	365	389	1528	576	1443	256	1059	275	826	948	1155	283	884	1067	568	643	1752	560	772
Minneapolis, MN	1458	956	251	698	1520	244	1723	564	1001	583	1135	1257	1266	591	1123	1376	459	932	1630	409	881
Mobile, AL	502	1372	954	988	1236	1413	705	839	624	1006	681	1290	478	749	178	413	819	449	1841	1039	430
Montgomery, AL	458	1412	1311	814	1325	1521	671	686	701	819	512	1133	709	590	255	379	867	348	2015	975	470
Nashville, TN	639	1167	712	536	1314	1136	900	385	698	534	429	973	795	302	422	592	590	174	1792	770	349
New Orleans, LA	632	1323	978	1077	1127	1494	843	916	519	1071	810	1436	367	857	193	551	857	607	1800	1114	430
New York City, NY	1054	1775	1070	620	2173	1450	1289	691	1557	706	561	101	1679	730	1192	957	1192	771	2520	1274	1235
Norfolk, VA	702	1800	1202	711	1998	1581	964	709	1382	802	227	471	1362	669	948	632	1179	412	2534	1354	1025
Oakland, CA	2831	1223	1742	2350	1194	1870	3041	2257	1723	2308	2809	2909	1957	2212	2270	2771	1799	2509	582	1604	1984
Oklahoma City, OK	1257	660	576	1030	708	989	1481	852	210	932	1118	1546	454	730	575	1181	373	847	1119	433	324
Omaha, NE	1402	559	146	726	1256	464	1604	634	634	640	1208	1321	949	616	914	1305	195	930	1249	57	690
Orlando, FL	81	1896	1363	1143	1735	1826	208	1059	1110	1188	648	1208	964	989	697	138	1266	665	2311	1452	965
Philadelphia, PA	914	1762	998	585	2075	1370	1127	562	1459	672	438	220	1581	624	1094	859	1134	646	2449	1260	1110
Phoenix, AZ	2101	802	1497	2019	438	1791	2244	1831	983	1906	2099	2523	1110	1719	1500	2100	1277	1845	284	1236	1379
Pittsburgh, PA	859	1475	770	304	1833	1112	1216	336	1241	397	438	486	1345	349	965	882	851	515	2181	965	899
Portland, Or	3018	1283	1816	2368	1661	1484	3204	2299	2003	2251	2823	2877	2369	2335	2518	3042	1809	2550	991	1641	2270
Providence, RI	1201	1961	1256	746	2335	1566	1459	799	1727	859	706	73	1849	892	1362	1127	1378	935	2683	1451	1395
Raleigh, NC	559	1694	1123	643	1800	1485	794	603	1184	754	73	624	1233	635	815	486	1086	356	2319	1263	851
Reno, NV	2758	1030	1606	2190	1183	1660	3008	2056	1608	2067	2591	2749	1932	2116	2143	2716	1606	2363	478	1411	1986
Richmond, VA	713	1904	1293	609	2023	1481	946	635	1333	722	191	455	2291	907	946	693	1205	440	2406	1249	963
Rochester, NY	1176	1637	932	424	2036	1249	1410	464	1452	499	600	324	1555	551	1183	1102	1062	710	2371	1135	1111
Saint Louis, MO	956	859	377	585	1238	872	1208	369	698	437	762	1030	835	251	495	859	251	497	1581	462	422
Saint Paul, MN	1458	956	251	698	1541	244	1753	564	987	583	1138	1257	1266	591	1160	1376	459	951	1630	408	881
Salt Lake City, UT	2283	519	1085	1679	892	1172	2578	1527	1184	1556	2059	2238	1460	1605	1742	2286	1095	1766	413	900	1462
San Antonio, TX	1175	975	1022	1500	576	1402	1378	1269	283	1353	1321	1965	203	1200	649	1086	795	1150	1273	916	592
San Diego, CA	2418	1054	1760	2419	721	1934	2621	2189	1332	2269	2457	2944	1484	2067	1783	2329	1627	2269	349	1573	1743
San Francisco, CA	2827	1233	1832	2360	1184	1886	3073	2304	1735	2318	2740	3019	1947	2224	2183	2781	1869	2549	592	1614	1994
Seattle, WA	3070	1371	1889	2299	1775	1440	3882	2202	2071	2221	2773	2918	2498	2229	2585	3090	1884	2553	1209	1636	2320
Shreveport, LA	903	1112	827	1069	844	1229	1144	909	228	1018	937	1519	271	827	223	814	624	729	1468	727	219
Spokane, WA	2811	1095	1556	2020	1686	1166	3014	1921	1978	1941	2503	2650	2222	1961	2205	2822	1727	2298	1119	1460	2092
Tallahassee, FL	259	1727	1216	957	1492	1598	462	871	867	1022	608	1223	721	818	421	170	1045	584	2068	1227	679
Tampa, FL	141	1858	1460	1200	1743	1849	268	1092	1118	1219	673	1240	972	1069	672	195	1296	730	2319	1477	958
Toledo, OH	1063	1272	567	65	1699	885	1289	105	1144	170	516	624	1249	243	876	989	717	449	1954	762	803
Tuscon, AZ	1999	835	1484	1938	316	1897	2271	1783	932	1856	2059	2433	1079	1668	1378	2010	1281	1755	389	1246	1257
Tulsa, OK	1156	714	471	916	788	972	1409	738	305	818	1037	1411	504	616	510	1167	283	782	1224	416	259
Washington, DC	802	1654	1054	506	1954	1322	1062	531	1338	608	309	341	1220	551	965	730	1046	554	2376	1184	832
West Palm Beach, FL	195	2157	1646	1305	1922	2028	41	1157	1297	1476	737	1339	1151	1176	851	284	1052	806	2498	1598	1101
Youngstown, OH	986	1421	737	239	1804	1038	1219	275	1225	340	482	470	1322	341	949	958	843	521	2124	923	876

	Los Angeles, CA	Louisville, KY	Memphis, TN	Miami, FL	Milwaukee, WI	Minneapolis, MN	Mobile, AL	Montgomery, AL	Nashville, TN	New Orleans, LA	New York City NY	Norfolk, VA	Oakland,CA	Oklahoma City, OK	Omaha, NE	Orlando, FL	Philadelphia, PA	Phoenix, AZ	Pittsburgh, PA	Portland, OR	Providence, RI	Raleigh, NC	Reno, NV	Richmond, VA	Rochester, NY	Saint Louis, MO	Saint Paul, MN	Salt Lake City, UT	San Antonio, TX	San Diego, CA	San Francisco, CA	Seattle, WA	Shreveport, LA	Spokane, WA	Tallahassee, FL	Tampa, FL	Toledo, OH	Tucson, AZ	Tulsa, OK	Washington, DC	West Palm Beach, FL	Youngstown, OH
Albany, NY	2911	868	1232	1439	933	1215	1322	1178	993	1453	146	505	2982	1523	1308	1249	251	2512	471	2869	178	656	2763	482	219	1028	1215	2290	1986	2855	2966	2855	1599	2652	1249	1281	633	2442	1409	378	1396	462
Albuquerque, NM	823	1332	1021	1994	1443	1256	1265	1345	1232	1187	1995	1905	1134	559	905	1751	1922	446	1654	1378	2156	1759	1056	1833	1857	1054	1362	621	684	787	1135	1500	868	1346	1508	1759	1526	486	674	1864	1938	1646
Amarillo, TX	1095	1041	721	1694	1143	1062	965	1045	932	875	1695	1632	1430	267	754	1451	1622	746	1354	1636	1856	1458	1345	1533	1557	754	1062	917	530	1078	1396	1805	568	1563	1208	1459	1220	656	336	1564	1638	1346
Atlanta, GA	2197	421	397	665	784	1105	340	164	243	493	855	551	2488	863	989	446	766	1810	712	2763	1027	397	2411	527	1015	588	1105	1900	965	2174	2511	2656	624	2367	268	476	641	1785	803	630	632	719
Austin, TX	1410	1022	658	1338	1203	1120	656	804	869	535	1728	1403	1786	414	847	1142	1630	1030	1412	2059	1898	1355	1775	1463	1623	806	1120	1341	81	1313	1776	2157	340	1981	899	1150	1315	908	462	1509	1329	1368
Baltimore, MD	2676	608	900	1095	794	1105	990	833	688	1136	201	237	2864	1322	1143	917	97	2311	245	2765	356	324	2562	155	300	827	1095	2051	1646	2714	2765	2686	1229	2417	932	949	454	2246	1208	41	1046	298
Billings, MT	1254	1550	1557	2580	1143	812	1854	1836	1640	1820	1926	2098	1218	1168	904	2277	2051	1220	1681	867	2238	2273	1021	1655	1922	1381	812	579	1600	1309	1239	815	1691	541	2306	2143	1557	1342	1293	2006	2736	1632
Birmingham, AL	2067	373	239	788	766	1088	269	93	195	352	1019	711	2321	701	904	545	880	1700	778	2571	1189	557	2363	699	965	539	1118	1825	895	2034	2371	2475	474	2469	302	553	673	1621	636	781	702	738
Boise, ID	837	1908	1833	2860	1777	1488	2143	2346	2059	2191	2571	2551	671	1451	1274	2695	2498	1022	2203	439	2701	2560	404	2594	2352	1727	1398	349	1709	1010	595	524	1912	369	2512	2763	2020	1144	1582	2441	2492	2090
Boston, MA	2993	976	1379	1516	1078	1362	1379	1232	1062	1525	203	560	3124	1659	1443	1297	327	2644	584	3149	41	713	2871	544	381	1184	892	2417	2052	2992	3133	2961	1618	2693	1312	1329	742	2571	1532	430	1426	568
Brownsville, TX	1678	1321	957	1580	1530	1456	851	1041	1168	730	2002	1735	2034	680	1249	2034	1954	1289	1713	2468	2222	1506	2068	1646	1891	1216	1565	1609	300	1574	2044	2521	644	2359	1094	1345	1622	1176	835	1787	1524	1695
Buffalo, NY	2587	543	908	1424	640	948	1184	1076	722	1273	390	569	2745	1242	1005	1306	397	2269	219	2677	454	721	2433	552	81	747	948	1922	1638	2613	2667	2531	1265	2263	1155	1346	309	2166	1128	429	1443	190
Charleston, SC	2521	608	689	630	1032	1316	607	464	576	727	787	454	2788	1176	1303	401	688	2222	778	2952	956	300	2765	462	871	884	1316	2254	1371	2505	2923	2960	945	2700	364	479	973	2100	1103	559	568	709
Charleston, WV	2394	258	653	1046	566	874	825	632	458	891	524	369	2600	1031	899	814	517	2045	211	2615	699	297	2407	251	495	544	870	1896	1419	2402	2616	2748	899	2503	868	903	284	2039	941	299	982	251
Charlotte, NC	2417	438	592	604	835	1143	575	415	399	721	625	341	2755	1069	1135	559	522	2061	504	2757	785	162	2570	280	689	689	1143	2059	1272	2423	2756	2765	885	2505	559	584	583	1913	989	334	673	502
Chicago, IL	1989	300	551	1338	92	405	908	762	474	925	794	851	2098	804	454	1127	757	1776	470	2140	924	802	1897	788	608	292	405	1386	1208	2306	2108	2043	916	1775	957	1143	243	1711	673	697	1289	413
Cincinnati, OH	2164	105	469	1086	388	696	712	561	283	810	628	601	2317	835	721	892	559	1808	291	2369	790	540	2201	503	502	340	696	1671	1208	2193	2329	2334	813	2066	706	908	203	1756	721	478	1051	275
Cleveland, OH	2392	349	713	1264	445	753	989	815	527	1078	446	493	2498	1047	824	1046	430	2045	128	2416	600	559	2238	583	268	552	753	1727	1443	2384	2408	2336	1070	2068	949	1091	114	1971	933	341	1192	74
Columbia, SC	2426	494	612	658	891	1276	555	379	458	701	715	412	2703	1091	1283	440	627	2025	572	2972	888	215	2626	390	789	737	1320	2115	1180	2389	2738	2971	833	2572	408	497	683	2080	1018	498	586	561
Columbus, OH	2254	211	575	1210	448	753	834	707	389	940	551	559	2391	909	795	997	460	1907	186	2478	713	453	2295	498	397	414	745	1711	1305	2277	2461	2408	592	2115	828	1513	138	1833	795	418	1146	170
Dallas, TX	1401	819	455	1321	1013	1013	592	677	666	530	1525	1359	1803	211	693	1078	1427	1013	1209	2059	1695	1152	1731	1313	1420	641	1013	1287	284	1369	1865	2203	196	1978	835	1086	1112	964	259	1306	1265	1193
Daytona Beach, FL	2407	801	749	259	1180	1458	502	458	639	632	1054	702	2831	1257	1402	81	914	2102	859	3018	1201	559	2758	713	1176	956	1458	2283	1175	2418	2827	3070	903	2811	259	141	1063	1999	1156	802	195	986
Denver, CO	1009	1127	1151	2131	1070	956	1372	1412	1167	1323	1775	1800	1223	660	559	1896	1762	802	1475	1283	1961	1694	1030	1904	1637	859	956	519	975	1054	1233	1371	1112	1095	1727	1858	1272	835	714	1654	2157	1421
Des Moines, IA	1654	591	599	1582	365	251	954	1131	712	978	1070	1202	1742	576	146	1363	1037	1479	770	1816	1256	1123	1606	1293	932	377	251	1085	1022	1760	1832	1889	827	1556	1216	1460	567	1484	471	1054	1646	737
Detroit, MI	2270	365	712	1386	389	698	988	814	536	1077	620	711	2350	1030	726	1143	585	2019	304	2368	746	643	2190	609	424	535	698	1679	1500	2419	2360	2299	1069	2020	957	1200	65	1938	916	506	1305	239
El Paso, TX	818	1467	1103	1958	1528	1520	1236	1325	1314	1127	2173	1998	1194	708	1256	1735	2073	438	1833	1661	2335	1800	1185	2023	2036	1238	1541	894	576	721	1184	1775	844	1686	1492	1743	1699	316	788	1954	1922	1804
Fargo, ND	1844	949	1224	1987	576	244	1413	1525	1138	1521	1450	1581	1870	989	464	1826	1370	1791	1112	1484	1566	1485	1660	1481	1249	872	244	1172	1402	1934	1886	1440	1229	1166	1598	1849	885	1897	972	1322	2028	1038
Fort Lauderdale, FL	2704	1078	989	24	1443	1723	705	671	900	843	1289	964	3041	1481	1604	208	1127	2244	1216	3204	1459	794	3008	946	1410	1208	1753	2578	1378	2621	3073	3382	1144	3014	462	268	1289	2271	1409	1062	41	1219
Fort Wayne, IN	2137	222	592	1326	256	564	839	686	385	916	691	709	2257	852	634	1059	604	1831	336	2299	799	603	2056	635	464	369	564	1527	1269	2189	2304	2202	909	1921	871	1092	105	1783	738	531	1157	275
Fort Worth, TX	1361	851	487	1353	1059	1001	624	701	698	519	1557	1382	1723	210	634	1110	1459	983	1241	2003	1727	1184	1608	1333	1452	698	987	1184	283	1332	1735	2071	228	1978	867	1118	1144	932	305	1338	1297	1225
Grand Rapids, MI	2148	373	690	1356	275	583	1006	819	534	1071	706	802	2308	932	640	1188	672	1906	397	2251	859	754	2067	722	499	437	583	1556	1353	2269	2318	2221	1018	1941	1022	1219	170	1856	818	608	1476	340
Greensboro, NC	2478	462	640	810	826	1135	681	512	429	810	561	227	2809	1118	1208	648	438	2099	438	2823	706	73	2591	191	600	762	1138	2059	1321	2457	2740	2773	937	2503	608	673	516	2059	1037	309	737	482
Hartford, CT	2829	867	1209	1427	948	1257	1290	1133	973	1436	101	471	2909	1546	1321	1208	220	2523	486	2877	73	624	2749	455	324	1030	1257	2238	1965	2944	3019	2918	1529	2656	1223	1240	624	2433	1411	341	1339	470
Houston, TX	1581	948	584	1207	1155	1266	478	709	795	367	1679	1362	1957	454	949	964	1581	1110	1345	2369	1849	1233	1932	2291	1555	835	1266	1460	203	1484	1947	2498	271	2222	721	972	1249	1079	504	1420	1151	1322
Indianapolis, IN	2075	129	470	1208	283	591	749	590	302	857	730	669	2212	730	616	989	624	1719	349	2335	892	635	2116	907	551	251	591	1605	1200	2067	2224	2229	827	1961	818	1069	243	668	616	551	1176	341
Jackson, MS	1880	575	211	907	884	1123	178	255	422	193	1192	948	2270	575	914	697	1094	1500	965	2518	1362	815	2143	946	1183	495	1160	1742	649	1783	2183	2585	223	2205	421	672	876	1378	510	965	851	949
Jacksonville, FL	2402	729	697	356	1067	1374	413	379	592	551	957	632	2771	1181	1305	138	859	2100	882	3030	1127	584	2716	693	1102	867	1374	2286	1086	2329	2781	3042	814	2822	170	195	989	2010	1167	730	284	958
Kansas City, MO	1589	519	470	1475	568	459	819	867	590	857	1192	1179	1799	373	195	1266	1134	1277	851	1809	1378	1086	1606	1205	1062	251	459	1095	795	1627	1869	1834	624	1727	1045	1296	717	1281	283	1052	144	843
Knoxville, TN	2201	246	385	859	643	932	449	348	174	607	753	412	2509	847	930	665	646	1845	515	2550	951	356	2363	440	710	497	935	1766	1150	2269	2549	2553	729	2298	584	730	449	1755	782	554	806	521
Las Vegas, NV	275	1861	1581	2570	1752	1630	1841	2015	1792	1800	2520	2534	582	1119	1249	2311	2449	284	2181	991	2683	2319	478	2406	2371	1581	1630	413	1273	349	592	1209	1468	1119	2068	2319	1954	389	1224	2376	2498	2124
Lincoln, NE	1476	730	647	1673	560	409	1039	975	770	1014	1274	1354	1604	433	57	1452	1260	1236	965	1641	1451	1263	1411	1249	1135	462	408	900	916	1573	1614	1636	727	1460	1227	1477	762	1246	416	1184	1598	923
Little Rock	1678	502	138	1208	772	881	430	470	349	430	1235	1025	1984	324	690	965	1110	1379	899	2270	1395	851	1986	963	1111	422	881	1462	592	1743	1994	2368	219	2092	679	958	803	1257	259	832	1101	876
Los Angeles, CA	0	2136	1816	2828	2238	1905	2013	2035	2027	1883	2790	2809	372	1354	1508	2585	2717	389	2449	989	2902	2554	511	2641	2400	1849	1905	672	1378	121	382	1159	1687	1406	2342	2578	2213	502	1459	2659	2772	2424
Louisville, KY	2136	0	364	1102	397	705	626	466	178	729	707	607	2333	738	671	907	664	1782	381	2298	421	525	2132	686	608	290	705	1638	1103	2119	2388	2320	721	2075	664	915	300	1697	633	533	1094	373
Memphis, TN	1816	364	0	1013	673	949	389	332	211	397	1095	876	2122	462	705	770	989	1444	795	2408	1257	712	2124	825	973	300	949	1613	730	1881	2132	2506	357	2230	527	778	665	1370	397	875	957	738
Miami, FL	2828	1102	1013	0	1435	1743	729	695	908	867	1313	988	3087	1524	1670	227	1215	2448	1248	3366	1483	818	3032	988	1435	1231	1743	2602	1402	2645	3097	3406	1130	3138	486	292	1293	2326	1483	1086	65	1264
Milwaukee, WI	2238	397	673	1435	0	332	981	859	571	1045	851	948	2171	884	503	1224	834	1873	567	2002	1021	899	1930	832	697	389	332	1419	1305	2109	2175	1970	1013	1702	1053	1240	332	1808	770	770	1386	510
Minneapolis, MN	1905	705	949	1743	332	0	1227	1281	892	1346	1160	1337	2065	803	381	1673	1126	1679	868	1670	1322	1241	1776	1237	1005	628	1	1475	1265	1975	2075	1638	985	1370	1354	1589	641	1702	705	1078	1737	794
Mobile, AL	2013	626	389	729	981	1227	0	176	462	146	1176	884	2351	786	1011	486	1078	1593	1050	2611	1346	738	2278	867	1273	673	1158	1903	697	1971	2361	2710	401	2342	243	494	940	1542	713	949	673	1005
Montgomery, AL	2035	466	332	695	859	1281	176	0	288	322	1010	715	2295	794	1037	452	930	1655	843	2632	1191	561	2456	792	1179	632	1281	1918	904	2127	2464	2838	478	2562	209	460	766	1633	765	794	639	831
Nashville, TN	2027	178	211	908	571	892	462	288	0	551	859	665	2374	673	735	689	761	1671	575	2376	1029	502	2189	614	770	323	892	1678	941	2092	2375	2384	669	2124	486	737	478	1581	608	632	875	543
New Orleans, LA	1883	729	397	867	1045	1346	146	322	551	0	1322	1054	2317	681	1021	624	1224	1540	1078	2505	1492	876	2278	1114	1362	681	1346	1842	551	1824	2327	2574	309	2409	381	632	1005	1419	657	1095	811	1095
New York, NY	2790	707	1095	1313	851	1160	1176	1010	859	1322	0	389	2876	1436	1208	1094	101	2425	381	2880	162	510	2635	366	320	941	1160	2124	1832	2773	2886	2837	1415	2569	1109	1126	556	2360	1331	252	1223	403
Norfolk, VA	2809	607	876	988	948	1337	884	715	665	1054	389	0	2957	1349	1362	770	268	2393	365	2968	527	197	2459	97	535	927	1337	2262	1606	2669	2967	2975	1203	2700	802	827	592	2271	1234	190	916	438
Oakland, CA	372	2333	2122	3087	2171	2065	2351	2295	2374	2317	2876	2957	0	1660	1596	2844	2913	744	2528	614	2974	2865	201	2988	2681	2003	2065	545	1734	493	9	777	2052	979	2601	2836	2293	878	1766	2772	3055	2463
Oklahoma City, OK	1354	738	462	1524	884	803	786	794	673	681	1436	1349	1660	0	495	1281	1363	998	1095	1946	1597	1200	1662	1287	1298	495	803	1151	478	1345	1670	2044	389	1768	1038	1289	961	908	105	1305	1468	1087
Omaha, NE	1508	671	705	1670	503	381	1110	1037	735	1021	1208	1362	1596	495	0	1421	1200	1427	908	1605	1394	1281	1395	1400	1078	446	381	947	949	1641	1605	1679	729	1403	1241	1492	705	1400	401	1151	1671	875
Orlando, FL	2585	907	770	227	1224	1673	486	452	689	624	1094	770	2844	1281	1421	0	1005	2205	1025	3123	1273	608	2789	776	1200	1030	1551	2359	1159	2402	2854	3163	920	2895	243	89	1086	2083	1240	876	194	1052
Philadelphia, PA	2717	664	989	1215	834	1126	1078	930	761	1224	101	268	2913	1363	1200	1005	0	2374	292	2830	259	412	2627	252	324	868	1126	2209	1734	2911	2923	2780	1270	2512	1020	1037	502	2287	1249	133	1134	357
Phoenix, AZ	389	1782	1444	2448	1873	1679	1593	1655	1671	1540	2425	2393	744	998	1427	2205	2374	0	2084	1322	2586	2172	754	2285	2281	1484	1808	673	989	357	754	1492	1282	1386	1962	2213	1950	122	1103	2367	2392	2061
Pittsburgh, PA	2449	381	795	1248	567	868	1050	843	575	1078	381	365	2528	1095	908	1025	292	2084	0	2538	559	519	2335	333	284	600	868	1824	1468	2441	2538	2513	1087	2190	932	998	227	2021	981	219	1111	65
Portland, OR	985	2298	2408	3366	2002	1670	2611	2632	2376	2505	2880	2968	614	1946	1605	3123	2830	1322	2538	0	3000	2903	616	3012	2676	2068	1670	764	2168	1078	624	170	2255	365	2880	3131	2311	1483	1987	2846	3310	2481
Providence, RI	2902	421	1257	1483	1021	1322	1346	1191	1029	1492	162	527	2974	1597	1394	1273	259	2586	559	3000	0	673	2814	511	381	1102	1322	2303	2002	2978	2984	2967	1585	2644	1288	1322	689	252	1483	397	1402	538
Raleigh, NC	2554	525	713	818	899	1241	738	561	502	876	510	197	2865	1200	1281	608	412	2172	519	2903	673	0	2716	175	600	835	1241	2205	1427	2529	2797	2911	538	2651	624	657	584	2124	1103	283	754	535
Reno, NV	511	2132	2124	3032	1930	1776	2278	2456	2189	2278	2635	2789	201	1662	1395	2789	2627	754	2335	616	2814	2716	0	2803	2489	1881	1776	511	1768	535	211	810	1927	770	2546	2797	2133	867	1702	2579	2976	2303
Richmond, VA	2641	686	825	988	832	1237	867	792	614	1114	366	97	2988	1287	1400	776	252	2285	333	3012	511	175	2803	0	455	976	1237	2324	1555	2643	2989	3029	1173	2761	794	827	630	2425	1222	114	924	662
Rochester, NY	2400	608	973	1435	697	1005	1273	1179	770	1362	320	535	2681	1298	1078	1200	324	2281	284	2676	381	600	2489	455	0	803	1005	1978	1686	2674	2691	2660	1361	2384	1208	1257	381	2222	1398	341	1346	265
Saint Louis, MO	1849	290	300	1231	389	628	673	632	323	681	941	927	2003	495	446	1030	868	1484	600	2068	1102	835	1881	976	803	0	628	1370	916	1840	2075	2076	624	1881	870	1030	466	1419	381	795	1241	592
Saint Paul, MN	1905	705	949	1743	332	1	1158	1281	892	1346	1160	1337	2065	803	381	1551	1126	1808	868	1670	1322	1241	1776	1237	1005	628	0	1475	1265	1975	2075	1638	985	1370	1354	1589	641	1702	705	1078	1737	794
Salt Lake City, UT	672	1638	1613	2602	1419	1475	1903	1918	1678	1842	2124	2262	545	1151	947	2359	2209	673	1824	764	2303	2205	511	2324	1978	1370	1475	0	1447	762	714	851	1563	706	2116	2318	1715	795	1223	2141	2490	1805
San Antonio, TX	1378	1103	730	1402	1305	1265	697	904	941	551	1832	1606	1734	478	949	1159	1734	989	1468	2168	2002	1427	1768	1555	1686	916	1265	1447	0	1274	1774	2255	474	2110	916	1151	1387	876	535	1605	1370	1477
San Diego, CA	121	2119	1881	2645	2109	1975	1971	2127	2092	1824	2773	2669	493	1345	1641	2402	2911	357	2441	1078	2978	2529	535	2643	2674	1840	1975	762	1274	0	527	1276	1565	1403	2213	2464	2604	405	1403	2733	2072	2456
San Francisco, CA	382	2388	2132	3097	2175	2075	2361	2464	2375	2327	2886	2967	9	1670	1606	2854	2923	754	2538	624	2984	2797	211	2989	2691	2075	2075	714	1774	527	0	787	2061	852	2611	2846	2415	868	1776	2949	3065	2569
Seattle, WA	1159	2343	2506	3406	1970	1638	2710	2838	2384	2574	2837	2975	777	2044	1679	3163	2780	1492	2513	170	2967	2911	810	3029	2660	2076	1638	851	2255	1276	787	0	2335	274	2920	3155	2231	1573	2034	2684	3388	2456
Shreveport, LA	1687	721	357	1130	1013	985	401	478	669	309	1415	1203	2052	389	729	920	1270	1282	1087	2255	1585	538	1927	1173	1361	624	985	1563	474	1565	2061	2335	0	2038	644	895	1099	1160	356	953	507	1081
Spokane, WA	1406	2075	2230	3138	1702	1370	2342	2562	2124	2409	2569	2700	979	1768	1403	2895	2512	1386	2190	365	2644	2651	770	2761	2384	1816	1370	706	2110	1403	852	274	2038	0	2652	2887	2100	1496	1727	2417	3196	2125
Tallahassee, FL	2342	664	527	486	1053	1354	243	209	486	381	1109	802	2601	1038	1241	243	1020	1962	932	2880	1288	624	2546	794	1208	795	1354	2116	916	2213	2611	2920	644	2652	0	251	900	1840	955	891	430	1005
Tampa, FL	2578	915	778	292	1240	1589	494	460	737	632	1126	827	2836	1289	1492	89	1037	2213	998	3131	1322	657	2797	827	1251	1030	1589	2318	1151	2464	2846	3155	895	2887	251	0	1143	2076	1182	908	219	1088
Toledo, OH	2213	300	665	1293	332	641	940	766	478	1005	556	592	2293	961	705	1086	502	1950	227	2311	689	584	2133	630	381	466	641	1715	1387	2604	2415	2231	1099	2100	900	1143	0	2051	867	438	1248	170
Tuscon, AZ	502	1697	1370	2326	1808	1702	1542	1633	1581	1419	2360	2271	878	908	1400	2083	2287	122	2021	1483	252	2124	867	2425	2222	1419	1702	795	876	405	868	1573	1160	1496	1840	2076	2051	0	1038	2254	2270	2003
Tulsa, OK	1459	633	397	1483	770	705	713	765	608	657	1331	1234	1766	105	401	1240	1249	1103	981	1987	1483	1103	1702	1222	1398	381	705	1223	535	1403	1776	2034	356	1727	955	1182	867	1038	0	1284	1167	964
Washington, DC	2659	533	875	1086	770	1078	949	796	632	1095	252	190	2772	1305	1151	876	133	2367	219	2846	397	283	2579	114	341	795	1078	2141	1605	2733	2949	2684	953	2417	891	908	438	2254	1284	0	1005	283
West Palm Beach, FL	2772	1094	957	65	1386	1737	673	639	875	811	1223	916	3055	1468	1671	194	1134	2392	1111	3310	1402	754	2976	924	1346	1241	1737	2490	1370	2072	3065	3388	507	3196	430	219	1248	2270	1167	1005	0	1167
Youngstown, OH	2424	373	738	1238	510	794	1005	831	543	1095	403	438	2463	1087	875	1052	357	2076	65	2481	527	535	2303	662	265	592	794	1877	1477	2432	2569	2456	1181	2125	1005	1088	170	2003	964	283	1167	0

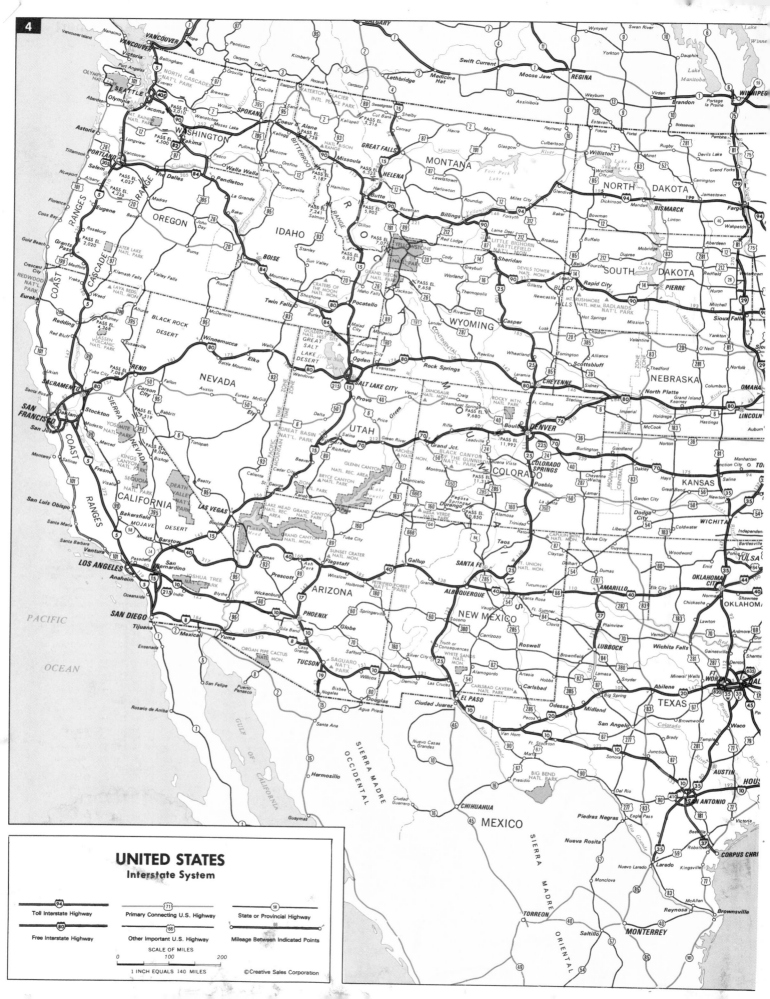

UNITED STATES
Interstate System

Toll Interstate Highway

Free Interstate Highway

Primary Connecting U.S. Highway

Other Important U.S. Highway

State or Provincial Highway

Mileage Between Indicated Points

SCALE OF MILES

0   100   200

1 INCH EQUALS 140 MILES

©Creative Sales Corporation

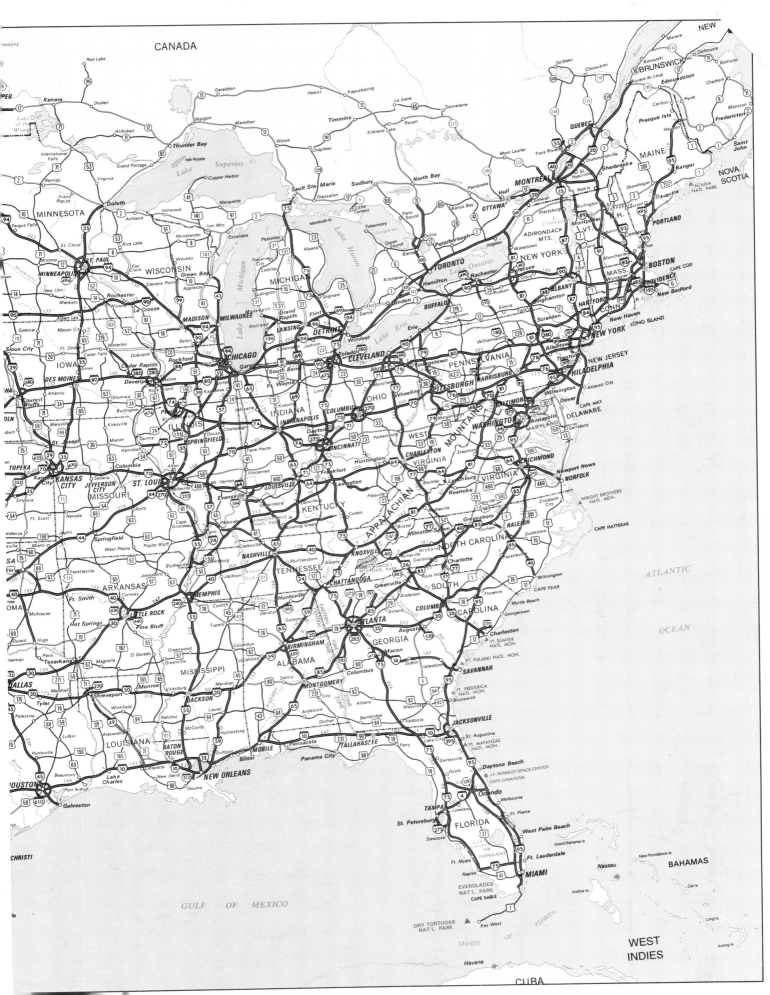

National Parks & Landmarks

USE ONLY FOR ORIENTATION TO NATIONAL PARKS AND LANDMARKS. FOR MORE DETAILED HIGHWAY INFORMATION, SEE INTERSTATE HIGHWAY MAP, PAGES 4-5, AND STATE MAP SECTION, PAGES 13-89.

QUEBEC

NEW BRUNSWICK

ONTARIO

MAINE

Kenora
Lake of the Woods
Thunder Bay
Voyageurs Nat'l Park
Isle Royale Nat'l Park
Pukaskwa Nat'l Park
Lake Superior
Apostle Islands Nat'l Lakeshore
Chippewa Nat'l Forest
Sault Ste. Marie
Pictured Rocks Nat'l Lakeshore
Sudbury
North Bay
Algonquin Prov. Park
Ottawa
Montreal
Quebec
Presque Isle
Roosevelt Campobello Int'l Park
Bangor
Acadia Nat'l Park
Augusta
Portland
Concord
N.H.
VT.
Adirondack Mtns.
Montpelier
White Mtns. Nat'l Forest

MINNESOTA
St. Paul
Minneapolis
Rochester
WISCONSIN
Madison
Milwaukee
Green Bay
MICHIGAN
Grand Rapids
Lansing
Sleeping Bear Dunes Nat'l Lakeshore
Manistee Nat'l Forest
Huron Nat'l Forest
Lake Huron
Toronto
Lake Ontario
Rochester
Syracuse
Albany
Boston
MASS.
Providence
R.I.
Cape Cod Nat'l Seashore
New Bedford
Hartford
CONN.
New Haven
New York
Fire Island Nat'l Seashore
Statue of Liberty Nat'l Monument

IOWA
Sioux City
Des Moines
Cedar Rapids
Rockford
Davenport
Chicago
Gary
South Bend
Ft. Wayne
Detroit
Windsor
Toledo
Cleveland
Akron
Youngstown
Pittsburgh
PENNSYLVANIA
Allegheny Nat'l Forest
Scranton
Allentown
Trenton
Philadelphia
Wilmington
NEW JERSEY
DELAWARE
Dover
Baltimore
Annapolis
Washington D.C.
MARYLAND
Assateague Island Nat'l Seashore

Omaha
Council Bluffs
Dodge House Nat'l Mon.
Topeka
Kansas City
Columbia
Jefferson City
St. Louis
MISSOURI
Springfield
ILLINOIS
Peoria
Springfield
INDIANA
Indianapolis
Hoosier Nat'l Forest
Cincinnati
OHIO
Columbus
Wayne Nat'l Forest
Mound City Group Nat'l Mon.
Wheeling
Charleston
WEST VIRGINIA
Monongahela Nat'l Forest
George Washington Nat'l Forest
Richmond
VIRGINIA
Norfolk
Newport News
Lynchburg
Roanoke
Petersburg Nat'l Battlefield
Wright Brothers Nat'l Memorial
Cape Hatteras Nat'l Seashore

KENTUCKY
Louisville
Frankfort
Lexington
Mammoth Cave Nat'l Park
Shawnee Nat'l Forest
Daniel Boone Nat'l Forest
Cumberland Gap Nat'l Hist. Park
Andrew Johnson Nat'l Mon.
Greensboro
Raleigh
Winston-Salem
NORTH CAROLINA
Uwharrie Nat'l Forest
Croatan Nat'l Forest
Cape Lookout Nat'l Seashore

MISSOURI
Springfield
Mark Twain Nat'l Forest
Kentucky Lake
Nashville
Knoxville
Great Smoky Mtns. Nat'l Park
TENNESSEE
Chattanooga
Charlotte
Cowpens Nat'l Battlefield
Kings Mtn. Nat'l Mil. Park
SOUTH CAROLINA
Columbia
Congaree Swamp Nat'l Mon.
Francis Marion Nat'l Forest

Tulsa
ARKANSAS
Ft. Smith
Ozark Nat'l Forest
Little Rock
Hot Springs Nat'l Park
Ouachita Nat'l Forest
Holly Springs Nat'l Forest
Memphis
William B. Bankhead Nat'l Forest
Birmingham
Talladega Nat'l Forest
Atlanta
Chattahoochee Nat'l Forest
Oconee Nat'l Forest
Augusta
Ft. Sumter Nat'l Mon.

Texarkana
Pine Bluff
Arkansas Post Nat'l Mon.
Tombigbee Nat'l Forest
Delta Nat'l Forest
MISSISSIPPI
Jackson
Bienville Nat'l Forest
Homochitto Nat'l Forest
Rocky Springs Nat'l Park
De Soto Nat'l Forest
ALABAMA
Montgomery
Columbus
Macon
GEORGIA
Conecuh Nat'l Forest
Ocmulgee Nat'l Mon.
Ft. Pulaski Nat'l Mon.
Savannah
Ft. Frederica Nat'l Mon.
Cumberland Island Nat'l Seashore

Tyler
Shreveport
Monroe
Sabine Nat'l Forest
Davy Crockett Nat'l Forest
Angelina Nat'l Forest
LOUISIANA
Baton Rouge
Sam Houston Nat'l Forest
Houston
Galveston
Lake Charles
New Orleans
Biloxi
Mobile
Pensacola
Panama City
Gulf Islands Nat'l Seashore
Apalachicola Nat'l Forest
Tallahassee
Osceola Nat'l Forest
Jacksonville
Castillo de San Marcos Nat'l Mon.
Ft. Matanzas Nat'l Mon.
Daytona Beach
Canaveral Nat'l Seashore
John F. Kennedy Space Center
Ocala Nat'l Forest
Orlando
FL TPK.
FLORIDA
Tampa
St. Petersburg
Lake Okeechobee
Desoto Nat'l Mon.
West Palm Beach
Ft. Myers
Naples
Ft. Lauderdale
Miami
Everglades Nat'l Park
Biscayne Nat'l Park
Dry Tortugas Nat'l Park

ATLANTIC OCEAN

GULF OF MEXICO

CENTRAL TIME ZONE
EASTERN TIME ZONE
ATLANTIC TIME ZONE

ALBERTA

Banff	J-4
Calgary	J-4
Camrose	H-5
Cardston	J-5
Drumheller	H-5
Edmonton	H-5
Edson	H-4
Fitzgerald	F-5
Fort Chipewyn	F-4
Ft. McMurray	G-5
Ft. Vermillion	F-4

Grande Centre	G-5
Grande Prairie	G-4
Habay	F-4
High Level	F-4
High River	J-4
Hinton	H-4
Jasper	H-4
Lethbridge	J-5
Medicine Hat	J-5
Peace Point	F-4
Peace River	G-4
Rainbow Lake	F-4

Red Deer	H-5
Rocky Mtn. House	H-4
Waterways	G-5
Wetaskiwin	H-4
Whitecourt	H-4

BRITISH COLUMBIA

Alert Bay	J-2
Atlin	F-2
Bella Coola	H-2
Campbell River	J-2

Cassiar	F-2
Courtnay	J-2
Cranbrook	J-4
Dawson Creek	G-3
Ft. Nelson	F-3
Ft. St. John	G-3
Hazelton	H-2
Kamloops	J-3
Kelowna	J-3
Kimberley	J-4
Kitimat	H-2
Masset	G-1
Nanaimo	J-2

Nelson	J-4
New Westminster	J-3
Ocean Falls	H-2
Penticton	J-4
Port Alberni	J-2
Port Alice	J-2
Powell River	J-3
Prince George	H-3
Prince Rupert	H-2
Quesnel	H-3
Revelstoke	J-4
Sandpit	H-1

Smithers	G-2
Stewart	G-2
Telegraph Creek	F-2
Trail	J-4
Ucluelet	J-2
Vancouver	J-3
Vernon	J-3
Victoria	J-3
Ware	G-3
Williams Lake	H-3

MANITOBA

Berens River	G-7
Brandon	H-7
Brochet	F-6
Churchill	F-7
Dauphin	H-7
Flin Flon	G-6
Gillam	F-7
Gods Lake	G-8
Grand Rapids	G-7
Island Lake	G-7

Lynn Lake	F-6
Norway House	G-7
Portage la Prairie	H-7
Selkirk	H-8
Snow Lake	G-7
S. Indian Lake	F-7
Swan River	H-7
The Pas	G-6
Thompson	G-7
Virden	J-7
Winnipeg	H-8

NEW BRUNSWICK

Bathurst	E-13
Campbellton	E-12
Chatam	E-13
Edmundston	F-12
Fredricton	F-13
Moncton	F-13
Newcastle	E-13
St. John	F-13
St. Stephen	F-13
Tracadie	E-13

Woodstock	F-13

NEWFOUNDLAND

Battle Harbour	C-13
Bonavista	C-14
Cartwright	C-12
Channel-Port aux Basques	D-14
Churchill Falls	D-12
Corner Brook	D-13
Gander	C-14

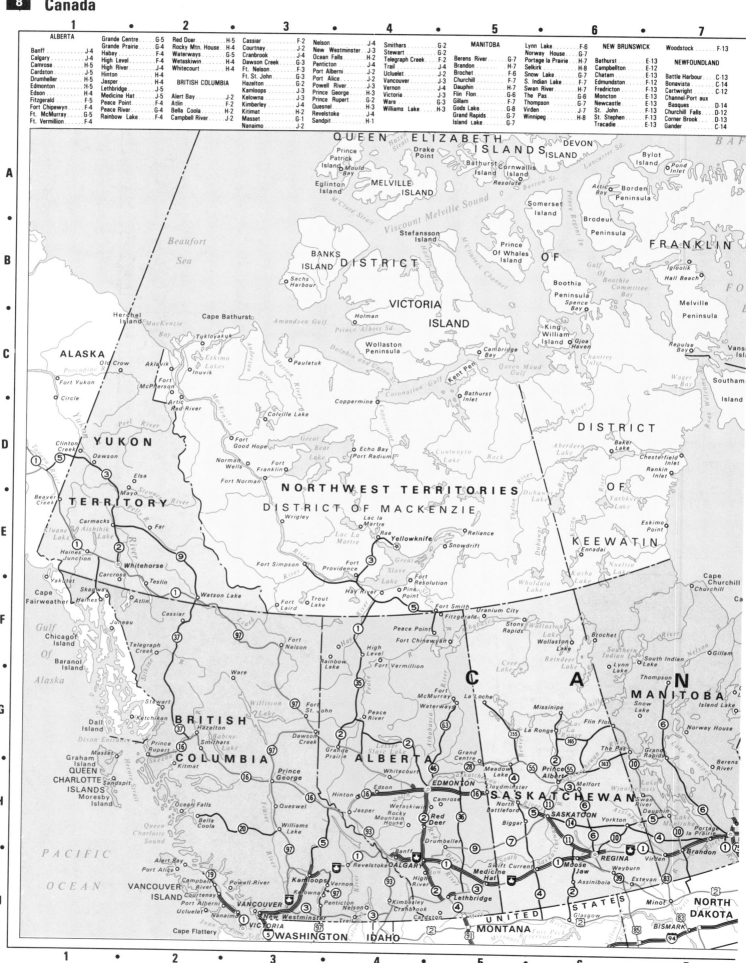

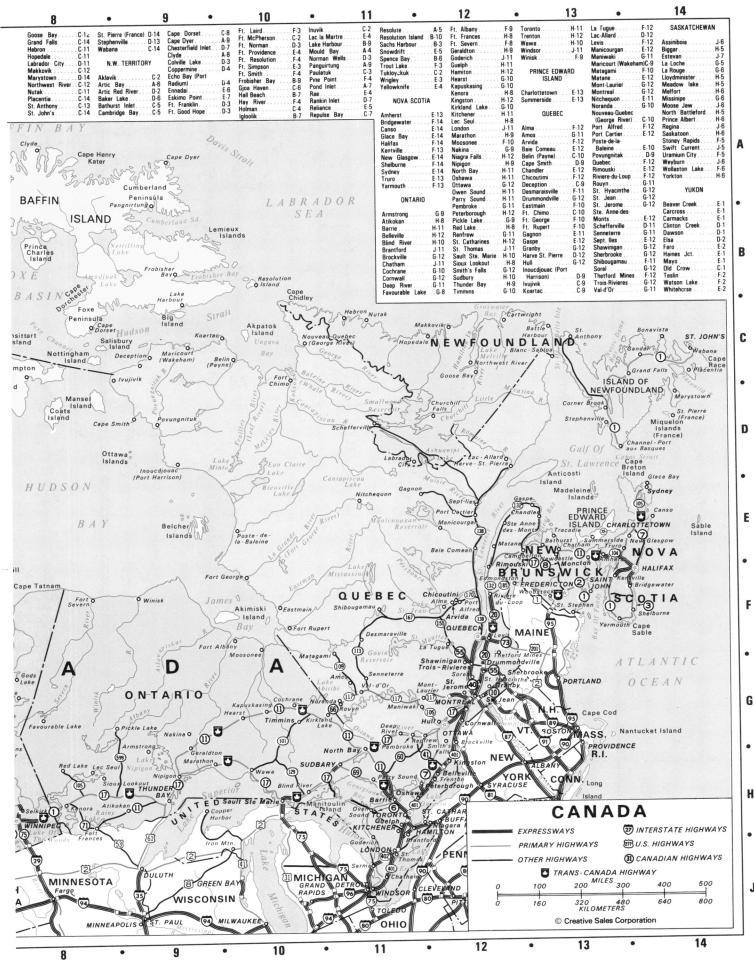

Goose Bay ... C-12
Grand Falls ... C-14
Hebron ... C-11
Hopedale ... C-11
Labrador City ... D-11
Makkovik ... C-12
Marystown ... D-14
Northwest River ... C-12
Nutak ... C-11
Placentia ... C-13
St. Anthony ... C-13
St. John's ... C-14

St. Pierre (France) ... D-14
Stephenville ... D-13
Wabana ... C-14

N.W. TERRITORY
Aklavik ... C-2
Artic Bay ... A-6
Artic Red River ... D-2
Baker Lake ... D-6
Bathurst Inlet ... C-5
Cambridge Bay ... C-5

Cape Dorset ... C-8
Cape Dyer ... A-9
Chesterfield Inlet ... D-7
Clyde ... A-8
Colville Lake ... D-3
Coppermine ... D-4
Echo Bay (Port Radium) ... D-4
Ennadai ... E-6
Eskimo Point ... E-7
Ft. Franklin ... D-3
Ft. Good Hope ... D-3

Ft. Laird ... F-3
Ft. McPherson ... C-2
Ft. Norman ... D-3
Ft. Providence ... E-4
Ft. Resolution ... F-4
Ft. Simpson ... F-4
Ft. Smith ... F-4
Frobisher Bay ... B-9
Gjoa Haven ... C-6
Hall Beach ... B-7
Hay River ... E-5
Holman ... C-3
Igloolik ... B-7

Inuvik ... C-2
Lac la Martre ... E-4
Lake Harbour ... B-9
Mould Bay ... A-4
Norman Wells ... D-3
Panguirtung ... A-9
Paulatuk ... C-3
Pine Point ... F-4
Pond Inlet ... A-7
Rae ... E-4
Rankin Inlet ... D-7
Reliance ... E-5
Repulse Bay ... C-7

Resolute ... A-5
Resolution Island ... B-10
Sachs Harbour ... B-3
Snowdrift ... E-5
Spence Bay ... B-6
Trout Lake ... F-3
Tukloyuktuk ... A-3
Wrigley ... E-3
Yellowknife ... E-4

NOVA SCOTIA
Amherst ... E-13
Bridgewater ... F-14
Canso ... E-14
Glace Bay ... E-14
Halifax ... F-14
Kentville ... F-13
New Glasgow ... E-14
Shelburne ... F-13
Sydney ... E-14
Truro ... E-13
Yarmouth ... F-13

ONTARIO
Armstrong ... G-9
Atikokan ... H-8
Barrie ... H-11
Belleville ... H-12
Blind River ... H-10
Brantford ... J-11
Brockville ... G-12
Chatham ... J-11
Cochrane ... G-10
Cornwall ... G-12
Deep River ... G-11
Favourable Lake ... G-8

Ft. Albany ... F-9
Ft. Frances ... H-8
Ft. Severn ... F-8
Geraldton ... H-9
Goderich ... J-11
Guelph ... H-11
Hamilton ... H-12
Hearst ... G-10
Kapuskasing ... G-10
Kenora ... H-8
Kingston ... H-12
Kirkland Lake ... G-10
Kitchener ... H-11
Lec Seul ... H-8
London ... J-11
Marathon ... H-9
Moosonee ... F-10
Nakina ... G-9
Niagra Falls ... H-12
Nipigon ... H-9
North Bay ... H-11
Oshawa ... H-12
Ottawa ... G-12
Owen Sound ... H-11
Parry Sound ... H-11
Pembroke ... G-11
Peterborough ... H-11
Pickle Lake ... G-9
Red Lake ... H-8
Renfrew ... G-11
St. Catharines ... H-12
St. Thomas ... J-11
Sault Ste. Marie ... H-10
Sioux Lookout ... H-8
Smith's Falls ... G-12
Sudbury ... H-10
Thunder Bay ... H-9
Timmins ... G-10

Toronto ... H-11
Trenton ... H-12
Wawa ... H-10
Windsor ... J-11
Winisk ... F-9

PRINCE EDWARD ISLAND
Charlottetown ... E-13
Summerside ... E-13

QUEBEC
Alma ... F-12
Amos ... F-12
Arvida ... F-12
Baie Comeau ... E-12
Belin (Payne) ... C-10
Cape Smith ... D-9
Chandler ... E-12
Chicoutimi ... F-12
Deception ... C-9
Desmaraisville ... F-11
Drummondville ... G-12
Eastmain ... F-10
Ft. Chimo ... C-10
Ft. George ... F-10
Ft. Rupert ... E-11
Gagnon ... E-11
Gaspe ... E-12
Granby ... G-12
Harve St. Pierre ... D-12
Hull ... G-12
Inoucdjouac (Port Harrison) ... D-9
Ivujivik ... C-9
Koartac ... C-9

La Tugue ... F-12
Lac-Allard ... D-12
Levis ... F-12
Manicouagan ... E-12
Maniwaki ... G-11
Maricourt (Wakeham)C-9
Matagami ... F-10
Matane ... E-12
Mont-Laurier ... G-12
Montreal ... G-12
Nitchequon ... E-11
Noranda ... G-11
Nouveau-Quebec (George River) ... C-10
Port Alfred ... F-12
Port Cartier ... E-12
Poste-de-la-Baleine ... E-10
Povungnitak ... D-9
Quebec ... F-12
Rimouski ... E-12
Riviere-du-Loup ... F-12
Rouyn ... G-11
St. Hyacinthe ... G-12
St. Jean ... G-12
St. Jerome ... G-12
Ste. Anne-des-Monts ... E-12
Schefferville ... D-11
Senneterre ... G-11
Sept. Iles ... E-12
Shawinigan ... G-12
Sherbrooke ... G-12
Shibougamau ... F-11
Sorel ... G-12
Thetford Mines ... F-12
Trois-Rivieres ... G-12
Val-d'Or ... G-11

SASKATCHEWAN
Assiniboia ... J-6
Biggar ... H-5
Estevan ... J-7
La Loche ... G-5
La Rouge ... G-6
Lloydminster ... H-5
Meadow lake ... H-5
Melfort ... H-6
Missinipe ... G-6
Moose Jaw ... J-6
North Battleford ... H-5
Prince Albert ... H-6
Regina ... J-6
Saskatoon ... H-6
Stoney Rapids ... F-5
Swift Current ... J-5
Uramium City ... F-5
Weyburn ... J-6
Wollaston Lake ... F-6
Yorkton ... H-6

YUKON
Beaver Creek ... E-1
Carcross ... E-1
Carmacks ... E-1
Clinton Creek ... D-1
Dawson ... E-2
Elsa ... D-2
Faro ... E-2
Haines Jct. ... E-1
Mayo ... E-1
Old Crow ... C-1
Teslin ... F-2
Watson Lake ... F-2
Whitehcrse ... E-2

CANADA

——— EXPRESSWAYS	㉗ INTERSTATE HIGHWAYS
——— PRIMARY HIGHWAYS	㉗ U.S. HIGHWAYS
——— OTHER HIGHWAYS	㉛ CANADIAN HIGHWAYS
TRANS-CANADA HIGHWAY	

MILES
0   100   200   300   400   500

KILOMETERS
0   160   320   480   640   800

© Creative Sales Corporation

Tijuana
Tecate
Mexicali
Yuma
San Luis
Ajo
ARIZONA
Tucson
Safford
Silver City
Alamogordo
Artesia
NEW MEXICO
Hobbs
Big Springs
Midland
Ensenada
BAJA CALIFORNIA
Sonorita
SONORA
Las Cruces
EL PASO
STATES
Odessa
San Felipe
Puerto Penasco
Nogales
Douglas
UNITED
CIUDAD JUAREZ
Pecos
Rankin
El Rosario
Caborca
Altar
Magdalena
Santa Ana
Agua Prieta
Cananea
CHIHUAHUA
Janos
Villa Ahumada
Carlsbad
Alpine
Sanders
Puerto de la Libertad
Bavispe
Nueva Casas Grandes
Moctezuma
Presidio
COAHUILA
Punta Prieta
Hermosillo
Sahuaripa
Madera
Buenaventura
Gallego
El Sauz
Ojinaga
Boquillas del Carmen
Rasarito
Bahía Kino
Tonichi
Ciudad Guerrero
Chihuahua
La Cuesta
Nacimiento
Gulf
Guaymas
Empalme
Rosario
Yécora
Cuauhtémoc
La Perla
Delicias
Sabina
San Ignacio
Santa Rosalía
Ciudad Obregón
Navojoa
Ciudad Camargo
Ocampo
Rosarito
El Fuerte
Sinaloa
Tameapa
Jiménez
Santa Barbara
Escalón
San Pedro de las Colonias
Parras
Los Mochis
Guasave
Hidalgo del Parral
La Cadena
Gómez Palacio
TORREÓN
Ejido Insurgentes
Topolobampo
M E X I C O
Durango
Tepehuanes
Abasolo
Cuencamé
Concepción del Oro
Camacho
El Medano
Altata
Culiacán
Cosalá
Canatlán
Camachy
La Paz
Eldorado
La Cruz
El Salto
Sombrerete
Río Grande
Todos Santos
San Jose del Cabo
Mazatlán
Villa Union
Durango
Fresnillo
Rosario
Zacatecas
Pacific
Tuxpan
Monte Escobedo
Los Corchos
Tepic
Aguascalientes
Jalpa
Lagos de Moreno
Las Varas
Moyahua
Tepatitlán
Irapuato
Puerto Vallarta
GUADALAJARA
Tlaquepaque
Ocotlán
Salamanca
El Tuito
JALISCO
Sahuayu
Autlán
Sayula
Ciudad Guzmán
Uruapan
Tomatlán
Ocean
Melaque
COLIMA
Colima
Apatzingán
Manzanillo
Arteaga
Playa Azul
Ixtapa

NAYARIT

AGUASCALIENTES

ZACATECAS

BAJA CALIFORNIA
BAJA CALIF SUR

Rio Grande

of
California

MEXICO

Cities and Towns

Abasolo	D-5
Acambaro	F-6
Acapulco	G-6
Acatlan	F-7
Acayucan	F-8
Agua Prieta	A-3
Aguascalientes	E-6
Altar	A-3
Altata	D-4
Alvarado	F-8
Apatzingan	F-6
Arcelia	F-6
Arriga	G-9
Arteaga	F-6
Arlixco	F-7
Autlan	F-5
Bahia Kino	B-2
Bavispe	B-4
Becal	E-10
Boquillas de Carmen	B-6
Buenaventura	B-4
Caborca	A-2
Camacho	D-6
Campeche	E-10
Cananea	A-3
Canatlan	D-5
Cardenas	F-9
Celaya	E-6
Celestun	E-10
Champoton	F-10
Chetumal	F-11
Chihuahua	B-5
Chilpancingo	F-7
China	C-7
Ciudad Acuna	B-6
Ciudad Camargo	C-5
Ciudad Guerrero	B-4
Ciudad Guzman	F-5
Ciudad Juarez	A-4
Ciudad Madero	E-7
Ciudad Mante	E-7
Ciudad Victoria	D-7
Ciudad de Carmen	F-9
Ciudad de Valles	E-7
Ciudad del Maiz	E-7
Coatzacoalcos	F-9
Colima	F-5
Comitan	G-9
Conception de Oro	D-6
Cordoba	F-8
Cosala	D-4
Cuauhtemoc	B-4
Cuencame	D-5
Cuernavaca	F-7
Culiacan	D-4
Delicias	B-5
Durango	D-5
Dzilam de Bravo	E-10
Ejido Insurgentes	C-3
El Fuerte	C-4
El Medana	D-3
El Rosario	A-1
El Sauz	B-4
El Tuito	E-5
Empalme	B-3
Ensanada	A-1
Escalon	C-5
Escarcega	F-10
Fresnillo	D-5
Gallego	B-4
Gomez Palacio	C-5
Guadalajara	E-5
Guasave	C-4
Guaymas	B-3
Hermosillo	B-3
Hidalgo del Parral	C-5
Hopelchen	E-10
Huajuapan de Leon	F-7
Iguala	F-7
Iturbide	F-10
Jalapa	F-8
Jalpa	E-5
Janos	A-4
Jimenez	C-5
Juchitan	G-8
La Cruz	D-4
La Cadena	C-5
La Cuesta	B-6
Lagos de Morena	E-6
La Paz	D-3
La Perla	B-5
La Pesca	D-7
La Piedad	E-6
Las Varas	E-5
Leon	E-6
Linares	D-7
Los Corchos	E-5
Los Mochis	C-3
Madera	B-4
Magdalena	A-3
Malpaso	G-9
Manuel	E-7
Manzanillo	F-5
Matamoros	C-7
Matehuala	D-6
Matias Romero	G-8
Mazatlan	D-4
Melaque	F-5
Merida	E-10
Mexicali	A-1
Mexico City	F-7
Miahuatlan	G-8
Mier	C-7
Minatitlan	F-8
Moctezuma	B-4
Molango	E-7
Moncloya	C-6
Monte Escobedo	E-5
Montemorelos	D-7
Monterrey	C-6
Morelia	F-6
Morelos	B-6
Moyahua	E-5
Nacimiento	C-6
Nautla	E-8
Navojoa	C-3
Nogales	A-3
Nueva Casas Grandes	B-4
Nueva Rosita	C-6
Nuevo Laredo	C-7
Oaxaca	G-8
Ocampo	C-6
Ocotlan	E-6
Ojinaga	B-5
Ometepec	G-7
Orizaba	F-8
Pachuca	E-7
Palenque	F-9
Papantla	E-7
Paraiso	F-9
Parras	C-6
Peto	E-10
Piedras Negras	B-6
Pijijiapan	G-9
Pinotepa Nacional	G-7
Piste	E-11
Playa Azul	F-6
Pochutla	G-8
Poza Pica	E-7
Progreso	E-10
Puebla	F-7
Puerto de la Libertad	B-2
Puerto Escondido	G-8
Puerto Juarez	E-11
Puerto Madero	G-9
Puerto Penasco	A-2
Punta Prieta	B-2
Queretaro	E-6
Rasarito	B-2
Reynosa	C-7
Rio Grande	D-6
Rio Lagartos	E-11
Rosario	C-3
Rosario	D-4
Sabinas	C-6
Sabinas Hidagalo	C-6
Sahuaripa	B-3
Salamanca	E-6
Salinas	E-6
Salina Cruz	G-8
Saltillo	C-6
San Andres Suxtla	F-8
San Cristobal	G-9
San Felipe	A-2
San Fernando	D-7
San Ignacio	C-2
San Jose del Cabo	D-3
San Luis	A-2
San Luis Potosi	E-6
San Pedro de las Colonias	C-6
Santa Ana	A-3
Santa Barbara	C-5
Santa Rosalia	C-2
Sayula	F-5
Sinaloa	C-4
Sombrerete	D-5
Sonorita	A-2
Soto La Marina	D-7
Tameapa	C-4
Tampico	E-7
Tapachula	G-9
Tapanatepec	G-9
Taxco	F-7
Teapa	F-9
Tecate	A-1
Tehuacan	F-7
Tehuantepec	G-8
Temporal	E-7
Tepatitlan	E-6
Tepehuanes	D-5
Tepic	E-5
Ticul	E-10
Tijuana	A-1
Tiquicheo	F-6
Tlaciaco	G-7
Tlaxcala	F-7
Tlaxiaco	F-7
Todos Santos	D-3
Toluca	F-7
Tomatian	F-5
Tonichi	B-3
Topolobampo	C-3
Torreon	C-5
Totolapan	G-8
Tulancingo	E-7
Tulum	E-11
Tuxpan	B-4
Tuxpan	E-7
Tuxtepec	F-8
Tuxtla Gutierrez	G-9
Uruapan	F-6
Valladolid	E-11
Veracruz	F-8
Villa Ahumada	A-4
Villagran	D-7
Villahermosa	F-9
Villa Union	D-4
Xcan	E-11
Yecora	B-4
Zacatal	F-9
Zacatecas	E-6
Zamora	F-6
Zihuatanejo	F-6
Zimapan	E-7
Zitacuaro	F-6

Map Labels

FT. WORTH
DALLAS
Snyder
Sweetwater
Abilene
Angelo
Brownwood
Waco
Temple
TEXAS
Austin
Junction
SAN ANTONIO
Del Rio
Uvalde
Eagle Pass
Brady
Victoria
Corpus Christi
Alice
Harlingen
Brownsville
Laredo
Nuevo Laredo
MONTERREY
Saltillo
Reynosa
Matamoros
China
Montemorelos
Linares
San Fernando
Villagrán
Soto La Marina
La Pesca
Ciudad Victoria
Ciudad Mante
Manuel
Ciudad Madero
Tampico
SAN LUIS POTOSÍ
Ciudad del Maiz
Ciudad de Valles
Temporal
TAMAULIPAS
NUEVO LEON
GUANAJUATO
Zimapan
Molango
Tuxpan
Poza Rica
Papantla
Nautla
QUERÉTARO
Querétaro
Celaya
Pachuca
Tulancingo
VERACRUZ
HIDALGO
Jalapa
MEXICO CITY
TLAXCALA
Tlaxcala
VERACRUZ
Toluca
Puebla
Cuernavaca
MORELOS
PUEBLA
Atlixco
Tehuacán
Orizaba
Cordoba
VERACRUZ
Alvarado
San Andrés Tuxtla
Paraiso
Coatzacoalcos
Villahermosa
TABASCO
Taxco
Arcelia
Iguala
Acatlán
Tuxtepec
Huajuapan de Leon
OAXACA
Zihuatanejo
Chilpancingo
GUERRERO
Tlaxiaco
Oaxaca
Minatitlan
Cardenas
Teapa
CHIAPAS
Malpaso
Tuxtla Gutiérrez
San Cristóbal de las Casas
Acapulco
Ometepec
Totolapan
Miahuatlán
Tehuantepec
Juchitán
Tapanatepec
Arriaga
Salina Cruz
Pijijiapan
Puerto Escondido
Pochutla
Pinotepa Nacional
Gulf of Tehuantepec
Tapachula
Puerto Madero
Quezaltenango
GUATEMALA
Ciudad del Carmen
Zacatal
Escárcega
Palenque
La Libertad
Comitan
BELIZE
Belize
Belmopan
Stann Creek
GUATEMALA
Puerto Barrios
Puerto Cortés
San Pedro Sula
HONDURAS
CAMPECHE
QUINTANA ROO
YUCATAN
MÉRIDA
Progreso
Dzilam de Bravo
Rio Lagartos
Celestun
Piste
Xcan
Chichen Itza
Valladolid
Cancun
COZUMEL
Ticul
Peto
Tulum
Becal
Campeche
Hopelchén
Champoton
Iturbide
Chetumal
Caribbean Sea
Gulf of Mexico
Bay of Campeche

STATE MAP LEGEND

ROAD CLASSIFICATIONS & RELATED SYMBOLS

Free Interstate Hwy.	—■——(90)——■—
Toll Interstate Hwy.	—■——(76)——■—
Divided Federal Hwy.	——(14)——
Federal Hwy.	——(20)——
Divided State Hwy.	——(31)——
State Hwy.	——(147)——
Other Connecting Road	----(258)----
Trans - Canada Hwy.	——ᗊ——
Point to Point Milage	— 17 —
State Boundaries	■ ■ ■ ■ ■ ■ ■ ■ ■

LAND MARKS & POINTS OF INTEREST

Indian Reservation		Desert	
National & State Forest or Wildlife Preserve		River, Lake, Ocean or other Drainage	
Military Installation		Urban Area	**Denver**
		Airport	✈
National & State Park or Recreation Area		State Capital	✱
		Park, Monument, University or other Point of Interest	■
Grassland		Roadside Table or Rest Areas	▲

ABBREVIATIONS

A.F.B. - Air Force Base	Mgmt. - Management	Prov. - Province	S. F. - State Forest
Hist. - Historical	Mon. - Monument	Rec. - Recreation	St. Pk. - State Park
Mem. - Memorial	Nat. - Natural	Ref. - Refuge	W.M.A. - Wildlife Management Area

CITIES & TOWNS - Type size indicates the relative population of cities and towns

Mapleton	Kenhorst	Somerset	Butler	Auburn	Harrisburg	Madison	Chicago
under 1000	1000-5,000	5,000-10,000	10,000-25,000	25,000-50,000	50,000-100,000	100,000-500,000	500,000 and over

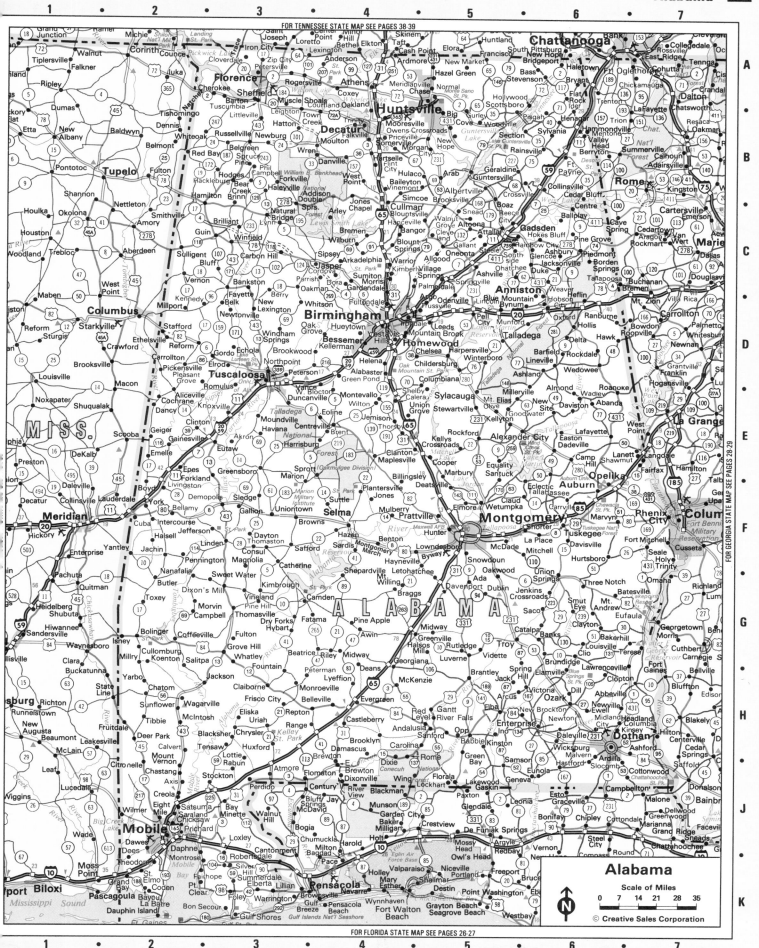

FOR GEORGIA STATE MAP SEE PAGES 28-29

Alabama

Scale of Miles

0   7   14   21   28   35

© Creative Sales Corporation

FOR CANADA MAP SEE PAGES 8-9

ALASKA

N.W. TERR.

YUKON

B.C.

Canada
United States

Arctic Ocean

Beaufort Sea

Chukchi Sea

Bering Sea

Gulf of Alaska

Pacific Ocean

RUSSIA USA

Anchorage
Fairbanks
Juneau

Barrow, Wainwright, Pt. Lay, Atkasuk, Umiat, Prudhoe Bay, Deadhorse, Beechey Point, Sagwon, Kaktovik, Gordon

Nome, Kotzebue, Kivalina, Point Hope, Noatak, Ambler, Kobuk, Shungnak, Selawik, Buckland, Deering, Candle

Galena, Ruby, Nulato, Kaltag, Koyukuk, Huslia, Hughes, Allakaket, Bettles, Wiseman

McGrath, Takotna, Flat, Sleetmute, Crooked Creek, Stony River, Lime Village, Farewell

Bethel, Napaskiak, Eek, Kwethluk, Akiachak, Tuluksak, Aniak, Chuathbaluk

Dillingham, Aleknagik, Manokotak, Togiak, Goodnews Bay, Platinum, Quinhagak, Kwigillingok

Naknek, King Salmon, Egegik, Pilot Point, Ugashik, Chignik, Perryville, Ivanof Bay

Kodiak, Old Harbor, Akhiok, Karluk, Larsen Bay, Port Lions, Ouzinkie

Cold Bay, King Cove, Sand Point, Squaw Harbor, False Pass, Akutan, Unalaska, Dutch Harbor, Nikolski

Homer, Seldovia, Seward, Kenai, Soldotna, Ninilchik, Hope, Whittier, Portage

Wasilla, Palmer, Willow, Talkeetna, Cantwell, Healy, Denali Nat'l Park and Preserve

Delta Junction, Tok, Northway, Chicken, Eagle, Circle, Central, Chatanika

Valdez, Cordova, Glennallen, Gakona, Gulkana, Copper Center, Chitina, McCarthy

Wrangell-St. Elias Nat'l Park and Preserve

Gates of the Arctic National Park & Preserve

Arctic Nat'l Wildlife Refuge

Yukon Flats Nat'l Wildlife Refuge

Kanuti N.W.R.

Koyukuk Nat'l Wildlife Refuge

Selawik Nat'l Wildlife Refuge

Kobuk Valley Nat'l Park

Noatak National Preserve

Cape Krusenstern Nat'l Mon.

Bering Land Bridge Nat'l Preserve

Yukon Delta Nat'l Wildlife Refuge

Togiak Nat'l Wildlife Refuge

Alaska Peninsula N.W.R.

Becharof Nat'l Wildlife Refuge

Katmai Nat'l Park & Preserve

Lake Clark Nat'l Park & Preserve

Kenai Fjords Nat'l Park

Chugach National Forest

Tongass Nat'l Forest

Glacier Bay Nat'l Park and Preserve

Kodiak Island

Saint Lawrence Island

Nunivak Island

St. Matthew Island

Pribilof Islands, St. Paul, St. George

Aleutian Islands, Near Islands, Fox Islands, Shumagin Is., Andreanof Islands, Rat Islands

YUKON: Whitehorse, Dawson, Mayo, Carmacks, Faro, Ross River, Teslin, Watson Lake, Old Crow, Fort McPherson

Inuvik, Tuktoyaktuk, Aklavik, Fort Good Hope, Norman Wells

Skagway, Haines, Yakutat, Gustavus, Hoonah, Sitka, Angoon, Kake, Petersburg, Wrangell, Ketchikan, Metlakatla, Hydaburg, Craig, Klawock

Prince Rupert, Fort Simpson

SEE MAIN MAP F1
SEE MAIN MAP E6

Anchorage inset:
Anchorage, Palmer, Wasilla, Houston, Willow, Chugiak, Eagle River, Whittier, Moose Pass, Seward, Hope, Soldotna, Kenai, Kasilof, Homer, Nikolski, Susitna, Chickaloon

Miles: 0 20 40

Alaska
Scale of Miles
0 40 80 120 160 200

© Creative Sales Corporation

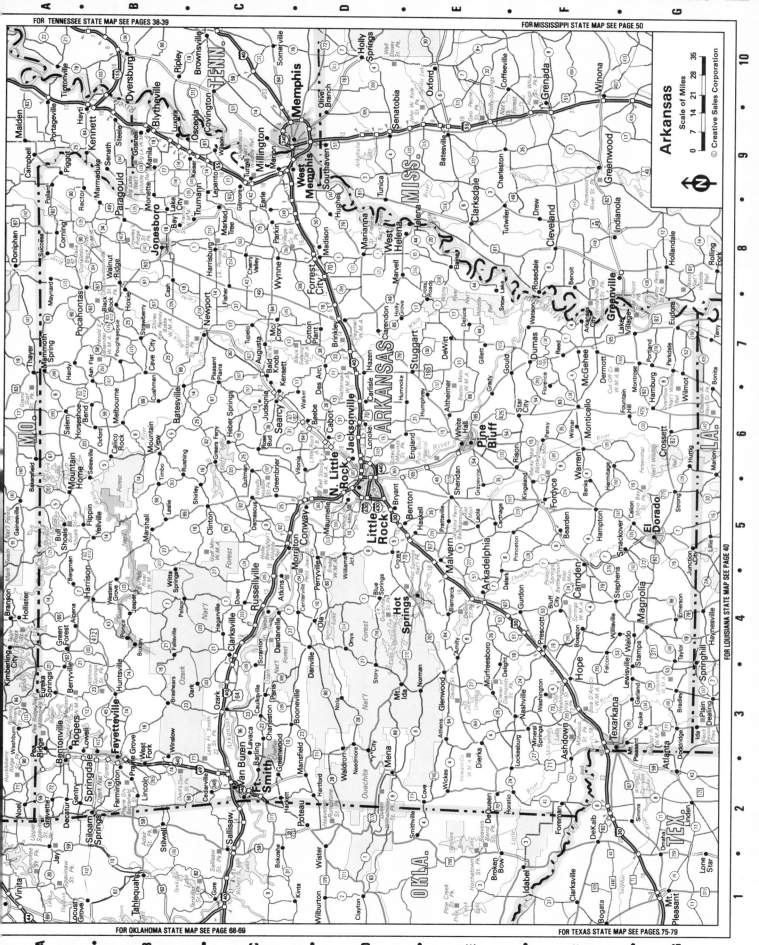

FOR TENNESSEE STATE MAP SEE PAGES 38-39
FOR MISSISSIPPI STATE MAP SEE PAGE 50
FOR OKLAHOMA STATE MAP SEE PAGE 68-69
FOR TEXAS STATE MAP SEE PAGES 75-79
FOR LOUISIANA STATE MAP SEE PAGE 40

Arkansas

Scale of Miles
0 7 14 21 28 35

© Creative Sales Corporation

FOR COLORADO STATE MAP SEE PAGES 22-23
FOR NEW MEXICO STATE MAP SEE PAGE 62
FOR UTAH STATE MAP SEE PAGES 80-81
FOR NEVADA STATE MAP SEE PAGE 54

UTAH

NEVADA

ARIZONA

Utah cities:
La Sal, La Sal Jct., Summit Pt., Manti-La Sal National Forest, Monticello, Eastland, Blanding, Bluff, Montezuma Creek, Aneth, Mexican Hat, Natural Bridges Nat'l Monument, Fry Canyon, Dark Canyon Wilderness Area, Canyonlands National Park, Hanksville, Bicknell, Lyman, Teasdale, Torrey, Grover, Boulder, Escalante, Henrieville, Cannonville, Tropic, Bryce, Bryce Canyon Nat'l Park, Widtsoe Jct. State Park, Antimony, Angle, Kingston, Junction, Circleville, Panguitch, Hatch, Ruby's Inn, Long Valley Jct., Alton, Mt. Carmel Jct., Mt. Carmel, Glendale, Orderville, Beaver, Greenville, Minersville, Adamsville, Paragonah, Parowan, Brian Head, Cedar City, Hamilton Fort, Kanarraville, Cedar Breaks Nat'l Monument, Dixie National Forest, Zion National Park, Springdale, Rockville, Virgin, La Verkin, Toquerville, Leeds, Hurricane, Washington, St. George, Santa Clara, Ivins, Shivwits, Gunlock, Veyo, Central, Pine Valley, New Harmony, Enterprise, Newcastle, Pinto, Summit, Enoch, Iron Sprs., Desert Mound, Lund, Beryl, Zane, Uvada, Modena, Newcastle

Nevada cities:
Ursine, Pioche, Panaca, Caliente, Elgin, Carp, Alamo, Mesquite, Bunkerville, Littlefield, Overton, Logandale, Glendale, Moapa, N. Las Vegas, E. Las Vegas, Las Vegas, Henderson, Boulder City

Arizona cities:
Teec Nos Pos, Rock Point, Round Rock, Many Farms, Chinle, Canyon de Chelly Nat'l Mon., Tsaile, Lukachukai, Cross Canyon, St. Michaels, Window Rock, Ganado, Greasewood (Lower), Kearns Canyon, Polacca, Cedar Springs, Indian Wells, Dilkon, Seba Dalkai, Sanders, Houck, Navajo, Chambers, Petrified Forest National Park, Sun Valley, Holbrook, Joseph City, Winslow, Leupp, Sunrise, Colorado River, Rough Rock, Red Lake, Cow Springs, Chilchinbito, Dinnehotso, Mexican Water, Tes Nez Iha, Kayenta, Tsegi, Oraibi, Old Oraibi, Second Mesa, Moenkopi, Tuba City, Tonalea, The Gap, Cedar Ridge, Page, Marble Canyon, Jacob Lake, Fredonia, Colorado City, Kanab, Cameron, Gray Mountain, Desert View, Grand Canyon, North Rim, Tusayan, Moqui, Valle, Flagstaff, Winona, Angell, Mountainaire, Munds Park, Lake Montezuma, McGuireville, Sedona, Cornville, Cottonwood, Clarkdale, Jerome, Prescott Valley, Prescott, Paulden, Chino Valley, Ash Fork, Williams, Bellemont, Parks, Pine Springs, Seligman, Yampai, Peach Springs, Truxton, Valentine, Hackberry, Nelson, Wikieup, Kingman, Goldroad, Oatman, Mohave, Yucca, Topock, Lake Havasu City, Bullhead City, Riviera, Golden Shores, Needles, Katherine, Cottonwood Cove, Cal Nev Ari, Laughlin, Temple Bar, Willow Beach, Dolan Springs, Chloride, Meadview, Lake Mead National Recreational Area, Grand Canyon National Park, Kaibab National Forest, Kaibab Indian Reservation, Havasupai Indian Reservation, Hualapai Indian Reservation, Navajo Indian Reservation, Hopi Indian Reservation, Petrified Forest, Hualapai Mtn. Park, Wobayuma Peak, Warm Springs Wilderness Area

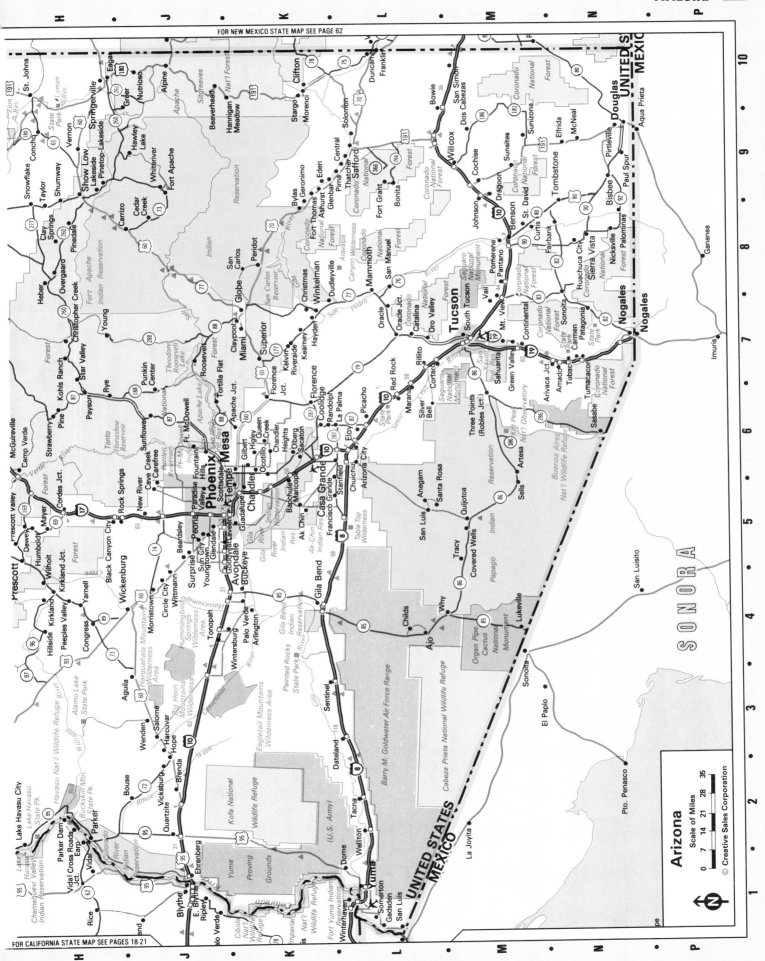

FOR NEW MEXICO STATE MAP SEE PAGE 62

FOR CALIFORNIA STATE MAP SEE PAGES 18-21

Arizona

Scale of Miles

0   7   14   21   28   35

© Creative Sales Corporation

N

FOR NEVADA STATE MAP SEE PAGE 54

FOR OREGON STATE MAP SEE PAGES 70-71

California

Scale of Miles

0 7 14 21 28 35

© Creative Sales Corporation

N

NEVADA

OREGON

CALIFORNIA

Reno
Sparks
Carson City
Fallon
Fernley
Wadsworth
Nixon
Silver Springs
Virginia City
Dayton
Wabuska
Eagle Picher
Gerlach
Pyramid Lake
Indian Reservation
Upper Alkali Lake (Seasonal)
Middle Alkali
Lower Klamath Lk.

Klamath Falls
Lakeview
Medford
Ashland
Talent
Jacksonville
Cave Junction
Brookings
Crescent City
Smith River
Gasquet
Ft. Dick
Requa
Klamath
Klamath Glen
Orick
Trinidad
McKinleyville
Arcata
Eureka
Fields Ldg.
Loleta
Ferndale
Fortuna
Rio Dell
Scotia
Alton
Carlotta
Hydesville
Redcrest
Weott
Petrolia
Capetown
Honeydew
Miranda
Redway
Redcrest
Garberville
Benbow
Bridgeville
Dinsmore
Mad River
Ruth
Alderpoint
Zenia
Covelo
Dos Rios
Laytonville
Westport
Rockport
Leggett
Piercy
Cummings
Longvale
Willits
Ukiah
Talmage
Calpella
Redwood Valley
Potter Valley
Upper Lake
Nice
Lucerne
Lakeport
Kelseyville
Hopland
Boonville
Philo
Navarro
Albion
Mendocino
Caspar
Ft. Bragg
Noyo
Manchester
Pt. Arena
Yorkville
Clearlake
Lower Lake
Middletown
Arbuckle
Williams
Colusa
Maxwell
Willows
Orland
Corning
Red Bluff
Los Molinos
Vina
Tehama
Gerber
Proberta
Paskenta
Stonyford
Sites
Grimes
Meridian
Live Oak
Gridley
Biggs
Richvale
Butte City
Princeton
Glenn
Artois
Hamilton City
Chico
Durham
Ordbend
Nord
Dairyville
Dales
Bend
Paynes Creek
Manton
Shingletown
Viola
Mineral
Mill Creek
Chester
Westwood
Susanville
Janesville
Milford
Herlong
Doyle
Vinton
Chilcoot
Loyalton
Sierraville
Calpine
Sattley
Sierra City
Downieville
Camptonville
Challenge
Brownsville
Oroville
Palermo
Thermalito
Paradise
Magalia
Stirling City
Butte Mdws.
Belden
Berry Creek
Forbestown
Clipper Mills
Rackerby
Dobbins
Marysville
Linda
Yuba City
Sutter
Gridley
Honcut
Olivehurst
Wheatland
Penn Valley
Grass Valley
Nevada City
Washington
Graniteville
North San Juan
Rough And Ready
Colfax
Gold Run
Emigrant Gap
Truckee
Soda Sprgs.
Kings Beach
Tahoe City
Tahoe Vista
Floriston
Boca
Portola
Blairsden
Graeagle
Quincy
Meadow Valley
Keddie
Twain
Greenville
Taylorsville
Crescent Mills
Canyon Dam
Almanor
Johnstonville
Litchfield
Standish
Wendel
Termo
Ravendale
Madeline
Likely
Alturas
Canby
Lookout
Adin
Bieber
Nubieber
Fall River Mills
McArthur
Burney
Round Mtn.
Montgomery Creek
Big Bend
Old Station
Whitmore
Inwood
Shingletown
Millville
Bella Vista
Palo Cedro
Project City
Enterprise
Anderson
Cottonwood
Olinda
Ono
Igo
Platina
Redding
Shasta
Summit City
Whiskeytown
French Gulch
Lakehead
Castella
Dunsmuir
Mt. Shasta
McCloud
Weed
Montague
Yreka
Hornbrook
Hilt
Grenada
Gazelle
Ft. Jones
Greenview
Etna
Callahan
Cecilville
Sawyers Bar
Forks Of Salmon
Somes Bar
Orleans
Weitchpec
Hoopa
Willow Cr.
Salyer
Burnt Ranch
Big Bar
Helena
Junction City
Weaverville
Lewiston
Douglas City
Hayfork
Trinity Ctr.
Peanut
Wildwood
Platina
Hamburg
Klamath River
Happy Camp
Seiad Valley
Mugginsville
Mugginsville
Scott Bar
Dorris
Macdoel
Tulelake
Newell
Tennant
Bray
Bartle
Pondosa
Bartle
Merrill
Malin
Bonanza

Klamath Nat'l Forest
Six Rivers Nat'l Forest
Shasta-Trinity Nat'l Forest
Lassen Nat'l Forest
Lassen Volcanic Nat'l Park
Modoc Nat'l Forest
Plumas Nat'l Forest
Tahoe Nat'l Forest
Mendocino Nat'l Forest
Humboldt Redwoods St. Pk.
Smith River Nat'l

Redwood Nat'l Park
Azalea State Park
Patrick's Pt. St. Beach
Prairie Creek Redwoods State Park
Del Norte Coast Redwoods St. Pk.
Jedediah Smith Redwoods St. Pk.
Richardson Grove St. Pk.
Sinkyone Wilderness St. Park
Standish-Hickey St. Rec. Area
Smithe Redwoods St. Reserve
Admiral Wm. Standley St. Rec. Area
Montgomery Woods St. Reserve
MacKerricher St. Park
Russian Gulch St. Park
Van Damme St. Park
Manchester St. Park
Mailliard Redwoods St. Park
Hendy Woods St. Park
Castle Crags St. Park
Lava Beds Nat'l Mon.
Lake Shasta
Trinity Lake
Eagle Lake
Honey Lk.
Pyramid Lk.
Lake Tahoe
Lake Oroville
Lake Almanor
Clear Lake
Lake Pillsbury
Lake Berryessa
Lake Mendocino
Lake Sonoma

Sacramento R.
Klamath R.
Trinity R.
Eel River
Pit River
Feather River
Yuba R.
Russian River
Mad River
Smith River

Samuel H. Boardman St. Park
Pelican St. Beach
Lake City
Davis Cr.
Ft. Bidwell
Cedarville
Eagleville
Willow Ranch
Wayside
Booth Wayside
Tub Springs Wayside

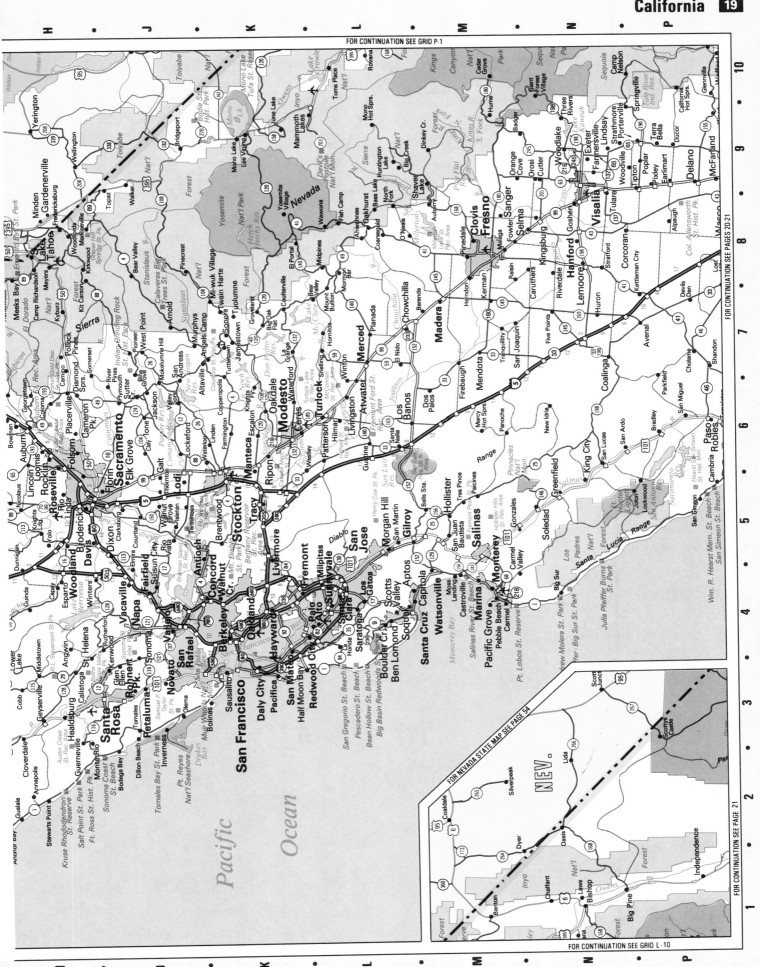

FOR CONTINUATION SEE GRID P-1

FOR CONTINUATION SEE PAGES 20-21

FOR CONTINUATION SEE PAGE 21

FOR NEVADA STATE MAP SEE PAGE 54

FOR CONTINUATION SEE GRID L-10

FOR CONTINUATION SEE PAGES 18-19

Pacific

Ocean

Carmel
Pt. Lobos St. Reserve
Carmel Valley
Gonzales
Soledad
Greenfield
Pinnacles Nat'l Mon.
Panoche
Tranquillity
San Joaquin
Malaga
Fowler
Sanger
Orange Cove
Badger
Giant Forest Village
Sequoia Nat'l Park
Raisin
Selma
Orosi
Cutler
Caruthers
Kingsburg
Woodlake
Three Rivers
Andrew Molera St. Park
Big Sur
Los Padres Nat'l Forest
King City
San Lucas
New Idria
Riverdale
Hanford
Lemoore
Goshen
Woodlake
Lake Kaweah
Pfeiffer - Big Sur St. Park
Santa Lucia Range
Julia Pfeiffer Burns St. Park
Coalinga
Huron
Stratford
Visalia
Farmersville
Exeter
Lindsay
Sequoia Nat'l Forest
San Ardo
Ft. Hunter Liggett
Jolon
Lockwood
Bradley
Parkfield
Avenal
Corcoran
Woodville
Strathmore
Porterville
Camp Nelson
San Simeon
Hearst San Simeon St. Hist. Mon.
San Miguel
Cholame
Kettleman City
Tipton
Poplar
Earlimart
Terra Bella
Springville
Tule River Ind. Res.
Wm. R. Hearst Mem. St. Beach
San Simeon St. Beach
Cambria
Paso Robles
Shandon
Devils Den
Alpaugh
Ducor
California Hot Sprs.
Nat'l Forest
Cayucos St. Beach
Cayucos
Templeton
Atascadero
Blackwells Corner
Lost Hills
Wasco
Delano
McFarland
Glennville
Kernville
Isabella Res.
Onyx
Atascadero St. Beach
Morro Bay
Santa Margarita
Simmler
Buttonwillow
Shafter
Bakersfield
Woody
Wofford Heights
Bodfish
Baywood Pk.
Morro Bay St. Park
Montana De Oro St. Park
San Luis Obispo
Pozo
McKittrick
Green Acres
Edison
Caliente
Nat'l Forest
Pismo Beach
Grover City
Arroyo Grande
Oceano
Nipomo
Twitchell Res.
Fellows
Ford City
Pumpkin Center
Lamont
Arvin
Keene
Tehachapi
Pismo St. Beach
San Luis Obispo Bay
Guadalupe
Orcutt
Santa Maria
Sisquoc
New Cuyama
Cuyama
Taft
Maricopa
Mojave
Pt. Sal St. Beach
Casmalia
Los Alamos
Madre Los Padres Mtns.
Frazier Pk.
Ft. Tejon St. Hist. Pk.
Gorman
Willow Sprs.
Surf
Vandenberg Air Force Base
Lompoc
La Purisima Mission St. Hist. Park
Los Olivos
Buellton
Solvang
Nat'l Forest
Castaic Lake St. Rec. Area
Palmdale
Gaviota St. Pk.
Gaviota
El Capitan St. Beach
Refugio St. Beach
Montecito
Summerland
Carpinteria
Ojai
Fillmore
Lake Piru
Castaic
Acton
Goleta
Santa Barbara
Carpenteria St. Beach
Emma Wood St. Beach
Santa Paula
Santa Clarita
Moorpark
San Fernando
San Miguel Is.
Santa Barbara Channel
Ventura
Oxnard
Port Hueneme
Saticoy
Simi Valley
Agoura Hills
Glendale
Pasadena
Santa Cruz Is.
Pt. Mugu St. Park
Thousand Oaks
Malibu
Beverly Hills
Leo Carrillo St. Beach
Santa Monica Mtns. Nat'l Rec. Area
Santa Monica
Los Angeles
Santa Rosa Is.
Anacapa Is.
Channel Islands National Park
Redondo Beach
Santa Monica Bay
Santa Barbara Is.
Rancho Palos Verdes
Long Beach
Huntington Beach
Newport Beach
Laguna
San Nicolas Is.
Santa Catalina Is.
Avalon
San Pedro Channel
Outer Santa Barbara Channel
San Clemente Is.

California
Scale of Miles
0 7 14 21 28 35
© Creative Sales Corporation
N

FOR NEVADA STATE MAP SEE PAGE 54

NEVADA

ARIZONA

CALIFORNIA

MEXICO

U.S.

FOR ARIZONA STATE MAP SEE PAGES 16-17

Lone Pine, Keeler, Panamint Sprs., Stovepipe Wells, Furnace Cr. Ranch, Panamint Range, Salt Cr., Death Valley, Lowest Point in North America 282 Ft. below sea level, Nat'l., Park, Olancha, Cartago, Owens Lk., Haiwee Res., Darwin, China Lake, Naval Weapons Sta., Little Lake, Inyokern, Ridgecrest, China Lake Naval Weapons Sta., Trona, Johannesburg, Randsburg, Red Mountain, Red Rock Canyon St. Park, Cantil, California City, Mojave, Boron, North Edwards, Edwards Air Force Base, Rodgers Lake, Saddleback Butte St. Pk., Lancaster, Pearblossom, Adelanto, Hinkley, Lenwood, Barstow, Yermo, Daggett, Helendale, Oro Grande, Newberry Sprs., Victorville, Apple Valley, Hesperia, Lucerne Valley, Phelan, Wrightwood, Los Angeles, Glendora, San Bernardino Nat'l Forest, Silverwood Lake St. Rec. Area, Fawnskin, Big Bear Lake, Yucca Valley, Bullion Mtns., Twentynine Pines Marine Corps Base, Cady Mtns., Ludlow, Amboy, Essex, Goffs, Fenner, Needles, Golden Shores, Topock, Lake Havasu City, Lake Havasu State Pk.

Keeler, Panamint Sprs., 136, 190, 395, 178, 14, 58, 395, 247, 18, 138, 330, 15, 40, 31, 66

Armagosa Valley, Mercury, Indian Springs, Death Valley Jct., Pahrump, Shoshone, Tecopa, Las Vegas, North Las Vegas, Henderson, Boulder City, Goodsprings, Jean, Nelson, Willow Beach, Cottonwood Cove, Searchlight, Nipton, Baker, Mohave, Ivanpah, Cima, Nationa, Mohave Mtns., Providence, Kelso, Providence Mtns. St. Rec. Area, Laughlin, Bullhead City, Kingman, McConnico, Chloride, Yucca, Black Mtns., Mohave Lake, Temple Bar, Mesquite, Glendale, Overton, Bunkerville, Lake Mead, Lake Mead Nat'l Rec. Area, Virgin R.

Toyabe Nat'l Forest, 373, 127, 178, 161, 160, 165, 164, 93, 168, 169, 15, 95, 515, 146, 163, 68, 40

San Bernardino, Yucaipa, Morongo Valley, Joshua Tree, Twentynine Palms, Riverside, Beaumont, Banning, Cabazon, Desert Hot Sprs., Thousand Palms, Palm Sprs., Indio, Coachella, Mecca, Palm Desert, La Quinta, Salton Sea St. Rec. Area, Desert Center, Blythe, Ripley, Ehrenberg, Palo Verde, Quartzsite, Vicksburg, Parker, Parker Dam, Earp, Vidal, Poston, Rice, Desert Shores, Salton City, Borrego Sprs., Ocotillo Wells St. Vehicular Rec. Area, Niland, Calipatria, Westmorland, Brawley, Glamis, Gunnery Range, Chocolate Mtns., Cibola Nat'l Wildlife Refuge, Imperial Nat'l Wildlife Refuge, Stone Cabin, Martinez Lake, Picacho St. Rec. Area, Imperial Dam

Pomona, Ontario, Riverside, Fullerton, Anaheim, Santa Ana, Corona, Perris, Romoland, San Jacinto, Hemet, Idyllwild, Sun City, Lake Elsinore, Murrieta, Temecula, Cahuilla, Cahuilla Ind. Res., Santa Rosa Mtns., Anza-Borrego, Borrego Sprs., Ocotillo Wells, Elmore, Alamorio, Alamorio, Imperial, Seeley, El Centro, Holtville, Heber, Calexico, Mexicali, Algodones, Galeana, Somerton, Yuma, Winterhaven, Dome, Tacna, Wellton

Oceanside, Carlsbad, Carlsbad St. Beach, Leucadia, Encinitas, Del Mar, La Jolla, San Diego, Coronado, Chula Vista, Imperial Beach, Tijuana, Rosarito, Metamuco, Vista, San Marcos, Escondido, Santa Ysabel, Julian, Ramona, Poway, Santee, El Cajon, Alpine, Jamul, Pine Valley, Mt. Laguna, Campo, Boulevard, Tecate, La Rumorosa, Colonia Progreso, Hermosillo, San Luis Rio Colorado, Cleveland Nat'l Forest, Fallbrook, Camp Pendleton, Pala, Pauma Valley, Palomar Mtn., San Onofre St. Beach, San Clemente, San Juan Capistrano, Dana Pt., Lake Forest, Cabrillo Nat'l Mon., Silver Strand St. Beach, Border Field St. Park, Rancho St. Park, Barrett, Morena Res., Dulzura

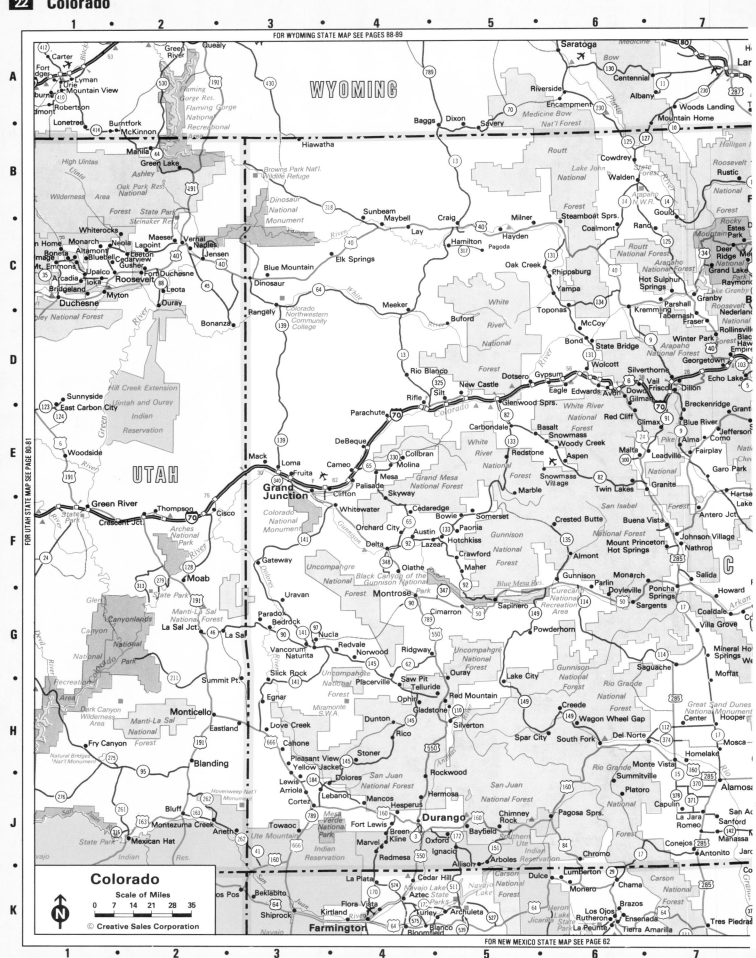

WYOMING

UTAH

Colorado

Scale of Miles

0 7 14 21 28 35

© Creative Sales Corporation

FOR WYOMING STATE MAP SEE PAGES 88-89

FOR NEBRASKA STATE MAP SEE PAGES 52-53

FOR KANSAS STATE MAP SEE PAGE 37

FOR OKLAHOMA STATE MAP SEE PAGES 68-69

NEBRASKA

KANSAS

COLORADO

NEW MEXICO

OKLA.

Grid references: 8 9 10 11 12 13 14 (top and bottom); A B C D E F G H J K (right side)

Laramie, Horse Creek, Federal, Tie Siding, Virginia Dale, The Forks Poudre Park, Bellvue, Fort Collins, Drake, Loveland, Estes Park, Pinewood Springs, Meeker Park, Lyons, Longmont, Boulder, Eldorado Springs, Westminster, Arvada, Black Hawk, Empire, Golden, Idaho Sprs., Lakewood, Englewood, Littleton, Conifer, Bailey, Shawnee, Deckers, Sedalia, Larkspur, Castle Rock, Franktown, Elizabeth, Kiowa

Cheyenne, Hillsdale, Burns, Pine Bluffs, Egbert, Carpenter, Burlington

Rockport, Nunn, Pierce, Ault, Windsor, Greeley, Eaton, Barnesville, Lucerne, Milliken, Evans, La Salle, Gilcrest, Platteville, Berthoud, Frederic, Lafayette, Brighton, Northglenn, Thornton, Commerce City, Watkins, Bennett, Strasburg, Deer Trail, Byers, Aurora, Denver, Greenwood Village, Parker, Agate

Briggsdale, Buckingham, Raymer, Stoneham, Merino, Atwood, Fleming, Sterling, Proctor, Iliff, Crook, Sedgwick, Ovid, Julesburg, Grant, Venango, Brandon, Amherst, Lamar, Holyoke, Paoli, Haxtun, Clarkville

Kimball, Dix, Potter, Bushnell, Sidney, Lodgepole, Big Springs, Brule, Ogallala, Chappell, Gurley

Horse Creek, Keystone, Sutherland, Paxton, North, Hershey, Madrid, Elsie, Grainton, Wallace, Dickens, Wellfl, Maywood, Hayes Center, Imperial, Enders, Hamlet, Champion, Wauneta, Palisade, Trenton, Stratton, Max, Benkelman, Culbertson, McCook, Haigler, Parks

Fort Morgan, Goodrich, Snyder, Brush, Weldona, Hillrose, Wiggins, Keenesburg, Roggen, Hudson, Prospect Valley, Lochbuie, Fort Lupton, Woodrow, Akron, Otis, Yuma, Eckley, Wray, Laird, Idalia, Joes, Cope, Last Chance, Lindon, Anton, Abarr, Idalia, Wheeler, St. Francis, McDonald, Bird City, Rexford, Gem, Colby, Brewster, Halford, Oakley, Winona, Russell Springs, Wallace, Leoti, Scott City

Goodland, Kanorado, Bethune, Burlington, Stratton, Vona, Seibert, Flagler, Arriba, Genoa, Limon, Hugo, Boyero, Matheson, Simla, Ramah, Calhan, Peyton, Punkin Center, Wild Horse, Firstview, Aroya, Kit Carson, Cheyenne Wells, Arapahoe, Sharon Springs

Monument, Palmer Lake, Woodland Park, Divide, Chipita Park, Manitou Sprs., Colorado Springs, Security-Widefield, Fountain, Falcon, Ellicott, Yoder, Rush, Fort Carson, Victor, Cripple Creek, Guffey, Florissant, Lake George, Hartsel, Westcreek

Canon City, Penrose, Florence, Parkdale, Royal Gorge, Texas Creek, Cotopaxi, Hillside, Wetmore, Pueblo, Pueblo West, Baxter, Boone, Olney Springs, Ordway, Crowley, Sugar City, Fort Lyon, McClave, Wiley, Lamar, Granada, Holly, Coolidge, Syracuse, Lakin, Holcomb, Deerfield, Cheney Center

Galatea, Eads, Brandon, Sheridan Lake, Towner, Tribune, Haswell, Chivington, Arlington, Bristol, Kornman, Carlton

Silver Cliff, Westcliffe, Beulah, Colorado City, Rye, Gardner, Farisita, Vineland, Avondale, Fowler, Manzanola, Rocky Ford, Cheraw, Swink, Las Animas, La Junta, Hawley, Toonerville, Two Buttes, Manter, Johnson City, Ulysses, Richfield, Moscow, Subl

Walsenburg, Pryor, La Veta, Cuchara, Aguilar, Tyrone, Model, Hoehne, Beshoar Jct., Thatcher, Timpas, Delhi, Kim, Utleyville, Pritchett, Springfield, Walsh, Vilas, Campo, Two Buttes, Lycan, Bartlett, Hugoton, Rolla

Blanca, Fort Garland, Monument Park, Stonewall, Janser, Segundo, Weston, Valdez, Trinidad, Starkville, Branson, Kenton, Sturgis, Surrey Hills, Hooker, Keyes, Eva, Four Corners, Guymon, Hardesty, Goodwell, Texhoma

San Luis, San Pablo, San Francisco, Chama, Garcia, Costilla, Amalia, Raton, Sugarite State Park, Folsom, Des Moines, Capulin, Boise City, Elkhart

Comanche National Grassland, Pike National Forest, Pawnee National Grassland, San Isabel National Forest, Kiowa National Grasslands, Cimarron Canyon

Comanche National Grassland, Two Buttes Res., Adobe Creek Res., John Martin Lake, Muddy Creek Res., Bonny Res., Flager State Wildlife Area, Ramah State W.A., Jackson Lake Res., Prewitt Res., Enders Res., Swanson Reservoir, North Sterling St. Park, Northeastern Jr. Coll., Summit Springs Battlefield, Beecher Island Battleground, Eastern Colorado Historical Society Museum, Site of Sand Creek Massacre, Otero Jr. Coll., Lake Meredith, Comanche National Grassland

Rivers: Platte River, South Platte River, Arkansas River, Republican River, Smoky Hill River, Purgatoire River, Apishapa River, Huerfano River, Cimarron River, Rio Grande

Highways: 80, 76, 70, 25, 287, 385, 40, 50, 34, 36, 24, 160, 87, 85, 6, 14, 71, 59, 86, 94, 96, 109, 350, 27, 23

1 2 3 4 5 6 7 8

FOR VERMONT STATE MAP SEE PAGE 55

FOR NEW YORK STATE MAP SEE PAGES 58-61

A B C D E F G H J K

N.H.
VT.
MASS.
N.Y.
CONN.

Long Island Sound

Troy
Albany
Rensselaer
Nassau
Stephentown
Chatham
Hudson
Hillsdale
Stanfordville
Amenia
Dover Plains
Poughquag
Pawling
Sherman
Brewster
Bedford
Cross River
Ridgefield
New Canaan
Norwalk
Darien
Stamford
Greenwich

Williamstown
North Adams
Adams
Cheshire
Pittsfield
Dalton
Hinsdale
Peru
Richmond
Lenox
West Stockbridge
Lee
Becket
West Becket
Stockbridge
Great Barrington
Monterey
Sheffield
New Marlborough
Sandisfield
Otis
Tolland
Norfolk
Colebrook
Winsted
Barkhamsted
New Hartford
North Canaan
Canaan
Salisbury
Sharon
Falls Village
Cornwall
Cornwall Bridge
Goshen
Torrington
Warren
Kent
Litchfield
Harwinton
Burlington
Farmington
Plymouth
Bristol
Morris
Bethlehem
Thomaston
Watertown
Washington
New Milford
Woodbury
Southbury
Brookfield
New Fairfield
Danbury
Bethel
Newtown
Monroe
Redding
Georgetown
Ridgefield
Salem Ctr.
Wilton
Weston
Westport
Fairfield
Bridgeport
Stratford
Milford
Trumbull
Shelton
Derby
Ansonia
Seymour
Oxford
Naugatuck
Waterbury
Southington
Cheshire
Wallingford
Hamden
Woodbridge
North Haven
New Haven
West Haven
East Haven
Branford
North Branford
Guilford
Madison
Clinton
Westbrook
Old Saybrook
Old Lyme

Pownal
Clarksburg
Berlin
Cherry Plain
Savoy
Windsor
Buckland
Hawley
Plainfield
Ashfield
Conway
Cummington
Worthington Ctr.
Chesterfield
Williamsburg
Whately
Hatfield
Northampton
Westhampton
Easthampton
Huntington
Russell
Montgomery
Blandford
Westfield
West Springfield
Agawam
Granville
Hartland
East Hartland
Granby
East Granby
Simsbury
Canton
Bloomfield
Avon
West Hartford
Hartford
Wethersfield
Newington
Rocky Hill
New Britain
Berlin
Cromwell
Middletown
Middlefield
Durham
Haddam
Killingworth
Essex
Deep River
Chester
Clinton
Old Lyme

Wilmington
Whitingham
Stamford
Readsboro
Florida
Charlemont
Shelburne Falls
Shelburne
Greenfield
Deerfield
Montague
Sunderland
Leverett
Amherst
Hadley
South Hadley
Belchertown
Granby
Holyoke
Chicopee
Springfield
Longmeadow
East Longmeadow
Hampden
Wales
Holland
Somers
Stafford
Enfield
Windsor Locks
Melrose
Ellington
Tolland
Vernon
Windsor
South Windsor
Manchester
East Hartford
Glastonbury
Andover
Coventry
Columbia
Hebron
Marlborough
East Hampton
Colchester
Salem
Bozrah
Norwich
Preston City
Ledyard Ctr.
New London
Waterford
Groton
Stonington
Mystic
Pawca...

Guilford
Leyden
Colrain
Heath
Bernardston
Gill
Northfield
Warwick
Orange
Athol
Millers Falls
Wendell
Petersham
Barre
Rutland
Hardwick
Ware
West Brookfield
North Brookfield
Brookfield
Warren
Palmer
Brimfield
Sturbridge
Southbridge
Dudley
Webster
Woodstock
Eastford
Ashford
Willington
Storrs
Chaplin
Hampton
Brooklyn
Canterbury
Scotland
Windham
Lebanon
Franklin
Jewett City
Hopeville
Voluntown
North Stonington

Swanzey
Troy
Winchester
Fitzwilliam
Royalston
Winchendon
Baldwinville
Gardner
Templeton
Westminster
Leominster
Princeton
West Boylston
Holden
Worcester
Leicester
Spencer
Oxford
Charlton
Southbridge
Auburn
Putnam
Pomfret
Killingly
Dayville
Sterling
Plainfield
Hopeville

Peterborough
Jaffrey
Rindge
Greenville
Ashby
Ashburnham
Fitchburg
Greenport
Southold
Shelter Island
Gardiners Island
Peconic
Montauk
Fishers Island

I-87 I-90 I-91 I-84 I-95 I-291 I-391 I-395 I-691

Connecticut
Massachusetts
Rhode Island

Scale of Miles
0   3   6   9   12   15

© Creative Sales Corporation

Florida
Scale of Miles
© Creative Sales Corporation
0 7 14 21 28 35

N

FOR GEORGIA STATE MAP SEE PAGES 28-29

Atlantic

Ocean

Gulf

of

Mexico

GEORGIA

Donalsonville
Bainbridge
Cairo
Thomasville
Quitman
Valdosta
Lakeland
Homerville
Okefenokee Nat'l Wildlife Refuge
Folkston
Kingsland
Saint Marys
Fernandina Beach
Hilliard
Callahan
Jacksonville
Atlantic Beach
Neptune Beach
Jacksonville Beach
St. Augustine
St. Augustine Beach
Baldwin
Orange Park
Green Cove Springs
Keystone Heights
Hastings
East Palatka
Palatka
Crescent City
Bunnell
Flagler Beach
Ormond By The Sea
Ormond Beach
Daytona Beach
Port Orange
New Smyrna Beach
Edgewater
Mims
Titusville
Cape Canaveral
Merritt Island
Cocoa Beach
Satellite Beach
Indian Harbour Beach
Melbourne
Palm Bay
Rockledge
Cocoa
W. Melbourne
Fellsmere
Sebastian
Gifford
Vero Beach
Yeehaw Junction

Tallahassee
Havana
Quincy
Gretna
Chattahoochee
Bloxham
Crawfordville
Sopchoppy
Carrabelle
Woodville
Lloyd
Monticello
Lamont
Perry
Greenville
Madison
Jasper
Live Oak
Lake City
White Springs
Day
Mayo
Branford
Old Town
Cross City
Suwanee
Cedar Key
Chiefland
Trenton
Bell
Fort White
High Springs
Alachua
Archer
Williston
Trenton
Reddick
Gainesville
Hawthorne
Micanopy
Ocala
Belleview
Dunnellon
Inverness
Crystal River
Homosassa Springs
Brooksville
Dade City
Bushnell
Wildwood
Leesburg
Eustis
Umatilla
DeLand
DeLeon Springs
DeBary
Deltona
Sanford
Winter Springs
Casselberry
Winter Park
Apopka
Mt. Dora
Orlando
Winter Garden
Lake Buena Vista
St. Cloud
Kissimmee
Haines City
Winter Haven
Lakeland
Plant City
Temple Terrace
Tampa
Brandon
Riverview
Bartow
Fort Meade
Frostproof
Avon Park
Lake Wales
Waverly
Zephyrhills
Dade City
Hudson
New Port Richey
Tarpon Springs
Dunedin
Clearwater
Largo
Treasure Island
St. Petersburg
St. Petersburg Beach
Sun City Center
Pembroke
Ocala Nat'l Forest

Okefenokee Nat'l Wildlife Refuge
Osceola Nat'l Forest
Steinhatchee W.M.A.

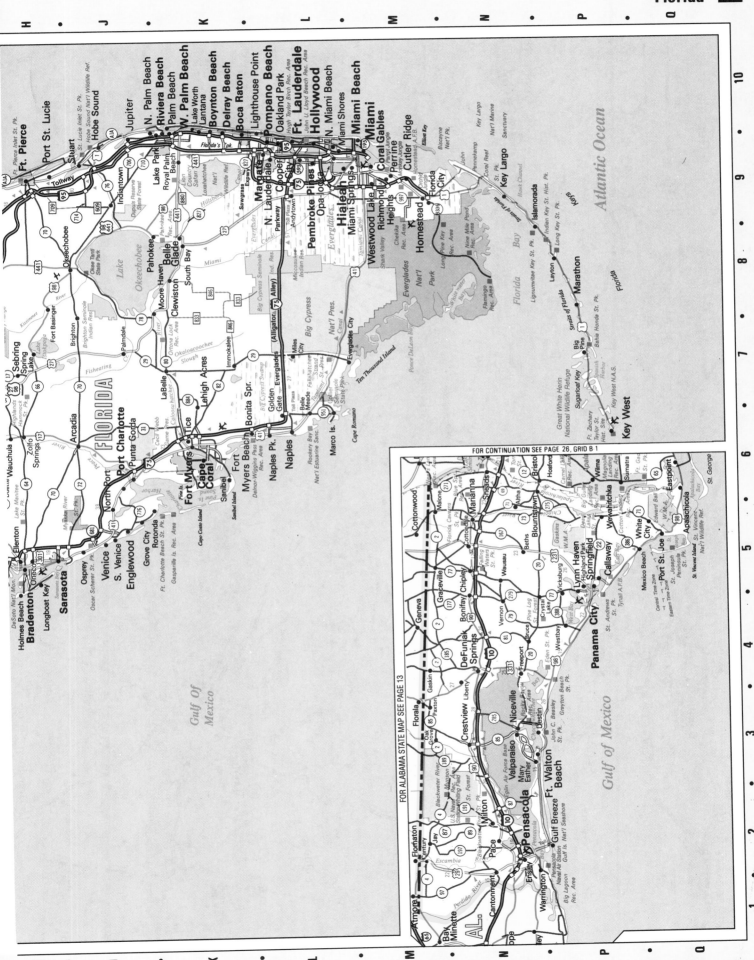

FOR CONTINUATION SEE PAGE 26, GRID B-1

FOR ALABAMA STATE MAP SEE PAGE 13

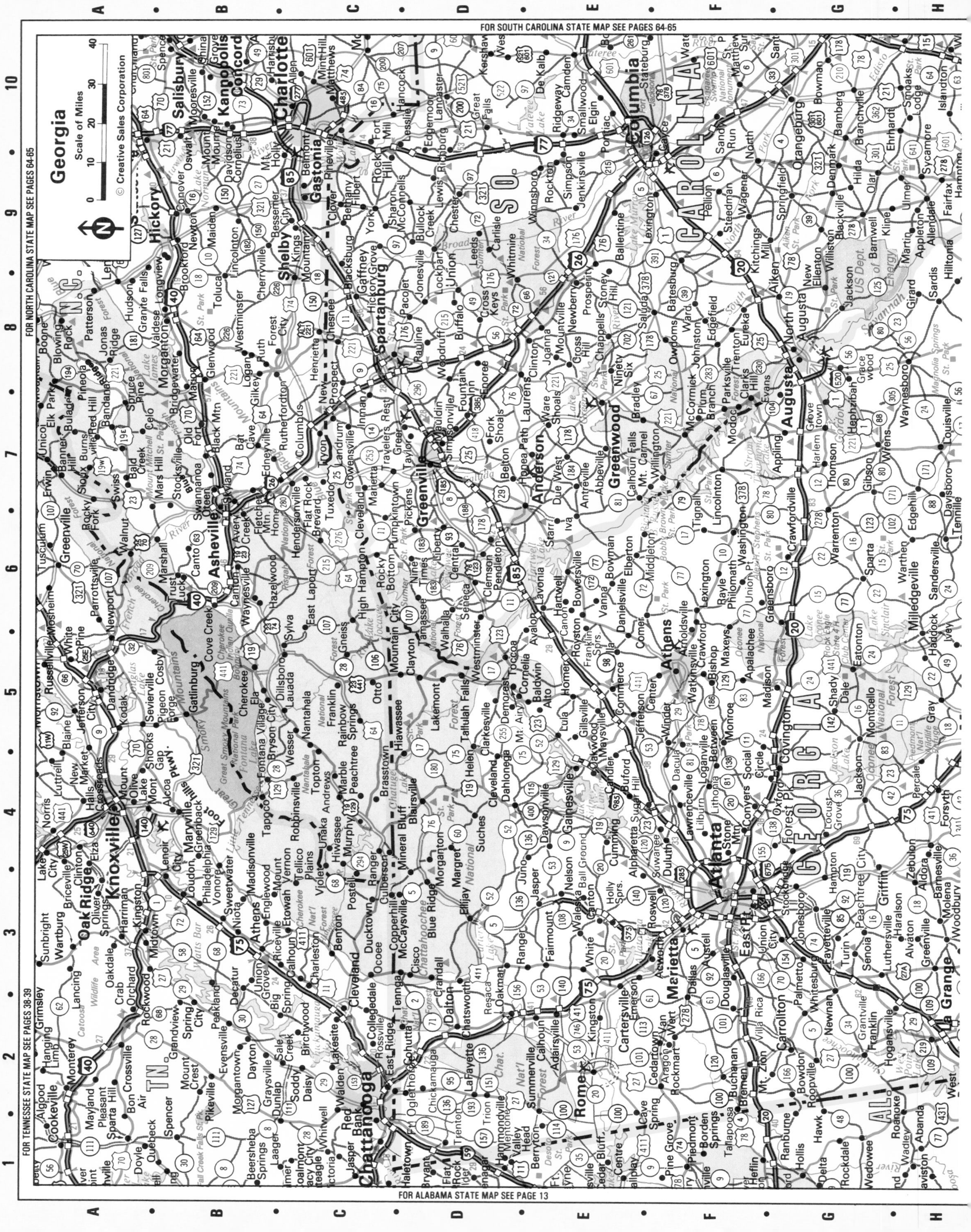

Georgia
Scale of Miles
0 10 20 30 40
© Creative Sales Corporation
FOR SOUTH CAROLINA STATE MAP SEE PAGES 64-65
FOR NORTH CAROLINA STATE MAP SEE PAGES 64-65
FOR TENNESSEE STATE MAP SEE PAGES 38-39
FOR ALABAMA STATE MAP SEE PAGE 13
Atlanta
Chattanooga
Knoxville
Asheville
Charlotte
Columbia
Augusta
Athens
Greenville
Spartanburg
Greenwood
Anderson
Gastonia
Hickory
Shelby
Salisbury
Kannapolis
Concord
Oak Ridge
Rome
Marietta
Dalton
La Grange
GEORGIA
CAROLINA
TN
AL

FOR FLORIDA STATE MAP SEE PAGES 26-27

FOR ALABAMA STATE MAP SEE PAGE 13

Hawaii

Scale of Miles

0 4 8 12 16 20

© Creative Sales Corporation

N

Maui

Nakalele Pt.
Honokahua
Lahaina
30
Honokahua
Kahakuloa Pt.
Waihee Pt.
Waihee
Kahului
Kahului Bay
Kaanapali
Puuwai
Pauwela Pt.
Puuwela
Paia
Spreckelsville
36
Puunene
311
Kihei
30
Waikapu
Wailuku
Maalaea
Olowalu
Heikli Pt.
Maalaea Bay
Kamaole Beach Park
Waiea
31
Makena
Iao Valley
Puukolii
Makawao
377
378
37
Haleakala Nat'l Park
Haleakala Crater
Keokea
Ulupalakua
Keonecio
Cape Hanamanioa
Nukuele Pt.
Pukauila Pt.
Kailua
Wailua
360
Kalahu Pt.
Hana
Waananapanapa St. Pk.
Muolea Pt.
Kipahulu
Kaupo
Apole Pt.
Alenuihaha Channel

Pacific Ocean

0 2 4 Miles

Molokai

Ilio Pt.
Lamaloa Head
Halawa
Cape Halawa
Mauna Loa
460
Kolo
Kahu Pt.
Makanalua Pen.
Kalaupapa
Kalae
Kualapuu
Kaunakakai
Kamiloloa
Kalae
Kikipua Pt.
450
Kamalo
Ualapue
Pukoo
Waialua
Pauwalu
Laau Pt.
Kaholi Channel
Pailolo Channel

Pacific Ocean

0 2 4 Miles

Kauai

Haena Pt.
Haena
Kalalau
56
Anahola
Lihue
50
Waimea
Mana
Kauai Channel

Niihau (Private)

Puuwai

Pacific Ocean

HAWAII

Kaiwi Channel

Honolulu Co.
Maui Co.

Kauai Co.
Honolulu Co.

Oahu

Kahuku
83
Kahana
Kaneohe
Kailua
H1
Waikiki
Pearl City
H2
Honolulu
Haleiwa
Makaha
Nanakuli

Pacific Ocean

Molokai

Halawa
450
Kamalo
Kaunakakai
Mauna Loa
460
Kualapuu

Lanai

Kualapuu
450
Kaumalapau
Koele
Lanai City
Keomuku
460
Mauna Loa

Maui

Halawa
Honokahua
Kahului
36
37
Lahaina
30
31
Ulupalakua
Hana
360
Haleakala Nat'l Park

Kahoolawe

Auau Channel
Kealaikahiki Channel
Kaka Pt.

Maui Co.
Hawaii Co.

Alenuihaha Channel

Hawaii

Upolu Pt.
Hawi
250
Niulii
Mahukona
270
Waiaka
Waimea
Kawaihae
Puako
190
Kalaoa
19
Keahole Pt.
Kailua
Keauhou
Napoopoo
Captain Cook
Honaunau
Honalo
Kainaliu
Keokea
Hookena
Papa
Milolii
Hoopuloa
11
Kauna Pt.
Hanamalo Pt.
Waiohinu
Waiahukini
Kaalualu
Ka Lae
Naalehu
Pahala
Honuapo
Kaaluaiu
11
Hawaii Volcanoes National Park
Punaluu Black Sands
Apua Pt.
Keaau
130
Pahoa
Kaimu
Kalapana
Black Sands Beach
Kurtistown
Mountain View
Glenwood
200
Keaau
Hilo
Rainbow Falls
Papaikou
Pepeekeo
Honomu
Hakalau
Honohina
Keaau
19
Ookala
Papaaloa
Paauilo
Honokaa
Kukuihaele
Waiakea
Paauhau
Pepeekeo Pt.
Mauna Kea 13,796 ft.
Mauna Loa 13,680 ft.
Waiakea
Pohoiki
Opihikao
Kalapana

Hawaii

Oahu

Kahuku Pt.
Kahuku
Laie
Hauula
Kahana
Kahana Bay
Sacred Falls
Punaluu
Kualoa Pt.
Kaneohe Bay
Mokapu Pt.
Kaneohe Marine Air Station
H3
Kaneohe
Waimanalo
72
Kailua
Makapuu Pt.
Makapuu Beach Park
Sea Life Park
Koko Head
Koko Head Park
Hawaii Kai
Diamond Head
Waikiki
92
Honolulu
H1
61
63
78
Aiea
99
Pearl City
Waipahu
H2
99
Wahiawa
Schofield Barracks
Mililani Town
750
Ewa
Makakilo City
Barbers Pt.
95
Kapolei
Waipio
Nanakuli
Maili
Waianae
780
Makaha
93
930
Dillingham Air Force Base
Kaena Pt.
Kahuku Pt.
Sunset Beach
Waialua
83
Haleiwa
Kaneohe
Pali Lookout
Puu Ualakaa
Waianae Range
Koolau Range
Kapuhi Pt.

Kauai Channel

Pacific Ocean

0 2 4 Miles

Kauai

Haena Pt.
Haena
Kalalau
Makaha Pt.
56
Kilauea
Hanalei
Moloaa
Anahola
Keelia
Kapaa
Wailua
56
580
583
Hanamaulu
Lihue
Lihue Airport
Nawiliwili
Ninini Pt.
50
Puhi
Koloa
Lawai
Kalaheo
Eleele
Port Allen
Hanapepe
Kaumakani
550
Waimea
Kekaha
Mana
Kokee State Park
Waimea Canyon
Mt. Waialeale 5,148 ft.
Makahuena Pt.
Koheo Pt.

Pacific Ocean

0 2 4 Miles

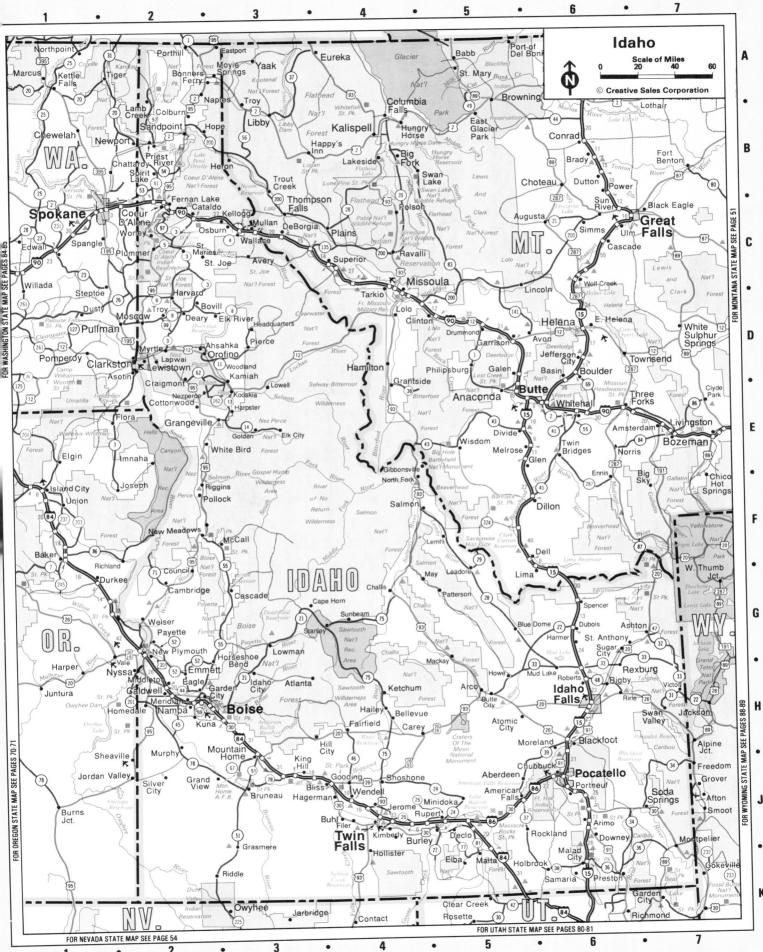

Idaho

Scale of Miles
0 20 40 60

© Creative Sales Corporation

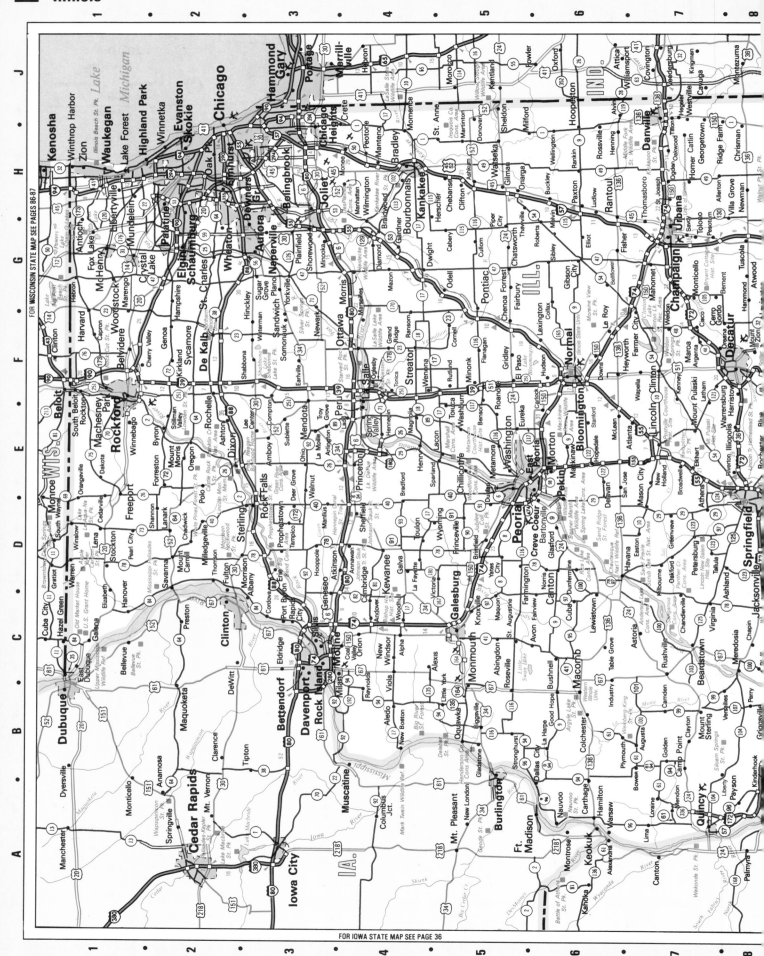

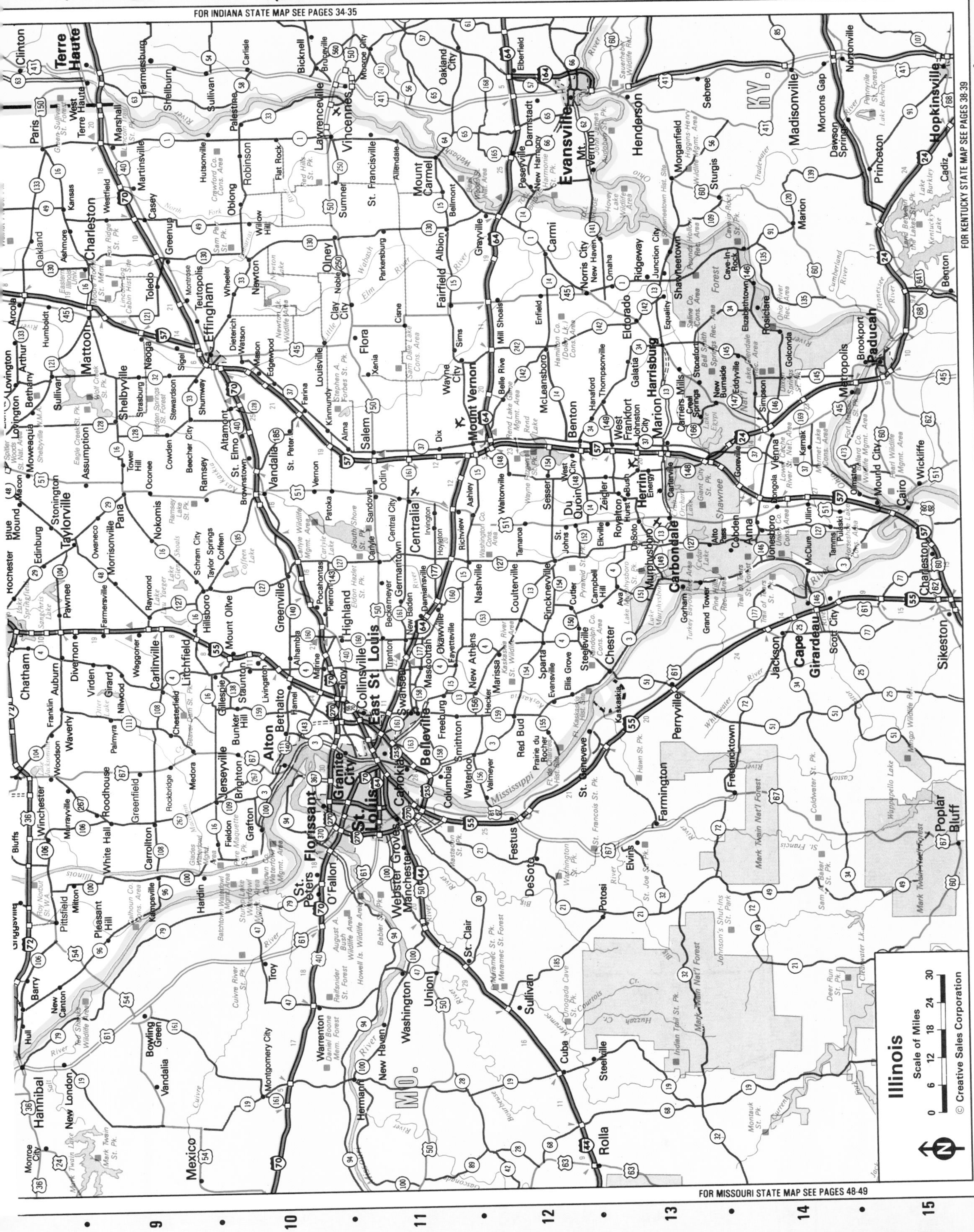

FOR INDIANA STATE MAP SEE PAGES 34-35
FOR KENTUCKY STATE MAP SEE PAGES 38-39
FOR MISSOURI STATE MAP SEE PAGES 48-49
Illinois
Scale of Miles
0 6 12 18 24 30
© Creative Sales Corporation
Terre Haute
Vincennes
Evansville
Henderson
Madisonville
Hopkinsville
Paducah
Effingham
Mattoon
Charleston
Olney
Centralia
Mount Vernon
Carbondale
Marion
Harrisburg
Belleville
East St. Louis
St. Louis
Alton
Cape Girardeau
Poplar Bluff
Hannibal
Mexico
Rolla
Washington
Farmington
Sikeston
Cairo
Metropolis
KY.
MO.

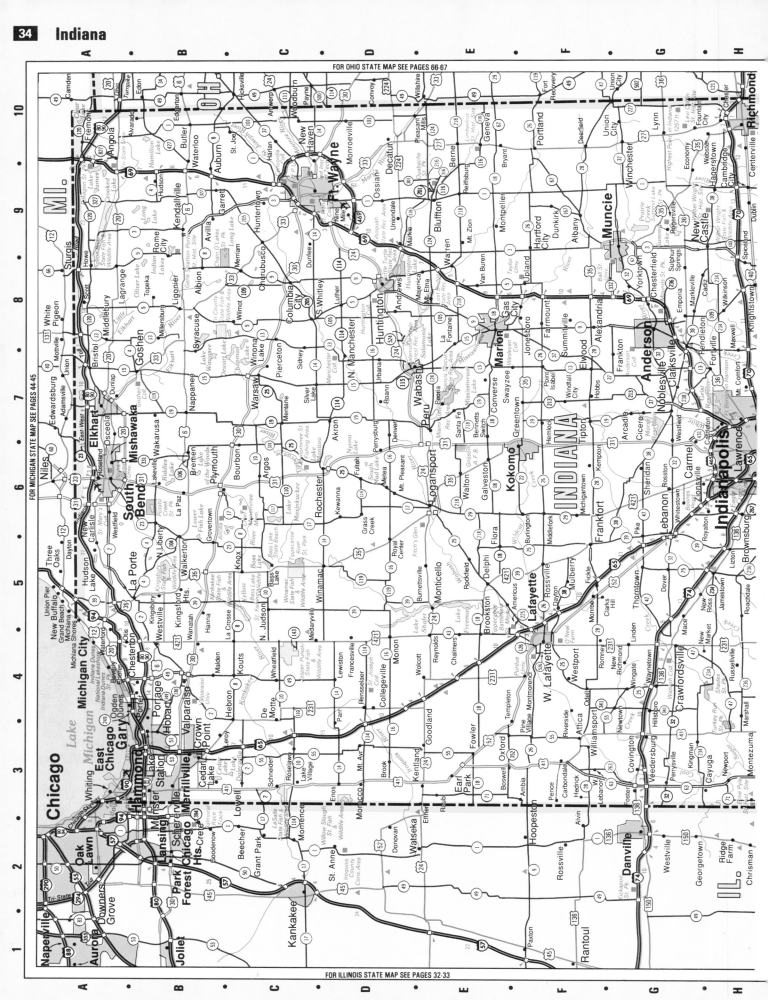

FOR OHIO STATE MAP SEE PAGES 66-67

FOR MICHIGAN STATE MAP SEE PAGES 44-45

FOR ILLINOIS STATE MAP SEE PAGES 32-33

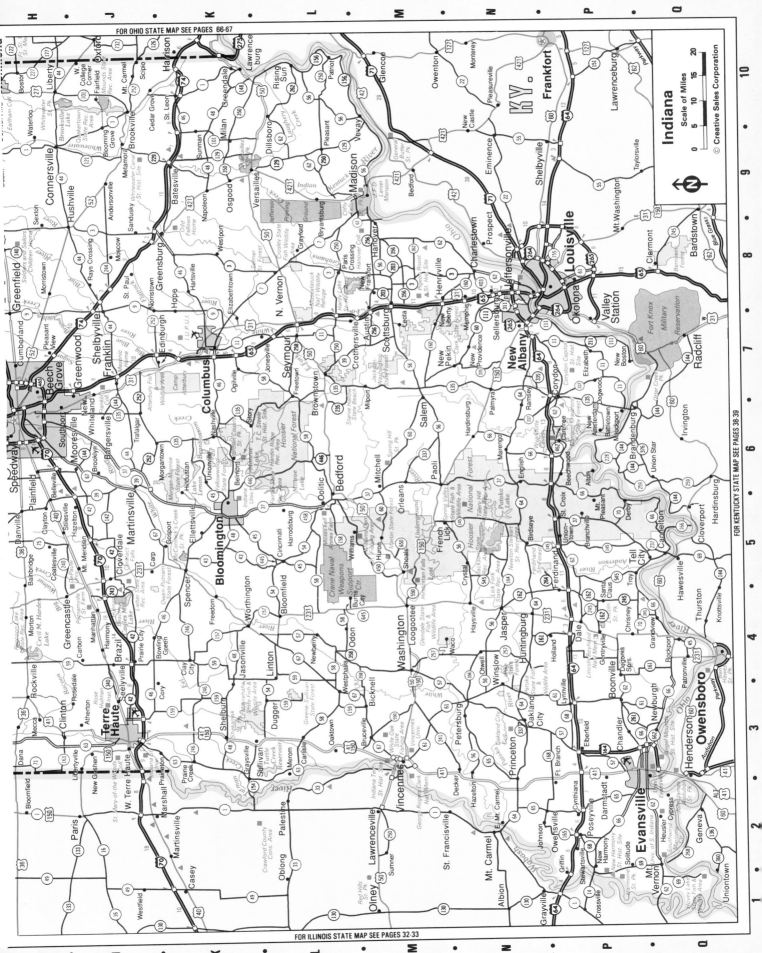

Indiana

Scale of Miles

© Creative Sales Corporation

KY. Frankfort

FOR KENTUCKY STATE MAP SEE PAGES 38-39

FOR WISCONSIN STATE MAP SEE PAGES 86-87
FOR ILLINOIS STATE MAP SEE PAGES 32-33
FOR MINNESOTA STATE MAP SEE PAGES 46-47
FOR MISSOURI STATE MAP SEE PAGES 48-49
FOR SOUTH DAKOTA STATE MAP SEE PAGE 74
FOR NEBRASKA STATE MAP SEE PAGES 52-53

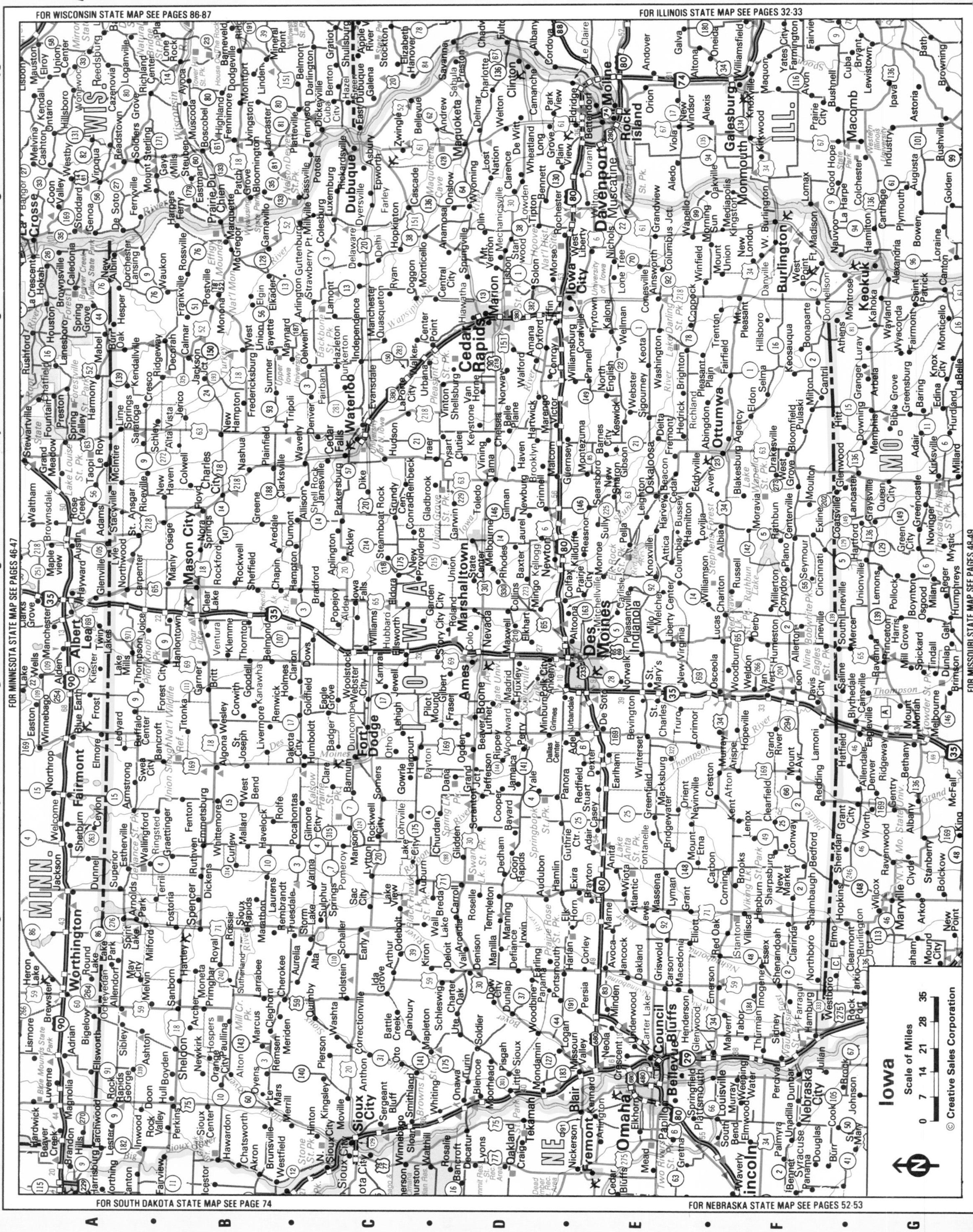

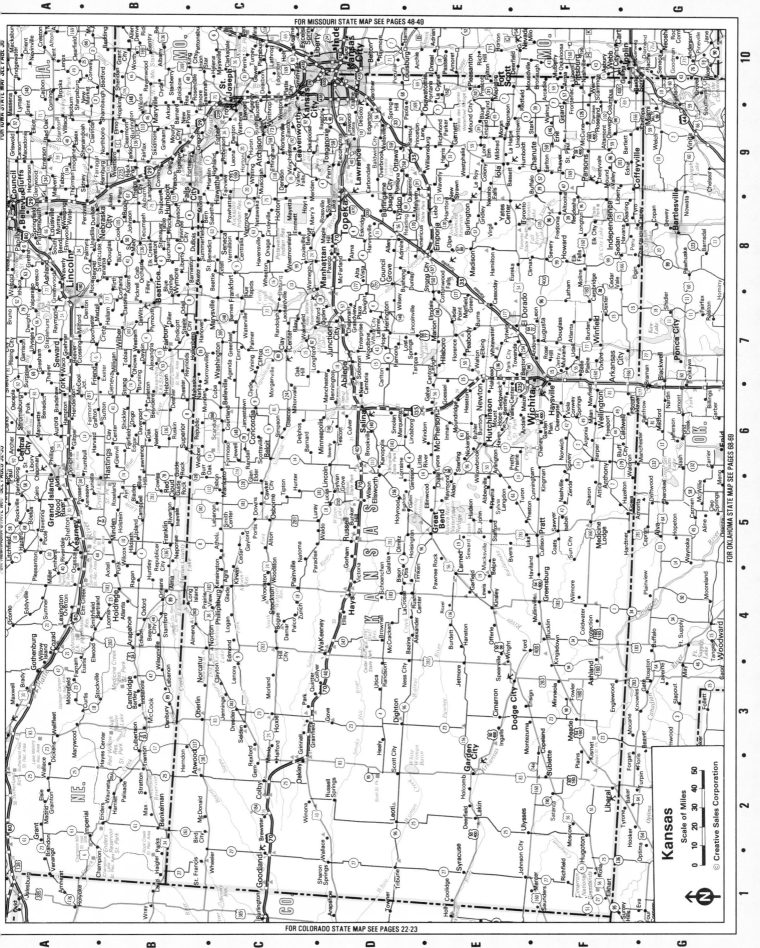

FOR OKLAHOMA STATE MAP SEE PAGES 68-69

Kansas

Scale of Miles

0   10   20   30   40   50

© Creative Sales Corporation

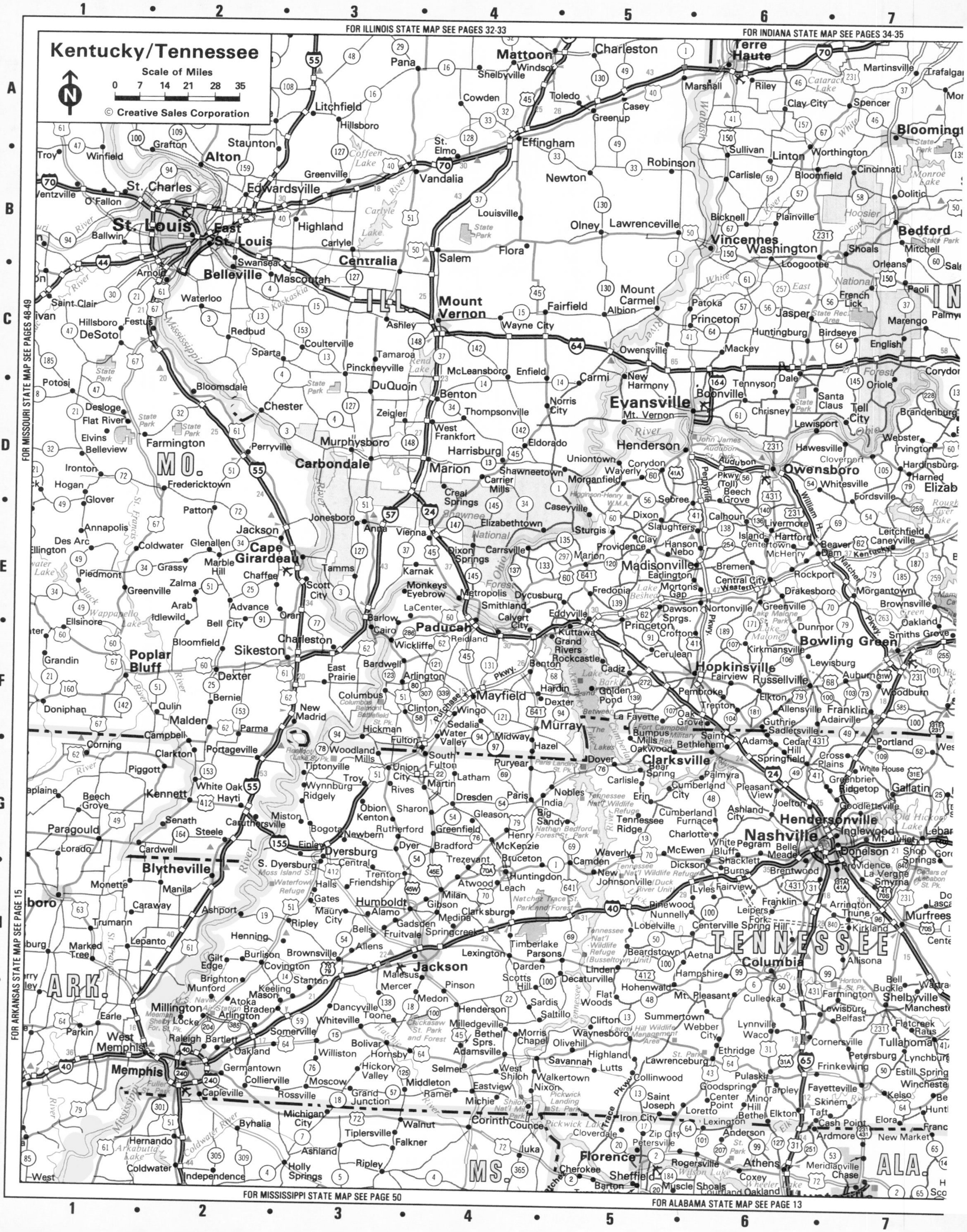

Kentucky/Tennessee

Scale of Miles

0 7 14 21 28 35

© Creative Sales Corporation

N

FOR ILLINOIS STATE MAP SEE PAGES 32-33
FOR INDIANA STATE MAP SEE PAGES 34-35
FOR MISSOURI STATE MAP SEE PAGES 48-49
FOR ARKANSAS STATE MAP SEE PAGE 15
FOR MISSISSIPPI STATE MAP SEE PAGE 50
FOR ALABAMA STATE MAP SEE PAGE 13

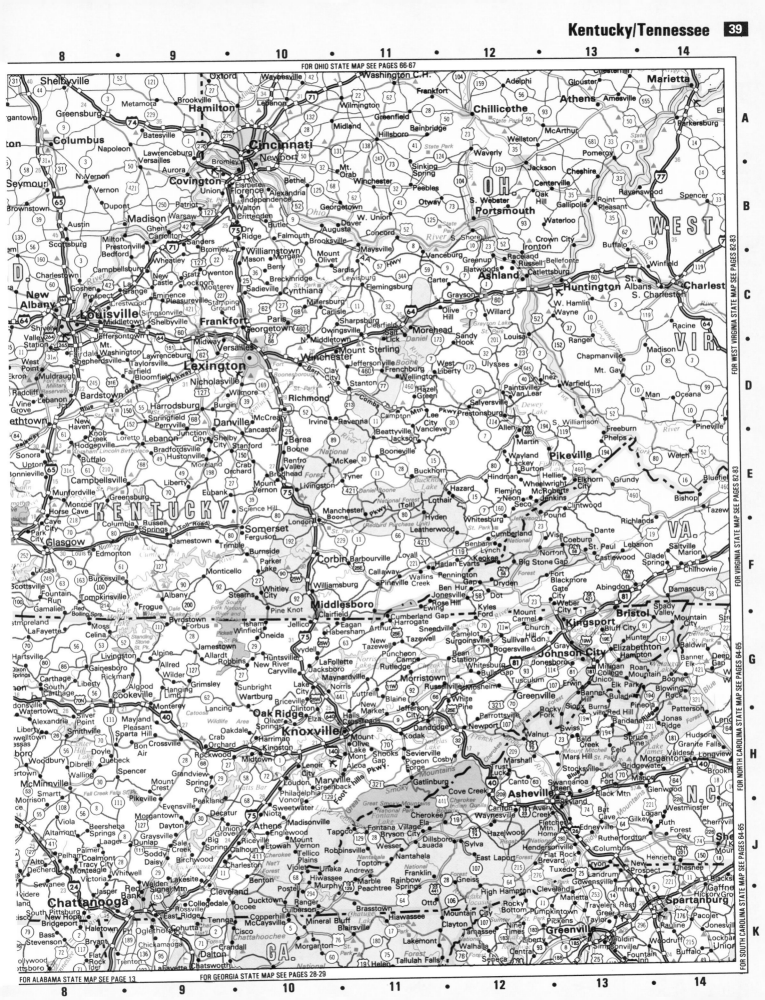

FOR OHIO STATE MAP SEE PAGES 66-67

FOR WEST VIRGINIA STATE MAP SEE PAGES 82-83

FOR VIRGINIA STATE MAP SEE PAGES 82-83

FOR NORTH CAROLINA STATE MAP SEE PAGES 64-65

FOR SOUTH CAROLINA STATE MAP SEE PAGES 64-65

FOR ALABAMA STATE MAP SEE PAGE 13

FOR GEORGIA STATE MAP SEE PAGES 28-29

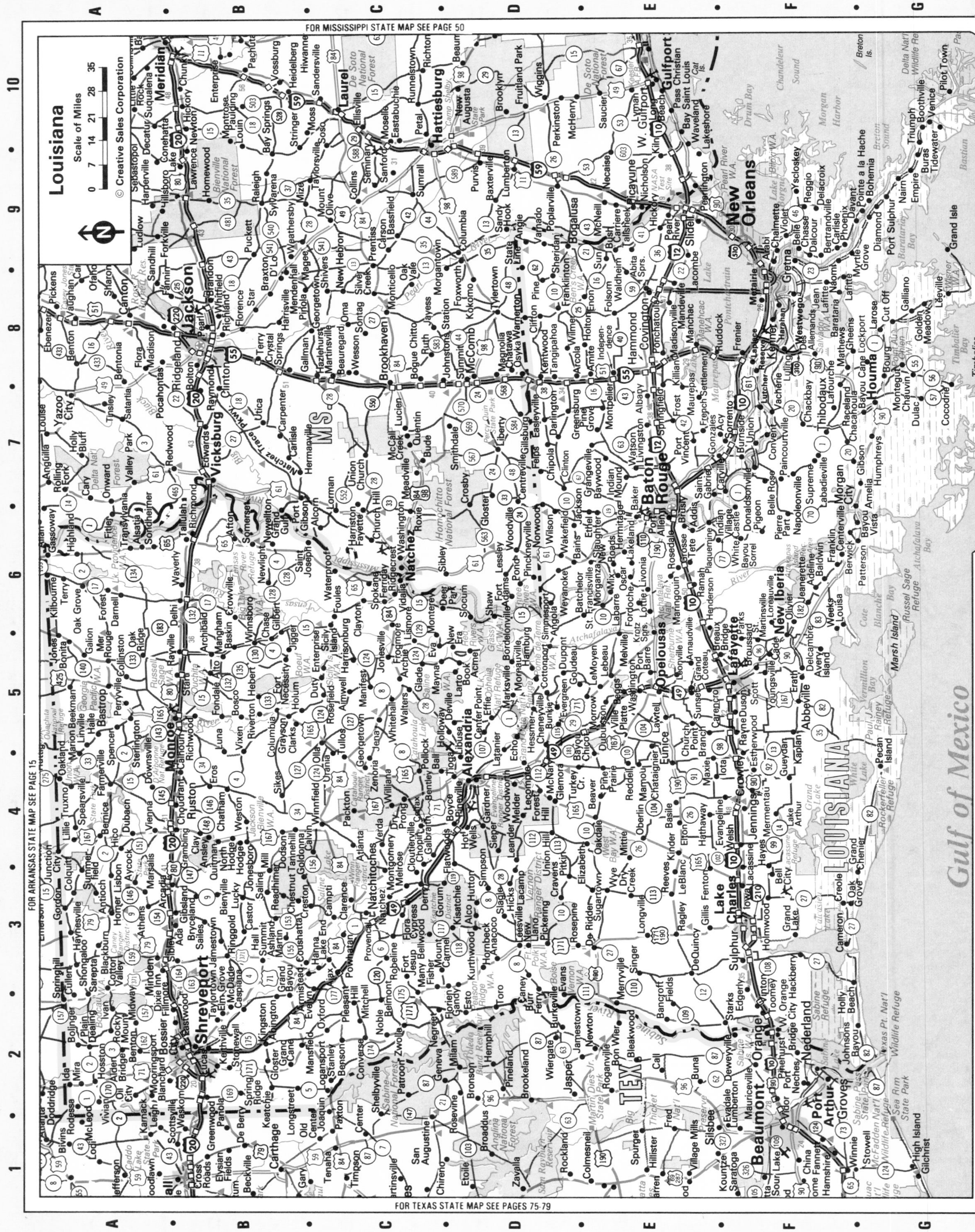

FOR MISSISSIPPI STATE MAP SEE PAGE 50

Louisiana

Scale of Miles

0 7 14 21 28 35

© Creative Sales Corporation

FOR ARKANSAS STATE MAP SEE PAGE 15

Gulf of Mexico

FOR TEXAS STATE MAP SEE PAGES 75-79

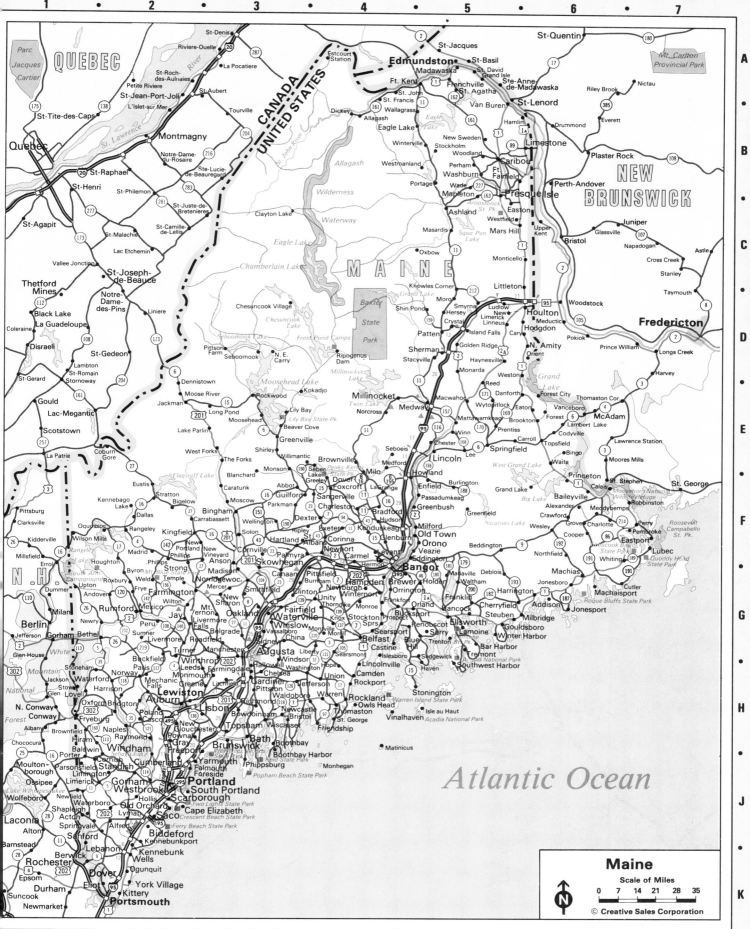

Maine
Scale of Miles
0 7 14 21 28 35
© Creative Sales Corporation

Atlantic Ocean

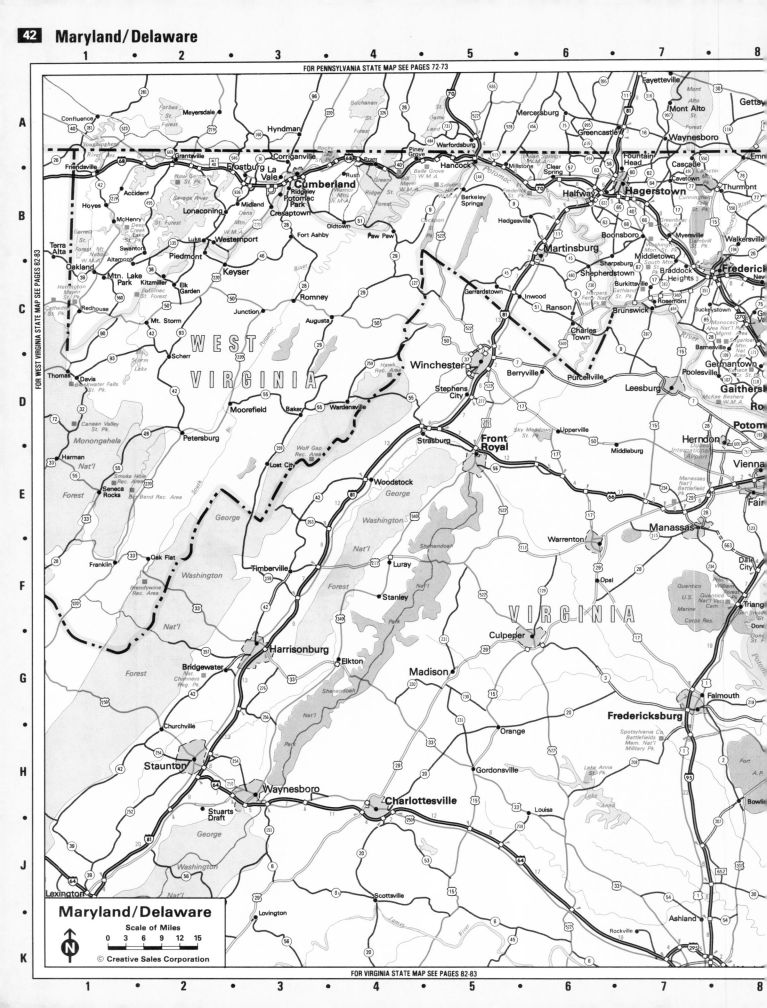

FOR PENNSYLVANIA STATE MAP SEE PAGES 72-73

FOR WEST VIRGINIA STATE MAP SEE PAGES 82-83

Maryland/Delaware

Scale of Miles

0 3 6 9 12 15

N

© Creative Sales Corporation

WEST VIRGINIA

VIRGINIA

FOR VIRGINIA STATE MAP SEE PAGES 82-83

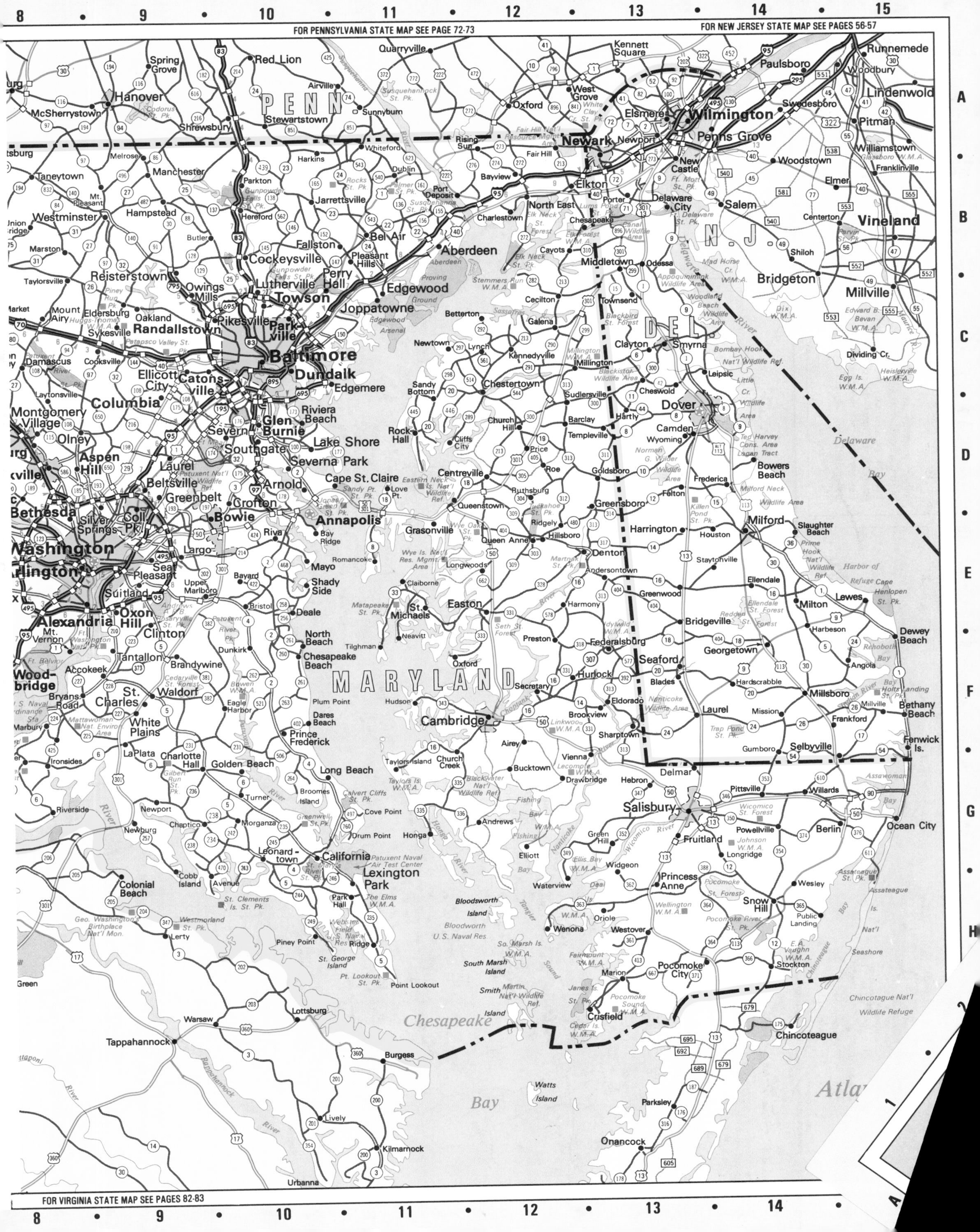

8
9
10
11
12
13
14
15
FOR PENNSYLVANIA STATE MAP SEE PAGE 72-73
FOR NEW JERSEY STATE MAP SEE PAGES 56-57
A
B
C
D
E
F
G
H
PENN
N. J.
DEL
MARYLAND
Red Lion
Spring Grove
Hanover
McSherrystown
Shrewsbury
Stewartstown
Quarryville
Airville
Sunnyburn
Kennett Square
West Grove
Oxford
Newark
Newport
Elsmere
Wilmington
Penns Grove
Paulsboro
Runnemede
Woodbury
Lindenwold
Swedesboro
Pitman
Williamstown
Woodstown
Franklinville
Elmer
Salem
Vineland
Centerton
Shiloh
Bridgeton
Millville
Dividing Cr.
Taneytown
Westminster
Manchester
Hampstead
Parkton
Hereford
Jarrettsville
Harkins
Whiteford
Dublin
Rising Sun
Fair Hill
Bayview
Elkton
North East
Charlestown
Port Deposit
Chesapeake City
Delaware City
New Castle
Porter
Bel Air
Fallston
Pleasant Hills
Aberdeen
Cockeysville
Reisterstown
Owings Mills
Lutherville
Towson
Perry Hall
Edgewood
Joppatowne
Pikesville
Parkville
Randallstown
Eldersburg
Mount Airy
Sykesville
Oakland
Baltimore
Dundalk
Edgemere
Ellicott City
Catonsville
Columbia
Damascus
Montgomery Village
Olney
Aspen Hill
Laurel
Beltsville
Greenbelt
Bowie
Crofton
Arnold
Severna Park
Severn
Southgate
Glen Burnie
Lake Shore
Riviera Beach
Bethesda
Silver Springs
Coll. Pk.
Washington
Arlington
Largo
Seat Pleasant
Suitland
Upper Marlboro
Alexandria
Oxon Hill
Mt. Vernon
Clinton
Tantallon
Brandywine
Accokeek
Woodbridge
Bryans Road
St. Charles
Waldorf
White Plains
LaPlata
Charlotte Hall
Ironsides
Riverside
Newport
Newburg
Chaptico
Morganza
Colonial Beach
Cobb Island
Avenue
Leonard-town
California
Lexington Park
Park Hall
Ridge
Piney Point
St. George Island
Point Lookout
Annapolis
Cape St. Claire
Riva
Mayo
Shady Side
Deale
North Beach
Chesapeake Beach
Dunkirk
Prince Frederick
Dares Beach
Long Beach
Golden Beach
Cove Point
Drum Point
Broomes Island
Cecilton
Galena
Betterton
Middletown
Odessa
Townsend
Clayton
Smyrna
Leipsic
Millington
Kennedyville
Chestertown
Newtown
Lynch
Sudlersville
Cheswold
Dover
Hartly
Barclay
Templeville
Camden
Wyoming
Church Hill
Rock Hall
Cliffs City
Price
Roe
Goldsboro
Centreville
Queenstown
Ruthsburg
Greensboro
Frederica
Felton
Bowers Beach
Grasonville
Queen Anne
Hillsboro
Ridgely
Harrington
Milford
Slaughter Beach
Houston
Denton
Staytonville
Ellendale
Claiborne
St. Michaels
Easton
Tilghman
Neavitt
Oxford
Preston
Federalsburg
Harmony
Andersontown
Greenwood
Bridgeville
Milton
Lewes
Harbeson
Georgetown
Seaford
Blades
Dewey Beach
Angola
Hurlock
Secretary
Eldorado
Hardscrabble
Millsboro
Cambridge
Brookview
Sharptown
Laurel
Mission
Frankford
Bethany Beach
Millville
Fenwick Is.
Selbyville
Gumboro
Delmar
Hudson
Taylors Island
Church Creek
Airey
Vienna
Bucktown
Drawbridge
Hebron
Pittsville
Willards
Salisbury
Fruitland
Powellville
Berlin
Ocean City
Andrews
Honga
Elliott
Green Hill
Widgeon
Princess Anne
Wesley
Snow Hill
Waterview
Wenona
Oriole
Westover
Public Landing
Pocomoke City
Marion
Stockton
Crisfield
Chincoteague
Bloodsworth Island
South Marsh Island
Smith Island
Chesapeake Bay
Warsaw
Lottsburg
Tappahannock
Burgess
Lively
Kilmarnock
Urbanna
Watts Island
Parksley
Onancock
Green
Atla
Delaware Bay
FOR VIRGINIA STATE MAP SEE PAGES 82-83

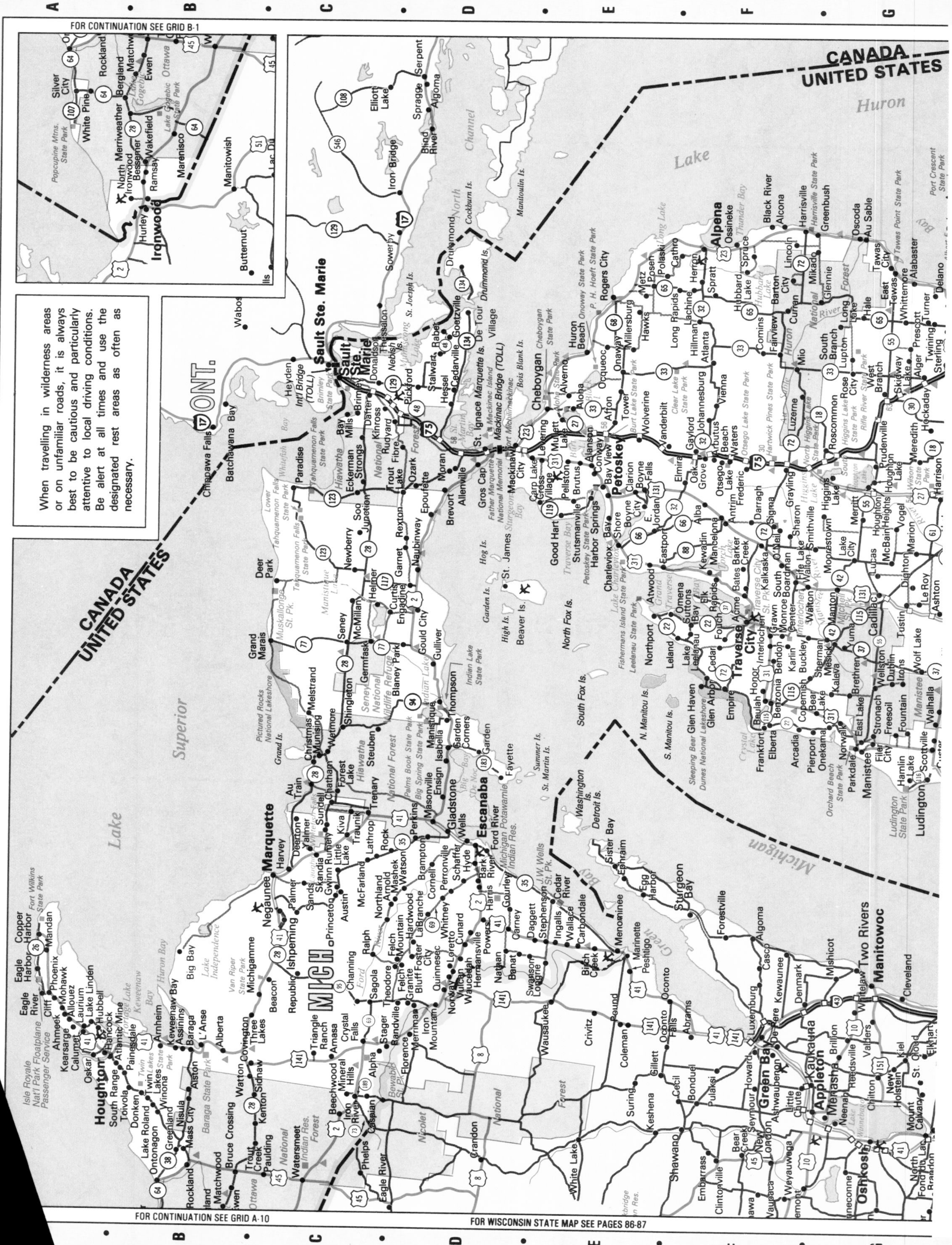

FOR CONTINUATION SEE GRID B-1

When travelling in wilderness areas or on unfamiliar roads, it is always best to be cautious and particularly attentive to local driving conditions. Be alert at all times and use the designated rest areas as often as necessary.

CANADA
UNITED STATES

ONT.

Sault Ste. Marie

Lake Superior

Lake Huron

Lake Michigan

Ironwood

Houghton

Marquette

Negaunee

Escanaba

Traverse City

Petoskey

Cheboygan

Alpena

Oscoda

Cadillac

Manistee

Ludington

Manitowoc

Green Bay

Appleton

Oshkosh

MICH

FOR CONTINUATION SEE GRID A-10

FOR WISCONSIN STATE MAP SEE PAGES 86-87

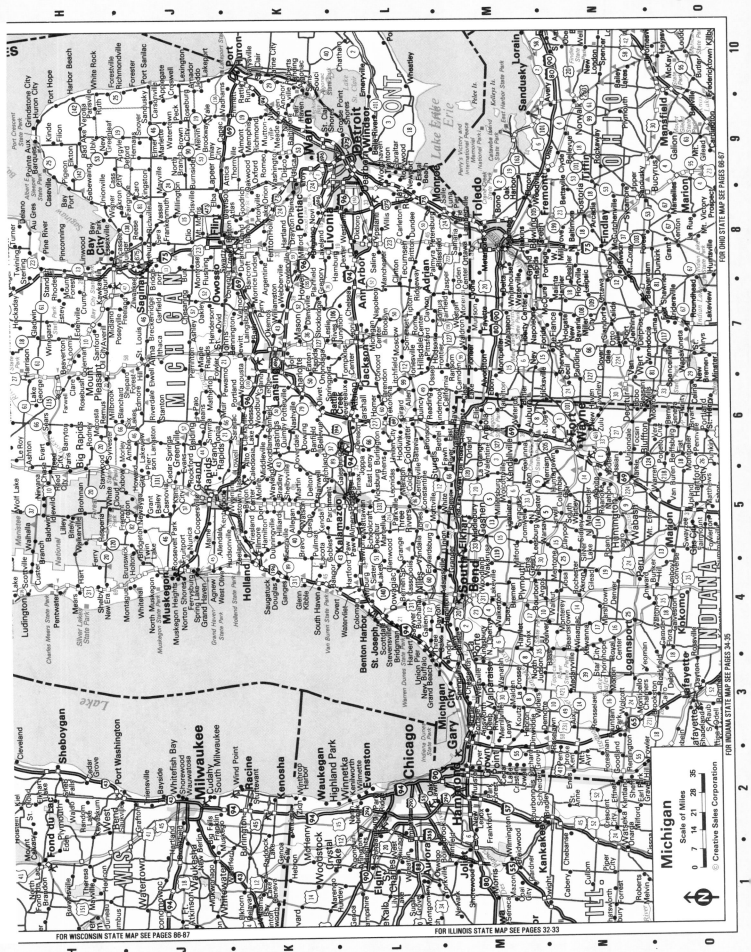

Michigan

Scale of Miles

0 7 14 21 28 35

© Creative Sales Corporation

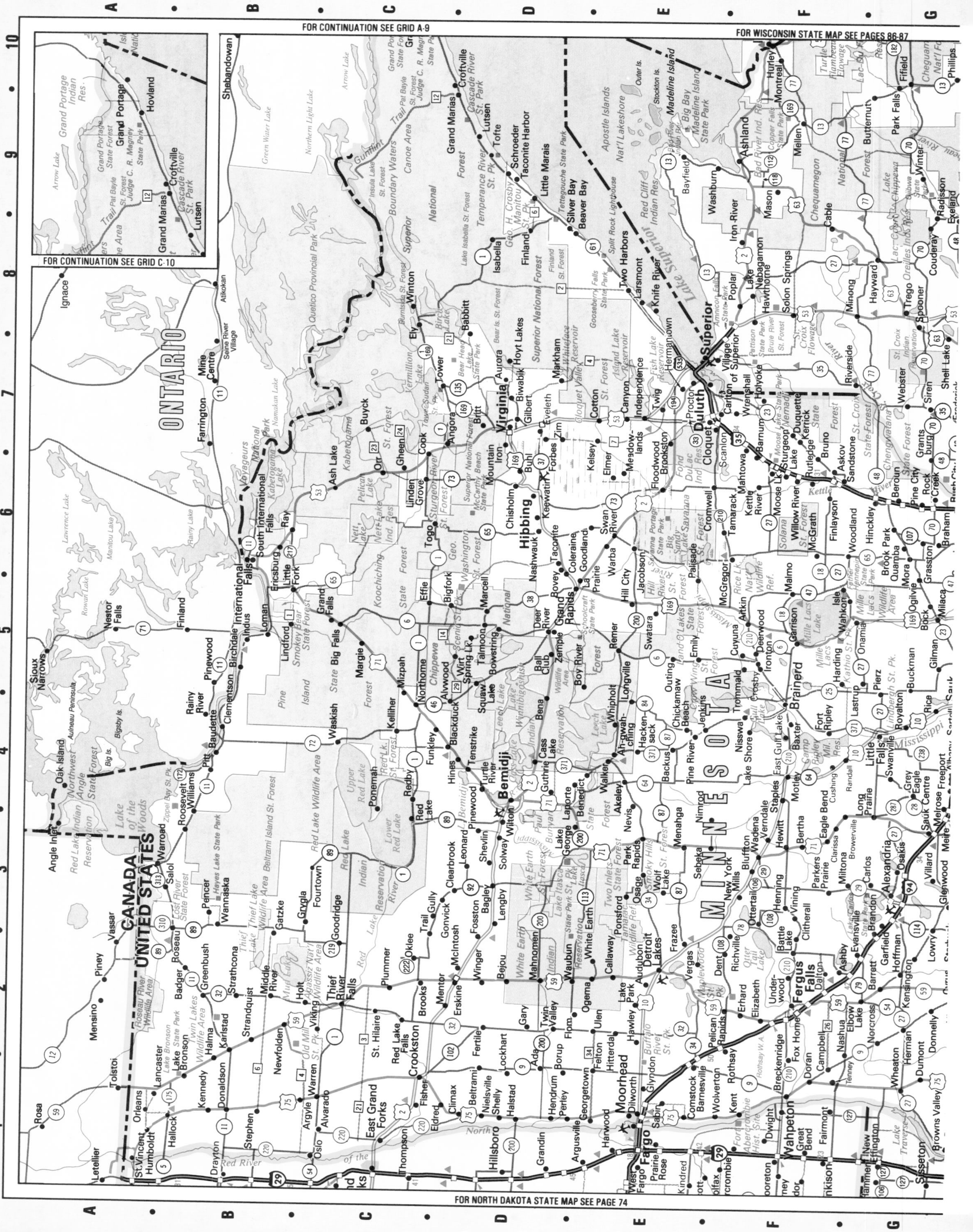

FOR CONTINUATION SEE GRID A-9
FOR WISCONSIN STATE MAP SEE PAGES 86-87
FOR CONTINUATION SEE GRID C-10
FOR NORTH DAKOTA STATE MAP SEE PAGE 74

MINNESOTA

ONTARIO

CANADA

UNITED STATES

Lake Superior

Lake of the Woods

Voyageurs National Park

Superior National Forest

Chippewa National Forest

Red Lake Indian Reservation

Leech Lake Indian Reservation

Mille Lacs

Duluth　Superior

Bemidji

Hibbing

Virginia

Fergus Falls

Moorhead　Fargo

Brainerd

Alexandria

Grand Portage Indian Res.

Grand Marais

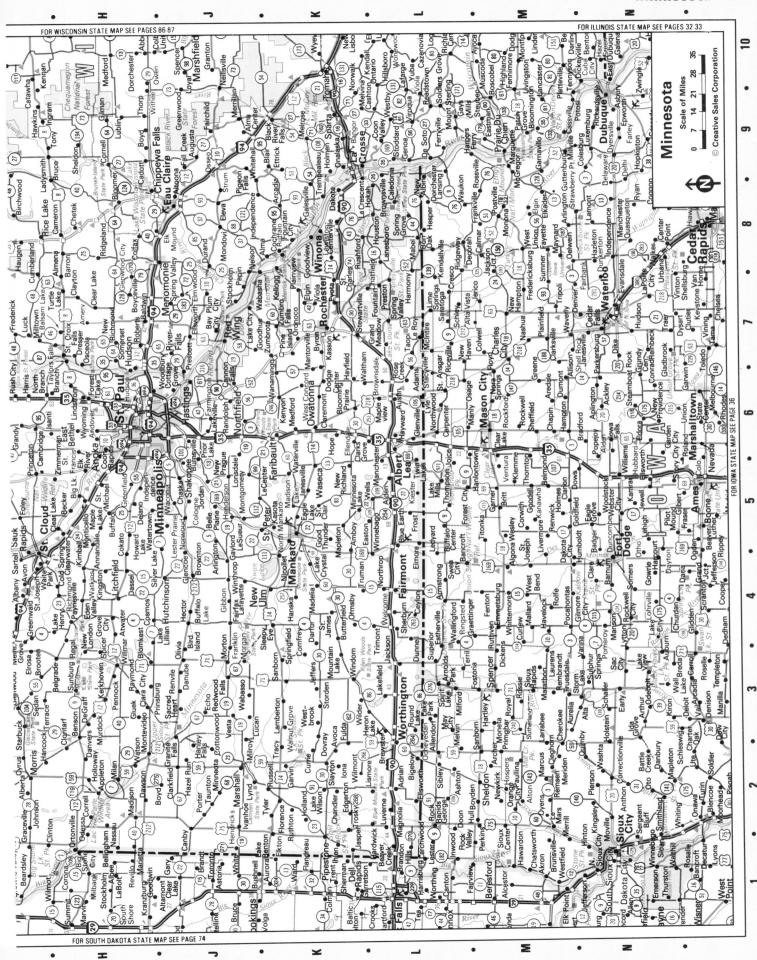

Minnesota

Scale of Miles

© Creative Sales Corporation

FOR WISCONSIN STATE MAP SEE PAGES 86-87

FOR ILLINOIS STATE MAP SEE PAGES 32 33

FOR IOWA STATE MAP SEE PAGE 36

FOR SOUTH DAKOTA STATE MAP SEE PAGE 74

FOR ILLINOIS STATE MAP SEE PAGES 32-33

FOR CONTINUATION SEE GRID D-1

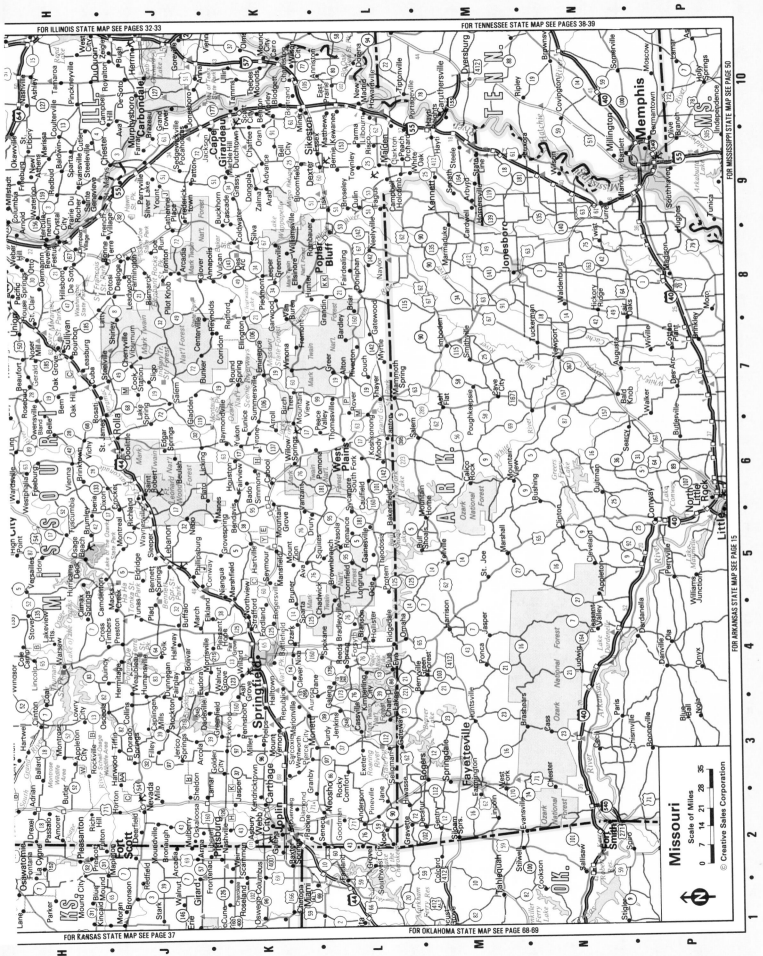

Missouri

Scale of Miles

0   7   14   21   28   35

© Creative Sales Corporation

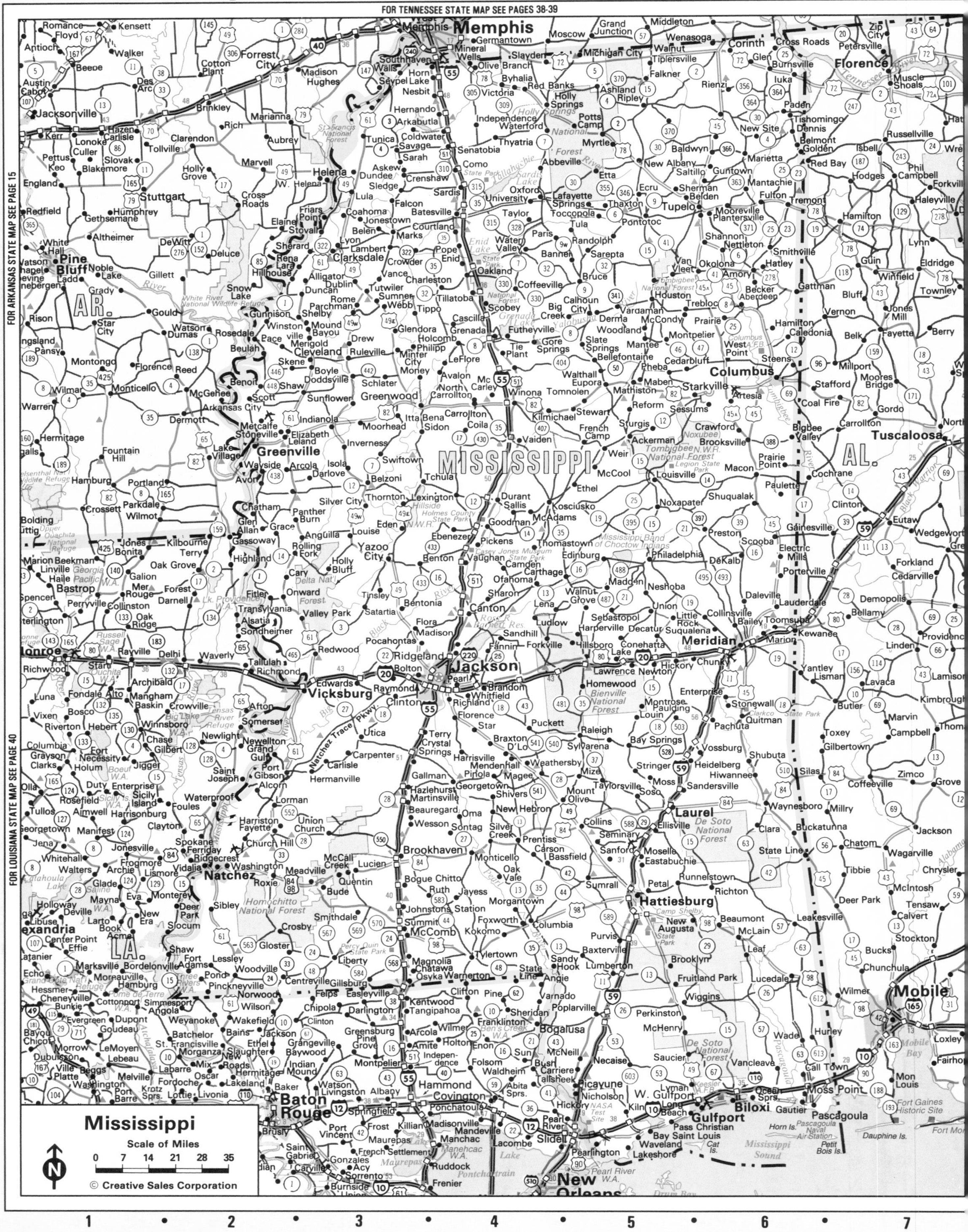

FOR TENNESSEE STATE MAP SEE PAGES 38-39

FOR ARKANSAS STATE MAP SEE PAGE 15

FOR LOUISIANA STATE MAP SEE PAGE 40

MISSISSIPPI

AR.

LA.

AL.

Mississippi

Scale of Miles

0 7 14 21 28 35

N

© Creative Sales Corporation

Memphis

Jackson

Vicksburg

Natchez

Meridian

Hattiesburg

Laurel

Columbus

Tupelo

Greenville

Greenwood

Corinth

Florence

Tuscaloosa

Mobile

Baton Rouge

New Orleans

Gulfport

Biloxi

Pascagoula

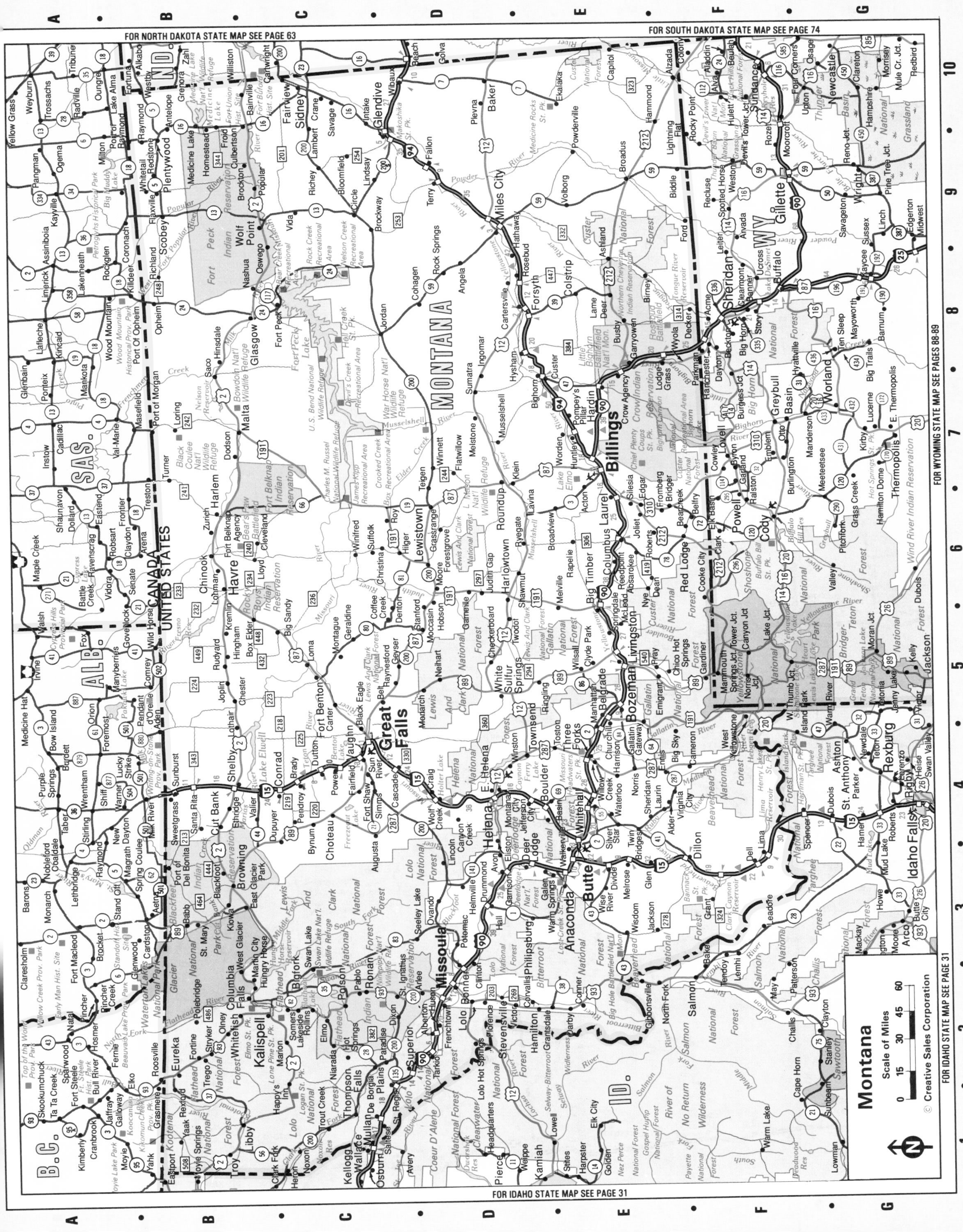

FOR NORTH DAKOTA STATE MAP SEE PAGE 63
FOR SOUTH DAKOTA STATE MAP SEE PAGE 74
FOR WYOMING STATE MAP SEE PAGES 88-89
FOR IDAHO STATE MAP SEE PAGE 31
FOR IDAHO STATE MAP SEE PAGE 31
Montana
Scale of Miles
0 15 30 45 60
© Creative Sales Corporation
MONTANA
CANADA
UNITED STATES
Great Falls
Billings
Missoula
Helena
Butte
Bozeman
Kalispell
Havre
Glasgow
Miles City
Glendive
Lewistown
Sheridan
Gillette
Idaho Falls
Rexburg
Cody

FOR SOUTH DAKOTA STATE MAP SEE PAGE 74

FOR WYOMING STATE MAP SEE PAGES 88-89

FOR COLORADO STATE MAP SEE PAGES 22-23

W Y

Mule Cr. Jct.
Gap
Hot Springs
Edgemont
Redbird
Cheyenne
Sharps Corner
Kyle
Long Valley
44
73
63
White River
Wood
183

Lance Creek
85
18
Provo
Angostura Res.
Angostura St. Rec. Area
Buffalo Gap National Grassland
Oelrichs
18
Oglala
Indian Reservation
Wounded Knee
Wounded Knee Battle Site
Allen
Martin
Batesland
Little
18
Parmelee
Okreek
Mission
63
44
53

Lusk
Node
Oglala National Grasslands
71
Whitney
Chadron
87
27
Pine Ridge
391
73
Merriman
Bowring Ranch St. Hist. Pk.
Eli
Cody
Nenzel
Kilgore
Crookston
Valentine
Rosebud
Saint Francis
Sioux Indian Museum
Rosebud Indian Reservation
Sparks
White
Lacreek National Wildlife Refuge
Lacreek Lake
Niobrara
12
Norder
83

Van Tassell
Harrison
Fort Robinson State Park
Crawford
Chadron St. Park
Pine Ridge Nebraska Nat'l Forest
20
385
Hay Springs
Rushville
87
250
Clinton
Gordon
61
20
Cottonwood Lake St. Pk.
Samuel R. McKelvie Nat'l Forest
Merritt Res.
Wood Lake
Keller St. Rec. A.
St. Rec. A.

Jay Em
85
White
Agate Fossil Beds Nat'l Mon.
Box Butte Res. St. Pk.
Marsland
Niobrara
Walgren Lake St. Pk.
Snake
River
Valentine Nat'l Wildlife Ref.
97
Johnsto
Ainsworth

Lingle
159
Torrington
Horse Creek Treaty Grounds
Hemingford
71
2
2
Alliance
Antioch
North Platte Nat'l Wildlife Ref.
Lakeside
Ellsworth
Bingham
Hyannis
North
61
Brownlee
Long Lake St. Rec. Area
Elsmere
7

Huntley
Yoder
Morrill
Mitchell
Lyman
Terrytown
Scottsbluff
Angora
2
Ashby
Whitman
Mullen
Seneca
Purdum
Halsey
83
NEBR

Hawk Sprs.
92
Gering
Minatare
26
Bayard
385
Thedford
Nebraska National Forest
Dunning
91

La Grange
Melbeta
McGrew
Wildcat Hills St. Rec. Area
Bridgeport St. Rec. Area
Crescent Lake National Wildlife Refuge
Dismal
River
2

Albin
Harrisburg
88
88
Bridgeport
Broadwater
61
Arthur
97
Tryon
Loup
2

85
Scotts Bluff Nat'l Mon.
Chimney Rock Nat'l. Hist. Site
92
Lisco
North Platte River
Oshkosh
26
Lewellen
Lake McConaughy State Park
92
Stapleton
Gandy
Arnold
92
Anselmo

Egbert
Bushnell
Kimball
Dix
Potter
30
385
Dalton
Gurley
27
Ash Hollow St. Hist. Pk.
LeMoyne
Lake Ogallala St. Rec. Area
Keystone
Buffalo Bill St. Pk.
97
Arnold Lake St. Rec. Area
40
Callawa
Bro
Bo

Oliver Res. St. Pk.
30
71
Lodgepole
Sidney
385
Lodgepole
Chappell
Big Springs
30
Brule
Ogallala
Paxton
Sutherland
Lake C.W. McConaughy
Sutherland Res.
Hershey
North Platte
Maxwell
47
Brady
30
Gothenburg
Willow Island
Cozad
21
Le

19
Sedgwick
Ovid
138
138
Julesburg
61
Grant
23
50
Sutherland Res. St. Rec. Area
Lake Malony St. Rec. Area
25
83
Platte
21

Briggsdale
Buckingham
Raymer
Crook
113
Proctor
Sterling Res.
138
385
Brandon
Venango
Madrid
Grainton
Elsie
Wallace
23
Dickens
Wellfleet
Gallager Canyon St. Rec. Area
Moorefield
47
21
Johnson
Lk. St. Rec. A.

Stoneham
Sterling
Willard
Merino
Atwood
76
Fleming
59
Haxtun
Paoli
176
Amherst
Holyoke
6
Champion Mill St. Hist. Site
Imperial
61
Marywood
25
Curtis
Farnam
Eustis
Johnson

Jackson Lake Res.
52
71
61
Clarkville
Champion
Champion Lake St. Rec. Area
Enders
Hayes Center
18
Stockville
Elwood
283
Smi

Orchard
Weldona
Snyder
Log Lane Village
6
63
Enders Reservoir St. Park
Wauneta
Hamlet
Red Willow Res. St. Park
Hugh Butler Lake
Medicine Creek St. Park
Cambridge
Bartley
Arapahoe
H

Wiggins
Fort Morgan
Brush
71
Akron
Otis
59
Eckley
Palisade
Culbertson
Indianola
McCook
47
Edison
Beaver City

Yuma
Woodrow
COL.
34
Wray
Stratton
17
34
Wilsonville
Stamfor
283

36
Last Chance
Lindon
Anton
Max
Swanson Reservoir
Trenton
25
Danbury
89
Lebanon
Creek
Harlan
Co. U.S. Arm

Cope
Joes
36
Idalia
St. Francis
161
Bird City
McDonald
Atwood
117
Herndon
Oberlin
Norcatur
Prairie Dog St. Pk.
Almena

Arikaree
River
Wheeler
27
Bonny Res.
Beaver
Herndon
Norton
Clayton
Dresden
Keith Sebelius Lake
Logan
Phi

River Bend
Limon
59
Genoa
Arriba
Seibert
Vona
Stratton
24
Burlington
Goodland
Brewster
184
Colby
Gem
Rexford
Selden
383
Lenora
Edmond
9

Hugo
70
Menlo
Halford
Hoxie
24
Morland
283
283

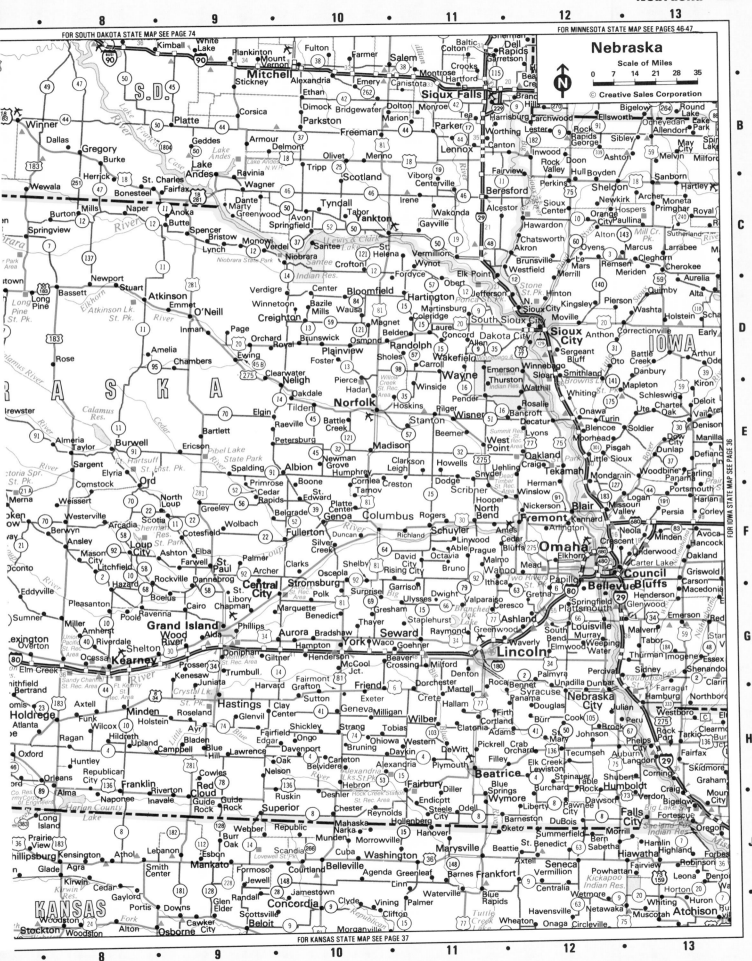

FOR OREGON STATE MAP SEE PAGES 70-71
FOR IDAHO STATE MAP SEE PAGE 31
FOR CALIFORNIA STATE MAP SEE PAGES 18-21

OR.   ID.

CA.   NEVADA   UT.   AZ.

Cities, towns and features:

Indian Res.
Modoc
Alkali Lake
Massacre Lake
Summit Lake Indian Reservation
Sheldon National Wildlife Refuge
McDermitt
Ft. McDermitt Indian Reservation
Humboldt National Forest
Riddle
Owyhee
Duck Valley Indian Reservation
Mountain City
Jarbridge
Contact
Jackpot
Sawtooth National Forest
Rogerson
Three Creek

Cedarville
Eagleville
High Rock Canyon
Orovada
Paradise Valley
Jack Creek
Tuscarora
Midas
Thousand Springs
Montello

Sulphur
Winnemucca
Golconda
Battle Mountain
Beowawe
Halleck
Deeth
Wells
Oasis
Wendover

Gerlach
Empire
Imlay
Mill City
Valmy
Carlin
Elko
Lamoille
Ruby Mountain Scenic Area
Wendover Range

Wendel
Herlong
Doyle
Sutcliffe
Pyramid Lake Indian Reservation
Eagle Picher Mine
Lovelock
Oreana
Unionville
Beowawe Geysers
Crescent Valley
Lee
Jiggs
Ruby Valley
Shantytown
Currie
Wenver Range
Desert Test Center
Dugway Proving Grounds
Goshute Indian Reservation
Cherry Creek
Lage's
Trout Cr.
Gandy

Honey Lake
Nixon
Wadsworth
Sparks
Reno
Fernley
Fallon
Stillwater Wildlife Management Area
Fallon Naval Air Station
Carson Sink
Austin
Eureka
Pony Express Station Site
Ruth
Ely
McGill
Baker
Great Basin National Park
Garrison

Squaw Valley
Virginia City
Silver City
Silver Springs
Cold Springs
Middle Gate
Ione
Toiyabe National Forest
Kimberly
East Ely
Lehman Caves Natl. Mon.
Major's Place
Wheeler Peak Scenic Area

Tahoe City
Lake Tahoe
Carson City
Weed Heights
Yerington
Schurz
Walker River Indian Res.
Gabbs
Carver's
Round Mountain
Duckwater
Preston
Lund
Currant
Pancake Range
Railroad Valley W.M.A.

Meeks Bay
Camp Richardson
Meyers
Wellington
Babbitt
Hawthorne
Luning
Mina
Warm Springs
Nyala
Adaven
Ursine
Pioche
Caselton
Panaca
Lund
Beryl

Bear Valley
Walker
Bridgeport
Coaldale
Tonopah
Goldfield
Rachel
Hiko
Ash Springs
Alamo
Caliente
Uvada

Yosemite National Park
June Lake
Lee Vining
Mono Lake
Benton
Dyer
Silver Peak
Lida
Gold Point
Scotty's Junction
Beatty
Mercury
Indian Springs
Glendale
Moapa
Mesquite
Bunkerville

Fish Camp
Sugar Pine
Mammoth Lakes
Toms Place
Bishop
Laws
Oasis
Death Valley
Death Valley Jct.
Cactus Springs
Overton
Valley of Fire State Park

Clovis
Fresno
Tulare
Round Valley
Independence
Lone Pine
Keeler
Shoshone
Blue Diamond
Goodsprings
Sandy
N. Las Vegas
Las Vegas
Henderson
Boulder City
Mead-Hoover Dam

Visalia
Hanford
Camp Nelson
Panamint Springs
Pioneer Point
Tecopa
Nelson
White Hills

Lost Hills
Delano
Oildale
Bakersfield
Onyx
Weldon
Inyokern
Westend
China Lake
Jean
Searchlight
Nipton
Cal Nev Ari
Laughlin
Kingman

Mojave
California City
Johannesburg
Boron
Edwards A.F.B.
Hinkley
Barstow
Yermo
Baker
Cima
Mohave

Nevada
Scale of Miles
0   20   40   60

© Creative Sales Corporation

N

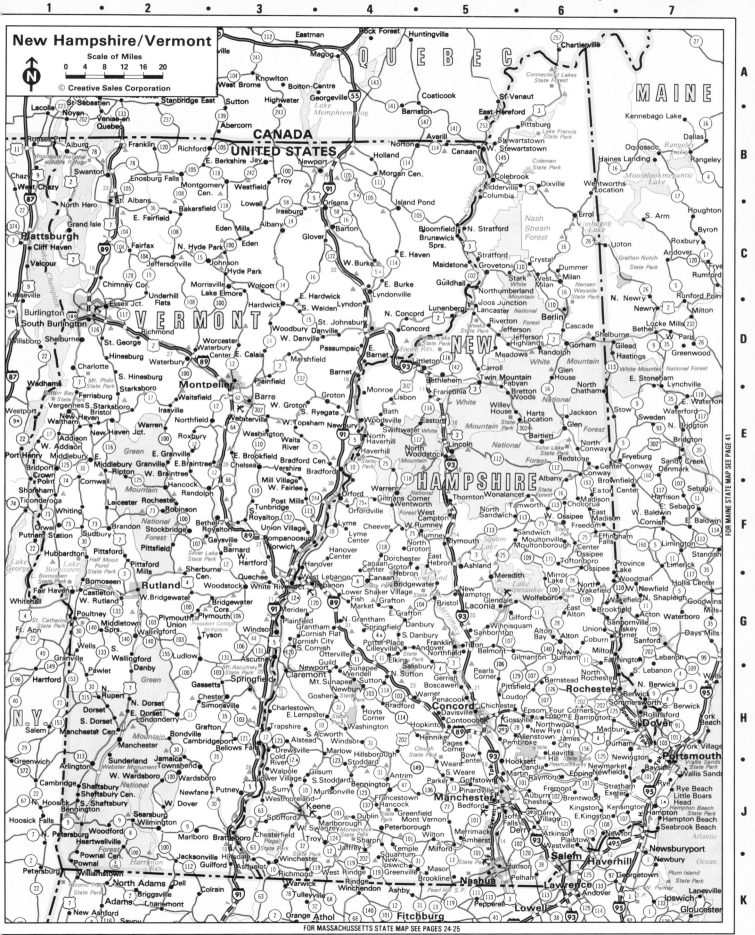

FOR NEW YORK STATE MAP SEE PAGES 58-61

FOR PENNSYLVANIA STATE MAP SEE PAGES 72-73

NEW YORK

PENNSYLVANIA

Ocean

Long Island Sound

Hudson River

Palisades

Peekskill, Ossining, Nyak, Tarrytown, White Plains, Mt. Vernon, Yonkers, Bergenfield, Tenafly, Englewood, Hackensack, Fort Lee, West New York, Union City, Hoboken, Jersey City, New York, Bayonne, Staten Is., Great Neck, Valley Stream, Atlantic Beach, Long Beach

Spring Valley, Central Valley, Monroe, Southfield, Florida, Warwick, Greenwood Lake, Vernon, West Milford, Ringwood, Wanaque, Pompton Lakes, Waldwick, Ridgewood, Fair Lawn, Hawthorne, Paterson, Passaic, Clifton, Nutley, Belleville, Bloomfield, Garfield, Newark, Elizabeth, Linden, Roselle, Carteret, Perth Amboy, South Amboy, Sayreville, South River, Highland Park, New Brunswick, Metuchen, Bound Brook, Somerville, Manville

Atlantic Highlands, Highlands, Sandy Hook, Rumson, Fair Haven, Shrewsbury, Eatontown, Oceanport, West Long Branch, Long Branch, Asbury Park, Bradley Beach, Belmar, Neptune, Freehold, Farmingdale, Red Bank, Keansburg, Keyport, Matawan, Holmdel, Colts Neck, Marlboro, Manalapan, Englishtown, Roosevelt, Cranbury, Hightstown, Robertsville

Sussex, Hamburg, Franklin, Ogdensburg, Sparta, Andover, Newton, Fredon, Branchville, Montague, Pt. Jervis, Stroudsburg, Scranton, Moscow, Sterling, Mt. Pocono, Bangor, Nazareth, Easton, Phillipsburg, Bethlehem, Allentown, Catasauqua, Northampton, Bath, Quakertown, Doylestown, Lansdale, Pottstown, Warminster, Newtown, Warrington

Hopatcong, Stanhope, Netcong, Budd Lake, Hackettstown, Allamuchy, Blairstown, Hope, Johnsonburg, Hainesburg, Belvidere, Oxford, Washington, Broadway, Hampton, Califon, High Bridge, Clinton, Lebanon, Flemington, Readington, Whitehouse, Bedminster, Peapack, Bernardsville, Mendham, Morristown, Hanover, Parsippany-Troy Hills, Dover, Wharton, Rockaway, Denville, Boonton, Montville, Kinnelon, Butler, Bloomingdale, Lincoln Park

Chester, Long Valley, Lambertville, Stockton, Frenchtown, Milford, Alpha, Bloomsbury, Wilson, Harmony, West Portal, Pittstown, Baptistown, Croton, Ringoes, Hopewell, Pennington, Lawrence, Princeton, Plainsboro, Monroe, South Brunswick, Trenton, Morrisville, Ewingville

Madison, Chatham, Summit, New Providence, Watchung, Plainfield, Dunellen, Warren, Liberty Corners, Raritan, Neshanic, Millstone, Rocky Hill, Kingston, Clarksville, Edinburg, Hamilton Sq.

East Orange, Orange, West Orange, Irvington, Maplewood, Westfield, Kenilworth, Roselle Park, Rahway, South Plainfield, Edison, Woodbridge, Old Bridge, Spotswood, Jamesburg, Helmetta

New Jersey

Scale of Miles

0 2.5 5 7.5 10 12.5

© Creative Sales Corporation

N

Atlantic

Atlantic Ocean

Delaware Bay

NEW JERSEY

DELAWARE

Manasquan • Point Pleasant Beach • Pt. Pleasant • Bay Head • Brielle • Mantoloking • Lavallette • Seaside Heights • Island Heights • Seaside Park • Ocean Gate • Island Beach St. Pk. • Barnegat Light • Harvey Cedars • Surf City • Ship Bottom • Beach Haven • Little Egg Harbor • Brigantine • Atlantic City • Ventnor City • Margate City • Longport • Somers Pt. • Ocean City • Sea Isle City • Avalon • Stone Harbor • North Wildwood • Wildwood • Wildwood Crest • Cape May • West Cape May • North Cape May • Villas • Rio Grande • Whitesboro

Lakewood • Whitesville • Lakehurst • Caseville • Toms River • Beachwood • Silverton • Cedar Grove • Gifford Park • Waretown • Barnegat • Manahawkin • Tuckerton • New Gretna • Port Republic • Smithville • Absecon • Pleasantville • Northfield • Linwood

Bordentown • Burlington • Beverly • Edgewater Park • Riverside • Riverton • Cinnaminson • Palmyra • Maple Shade • Moorestown • Mt. Holly • Lumberton • Medford • Medford Lakes • Red Lion • Pemberton • Wrightstown • Fort Dix • McGuire A.F.B. • Browns Mills • Columbus • Crestwood Village • Whiting • Manchester • Chatsworth • Tabernacle • Atsion • Speedwell • Cedar Bridge • Green Bank • Egg Harbor City • Elwood • Hammonton • Mays Landing • Weymouth • Estell Manor • Corbin City

Philadelphia • Camden • Collingswood • Haddonfield • Audubon • Bellmawr • Runnemede • Stratford • Lindenwold • Berlin • Pine Hill • Clementon • Gibbsboro • Glassboro • Pitman • Clayton • Williamstown • Franklinville • Winslow • Folsom • Buena • Vineland • East Vineland • Newfield • Malaga • Elmer • Pole Tavern • Woodbine • South Dennis • North Dennis • Marshallville • Belleplain • Seaville • Ocean View

Gloucester City • National Park • Westville • Woodbury • Woodbury Heights • Wenonah • Mantua • Mickleton • Swedesboro • Mullica Hill • Woodstown • Sharptown • Alloway • Quinton • Salem • Pennsville • Carneys Pt. • Deepwater • Pennsgrove • Deerfield • Seabrook • Centerton • Carlls Corner • Goulddtown • Bridgeton • Shiloh • Millville • Port Elizabeth • Cumberland • Port Norris • Maurice River • Dividing Creek • Fairton • Cedarville • Bay Point

King of Prussia • Newtown Square • West Chester • Phoenixville • Norristown • Conshohocken • Darby • Elsmere • Wilmington • New Castle • Newport • Delaware City • Smyrna • Dover • Camden • Magnolia • Frederica • Milford • Bowers Beach • Houston • Felton • Viola • Harrington • Slaughter Beach

FOR DELAWARE STATE MAP SEE PAGES 42-43

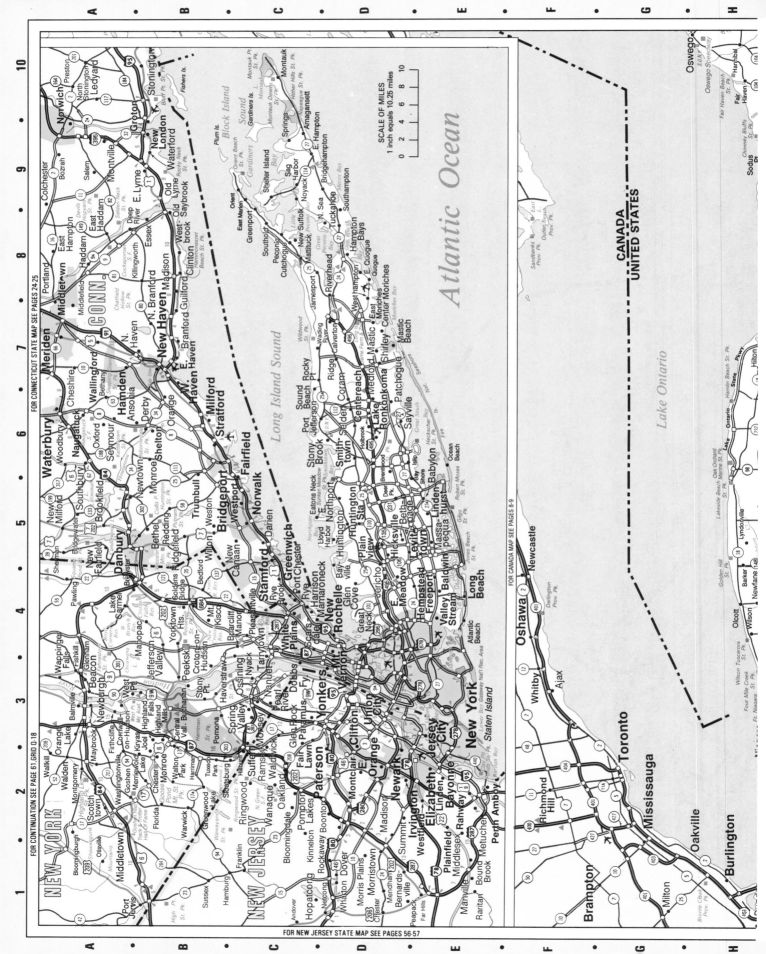

FOR CONNECTICUT STATE MAP SEE PAGES 24-25

FOR CONTINUATION SEE PAGE 61, GRID O-18

FOR CANADA MAP SEE PAGES 8-9

FOR NEW JERSEY STATE MAP SEE PAGES 56-57

SCALE OF MILES
1 inch equals 10.25 miles
0 2 4 6 8 10

Atlantic Ocean

Long Island Sound

Lake Ontario

CANADA
UNITED STATES

NEW YORK

NEW JERSEY

CONN.

FOR CONTINUATION SEE PAGE 61

NEW YORK

PENNSYLVANIA

ONTARIO

CANADA / UNITED STATES

Lake Erie

Lake Ontario

New York
Scale of Miles
0 4 8 12 16 20

© Creative Sales Corporation

FOR PENNSYLVANIA STATE MAP SEE PAGES 72-73

Oswego Speedway

Burlington, Hamilton, Stoney Creek, Grimsby, St. Catherines, Thorold, Niagara Falls, Welland, Port Colborne, Dunnville

Niagara-on-the-Lake, Youngstown, Lewiston, Niagara Falls, Tonawanda, N. Tonawanda, Kenmore, Buffalo, Lackawanna, Blasdell, Hamburg, Orchard Pk., Fort Erie

Olcott, Wilson, Newfane, Lockport, Middleport, Medina, Barker, Lyndonville, Albion, Holley, Brockport, Spencerport, Churchville, Bergen, Elba, Batavia, Oakfield, Akron, Corfu, Alden, Lancaster, Depew, Williamsville, Clarence Center

Sodus Pt., Sodus, Wolcott, Clyde, Lyons, Newark, Palmyra, Macedon, Fairport, Webster, Greece, Rochester, Hilton, E. Rochester, Pittsford, Scottsville, Caledonia, LeRoy, Avon, Lima, Victor, Honeoye Falls, Canandaigua, Manchester, Clifton Sprs., Shortsville, Holcomb

Fair Haven, Red Creek, Port Byron, Weedsport, Auburn, Seneca Falls, Waterloo, Geneva, Union Springs, Cayuga, Aurora, Ovid, Willard, Lodi, Interlaken, Trumansburg, Penn Yan, Dundee, Keuka Park, Prattsburg, Naples, Springwater, Wayland, Dansville, Nunda, Mt. Morris, Geneseo, Leicester, Perry, Castile, Silver Springs, Warsaw, Wyoming, Attica, Alexander, Darien

Horseheads, Elmira Hts., Elmira, Southport, Corning, Riverside, Gang Mills, Painted Post, Addison, Woodhull, Jasper, Canisteo, Hornell, N. Hornell, Almond, Alfred, Andover, Avoca, Cohocton, Bath, Savona, Hammondsport, Watkins Glen, Montour Falls, Odessa, Burdett, Millport

Troy, Canton, Blossburg, Mansfield, Wellsboro, Galeton, Coudersport, Port Allegany, Smethport, Mt. Jewett, Kane, Warren, Clarendon, Youngsville, Bradford, Eldred, Portville, Olean, Allegany, Salamanca, Little Valley, Randolph, E. Randolph, Frewsburg, Jamestown, Celoron, Lakewood, Falconer, Cherry Creek, Sinclairville, Cassadaga, Fredonia, Dunkirk, Brocton, Westfield, Mayville, Sherman, Corry, Union City, Bemus Pt.

Cuba, Bolivar, Friendship, Belmont, Wellsville, Richburg, Shinglehouse, Limestone, Weston Mills, Franklinville, Machias, Delevan, Yorkshire, Arcade, Springville, Gowanda, Cattaraugus, Ellicottville, Great Valley

Liberty, Emporium, Johnsonburg

National Forest

Allegheny Indian Reservation

Cattaraugus Indian Reservation

Seneca Indian Reservation

N.Y. State Thruway

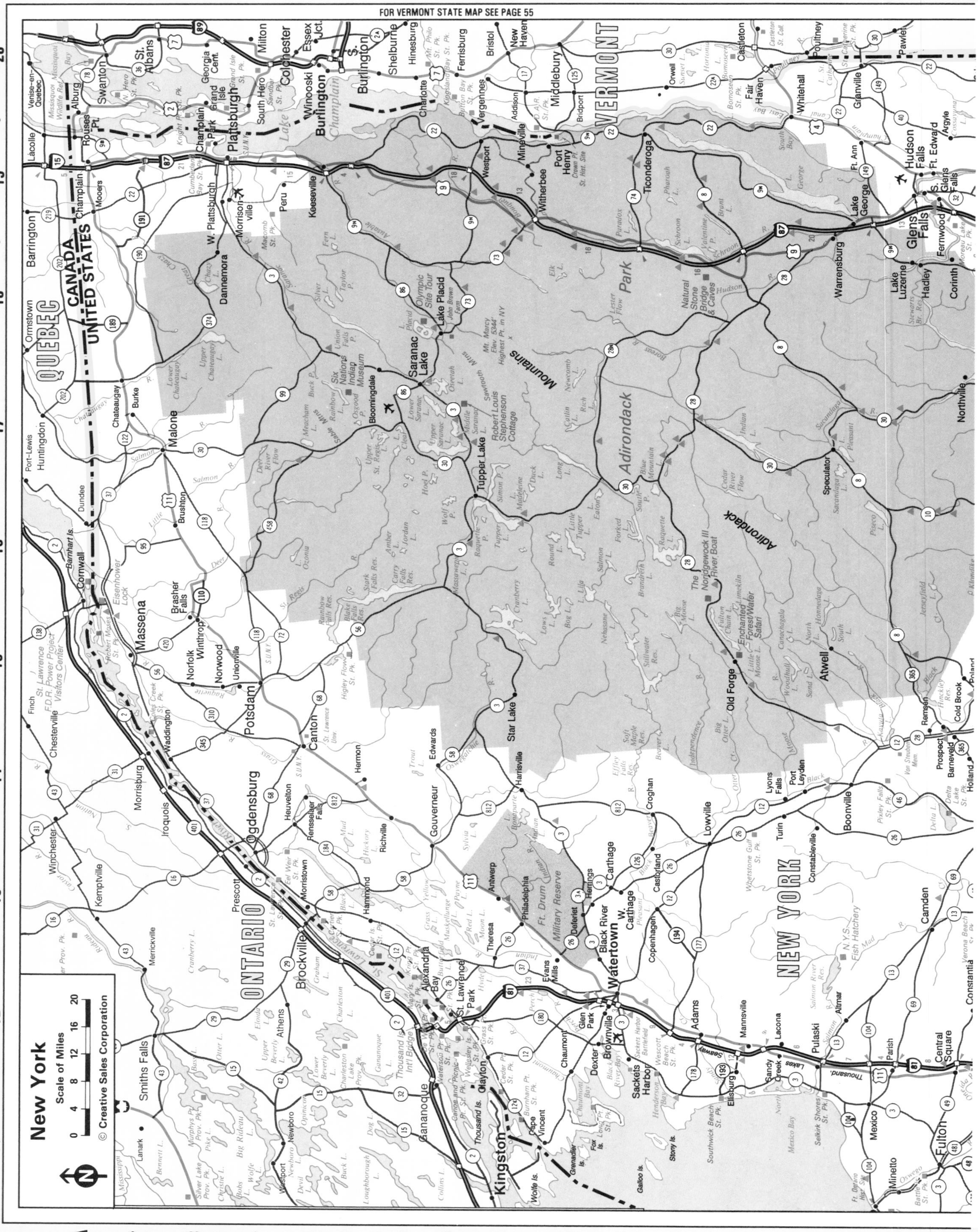

FOR VERMONT STATE MAP SEE PAGE 55

New York

Scale of Miles

0 4 8 12 16 20

© Creative Sales Corporation

N

QUEBEC

CANADA
UNITED STATES

ONTARIO

VERMONT

NEW YORK

Adirondack Park

Adirondack Mountains

Lake Champlain

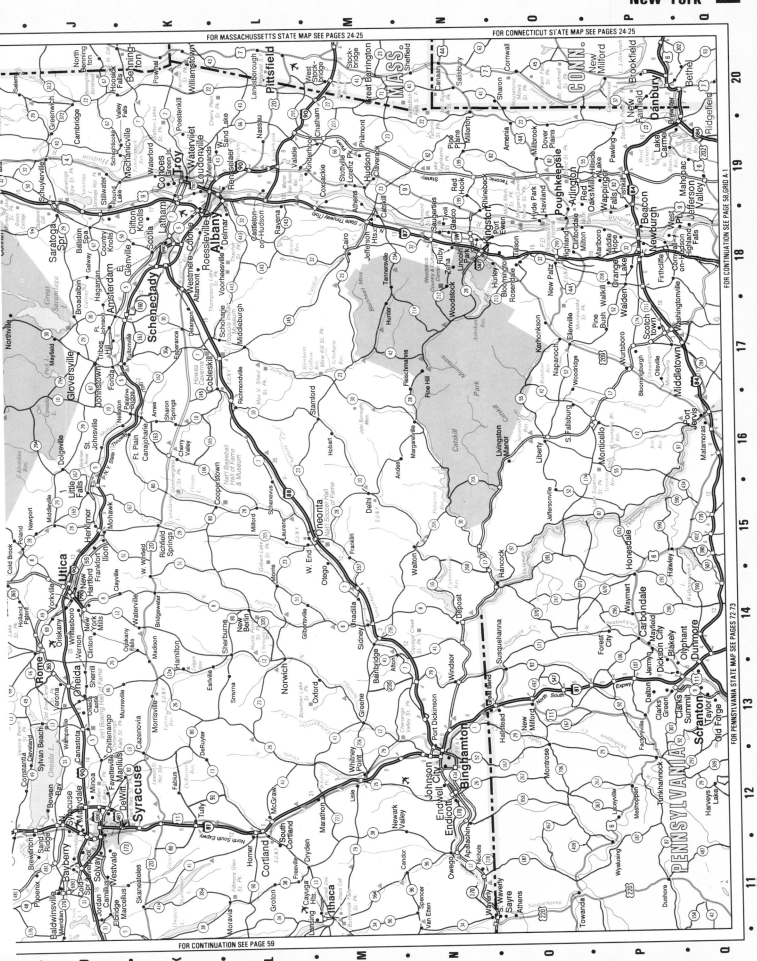

FOR MASSACHUSSETTS STATE MAP SEE PAGES 24-25

FOR CONNECTICUT STATE MAP SEE PAGES 24-25

FOR CONTINUATION SEE PAGE 58, GRID A-1

FOR PENNSYLVANIA STATE MAP SEE PAGES 72-73

FOR CONTINUATION SEE PAGE 59

FOR COLORADO STATE MAP SEE PAGES 22-23

FOR UTAH STATE MAP SEE PAGE 80-81

FOR ARIZONA STATE MAP SEE PAGES 16-17

CO.

NEW MEXICO

TEX.

CHIHUAHUA

UNITED STATES
MEXICO

New Mexico

Scale of Miles

0 10 20 30 40 50

N

Creative Sales Corporation

Cahone · Pleasant View · Yellow Jacket · Lewis · Arriola · Dolores · Stoner · Rockwood · Spar City · South Fork · Del Norte · Monte Vista · Homelake · Mosca · Waisenburg · Thatcher · Springfield · Pritchett

Cortez · Lebanon · Mancos · Hesperus · Durango · Summitville · Platoro · Capulin · Alamosa · Blanca · Fort Garland · La Veta · Cuchara · Hoehne · Model · Tobe · Kim · Utleyville · Comanche

Towaoc · Fort Lewis · Chimney Rock · Pagosa Spgs. · La Jara · Romeo · San Luis · Chama · San Pablo · Weston · Valdez · Starkville · Branson · Kenton

Shiprock · Kirtland · Aztec · Bloomfield · Lumberton · Chama · Costilla · Cerro · Red River · Questa · Raton · Capulin · Des Moines · Seneca · Felt

Farmington · Turley · Archuleta · Monero · Brazos · Los Ojos · Tres Piedras · Amalia · Ute Park · Maxwell · Springer · Abbott · Clapham · Sedan · Texline

Blanco Trading Post · Nageezi · Lindrith · Gallina · La Madera · El Rito · Ojo Caliente · Embudo · Chacon · Miami · Ocate · Mills · Roy · Solano · Hayden · Amistad

Gallup · Crownpoint · White Horse · Torreon · Jemez Springs · Los Alamos · Santa Cruz · Chimayo · Las Vegas · Wagon Mound · Mosquero · Nara Visa

Thoreau · Ambrosia Lake · San Mateo · Cuba · Cochiti Lake · Santa Fe · Pecos · Romeroville · Variadero · Conchas · Logan · Tucumcari

Grants · Milan · Laguna · Bernalillo · Rio Rancho · Placitas · Golden · Pueblo · Dilia · Santa Rosa · Newkirk · Cuervo · Montoya · San Jon · Wheatland

Albuquerque · Tijeras · Moriarty · Clines Corners · Encino · Vaughn · Pastura · McAlister · Grady · Forrest · Broadview · Bellview

Los Lunas · Belen · Tome · Estancia · Willard · Duran · Ramon · Fort Sumner · Tolar · Melrose · St. Vrain · Clovis · Portales

Socorro · Magdalena · San Antonio · Bingham · Gran Quivira · Corona · Mesa · Kenna · Elida · Dora · Causey

Trinity Site · World's First Atomic Explosion (July 16, 1945-Closed to Public) · White Sands Missile Range · Carrizozo · Capitan · Lincoln · Roswell · Caprock · Tatum

Truth or Consequences · Elephant Butte · Ruidoso · Alto · Hondo · Picacho · Dexter · Hagerman · Lovington · Knowles

Silver City · Hillsboro · Caballo · Alamogordo · Cloudcroft · Artesia · Hobbs

Las Cruces · Mesilla · Organ · White Sands Missile Range · Carlsbad · Jal

Deming · Columbus · Anthony · El Paso · Juarez

Lordsburg · Animas · Hachita · Rodeo

CHIHUAHUA

FOR MINNESOTA STATE MAP SEE PAGES 46-47

FOR SOUTH DAKOTA STATE MAP SEE PAGE 74

FOR MONTANA STATE MAP SEE PAGE 51

North Dakota

Scale of Miles

0 10 20 30 40 50

© Creative Sales Corporation

N

CANADA
UNITED STATES

SASKATCHEWAN

MANITOBA

MINNESOTA

MONTANA

SOUTH DAKOTA

NORTH DAKOTA

Bismarck

Fargo

Grand Forks

Devils Lake

Dickinson

Williston

Minot

Jamestown

Valley City

Aberdeen

Mobridge

Moorhead

FOR KENTUCKY STATE MAP SEE PAGES 38-39
FOR VIRGINIA STATE MAP SEE PAGES 82-83
FOR TENNESSEE STATE MAP SEE PAGES 38-39
FOR GEORGIA STATE MAP SEE PAGES 38-29

KY.
VIR.
TENN
NORTH CAROLINA
SOUTH CAROLINA
GEORGIA

Middlesboro
Corbin
Knoxville
Asheville
Bristol
Kingsport
Johnson City
Winston-Salem
High Point
Statesville
Hickory
Salisbury
Kannopolis
Concord
Charlotte
Gastonia
Spartanburg
Greenville
Anderson
Greenwood
Columbia
Sumter
Augusta
Aiken
Atlanta
Athens
Macon
Warner Robins
Savannah
Hilton Head Island

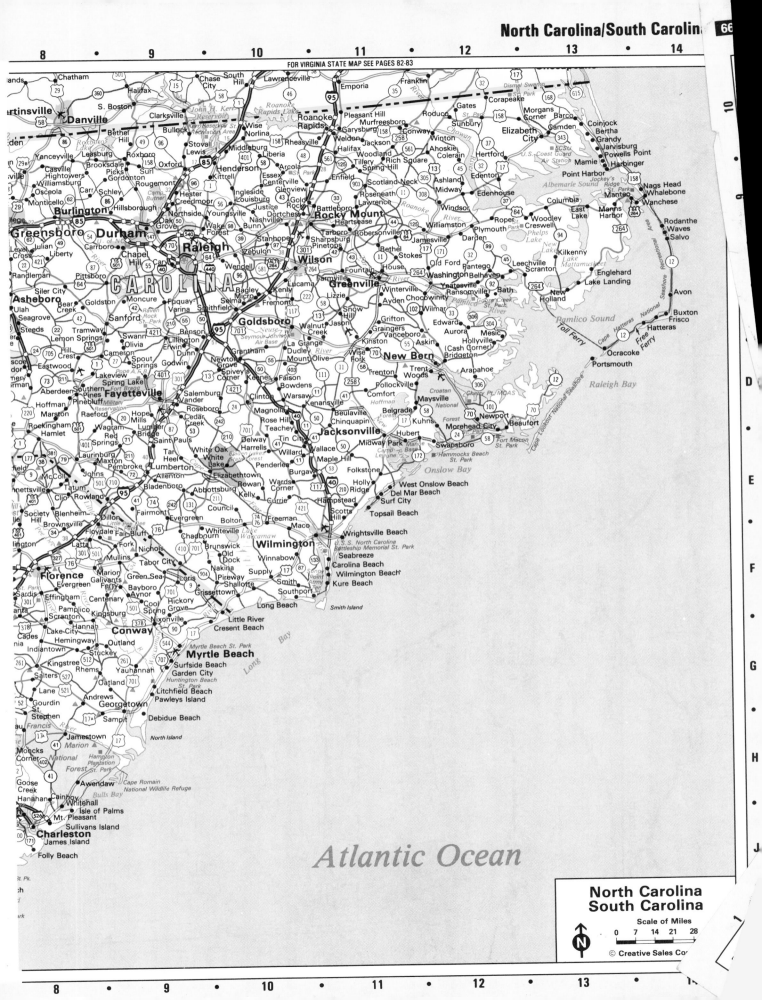

FOR PENNSYLVANIA STATE MAP SEE PAGES 72-73

FOR MICHIGAN STATE MAP SEE PAGES 44-45

FOR MICHIGAN STATE MAP SEE PAGES 44-45

FOR INDIANA STATE MAP SEE PAGES 34-35

CANADA
UNITED STATES

ONTARIO

MICHIGAN

OHIO

Lake Erie

Lake Huron

Lake St. Clair

Selected cities and towns:

Norwich, Otterville, Delhi, Mt. Elgin, Holbrook, Ingersoll, Dorchester, London, St. Thomas, Talbotville, Port Stanley, Port Bruce, Port Burwell, Tillsonburg, Brownsville, Aylmer, Sparta, Melbourne, W. Lorne, Dutton, Wardsville, Ridgetown, Morpeth, Blenheim, Charing Cross, Wheatley, Leamington, Kingsville, Essex, Harrow, Amherstburg, Windsor, Chatham, Wallaceburg, Dresden, Thamesville, Bothwell, Newbury, Glencoe

Sarnia, Pt. Edward, Port Huron, Marysville, St. Clair, Marine City, Algonac, Mt. Clemens, St. Clair Shores, Grosse Pointe Woods, Grosse Pointe Park, Detroit, Dearborn, Windsor

Flint, Mt. Morris, Burton, Grand Blanc, Davison, Lapeer, Imlay City, Almont, Romeo, Rochester, Pontiac, Auburn Hills, Troy, Sterling Hts., Warren, Royal Oak, Southfield, Farmington Hills, Livonia, Westland, Taylor, Inkster, Romulus, Belleville, Ypsilanti, Ann Arbor, Saline, Milan, Dexter, Chelsea, Brighton, Howell, Fowlerville

E. Lansing, Lansing, Mason, Stockbridge, Jackson, Albion, Homer, Hillsdale, Jonesville, Reading, Quincy, Coldwater, Hudson, Adrian, Tecumseh, Clinton, Blissfield, Morenci, Fayette, Lyons, Wauseon, Archbold, Bryan, Edgerton, Defiance, Napoleon, Holgate, Paulding, Van Wert, Celina, St. Marys, Lima, Delphos, Ottawa, Findlay, Bowling Green, Toledo, Maumee, Perrysburg, Oregon, Sylvania, Northwood, Genoa, Elmore, Fremont, Fostoria, Tiffin, Bucyrus, Marion, Upper Sandusky, Kenton, Ada, Bluffton

Sandusky, Huron, Vermilion, Lorain, Elyria, Sheffield Lake, Avon Lake, Westlake, Lakewood, Cleveland, Cleveland Hts., Shaker Hts., Garfield Hts., Parma, Berea, Strongsville, Brunswick, Medina, Wooster, Ashland, Mansfield, Shelby, Crestline, Galion, Bellville, Loudonville, Millersburg, Orrville, Wadsworth, Barberton, Norton, Akron, Cuyahoga Falls, Stow, Kent, Ravenna, Tallmadge, Canton, Massillon, Dalton, Dover, Strasburg, Sugar Creek

Willoughby, Eastlake, Willowick, Euclid, Mentor, Mentor-on-the-Lake, Fairport Harbor, Madison, Geneva, Geneva-on-the-Lake, Ashtabula, N. Kingsville, Conneaut, Andover, Jefferson, Cortland, Warren, Niles, Girard, Youngstown, Campbell, Struthers, Canfield, Columbiana, Salem, Alliance, Minerva, Carrollton, Lisbon, E. Liverpool, Hubbard

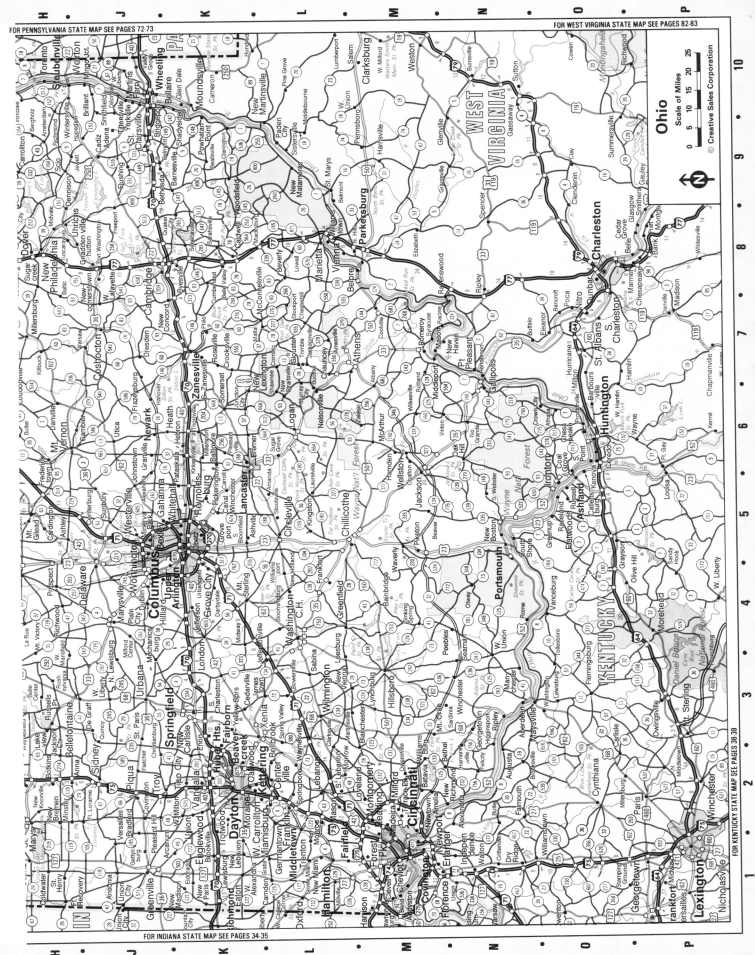

FOR PENNSYLVANIA STATE MAP SEE PAGES 72-73

FOR WEST VIRGINIA STATE MAP SEE PAGES 82-83

Ohio

Scale of Miles

© Creative Sales Corporation

FOR INDIANA STATE MAP SEE PAGES 34-35

FOR KENTUCKY STATE MAP SEE PAGES 38-39

FOR COLORADO STATE MAP SEE PAGES 22-23
FOR KANSAS STATE MAP SEE PAGE 37
FOR NEW MEXICO STATE MAP SEE PAGE 62
FOR TEXAS STATE MAP SEE PAGES 75-79

COLORADO

KANSAS

Dodge City

Johnson City

Greensburg

Cullison

Pritchett · Bartlett · Springfield
Vilas
Kim · Utleyville · Campo
Comanche National Grassland

Montezuma · Sublette · Bucklin
Minneola
Meade · Coldwater
Kismet · Protection · Ashland

Richfield · Hugoton

Elkhart · Liberal · Englewood

Kenton · Sturgis · Surrey Hills · Hough · Tyrone · Floris · Mocane · Knowles · Buffalo · Lookout · Plainview
Black Mesa St. Pk.
Boise City · Hooker · Turpin · Forgan · Gate · Rosston · Selman · Edith · Tegarden · Cora
Wheeless · Four Corners · Eva · Optima · Boyd · Laverne · May · Freedom · Brace · Hopeton
Kiowa National Grasslands
Guymon · Griggs · Goodwell · Bryan's Corner · Balko · Elmwood · Slapout · Ft. Supply · Belva · Curtis · Quinlan
Felt · Hardesty · Gray · Catesby · Mooreland · Woodward
Clayton · Texhoma · Perryton · Booker · Darrouzett · Follett · Fargo · Gage · Shattuck · Goodwin · Mutual · Chester · Seiling
Rita Blanca Nat'l Grassland · Stratford · Gruver · Waka · Farnsworth · Lipscomb · Higgins · Arnett · Vici · Cestos · Camargo · Taloga
Sedan · Spearman · Glazier · Durham · Crawford · Angora · Leedey · Rhea · Putnam · Oakwood
Dalhart · Cactus · Etter · Sunray · Morse · Canadian · Roll · Aledo · Burmah
Hartley · Dumas · Stinnett · Miami · Reydon · Cheyenne · Hammon · Arapaho · Clinton
Channing · Masterson · Sanford · Borger · Phillips · Pampa · New Mobeetie · Briscoe · Rankin · Dempsey · Elk City · Foss · Corn
Boys Ranch · Tascosa · Fritch · Bunavista · Skellytown · White Deer · Kings Mill · Mobeetie · Wheeler · Sweetwater · Sayre · Doxey · Bessie
Adrian · Vega · Amarillo · Panhandle · Lefors · Kellerville · McLean · Lela · Twitty · Erick · Carter · Retrop · Cordell
Glenrio · Wildorado · Bushland · Lark · Conway · Groom · Alanreed · Shamrock · Texola · Dill City · Rocky
San Jon · Endee · Canyon · Goodnight · Claude · Ashtola · Dozier · Samnorwood · Willow · Granite · Lone Wolf · Hobart
Wheatland · Bellview · Hereford · Umbarger · Dawn · Clarendon · Lelia Lake · Hedley · Quail · Vinson · Reed · Mangum · Cooperton
Summerfield · Friona · Nazareth · Happy · Wayside · Brice · Memphis · Lakeview · Newlin · Estelline · Hollis · Gould · Duke · Altus · Snyder
Clovis · Farwell · Texico · Dimmitt · Hart · Tulia · Silverton · Parnell · Childress · Lincoln · Olustee · Creta · Elmer · Roosevelt
Portales · Arch · Muleshoe · Earth · Springlake · Olton · Aiken · Lockney · Quitaque · Turkey · Northfield · Tell · Kirkland · Goodlett · Quanah · Tipton · Frederick
Rogers · Needmore · Circle Back · Sudan · Amherst · Littlefield · Spade · Floydada · Matador · Paducah · Crowell · Thalia · Vernon · Lockett
Enochs · Bula · Anton · Petersburg · Abernathy · Glenn · Dumont · Finney · Rayland · Harrold
Maple · Morton · Whitharral · Shallowater · New Deal · Idalou · Ralls · McAdoo · Guthrie · Vera · Red Springs · Mankins
Bledsoe · Lehman · Whiteface · Levelland · Hurlwood · Smyer · Lorenzo · Dickens · Benjamin · Seymour
Bronco · Sundown · Wolfforth · Lubbock · Posey · Spur · Knox City · Munday · Goree · Bomarton · Olney
Ropesville · New Home · Slaton · Kalgary · Girard · Jayton · Rochester · Weinert · Megargel
Southland · Wilson · Swenson · Old Glory · Haskell · Throckmorton · Newcastle
Meadow · Tahoka · Post · Clairemont · Rule · Aspermont · Sagerton · Woodson
Grassland · Draw · Justiceburg · Old · Stamford · South Bend
O'Donnell · Fluvanna

TEXAS

N.M.
Nara Visa
Logan

Lake Meredith National Recreation Area
Alibates Nat'l Mon.

Palo Duro Canyon State Park
Buffalo Lake Nat'l Wildlife Refuge
Muleshoe Nat'l Wildlife Refuge
Mackenzie State Park
Caprock Canyons State Park
Reese AFB
Quartz Mt. St. Pk.
Great Plains St. Pk.
Copper Breaks State Park
Wichita Mts. W.R.
Lake Kemp
Lake Stamford

Palo Duro Canyon State Park

Oklahoma
Scale of Miles
0 7 14 21 28 35
© Creative Sales Corporation

FOR KANSAS STATE MAP SEE PAGE 37

When travelling on highways in states where there are long stretches of open space, it is important to watch your speed. The 65 mile per hour speed limit applies only to rural areas where it is clearly marked. Drivers should always observe the posted speed limit. Remember, speed kills, so take it easy.

FOR MISSOURI STATE MAP SEE PAGES 48-49

FOR ARKANSAS STATE MAP SEE PAGE 15

FOR TEXAS STATE MAP SEE PAGES 75-79

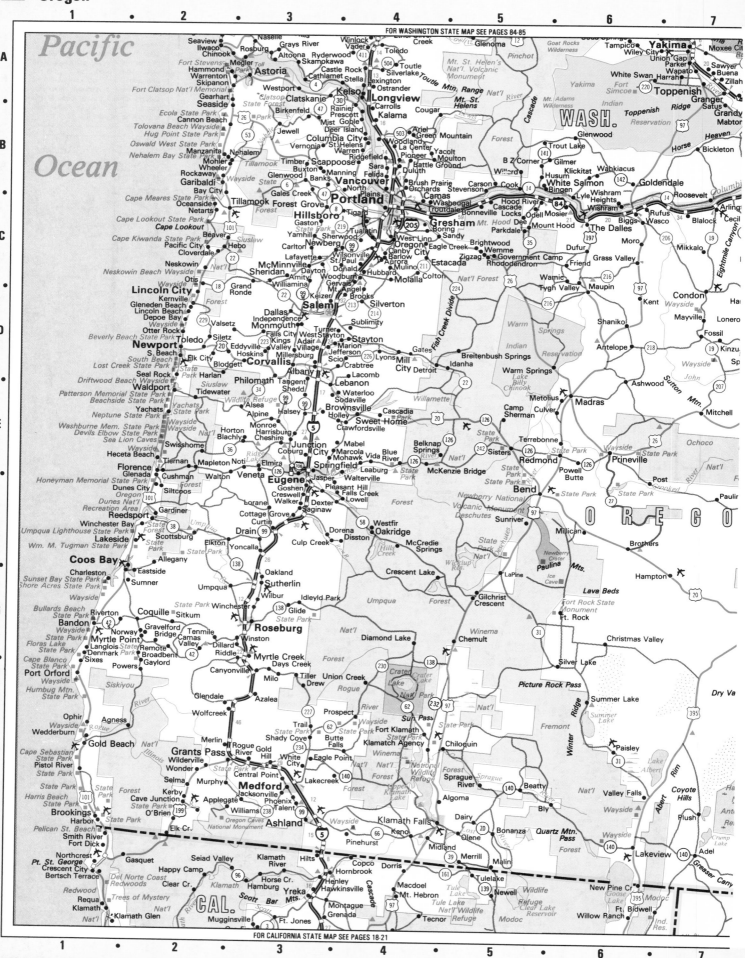

FOR WASHINGTON STATE MAP SEE PAGES 84-85

FOR IDAHO STATE MAP SEE PAGE 31

Vernita U.S. Dept. of Energy Basin City Connell Hay Penawawa Pullman Moscow Deary Troy National Forest
Outlook Sunnyside Mesa Ringold Kahlotus Riparia Hooper Illia Wawawai Almota Joel Kendrick Dworshak Reservoir Headquarters
West Richland Glade Page Eltopia Ayer Pleasant View Starbuck Gould City Dodge Pomeroy Patwawpa Uniontown Genesee Cavendish Ahsahka Grangemont Pierce
Benton City Pasco Burbank Clyde Eureka Prescott Dayton Pataha Clarkston Spalding Lenore Myrtle Reck Orofino Greer Weippe Selway-Bitterroot
Richland Kennewick Wallula Lowden Sudbury Dixie Waitsburg Cloverland Asotin Lewistown Lapwai Gifford Mohler Nezperce Kamiah Clearwater
Prosser Hills Finley Hover Touchet College Place Walla Walla Rogersburg Waha Craigmont Ferdinand Kooskia Mountains Crags Wilderness
Paterson Plymouth McNary Umatilla Umapine Milton-Freewater Troy Flora Greencreek Cottonwood Stites Harpster Lowell National
Irrigon Boardman Hermiston Stanfield Helix Weston Wallowa Flora Keuterville Fenn Grangeville Mount Idaho Selway
Echo Adams Athena Weston Umatilla Nat'l Forest Wenaha Tucannon Wilderness White Bird Golden Elk City
Pendleton Mission Gibbon Minam Elgin Wallowa Lostine Imnaha Hell's Canyon Lucile Orogrande Forest
Pilot Rock Meacham Kamela Summerville Imbler Enterprise Joseph Riggins Dixie Salmon River Breaks Primitive Area
Ukiah Alicel Island City Cove Pollock Payette Gospel Hump Wilderness Idaho
La Grande Union Telocaset Homestead Cuprum Burgdorf Warren Primitive
Meadow Br. Pass Ritter North Powder Haines Medical Springs Tamarack New Meadows Meadows Area
Kimberly Monument Long Creek Granite Sumpter Baker City Halfway McCall Lake Fork Yellow Pine Stibnite
Hamilton Fox Austin Greenhorn Whitney Pleasant Valley New Bridge Richland Fruitvale Donnelly Warm Lake
Dayville Prairie City Bridgeport Durkee Cambridge Starkey Council Casacade Cape Horn
Mount Vernon Canyon City John Day Unity Ironside Brogan Midvale Indian Valley Sunbeam Stanley
Seneca Jamieson Willow Creek Huntington Weiser Smiths Ferry Banks Crouch Garden Valley Lowman Centerville Placerville Pioneerville Idaho City Atlanta
Westfall Vale Ontario Payette Jct. Payette New Plymouth Montour Gardena Ketch
Drewsey Drinkwater Pass Harper Nyssa Fruitland Sweet Horse Shoe Bend
Burns Hines Juntura Owyhee Parma Emmett Pearl Eagle Garden Valley Corral
Riley Lawen Crane Roswell Notus Middleton Star Meridian Boise Pine Fairfield
Warm Springs Valley New Princeton Adrian Wilder Caldwell Nampa Mayfield Hill City
Diamond Malheur Caves Homedale Marsing Kuna Bowmont Melba Orchard Mountain Home
Frenchglen Sheaville The Craters Reynolds Murphy Oreana Silver City Grand View Bruneau Glenns Ferry King Hill Bliss Tuttle
Fields Jordon Valley Lava Beds Hammett Bruneau Hot Sprs. Hagerman Good
Arock Rome Triangle Grasmere Castleford Buhl Filer Twin F
Burns Jct. Riddle Hollister

Denio Denio Junction Fort McDermitt Indian Reservation McDermitt Duck Valley Owyhee

FOR NEVADA STATE MAP SEE PAGE 54

IDAHO

NV.

Oregon
Scale of Miles
0 7 14 21 28 35

© Creative Sales Corporation

FOR NEW YORK STATE MAP SEE PAGES 58-61

FOR OHIO STATE MAP SEE PAGES 66-67

FOR WEST VIRGINIA STATE MAP SEE PAGES 82-83

FOR MARYLAND STATE MAP SEE PAGES 42-43

Lake Erie

Presque Isle St. Pk.

Erie

PENNSYLVANIA

Allegheny National Forest

Gowanda • Springville • Lime Lake • Fillmore • Canaseraga
Fredonia • Brocton • Machias • Houghton • Arkport
Westfield • Mayville • Cassadaga • Cherry Creek • Cattaraugus • Franklinville • Angelica • Almond
N. East • Sherman • Randolph • E. Randolph • Ellicottville • Belmont
Wesleyville • Panama • Lakewood • Celoron • **Jamestown** • Salamanca • Cuba • Friendship • Andover • Wellsville
Fairview • Frewsburg • Allegany • Olean • Richburg • Stannards
Lake City • Girard • McKean • Wattsburg • Sugar Grove • Webb's Ferry • Bradford • Eldred • Shinglehouse • Oswayo
Conneaut • Platea • Cranesville • Waterford • Union City • Warren • Smethport • Port Allegany • Coudersport
Albion • Springboro • Edinboro • Mill Village • Corry • Youngsville • Clarendon • Mt. Jewett • Austin
Andover • Conneautville • Cambridge Springs • Spartansburg • Centerville • Kane • Sizerville
Linesville • Venango • Saegertown • Townville • Tidioute • Wilcox • Emporium
Meadville • Blooming Valley • Hydetown • Titusville • Russell City • Johnsonburg • Renovo
Cochranton • Pleasantville • Oil City • Tionesta • Ridgway • St. Marys • Driftwood • Westport
Greenville • New Lebanon • Sugarcreek • Cooperstown • Rouseville • Clarion • Brockway • Clearfield
Sharon • Hermitage • Franklin • Stoneboro • Jackson Center • Knox • Strattanville • Brockway • Du Bois • Clearfield • Snow Shoe • Milesburg
Farrell • Mercer • Clintonville • Emlenton • St. Petersburg • Corsica • Brookville • Reynoldsville • Curwensville • Bellefonte
Youngstown • New Wilmington • Grove City • Harrisville • Parker • Callensburg • Sligo • Summerville • Sykesville • Philipsburg • Chester Hill • State College
New Castle • Slippery Rock • Bruin • Rimersburg • New Bethlehem • Hawthorn • Big Run • Lumber City • Osceola Mills • Port Matilda
Ellwood City • Harmony • Butler • Petrolia • Karns City • E. Brady • S. Bethlehem • Punxsutawney • Glen Campbell • Newburg • Houtzdale • Centre Hall
Beaver Falls • New Brighton • Zelienople • Evans City • Saxonburg • Dayton • Marion Center • Cherry Tree • Irvona • Ramey
New Beaver • Monaca • Conway • Mars • Freeport • Kittanning • Ford City • Rural Valley • Creekside • Clymer • Barnesboro • Hastings • Patton • Tyrone
Beaver • Aliquippa • Economy • Brackenridge • Indiana • Spangler • Carrolltown • Bellwood • Altoona
Midland • Ambridge • Franklin Park • New Kensington • Lower Burrell • Apollo • Homer City • Ebensburg • Nanty-Glo • Loretto • Gallitzin • Petersburg • Huntingdon
Coraopolis • Bellevue • Oakmont • Plum • Vandergrift • Avonmore • Saltsburg • Cresson • Ashville • Hollidaysburg • Williamsburg
Pittsburgh • Wilkinsburg • Murrysville • Blairsville • Seward • Portage • Lily • Cassandra • Duncansville • Mill Creek • Mt. Union
Carnegie • Dormont • W. Mifflin • Monroeville • New Alexandria • Bolivar • New Florence • S. Fork • Summerhill • Roaring Spring • Marklesburg • Shirleysburg
Bridgeville • Bethel Park • McKeesport • White Oak • Jeanette • Derry • Brownstown • **Johnstown** • Woodbury • Martinsburg • Orbisonia • Saltillo
Canonsburg • Clairton • Youngwood • Greensburg • **Latrobe** • Westmont • Geistown • Scalp Level • Windber • Dudley • Three Gap Springs
Washington • Jefferson • New Eagle • W. Newton • Scottdale • Ligonier • Benson • Hopewell • Broad Top City • Kittatinny Tunnel
Houston • Donora • Mt. Pleasant • Jennerstown • Boswell • Pleasantville • Everett • Tuscarora Tunnel
Monessen • Charleroi • Belle Vernon • N. Belle Vernon • Connellsville • Stoystown • Central City • New Paris • Bedford • Breezewood • Chambersburg
California • Brownsville • S. Connellsville • Somerset • Berlin • Mann's Choice • McConnellsburg • Mercersburg
Marianna • Rices Landing • New Salem • Dunbar • Rockwood • Garrett • Meyersdale • Hyndman • Rainsburg • Greencastle
Waynesburg • Carmichaels • **Uniontown** • Ohiopyle • Ursina • Salisbury • Wellersburg • Hancock • Hagerstown
Masontown • Greensboro • Fairchance • Smithfield • Addison • Lonaconing • Frostburg • **Cumberland** • Williamsport
Point Marion • Star City • Friendsville • Grantsville • Accident • Midland • Barton
Morgantown • Westover • **WV** • **MD**

Lake Erie • Chautauqua L. • Allegheny Res. • Kinzua Bridge • Pymatuning Res.

Pennsylvania
Scale of Miles
0 5 10 15 20 25
© Creative Sales Corporation
N

FOR NEW YORK STATE MAP SEE PAGES 58-61

NEW YORK

FOR NEW JERSEY STATE MAP SEE PAGES 56-57

Avoca, Bath, Hammondsport, Watkins Glen, Montour Falls, Ithaca, Dryden, Oxford, Greene, Sidney, Unadilla, Walton, Andes, Margaretville

Painted Post, Corning, Horseheads, Elmira Hts., Odessa, Spencer, Van Etten, Candor, Newark Valley, Owego, Endwell, Endicott, Binghamton, Windsor, Deposit, Afton, Bainbridge, Oquaga Creek St. Pk., Cannonsville Res., Pepacton Res., Catskill P.

Addison, Woodhull, S. Corning, Southport, Elmira, Waverly, S. Waverly, Athens, Sayre, Nichols, Apalachin, Johnson City, Great Bend, Oakland, Lanesboro, Susquehanna, Hancock, Livingston Manor

Knoxville, Elkland, Tioga, Roseville, Sylvania, Troy, Burlington, Monroe, Towanda, Le Raysville, Montrose, New Milford, Liberty, Jeffersonville, Monticello

Westfield, Galeton, Wellsboro, Blossburg, Canton, Alba, West Burlington, Monroeton, Wyalusing, Meshoppen, Nicholson, Hop Bottom, Union Dale, Forest City, Carbondale, Honesdale

Grand Canyon of Pennsylvania, Leonard Harrison St. Pk., Oleana, Liberty, Dushore, New Albany, Tunkhannock, Factoryville, Dalton, Jermyn, Archbald, Waymart, Hawley, Matamoras

Williamsport, Montoursville, S. Williamsport, Jersey Shore, Dubois town, Watsontown, Milton, Danville, Bloomsburg, Berwick, Nanticoke, Scranton, Taylor, Old Forge, Clarks Summit, Dickson City, Blakely, Olyphant, Dunmore, Moosic, Pittston, Kingston, Wilkes-Barre, Moscow, Milford

Lock Haven, Flemington, Mill Hall, Beech Creek, Loganton, Carrol, Lewisburg, Mifflinburg, Sunbury, Northumberland, Shamokin Dam, Selinsgrove, Shamokin, Mt. Carmel, Frackville, Shenandoah, Mahanoy City, Tamaqua, Hazleton, Freeland, White Haven, Mt. Pocono, E. Stroudsburg, Stroudsburg, Newton

Harrisburg, Hershey, Palmyra, Lebanon, Myerstown, Reading, Wyomissing, Pottstown, Norristown, Philadelphia, Allentown, Bethlehem, Easton, Phillipsburg, Washington, Trenton, Levittown, Bristol, Camden

Carlisle, Mechanicsburg, New Cumberland, Middletown, Elizabethtown, Mt. Joy, Manheim, Lititz, Ephrata, Lancaster, Columbia, Coatesville, W. Chester, Media, Chester, Wilmington, Newark, DE, NJ

Shippensburg, Newville, Newburg, Dillsburg, York, Dover, Red Lion, Quarryville, Oxford, Elkton

Gettysburg, Hanover, Waynesboro, Emmitsburg, Taneytown, Westminster, Bel Air

FOR MARYLAND STATE MAP SEE PAGES 42-43
FOR DELAWARE STATE MAP SEE PAGE 42-43

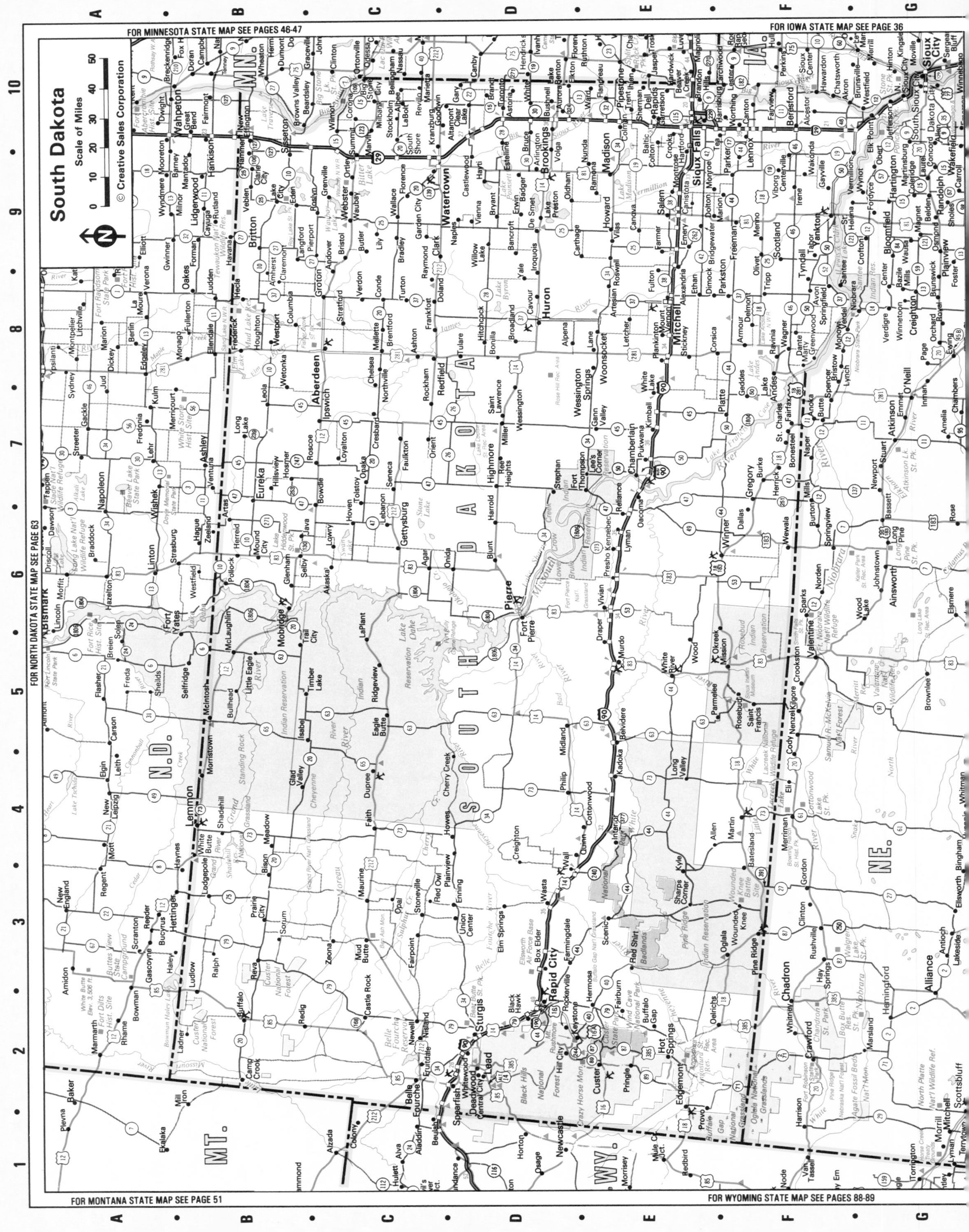

FOR MINNESOTA STATE MAP SEE PAGES 46-47
FOR IOWA STATE MAP SEE PAGE 36
FOR NORTH DAKOTA STATE MAP SEE PAGE 63

South Dakota

Scale of Miles

0 10 20 30 40 50

© Creative Sales Corporation

N

MN

IA

N.D.

MT.

WY.

NE.

SOUTH DAKOTA

Sioux Falls · Watertown · Brookings · Madison · Huron · Mitchell · Yankton · Aberdeen · Pierre · Fort Pierre · Rapid City · Sturgis · Deadwood · Lead · Spearfish · Belle Fourche · Mobridge · Lemmon · Chamberlain · Winner · Valentine · Chadron

FOR MONTANA STATE MAP SEE PAGE 51
FOR WYOMING STATE MAP SEE PAGES 88-89

Texas

Scale of Miles

0 8 16 24 32 40

© Creative Sales Corporation

N

NEW MEXICO

TEXAS

UNITED STATES

MEXICO

CHIHUAHUA

Engle

Ancho
Jicarilla
Lincoln National Forest
Carrizozo
White Oaks
Pine Lodge
Arabela
Capitan
Lincoln
San Patricio
Angus
Alto
Ruidoso Downs
Hondo
Tinnie
Picacho
Sunset
Ruidoso
Bent
Mescalero
Apache Mescalero Indian Reservation
Tularosa
Elk Silver
La Luz
High Rolls
Cloudcroft
Alamogordo
White Sands Nat'l Mon.
Sacramento
Elk
Mayhill
Weed
Lincoln National Forest
Dunken
Hope
Pinon
Orogrande
White Sands Missile Range
Fort Bliss Military Reservation

Mesa
Roswell
Dexter
Greenfield
Hagerman
Lake Arthur
Artesia
Riverside
Atoka
Loco Hills
Seven Rivers
Lake McMillan
Carlsbad
Black River Village
Loving
Malaga
Whites City
Carlsbad Caverns
Carlsbad Caverns National Park

Elida
Rogers
Needmore
Fieldton
Sudan
Dora
Pep
Goodland
Enochs
Maple
Morton
Littlefield
Muleshoe Nat'l Wildlife Refuge
Whitharral
Milnesand
Bledsoe
Lehman
Whiteface
Levelland
Crossroads
Sundown
Bronco
Brownfield
McDonald
Hilburn City
Lovington
Denver City
Seagraves
Wellman
Loop
Welc
Humble City
Knowles
Hobbs
Monument
Nadine
Seminole
Oil Center
Eunice
Patricia
Frankel City
Jal
Gardendale
Midland
Kermit
Notrees
Odessa
Wink
Monahans Sandhills State Park
Penwell
Pyote
Monahans
Pecos
Barstow
Wickett
Royalty
Crane
Grandfalls
Imperial
Toyah
Coyanosa
McCamey
Balmorhea State Park
Saragosa
Balmorhea
Fort Stockton
Girvin
Bakersfield
Iraa
Shef

Rincon
Hill
Dona Ana
Organ
Fairacres
Las Cruces
Mesilla
San Miguel
La Mesa
Mesquite
Chamberino
Berino
Chaparral
Anthony
Newman
Franklin Mt. St. Pk.
Canutillo
Univ. of Texas at El Paso
Magoffin House State Park
El Paso
Socorro
Clint
Ciudad Juarez
San Elizario
Fabens
Tornillo
Horizon City
Acala
Fort Hancock
McNary
Sierra Blanca
Allamore
Van Horn
Lobo
Valentine
Davis Mountains State Park
Fort Davis
Marfa
Alpine
Plata
Shafter
Ojinaga
Fort Leaton State Park
Redford
Terlingua
Study Butte
Chisos Basin
Big Bend National Park
Boquillas del Carmen

Huenco Tanks State Park
El Paso Gap
Dell City
Cornudas
Salt Flat
Guadalupe Mtns. National Park
Red Bull Lake
Orla
Mentone

Chihuahua

FOR CONTINUATION SEE PAGE 76
FOR CONTINUATION SEE PAGE 78

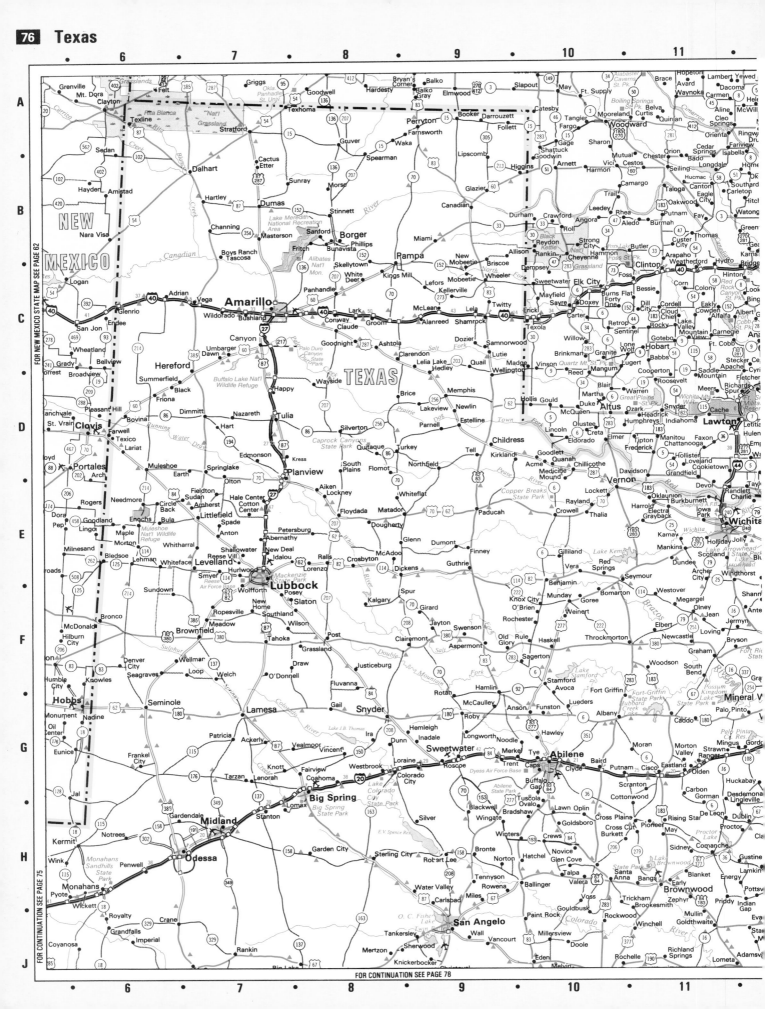

FOR NEW MEXICO STATE MAP SEE PAGE 62

FOR CONTINUATION SEE PAGE 75

Texas

Scale of Miles
0 8 16 24 32 40

N

© Creative Sales Corporation

FOR OKLAHOMA STATE MAP SEE PAGES 68-69

FOR ARKANSAS STATE MAP SEE PAGE 15

FOR LOUISIANA STATE MAP SEE PAGE 40

FOR CONTINUATION SEE PAGE 79

OKLAHOMA

ARKANSAS

TEXAS

LA.

Major cities and places shown include: Enid, Oklahoma City, El Reno, Yukon, Shawnee, Stillwater, Guthrie, Edmond, Norman, Chickasha, Duncan, Ardmore, Ada, Pauls Valley, Sulphur, Durant, Denison, Sherman, Gainesville, Denton, Fort Worth, Arlington, Dallas, Irving, Garland, Richardson, Mesquite, Grand Prairie, Cleburne, Corsicana, Waco, Tulsa, Broken Arrow, Sapulpa, Muskogee, McAlester, Henryetta, Okmulgee, Fort Smith, Tahlequah, Fayetteville, Paris, Greenville, Sulphur Sprs, Commerce, Mt. Pleasant, Texarkana, Marshall, Longview, Tyler, Kilgore, Henderson, Carthage, Nacogdoches, Lufkin, Palestine, Jacksonville, Athens, Shreveport, Minden

FOR CONTINUATION SEE PAGE 76
FOR CONTINUATION SEE PAGE 75

Rankin
Mertzon
Eden
Rochelle
Richland Springs
Lometa
Adamsville
McCamey
Big Lake
Knickerbocker
Christoval
Melvin
Brady
San Saba
Copp
Lampasa
Girvin
Barnhart
Calf Creek
Voca
Fredonia
Cherokee
Tow
Buchanan
Fort Stockton
Bakersfield
Iraan
Menard
Hext
Katemcy
Pontotoc
Valley Spring
Bluffton
Buchanan Dam
Eldorado
Fort McKavett State Park
Fort McKavett
London
Grit
Mason
Llano
Mico Lake
Longho
Sheffield
Fort Lancaster State Park
Ozona
Sonora
Roosevelt
Junction
Segovia
Loyal Valley
Cherry Spring
Kingsland
Marble Falls
Spicew
Doss
Willow City
Round Mountain
Sanderson
Juno
Telegraph
Harper
Fredericksburg
Johnson City
Stonewall
Hye
Dryden
Loma Alta
Rocksprings
Mountain Home
Hunt
Ingram
Kerrville
Comfort
Luckenbach
Blanco
Langtry
Carta Valley
Barksdale
Camp Wood
Center Pt.
Sisterdale
Spring Branch
Ne
Brau
Comstock
Amistad National Recreation Area
Vanderpool
Camp Verde
Medina
Pipecreek
Lost Maples State Park
Bandera
Tarpley
Utopia
Leon Springs
Convers
Sch
Del Rio
Ciudad Acuna
Fort Clark Springs
Brackettville
Concan
Riomedina
Castroville
Mico
Lake Hills
San
Spofford
Dabney
Blewett
Uvalde
Knippa
D'Hanis
Sabinal
Hondo
Natalia
Lytle
Devine
Somerset
Leming
Querpado
Normandy
Frio Town
Moore
Bigfoot
Poteet
Jourdanton
Pleasant
Eagle Pass
Piedras Negras
Crystal City
La Pryor
Batesville
Derby
Dilley
Charlotte
Christine
Hindes
Campbellton
Whitsett
Brundage
Big Wells
Woodward
Millett
Los Angeles
Fowlerton
Tilden
Three Rivers
Carrizo Springs
Asherton
Cotulla
Calliham
George We
Catarina
Artesia Wells
TEXAS
Nueces
Nueva Rosita
Encinal
Freer
San Diego
Ora
San
Benavides
Oilton
Realitos
Concepcion
COAHUILA
Laredo St. Univ.
Lake Casa Blanca State Park
Nuevo Laredo
Laredo
Mirando City
Bruni
Ramirez
Hebbronville
UNITED STATES
MEXICO
San Ygnacio
Escobas
Randado
Bustamante
Monclova
Lopeno
Falcon
La Gloria
Santa Ele
San Isidr
Sabinas Hidalgo
Nuevo Guerrero
Falcon State Park
El Sauz
La Reforma
Cd. Mier
Roma
Rio Grande City
Edinbu
NUEVO LEON
Cd. Camargo
La Grulla
Sullivan City
La Joya
Mission
Presa De El Azucar
Bentson-Rio Grande Valley State Park
Hidalgo
San Pedro de las Colonias
Reynosa
Monterrey

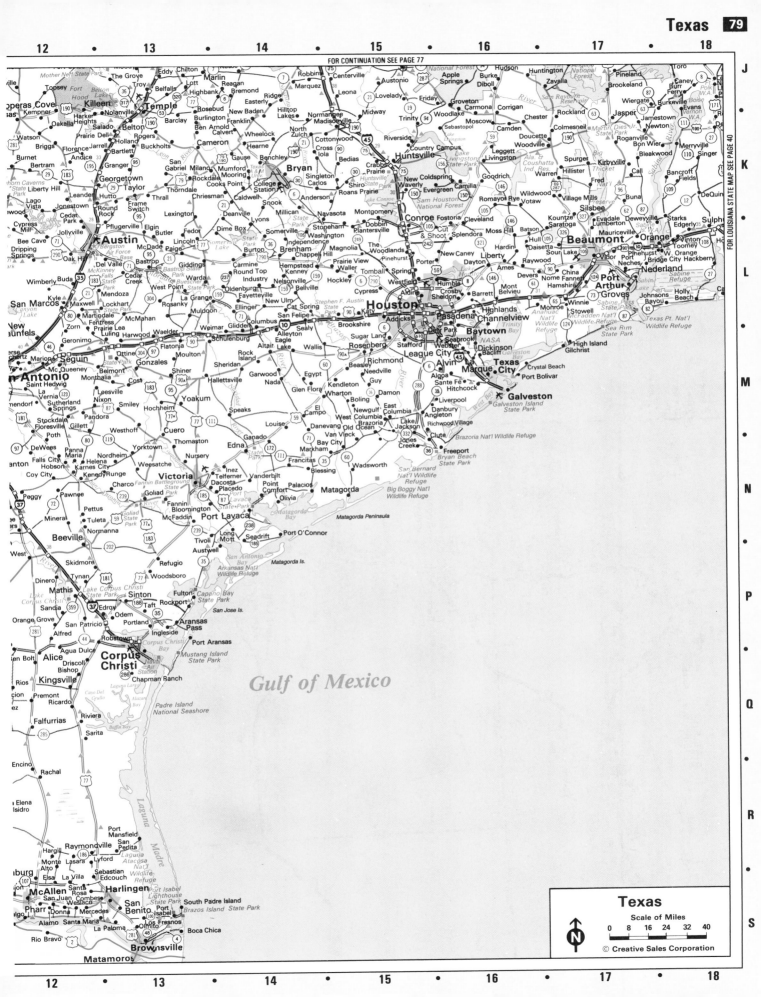

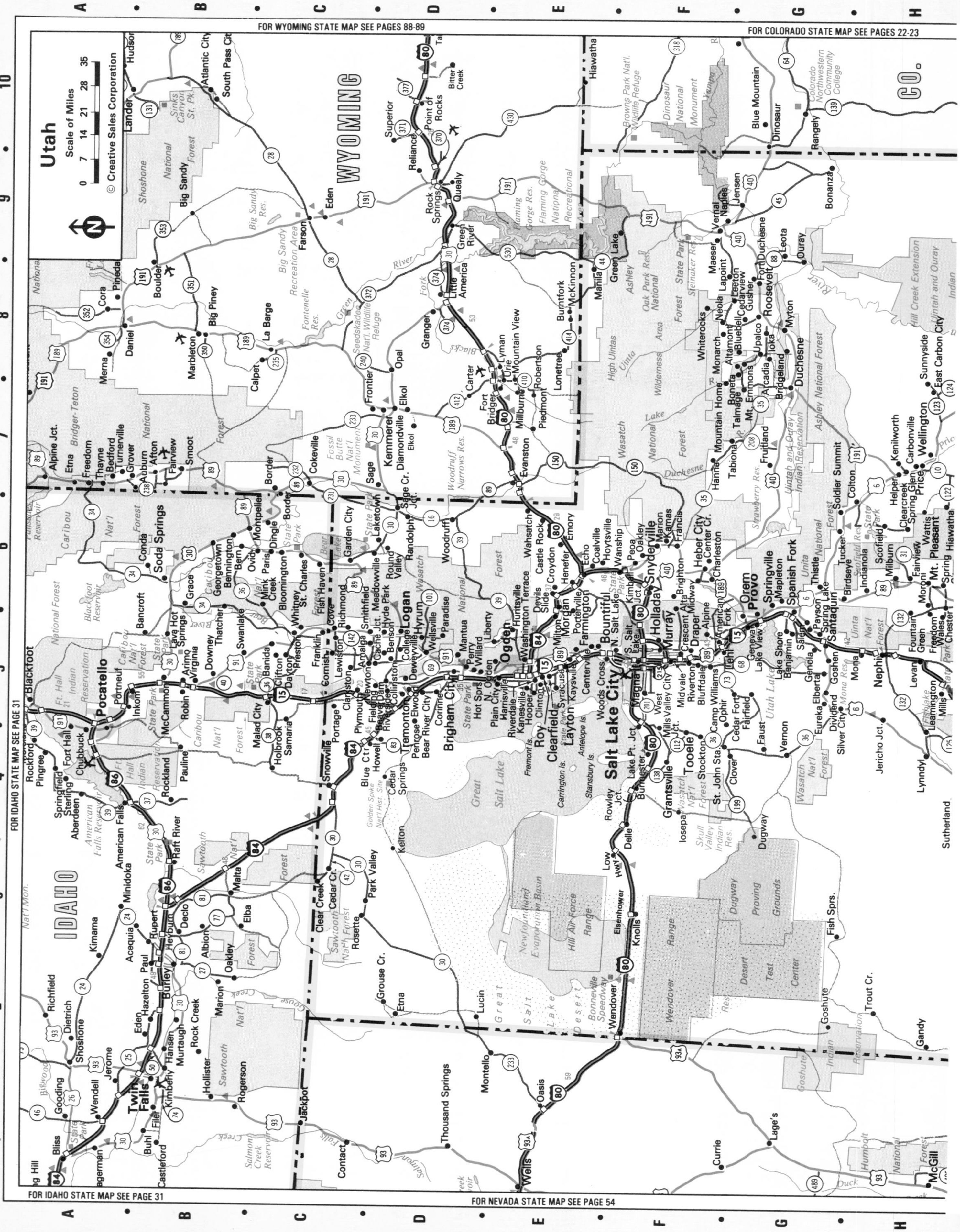

FOR WYOMING STATE MAP SEE PAGES 88-89
FOR COLORADO STATE MAP SEE PAGES 22-23

Utah

Scale of Miles

0 7 14 21 28 35

© Creative Sales Corporation

N

WYOMING

IDAHO

CO.

Great Salt Lake

Great Salt Lake Desert

Salt Lake City

Ogden

Provo

Orem

Pocatello

Blackfoot

Twin Falls

Burley

Rock Springs

Green River

Evanston

Logan

Brigham City

Vernal

Dinosaur

Tooele

Nephi

Spanish Fork

Bonneville Speedway

Wendover

FOR IDAHO STATE MAP SEE PAGE 31
FOR IDAHO STATE MAP SEE PAGE 31
FOR NEVADA STATE MAP SEE PAGE 54

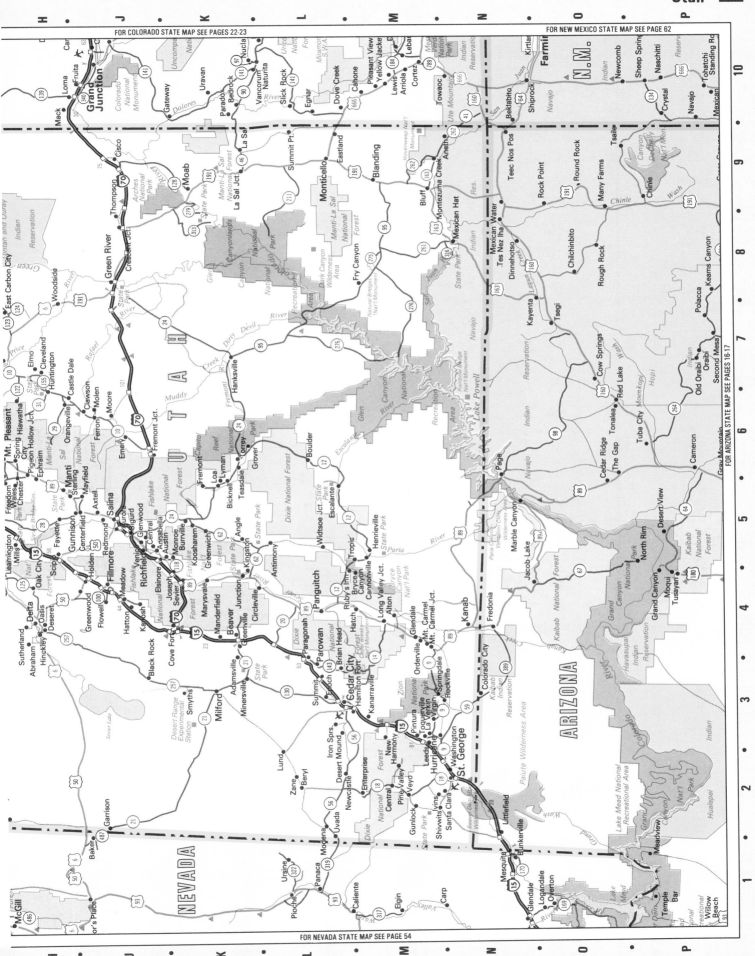

FOR COLORADO STATE MAP SEE PAGES 22-23
FOR NEW MEXICO STATE MAP SEE PAGE 62
FOR ARIZONA STATE MAP SEE PAGES 16-17

FOR OHIO STATE MAP SEE PAGES 66-67

FOR PENNSYLVANIA STATE MAP SEE PAGES 72-73

FOR OHIO STATE MAP SEE PAGES 66-67

FOR KENTUCKY STATE MAP SEE PAGES 38-39

OHIO

WEST VIRGINIA

KENTUCKY

TENN.

Columbus

Pittsburgh

Wheeling

Morgantown

Charleston

Parkersburg

Huntington

Ashland

Portsmouth

Beckley

Roanoke

Blacksburg

Bluefield

Bristol

Kingsport

Danville

Newark   **Zanesville**   **Lancaster**   **Logan**   **Marietta**   **Athens**   **Chillicothe**   **Jackson**

Marion   **Mt. Vernon**   **Delaware**   **Coshocton**   **New Philadelphia**

Weirton   **McKeesport**   **Bethel Park**   **Washington**   **Monessen**

Clarksburg   **Fairmont**   **Bridgeport**   **Elkins**

Williamson   **Logan**   **Lynchburg**

Welch   **Princeton**   **Pulaski**   **Radford**   **Christiansburg**

Wytheville   **Marion**   **Martinsville**

Virginia West Virginia
Scale of Miles
0 7 14 21 28 35
© Creative Sales Corporation

FOR PENNSYLVANIA STATE MAP SEE PAGES 72-73

FOR NEW JERSEY STATE MAP SEE PAGES 56-57

FOR DELAWARE STATE MAP SEE PAGE 42-43

FOR NORTH CAROLINA STATE MAP SEE PAGES 64-65

PENN.
MD.
VIRGINIA
N.J.
DEL.
N.C.
Atlantic Ocean
Chesapeake Bay

Altoona, Johnstown, Huntingdon, Carrolltown, Homer City, Ebensburg, Duncansville, Hollidaysburg, Roaring Spring, Windber, Westmont, Boswell, Central City, Somerset, Myersdale, Hyndman, Bedford, Everett, Napier, Breezewood, McConnellsburg, Chambersburg, Shippensburg, Fayetteville, Mont Alto, Waynesboro, Greencastle, Gettysburg, Hanover, McSherrystown, Shrewsbury, York, Columbia, Lancaster, Ephrata, Manheim, Hershey, Harrisburg, Camp Hill, Carlisle, Newville, Boiling Springs, Mt. Holly Spr., Dillsburg, East Berlin, Spring Grove, Red Lion, Oxford, West Grove, Quarryville, Millersville, Coatesville, Phoenixville, Willow Grove, Glenside, Philadelphia, Westchester, Chester, Elsmere, Wilmington, Newark, Rising Sun, North East, Elkton, Aberdeen, Edgewood, Middletown, Townsend, Smyrna, Clayton, Dover, Camden, Harrington, Felton, Frederica, Greenwood, Milford, Lewes, Milton, Ellendale, Georgetown, Frankford, Selbyville, Laurel, Delmar, Salisbury, Fruitland, Snow Hill, Princess Anne, Westover, Chincoteague

Cumberland, Hagerstown, Hancock, Warfordsburg, Grantsville, Ridgeley, Keyser, Piedmont, Romney, Paw Paw, Martinsburg, Shepherdstown, Charles Town, Ranson, Inwood, Winchester, Stephens City, Middletown, Berryville, Purcellville, Leesburg, Frederick, Mt. Airy, Catonsville, Columbia, Baltimore, Parkville, Edgemere, Rock Hall, Chestertown, Centreville, Queenstown, Grasonville, Easton, St. Michaels, Cambridge, Hurlock, Seaford

Moorefield, Petersburg, Wardensville, Baker, Strasburg, Woodstock, New Market, Mt. Jackson, Timberville, Broadway, Luray, Stanley, Shenandoah, Elkton, Front Royal, Marshall, Warrenton, Sperryville, Culpeper, Remington, Madison, Gordonsville, Orange, Manassas, Fairfax, Vienna, Arlington, Washington, Alexandria, Woodbridge, Dale City, Herndon, Bethesda, Silver Spring, Greenbelt, Annapolis, Southgate, Chesapeake Beach, Prince Frederick, Leonardtown, Lexington Pk., Montrose, St. Charles, La Plata, White Plains, Waldorf, Colonial Beach, Oak Grove, Warsaw, Tappahannock, Lottsburg, Burgess, Lancaster, Kilmarnock, Irvington, Tangier, Saxis, Parksley, Onancock, Onley, Mappsville, Belle Haven, Exmore, Nassawadox

Harrisonburg, Dayton, Bridgewater, Verona, Staunton, Waynesboro, Crozet, Charlottesville, Scottsville, Zion, Palmyra, Louisa, Cuckoo, Gum Spr., Ashland, Hanover, Mechanicsville, Richmond, Bon Air, Powhatan, Chester, Sandston, West Point, Gloucester, Gloucester Pt., Seaford, Poquoson, Hampton, Newport News, Norfolk, Portsmouth, Virginia Beach, Chesapeake, Suffolk, Williamsburg, Surry, Smithfield, Windsor, Cape Charles, Cheriton, Eastville, Mathews, Deltaville, Gwynn, King & Queen C.H., Urbanna, King William, Central Garage

Buena Vista, Lexington, Lovingston, Shipman, Amherst, Madison Hts., Buckingham, Dillwyn, Cumberland, Farmville, Appomattox, Hampden-Sydney, Pamplin City, Rustburg, Gladys, Altavista, Hurt, Brookneal, Gretna, Chatham, South Boston, Halifax, Volens, Wylliesburg, Chase City, Boydton, Clarksville, South Hill, La Crosse, Brodnax, Lawrenceville, Kenbridge, Victoria, Keysville, Drakes Branch, Blackstone, Crewe, Burkeville, Amelia, Powhatan, Colonial Hts., Petersburg, Hopewell, Waverley, Wakefield, Sussex, McKenney, Jarratt, Emporia, Franklin, Courtland, Roanoke Rapids, Murfreesboro, Garysburg, Pleasant Hill

Mt. Storm, Scherr, Junction, Augusta, Lost City, Oak Flat, Brandywine Rec. Area, Smoke Hole Rec. Area, Stuarts Draft

Raystown Lake, Blue Knob St. Pk., Shawnee St. Pk., Gifford Pinchot St. Pk., Codorus St. Pk., Michaux St. Forest, Catoctin Mtn. Park, Cunningham Falls St. Pk., George Washington Nat'l Forest, Shenandoah Nat'l Park, Sky Meadows St. Pk., Manassas Nat'l Battlefield Pk., Quantico U.S. Marine Corps Res., Lake Anna St. Pk., Pocahontas St. Forest, Lake Chesdin, Fort Pickett, Fort Eustis, Blackwater Nat'l Wildlife Rfg., Chesapeake Bay Bridge Tunnel Toll

1 2 3 4 5 6 7 8

BRITISH COLUMBIA
Vancouver Island

Barkleys Sound
Nitinat Lake
Ladysmith
Duncan
Sidney
Port Renfrew
Friday Harbor
Victoria
Sooke
Neah Bay
Ozette
Sappho
Forks
La Push
Fairholm
Joyce
Port Angeles
Sequim
Port Townsend
Coupeville
Oak Harbor
Discovery Bay

CANADA
U.S.
Strait of Juan De Fuca
Strait of Georgia

White Rock
Blaine
Langley
Mission
Sumas
Lynden
Ferndale
Everson
Bellingham
Deming
Mount Baker
Acme
Wickersham
Lyman
Hamilton
Concrete
Rockport
Sedro-Woolley
Burlington
Mount Vernon
La Conner
Anacortes
Stanwood
Arlington
Darrington
Marysville
Granite Falls
Everett
Lake Stevens
Mukilteo
Snohomish
Sultan
Gold Bar
Index
Monroe
Duvall
Carnation
Skykomish
Lynnwood
Edmonds
Bothell
Seattle
Kirkland
Redmond
Bellevue
Bremerton
Mercer Island
Renton
Issaquah
North Bend
Poulsbo
Bainbridge Island
Port Orchard
Kent
Black Diamond
Hyak
Des Moines
Auburn
Salmon
Gig Harbor
Tacoma
Sumner
Enumclaw
Fircrest
Bonney Lake
Buckley
Steilacoom
Puyallup
Orting
Carbonado
Greenwater
Olympia
Lacey
Tumwater
Roy
Yelm
Eatonville
Shelton
Union
Hoodsport
Eldon
Neilton
Taholah
Pacific Beach
Copalis Beach
Ocean Shores
Westport
Aberdeen
Hoquiam
Montesano
Elma
McCleary
Oakville
Rochester
Tenino
Rainier
North Cove
Raymond
South Bend
Menlo
Lebam
Pe Ell
Bucoda
Centralia
Chehalis
Napavine
Klaus
Morton
Glenoma
Randle
Packwood
Winlock
Vader
Toledo
Mossyrock
Ocean Park
Long Beach
Ilwaco
Naselle
Rosburg
Ryderwood
Castle Rock
Silver Lake
Mt. St. Helens
Trout Lake
Astoria
Warrenton
Seaside
Cannon Beach
Manzanita
Cathlamet
Stella
Kelso
Longview
Clatskanie
Kalama
Woodland
La Center
Ridgefield
Battle Ground
Yacolt
Stevenson
Bonneville Dam
Hood River
White Salmon
Bingen
Klickitat
Husum
Garibaldi
Tillamook
Forest Grove
Vancouver
Camas
Washougal
The Dalles
Hillsboro
Gresham
Portland
Oregon City
Newberg
Sandy
Dufur

Olympic National Park
Olympic Nat'l Forest
Mt. Rainier Nat'l Park
Snoqualmie Nat'l Forest
Gifford Pinchot Nat'l Forest

Pacific Ocean
Willapa Bay
Grays Harbor
Columbia R.

Washington
Scale of Miles
0 6 12 18 24 30

N

© Creative Sales Corporation

1 2 3 4 5 6 7 8

WASHINGTON

CANADA
U.S.

BC

OREGON

IDAHO

FOR IDAHO STATE MAP SEE PAGE 31

Manning Prov. Pk.
Cathedral Prov. Pk.
Pasayten Wilderness
Ross Lake
Okanogan
Osoyoos
Greenwood
Grand Forks
Rossland
Trail
Montrose
Christina Lake
Osoyoos Lake Vets. Mem. St. Pk.
Similkameen Dam
Oroville
Danville
Northport
Boundary
Boundary Dam
Colville
Metaline Falls
Metaline
Nat'l
Forest
Nordman
Palmer Lk.
Okanogan
Tonasket
Wauconda
Republic
Orient
Marcus
Kettle Falls
Bossburg
Ione
Priest Lake St. Pk.
Priest Lake
Kaniksu
National
Forest
Conconully St. Pk.
Conconully
Riverside
Omak
Okanogan
Disautel
Colville
Colville
Addy
Cusick
Sandpoint
Omak Lake
Indian
Res.
Gifford
Chewelah
National
Forest
Kaniksu
Nat'l
Forest
Albeni Falls Dam
Newport
Priest River
Oldtown
Pend Oreille Round Lake St. Pk.
Spirit Lake
Bayview
Athol
Winthrop
Twisp
Pearrygin Lake St. Pk.
Brewster
Pateros
Bridgeport
Chief Joseph Dam
Bridgeport St. Pk.
Elmer City
Coulee Dam
Keller
Free Ferry
Springdale
Clayton
Deer Park
Mt. Spokane St. Pk.
Spirit Lake
Twin Lakes
Rathdrum
Hayden Lake
Farragut St. Pk.
Spirit Lake
Lake Chelan Nat'l Rec. Area
Sawtooth Wilderness
Methow
25 Mile Creek St. Pk.
Alta Lake St. Pk.
Manson
Wells Dam
Grand Coulee Dam
Electric City
Grand Coulee
Steamboat Rock St. Pk.
Spokane Indian Res.
Little Falls Dam
Long Lake Dam
Post Falls
Coeur D'Alene
Telma
Chelan
Lake Chelan Dam
Mansfield
Withrow
Banks Lake
Wilbur
Creston
Davenport
Reardan
Spokane
Airway Heights
Millwood
Coeur D'Alene
Leavenworth
Entiat
Waterville
Dry Falls Dam
Hartline
Almira
Medical Lake
Cheney
Rockford
Coeur D'Alene Lake
Cashmere
Rocky Reach Dam
Lincoln Rock St. Pk.
Lenore Lake
Lake Lenore Caves St. Pk.
Coulee City
Sun Lakes St. Pk.
Harrington
Edwall
Spangle
Waverly
Fairfield
Plummer
Wenatchee
East Wenatchee
Rock Island
Rock Island Dam
Soap Lake
Summer Falls St. Pk.
Wilson Creek
Krupp
Odessa
Rosalia
Tekoa
Latah
WASHINGTON
Appleyard
Wenatchee Hts.
Squilchuck St. Pk.
Ephrata
Quincy
Crescent Bar
Winchester Res.
Moses Lake St. Pk.
Moses Lake
Ritzville
Lamont
St. John
Rock Lake
Steptoe Butte St. Pk.
Oakesdale
Farmington
Roslyn
Cle Elum
Ellensburg
Kittitas
Vantage
George
Moses Lake Dam
Potholes Res.
O'Sullivan Dam
Warden
Lind
Sprague
Steptoe
Garfield
Palouse
Potlatch
Naches
Tieton
Selah
Wanapum St. Pk.
Wanapum Dam
Royal City
Frenchman Hills Lakes
Potholes St. Pk.
Columbia Nat'l Wildlife Refuge
La Crosse
Dusty
Endicott
Colfax
Albion
Yakima
Union Gap
Moxee City
U.S. Military Reservation Yakima Firing Range
Priest Rapids Dam
Yakima Sportsman's St. Pk.
Saddle Mtn. Nat'l Wildlife Refuge
Mattawa
Othello
Hatton
Washtucna
Pullman
Moscow
Wapato
Sunnyside Dam
Zillah
Granger
Sunnyside
U.S. Dept. of Energy
Hanford Site
Connell
Mesa
Kahlotus
Lower Granite Dam
Central Ferry St. Pk.
Colton
Uniontown
Genesee
Harrah
White Swan
Toppenish
Grandview
Mabton
Prosser
Granger
Benton City
West Richland
Richland
Pasco
Kennewick
Eureka
Little Goose Dam
Dodge
Pomeroy
Clarkston
Lewiston
Asotin
Craigmon
Nez Perce Indian Res.
Bickleton
Juniper Dunes Wilderness
Lower Monumental Dam
Starbuck
Dayton
Camp William T. Wooten St. Pk.
Umatilla Nat'l Forest
Wallula
Prescott
Waitsburg
Wenaha
Hells Gate St. Pk.
Anatone
Winchester Lake St. Pk.
Goldendale
Roosevelt
Boardman
Hermiston
Stanfield
Pendleton
College Place
Walla Walla
Whitman Mission Nat'l Hist. Site
Milton-Freewater
Athena
Lewis & Clark Trail St. Pk.
Fields Spring St. Pk.
Wilderness
Hells Canyon
Wasco
Moro
John Day Dam
Arlington
Ione
Lexington
Heppner
Pilot Rock
Umatilla Indian Res.
Elgin
Wallowa
Enterprise
Joseph
Nat'l Forest
Whitman
Wallowa
Hells Canyon Nat'l Rec. Area
McNary Dam
Umatilla Nat'l Wildlife Refuge
Cold Springs Wildlife Refuge
Crow Butte St. Pk.

FOR MICHIGAN STATE MAP SEE PAGES 44-45

United States Citizens Visiting Canada

All persons entering Canada must report to the Canadian Immigration and Customs Office at the Port of Entry and secure required permits for admission for their person and possessions. The transportation of plants and produce is rigidly controlled. Check with customs officials for complete regulations and requirements.

Canadian Citizens Visiting the United States

Passports or visas are not required of Canadian citizens or British subjects residing in Canada entering the United States for a period of six months or less, however, evidence of citizenship is required. Check with customs officials for complete regulations and requirements.

The Interstate Highway System in and around the Chicago area is confusing to many people. It is helpful to remember that, in most cases, Interstate Highways running north and south have odd numbers, and Interstate Highways running east and west have even numbers

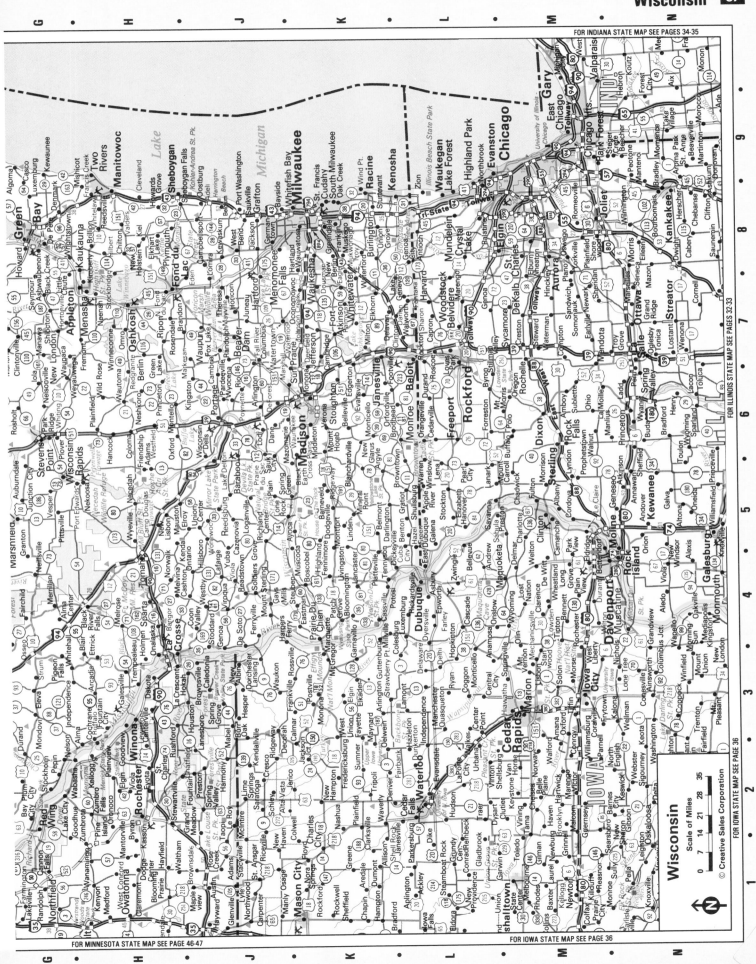

FOR INDIANA STATE MAP SEE PAGES 34-35

FOR ILLINOIS STATE MAP SEE PAGES 32,33

FOR IOWA STATE MAP SEE PAGE 36

FOR MINNESOTA STATE MAP SEE PAGE 46-47

FOR IOWA STATE MAP SEE PAGE 36

Wisconsin

Scale of Miles

0 7 14 21 28 35

© Creative Sales Corporation

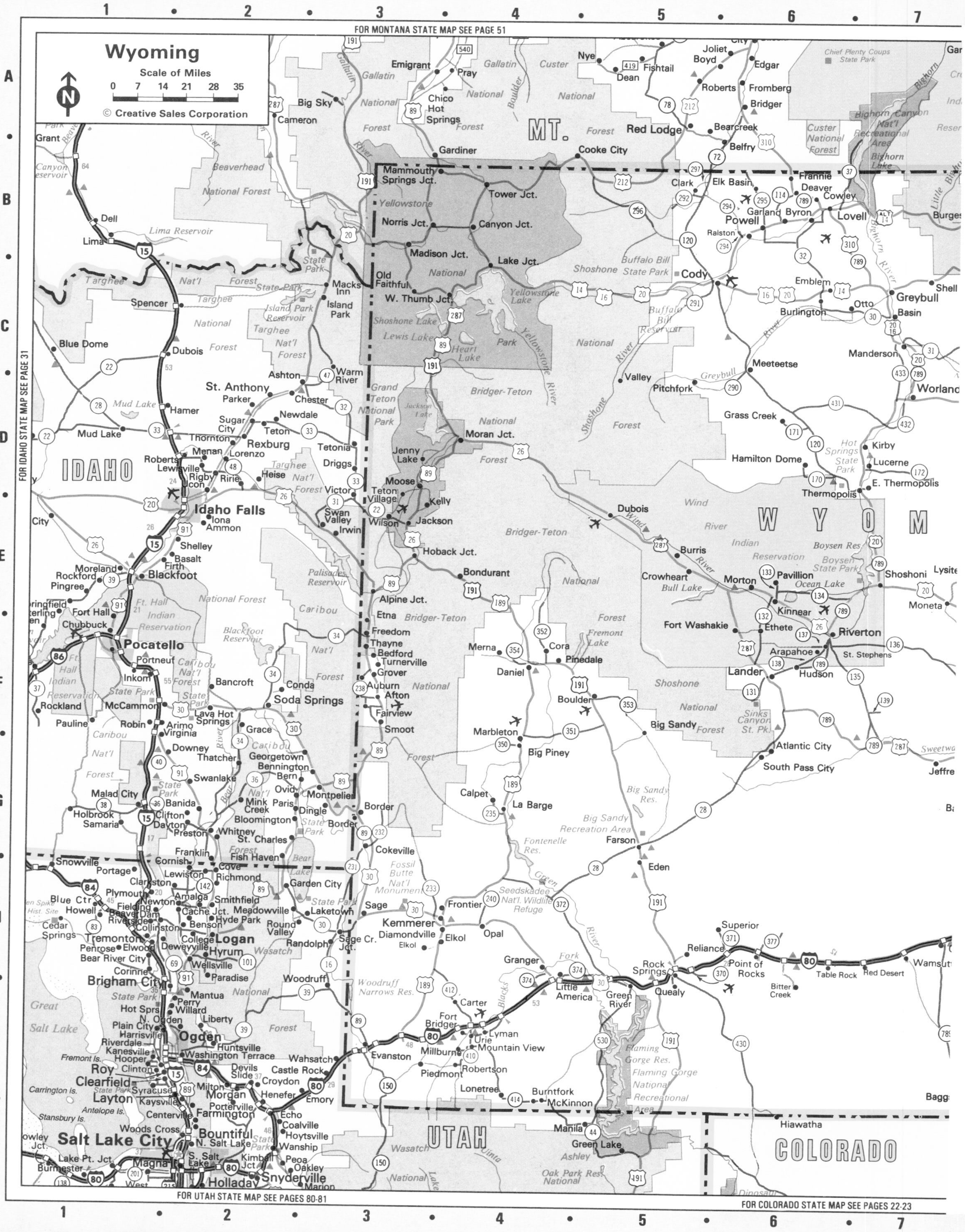

Wyoming

Scale of Miles

0 7 14 21 28 35

© Creative Sales Corporation

N

FOR MONTANA STATE MAP SEE PAGE 51

FOR IDAHO STATE MAP SEE PAGE 31

W Y O M

IDAHO

MT.

Yellowstone National Park

Grand Teton National Park

UTAH

COLORADO

FOR COLORADO STATE MAP SEE PAGES 22-23

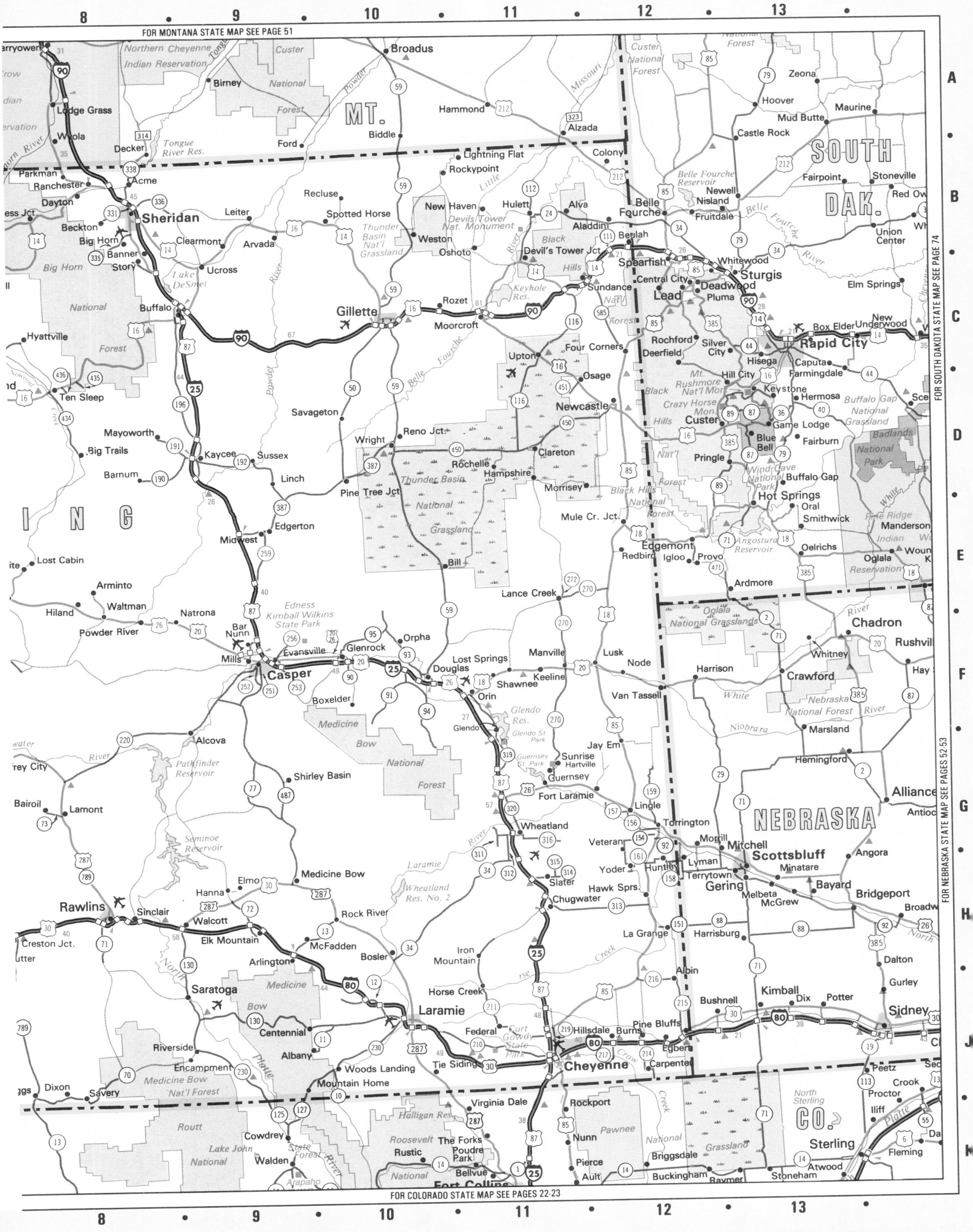
8
9
10
11
12
13
FOR MONTANA STATE MAP SEE PAGE 51
FOR SOUTH DAKOTA STATE MAP SEE PAGE 74
FOR NEBRASKA STATE MAP SEE PAGES 52-53
FOR COLORADO STATE MAP SEE PAGES 22-23
A
B
C
D
E
F
G
H
J
K
MT.
SOUTH
DAK.
NEBRASKA
CO.
I N G
Northern Cheyenne
Indian Reservation
Custer
National
Forest
Broadus
Birney
Hammond
Alzada
Biddle
Ford
Decker
Tongue
River Res.
Lodge Grass
Wyola
Parkman
Ranchester
Dayton
Acme
Sheridan
Big Horn
Banner
Story
Beckton
Clearmont
Ucross
Leiter
Arvada
Recluse
Spotted Horse
Thunder
Basin
Nat'l
Grassland
Lightning Flat
Rockypoint
Colony
New Haven
Hulett
Alva
Devils Tower
Nat. Monument
Aladdin
Belle Fourche
Beulah
Weston
Oshoto
Devil's Tower Jct.
Black
Hills
Spearfish
Sundance
Central City
Lead
Deadwood
Pluma
Sturgis
Whitewood
Keyhole
Res.
Gillette
Rozet
Moorcroft
Buffalo
Big Horn
National
Forest
Hyattville
Ten Sleep
Lake
DeSmet
Upton
Four Corners
Osage
Newcastle
Rochford
Deerfield
Silver
City
Hill City
Hisega
Rapid City
Box Elder
New
Underwood
Caputa
Farmingdale
Keystone
Hermosa
Mt.
Rushmore
Nat'l Mon.
Crazy Horse
Mon.
Custer
Game Lodge
Fairburn
Blue
Bell
Pringle
Wind Cave
National
Park
Buffalo Gap
Hot Springs
Oral
Smithwick
Buffalo Gap
National
Grassland
Badlands
National
Park
Savageton
Reno Jct.
Wright
Rochelle
Hampshire
Clareton
Morrisey
Pine Tree Jct.
Thunder Basin
National
Grassland
Mayoworth
Big Trails
Kaycee
Sussex
Barnum
Linch
Edgerton
Midwest
Bill
Mule Cr. Jct.
Black Hills
National
Forest
Edgemont
Redbird
Igloo
Provo
Angostura
Reservoir
Oelrichs
Oglala
Pine Ridge
Manderson
Indian
Reservation
Ardmore
Lost Cabin
Arminto
Waltman
Hiland
Powder River
Natrona
Bar Nunn
Edness
Kimball Wilkins
State Park
Evansville
Mills
Casper
Glenrock
Orpha
Lance Creek
Oglala
National Grasslands
Chadron
Whitney
Rushville
Hay
Lost Springs
Douglas
Shawnee
Keeline
Manville
Lusk
Node
Van Tassell
Harrison
Crawford
Nebraska
National Forest
Niobrara
Marsland
Hemingford
Alliance
Boxelder
Orin
Glendo
Res.
Glendo St.
Park
Medicine
Bow
National
Forest
Alcova
Pathfinder
Reservoir
Shirley Basin
Jay Em
Sunrise
Hartville
Guernsey
St. Park
Guernsey
Fort Laramie
Lingle
Torrington
Bairoil
Lamont
Seminoe
Reservoir
Wheatland
Veteran
Morrill
Mitchell
Scottsbluff
Minatare
Angora
Lyman
Huntley
Terrytown
Gering
Bayard
Melbeta
McGrew
Bridgeport
Yoder
Hawk Sprs.
Chugwater
Slater
Wheatland
Res. No. 2
Medicine Bow
Elmo
Hanna
Rawlins
Sinclair
Walcott
Elk Mountain
Rock River
McFadden
Creston Jct.
Arlington
Bosler
Iron
Mountain
La Grange
Harrisburg
Dalton
Gurley
Albin
Saratoga
Medicine
Bow
Centennial
Laramie
Horse Creek
Kimball
Dix
Potter
Bushnell
Sidney
Pine Bluffs
Burns
Hillsdale
Egbert
Federal
Curt
Gowdy
State
Park
Riverside
Encampment
Albany
Tie Siding
Cheyenne
Carpenter
Woods Landing
Mountain Home
Medicine Bow
Nat'l Forest
Dixon
Savery
Peetz
Crook
Proctor
Iliff
North
Sterling
Virginia Dale
Rockport
Halligan Res.
Routt
National
Forest
Lake John
Cowdrey
Walden
Roosevelt
National
Rustic
The Forks
Poudre
Park
Bellvue
Fort Collins
Nunn
Pierce
Ault
Pawnee
National
Grassland
Briggsdale
Buckingham
Raymer
Stoneham
Sterling
Atwood
Fleming
Zeona
Hoover
Maurine
Mud Butte
Castle Rock
Fairpoint
Stoneville
Belle Fourche
Reservoir
Newell
Nisland
Fruitdale
Union
Center
Elm Springs
Red Owl

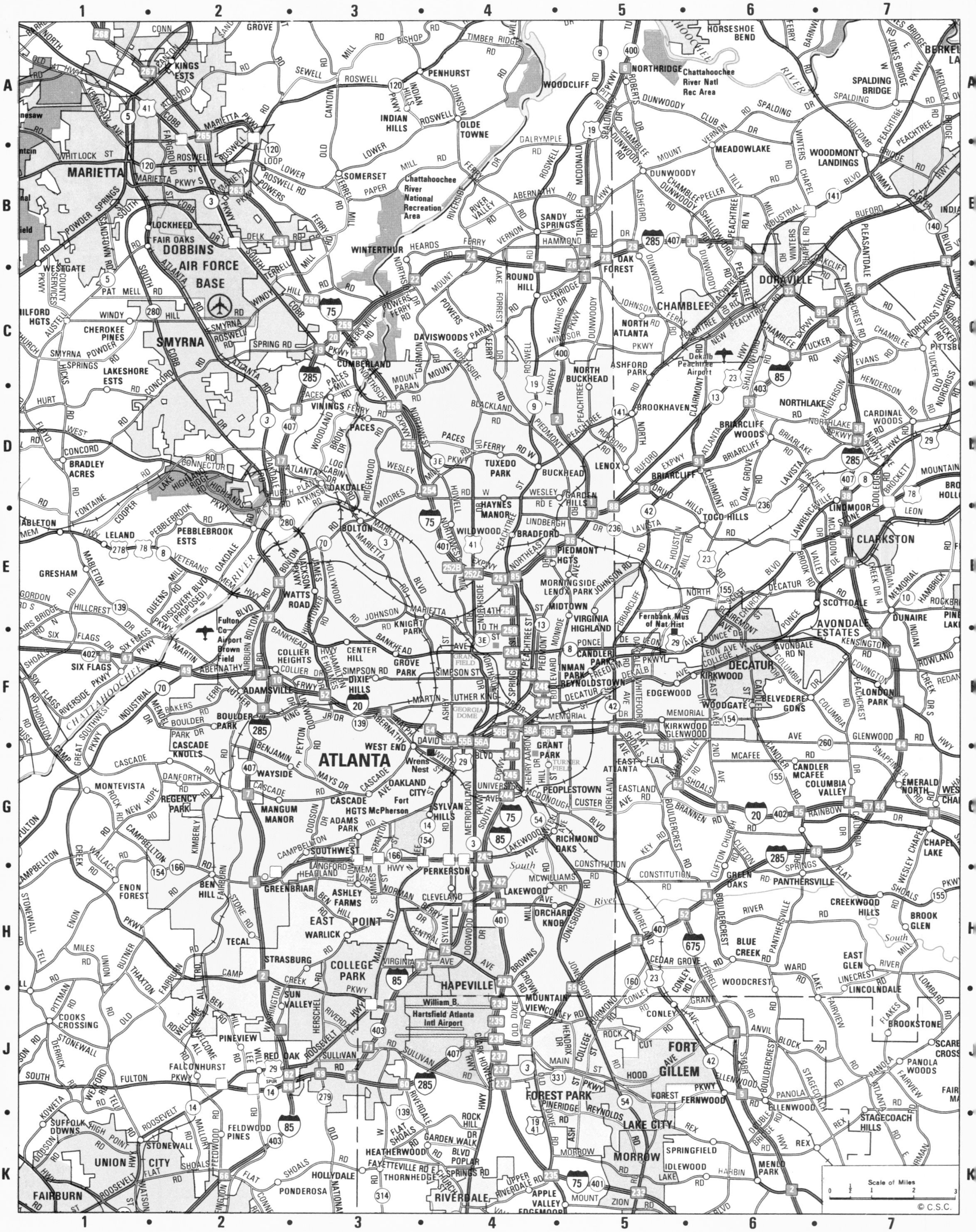

MARIETTA
KINGS ESTS
DOBBINS AIR FORCE BASE
SMYRNA
CHEROKEE PINES
LAKESHORE ESTS
CUMBERLAND
VININGS
PACES
INDIAN HILLS
OLDE TOWNE
PENHURST
WOODCLIFF
NORTHRIDGE
Chattahoochee River Natl Rec Area
HORSESHOE BEND
SPALDING BRIDGE
MEADOWLAKE
WOODMONT LANDINGS
Chattahoochee River National Recreation Area
SANDY SPRINGS
WINTERTHUR
ROUND HILL
OAK FOREST
CHAMBLEE
DORAVILLE
NORTH ATLANTA
NORTH BUCKHEAD
Dekalb Peachtree Airport
BROOKHAVEN
NORTHLAKE
CARDINAL WOODS
BRIARCLIFF WOODS
LENOX
BUCKHEAD
TUXEDO PARK
HAYNES MANOR
BRADFORD
PIEDMONT HGTS
MORNINGSIDE LENOX PARK
MIDTOWN
VIRGINIA HIGHLAND
Fernbank Mus of Nat Hist
TOGO HILLS
LINDMOOR
CLARKSTON
SCOTTDALE
AVONDALE ESTATES
DUNAIRE
DECATUR
KIRKWOOD
EDGEWOOD
WOODGATE
BELVEDERE GDNS
LONDON PARK
CANDLER PARK
INMAN PARK
REYNOLDSTOWN
GRANT PARK
PEOPLESTOWN
EAST ATLANTA
CANDLER MCAFEE
COLUMBIA VALLEY
EMERALD NORTH
ATLANTA
GEORGIA DOME
WEST END
Wrens Nest
OAKLAND CITY
Fort McPherson
SYLVAN HILLS
CASCADE HGTS
ADAMS PARK
MANGUM MANOR
REGENCY PARK
CASCADE KNOLLS
WAYSIDE
ADAMSVILLE
BOULDER PARK
DIXIE HILLS
GROVE PARK
CENTER HILL
COLLIER HEIGHTS
KNIGHT PARK
WATTS ROAD
BOLTON
OAKDALE
Fulton Co Airport Brown Field
SIX FLAGS
BRADLEY ACRES
PEBBLEBROOK ESTS
GRESHAM
MONTEVISTA
ENON FOREST
BEN HILL
GREENBRIAR
ASHLEY FARMS
EAST POINT
WARLICK
PERKERSON
LAKEWOOD
ORCHARD KNOB
RICHMOND OAKS
TECAL
STRASBURG
COLLEGE PARK
HAPEVILLE
William B. Hartsfield Atlanta Intl Airport
MOUNTAIN VIEW
SUN VALLEY
COOKS CROSSING
PINEVIEW
RED OAK
FALCONHURST
FOREST PARK
FORT GILLEM
LAKE CITY
MORROW
RIVERDALE
HEATHERWOOD
ROCK HILL
HOLLYDALE
PONDEROSA
FELDWOOD PINES
UNION CITY
FAIRBURN
SUFFOLK DOWNS
GREEN OAKS
PANTHERSVILLE
CREEKWOOD HILLS
BROOK GLEN
BLUE CREEK
EAST GLEN
LINCOLNDALE
BROOKSTONE
PANOLA WOODS
STAGECOACH HILLS
ELLENWOOD
FERNWOOD
SPRINGFIELD
IDLEWOOD
MENLO PARK
APPLE VALLEY
Scale of Miles
0 1/2 1 2 3
© C.S.C.

Scale of Miles

0 1 2 3

© C.S.C.

SAYRE
KILGORE
LINN CORSSING
DIVIDE STATION
MT. OLIVE
GARDENDALE
NEW CASTLE
PINSON
GREENS STATION
CHALKVILLE
CENTER POINT
BESSIE
CARDIFF
ALDEN
GRAYSVILLE
BROOKSIDE
FIELDSTOWN
MINERAL SPRINGS
FULTONDALE
ROBINWOOD
LINDBERGH
ADAMSVILLE
REPUBLIC
KETONA
ROEBUCK PLAZA
UNION GROVE
COALBURG
WALKER CHAPEL
LEWISBURG
TARRANT CITY
ALTON
BAY VIEW
DOCENA
MULGA
IRONDALE
JEFFERSON PARK
MAYTOWN
SYLVAN SPRINGS
EDGEWATER
BIRMINGHAM
OVERTON
GRANTS MILL
PLEASANT GROVE
FAIRFIELD
ISHKOODA
MOUNTAIN BROOK
HOMEWOOD
MIDFIELD
DOLOMITE
BROWNSVILLE
OXMOOR
WENONAH
CAHABA HEIGHTS
BRIGHTON
HUEYTOWN
LIPSCOMB
SHANNON
VESTAVIA HILLS
ROCKY RIDGE
BESSEMER
HOOVER
PATTON CHAPEL
JEFFERSON CO.
SHELBY CO.
MUSCODA
NEW HOPE
EASTERN VALLEY
ACTION
MC CALLA
MORGAN
GREENWOOD
ELVIRA
CHELSEA
Oak Mountain State Park
GENERY
HELENA
PELHAM

Civic Center
Museum of Art
Civil Rights Inst.
U.A.B.
University of Alabama Medical Center
Vulcan Statue
Samford University
Lake Shore Dr.
Southern Museum of Flight
Birmingham Municipal Airport
Sloss Furnaces
Birmingham Sou. College
Miles College
Ruffner Mtn. Nature Ctr.
Lake Purdy

Scale of Miles
0   1   2   3

N

© C.S.C.

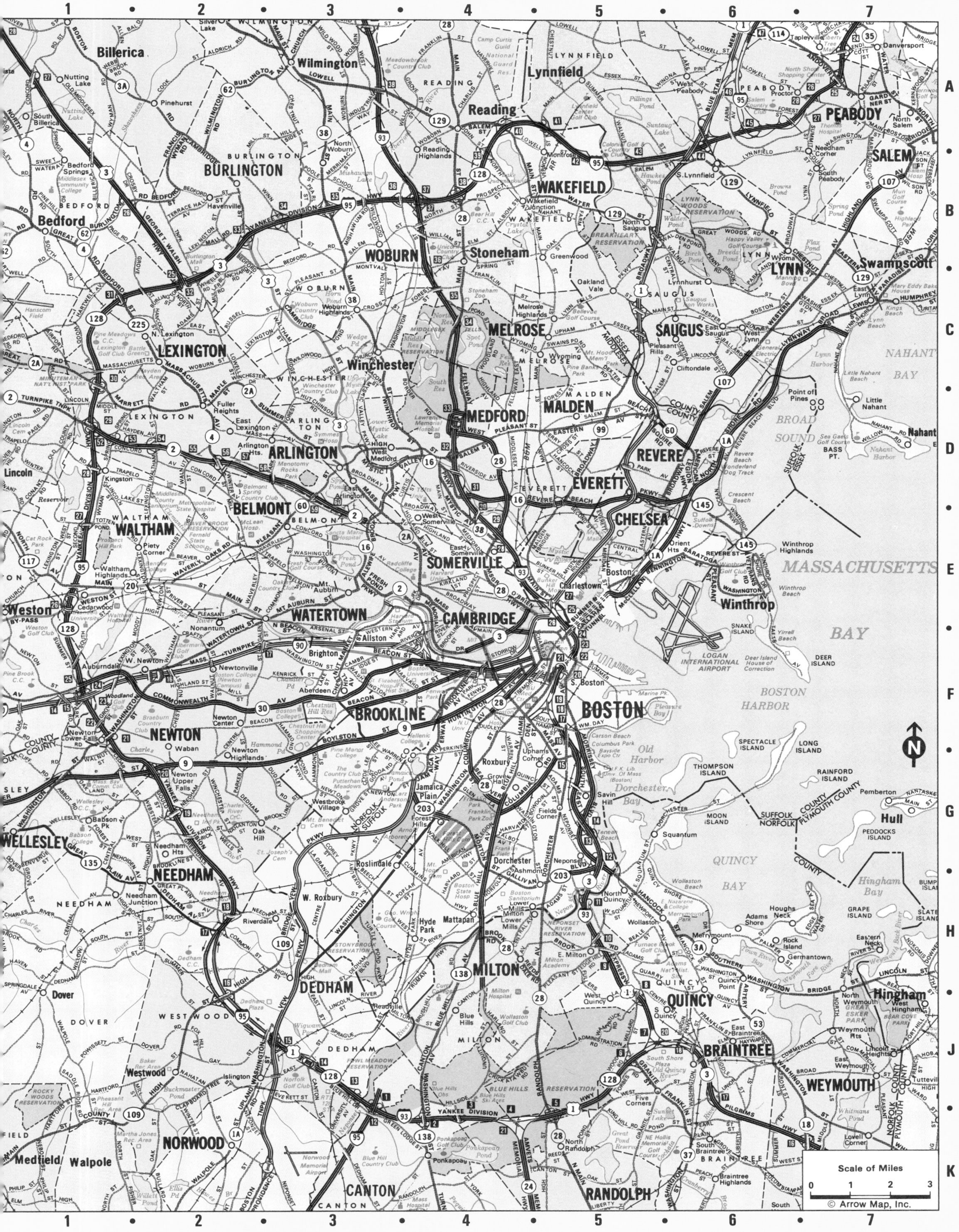
Billerica
Wilmington
Reading
Lynnfield
Peabody
Danversport
Burlington
Wakefield
Salem
Bedford
Woburn
Stoneham
Lynn
Swampscott
Saugus
Lexington
Melrose
Winchester
Nahant
Nahant Bay
Medford
Malden
Arlington
Revere
Broad Sound
Lincoln
Everett
Belmont
Chelsea
Waltham
Somerville
Massachusetts Bay
Winthrop
Weston
Watertown
Cambridge
Logan International Airport
Brighton
Allston
Boston Harbor
Brookline
Boston
Newton
Jamaica Plain
Roxbury
Dorchester Bay
Wellesley
Hull
Needham
Roslindale
Dorchester
Quincy Bay
Mattapan
Hyde Park
Milton
Dover
Dedham
Quincy
Hingham
Braintree
Westwood
Weymouth
Norwood
Randolph
Canton
Medfield
Walpole
Blue Hills Reservation
Scale of Miles
0 1 2 3
© Arrow Map, Inc.

1   2   3   4   5   6   7

A

NIAGARA FALLS
ECHOTA
BERKHOLTZ
BEACH RIDGE
PENDLETON
RAPIDS
MILLERSPORT
NIAGARA FALLS
ST. JOHNSBURG
NASHVILLE
HOFFMAN
WENDELVILLE
LA SALLE
SAWYER
Lundy's Lane Battleground
McLeod Rd.
Convention Center
ELSERS CORNERS

B

CHIPPAWA
SANDY BEACH
PEACH HAVEN
EDGEWATER
WURLITZER PARK
MARTINSVILLE
NORTH TONAWANDA
E. Robinson
GETZVILLE
EAST AMHERST
SWORMVILLE
Chippawa Battle Monument
Big Six Mile Creek Park
Whitehaven
Marshall Rd.
Bossert Rd.
CLARENCE CENTER

C

SNYDER
GRANDYLE VILLAGE
TONAWANDA
KENMORE
NORTH BAILEY
AMHERST
EGGERTSVILLE
SNYDER
WILLIAMSVILLE
HARRIS HILL
Sheridan Park
Sheridan
Englewood
S.U.N.Y. Buffalo
New York
State
Thruway

D

STEVENSVILLE
SNYDER
FERRY VILLAGE
FORT ERIE NORTH
Fort Erie Airport
Beaver Island State Park
Scajaquada Expwy.
SUNY Coll Buffalo
Buffalo Zoo
Kensington Expwy.
Buffalo International Airport
DEPEW
LANCASTER
BOWMANSVILLE
Fort Erie Race Track

E

POINT ABINO
RIDGEWAY
CRESCENT PARK
ERIE BEACH
FORT ERIE
Buffalo Museum of Science
Walden
SLOAN
CHEEKTOWAGA
BELLEVUE
War Mem. Stadium
Broadway

F

THUNDER BAY
CRYSTAL BEACH
Crystal Beach
Waverly Beach
Crescent Beach
BUFFALO
GARDENVILLE
BLOSSOM
ELMA
WEST SENECA
EAST SENECA
EBENEZER
ELMA CENTER
Botanical Gardens

G

Lake Erie
LACKAWANNA
BLASDELL
WOODLAWN
WINDOM
EAST HAMBURG
WEBSTER CORNERS
SPRINGBROOK
CANADA
UNITED STATES
ONTARIO
NEW YORK
WELLAND CO. ERIE CO.
Orchard Park Airport
Proner Airport

H

BAY VIEW
ATHOL SPRINGS
LOCKSLEY PARK
MT. VERNON
WANAKAH
CARNEGIE
BIG TREE
ORCHARD PARK
DUELLS CORNERS
ELLICOTT
ELLICOTT HEIGHTS
South Shore C.C.
Orchard Park C C

J

HIGHLAND-ON-THE-LAKE
LAKE VIEW
CLIFTON HEIGHTS
PINEHURST
SCRANTON
ARMOR
HAMBURG
WATER VALLEY
JEWETTVILLE
GRIFFINS MILLS
WEST FALLS
Eighteen Mile Creek
Erie Co. Fairgrounds
Chestnut Ridge Park

K

ANGOLA-ON-THE-LAKE
JERUSALEM CORNERS
DERBY
NORTH EVANS
EDEN VALLEY
NORTH BOSTON
PATCHIN
EAST EDEN
EVANS

Scale of Miles
0   1   2   3

© C.S.C.

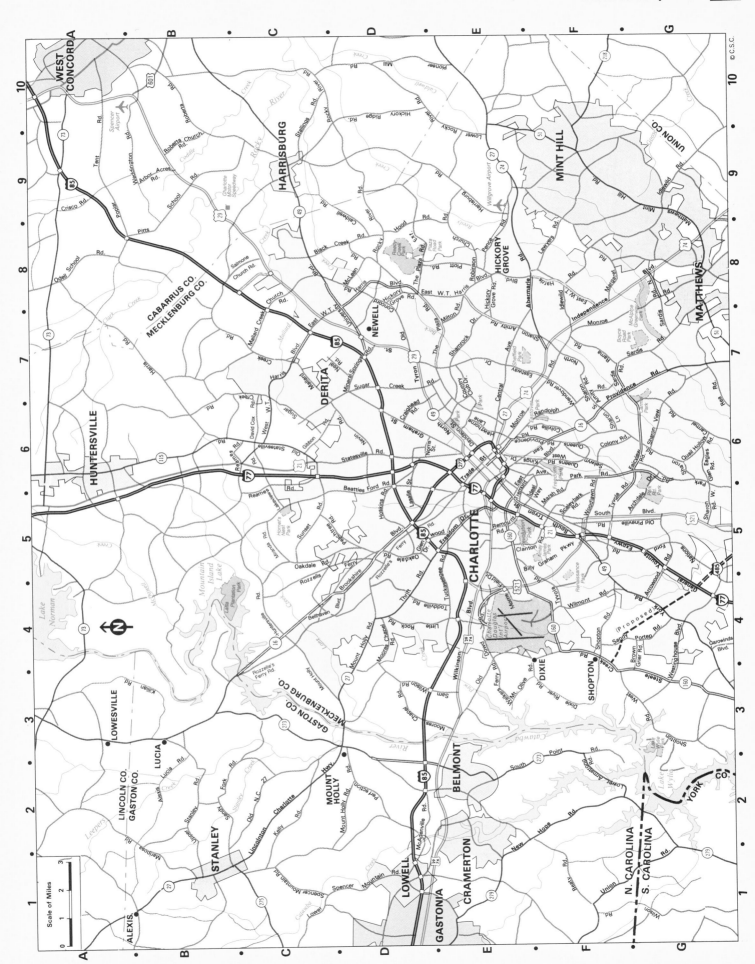

WONDER LAKE
Greenwood
Wonder Lake
McHENRY
Woodstock
Ringwood
Solon Mills
Johnsburg
McCullom Lake
Lilymoor
FOX LAKE
Fox Lake Hills
Lindenhurst
Venetian Village
Lake Villa
Round Lake Heights
Round Lake Beach
Round Lake Park
Round Lake
Hainesville
GRAYSLAKE
Lakemoor
Volo
Wauconda
Mundelein
Ivanhoe
Fremont Center
Crystal Lake
Lakewood
Prairie Grove
Burtons Bridge
Island Lake
Fox River Valley Gardens
Cary
Fox River Grove
Oakwood Hills
Lake in the Hills
Tower Lakes
North Barrington
Lake Barrington
Lake Zurich
Hawthorn Woods
Kildeer
Long Grove
Deer Park
HUNTLEY
Gilberts
Starks
Barrington Hills
Barrington
Inverness
PALATINE
Buffalo Grove
ARLINGTON HEIGHTS
Rolling Meadows
PINGREE GROVE
Udina
Plato Center
Bowes
Carpentersville
East Dundee
West Dundee
Sleepy Hollow
ELGIN
South Elgin
HOFFMAN ESTATES
South Barrington
Harper College
Palatine
SCHAUMBURG
Streamwood
Hanover Park
Bartlett
Roselle
Keeneyville
Medinah
ELK GROVE VILLAGE
ITASCA
Wood Dale

McHENRY CO.
LAKE CO.
KANE CO.
COOK CO.
LAKE COUNTY
COOK COUNTY

LAKE MICHIGAN

LAKE MICHIGAN

INDIANA

ILLINOIS

EAST CHICAGO

HAMMOND

GARY

GRIFFITH

MERRILLVILLE

CROWN POINT

MARQUETTE PARK

Grand Calumet River Lagoon

Purdue Univ. Regional Campus

Indiana Univ. Regional Campus

WAUKEGAN

ZION

BEACH PARK

WADSWORTH

GURNEE

NORTH CHICAGO

ILLINOIS BEACH STATE PARK

Great Lakes Naval Training Station

LIBERTYVILLE

LAKE FOREST

Lake Forest College

LAKE BLUFF

VERNON HILLS

DEERFIELD

HIGHLAND PARK

GLENCOE

NORTHBROOK

WHEELING

NORTHFIELD

WINNETKA

KENILWORTH

GLENVIEW

WILMETTE

Glenview N.A.S. (Closed)

MORTON GROVE

MOUNT PROSPECT

DES PLAINES

PARK RIDGE

NILES

SKOKIE

EVANSTON

National College of Education

Kendall College
Northwestern University

Loyola University

ROSEMONT

BENSENVILLE

CHICAGO O'HARE INTERNATIONAL AIRPORT

HARWOOD HEIGHTS

CONTINUED ON PAGE 105, GRID L-8

N

Scale of Miles
0   1   2   3

© A.M.C.

ELBURN
Wasco
La Fox
KESLINGER RD.
Lake Campton
EMPIRE RD.
Baldmond
Kaneville
GENEVA
ST. CHARLES
DuPage County Airport
Kane County Fairgrounds
WEST CHICAGO
Prince Crossing
Hawthorne La.
BLOOMINGDALE
Gloverdale
CAROL STREAM
GLENDALE HEIGHTS
ADDISON
WOOD DALE
BATAVIA
Mooseheart
NORTH AURORA
Merywood
WARRENVILLE
WHEATON
Wheaton College
GLEN ELLYN
LOMBARD
VILLA PARK
OAK
Flowerfield
York Center
Highland Hills
College of DuPage
Morton Arboretum
Herrick Lake
SUGAR GROVE
AURORA
Aurora University
Indian Trail
Eola
NAPERVILLE
North Central College
Illinois Benedictine College
LISLE
DOWNERS GROVE
FERMI LAB
Kress Creek
MONTGOMERY
Frontenac
Wheatland
Eola
WOODRIDGE
OSWEGO
Wolfs
BOLINGBROOK
Lily Cache
ARGONNE NATIONAL LABORATORY
YORKVILLE
Normantown
ROMEOVILLE
LEMONT
DES PLAINES
PLAINFIELD
Renwick
Lake Renwick
Lewis University
LOCKPORT
Statesville Correctional Center
Caton Farm
CREST HILL
SOUTH LOCKPORT
Fairmont
Rosalind
Ridgewood
JOLIET
College of St. Francis
Joliet Junior College
SHOREWOOD
ROCKDALE
Ingalls Park
Preston Heights
NEW LENOX
Lisbon Center
Plattville
MINOOKA
KENDALL CO.
GRUNDY CO.
WILL COUNTY
DU PAGE COUNTY
KANE CO.
DuPAGE CO.
DALL CO.
NE CO.

Scale of Miles
0 1 2 3

© A.M.C.

Dunlap

FOREST PARK

Greenhills

Springdale

E. Kemper

Sharonville

Glendale

Woodlawn

EVENDALE

BLUE ASH

CINCINNATI BLUE ASH AIRPORT

Univ. of Cinci. Raymond Walters Campus

Lincoln Hts.

WYOMING

Lockland

Reading

Arlington Hts.

AMBERLEY

Deer Park

French Mem. Park

Mt. Healthy

North College Hill

Silverton

Golf Manor

Madeira

Spring Grove Cemetery

La Boiteaux Woods

Mt. Airy Forest

ELMWOOD PL

Cheviot

NORWOOD

Fairfax

Mariem

St. Bernard

Zoological Gardens

Univ. of Cincinnati

Xavier Univ.

Ault Park

Observatory

CINCINNATI

Bridgetown

Burnet Woods

Turkey Ridge Park

Aims Park

Rapid Run Park

Dayton

LUNKEN AIRPORT

Art Museum

Eden Park

City Hall

Sabin Convention Center

Bellevue

Ft. Thomas

College of Mount St. Joseph

Embshoff Woods & Nature Preserve

Ludlow

Bromley

COVINGTON

Newport

Ft. Thomas

Constance

Devou Park

Park Hills

Wilder

Southgate

Villa Hills

Fort Wright

Kenton Vale

Crescent Springs

Highland Hts.

Cold Spring

River Downs Race Track

Crescent Park

Fort Mitchell

Lakeside Park

Lakeview

Erlanger

Crestview Hills

CINCINNATI & NORTHERN KENTUCKY INT'L AIRPORT

OHIO River

KENTUCKY

OHIO

Scale of Miles

0   1   2   3

© C.S.C.

Lake Erie

CLEVELAND

LAKEWOOD

ROCKY RIVER

FAIRVIEW PARK

BROOKLYN

BROOK PARK

BEREA

MIDDLEBURG HEIGHTS

PARMA HEIGHTS

PARMA

NORTH ROYALTON

STRONGSVILLE

BROADVIEW HEIGHTS

SEVEN HILLS

INDEPENDENCE

VALLEY VIEW

NEWBURGH HEIGHTS

BROOKLYN HEIGHTS

CUYAHOGA HEIGHTS

GARFIELD HEIGHTS

MAPLE HEIGHTS

BRECKSVILLE

SAGAMORE HILLS

WALTON HILLS

OAKWOOD

BEDFORD

BEDFORD HTS.

SOLON

GLENWILLOW

NORTHFIELD

MACEDONIA

TWINSBURG

BOSTON HEIGHTS

HUDSON

STOW

PENINSULA

EVERETT

CUYAHOGA FALLS

BOTZUM

AKRON

GHENT

BATH CENTER

BATH

GRANGER

REMSEN CORNERS

WEYMOUTH

ABBEYVILLE

BRUNSWICK

HINCKLEY

RICHFIELD

EUCLID

WICKLIFFE

WILLOUGHBY HILLS

RICHMOND HEIGHTS

SOUTH EUCLID

HIGHLAND HTS.

LYNDHURST

MAYFIELD HEIGHTS

EAST CLEVELAND

CLEVELAND HEIGHTS

UNIVERSITY HEIGHTS

SHAKER HEIGHTS

BEACHWOOD

PEPPER PIKE

WOODMERE

MORELAND HILLS

ORANGE

WARRENSVILLE HEIGHTS

NORTH RANDALL

BRATENAHL

Scale of Miles
0   1   2   3

© CSC

1 2 3 4 5 6 7

A

Moore
Hyatts
HYATTS
Shanahan
Hollenback
Rome Corners
GALENA
Vans Valley
Duffy
Home
Platt
North
Rest Area
Trenton
Merchant
RATHBONE
745
257
Taggert
Columbus
Lewis Center
Alum Creek Lake
37
605

JEROME
42
Cook
Concord
Harriott
Steitz
Rutherford
315
Perry
W. Orange
E. Orange
LEWIS CENTER
S. Lackey
Alum Creek State Rec. Area
Jaycox
Lewis Center
AFRICA
Africa
Freeman
Big Walnut
Maxtown
Woodtown
CENTER VILLAGE
Center Village
HARLEM
Gorsuch
Robins

SHAWNEE HILLS
Powell
750
Smoky Row
Jewett
Carriage
Powell
Polaris
POWELL
Highbanks Metro Park
Pike
Polaris Pkwy.
Hanawalt
WESTERVILLE
Smothers
Tussic Street
Sunbury
Otterbein College
Hoover Dam Park
Red Bank
Fancher
Bevelheimer
Green-Cook
605
62

DELAWARE CO. FRANKLIN CO.
Summit View
MOUNT AIR
Hard
Bright Rd.
745
Nicklaus
JACK
FRWY.
Snouffer
FLINT
Lazelle Rd.
Worthington-Galena
Sharon Woods Metro Park
Schrock Rd.
Walnut
St.
Inniswood Metro Gardens
Hempstead
Hoover
Warner
Central College
161
62

KILEVILLE
161
Plain City
Post
Indian Run
JACK
161
LINWORTH
Dublin-Granville
Antrim Park
WORTHINGTON
710
161
Dempsey
HUBER RIDGE
Cherry Bottom Rd.
Cubbage Rd.
Lee
Warner
NEW ALBANY
161

DUBLIN
Shier Rings
Avery
Rings
Tuttle
Case
Don Scott Airport
Godown Rd.
Linworth
Brandy Meadows Park
RIVERLEA
MINERVA PARK
Minerva Lake Rd.
3
Sunbury
GOULD PARK
Thompson
Blendon Woods Metro Park
Clark
GAHANNA
Headley Rd.
Havens

AMLIN
Houchard
Cosgray
Rings
Dublin Rd.
Bethel
Henderson
Morse
High
CLINTON
Ferris Rd.
Karl
Innis
McCutchen
Agler
270
McCutcheon Rd.
Morse
Gahanna Woods Park
Haven's Corner

HAYDEN
HILLARD
270
Davidson
Hillard-Cem.
Fishinger
UPPER ARLINGTON
McCoy
Reed
Kenny
Highland
Whetstone Park Columbus Park
Port of Roses
23
Oakland Park
N. Broadway
Innis Park
Agler
Rd.
Styger
Hamilton
62

Scioto-Darby Creek
33
Hayden Run
Scioto
Columbus
Cooke
Weber
Indianola
Hudson
Ohio History Museum
Mock Park
Columbus Intl Gateway
Prt Columbus Intl. Airport
317
BLACKLICK

MUDSOCK
Davis
Darby Creek
Robert
Scioto-Darby Creek Frwy.
Maryville
Lane
Northwest
Summit
St.
Ohio State Univ.
Ohio Stadium
Seventeenth Ave.
Ohio Dominican College
Woodland
Cassady Ave.
Columbus-Millersburg
670
16

Robert's
Feder
Rome-Hilliard
Walcott
Nicklaus
Trabue
SAN MARGHERITA
Hague
5th
North Star
MARBLE CLIFF
GRANDVIEW HEIGHTS
670
Leonard
BEXLEY
Nelson
WHITEHALL
St.
40

NEW ROME
National
ALTON
Darby Dan Airport
70
Fisher Rd.
VALLEY VIEW
Ave.
Broad
670
33
State Capital
Broad
COLUMBUS
Capital University
Main
Ave.
REYNOLDSBURG
256
70

Amny
40
Sullivant Ave.
Sullivant
Ave.
Cooper Stadium
62
3
71
23
Lou Berliner Park
Livingston
Champion
Lockbourne
James
Alum Creek
Big Walnut Park
Blacklick Woods Metro Park
McNaughten
70

Georgesville
BRIGGSDALE
Frank
Grove City Monteney Airport
104
Marion
Champion
Refugee
Winchester
Natzger Park
BRICE
Refugee
71

GALLOWAY
Galloway
Bolton Field
Alkire
Brown
Dyer
270
Three Rivers Park
Helser Park
Shannon Rd.
Wright

GEORGEVILLE
Columbus South West Airport
Alkire
Johnson
Bixby
Big Run South
URBANCREST
Home Rd.
Gantt Rd.
Williams
Groveport
OBETZ
FRWY.
JACK
NICKLAUS
GROVEPORT
317
33
Pike
Pickerington Ponds Wetlands Wildlife Area

Battelle
Darby Creek Metro Park
City
GROVE CITY
Columbus St.
Stringtown
White
Rd.
Parson's
JACK
Rathmell
Bixby
CANAL WINCHESTER
Groveport Rd.
674

DARBYDALE
665
PLEASANT CORNERS
London-Groveport
Beatty
Orders
Haughn
Holton
Western
REESE
Rohr
Creek
Bixby
London Groveport
Lithopolis
WATERLOO

Opossum Run
Boyd
Gay
Harrisburg
71
SHADEVILLE
317
Lockbourne
London Groveport
N
Richardson
Oregon
LITHOPOLIS
Elder

HARRISBURG
62
3
ORIENT
FRANKLIN CO. PICKAWAY CO.
Borror
Cols-Chillicothe
Young
23
LOCKBOURNE
Rowe
Vause
Rickenbacker Air Force Base
Pontus
Lancaster
U.S. Military Res.

104
762

Scale of Miles
0 1 2 3

© C.S.C.

Scale of Miles

© C.S.C.

N

Denver International Airport

Toll Plaza

Rocky Mountain Arsenal Wildlife Refuge

AURORA

Monaghan Rd.

Powhatan Ave.

Jewell

30

Buckley Air National Guard Base

Plains Conservation Center

Aurora Fairgrounds

Smoky Hill Rd.

Ireland Way

E-470 Toll Plaza

Centennial Airport

ARAPAHOE COUNTY
DOUGLAS COUNTY

GRANDVIEW ESTATES

Lincoln Ave.

THORNTON

WESTMINSTER

FEDERAL HEIGHTS

ARVADA

WHEAT RIDGE

GOLDEN

PLEASANT VIEW

LAKEWOOD

EDGEWATER

MOUNTAIN VIEW

COMMERCE CITY

DUPONT

WELBY

DENVER

GLENDALE

AURORA

ENGLEWOOD

SHERIDAN

CHERRY HILL VILLAGE

GREENWOOD VILLAGE

LITTLETON

BOW MAR

COLUMBINE VALLEY

MORRISON

IDLEDALE

INDIAN HILLS

TINY TOWN

TWIN FORKS

FENDERS

Coors Field

Mile High Stadium

McNichols Arena

Cherry Creek State Park

Cherry Creek Reservoir

Chatfield State Park

Chatfield Lake

Standley Lake

Marston Lake

Bear Creek Lake

Red Rocks Park

Mount Falcon County Park

Jefferson Co. Park

Camp George West (National Guard)

Apex County Park

U.S. Atomic Energy Commission (Rocky Flats Plant)

Denver Coliseum

City Park

Zoo & Mus.

Botanic Gardens

State Capitol

Park Hill G.C.

Washington Park

Denver University

Federal Correctional Institute

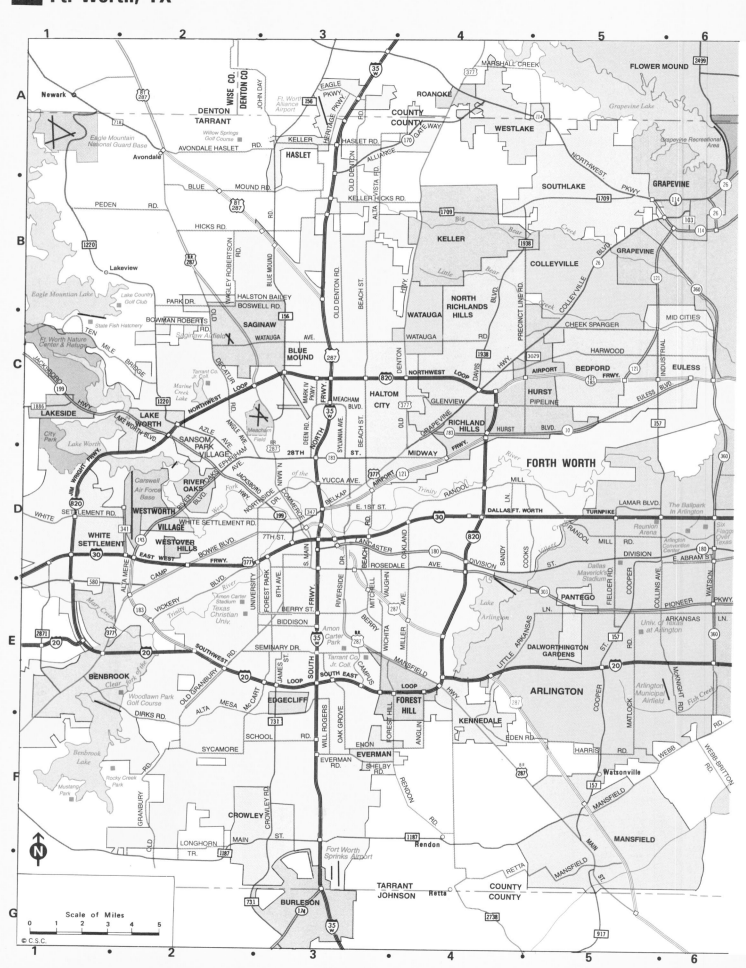

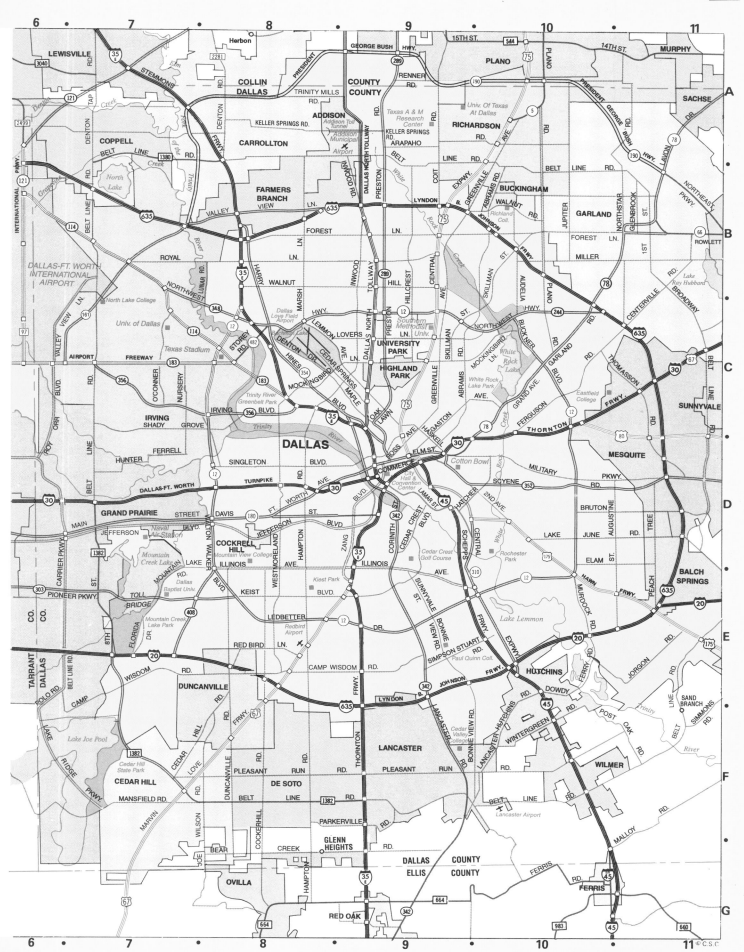

WATERFORD TWP.

PONTI

MILFORD

SYLVAN LAKE

KEEGO HARBOR

ORCHARD LAKE

WOLVERINE LAKE

BLO

WALLED LAKE

NEW HUDSON

WIXOM

FRANKLIN

BE HI

SOUTH LYON

FARMINGTON HILLS

NOVI

FARMINGTON

SOUTHFIELD

NORTHVILLE

LIVINGSTON CO. OAKLAND CO.
WASHTENAW CO.

REDFORD TWP.

SALEM

LIVONIA

PLYMOUTH

JEFFRIES FRWY.

WESTLAND

GARDEN CITY

DEARBORN HTS.

ANN ARBOR

CANTON TWP.

INKSTER

WAYNE

YPSILANTI

ROMULUS

Willow Run Airport

BELLEVILLE

Detroit Metropolitan Wayne County Airport

TA

LIVINGSTON CO. OAKLAND CO.

OAKLAND CO. WAYNE CO.

WASHTENAW CO. WAYNE CO.

Island Lake State Recreation Area

Kensington Metropark

Maybury State Park

Proud Lake State Recreation Area

Highland State Recreation Area

Lower Huron Metropark

AUBURN HILLS
ROCHESTER HILLS
UTICA
TROY
STERLING HEIGHTS
CLINTON TWP
MOUNT CLEMENS
BIRMINGHAM
CLAWSON
FRASER
ROYAL OAK
MADISON HEIGHTS
WARREN
ST. CLAIR SHORES
ROSEVILLE
LATHRUP VILLAGE
BERKLEY
HUNTINGTON WOODS
CENTER LINE
EAST DETROIT
HAZEL PARK
OAK PARK
FERNDALE
HARPER WOODS
GROSSE POINTE SHORES
GROSSE POINTE WOODS
HIGHLAND PARK
DETROIT
HAMTRAMCK
GROSSE POINT FARMS
GROSSE POINTE
GROSSE POINTE PARK
U.S.A.
CANADA
DEARBORN
WINDSOR
TECUMSAH
MELVINDALE
ALLEN PARK
RIVER ROUGE
ECORSE
LA SALLE
LINCOLN PARK
SOUTH GATE
WYANDOTE
Anchor Bay
Lake St. Claire
Metro Beach Metropark
Berz-Macomb Airport
Rochester-Utica State Rec. Area
Oakland Troy Airport
State Fair Grounds
Palmer Park
Univ. of Detroit
Detroit City Airport
Wayne St. Univ.
Tiger Stadium
Belle Isle Park
Windsor Airport
MACOMB CO.
WAYNE CO.
OAKLAND CO.
ESSEX CO.
MICH.
ONT.
Scale of Miles
0 1 2 3

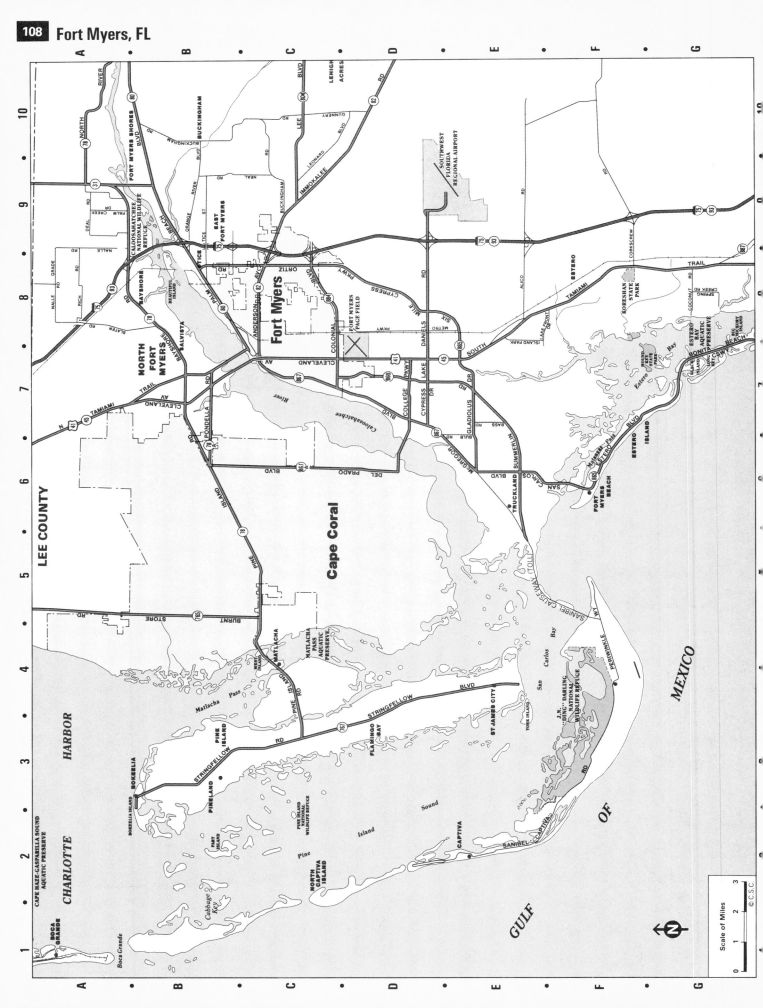

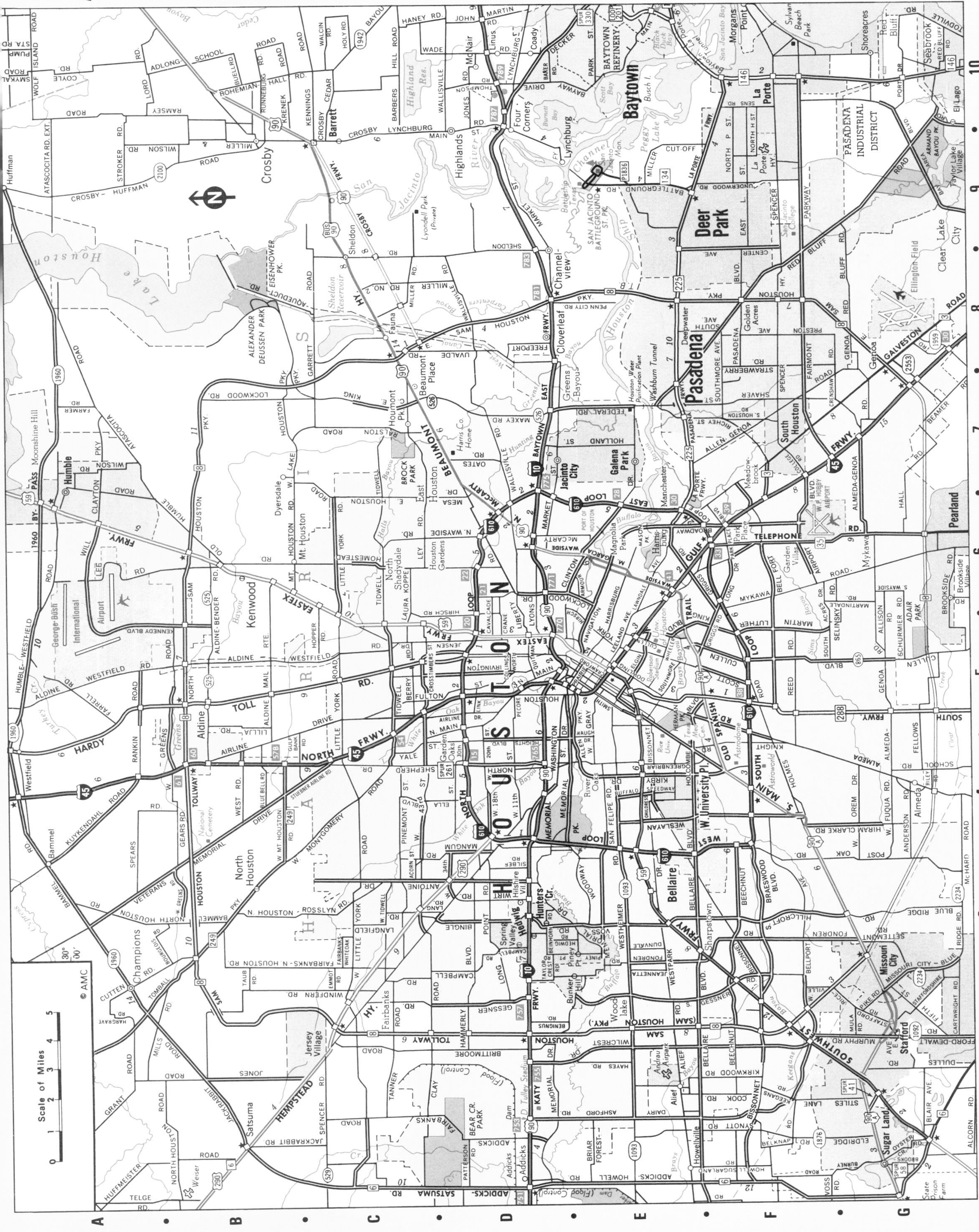
HOUSTON
Baytown
Pasadena
Deer Park
La Porte
Humble
Crosby
Barrett
Highlands
Channelview
Cloverleaf
Galena Park
Jacinto City
South Houston
Bellaire
West University Pl.
Missouri City
Stafford
Sugar Land
Pearland
Aldine
Kenwood
North Houston
Jersey Village
Champions
Satsuma
Addicks
Alief
Sheldon
Huffman
Lake Houston
George Bush International Airport
W. P. Hobby Airport
Ellington Field
San Jacinto Battleground St. Pk.
Pasadena Industrial District
Astrodome
Scale of Miles
© AMC

1 2 3 4 5 6

A

White

Carmel

116TH ST.

116TH. ST.

Fishers

Eagle Village

334

Zionville

52
421

Metropolitan Airport

465

31

52
421

465

HAMILTON CO.
MARION CO.

96TH ST.

37

A

65

B

86TH ST.

86TH ST.

Nora

Sahm Park

Allisonville

Castleton

82ND ST.

Fairbanks Hosp.

465

79TH ST.

79TH ST.

Williams Creek

Castleton
Square S.C.

Traders Point

71ST ST.

Augusta

Meridian Hills

71ST ST.

71ST ST.

31

ZIONSVILLE RD.

TOWNSHIP LINE RD.

DITCH RD.

73RD ST.

Ravenswood

65TH ST.

Hillcrest C.C.

Eagle Creek Pk.

New Augusta

62ND ST.

Shore Acres

62ND ST.

SOUTH RIVER RD.

Fort Harrison State Park

B

North Westway Park

Little Eagle Creek

56TH

North Crows Nest

FOX HILL DR.

KESSLER

Glendale S.C.

ALLISONVILLE RD.

KESSLER BLVD.

Camp Belzer

Indianapolis Colts Training Facility

Washington Park North Cemetery

Highland Country Club

Crows Nest

KEYSTONE AVE.

State School For The Deaf

56TH ST.

Cathedral H.S.

Lawrence Central H.S.

Fort Benjamin Harrison

C

Eagle Creek Reservoir

LAFAYETTE RD.

HIGH SCHOOL RD.

GUION RD.

Broadmoor Country Club

Highwood

Rocky Ripple

Spring Hills

Butler University

46TH ST.

Pleasant Run

Arlington H.S.

Lawrence

PENDLETON PIKE

67

36

37
67

C

Clermont

136

Eagle Creek Airport

34TH ST.

Wynnedale

Woodstock

Crown Hill Cem.

N. MERIDIAN ST.

COLLEGE ST.

State Fairgrounds

FALL CR. PKWY.

38TH ST.

SHADELAND AVE.

74

Moller

GEORGETOWN RD.

TIBBS RD.

Marion College

Coffin G.C.

30TH ST.

South Grove G.C.

34TH ST.

SHERMAN DR.

MASSACHUSETTS

70

ARLINGTON AVE.

Chrysler Corp.

52
421

D

Indianapolis Country Club

21ST ST.

134

Camp Dellwood

Speedway H.S.

Indianapolis Motor Speedway

25TH ST.

16TH ST.

Benjamin Harrison Memorial

21ST ST.

16TH ST.

10TH ST.

EMERSON AVE.

Pleasant Run G.C.

Indiana St. Police Hqts.

COUNTRY CLUB RD.

SCHOOL RD.

Speedway

10TH ST.

COLLEGE ST.

RURAL ST.

MICHIGAN ST.

YORK ST.

Warren Park

D

465

Tremont

36

INDIANAPOLIS

ROCKVILLE RD.

Thatcher Golf Course

Indiana Univ. Medical Center

I.U.P.U.I.

War Memorial

NEW YORK ST.

40

E

GIRLS SCHOOL RD.

Ben Davis

Mickeyville

Central State Hosp.

White River St. Pk.

Indianapolis Zoo

State Capitol

Victory Field

RCA Dome

WEST ST.

DELAWARE ST.

Nat'l Track & Field Hall Of Fame

Union Station Market Place

WASHINGTON

Willard Park

65

70

ENGLISH AVE.

ENGLISH AVE.

Ford Assembly Plant

HENDRICKS COUNTY

MARION COUNTY

WASHINGTON

40

Bridgeport

BEN DAVIS ST.

70

MORRIS ST.

MINNESOTA

Indiana Nat'l Guard

Union Stock Yards

MERIDIAN ST.

MADISON AVE.

Conseco Fieldhouse

PROSPECT

SOUTHEASTERN ST.

W. RAYMOND ST.

POST RD.

52

Raymond Park

E

Six Points

LYNHURST DR.

HOLT RD.

TIBBS AVE.

W. AVE.

KEYSTONE AVE.

Sarah Shank G.C.

Marion County Fair Grounds

Indianapolis International Airport

Mars Hill

Maywood

HARDING ST.

TROY AVE.

St. Francis Hospital

Five Points

FISHER RD.

74

421

KENTUCKY AVE.

36
40

Beech Grove

Hanna

F

74

Decatur Central H.S.

HIGH SCHOOL RD.

MANN RD.

White River

37
67

HANNA AVE.

Univ. of Indianapolis

THOMPSON RD.

Edgewood

SHELBYVILLE RD.

465

40

31
36

465

74

Wanamaker

Franklin Central H.S.

N

F

70

Valley Mills

67

THOMPSON RD.

EPLER AVE.

BLUFF RD.

EAST ST.

135

37

65

Homecroft

31

G

Camby

CAMBY RD.

MOORESVILLE RD.

Antrim

EDGEWOOD AVE.

SOUTHPORT RD.

MADISON AVE.

Southport

West Newton

South Westway Park

STOP 11 RD.

Glenns Valley

Carl Smock Park

Scale of Miles
0 5 1 2 3

MARION COUNTY

© C.S.C.

1 2 3 4 5 6

G

SCALE IN MILES
0   1½   3
0   1.5   3
SCALE IN KILOMETERS
©1999 TRAKKER MAPS, INC.

Thomas Creek

To Waycross

115

95

JACKSONVILLE
INTERNATIONAL
AIRPORT

ARNOLD RD

YELLOW BLUFF RD

STARRATT RD

NASSAU CO.
DUVAL CO.

River

Amelia Island

A1A

Atlantic Ocean

A

B

NEW KINGS RD

LEM TURNER RD

PECAN PARK RD

OWENS RD

AIRPORT RD

DUVAL RD

TERRELL RD

9

17

5

DUVAL STATION RD

STARRATT RD

NEW BERLIN RD

CEDAR POINT RD

Nassau Sound

C

104

115

DUNN AV

BROWARD RD

MAIN ST N

EASTPORT RD

295

9A

105

HECKSCHER DR

Fort George River

FORT GEORGE CULTURAL CENTER

Fort George Inlet

A1A

1

117

106

TROUT RIVER BLVD

SOUTEL DR

Broward

Trout River

ANNHEUSER BUSCH BREWERY TOUR

163

Dunn Cr

Clapboard Cr

St Johns River

D

295

23

115A

MONCRIEF RD

EDGEWOOD AV

JACKSONVILLE ZOO

111

Blount Island

105

Mill Cove

MAYPORT U.S. NAVAL AIR STATION

A1A

HANNA STATE PARK

E

PRITCHARD RD

9A

103

15

CSX

OLD KINGS RD

15

NEW KINGS RD

111

17

ALT 1

1

115

FT CAROLINE

MERRILL RD

GILMORE HTS RD

RD

MONUMENT RD

MT PLEASANT RD

GRAIG MUNICIPAL AIRPORT

10

F

21B

21D

JACKSONVILLE UNIVERSITY

ARLINGTON RD

ALT 90

115

ATLANTIC BLVD

ATLANTIC BEACH

COMMONWEALTH AV

BEAVER ST

129

8

CIVIC AUDITORIUM

CONVENTION CENTER

MUSEUM OF SCIENCES

ALLTEL STADIUM

10

NEPTUNE BEACH

NORMANDY BLVD

US

10

228

PARK ST

211

JACKSONVILLE

EMERSON ST

95

228

ALT 90

90

212

St Johns Bluff RD

BEACH BLVD

San Pablo RD

90   212

JACKSONVILLE BEACH

G

HERLONG RD

FOURAKER

CASSAT AV

ORTEGA BLVD

ROOSEVELT BLVD

13

AUGUSTINE BLVD

9

109

208

WILSON BLVD

21

RD

Ortega River

TIMUQUANA RD

UNIVERSITY BLVD

St Johns River

202

J. TURNER BUTLER BLVD

SOUTHSIDE BLVD

202

DUVAL COUNTY
ST JOHNS COUNTY

H

295

RICKER RD

MORSE AV

TOWNSEND RD

JAMMES RD

BLANDING BLVD

15

17

JACKSONVILLE NAVAL AIR STATION

PHILLIPS HWY

1

BAY MEADOWS RD

152

SUNBEAM RD

115

J

To Gainesville

9A

DUVAL CLAY COUNTY

BUCKMAN BRIDGE

295

9A

OLD ST AUGUSTINE RD

95

1

K

21

17

13

9

1   2   3   4   5   6   7

N

Mosby

Major Places / Labels

Kansas City International Airport

Ferrelview

Weatherby Lake

Parkville

Riverside

Gladstone

Oakview

Liberty

Glenaire

Pleasant Valley

Claycomo

Randolph

Birmingham

Sugar Creek

Kansas City Kansas

Kansas City

Independence

Blue Summit

Shawnee

Merriam

Mission

Roeland Park

Fairway

Countryside

Mission Hills

Prairie Village

Overland Park

Lenexa

Leawood

Raytown

Unity Village

Lee's Summit

Lake Quivira

Westwood

Military Golf Course

Swope Park

Zoo

Scale of Miles

0 1 2 3 4

© C.S.C.

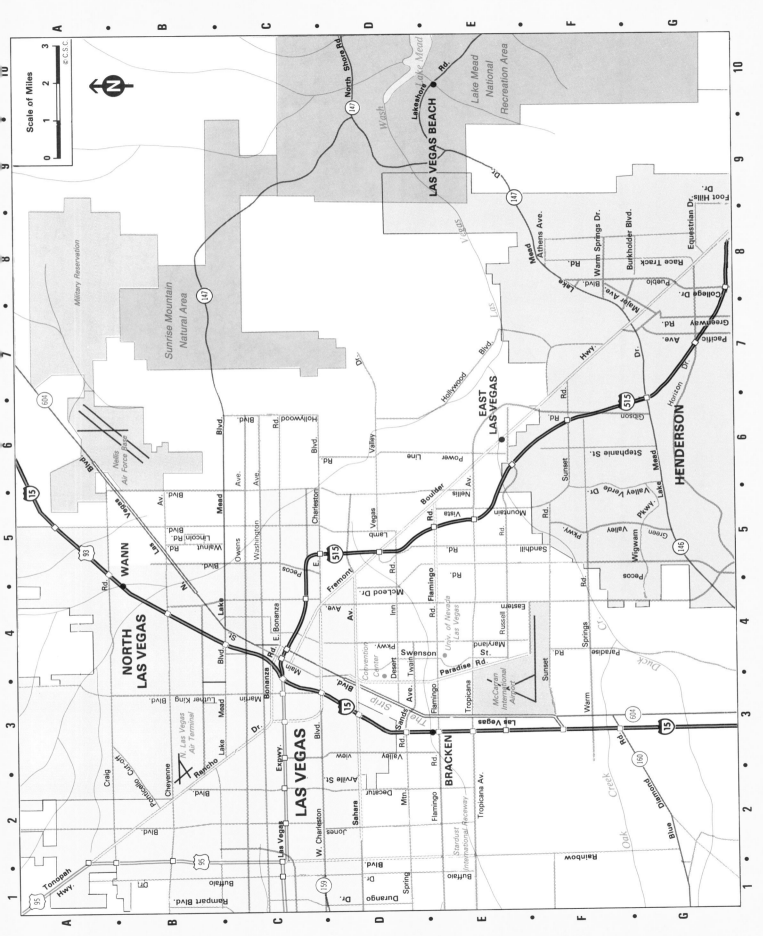

ANGELES NATIONAL FOREST

VETTER PK. + 5908
JOSEPHINE PK. 5558
STRAWBERRY PK. + 6164
SAN GABRIEL PK. 6161
BROWN MTN. 4454
MT. HARVARD 5440
CONDOR PK. 5439
MT. LUKENS 5074

VERDUGO MOUNTAINS
VERDUGO PK. + 3126

GLENDALE
BURBANK
BRAND PARK
GRIFFITH PARK

ALTADENA
PASADENA
SOUTH PASADENA
SIERRA MADRE
SAN MARINO
ALHAMBRA
TEMPLE CITY
EL MONTE
ROSEMEAD
SAN GABRIEL
MONTEREY PARK
MONTEBELLO
PICO-RIVERA
COMMERCE
BELL GARDENS
MAYWOOD
BELL
HUNTINGTON PARK
FLORENCE PARK
HYDE PARK
EXPOSITION PARK

LOS ANGELES

SANTA MONICA MOUNTAINS
SAN VICENTE MTN. 1960

HOLLYWOOD
NORTH HOLLYWOOD
STUDIO CITY
UNIVERSAL CITY
SHERMAN OAKS
ENCINO
TARZANA
RESEDA
NORTHRIDGE
PANORAMA CITY
VAN NUYS
MISSION HILLS
SAN FERNANDO
SUN VALLEY
CANOGA PARK
WOODLAND HILLS

BEVERLY HILLS
CENTURY CITY
WESTWOOD
BEL AIR
CULVER CITY
BALDWIN HILLS
SANTA MONICA
PACIFIC PALISADES

PACIFIC OCEAN

Will Rogers State Park
Topanga Beach
Las Tunas State Beach

Scale of Miles
0 1 2 3

N

SANTA FE SPRINGS
NORWALK
DOWNEY
BELL GARDENS
BELL
CUDAHY
MAYWOOD
HUNTINGTON PARK
SOUTH GATE
LYNWOOD
PARAMOUNT
BELLFLOWER
LAKEWOOD
ARTESIA
CYPRESS
LOS ALAMITOS NAVAL AIR STATION
U.S. NAVAL WEAPONS STATION
SEAL BEACH
LONG BEACH
COMPTON
WATTS
INGLEWOOD
HAWTHORNE
GARDENA
LAWNDALE
TORRANCE
CARSON
LOMITA
MANHATTAN BEACH
HERMOSA BEACH
REDONDO BEACH
EL SEGUNDO
MARINA DEL REY
VENICE
TERMINAL ISLAND
SAN PEDRO
PALOS VERDES ESTATES
ROLLING HILLS ESTATES
ROLLING HILLS
PALOS VERDES
FLATROCK PT.
PALOS VERDES PT.
PT. VINCENTE
LONG PT.
PT. FERMIN
Pacific Ocean

SAN BERNARDINO NATIONAL FOREST

+ HARRISON MTN. 4743

+ McKINLEY MTN. 3795

MT. SALLY 5408

ANGELES NATIONAL FOREST

+ MT. BLISS 3725

Falling Springs

SAN BERNARDINO

REDLANDS

NORTON AIR FORCE BASE

COLTON

RIALTO

FONTANA

ONTARIO INTERNATIONAL AIRPORT

UPLAND

MONTCLAIR

ONTARIO

CHINO

CALIFORNIA INSTITUTE FOR MEN

CLAREMONT

POMONA

LOS ANGELES COUNTY FAIRGROUNDS

PUDDINGSTONE RESERVOIR STATE REC. AREA

U.S. NAVAL ORDNANCE PLANT

SAN DIMAS

GLENDORA

AZUSA

DUARTE

MONROVIA

ARCADIA

BALDWIN PARK

COVINA

WEST COVINA

LA PUENTE

SAN JOSE HILLS

CALIF. STATE POLYTECHNIC UNIV.

Diamond Bar

WORKMAN HILL 1387

PUENTE HILLS

WHITTIER

LOS ANGELES COUNTY / SAN BERNARDINO COUNTY

For continuation of inset, see main map

Scale of Miles
0 1 2 3

RIVERSIDE

HOME GARDENS

NORCO

CORONA

CLEVELAND NATIONAL FOREST

EL CERRITO

CHINO HILLS

CALIFORNIA INSTITUTE FOR MEN

CHINO AIRPORT

CALIF. INST. FOR WOMEN

PRADO FLOOD CONTROL BASIN

RIVERSIDE COUNTY
ORANGE COUNTY

SAN BERNARDINO COUNTY

LOS ANGELES COUNTY
ORANGE COUNTY

Silverado

Modjeska Canyon

Trabuco Canyon

Lake Forest

El Toro

EL TORO U.S.M.C. AIR STATION

IRVINE

UNIV. OF CALIFORNIA IRVINE CAMPUS

SANTA ANA

TUSTIN

ORANGE

SANTA ANA U.S.M.C. AIR FACILITY

COSTA MESA

NEWPORT BEACH

YORBA LINDA

PLACENTIA

BREA

LA HABRA

FULLERTON

BUENA PARK

ANAHEIM

GARDEN GROVE

DISNEYLAND

STANTON

WESTMINSTER

FOUNTAIN VALLEY

HUNTINGTON BEACH

LA MIRADA

WORKMAN HILL 1387

WORKMAN HILL

Santa Ana Canyon

Santiago Res.

Villa Park Res.

New Albany

Clarksville

Jeffersonville

LOUISVILLE

Shively

Matthews

Broadfields

Rolling Fields

Mockingbird Valley

Druid Hills

Dutchmanns

West Buechel

Lynnview

Minor Lane Hts

OHIO RIVER

INDIANA
KENTUCKY

Shawnee Park

Commonwealth Park

Gibson

Cherokee Park

Seneca Park

Big Springs G.C.

Bowman Field

George Rodgers Clark Bridge

J.F. Kennedy Mem. Bridge

Sherman Minton Bridge

Bandman Park

Cave Hill Cemetery

St. Calvary Cemetery

Churchill Downs

Kentucky State Fair & Exposition Center

U.S. Navy Ordnance Plant

Iroquis Park

Palatka

Standford Field

Audubon Park

Audubon C.C.

Parkway Village

Trevilian Park

Zoological Gardens

General Electric Appliance Park

Ford Car Plant

Camp Ground

RIVERSIDE PKWY.

WATTERSON EXPWY.

HENRY WATTERSON EXPWY.

DUTCHMANNS EXPWY.

Scale of Miles
0 1 2 3

N

© C.S.C.

Scale of Miles
© C.S.C.

ARLINGTON
BOLTON
GILDFIELD
BRUNSWICK
LENOW
PISGAH
FISHERVILLE
COLLIERVILLE
BAILEY
TENNESSEE
MISSISSIPPI
MINERAL WELLS
CORDOVA
ELMORE PARK
GERMANTOWN
FOREST HILL
ELLENDALE
BARTLETT
SPRING LAKE
SHELBY FARMS
Penal Farm
Shelby County
Wolf River
CAPLEVILLE
RALEIGH
EGYPT
LUCY
WOODSTOCK
MEMPHIS
South Western University
Overton Park
Memphis State University
Audubon Park
OAKVILLE
PLUM POINT
Shelby County Airport
Memphis International Airport
McKellar Park
BENJESTOWN
Firestone Park
Gen. DeWitt Spain Downtown Airport
WHITEHAVEN
RAMSEY
Meeman Shelby Forest State Park
Mississippi River
SHELBY CO.
CRITTENDEN CO.
Robinson Crusoe Island
Chicken Island
Presidents Island
Fuller State Park
Boxtown
Coro Lake
Robco Lake
REDMAN POINT
ST. CLAIR
MOUND CITY
BLANTON
Ingram Blvd.
WEST MEMPHIS
HULBERT
WYANOKE
TENNESSEE
ARKANSAS
Broadway
GAMMON
HARVARD
MARION
SHELBY CO.
DE SOTO CO.
LAKE VIEW
North Horn Lake

Map continues on this page G-2

Scale of Miles

0 1 2 3

©TRAKKER MAPS INC.

MEEKER
GERMANTOWN
MEQUON
COLGATE
WASHINGTON CO.
WAUKESHA CO.
Donges Bay
Ozaukee Co.
Milwaukee Co.
BROWN DEER
RIVER HILLS
BAYSIDE
Schlitz Audubon Ctr.
MENOMONEE FALLS
Menomonee
Dretzka Park & G.C.
FOX POINT
Plainview
Menomonee Park & G.C.
LANNON
Good Hope
Brown Deer
Bradley
Dean
GLENDALE
Good Hope
SUSSEX
W. Mill
W. Mill
Mill
Bender
WHITEFISH BAY
Silver Spring
Silver Spring
Villard
SHOREWOOD
Town Line
Lisbon
BUTLER
Timmerman Airport
Hampton
Keefe Av.
University of Wisconsin (Milwaukee)
PEWAUKEE
Capitol
Capitol
Lisbon
Burleigh
Burleigh
Edgewood
Lake Park
DUPLAINVILLE
Burleigh
BROOKFIELD
Brookfield City Park
North
North
Sherman
McKinley Park
ELM GROVE
Mayfair
WAUWATOSA
Milwaukee County Zoo
Vliet
MILWAUKEE
City Hall
Prospect
WAUKESHA
Gebhardt
Blue Mound
Watertown Plank
Wisconsin
Blue Mound
Highland
Wells
Marquette Univ.
East-West Freeway
State Fair Park
Miller Field
Stadium
Greenfield
WEST MILWAUKEE
Lake Michigan
Greenfield G.C.
Greenfield Park
National
Lincoln
Lincoln
Jackson Park
SAINT FRANCIS
NEW BERLIN
Cleveland
WEST ALLIS
Oklahoma
Morgan
Holt
Beloit
Howard
Forest Home
Thompson
Sunny Slope
Airport
GREENFIELD
Morgan
CUDAHY
Lawnsdale
Layton
Edgerton
General Mitchell International Airport
Sheridan Park
HALES CORNERS
GREENDALE
Whitnall Park
Grobschmidt Park
College
SOUTH MILWAUKEE
Glengary
College
Root River Pkwy
Grant Park
VERNON
W. Janesville
Rawson
MUSKEGO
Little Muskego Lake
Corners
Drexel
OAK CREEK
Muskego Co. Park
Root River Pkwy
Puetz
BIG BEND
Big Muskego Lake
Ryan
FRANKLIN
Oakwood G.C.
Rainbow Airport
Oakwood
Bender Park
Kee Nong Go Mong Lake
WAUSHEKA CO.
RACINE CO.
MILWAUKEE CO.
RACINE CO.
TICHIGAN
UNION CHURCH
CADDY VISTA
Seven Mile
Wind Lake
Tichigan Lake
KNEELAND
HUSHER
Waubeesee Lake
Six Mile
Six Mile
TABOR
Five and a Half Mile
RAYMOND
CALEDONIA
BUENA PARK
Five Mile
NORTH CAPE
THOMPSONVILLE

Scale of Miles
0   1   2   3
© C.S.C.

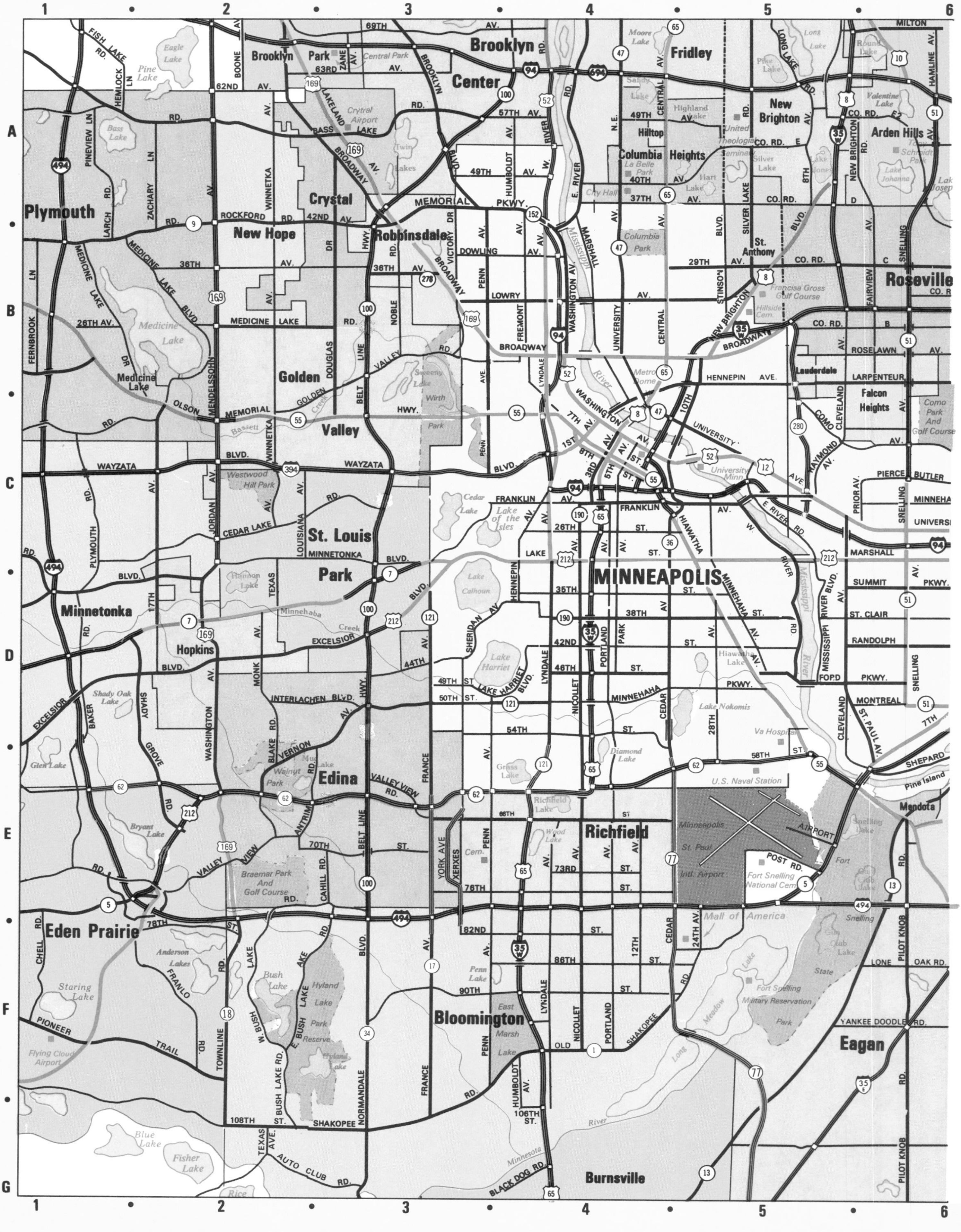

Brooklyn Park
Brooklyn Center
Fridley
New Brighton
Arden Hills
Hilltop
Columbia Heights
Plymouth
New Hope
Crystal
Robbinsdale
St. Anthony
Roseville
Golden Valley
Lauderdale
Falcon Heights
St. Louis Park
Minnetonka
Hopkins
MINNEAPOLIS
Edina
Richfield
Mendota
Eden Prairie
Bloomington
Eagan
Burnsville
Fish Lake
Eagle Lake
Pine Lake
Bass Lake
Medicine Lake
Moore Lake
Sandy Lake
Highland Lake
Long Lake
Round Lake
Pike Lake
Valentine Lake
Twin Lakes
Silver Lake
Lake Johanna
Lake Josephine
Crytral Airport
Central Park
United Theological Seminary
La Belle Park
City Hall
Columbia Park
Francisca Gross Golf Course
Hillside Cem.
Metro Dome
University Minn
Como Park And Golf Course
Sweeny Lake
Wirth Park
Bassett Creek
Westwood Hill Park
Cedar Lake
Lake of the Isles
Lake Calhoun
Lake Harriet
Hiawatha Lake
Lake Nokomis
Diamond Lake
Grass Lake
Wood Lake
Va Hospital
U.S. Naval Station
Minneapolis St. Paul Intl. Airport
Fort Snelling National Cem
Fort Snelling Military Reservation State Park
Snelling Lake
Gun Club Lake
Mall of America
Shady Oak Lake
Glen Lake
Hannon Lake
Mud Lake
Walnut Park
Minnehaha Creek
Bryant Lake
Braemar Park And Golf Course
Anderson Lakes
Staring Lake
Bush Lake
Hyland Lake Park Reserve
Penn Lake
East Bloomington Marsh Lake
Long Meadow Lake
Flying Cloud Airport
Blue Lake
Fisher Lake
Rice
Minnesota River
Mississippi River
494
694
94
394
35W
35E
169
212
52
10
8
12
100
65
47
55
7
62
121
77
13
5
18
17
34
1
36
190
280
51
152
9
FRANKLIN AV.
LAKE ST.
HIAWATHA AV.
MINNEHAHA AV.
HENNEPIN AV.
NICOLLET
LYNDALE AV.
PORTLAND AV.
CEDAR AV.
WAYZATA BLVD.
EXCELSIOR BLVD.
OLSON MEMORIAL HWY.
ROCKFORD RD.
BROADWAY
UNIVERSITY AV.
WASHINGTON AV.
CENTRAL AV.
SNELLING AV.
CLEVELAND AV.
LARPENTEUR AV.
MARSHALL
SUMMIT
ST. CLAIR
RANDOLPH
FORD PKWY.
MONTREAL
SHEPARD
78TH ST.
82ND ST.
86TH ST.
90TH ST.
98TH
106TH ST.
108TH ST.
OLD SHAKOPEE RD.
BLACK DOG RD.
AUTO CLUB RD.
PIONEER TRAIL
YANKEE DOODLE RD.
PILOT KNOB RD.
LONE OAK RD.
NORMANDALE BLVD.
FRANCE AV.
YORK AVE
XERXES
PENN AV.
VALLEY VIEW RD.
VERNON
INTERLACHEN BLVD.
MINNETONKA BLVD.
CEDAR LAKE RD.
MEDICINE LAKE RD.
36TH AV.
26TH AV.
LOWRY AV.
DOWLING AV.
37TH AV.
40TH
49TH AV.
57TH AV.
62ND AV.
63RD AV.
69TH AV.
MILTON
1
2
3
4
5
6
A
B
C
D
E
F
G

Shoreview

Snail Lake

Vadnais Heights

McMenemy

Gem Lake

White Bear Lake

Mahtomedi

Birchwood

Willernie

CEDAR AV.

75TH ST.

DALLWOOD RD.

KEATS AVE. N.

MANNING TR.

White Bear Lake

Lake Owasso

Little Canada

Kohlman Lake

Gervais Lake

Maplewood

North St. Paul

Silver Lake

Pine Springs

Lake De Montreville

Lake Jane

JANE

ELMO RD.

40TH ST. N.

30TH ST. N.

Roselawn

Larpenteur

Roseland Cem.

Elmhurst Cem.

Arlington

Maryland

Lake Phalen

Phalen Park Golf Course

Frost Av.

Larpenteur Av.

Prosperity

McKnight

Beaver Lake

Oakdale

Lake Elmo

Sunfish Lake

Eagle Point Lake

ST. PAUL

Como

Calvary Cem.

Oakland Cem.

Como Park Golf Course

Pierce Butler Rte.

Minnehaha

University

Concordia Coll.

Dayton Av.

Summit Av.

State Off. Bldg.

Ramsey Hosp.

Maryland

Minnehaha

White Bear Av.

Union Cem.

Harvester

Minnehaha

Landfall

HUDSON RD.

10TH ST.

Markgrafs Lake

Civic Center

St. Paul Downtown Airport (Holman Field)

George St.

Annapolis

Burns Av.

Upper Afton

Lower Afton

Linwood Av.

Highwood Av.

Battle Creek Lake

Brookview

Radio

Lower Afton

Valley Creek

Woodbury

Powers Lake

St. Johns Dr.

Colby Lake

Afton

Lilydale

Highland Park Golf Course

Butler

Charlton

Wentworth

West St. Paul

Thompson Av.

South St. Paul

Pigs Eye Lake

Burlington Rd.

Point Douglas

Carver Av.

Steeple View Rd.

Bailey

40TH ST. S.

Mendota

Mendota Heights

Resurrection Cem.

Sunfish Lake

Rogers Lake

Delaware

Southview Blvd.

Newport

Military

Tower

Dale

Glen Rd.

Woodlane

Keats

Cottage

Manning

70TH
LONE

Yankee Doodle Rd.

Alverno Av.

Inver Grove

So. St. Paul Municipal Airport

Babcock

Cahill

70TH

65TH

70TH

80TH

St. Paul Park

Hastings

Cottage Grove

Jamaica Av.

Military

Heights

Diffley Rd.

College Tr.

Inver Grove Tr.

Cuneen Tr.

Concord Tr.

Rich Valley

100TH ST. S.

105TH ST.

Mississippi River

Scale of Miles 0 1 2

© C.S.C.

N

NASHVILLE

MOUNT ZION
AMORE
AVONDALE
SAUNDERSVILLE
HENDERSONVILLE
UNION HILL
GOODLETTSVILLE
LICKTON
JOELTON
GERMANTON
WHITES CREEK
LITTLE CREEK
MADISON
RAYON CITY
OLD HICKORY
HOPEWELL
LAKEWOOD
GREEN MILL
MOUNT JULIET
WILSON DAVIDSON
HERMITAGE HILLS
SUMNER CO.
DAVIDSON CO.
WILSON CO.
DAVIDSON CO.
DONELSON
SEVEN POINTS
SMITH SPRINGS
RURAL HILL
FOSTER CORNERS
BROOKLIN
ANTIOCH
UNA
KIMBRO
LA VERGNE
WRENCOE
BEACON
OGLESBY
TUSCULUM
PARAGON MILL
PROVIDENCE
BERRY HILL
OAK HILL
BRENTWOOD
FOREST HILLS
BELLE MEADE
WEST MEADE
VAUGLANS GAP
PASQUO
GOWER
BELLEVUE
RICHLAND
INGLEWOOD
MARROWBONE
RUTHERFORD CO.
CHEATHAM CO.
DAVIDSON CO.
DAVIDSON CO.
WILLIAMSON CO.

Scale of Miles
0   1   2   3

© C.S.C.

N

NEW YORK
NEW JERSEY

CHAPPAQUA · THORNWOOD · HAWTHORNE · VALHALLA · WHITE PLAINS · MAMARONECK · LARCHMONT

PLEASANTVILLE · BRIARCLIFF MANOR · MT. PLEASANT · ELMSFORD · GREENBURGH · SCARSDALE · EASTCHESTER · NEW ROCHELLE · PELHAM · PELHAM MANOR

OSSINING · POCANTICO HILL · EAST VIEW · HILLSIDE · WHITE PLAINS · ARDSLEY · IRVINGTON · MOUNT VERNON · BRONX

ARCHVILLE · TARRYTOWN · N. TARRYTOWN · DOBBS FERRY · HASTINGS-ON-HUDSON · YONKERS

UPPER NYACK · NYACK · S. NYACK · GRANDVIEW-ON-HUDSON · PIERMONT · SPARKILL · PALISADES · ROCKLEIGH · ALPINE · RIVERDALE

VALLEY COTTAGE · CENTRAL NYACK · BLAUVELT · ORANGETOWN · ORANGEBURG · NORTHVALE · NORWOOD · CLOSTER · DEMAREST · CRESSKILL · ENGLEWOOD CLIFFS

CLARKSTOWN · BARDONIA · OLD TAPPAN · HARRINGTON · HAWORTH · DUMONT · BERGENFIELD · TENAFLY · ENGLEWOOD · LEONIA · PALISADES PK. · FORT LEE · LITTLE FERRY

MT. IVY · HILLCREST · SPRING VALLEY · NEW HEMPSTEAD · RIVER VALE · WESTWOOD · EMERSON · ORADELL · RIVER EDGE · NEW MILFORD · HACKENSACK · BOGOTA · TETERBORO · MOONACHIE

PEARL RIVER · MONTVALE · PARK RIDGE · WOODCLIFF LAKE · HILLSDALE · WASHINGTON TWP. · PARAMUS · ROCHELLE PK. · MAYWOOD · SADDLE BROOK · HASBROUCK HTS. · WALLINGTON · WOOD RIDGE

LADENTOWN · WESLEY HILLS · VIOLA · MONSEY · UPPER SADDLE RIVER · SADDLE RIVER · HO-HO-KUS · FAIR LAWN · LODI · GARFIELD · PASSAIC

TALLMAN · AIRMONT · ALLENDALE · WALDWICK · MIDLAND PARK · RIDGEWOOD · GLEN ROCK · ELMWOOD PARK · CLIFTON

SUFFERN · MAHWAH · RAMSEY · WYCKOFF · HAWTHORNE · PROSPECT PK. · PATERSON · WEST PATERSON

SLOATSBURG · RAMAPO · HILLBURN · NORTH HALEDON · HALEDON · LITTLE FALLS TWP. · ESSEX CO.

TUXEDO PARK · MAHWAH · FRANKLIN LAKES · WAYNE TWP. · WAYNE · BORO OF TOTOWA · CEDAR GROVE

HEWITT · RINGWOOD · ERSKINE · OAKLAND · POMPTON LAKES · NORTH CALDWELL · FAIRFIELD · WEST CALDWELL

BORO OF RINGWOOD · BORO OF WANAQUE · BORO OF BLOOMINGDALE · RIVERDALE · LINCOLN PARK · PEQUANNOCK

HARRIMAN STATE PARK · PALISADES INTERSTATE PARK

ROCKLAND CO. · ORANGE CO. · PASSAIC CO. · BERGEN CO. · WESTCHESTER CO. · BRONX CO.

Hudson River · Tappan Zee · Tappan Zee Bridge

Scale of Miles

© C.S.C.

Ocean

Atlantic

QUEENS

BROOKLYN

MANHATTAN

STATEN ISLAND

NEW YORK

NEW JERSEY

NEWARK

JERSEY CITY

BAYONNE

ELIZABETH

NASSAU CO.

BRONX CO.

MANHATTAN CO.

HUDSON CO.

ESSEX CO.

UNION CO.

MIDDLESEX CO.

RICHMOND CO.

KINGS CO.

QUEENS CO.

FLUSHING

JAMAICA

FOREST HILLS

RICHMOND HILL

OZONE PARK

E. NEW YORK

CANARSIE

FLATBUSH

BENSON HURST

CONEY ISLAND

BAY RIDGE

GREEN POINT

ASTORIA

LONG ISLAND CITY

MASPETH

JACKSON HTS.

COLLEGE POINT

BAYSIDE

GREAT NECK EST.

SADDLE ROCK

INWOOD

SPRINGFIELD GDNS.

NEPONSIT

WEEHAWKEN

UNION CITY

HOBOKEN

SECAUCUS

WEST NEW YORK

NORTH BERGEN

GUTTENBERG

EDGEWATER

CLIFFSIDE PK.

FAIRVIEW

RIDGEFIELD

CARLSTADT

WOODRIDGE

RUTHERFORD

EAST RUTHERFORD

LYNDHURST

NORTH ARLINGTON

KEARNY

HARRISON

E. NEWARK

BELLEVILLE

NUTLEY

BLOOMFIELD

GLEN RIDGE

MONTCLAIRE

VERONA

ROSELAND

LIVINGSTON TWP.

WEST ORANGE

ORANGE

EAST ORANGE

MAPLEWOOD TWP.

MILLBURN

MILBURN TWP.

IRVINGTON

HILLSIDE TWP.

UNION TWP.

SPRINGFIELD TWP.

KENILWORTH

BORO OF KENILWORTH

ROSELLE PARK

BOROUGH OF ROSELLE

CRANFORD

BORO OF GARWOOD

CLARK TWP.

WESTFIELD

RAHWAY

LINDEN

CARTERET

PORT READING

SEWAREN

WOODBRIDGE

AVENEL

COLONIA

ISELIN

FORDS

PERTH AMBOY

HUGUENOT

HUGUENOT BEACH

ROSSVILLE

GREAT KILLS

NEW DORP

NEW DORP BEACH

DONGAN HILLS

CASTLETON CORNERS

NEW BRIGHTON

WILLOW BROOK

CHELSEA

PORT RICHMOND

BROOKLYN

Newark International Airport

F. Kennedy International Airport

Floyd Bennett Field

Hudson River

East River

Kill Van Kull

Arthur Kill

Raritan River

Upper New York Bay

Lower New York Bay

Jamaica Bay

Gateway National Recreational Area

Verrazano Narrows Bridge

Throgs Neck Bridge

Triborough Bridge

Brooklyn Bridge

Manhattan Bridge

Williamsburg Bridge

Holland Tunnel

Lincoln Tunnel

Cross Bay Bridge (Toll)

Marine Parkway Bridge

Goethals Bridge

Bayonne Bridge

Outerbridge Crossing

Pulaski Skyway

Statue of Liberty National Monument

Liberty Is.

Ellis Is.

Governors Is.

Randalls Is.

Wards Is.

Rikers Is.

Roosevelt Island

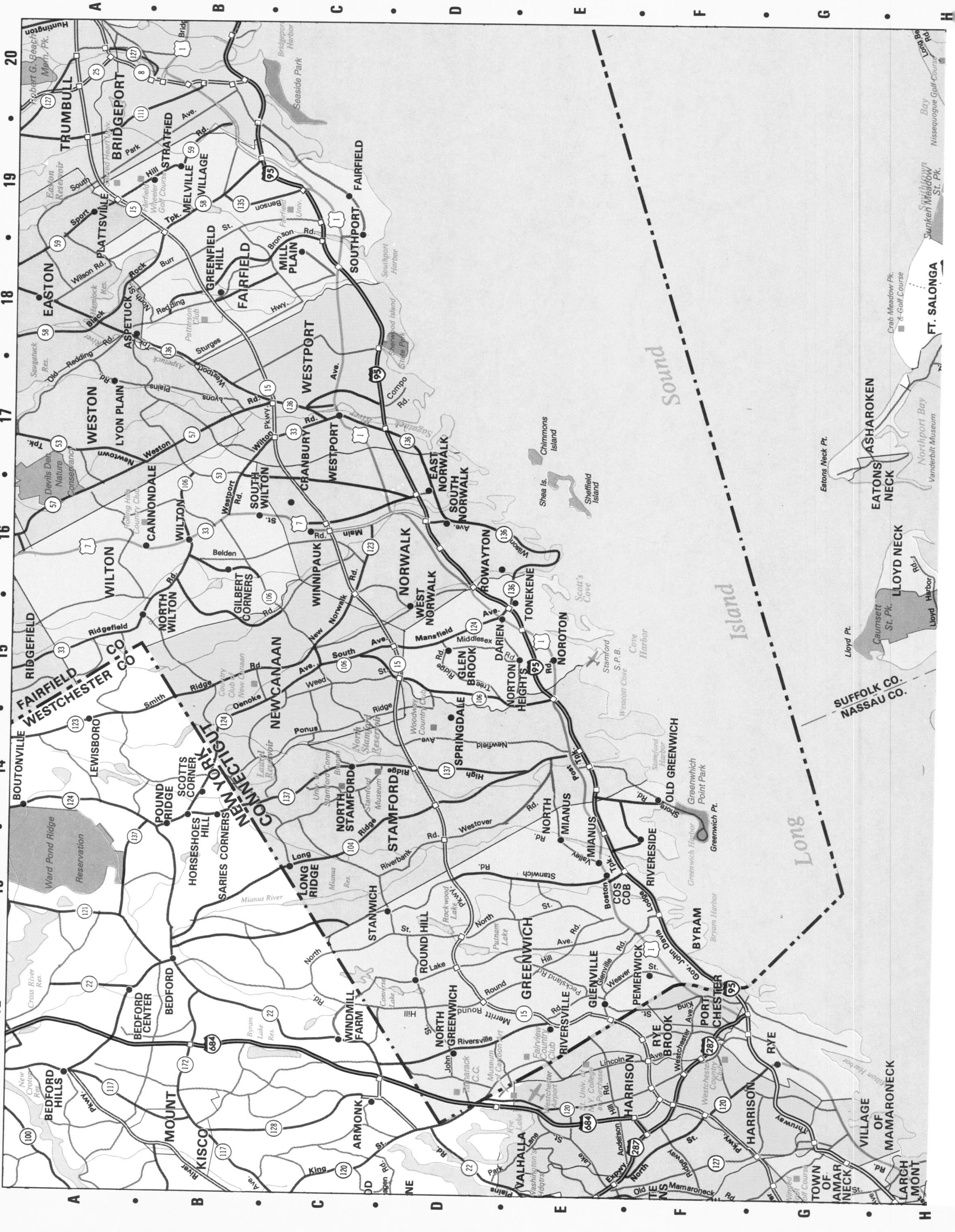
BRIDGEPORT
TRUMBULL
STRATFIELD
EASTON
FAIRFIELD
SOUTHPORT
WESTPORT
WESTON
WILTON
NORWALK
SOUTH NORWALK
EAST NORWALK
ROWAYTON
DARIEN
NEW CANAAN
STAMFORD
GREENWICH
OLD GREENWICH
COS COB
BYRAM
PORT CHESTER
RYE
RYE BROOK
HARRISON
ARMONK
MOUNT KISCO
BEDFORD
POUND RIDGE
LEWISBORO
VALHALLA
Long Island Sound
FAIRFIELD CO.
WESTCHESTER CO.
SUFFOLK CO.
NASSAU CO.
NEW YORK
CONNECTICUT
LLOYD NECK
EATONS NECK
ASHAROKEN
FT. SALONGA
VILLAGE OF MAMARONECK
LARCHMONT

Scale of Miles

© C.S.C.

0 1 2 3
20

N

Ocean

Atlantic

Long Island Sound

Great South Bay

Fire Island

SAN REMO
KINGS PARK
SMITHTOWN
SMITHTOWN TWP.
VILLAGE OF THE BRANCH
VILLAGE OF ISLANDIA
HAUPPAUGE
CENTRAL ISLIP
ISLIP
ISLIP TWP.
EAST ISLIP
BAY SHORE
MIDDLEVILLE
VERNON VALLEY
EAST NORTHPORT
GREEN LAWN
ELWOOD
BRENTWOOD
EAST BRENTWOOD
NORTH BAY SHORE
BRIGHT WATERS
WEST BAY SHORE
WEST ISLIP
DUNEWOOD
SALTAIRE
OAK BEACH
CENTERPORT
EAST NORTHPORT
HUNTINGTON
HUNTINGTON BAY
HALESITE
HUNTINGTON TWP.
SOUTH HUNTINGTON
HUNTINGTON STATION
MELVILLE
WYANDANCH
DEER PARK
BABYLON TWP.
WEST BABYLON
BABYLON
NORTH AMITYVILLE
AMITYVILLE
LINDENHURST
COPIAGUE
LLOYD HARBOR
COLD SPRING HARBOR
LAUREL HOLLOW
WOODBURY
OLD BETHPAGE
PLAINVIEW
FARMINGDALE
SOUTH FARMINGDALE
NORTH AMITYVILLE
COVE NECK
OYSTER BAY COVE
SYOSSET
LOCUST GROVE
MUTTONTOWN
PLAINVIEW
BETHPAGE
HICKSVILLE
MASSAPEQUA
MASSAPEQUA PK.
SEAFORD
BAYVILLE
MILL NECK
MATINECOCK
UPPER BROOKVILLE
OYSTER BAY
NORWICH
BROOKVILLE
OLD BROOKVILLE
JERICHO
NEW CASSEL
LEVITTOWN
EAST MEADOW
BELLMORE
MERRICK
WANTAGH
LATTINGTOWN
LOCUST VALLEY
SEA CLIFF
GLEN HEAD
OLD BROOKVILLE
ROSLYN HARBOR
EAST HILLS
ROSLYN HILLS
OLD WESTBURY
WESTBURY
UNIONDALE
ROOSEVELT
FREEPORT
BALDWIN
OCEANSIDE
GLEN COVE
MANOR HAVEN
PORT WASHINGTON NORTH
PORT WASHINGTON
FLOWER HILL
MANHASSET
NORTH HILLS
SEARINGTOWN
WILLISTON PK.
MINEOLA
NEW GARDEN CITY
HEMPSTEAD
ROCKVILLE CENTER
MALVERNE
LYNBROOK
EAST ROCKAWAY
HEWLETT
WOODS BURG
LIDO BEACH
SANDS POINT
KINGS POINTS
GREAT NECK
PLANDOME
MANOR
SADDLE ROCK
KENSINGTON
UNIVERSITY GARDENS
GREAT NECK
BAYSIDE
NORTH NEW HYDE PARK
NEW HYDE PARK
FLORAL PARK
ELMONT
VALLEY STREAM
WOODMERE
CEDAR HURST
LAWRENCE
ATLANTIC BEACH
NASSAU CO.
QUEENS CO.
JAMAICA
ROSEDALE
SPRINGFIELD GDNS.
EDGEMERE

Nassau Co.
Suffolk Co.

OYSTER BAY
HEMPSTEAD HARBOR
MANHASSET BAY
LITTLE NECK BAY

JONES IS.
MEADOW IS.
JONES BEACH STATE PARK
FIRE ISLAND
Robert Moses Causeway
Robert Moses State Park
J.F.K. Mem. Wildlife Sanctuary

Routes: 25, 25A, 24, 27, 27A, 107, 110, 106, 105, 115, 109, 111, 231, 135, 101, 347, 454

I-495 Long Island Expwy.
Southern State Pkwy.
Northern State Pkwy.
Meadowbrook State Pkwy.
Wantagh State Pkwy.
Sagtikos State Pkwy.
Sunken Meadow Pkwy.
Bethpage St. Pkwy.
Eisenhower Pk.

Republic Airport
Bethpage Airport
Grumman

Belmont Lake State Park
Caumsett State Park
Sunken Meadow

Sagamore Hill Nat'l Historic Site

POQUOSON

NEWPORT NEWS

HAMPTON

NASA

LANGLEY AIR FORCE BASE

Plum Tree Island Wildlife Refuge

Plumtree Point

Grandview Park

Salt Ponds

CHESAPEAKE BAY

Fort Monroe

Walker Airfield

Fort Wool

WILLOUGHBY

Willoughby Bay

Bellinger

Norfolk Naval Air Station

OCEAN VIEW

NORFOLK

Norfolk International Airport

USN Little Creek Amphibious Base

LYNNHAVEN ROADS

Lynnhaven Inlet

Lynnhaven Bay

Little Neck

KINGS GRANT

HAMPTON ROADS

Newport News Point

Fishing Point

Ragged Island Creek

Batten Bay

JAMES RIVER

CRITTENDEN

NANSEMOND RIVER

Craney Island Supply Depot

TWIN PINES

CRANEY HEDGEROW CEDAR LN

CHURCHLAND

PORTSMOUTH

SUFFOLK

BOWERS HILL

Portsmouth Chesapeake Airport

CRADDOCK

GREENWOOD

PORTLOCK

SOUTH NORFOLK

DEEP CREEK

SAINT MICHAEL

INDIAN RIVER

COLLEGE PARK

VIRGINIA BEACH

Little Creek Reservoir

Stumpy Lake

GREEN RUN

GREAT DISMAL SWAMP NATIONAL WILDLIFE REFUGE

CHESAPEAKE

GREAT BRIDGE

FENTRESS

US Naval Airfield Fentress Station

Scale of Miles

© ADC of Alexandria

N

Lake Maury

WARWICK

James River Bridge

Elizabeth River

Lafayette River

Southern Branch Elizabeth River

Western Branch Elizabeth River

Eastern Branch Elizabeth River

Albemarle Canal

Nansemond River

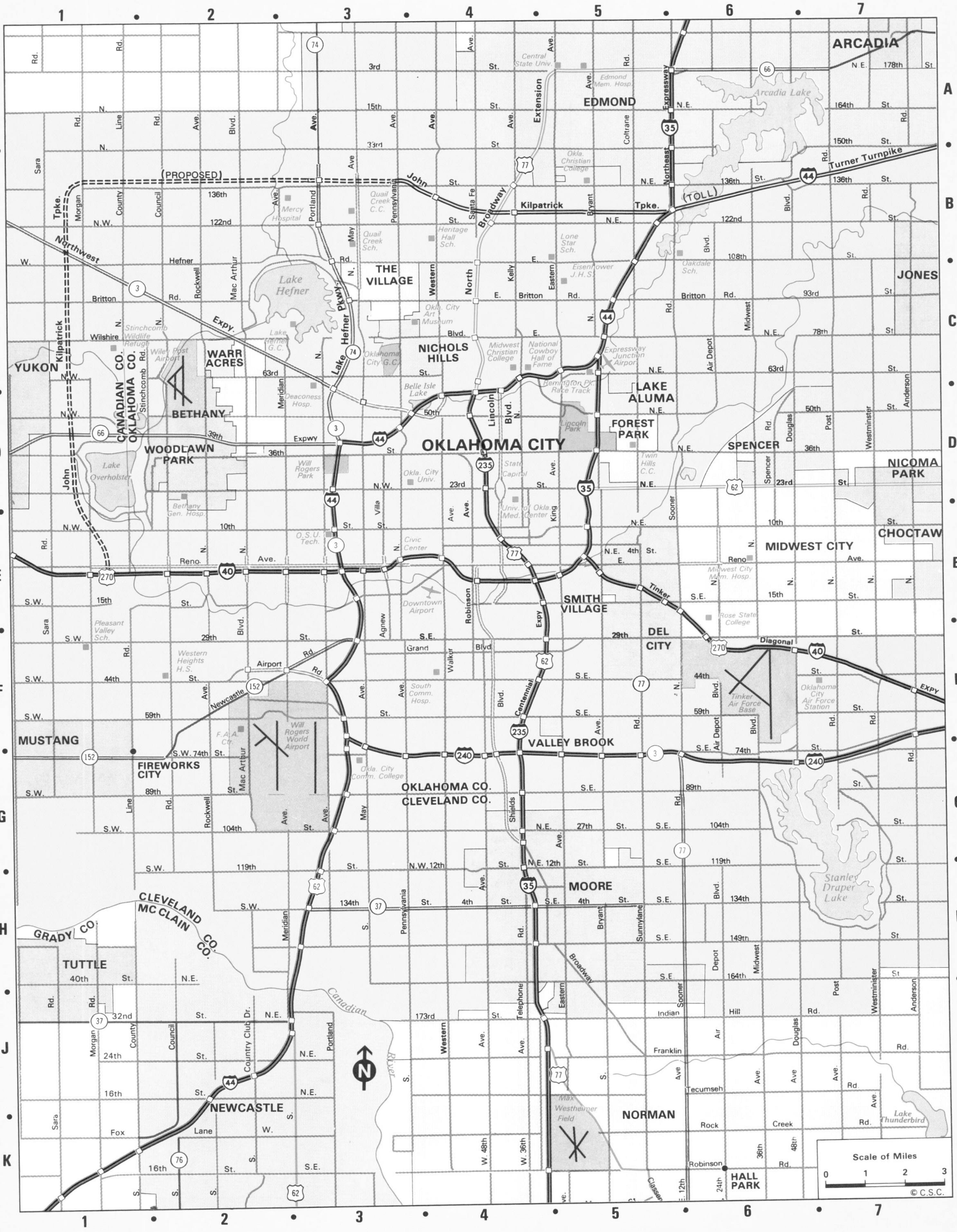
ARCADIA
Arcadia Lake
EDMOND
Central State Univ.
Edmond Mem. Hosp.
Okla. Christian College
Turner Turnpike
Kilpatrick Tpke.
John Kilpatrick
(PROPOSED)
(TOLL)
Mercy Hospital
Quail Creek C.C.
Quail Creek Sch.
Heritage Hall Sch.
Lone Star Sch.
Eisenhower J.H.S.
Oakdale Sch.
Lake Hefner
Lake Hefner G.C.
Lake Hefner Pkwy.
THE VILLAGE
Okla. City Art Museum
JONES
Northwest Expy.
Stinchcomb Wildlife Refuge
Wiley Post Airport
YUKON
WARR ACRES
NICHOLS HILLS
Midwest Christian College
National Cowboy Hall of Fame
Expressway Junction Airport
Oklahoma City G.C.
Belle Isle Lake
Remington Pk. Race Track
Deaconess Hosp.
LAKE ALUMA
CANADIAN CO.
OKLAHOMA CO.
BETHANY
Lincoln Park
FOREST PARK
WOODLAWN PARK
OKLAHOMA CITY
SPENCER
NICOMA PARK
Lake Overholster
Will Rogers Park
State Capitol
Twin Hills C.C.
Okla. City Univ.
Bethany Gen. Hosp.
Univ. of Okla. Med. Center
O.S.U. Tech.
Civic Center
CHOCTAW
MIDWEST CITY
Midwest City Mem. Hosp.
Downtown Airport
SMITH VILLAGE
Pleasant Valley Sch.
Rose State College
DEL CITY
Western Heights H.S.
Tinker Air Force Base
Oklahoma City Air Force Station
Diagonal Expy.
South Comm. Hosp.
MUSTANG
F.A.A. Ctr.
Will Rogers World Airport
VALLEY BROOK
FIREWORKS CITY
Okla. City Comm. College
OKLAHOMA CO.
CLEVELAND CO.
Stanley Draper Lake
MOORE
CLEVELAND CO.
MC CLAIN CO.
GRADY CO.
TUTTLE
Canadian River
NEWCASTLE
Max Westheimer Field
NORMAN
Lake Thunderbird
HALL PARK
Scale of Miles
0 1 2 3
© C.S.C.

1 2 3 4 5 6 7

A

B

C

D

E

F

G

H

J

K

Flightland Airport

NASHVILLE

WASHINGTON CO.
DOUGLAS CO.

Horseshoe Lake

HONEY CREEK

Dutch Hall Rd.

Pawnee Rd.

BENNINGTON

Bennington

Northern Hills Dr.

North Omaha Airport

McKinley

Skyranch Airport

Glen Cunningham Lake and Recreation Area

DEBOLT

Dodge Park

CLARA

Jackson

CRESCENT

WESTON

Standing Bear Lake and Recreation Area

Ida

Fort

Tranquility Park

Omaha Country Club

SORENSON PKWY.

Hartman Ave.

Benson Park

Ames

Miller Park

Redick Ave.

John J. Pershing Dr.

STORZ EXPWY.

River

Omaha Airport

Rainbow Rd.

Lewis & Clark Monument

Maple

Blondo

Miracle Hill Golf Course

Dodge

BOYS TOWN

Pacific

Fontenelle Park

Nebraska School for the Deaf

Western Baptist Bible College

Fort

Carter

Locust

Levi Carter Park

Carter Lake

Epley Airfield

CARTER LAKE

Lincoln Monument

Iowa Western Community College

McPherson Ave.

OMAHA

Memorial Park

University of Nebraska at Omaha

Elmwood Park

Happy Hollow Country Club

College of St. Mary

Cumming

Dodge

Leavenworth

Center

Creighton U.

Joslyn Art Museum

Dodge Park

West Broadway

9th

Nebraska Ave.

23rd

16th

COUNCIL BLUFFS

Pierce St.

Pomona Ave.

Millard Airport

MILLARD

Highland

Main St.

RALSTON

MAY

Seymour Smith Park

DOUGLAS CO
SARPY CO

Grover

F St.

Ed Creighton Blvd.

Martha St.

480

Rosenblatt Stadium

H. Doorly Zoo

Spring Lake Park

Missouri Ave.

34th Ave.

So. Omaha

Lake Manawa

Lake Manawa State Park

DUMFRIES

CHALCO

LA VISTA

Applewood Golf Course

Harrison

Giles

Giles Rd.

Childs Rd.

Mount Vernon Garden

Marian Park

Gifford

Fontenelle Forest

Missouri

POTTAWATTAMIE CO
MILLS CO

PAPILLION

South Omaha Airport

Lincoln

Cornhusker Dr.

BELLEVUE

131

Schram Rd.

Capehart Rd.

GILMORE
FORT CROOK

Harlan

Mission Ave.

Offutt Air Force Base

Fairview

RICHFIELD

CAPEHART

Platteview Rd.

SPRINGFIELD

NEBRASKA
IOWA

SARPY CO.
CASS CO.

Platte River

PACIFIC CITY

GLENWOOD

CULLOM

OREAPOLIS

CEDAR CREEK
MEADOW

PLATTSMOUTH

PACIFIC JUNCTION

Scale of Miles
0 1 2 3

© C.S.C.

Lake Monroe

Johns River

441

46

46

46

17

SANFORD

CELERY AV

GENEVA AV

PAOLA RD

CENTRAL FLORIDA REGIONAL AIRPORT

A

500

LAKE ORANGE

LAKE

LAKE MARY

Crystal Lake Mary

Belair Lake

SANFORD AV

Lake Jesup

ONDICH RD

KELLY PARK RD

ROUND

SORRENTO

PONKAN RD

COUNTY COUNTY

4

400

BLVD

92

15

600

CENTRAL FLORIDA GREENEWAY

B

ZELLWOOD

WEKIWA SPRINGS STATE PARK

Wekiva Swamp

Wekiva River

LAKE WOODS

MARKHAM

LONGWOOD

OLD ORLANDO HWY

SANFORD OVIEDO RD

WINTER SPRINGS

434

FLORIDA AV

ALOMA AV

APOPKA

PLYMOUTH

ROCK SPRINGS RD

434 BLVD

LONGWOOD AV

ALTAMONTE SPRINGS

CASSELBERRY

TUSKAWILLA

OVIEDO

C

437

BINION RD

OCOEE APOPKA RD

APOPKA BLVD

441

SEMORAN

500

ORANGE SEMINOLE

436

FOREST CITY

Lake Howell

Little Howell Lake

CHULU RD

SEMINOLE ORANGE

434

Lake Price

D

437

MAGNOLIA PARK

CLARCONA

CLARCONA OCOEE RD

EDGEWATER DR

500

EATONVILLE

17

92

MAITLAND

WINTER PARK

Lake Osceola

Lake Maitland

Bear Gulley Lake

GOLDENROD RD

Lake Irma

ORLANDO SPORT STAD

Lake Baldwin

COLONIAL

DEAN RD

DR

420

Lake Apopka

OCOEE

WINTER GARDEN

SILVER STAR RD

BEN WHITE RACEWAY

Lake Wekiva

Lake Fairview

GARDEN

Lake Mizell

Lake Berry

Lake Nue

Lake Virginia

15

600

50

Barton Lake

425

OAKLAND

To Leesburg

50

W. B. BILL McGEE HWY

PRINCETON HOSPITAL

Lake Lawne

423

Orlando Executive Airport

EAST-WEST EXPRESS WAY

LAKE

UNDERHILL RD

E

545

265

267

FLORIDA'S TURNPIKE

WINTER GARDEN RD

526

CITRUS BOWL

Lake Mann

ARENA

527

CHURCH STREET STATION

CURRY FORD RD

436

552

John's Lake

439

MAGUIRE

Turkey Lake

Clear Lake

ORLANDO

15

551

535

TILDEN RD

WINDERMERE

Lake Down

CONROY

439

Lake Holden

Little Lake Conway

506

15

F

Huckleberry Lake

Lake Butler

WINTER GARDEN VINELAND RD

Lake Blanche

Lake Tibet

Lake Sheen

UNIVERSAL STUDIOS

439

KIRKMAN

4

400

JOHN YOUNG PARKWAY

OAK RIDGE RD

ORANGE

BLOSSOM TRAIL

EDGEWOOD

BELLE ISLE

Lake Conway

McCOY RD

BEELINE EXPRESSWAY

To Cape Canaveral

APOPKA - VINELAND RD

Lake Palmia

482

Big Sand Lake

Spring Lake

WET 'N WILD

ORLANDO CENTRAL PARK

BEELINE EXPWY

ORLANDO INTERNATIONAL AIRPORT

MOSS PARK RD

G

MAGIC KINGDOM

THE DISNEY INN

Bay Lake

South Lake

Pocket Lake

Lake Mabel

TURKEY LAKE RD

SEA WORLD

ORANGE COUNTY CONVENTION-CIVIC CENTER

423

528

254

4

17

TAFT

ST

TERMINAL

AIRPORT BLVD

Lake Nona

Mud Lake

Red Lake

Buck Lake

BOGGY CREEK RD

GREENEWAY

NARCOOSSEE

Lake Whippoorwill

Lake Hart

WALT DISNEY WORLD RESORT

535

CONTEMPORARY RESORT

GRAND FLORIDIAN

EPCOT

BUENA VISTA

Village Resort

HOTEL PLAZA BLVD

INTERNATIONAL DRIVE

CENTRAL FLORIDA PKWY

JOHN YOUNG PARKWAY

92

441

527

527 A

Lake Mary Jane

H

545

ORLANDO VACATION RESORT

ANIMAL KINGDOM

DISNEY-MGM STUDIOS

WORLD DR

Lake Bryan

Lake Willis

500

600

GATORLAND

FLORIDA

ORANGE OSCEOLA

COUNTY COUNTY

Boggy Creek RD

East Lake Tohopekaliga

Fells Cove

Hinden Lake

LAKE ORANGE

To US 27

OSCEOLA PKWY

TOLL

192

530

IRLO BRONSON MEMORIAL HWY

KISSIMMEE VIEW

BERMUDA AV

249

BUENAVENTURA LAKES

TURNPIKE

BOGGY CREEK RD

Lake Myrtle

NARCOOSSEE

J

CELEBRATION

4

400

LAKE WILSON RD

KISSIMMEE

ALLIGATOR SAFARI ZOO

MEDIEVAL TIMES

POINCIANA BLVD

192

441

NEPTUNE

500

FORTUNE RD

244

PARTIN SETTLEMENT RD

RUNNYMEDE

15

Lake Center

NOVA

POLK OSCEOLA

COUNTY COUNTY

To Tampa

To Haines City

600

ORANGE BLOSSOM TRAIL

KISSIMMEE MUNICIPAL AIRPORT

17

KINGS HWY

LAKE SHORE BLVD

10 ST

242

Lake Tohopekaliga

532

Coon Lake

Trout Lake

K

Scale of Miles

0   1½   3 Miles

0   1½   3 Kilometers

© TRAKKER MAPS INC.

INTERCESSION CITY

CAMPBELL CITY

Lake Tohopekaliga

ST CLOUD

192

IRLO BRONSON

Alligator Lake

Lake Lizzie

Live Oak Lake

Scale of Miles

© ADC of Alexandria

A

B

C

D

E

F

G

1 2 3 4 5 6

Beardsley Canal
McMicken Dam Outlet Canal

DYNAMITE RD.

JOMAX RD.

HAPPY VALLEY RD.

PINNACLE PEAK RD.

Cave Creek Dam

Deer Valley Airport

Arizona Veterans Mem. Cemetery

PINNACLE PEAK RD.

Currys Corner

Peoria

83RD AVE.

BEARDSLEY RD.

Adobe
Deer Valley RD.

BEARDSLEY RD.

Paradise Valley Community College

Paradise Valley Park

Suprise

Beardsley

Sun City West

W. UNION HILLS

AGUA FRIA FRWY.

UNION HILLS RD.

UNION HILLS RD.

BELL

Paradise City

RD.

Turf Paradise Race Track

Scottsdale Mun. Airport

GREENWAY RD.

GREENWAY RD.

75TH AVE.

67TH AVE.

GREENWAY

American Inst. for Foreign Trade

RD.

Moon Valley C.C.

32ND ST.

GREENWAY

40TH ST.

56TH ST.

Scottsdale

WADDELL AVE.

Litchfield

THUNDERBIRD

THUNDERBIRD

Century C.C.

HAYDEN

El Mirage

Sun City

101

CACTUS AVE.

ASU West

Cactus Pk.

Metro Center

BLACK CANYON HWY.

North Mountain Park

CACTUS

7TH ST.

64TH ST.

Youngstown

59TH AVE.

43RD AVE.

PEORIA AVE.

Arizona Canal

19TH AVE.

24TH ST.

SHEA

Scottsdale

OLIVE AVE.

DUNLAP

GRAND AVE.

Glendale Com. Col.

NORTHERN

35TH AVE.

Royal Palm Mobile Pk.

Phoenix Mountain Preserve

Squaw Peak Park

Paradise Valley

Paradise Valley G.C.

AVE.

Glendale

NORTHERN

Glendale

GLENDALE

PHOENIX

LINCOLN

MOCKINGBIRD LN.

Luke Air Force Base

MIRAGE

Glendale Municipal Airport

Rosthaven Cem.

BETHANY HOME RD.

BETHANY

Holiday Pk.

7TH AVE.

CENTRAL

16TH ST.

HOME RD.

Arizona Biltmore

McDONALD DR.

CAMELBACK

60

Litchfield Park

New Agua Fria River

101

CAMELBACK RD.

Grand Canyon Col.

27TH AVE.

Mun. G.C.

CAMELBACK

24TH ST.

SQUAW PEAK

CAMELBACK

Avondale

INDIAN SCHOOL

Eloso Pk.

INDIAN SCHOOL RD.

V.A. Hospital

51

INDIAN SCHOOL

Arizona C.C.

Scottsdale

HAYDEN RD.

McDOWELL

THOMAS

RD.

Encanto Golf Course & Park

Phoenix C.C.

32ND ST.

44TH ST.

56TH ST.

INVERGORDON RD.

RD.

Irrigation District

Canal

McDOWELL

Heard Mus.

County Hospital

RED MT.

Military Res.

Arizona C.C.

Desert Botanical Gardens

McDOWELL

PAPAGO FRWY.

83RD AVE.

VAN BUREN

51ST AVE.

State Fair Grounds

Papago Frwy.

VAN BUREN

State Hospital

202

Phoenix Greyhound

153

Papago Park

Zoological Park

10

Goodyear

PAPAGO ST.

67TH AVE.

75TH AVE.

State Capitol

Mun. Bldg.

BankOne Ballpark

WASHINGTON ST.

SKY HARBOR BLVD.

Sun Devil Stadium

Tempe Park

University

Avondale

Cashion

BUCKEYE

LOWER BUCKEYE RD.

Tolleson

107TH AVE.

91ST AVE.

59TH AVE.

17

America West Arena

60

Sky Harbor Int'l. Airport

143

Arizona State Univ.

APACHE

BROADWAY

Goodyear Airfield

115TH AVE.

BROADWAY RD.

43RD AVE.

16TH ST.

24TH ST.

32ND ST.

40TH ST.

48TH ST.

Maricopa

10

PRIEST DR.

MIL AVE.

RURAL RD.

Tempe

BULLARD

SOUTHERN AVE.

Salt River

35TH AVE.

27TH AVE.

19TH AVE.

7TH AVE.

CENTRAL

7TH ST.

Manzanita Speedway

SOUTHERN

Western Canal

60

Casey Abbott Semi-Regional Park

BASE LINE RD.

DOBBINS RD.

Laveen

59TH AVE.

51ST AVE.

Phoenix Police Academy

Thunderbird C.C.

CANYON RD.

Guadalupe

GUADALUPE RD.

Ahwatukee

GUADALUPE RD.

ESTRELLA MOUNTAIN REGIONAL PARK

Gila River

ELLIOT RD.

ESTRELLA DR.

Las Ramadas Picnic Area

STEHPEN RD.

MATHER RD.

TELEGRAPH PASS

BUENA VISTA RD.

Gila Valley Lookout

ELLIOT

WARNER

48TH ST.

56TH ST.

KYRENE

MC CLINTOCK DR.

Chandler

SAN JUAN RD.

PHOENIX SOUTH MOUNTAIN PARK

International Harvester Proving Ground

RAY RD.

CANAL

Highland

PECOS RD.

WILLIAMS RD.

N

GILA RIVER

MARICOPA CO. PINAL CO.

INDIAN

RESERVATION

10

347

PIMA FREEWAY

Goodyear Air Force Mil. Field

Scale of Miles
0 1 2 3 4 5

© C.S.C.

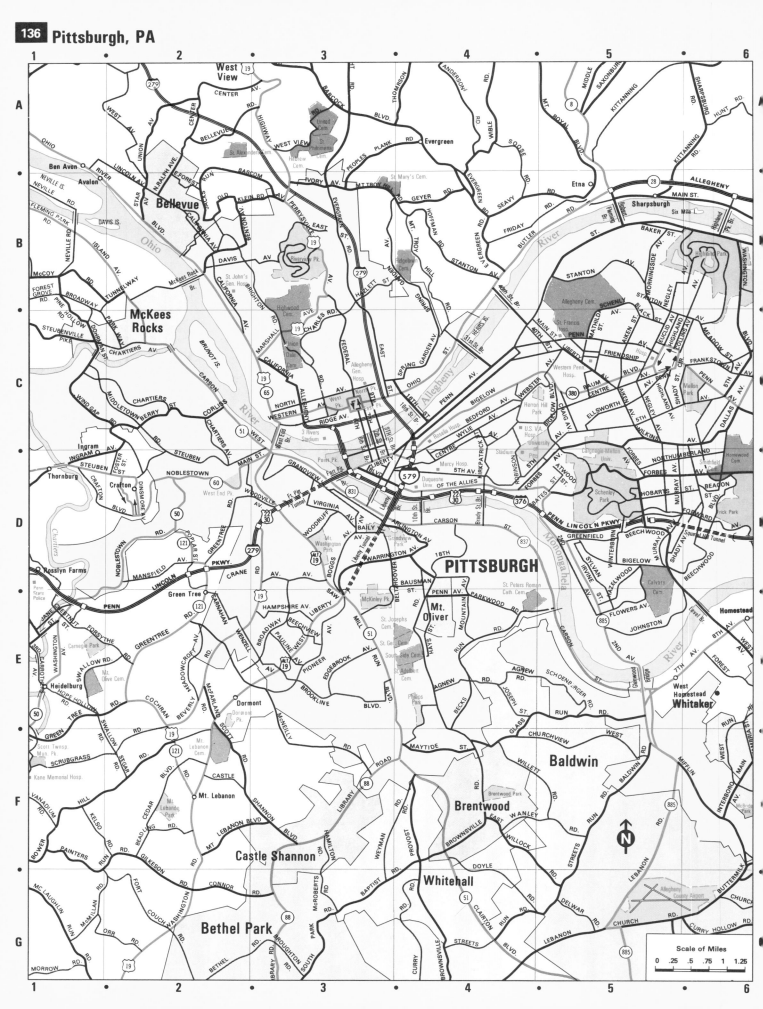

MULTNOMAH COUNTY
CLARK COUNTY

VANCOUVER

E. MILL PLAIN BLVD.

SKYLINE BLVD.
NEWBERRY RD.
SUAVE
ISLAND RD.
MULTNOMAH
GILLIMAN
LOOP
MARINE DR.
HAYDEN ISLAND

Pearson Field

N.W. SKYLINE BLVD.
GERMANTOWN RD.
COLUMBIA BLVD.
LOMBARD ST.
N. FESSENDEN ST.
N. COLUMBIA

Columbia

Exposition Center
Delta Park

Portland Yacht Club
Tomahawk Island
Delta Park

Columbia River

Tyee Yacht Club

Rose City Yacht Club

WASHINGTON
OREGON

Columbia River Yacht Club

N

Forest Park

N. LOMBARD ST.
N. WILLAMETTE
N. PORTSMITH AVE.
WILLIS BLVD.
N. PENINSULAR AVE.
N. DENVER
BLVD.

Columbia Park

Columbia Edgewater G.C.

Riverside G.C.

N.E. MARINE RD.

Portland Int'l Airport

Portland Air Force Base

Broadmoor G.C.

Colwood G.C.

Willamette River

Univ. of Portland

Swan Island

N. PORTLAND AVE.
Peninsula Park

N. GREELEY
N. INTERSTATE AVE.
N.E. COLUMBIA BLVD.
N.E. LOMBARD
N.E. SUNDERLAND

N.E.
KILLNGSWORTH ST.

Alberta Park

PORTLAND

YEON AVE.

N.W. VAUGHN ST.

99E

N.E. FREMONT ST.

N.E. 33RD AVE.
N.E. 39TH
THE ALAMEDA
N.E. 42ND AVE.
N.E. 57TH
N.E. CULLY RD.

Rose City G.C.

MacLeay Park

Broadway Bridge

Fremont Bridge

UNION

N.E. BROADWAY
N.E. HALSEY ST.

BRONSON RD.
CORNELL RD.
CORNELL RD.
CORNELL RD.

N.W. 23RD AVE.
N.W. 19TH AVE.

Memorial Coliseum

SANDY
N.E.
GLISAN
ST.

BURNSIDE

84

174TH AVE.
WALKER

N.W.
SKYLINE BLVD.
BARNES

Portland State Univ.

405

S.E. STARK ST.
S.E. BELMONT ST.

Mt. Tabor Park

170TH AVE.
JENKINS
MURRAY
WALKER RD.
BARNES RD.
CEDAR HILLS BLVD.
West Slope
CENTER RD.

Zoological Gardens and Museum

W. HUMPHREY
S.W. VISTA AVE.
W. BROADWAY DR.

S.E. MORRISON ST.

S.E. HAWTHORNE BLVD.

S.E. DIVISION ST.

S.E. 28TH AVE.
39TH
POWELL
62ND
71ST

Warner Pacific College

8
FARMINGTON RD.
Raleigh Hills
BEAVERTON-HILLSDALE

S.W. FATTON
S.W. FAIRMONT
BROADWAY DR.
Council Crest
Univ of Oregon Med. Sch.

Ross Is. Bridge

Ross Island

S.E. FOSTER RD.

10
AVE.
ALLEN BLVD.
WESTERN AVE.
FERRY

HAMILTON ST.
S.W. SHATTUCK RD.
DOSCH RD.
SUNSET BLVD.
CAMERON RD.
Hillsdale
S.W. VERMONT ST.

TERWILLIGER BLVD.
MACADAM AVE.
BALDOCK FWY.

S.E. 13TH
S.E. 17TH
Harktack Island
Pioneer Park

HOLGATE
S.E. 52ND
S.E. HAROLD

Reed College

WOODSTOCK BLVD.

DENNEY RD.
217
HALL BLVD.
SCHOLLS BLVD.
OLESON RD.

Gabriel Park

AVE.
Multnomah

S.W. MULTNOMAH BLVD.

Eastmoreland Golf Course

S.E. TOLMAN ST.
72ND
S.E. FLAVEL DR.

170TH RD.
HART RD.
MURRAY
WEIR RD.

BEAVERTON

TAYLORS
80TH AVE.
GARDEN RD.
HOME RD.
45TH AVE.
S.W. BARBUR BLVD.

R.H.

Waverly C.C.

JOHNSON

S.E. STROW BRIDGE
LINWOOD

Kendall
ALBERTA ST.

BELL
32ND

Metzger

OAK ST.
CAPITAL HWY.
FERRY
99W
S.W. 35TH AVE.
TAYLORS
FER FRY RD.

BOONES

Riverside C.C.

99E
MILWAUKIE

HARRISON ST.
RAILROAD
KING RD.

REUSSER RD.
SCHOLLS FERRY RD.
OLD SCHOLLS FERRY RD.
TIGARD

WASHINGTON CO.

Portland Comm. College
MULTNOMAH

KERR

STEPHENSON ST.

Lewis & Clark College

Tryon Creek State Park

WILLAMETTE

LAKE RD.
224
ALDERCREST
HARRISON ST.
AVE.
HARMONY RD.

210
217
99W
PACIFIC HWY.
KRUSE WAY
BONITA RD.
LAKE OSWEGO

COUNTRY CLUB RD.

Lake Oswego C.C.

Oak Grove

OATFIELD RD.
HILL RD.
N. Clackamas Central Park
WEBSTER RD.

BEEF BEND RD.
KING CITY
DURHAM RD.

CARMEN DR.
Lake Grove
Waluga Park

Oswego Lake

OAK GROVE BLVD.
CONCORD RD.
THIESSEN

RIVER RD.

DURHAM
TUALATIN

99W
5
CLACKAMAS CO.

STAFFORD RD.
ROSE MONT

PORTLAND AVE.
43
Maryhurst College
WEST LINN

Scale of Miles
0   .5   1   1.5

© C.S.C.

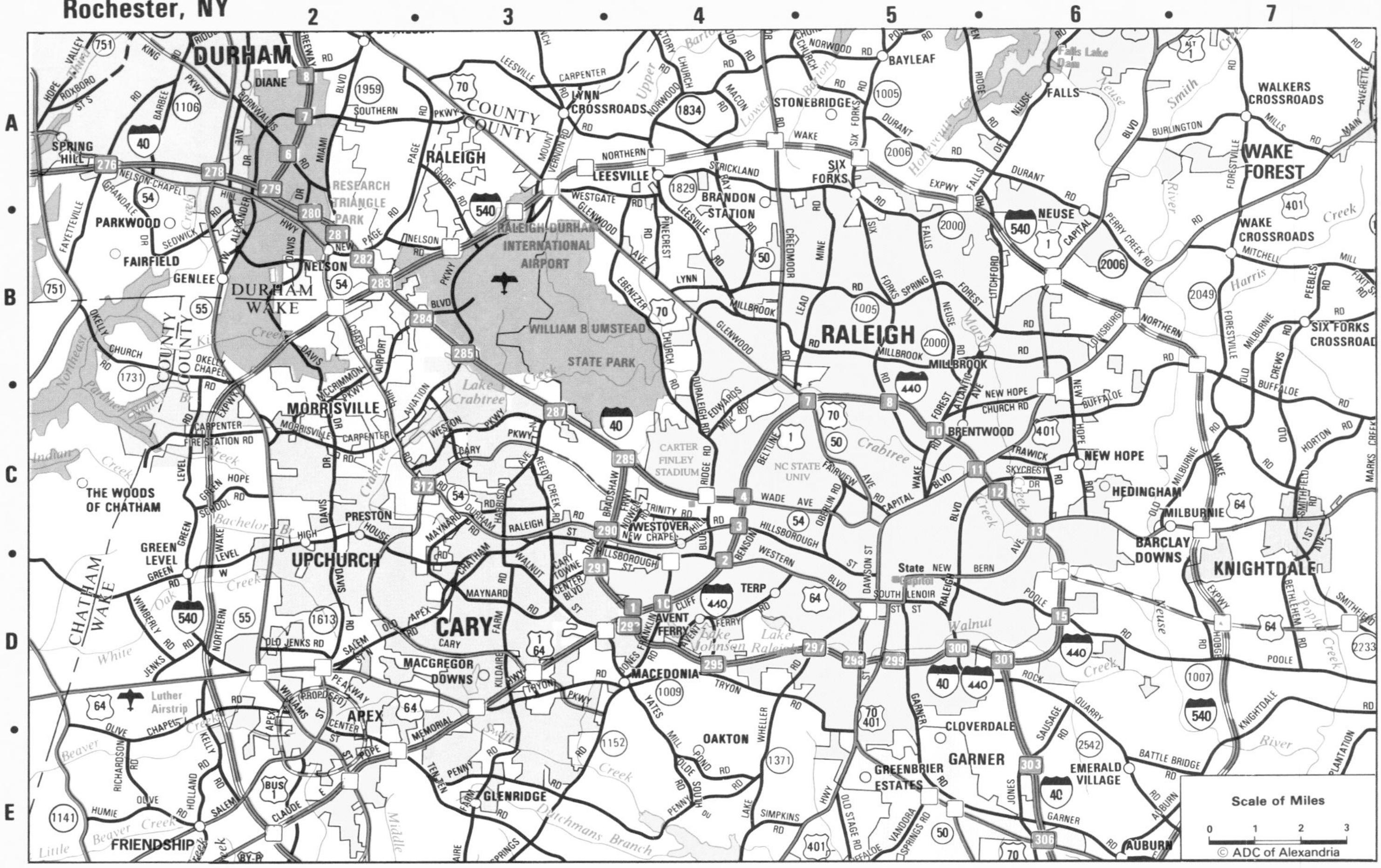
DURHAM
DIANE
SPRING HILL
PARKWOOD
FAIRFIELD
GENLEE
NELSON
DURHAM
WAKE
RESEARCH TRIANGLE PARK
RALEIGH-DURHAM INTERNATIONAL AIRPORT
WILLIAM B UMSTEAD STATE PARK
LYNN CROSSROADS
LEESVILLE
BRANDON STATION
STONEBRIDGE
SIX FORKS
BAYLEAF
FALLS
WALKERS CROSSROADS
WAKE FOREST
NEUSE
WAKE CROSSROADS
SIX FORKS CROSSROAD
RALEIGH
MILLBROOK
BRENTWOOD
NEW HOPE
HEDINGHAM
MILBURNIE
BARCLAY DOWNS
KNIGHTDALE
MORRISVILLE
THE WOODS OF CHATHAM
GREEN LEVEL
UPCHURCH
PRESTON
CARTER FINLEY STADIUM
NC STATE UNIV
WESTOVER
CARY
CHATHAM
WAKE
COUNTY
MACGREGOR DOWNS
APEX
Luther Airstrip
MACEDONIA
AVENT FERRY
TERP
Lake Johnson
Lake Raleigh
State Capitol
OAKTON
CLOVERDALE
GARNER
GREENBRIER ESTATES
EMERALD VILLAGE
GLENRIDGE
FRIENDSHIP
AUBURN
Scale of Miles
0 1 2 3
© ADC of Alexandria

GRAND VIEW HEIGHTS
HILTON
CRESCENT BEACH
RIGNEY BLUFF
Lake Ontario
Scale of Miles
0 1 2 3
© C.S.C.
N
PARMA CENTER
NORTH GREECE
FOREST LAWN
OKLAHOMA BEACH
Durand Eastman Park
PARMA CORNERS
WEST GREECE
GREECE
WEST WEBSTER
WEBSTER
UNION HILL
IRONDEQUOIT
Irondequoit Bay
SOUTH GREECE
SPENCERPORT
ROSELAND
OGDEN CENTER
ROCHESTER
PENFIELD CENTER
GATE
WEST WALWORTH
PENFIELD
EAST PENFIELD
EAST ROCHESTER
NORTH CHILI
CHILI CENTER
BRIGHTON
WEST CHILI
CRITTENDEN
PITTSFORD
FAIRPORT
WAYNEPORT

Scale of Miles
0 1 2 3
© ADC of Alexandria

Scale of Miles
0 1 2 3 4

© C.S.C.

St. Charles
St. Louis County
St. Charles County

Florissant
Black Jack
Hazelwood
Bridgeton
Berkeley
Ferguson
Dellwood
Bellefontaine Neighbors
Riverview
Moline Acres
Jennings
Normandy
Cool Valley
Bellerive
Northwoods
Velda City
Pagedale
Wellston
University City
Olivette
Overland
St. Ann
St. John
Breckenridge Hills
Charlack
Bel-Ridge
Bel-Nor
Vinita Park
Hanley Hills
Maryland Heights
Creve Coeur
Frontenac
Ladue
Clayton
Richmond Heights
Brentwood
Maplewood
Des Peres
Town and Country
Huntleigh
Warson Woods
Rock Hill
Webster Groves
Glendale
Kirkwood
Oakland
Shrewsbury
Crestwood
Sunset Hills
Fenton
Marlborough
Grantwood Village
Wilbur Park
Green Park
St. George
Bella Villa
Lakeshire

ST. LOUIS
East St. Louis
Brooklyn
National City
Madison
Venice
Granite City
Sauget
Cahokia
Dupo
East Carondelet
North Dupo
Columbia

Missouri / Illinois
Mississippi River
Missouri River
Meramec River

St. Louis County
St. Clair County
Madison County
St. Louis County / Jefferson Co.
St. Clair County / Monroe County
Monroe County

Arnold

Lambert–St. Louis International Airport
Forest Park
Washington University
St. Louis University
Missouri Botanical Gardens
Jefferson Barracks Historical Park
National Museum of Transportation

N

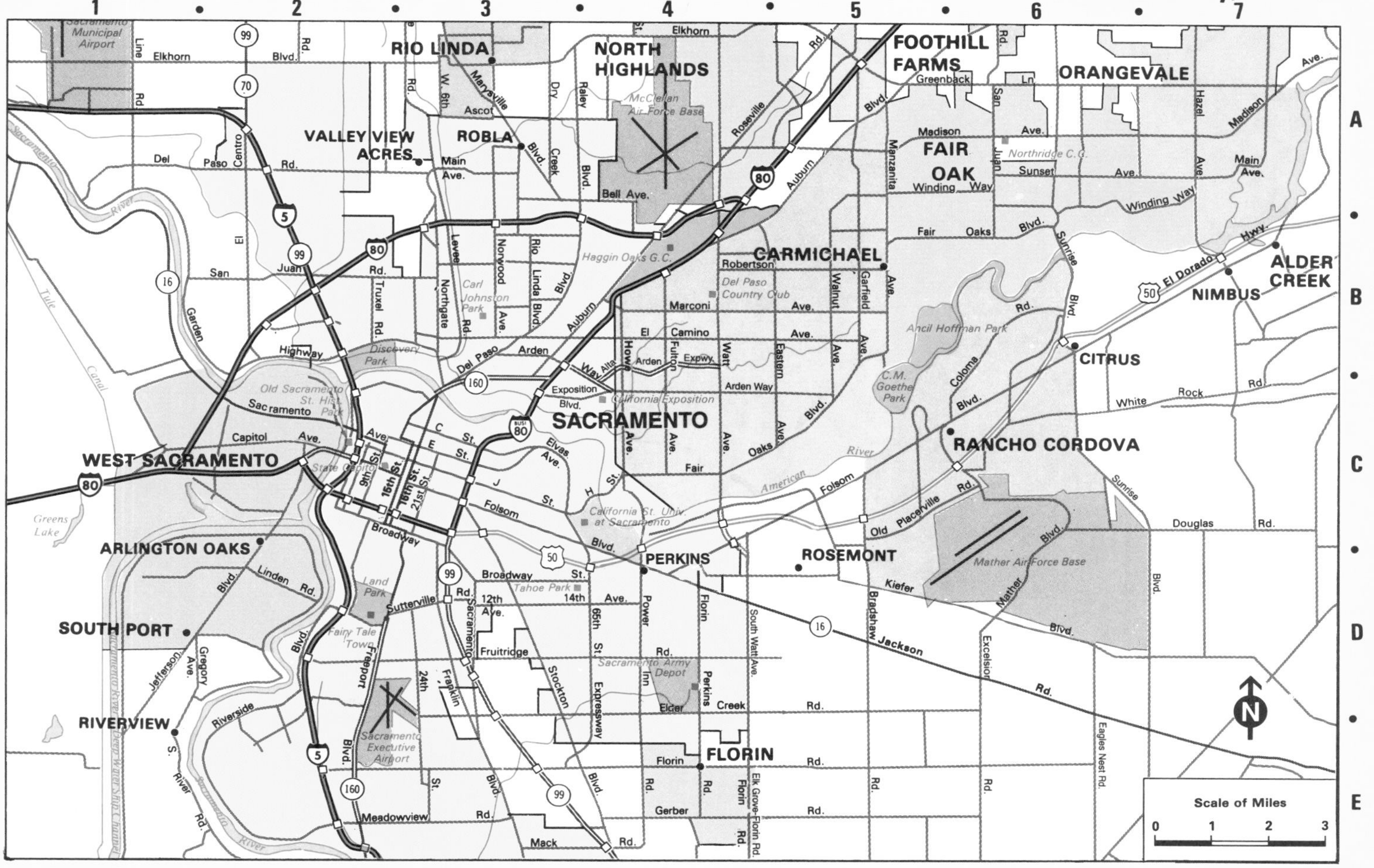
RIO LINDA
NORTH HIGHLANDS
FOOTHILL FARMS
ORANGEVALE
VALLEY VIEW ACRES
ROBLA
FAIR OAK
McClellan Air Force Base
Sacramento Municipal Airport
CARMICHAEL
ALDER CREEK
NIMBUS
CITRUS
SACRAMENTO
WEST SACRAMENTO
RANCHO CORDOVA
ARLINGTON OAKS
PERKINS
ROSEMONT
Mather Air Force Base
SOUTH PORT
RIVERVIEW
FLORIN
Sacramento Executive Airport
Sacramento Army Depot
California Exposition
California St. Univ. at Sacramento
Haggin Oaks G.C.
Del Paso Country Club
Ancil Hoffman Park
Discovery Park
Land Park
Fairy Tale Town
Tahoe Park
Northridge C.C.
State Capitol
American River
Sacramento River
Scale of Miles
0 1 2 3

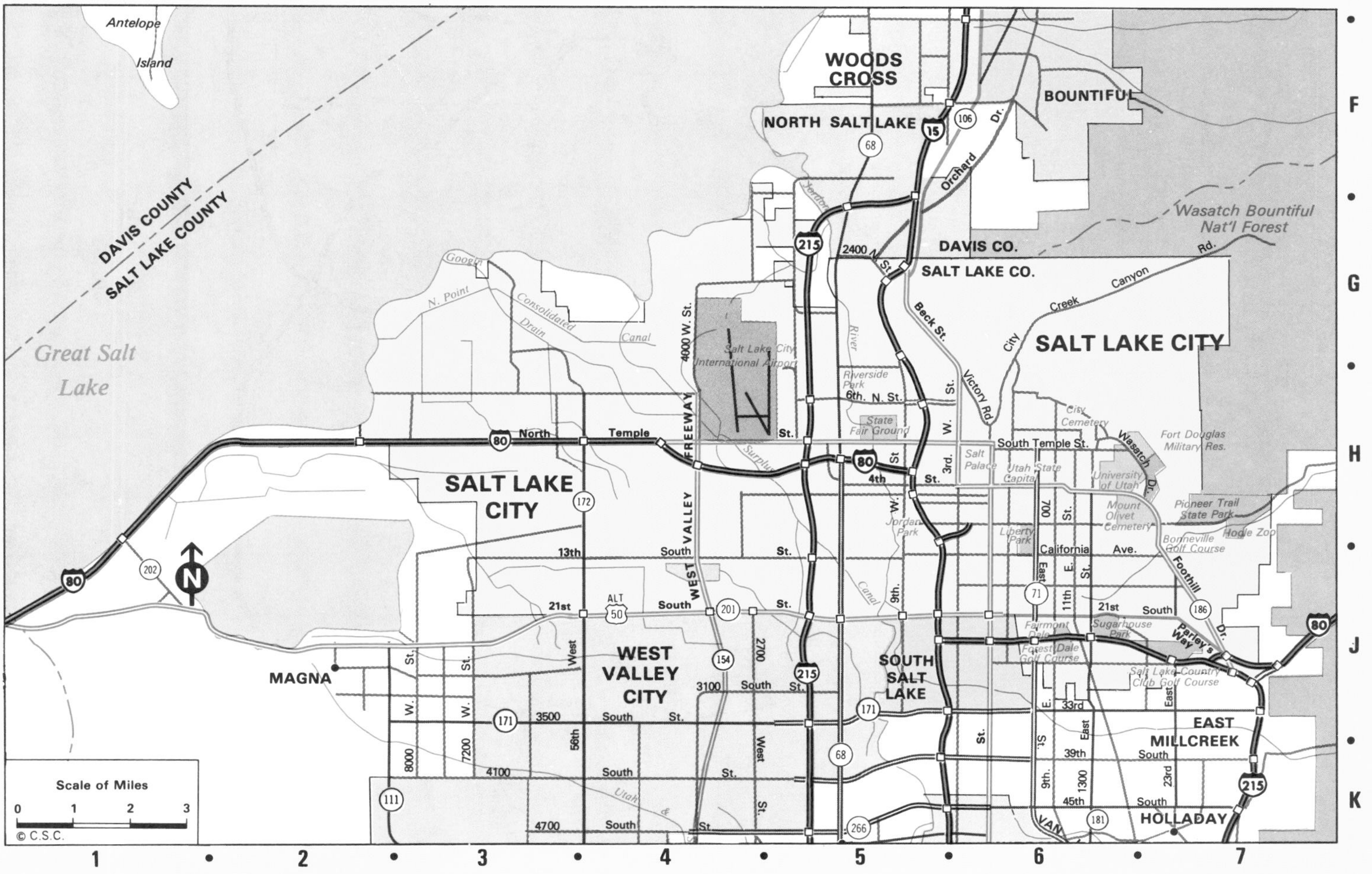
Antelope Island
Great Salt Lake
DAVIS COUNTY
SALT LAKE COUNTY
WOODS CROSS
BOUNTIFUL
NORTH SALT LAKE
Wasatch Bountiful Nat'l Forest
DAVIS CO.
SALT LAKE CO.
SALT LAKE CITY
Salt Lake City International Airport
Riverside Park
State Fair Ground
City Cemetery
Fort Douglas Military Res.
Salt Palace
Utah State Capitol
University of Utah
Pioneer Trail State Park
Jordan Park
Liberty Park
Mount Olivet Cemetery
Bonneville Golf Course
Hogle Zoo
SALT LAKE CITY
WEST VALLEY CITY
MAGNA
SOUTH SALT LAKE
Fairmont Park
Sugarhouse Park
Forest Dale Golf Course
Salt Lake Country Club Golf Course
EAST MILLCREEK
HOLLADAY
Scale of Miles
0 1 2 3
© C.S.C.

GREY FOREST
HELOTES
Camp Bullis Military Reservation
Univ. of Texas at San Antonio
SHAVANO PARK
HOLLYWOOD PARK
HILL COUNTRY VILLAGE
BRACKEN
SELMA
LIVE OAK
CONVERSE
WINDCREST
CASTLE HILLS
San Antonio International Airport
LEON VALLEY
S. Texas Medical Center
BALCONES HEIGHTS
ALAMO HEIGHTS
OLMOS PARK
TERRELL HILLS
KIRBY
St. Mary's University
Assumption Seminary
Brooke Army Medical Center
Fort Sam Houston
Alamo Stadium
Trinity University
SAN ANTONIO
Our Lady of the Lake College
San Fernando Cem.
The Alamo
City Hall
MARTINEZ
GARDENDALE
CHINA GROVE
Joe Freeman Coliseum
Martindale Army Airfield
Lackland Training Annex
Lackland AFB
Kelly AFB
East Kelly AFB
Lions Park
Pecan Valley G.C.
San Antonio State Hospital
Aerospace Med. Cent.
Brooks AFB
Mission
Stinson Field
MACDONA
MANGUS CORNER
VON ORMY
SOUTHTON
BUENA VISTA
Mitchell Lake
Blue Wing Lake
CASSIN
ELMENDORF
Braunig Lake
Medina River
SOMERSET
Dixon
LOSOYA
THELMA
BEXAR CO.
ATASCOSA CO.

Scale of Miles
0   1   2   3

© C.S.C.

SOLANA BEACH

DEL MAR

Del Mar Heights Rd.

Torrey Pines State Park

SORRENTO

University of California San Diego Campus

Scripps Institute of Oceanography

La Jolla Caves

LA JOLLA

La Jolla G.C.

Prospect

Nautilus St.

Pacific Beach

MISSION BEACH

Mission Bay G.C.

Mission Bay Yacht Club

Sea World Aquatic Park

Ocean Beach

Pointe Loma Coll.

U. S. International U.

SAN DIEGO

Mira Mesa Blvd.

MIRAMAR

Miramar G.C.

Miramar Naval Air Station

Camp Elliott

U.S. Air Force Reservation

POWAY

Powers Airport

FERNBROOK

EUCALYPTUS HILLS

MORENO

LAKESIDE

LAKEVIEW

WINTER GARDENS

JOHNSTOWN

GLENVIEW

SANTEE

Carlton Oaks G.C.

Gillespie Field

Fletcher Hills G.C.

EL CAJON

Clairemont General Hosp.

San Diego Mesa Coll.

Montgomery Field

Tierra

U.S. Naval Recreational Facilities

San Diego State Univ.

LA MESA

JAMACHA JUNCTION

JAMACHA

SPRING VALLEY

LEMON GROVE

DICTIONARY HILL

LA PRESA

Sweetwater Reservoir

BALBOA PARK

Zoo

Laurel

Pershing Dr.

Balboa Park

San Diego International Airport

Naval Training Center

U.S.M.C. Base

CORONADO

North Island Naval Air Station

U. S. Military Reservation

Cabrillo Nat'l. Mon.

NATIONAL CITY

LINCOLN ACRES

SUNNYSIDE

LYNWOOD HILLS

Southwestern College

San Diego Naval Station

U.S. Naval Amphibious Base

HARBOR SIDE

CHULA VISTA

Silver Strand State Beach

Imperial Beach Naval Radio Station

IMPERIAL BEACH

Imperial Beach Naval Air Station

SAN DIEGO

U.S. Immigration Detention Facility

Brown Field

OTAY MESA

Upper Otay Reservoir

Lower Otay Reservoir

Pacific Ocean

San Diego Bay

San Vicente Reservoir

Miramar Reservoir

Murray Reservoir

Scale of Miles
0 1 2 3

© C.S.C.

N

SAN PABLO BAY

STATE GAME REFUGE

MT. DIABLO STATE PARK

Chipps Island
Pittsburg
Sacramento River
Shore Acres
U.S. NAVAL MAGAZINE PORT CHICAGO
Clyde
Seal Islands
Avon
Benicia
Pomona
Crockett
Rodeo
Hercules
Pinole
Martinez
Concord
Pleasant Hill
Walnut Creek
Lafayette
Danville
San Ramon
SAN RAMON VALLEY
BOLLINGER CANYON
CULL CANYON
Anthony Chabot Regional Park
Las Trampas Regional Park
St. Mary's College
Moraga
Rheem
Redwood Regional Park
Robert Sibley Regional Park
Briones Regional Park
Charles Lee Tilden Reg. Park
Wildcat Canyon Regional Park
San Pablo Res.
Upper San Leandro Res.
El Cerrito
Albany
Berkeley
U.C. Berkeley
University of California
Emeryville
Piedmont
OAKLAND
Alameda
Oakland Metropolitan International Airport
Alameda Naval Air Station
Oakland Naval Supply Center
Yerba Buena Island
Treasure Island
Brooks Is.
Angel Island State Park
Alcatraz Island
Tiburon
Belvedere
Sausalito
San Rafael
Richmond
RICHMOND SAN RAFAEL BRIDGE (TOLL)
OAKLAND BAY BRIDGE
SAN FRANCISCO
Chinatown
Candlestick Park
GOLDEN GATE BRIDGE (TOLL)
Hunters Point Naval Shipyard
CARQUINEZ STRAIT
SAN PABLO STRAIT

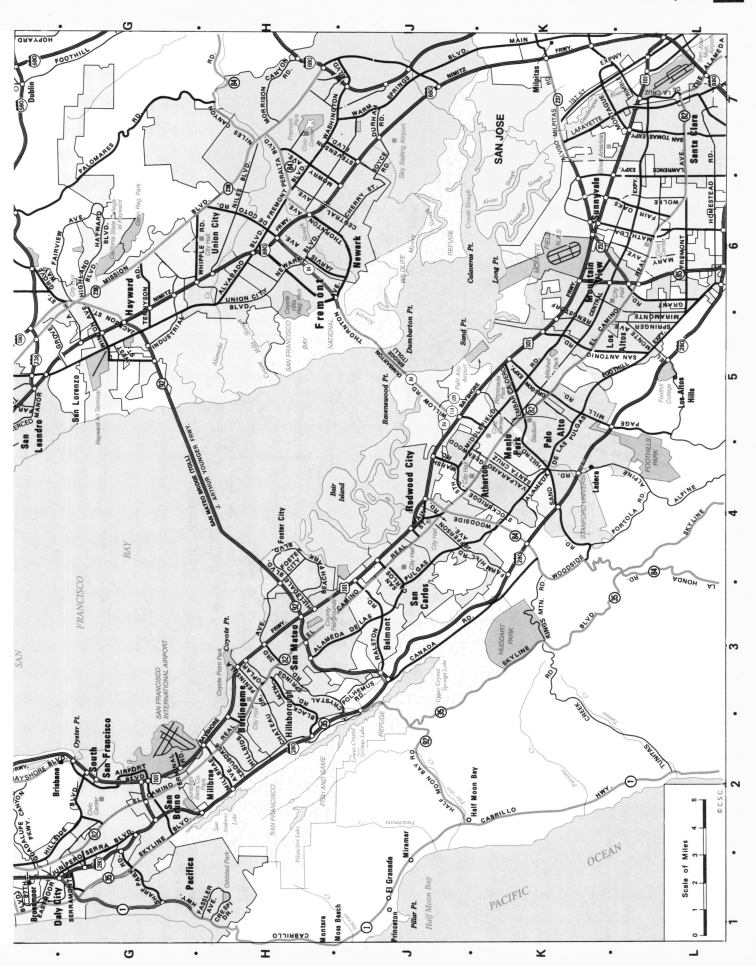

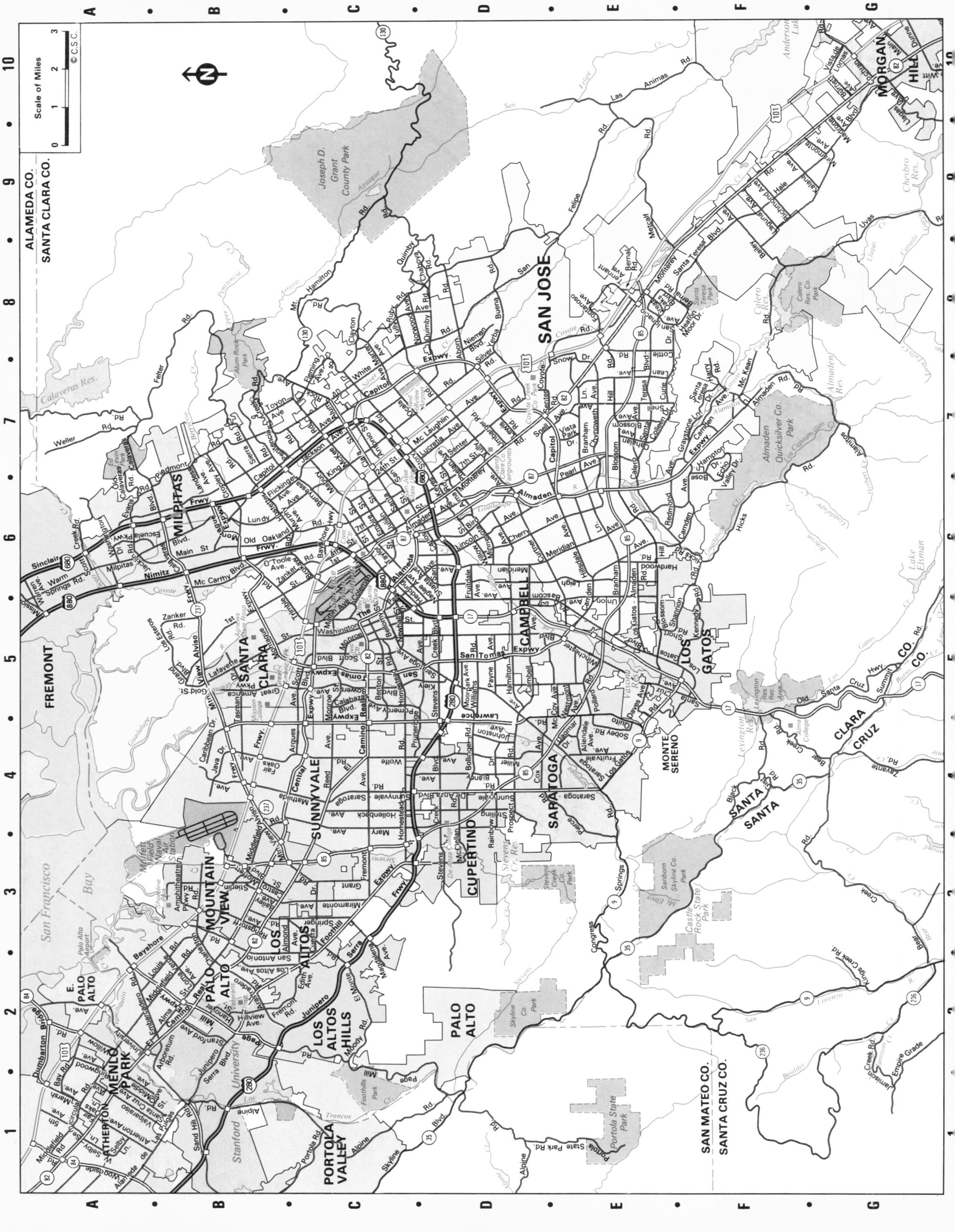
Scale of Miles
©C.S.C.
ALAMEDA CO.
SANTA CLARA CO.
SAN MATEO CO.
SANTA CRUZ CO.
SAN JOSE
FREMONT
MILPITAS
SANTA CLARA
SUNNYVALE
MOUNTAIN VIEW
CUPERTINO
CAMPBELL
SARATOGA
LOS GATOS
MONTE SERENO
LOS ALTOS
LOS ALTOS HILLS
PALO ALTO
E. PALO ALTO
MENLO PARK
ATHERTON
PORTOLA VALLEY
MORGAN HILL
Joseph D. Grant County Park
Alum Rock Park
Calaveras Res.
Almaden Quicksilver Co. Park
Calero Res. Co. Park
Sanborn Skyline Co. Park
Castle Rock State Park
Portola State Park
Skyline Co. Park
Stevens Creek Co. Park
Foothills Park
Moffett Field Naval Air Station
Stanford University
San Francisco Bay
Lexington Res.
Vasona Res.
Chesbro Res.
Lake Elsman
Almaden Res.
Anderson Lake

Scale of Miles
0 1 2 3
© C.S.C.

N

1 2 3 4 5 6 7

EDMONDS
LYNNWOOD
KINGSTON
WOODWAY
MOUNTLAKE TERRACE
BRIER
MALTBY
Appletree Cove
Jefferson Pt. Rd.
Tulin Rd.
Edmunds Point
196th St.
Main St.
212th
220th St.
84th Ave.
9th Ave.
Richmond
Beach N.E.
Lake Ballinger
Ballinger Way
Cedar Way
Larch
228th St. S.W.
Canyon Park Rd.
228th St.
45th Ave. N.E.
175th Ave.
Woodinville
Duvall
SNOHOMISH CO.
KING CO.
Paradise Lake Rd.
Echo Lake Rd.
Lost Lake Rd.
Welch Rd.
Fales Rd.

Puget Sound
KENMORE
BOTHELL
WOODINVILLE
SHORELINE
LAKE FOREST PARK
St. Edward State Park
N. 175th St.
170th St.
Simonds Rd. N.E.
Juanita-Woodinville Rd. N.E.
100th Ave.
Cottage Lake
Bothell Rd.
Sammamish

Carkeek Park
N. 145th St.
N. 130th St.
N. 105th St.
1st Ave.
Lake City Way
513
N.E. 132nd St.
N.E. 124th St.
N.E. 116th St.
202
116th Ave.
KIRKLAND
REDMOND
Novelty Hill Rd.

ROLLINGBAY
Golden Gardens Park
Shilshole Bay
West Point
Discovery Park
Murden Cove
Bainbridge Island
Eagle Harbor
85th
65th St.
15th Ave.
Greenwood Ave.
Green Lake
45th
Market St.
N.E. 65th St.
35th Ave.
Sand Point Way
Magnuson Park
University of Washington
908
Bridle Trails State Park
132nd Ave. N.E.
140th Ave. N.E.
148th Ave. N.E.
196th Ave. N.E.
208th Ave. N.E.
228th Ave. N.E.
202

Seaview Ave.
Holman Rd.
Roosevelt
Seattle-Victoria Ferry
5
N.E. Pacific
Northlake Blvd.
Lake Union
HUNTS PT.
Evergreen Point Floating Bridge (Toll)
520
N.E. 1st St.
104th Ave. S.E.
Bellevue-Redmond
Northup Rd.
Lake Sammamish
Inglewood Hill Rd.

Seattle-Winslow Ferry
Gilman Ave. W.
15th Ave. W.
Thorndyke Ave.
U.S. Naval Supply Depot
Queen Anne Ave.
Elliott Ave.
Aurora
10th Ave.
Madison St.
Lake Washington Blvd.
76th Ave.
84th Ave.
92nd St.
MEDINA
CLYDE HILL
8th St.
BELLEVUE
W. Lake Sammamish
Phantom Lake
S.E. 24th St.
Pine Lake

Sherwood Forest
Country Club Rd.
SEATTLE
Safeco Field
Elliott Bay
E. Yesler Way
23rd
Empire Way
Rainier Ave.
90
Lake Washington Floating Bridge
BEAUX ARTS
MERCER ISLAND
Seward Park
S.E. 40th St.
East Mercer Way
Kathleen Rd.
405
Newport Way
EASTGATE
184th Ave. S.E.
S.E. 60th St.
Lake Sammamish State Park
90

Bremerton-Seattle Ferry
Alki Beach Park
Alki Point
S.W. Admiral Way
California Ave.
Fauntleroy Ave.
4th Ave. S.
15th Ave. S.
West Seattle Freeway
99
King Co.
NEWCASTLE
New Castle Rd.
S.E. 60th St.
Coal field Way
ISSAQUAH
900
Issaquah-Hobart Rd.

SOUTH-WORTH
VASHON HEIGHTS
Vashon-Southworth Ferry
Fauntleroy-Vashon Ferry
Lincoln Park
35th Ave. S.W.
Delridge Way
S.W. Holden
BURIEN
509
5
99
SKYWAY
N. 30th St.
S.E. 38th Ave.
Renton-Issaquah Rd.
148th Ave.
164th Ave.
Coalfield Issaqua Rd.
Cedar Grove Rd.

18th Ave. S.W.
Ambaum Blvd. S.W.
1st Ave.
152nd St.
Military Rd.
599
900
TUKWILA
W. Valley Hwy.
RENTON
169
128th
S.E.
Lake Desire
Otter Lake

S.W. 168th St.
S.W. 176th St.
Maplewild Ave. S.W.
S.W. Barton
S.W. Henderson
Des Moines
518
99
Seattle Tacoma Int'l Airport
S. 176th St.
181
515
180th St.
167 Hwy.
140th Ave. S.E.
S.E. 192nd St.
Petrovitsky Rd.
Lake Youngs

NORMANDY PARK
91st Ave. S.W.
S.W. 196th St.
204th St. S.W.
220th St. S.W.
PORTAGE
Tramp Harbor
SEATAC
200th St.
S. 188th St.
KENT
509
S. 216th St.
208th St.
224th St.
116th Ave. S.E.
132nd Ave. S.E.
148th Ave. S.E.
179th Ave. S.E.

VASHON ISLAND
S.W. 232nd St.
248th St. S.W.
DES MOINES
MAURY ISLAND
Wick Rd.
516
228th St.
167
S.E. 240th St.
Kent
North Rd.
240th St.
MAPLE VALLEY
169
18

TARPON SPRINGS

CLEARWATER

CLEARWATER BEACH

DUNEDIN

OZONA

CRYSTAL BEACH

PALM HARBOR

SAFETY HARBOR

OLDSMAR

CITRUS PARK

TAMPA

BELLEAIR

BELLEAIR BEACH

BELLEAIR SHORES

BELLEAIR BLUFFS

LARGO

INDIAN ROCKS BEACH

INDIAN SHORES

REDINGTON SHORES

NORTH REDINGTON BEACH

REDINGTON BEACH

MADEIRA BEACH

SEMINOLE

PINELLAS PARK

KENNETH CITY

TREASURE ISLAND

SOUTH PASADENA

GULFPORT

ST. PETERSBURG

ST. PETE BEACH

RUSKIN

SUN CITY

BUCKEYE

MOCCASSIN

Gulf of Mexico

Tampa Bay

Hillsborough Bay

St. Petersburg-Clearwater International Airport

Tampa International Airport

Macdill Airforce Base

Fort De Soto County Park

Egmont Key National Wildlife Refuge

Honeymoon Island

Caladesi Island State Park

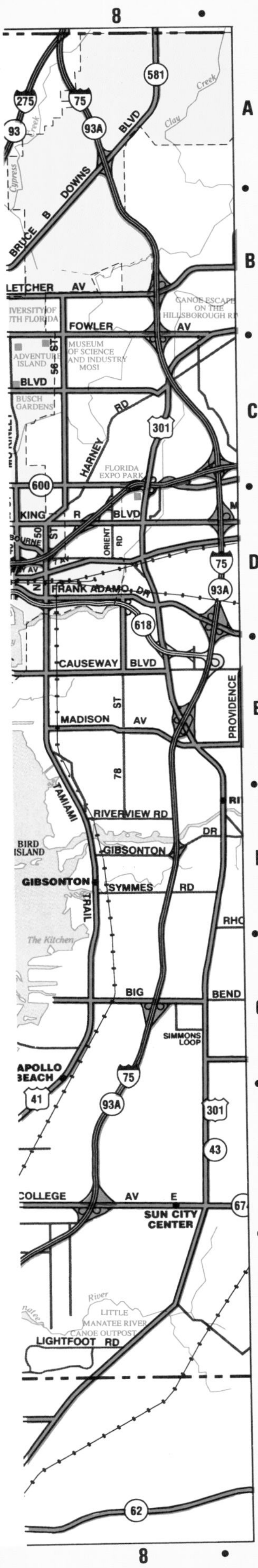

Scale of Miles
0 1 2 3
© C.S.C.

N

Coronado National Forest

Airport

Tucson Florence Hwy.

Naranja
Lambert Ln.
Linda Vista Blvd.
Thornydale Rd.
Magee
Overton
La Cholla
Romero Rd.
Sage St.
Magee
Northern Rd.
Hardy
Cortaro Farms Rd.
Casa Grande Hwy.
Ina Rd.
Orange Grove Dr.
Skyline Dr.
Alvernon Way
Sunrise
Kolb
Snyder
Shannon
La-Chola
La Canada
Campbell Ave.
Hacienda Del Sol
Pontatoc Rd.
Crawcroft
Sabino Canyon Rd.
Sunset Rd.
Camino De Questa
Del Cerro
Ruthrauff Rd.
Rillito
JAYNES
77
River Rd.
River Rd.
El Camino
Silverbell
Freeway Airport
Wetmore
Roger Rd.
Prince
Swan
River
Rd.
Cloud Rd.
Bear Canyon Rd.
El Morago Dr.
Flowing Wells Rd.
Fairview Ave.
Oracle Ave.
N-1st Ave.
Wrightstown
Sweet
Water
Goret Rd.
Stone Ave.
Ft. Lowell
Ft. Lowell Rd.
Dodge Blvd.
Ft. Lowell Rd.
Ironwood Hill Dr.
Grant Rd.
Miracle Mile
77
Miracle Mile
Rd.
Tangue
Verde
Blvd.
Greasewood Rd.
Shannon Rd.
W. Speedway Blvd.
Speedway
TUCSON Blvd.
Campbell
Speedway Blvd.
Pantano
W. Anklam Rd.
Marys Rd.
University of Arizona
Club
Alvernon
Wilmot Rd.
Camino Seco
W. Congress
Broadway
Randolph Park Municipal Golf Course
22nd St.
22nd
22nd
St.
San Juan Trail
Silver Lake Rd.
Davis-Monthan Air Force Base
36th St.
36th St.
Aviation Way
Fairfield Strav
Golf
Links Rd.
John F. Kennedy Park
Downtown Airport
Country Club Blvd.
Crawcroft
Kolb Rd.
Escalante Rd.
Lachola Blvd.
Ajo Hwy
86
Veterans Hospital
Verde
Irvington
Irvington
Tucson Ajo Hwy.
SOUTH TUCSON
De Oeste
Dakota
Valley Rd.
Drexel
Ave.
S. Park Ave.
Palo Verde Way
Tucson-Benson Hwy.
Valencia Blvd.
LITTLETOWN
Cardinal
Valencia Rd.
Valencia
EMERY PARK
Alvernon
Wilmot
Valen
pio
10
Mission Rd.
12th Ave.
6th Ave.
Missiondale
19
Tucson International Airport
Los Reales Rd.
Access
Vail Rd.
Rita Rd.
Tucson
Missions Hwy.
San Xavier Indian Reservation
Hughes
19
San Xavier Indian Reservation
19

(Inset, left — grid 8)

93 275 581 75
93A BLVD
Creek
Clay
Cypress Creek
BRUCE B DOWNS
LETCHER AV
FOWLER AV
UNIVERSITY OF SOUTH FLORIDA
CANOE ESCAPE ON THE HILLSBOROUGH R.
MUSEUM OF SCIENCE AND INDUSTRY MOSI
ADVENTURE ISLAND
BLVD
BUSCH GARDENS
HARNEY RD
301
FLORIDA EXPO PARK
600
KING R BLVD
ORIENT RD
75
FRANK ADAMO DR
93A
618
CAUSEWAY BLVD
MADISON AV
PROVIDENCE
RIVERVIEW RD DR
GIBSONTON
78
RI
GIBSONTON
SYMMES RD
BIRD ISLAND
TAMIAMI TRAIL
RHO
The Kitchen
BIG BEND
SIMMONS LOOP
41 75 93A 301
APOLLO BEACH
US 43
COLLEGE AV E
67
SUN CITY CENTER
River
LITTLE MANATEE RIVER
LITTLE CANOE OUTPOST
LIGHTFOOT RD
62

Scale of Miles

© ADC of Alexandria

WASHINGTON D.C.

MARYLAND

VIRGINIA

POTOMAC RIVER

ANACOSTIA RIVER

ANDREWS AIR FORCE BASE

SCIENCE CENTER

NATIONAL AGRICULTURAL RESEARCH CENTER

BELTSVILLE

GREENBELT

COLLEGE PARK

HYATTSVILLE

SILVER SPRING

TAKOMA PARK

BETHESDA

GEORGETOWN

ROSSLYN

ARLINGTON

ALEXANDRIA

FALLS CHURCH

SEVEN CORNERS

ANNANDALE

SPRINGFIELD

FRANCONIA

TYSONS CORNER

VIENNA

FAIRFAX

BURKE

MC LEAN

GREAT FALLS

POTOMAC

ROCKVILLE

KENSINGTON

WHEATON

GARRETT PARK

CHEVY CHASE

COLESVILLE

WHITE OAK

DEER PARK

NEW CARROLLTON

LANDOVER

LANDOVER HILLS

CHEVERLY

FAIRMOUNT HGTS

SEAT PLEASANT

CAPITOL HEIGHTS

DISTRICT HEIGHTS

MORNINGSIDE

FOREST HEIGHTS

OXON HILL

CLINTON

CAMP SPRINGS

SUITLAND

LARGO

GLENARDEN

BLADENSBURG

RIVERDALE

COTTAGE CITY

COLMAR MANOR

MOUNT RAINIER

BRENTWOOD

UNIVERSITY PARK

BERWYN HGTS

LANHAM

SEABROOK

BOWIE

LAUREL

PATUXENT

ANACOSTIA NAVAL STATION

BOLLING AFB

CRYSTAL CITY

ARLINGTON NATIONAL CEMETERY

PENTAGON

BAILEY'S CROSSROADS

MERRIFIELD

RAVENSWORTH

FORT BELVOIR

POTOMAC RIVER

INDEX
To The United States
Index to Canadian Cities and Towns on Pages 8-9.
Index to Mexican Cities and Towns on Page 11.

ALABAMA
Page 13
Population: 3,893,888
Capital: Montgomery
Land Area: 50,767 sq. mi.

Abanda . . . E-6
Abbeville . . . H-6
Action . . . Pg. 92, J-4
Ada . . . G-5
Adamsville . . . Pg. 92, J-2
Addison . . . B-4
Akron . . . E-3
Alabaster . . . D-4
Albertville . . . C-5
Alden . . . Pg. 92, C-2
Aldrich . . . C-4
Alexander City . . . E-5
Aliceville . . . C-5
Allgood . . . C-5
Almond . . . C-5
Altoona . . . C-5
Andalusia . . . H-4
Anderson . . . A-4
Anniston . . . C-5
Arab . . . B-5
Arcus . . . H-6
Ardilla . . . H-6
Ardmore . . . A-4
Argo . . . D-5
Arkadelphia . . . C-4
Arley . . . C-4
Ashbury . . . C-6
Ashford . . . H-7
Ashland . . . D-6
Ashville . . . C-5
Athens . . . A-4
Atmore . . . J-3
Attalla . . . C-5
Auburn . . . F-6
Awin . . . G-4
Axis . . . J-2
Babbie . . . H-5
Bailyton . . . B-4
Bakerhill . . . G-6
Ballplay . . . C-6
Bangor . . . C-4
Banks . . . G-6
Bankston . . . C-3
Barfield . . . D-6
Barton . . . A-3
Bass . . . A-6
Batesville . . . G-7
Bay Minette . . . J-3
Bay View . . . Pg. 92, D-2
Bayou LaBatre . . . K-2
Bear Creek . . . B-3
Beatrice . . . G-3
Belgreen . . . B-3
Belk . . . D-3
Bellamy . . . F-2
Belleville . . . H-4
Benton . . . F-4
Berry . . . C-3
Bessemer . . . D-4
Vicinity . . . Pg. 92, H-2
Bessie . . . Pg. 92, C-1
Big Cove . . . B-5
Billingsley . . . E-4
Birmingham . . . C-4
Vicinity . . . Pg. 92
Blacksher . . . H-3
Blount Springs . . . C-4
Blountsville . . . C-4
Blue Mountain . . . D-5
Bluff . . . C-3
Boaz . . . C-5
Bolinger . . . G-2
Bon Secour . . . K-3
Borden Springs . . . C-6
Boyd . . . F-2
Braggs . . . G-4
Brantley . . . H-5
Bremen . . . C-4
Brent . . . E-4
Brewton . . . J-4
Bridgeport . . . A-6
Brighton . . . Pg. 92, G-2
Brilliant . . . C-3
Brinn . . . B-3
Brooklyn . . . H-4
Brookside . . . Pg. 92, C-3
Brooksville . . . C-5
Brookwood . . . D-3
Browns . . . F-4
Brownsville . . . Pg. 92, G-6
Brundidge . . . G-6
Bryant . . . A-6
Butler . . . G-2
Bynum . . . D-5
Cahaba Heights . . . Pg. 92, G-6
Calera . . . E-4
Calvert . . . H-2
Camden . . . G-4
Campbell . . . G-3
Camphill . . . E-6
Carbon Hill . . . C-3
Cardiff . . . Pg. 92, C-2
Carrollton . . . D-2

Carrville . . . F-6
Castleberry . . . H-4
Catalpa . . . G-6
Catherine . . . F-3
Cedar Bluff . . . B-6
Center Point . . . Pg. 92, C-6
Centre . . . C-6
Centreville . . . E-4
Chalkville . . . Pg. 92, B-7
Chastang . . . J-2
Chatom . . . H-2
Chelsea . . . Pg. 92, J-7
Cherokee . . . A-3
Chickasaw . . . J-2
Childersburg . . . D-5
Chrysler . . . H-3
Citronelle . . . H-2
Claiborne . . . H-3
Clanton . . . E-4
Claud . . . F-5
Clayton . . . G-6
Cleveland . . . C-5
Clinton . . . E-2
Clio . . . G-6
Clopton . . . H-6
Cloverdale . . . A-3
Coalburg . . . Pg. 92, D-3
Cochrane . . . E-2
Coden . . . K-2
Coffeeville . . . G-2
Collinsville . . . B-6
Columbia . . . H-7
Columbiana . . . D-5
Consul . . . F-3
Cooper . . . E-5
Cordova . . . C-4
Cottonwood . . . J-6
Courtland . . . B-4
Coxey . . . A-4
Creola . . . J-2
Crossville . . . B-6
Cuba . . . F-2
Cullman . . . C-4
Cullomburg . . . G-2
Dadeville . . . E-6
Damascus . . . H-4
Dancy . . . E-2
Danville . . . B-4
Daphne . . . J-3
Dauphin Island . . . K-2
Davenport . . . E-6
Daviston . . . E-6
Davisville . . . F-6
Dawes . . . J-2
Dayton . . . F-3
Deans . . . H-4
Deatsville . . . F-5
Decatur . . . B-4
Deer Park . . . H-2
Dees . . . K-2
Delta . . . D-6
Demopolis . . . F-3
Dill . . . H-6
Divide Station . . . Pg. 92, B-3
Dixie . . . J-4
Dixons Mill . . . G-2
Dixonville . . . J-4
Docena . . . Pg. 92, E-2
Dolomite . . . Pg. 92, H-2
Dora . . . H-7
Dothan . . . H-7
Double Springs . . . C-3
Dry Forks . . . G-3
Dublin . . . G-5
Duke . . . C-6
Duncanville . . . E-3
E. Brewton . . . J-4
Eastern Valley . . . Pg. 92, J-2
Easton . . . E-6
Echola . . . D-3
Eclectic . . . F-6
Edgewater . . . Pg. 92, E-2
Eight Mile . . . H-2
Elamville . . . H-6
Elba . . . K-3
Elberta . . . K-3
Elias . . . H-3
Eliska . . . H-3
Elmore . . . F-5
Elrod . . . D-3
Elvira . . . Pg. 92, K-3
Emelle . . . E-2
Enterprise . . . H-5
Eoline . . . E-4
Epes . . . E-2
Equality . . . F-5
Ethelsville . . . D-2
Eufaula . . . J-6
Eunola . . . J-6
Eutaw . . . E-3
Evergreen . . . H-4
Ewell . . . J-6
Fairfax . . . E-7
Fairfield . . . Pg. 92, F-1
Vicinity . . . Pg. 92, F-2
Fairhope . . . K-2
Fatama . . . G-4
Fayette . . . D-3
Fieldstown . . . Pg. 92, C-4
Flat Rock . . . A-6

Flint City . . . B-4
Flomaton . . . J-4
Florala . . . J-5
Florence . . . A-3
Foley . . . K-3
Forkland . . . F-2
Forkville . . . B-3
Fort Mitchell . . . F-7
Fort Payne . . . B-6
Fountain . . . H-3
Francisco . . . A-5
Frisco City . . . H-3
Fruitdale . . . H-2
Fulton . . . G-3
Fultondale . . . D-4
Vicinity . . . Pg. 92, C-4
Gadsden . . . C-5
Gainesville . . . E-2
Gallant . . . C-5
Gallion . . . F-3
Gantt . . . H-4
Gardendale . . . C-4
Vicinity . . . Pg. 92, B-5
Geiger . . . E-2
Genery . . . Pg. 92, K-3
Geneva . . . J-6
Georgiana . . . H-4
Geraldine . . . B-5
Glencoe . . . C-6
Goodwater . . . E-5
Gordo . . . D-3
Grand Bay . . . K-2
Grants Mill . . . Pg. 92, F-7
Graysville . . . Pg. 92, C-3
Green Bay . . . H-5
Green Pond . . . D-4
Greens Station . . . Pg. 92, C-6
Greensboro . . . E-3
Greenville . . . G-5
Greenwood . . . Pg. 92, K-2
Grove Hill . . . G-3
Guin . . . C-3
Gulf Shores . . . K-3
Guntersville . . . C-5
Gurley . . . B-5
Vicinity . . . Pg. 92, C-7
Hackleburg . . . B-3
Haleyville . . . B-3
Halsell . . . F-2
Halsos Mill . . . H-3
Hamilton . . . B-2
Hammondville . . . B-6
Hanceville . . . C-4
Harpersville . . . D-5
Harrisburg . . . E-3
Hartford . . . J-6
Hartselle . . . B-4
Hatton . . . B-3
Havana . . . E-3
Hawk . . . D-6
Hayneville . . . G-4
Hazel Green . . . A-5
Hazen . . . F-3
Headland . . . H-7
Helena . . . Pg. 92, J-4
Vicinity . . . Pg. 92, K-4
Henagar . . . B-6
Hobson City . . . D-6
Hodges . . . B-3
Hokes Bluff . . . C-6
Hollis . . . D-6
Hollywood . . . A-6
Holt . . . D-3
Holy Trinity . . . F-7
Homewood . . . Pg. 92, F-4
Vicinity . . . Pg. 92, F-4
Hoover . . . Pg. 92, H-4
Hueytown . . . C-4
Vicinity . . . Pg. 92, G-1
Hulaco . . . B-4
Hunter . . . F-5
Huntsville . . . A-5
Hurtsboro . . . F-6
Huxford . . . H-3
Hybart . . . G-3
Ider . . . B-6
Ino . . . H-5
Intercourse . . . F-2
Irondale . . . D-4
Vicinity . . . Pg. 92, E-7
Ishkooda . . . Pg. 92, G-3
Isney . . . G-2
Jachin . . . F-2
Jack . . . H-5
Jackson . . . H-3
Jacksonville . . . C-6
Jasper . . . C-4
Jefferson . . . F-2
Jefferson Park . . . Pg. 92, E-7
Jemison . . . E-4
Jenkins Crossroads . . . F-4
Jones . . . F-5
Jones Chapel . . . C-4
Kellerman . . . D-4
Kelly's Crossroads . . . E-5
Kellyton . . . E-5
Kennedy . . . C-3
Ketona . . . Pg. 92, D-5
Kilgore . . . Pg. 92, B-1
Kimberly . . . C-4
Kimbrough . . . G-3
Kinsey . . . H-6

Kinston . . . H-5
Knoxville . . . E-3
Koenton . . . H-2
La Place . . . F-6
Lafayette . . . E-6
Lanett . . . E-7
Langdale . . . E-7
Lawrenceville . . . D-5
Leeds . . . D-5
Leighton . . . A-3
Letohatchee . . . G-4
Lewisburg . . . Pg. 92, D-4
Lexington . . . A-3
Lillian . . . K-3
Lincoln . . . D-5
Lindbergh . . . Pg. 92, J-4
Linden . . . F-3
Lineville . . . D-6
Linn Crossing . . . Pg. 92, B-2
Lipscomb . . . Pg. 92, H-3
Littleville . . . B-3
Livingston . . . F-2
Lockhart . . . J-5
Lottie . . . H-3
Louisville . . . G-6
Lowndesboro . . . F-5
Loxley . . . K-3
Luverne . . . G-5
Lyefflon . . . H-4
Lynn . . . C-3
Magnolia . . . F-3
Malvern . . . J-6
Maplesville . . . E-4
Marbury . . . E-5
Marion . . . E-3
Marvyn . . . F-6
Maytown . . . Pg. 92, E-2
McCalla . . . Pg. 92, J-1
McDade . . . F-5
McIntosh . . . H-2
McKenzie . . . H-5
Mentone . . . B-6
Meridianville . . . A-5
Midfield . . . Pg. 92, G-3
Midland City . . . H-6
Midway . . . G-4
Midway . . . G-5
Millerville . . . E-5
Millport . . . D-2
Millry . . . G-2
Mineral Springs . . . Pg. 92, C-3
Mitchell . . . F-6
Mobile . . . J-2
Monroeville . . . H-4
Monrovia . . . $UP
Montevallo . . . E-4
Montgomery . . . F-5
Montrose . . . K-2
Mooresville . . . B-4
Morgan . . . Pg. 92, J-3
Morgan City . . . B-5
Morris . . . C-4
Morvin . . . G-3
Moulton . . . B-4
Moundville . . . E-3
Mount Andrew . . . G-6
Mount Olive . . . E-5
Vicinity . . . Pg. 92, B-4
Mount Vernon . . . J-2
Mount Willing . . . G-4
Mountain Brook . . . D-4
Vicinity . . . Pg. 92, F-5
Mulberry . . . E-4
Mulga . . . Pg. 92, E-1
Munford . . . D-6
Muscle Shoals . . . A-3
Muscoda . . . Pg. 92, H-2
Nanafalia . . . G-2
Natural Bridge . . . B-3
New Brockton . . . H-5
New Castle . . . Pg. 92, B-5
New Hope . . . B-5
Vicinity . . . Pg. 92, J-6
New Lexington . . . D-3
New Market . . . A-5
Newburg . . . B-3
Newsite . . . E-6
Newton . . . H-6
Newtonville . . . D-3
Newville . . . H-6
Northport . . . D-3
Oak Grove . . . C-4
Oakland . . . B-4
Oakman . . . C-3
Oakwood . . . F-5
Odenville . . . C-5
Ohatchee . . . C-5
Omaha . . . G-7
Oneonta . . . C-5
Opelika . . . E-6
Opp . . . H-5
Overton . . . Pg. 92, F-6
Owens Crossroads . . . B-5
Oxford . . . D-6
Oxmoor . . . Pg. 92, G-3
Ozark . . . H-6
Palmerdale . . . C-4
Parrish . . . C-3
Patton Chapel . . . Pg. 92, H-5
Pelham . . . Pg. 92, K-4
Pell City . . . D-5

Pennington . . . F-2
Perdido . . . J-3
Peterman . . . H-3
Peterson . . . D-3
Petersville . . . A-3
Phenix City . . . F-7
Phil Campbell . . . B-3
Pickensville . . . D-2
Piedmont . . . C-6
Pine Apple . . . G-4
Pine Grove . . . C-6
Pine Hill . . . G-3
Pinson . . . Pg. 92, B-6
Pisgah . . . B-6
Plantersville . . . F-4
Pleasant Grove . . . D-2
Vicinity . . . Pg. 92, F-1
Prattville . . . F-5
Priceville . . . B-4
Prichard . . . J-2
Pt. Clear . . . K-2
Rabun . . . J-3
Rainbow City . . . C-5
Rainsville . . . B-6
Ranburne . . . D-6
Range . . . H-3
Red Bay . . . B-2
Red Level . . . H-4
Reece City . . . C-5
Reform . . . D-3
Repton . . . H-3
Republic . . . Pg. 92, D-3
Riley . . . G-4
River Falls . . . H-4
River View . . . E-6
Roanoke . . . E-6
Robertsdale . . . K-3
Robinwood . . . Pg. 92, C-5
Rockdale . . . D-6
Rockford . . . E-5
Rocky Ridge . . . Pg. 92, H-5
Roebuck Plaza . . . Pg. 92, D-7
Rogersville . . . A-3
Rome . . . H-5
Romulus . . . E-3
Russellville . . . B-3
Rutledge . . . G-5
Saco . . . G-6
Safford . . . C-5
Saint Elmo . . . K-2
Salitpa . . . G-3
Samson . . . H-5
Sanford . . . H-5
Santuck . . . E-5
Saraland . . . J-2
Sardis . . . F-4
Satsuma . . . J-2
Sayre . . . Pg. 92, A-2
Scottsboro . . . B-5
Seale . . . F-7
Section . . . B-5
Selma . . . F-4
Shannon . . . Pg. 92, H-3
Shawmut . . . A-3
Sheffield . . . A-3
Shelby . . . D-5
Shepardville . . . G-4
Shorter . . . F-6
Vicinity . . . Pg. 92, B-4
Silver Hill . . . K-3
Simcoe . . . B-4
Sipsey . . . C-4
Sledge . . . Pg. 92, F-4
Slocomb . . . J-6
Smut Eye . . . G-6
Snead . . . C-5
Snowdoun . . . F-5
Somerville . . . B-4
Southside . . . C-5
Spring Hill . . . H-6
Springville . . . C-5
Sprott . . . E-3
Spruce Pine . . . B-3
Stafford . . . C-5
Steele . . . C-5
Stevenson . . . A-6
Stewartville . . . E-5
Stockton . . . J-3
Sulligent . . . C-2
Sumiton . . . C-4
Summerdale . . . K-3
Sunflower . . . H-2
Suttle . . . F-4
Sweet Water . . . G-3
Sylacauga . . . E-5
Sylvan Springs . . . Pg. 92, E-1
Sylvania . . . B-6
Talladega . . . D-5
Tallassee . . . F-6
Tarrant City . . . Pg. 92, D-5
Tensaw . . . H-3
Terese . . . K-2
Theodore . . . K-2
Thomaston . . . F-3
Thomasville . . . G-3
Thorsby . . . E-4
Three Notch . . . G-6
Tibbie . . . H-2
Town Creek . . . B-4
Toxey . . . G-2
Trinity . . . B-4
Troy . . . G-5

Trussville . . . D-5
Tuscaloosa . . . D-3
Tuscumbia . . . A-3
Tuskegee . . . F-6
Union Grove . . . E-5
Vicinity . . . Pg. 92, D-1
Union Springs . . . G-6
Uniontown . . . F-3
Uriah . . . H-3
Valley Head . . . B-6
Vance . . . E-3
Vernon . . . C-2
Vestavia Hills . . . D-4
Vicinity . . . Pg. 92, G-5
Victoria . . . H-6
Vidette . . . G-5
Village Springs . . . C-5
Vineland . . . G-3
Vinemont . . . B-4
Wadley . . . E-6
Wagarville . . . H-2
Walker Chapel . . . Pg. 92, C-4
Walnut Grove . . . C-5
Walnut Hill . . . E-6
Warrior . . . C-4
Weaver . . . C-6
Wedowee . . . D-6
Wenonah . . . Pg. 92, G-3
West Blockton . . . D-4
West Point . . . B-4
Wetumpka . . . F-5
Whatley . . . G-3
Whiteoak . . . B-2
Whitson . . . D-3
Wicksburg . . . H-6
Wilburn . . . C-4
Wilmer . . . J-2
Wilton . . . E-4
Windham Springs . . . D-3
Winfield . . . C-3
Wing . . . J-4
Winterboro . . . D-5
Woodville . . . B-5
Wren . . . B-3
Yantley . . . F-2
Yarbo . . . H-2
York . . . F-2
Zip City . . . A-3

ALASKA
Page 14
Population: 401,851
Capital: Juneau
Land Area: 570,883 sq. mi.

Akhiok . . . F-5
Akolmiut . . . D-4
Akulurak . . . D-4
Akutan . . . F-2
Alakanuk . . . C-4
Alaktak . . . A-7
Aleknagik . . . E-4
Alice Arm . . . H-10
Allakaket . . . C-6
Ambler . . . B-6
Anaktuvuk Pass . . . B-7
Anchorage . . . E-6
Inset Map . . . B-2
Anderson . . . D-7
Angoon . . . G-9
Aniak . . . D-4
Anvik . . . D-4
Arctic Village . . . C-8
Atka . . . H-8
Atkasuk . . . A-6
Attu . . . G-9
Baranof . . . A-7
Barrow . . . A-7
Beaver . . . C-7
Beechey Pt . . . A-7
Bethel . . . D-4
Bettles . . . C-7
Big Delta . . . D-7
Big Port Walter . . . G-9
Black . . . D-7
Brevig Mission . . . B-4
Buckland . . . C-5
Candle . . . C-5
Cantwell . . . D-7
Cape Romanzof . . . D-3
Cape Yakataga . . . F-8
Caro . . . C-7
Chalkyitsik . . . C-8
Chatanika . . . D-7
Chenik . . . E-5
Chevak . . . D-4
Chickaloon . . . H-10
Inset Map . . . A-2
Chicken . . . D-8
Chignik . . . F-5
Chitina . . . E-7
Christian . . . C-8
Christochina . . . E-7
Chugiak . . . B-2
Circle . . . C-7
Circle Hot Springs . . . D-8
Clarks Pt . . . E-4
College . . . D-7
Copper Center . . . E-7

Cordova . . . E-7
Craig . . . H-9
Crooked Creek . . . D-5
Deadhorse . . . B-7
Deering . . . B-5
Delta Junction . . . D-7
Dillingham . . . E-4
Donnelly . . . D-7
Dot Lake . . . D-8
Douglas . . . G-9
Dutch Harbor . . . F-2
Eagle . . . D-8
Eagle River . . . E-6
Inset Map . . . B-2
Edna Bay . . . H-9
Eek . . . E-4
Egavic . . . C-5
Elfin Cove . . . G-9
Emmonak . . . C-4
English Bay . . . F-6
Eureka . . . D-7
Fairbanks . . . D-7
False Pass . . . F-3
Farewell . . . D-6
Flat . . . D-5
Fort Yukon . . . C-7
Gakona . . . E-7
Galena . . . C-5
Gambell . . . C-3
Glen Alps . . . E-6
Glennallen . . . C-5
Golovin . . . C-5
Goodnews Bay . . . E-4
Gordon . . . B-8
Grayling . . . D-4
Gulkana . . . E-7
Gustavus . . . G-8
Haines . . . F-9
Hawk Inlet . . . G-9
Healy . . . D-7
Homer . . . E-6
Inset Map . . . C-1
Hoonah . . . G-8
Hooper Bay . . . D-3
Hope . . . E-6
Inset Map . . . B-2
Houston . . . A-2
Hughes . . . C-6
Huslia . . . C-6
Hydaburg . . . H-9
Itulilick . . . G-9
Juneau . . . G-9
Kachemak . . . E-6
Kake . . . G-9
Kaktovik . . . B-8
Kalla . . . C-5
Kaltag . . . C-5
Karluk . . . E-5
Kashegelok . . . E-5
Kasilof . . . E-6
Inset Map . . . B-1
Kaskanak . . . E-5
Katalla . . . F-7
Kenai . . . E-6
Ketchikan . . . H-10
Kiana . . . B-5
Kinegnak . . . E-4
King Cove . . . F-3
King Salmon . . . E-5
Kipnuk . . . E-4
Kivalina . . . B-5
Klawock . . . H-9
Knik . . . B-2
Kobuk . . . C-6
Kodiak . . . E-5
Kokrines . . . C-6
Koliganek . . . E-5
Kotlik . . . C-4
Kotzebue . . . B-5
Koyuk . . . C-5
Koyukuk . . . C-5
Kuliuk . . . F-5
Kwethluk . . . D-4
Kwigillingok . . . E-4
Larsen Bay . . . E-5
Latouche . . . F-7
Levelock . . . E-5
Lime Village . . . E-5
Livengood . . . D-6
Long . . . D-6
Lower Tonsina . . . E-7
Manley Hot Springs . . . D-6
Manokotak . . . E-4
McCarthy . . . E-8
McGrath . . . D-5
McKinley Park . . . D-7
Medfra . . . D-6
Mekoryuk . . . D-3
Mentasta Lake . . . E-7
Metlakata . . . H-10
Minto . . . D-7
Moose Pass . . . B-2
Mount Edgecumbe . . . G-9
Mountain Village . . . D-4
Naknek . . . E-5
Napakiak . . . D-4
Napaskiak . . . D-4
Nenana . . . D-7
New Stuyahok . . . E-5
Newhalen . . . E-5
Nikolai . . . D-6
Nikolski . . . F-1

Noatak . . . B-5
Nogamut . . . E-5
Nome . . . C-4
Nondalton . . . E-5
Noorvik . . . B-5
North Pole . . . D-7
Northeast Cape . . . C-4
Northway . . . E-8
Nulato . . . C-5
Old Harbor . . . F-5
Ooliktok . . . A-7
Ouzinkie . . . F-6
Palmer . . . E-7
Inset Map . . . A-2
Pedro Bay . . . E-5
Pelican . . . G-9
Perryville . . . F-4
Petersburg . . . E-6
Pilgrim Springs . . . C-4
Pilot Point . . . F-4
Inset Map . . . D-4
Platinum . . . E-4
Point Hope . . . A-5
Point Lay . . . A-5
Porcupine . . . F-9
Port Alexander . . . G-9
Port Lions . . . F-5
Portlock . . . F-6
Prudhoe Bay . . . B-8
Quinhagak . . . E-4
Rampart . . . C-7
Rampart House . . . C-8
Richardson . . . D-7
Ruby . . . C-6
Russian Mission . . . D-4
Sagwon . . . B-7
Salchaket . . . D-7
Sand Pt . . . F-4
Saroonga . . . C-3
Selawik . . . B-5
Seward . . . E-6
Inset Map . . . C-2
Shageluk . . . D-5
Shaktoolik . . . C-5
Shishmaref . . . B-4
Shungnak . . . B-6
Sinuk . . . C-4
Sitka . . . G-9
Skagway . . . F-9
Sleetmute . . . D-5
Soldotna . . . E-6
Inset Map . . . B-1
Squaw Harbor . . . G-3
St. George . . . E-2
St. Marys . . . D-4
St. Michael . . . C-5
St. Paul . . . E-2
Stebbins . . . C-5
Stevens Village . . . C-7
Stony River . . . D-5
Stuyahok . . . D-5
Susitna . . . B-2
Takotna . . . D-5
Talkeetna . . . E-7
Tanalian Pt . . . E-5
Tanana . . . C-6
Tatitlek . . . E-7
Teller . . . C-4
Tetlin . . . E-8
Tetlin Junction . . . E-8
Togiak . . . E-4
Tok . . . D-8
Toksook Bay . . . D-4
Tonsina . . . E-7
Tuluksak . . . D-4
Tununak . . . D-3
Tyonek . . . E-6
Inset Map . . . B-1
Ugashik . . . F-5
Umiat . . . B-7
Unalakleet . . . C-5
Unalaska . . . F-2
Valdez . . . E-7
Venetie . . . C-8
Wainwright . . . A-6
Wales . . . B-4
Wasilla . . . A-2
Wasilla . . . E-6
White Mountain . . . C-5
Whittier . . . E-6
Willow . . . A-1
Inset Map . . . A-1
Wiseman . . . C-7
Wrangell . . . G-10
Yakutat . . . F-8

ARIZONA
Pages 16-17
Population: 2,718,215
Capital: Phoenix
Land Area: 113,508 sq. mi.

Aguila . . . J-
Ajo . . . L-
Ak Chin . . . K-
Alpine . . . J-
Amado . . . N-
Anegam . . . L-

ARIZONA

Angell F-7
Apache Jct. K-6
Arivaca Jct. N-7
Arizona City L-6
Arlington K-4
Artesia M-6
Ash Fork F-5
Ashurst K-9
Avondale K-5
  Vicinity . . . . Pg. 135, E-2
Bagdad G-4
Bapchule K-6
Beaverhead J-10
Bellemont F-6
Benson M-8
Bisbee N-9
Black Canyon City . . . H-5
Bonita L-9
Bouse J-2
Bowie M-10
Brenda J-2
Buckeye K-5
Bullhead City F-2
Bylas K-9
Cameron E-7
Camp Verde H-6
Carefree J-6
Carmen N-7
Carrizo J-8
Casa Grande K-6
Cashion . . . . . . Pg. 151, E-2
Catalina L-7
Cave Creek J-6
Cedar Creek J-6
Cedar Ridge D-7
Cedar Springs F-8
Central L-9
Chambers F-9
Chandler K-6
  Vicinity . . . . Pg. 135, F-6
Chandler Heights K-6
Chilchinbito D-9
Childs L-4
Chinle E-10
Chino Valley G-5
Chloride F-2
Christmas K-8
Christopher Creek H-7
Chuichu L-6
Circle City J-4
Clarkdale G-5
Clay Spring H-8
Claypool K-7
Clifton K-10
Cochise M-9
Colorado City C-4
Concho H-9
Congress H-4
Continental M-7
Coolidge K-6
Cordes Jct. H-5
Cornville G-6
Cortaro L-7
Cottonwood G-6
Covered Wells M-5
Cow Springs D-8
Cross Canyon E-10
Curtis M-8
Dateland K-3
Desert View E-6
Dewey H-5
Dilkon F-8
Dinnehotso D-9
Dolan Springs F-2
Dome L-2
Dos Cabezas M-10
Douglas N-10
Dragoon M-9
Dudleyville L-8
Duncan L-10
Eager H-10
Eden K-9
Ehrenberg J-2
Elfrida N-9
Eloy L-6
Fairbank N-8
Flagstaff F-6
Florence K-7
Florence Jct. K-7
Fort Apache J-9
Fort Defiance E-10
Fort Grant L-9
Fort McDowell J-6
Fort Thomas K-9
Fountain Hills J-6
Francisco Grande K-5
Franklin L-10
Fredonia C-5
Gadsden L-1
Ganado F-9
Gila Bend K-4
Gilbert K-6
Glendale J-5
  Vicinity . . . . Pg. 135, C-3
Globe K-8
Golden Shores G-2
Goldroad F-2
Goodyear K-5
  Vicinity . . . . Pg. 135, E-1
Grand Canyon E-5
Gray Mountain E-7
Greasewood (Lower) . . F-9
Green Valley M-7
Greer J-10
Guadalupe K-5
  Vicinity . . . . Pg. 135, F-5
Hackberry F-3
Hannigan Meadow . . . K-10
Harcuvar J-3
Hawley Lake J-9
Hayden K-7
Heber H-8
Higley K-6
Hillside H-4
Holbrook G-8

Hope J-3
Hotevilla E-8
Houck F-10
Huachuca City N-8
Humboldt H-5
Indian Wells F-8
Jacob Lake D-5
Jerome G-5
Johnson M-8
Joseph City G-8
Katherine F-2
Kayenta D-8
Keams Canyon E-9
Kearny K-7
Kelvin K-7
Kingman F-2
Kirkland H-4
Kirkland Jct. H-5
Kohls Ranch H-7
La Palma L-6
Lake Havasu City G-2
Lake Montezuma G-6
Lakeside H-9
Laveen K-5
  Vicinity . . . . Pg. 135, F-3
Leupp F-7
Litchfield Park J-5
Littlefield C-3
Littletown . . . . . Pg. 149, L-8
Lukeville M-4
Lupton F-10
Mammoth L-8
Many Farms D-10
Marana L-6
Marble Canyon D-6
Maricopa K-5
Mayer H-5
McGuireville G-6
McNeal N-9
Meadview E-2
Mesa J-6
Mexican Water C-9
Miami K-7
Moenkopi E-7
Moqui E-5
Morenci K-10
Morristown J-4
Mountainaire G-6
Mt. View M-7
Munds Park G-6
Naco N-8
Navajo G-10
Nelson F-3
New River J-5
Nicksville N-8
Nogales N-7
North Rim D-6
Nutrioso J-10
Oatman G-2
Ocotillo K-6
Olberg K-6
Old Oraibi E-8
Oracle L-7
Oracle Jct. L-7
Oraibi E-8
Oro Valley L-7
Overgaard H-8
Page C-7
Palm Springs K-6
Palo Verde K-4
Palominas N-8
Pantano M-8
Paradise City . . . Pg. 135, B-5
Paradise Valley J-5
  Vicinity . . . . Pg. 135, C-5
Parker H-2
Parks F-6
Patagonia N-7
Paul Spur N-9
Paulden G-5
Payson H-6
Peach Springs F-4
Peeples Valley H-4
Peoria J-5
  Vicinity . . . . Pg. 135, B-2
Peridot K-8
Phoenix J-6
  Vicinity . . . . . Pg. 135
Picacho L-6
Pima L-9
Pine H-6
Pine Springs F-5
Pinedale H-8
Pinetop H-9
Pirtleville N-9
Polacca E-8
Pomerene M-8
Prescott G-5
Prescott Valley G-5
Punkin Center J-7
Quartzite J-2
Queen Creek K-6
Quijotoa M-5
Randolph K-6
Red Lake D-7
Red Rock L-7
Rillito L-7
Riverside K-7
Riviera F-2
Rock Point D-10
Rock Springs J-5
Roosevelt J-7
Rough Rock D-9
Round Rock D-10
Rye H-7
Sacaton K-6
Safford L-9
Sahuarita M-7
Saint David M-9
Saint Johns H-10
Saint Michaels F-10
Salome J-3
San Carlos K-8
San Luis (Yuma Cty) . . L-1
San Luis (Pima Cty) . . L-5

San Manuel L-8
San Simon M-10
Sanders F-10
Sasabe N-6
Scottsdale J-6
  Vicinity . . . . Pg. 135, D-6
Seba Dalkai E-8
Second Mesa E-8
Sedona G-6
Seligman F-4
Sells M-5
Sentinel K-3
Shonto D-8
Show Low H-9
Shumway H-9
Sierra Vista N-8
Silver Bell N-6
Snowflake H-9
Solomon L-9
Somerton L-1
Sonoita N-7
South Tuscon M-7
  Vicinity . . . . Pg. 149, G-8
Springerville H-10
Stanfield L-6
Star Valley H-7
Stargo K-10
Strawberry H-7
Sun City J-5
  Vicinity . . . . Pg. 135, C-2
Sun City West J-5
  Vicinity . . . . Pg. 135, B-1
Sun Lake K-6
Sun Valley G-9
Sunflower J-6
Sunizona M-9
Sunsites M-9
Superior K-7
Surprise J-5
  Vicinity . . . . Pg. 135, B-1
Tacna L-2
Taylor H-9
Teec Nos Pas D-10
Tempe K-6
  Vicinity . . . . Pg. 135, E-6
Tes Nez Iha C-9
Thatcher L-9
The Gap D-7
Three Points (Robles) . . M-6
Tolleson . . . . . . Pg. 135, E-2
Tombstone N-9
Tonalea D-7
Tonopah J-4
Topock G-2
Tortilla Flat J-7
Tracy M-5
Truxton F-3
Tsaile D-10
Tsegi D-8
Tuba City E-7
Tubac N-7
Tucson M-7
  Vicinity . . . . . Pg. 149
Tumacacori N-7
Tusayan E-5
Vail M-8
Valentine F-3
Valle E-5
Vernon H-9
Vicksburg J-2
Wellton L-2
Wenden J-3
Whiteriver J-9
Why M-4
Wickenburg J-4
Wikieup G-3
Wilhoit H-5
Willcox M-9
Williams F-5
Window Rock F-10
Winkelman K-8
Winona F-7
Winslow H-7
Wintersburg K-4
Wittmann J-4
Yampai F-3
Yarnell H-4
Young H-7
Youngtown J-5
  Vicinity . . . . Pg. 135, C-2
Yucca G-2
Yuma L-1

ARKANSAS
Page 15
Population: 2,286,435
Capital: Little Rock
Land Area: 52078 sq. mi.

Alpena A-4
Altheimer E-6
Amity E-4
Arkadelphia E-4
Arkansas City F-7
Ash Flat A-7
Ashdown F-3
Athens E-3
Atkins C-4
Augusta C-7
Bald Knob C-6
Banks F-5
Barling C-2
Batesville B-6
Bay B-8
Bearden E-5
Beebe D-6
Benton D-5
Bentonville A-3
Bergman A-4
Berryville A-3
Bismark E-4
Black Rock B-7

Blue Springs D-4
Bluff City F-4
Blytheville B-9
Booneville C-3
Boxley B-4
Bradley G-3
Brashears B-3
Brinkley D-7
Bryant D-5
Bull Shoals A-5
Cabot D-6
Calico Rock B-6
Calion F-5
Camden F-4
Carlisle D-6
Carthage E-5
Cash B-8
Caulksville C-3
Cave City B-7
Cedarville C-2
Centerville C-4
Charleston C-3
Cherry Valley C-8
Clarksville C-4
Clinton C-5
Conway C-5
Corning A-8
Cotton Plant D-7
Cove E-2
Crossett G-6
Crossroads E-7
Crows D-5
Cushman B-6
Dalark E-4
Damascus C-5
Danville D-4
Dardanelle C-4
DeQueen E-2
DeWitt E-7
Decatur A-2
Delight E-3
Deluce E-3
Dermott F-7
Des Arc D-7
Dierks E-3
Dodridge G-3
Dover C-4
Dumas F-7
Earle C-8
El Dorado G-5
Elaine E-8
Emerson G-4
England D-6
Eudora G-8
Eureka Springs A-3
Falcon F-4
Fallsville B-4
Farmington B-2
Fayetteville B-3
Fisher C-7
Flippin A-5
Florence F-6
Fordyce F-5
Foreman F-2
Forrest City D-8
Fouke G-3
Fountain Hill F-6
Ft. Smith C-2
Garland G-3
Gentry A-2
Gillett E-7
Gilmore C-8
Glenwood E-3
Gosnell B-9
Gould E-7
Grady E-6
Grapevine E-5
Gravette A-2
Green Forest A-4
Greenbrier C-5
Greenwood C-2
Greers Ferry C-6
Gurdon E-4
Hackett C-2
Hagarville C-4
Hamburg G-6
Hampton F-5
Hardy A-7
Harrisburg C-8
Harrison A-4
Hartford C-2
Haskell E-5
Hazen D-7
Heber Springs D-8
Helena D-8
Hermitage F-5
Holly Grove D-7
Hope F-3
Horatio E-2
Horseshoe Bend A-6
Hot Springs D-4
Hoxie B-7
Hughes D-8
Humnoke E-6
Humphrey E-6
Huntsville B-3
Huttig G-6
Jacksonville D-6
Jasper B-4
Jonesboro B-8
Judsonia C-6
Junction City G-5
Keiser B-9
Kensett C-6
Kingsland F-5
Lake City B-8
Lake Village F-7
Lavaca C-2
LePanto C-8
Lead Hill A-5
Leslie B-5
Lewisville F-3
Lincoln B-2
Little Rock D-5
Lockesburg E-3

Lonoke D-6
Lowell A-3
Luxora B-9
Madison D-8
Magnolia G-4
Malvern E-5
Mammoth Spring A-7
Manila B-9
Mansfield C-2
Marianna D-8
Marion C-9
Marked Tree C-8
Marmaduke B-8
Marshall B-5
Marvell D-8
Maumelle D-5
Maynard A-7
McCrory C-7
McGehee F-7
Melbourne B-6
Mena D-2
Mineral Springs F-3
Monette B-8
Monticello F-6
Montrose G-8
Morrilton C-5
Mountain Home A-5
Mountain View B-6
Mt. Ida D-3
Mt. Pleasant B-6
Murfreesboro E-3
N. Little Rock D-5
Nashville E-3
Needmore D-3
Newport C-7
Nola D-3
Norman D-3
Oark B-3
Ola D-4
Onyx B-9
Osceola B-9
Oxford B-6
Ozark C-3
Pansy F-6
Paragould B-8
Paris C-3
Parkdale G-8
Parkin C-8
Pea Ridge A-3
Pelsor B-4
Perryville D-5
Piggot A-9
Pine Bluff E-6
Pleasant Plains C-7
Pocahontas A-7
Pollard A-9
Ponca B-4
Portland G-7
Poughke B-7
Prairie Grove B-2
Prattsville E-5
Prescott F-4
Princeton E-5
Quitman C-6
Rector A-8
Reed F-7
Rison E-6
Rogers A-3
Rose Bud C-6
Rosston F-4
Rushing B-6
Russellville C-4
Salem A-6
Salesville A-6
Scranton C-4
Searcy C-6
Sherdian E-5
Shirley C-5
Siloam Springs A-2
Smackover F-5
Snow Lake E-7
Springdale A-2
St. Francis G-4
Star City E-6
Stephens F-4
Story D-3
Strawberry B-7
Strong G-5
Stuttgart D-7
Success A-8
Taylor G-4
Texarkana F-3
Timbo B-5
Trumann B-8
Tupelo C-7
Turrell C-9
VanBuren C-2
Vilonia C-6
Waldo G-4
Waldron D-2
Walker C-6
Walnut Ridge B-8
Warren F-6
Washington F-3
Watson F-7
West Fork B-2
West Helena D-8
West Memphis C-9
Western Grove B-4
White Hall E-6
Wickes E-2
Williams Jct. D-5
Willisville F-4
Wilmar F-6
Wilmot G-8
Wilson B-9
Winslow B-3
Witt Springs B-4
Wynne C-8
Y City D-3
Yellville B-5

CALIFORNIA

CALIFORNIA
Pages 18-21
Population: 23,667,902
Capital: Sacramento
Land Area: 156,299 sq. mi.

Acton S-10
Adelanto S-11
Adin C-7
Agoura Hills . . . . Pg. 144, A-2
Ahwahnee L-8
Alameda . . . . . . Pg. 144, C-3
Alamorio V-15
Albany . . . . Pg. 144, C-3
Albion G-2
Alder Creek . . . . Pg. 141, B-7
Alder Springs F-3
Alderpoint E-2
Alhambra . . . . . . Pg. 114, C-5
Alleghany F-6
Almanor E-6
Alpaugh P-8
Alpine V-12
Alta Loma . . . . . Pg. 116, C-10
Altadena . . . . . . Pg. 114, B-6
Altaville J-6
Alton D-1
Alturas C-7
Amboy S-15
Anaheim T-11
  Vicinity . . . . Pg. 117, G-7
Anderson D-4
Angels Camp J-7
Angwin H-3
Annapolis H-2
Antioch J-4
Apple Valley S-12
Aptos L-4
Arbuckle G-4
Arcadia . . . . Pg. 116, C-7
Arcata C-1
Arlington Oaks . . . Pg. 141, D-2
Arnold J-7
Arroyo Grande Q-6
Artesia . . . . Pg. 115, F-4
Artois F-4
Arvin Q-9
Atascadero P-6
Atherton . . . . . . Pg. 146, A-1
Atwater L-6
Auberry L-8
Auburn H-6
Avalon U-10
Avenal N-7
Avon . . . . Pg. 144, A-4
Azusa . . . . Pg. 116, C-8
Badger N-8
Baker Q-14
Bakersfield Q-9
Balboa Park . . . . Pg. 143, F-4
Baldwin Park . . . Pg. 116, C-7
Banning T-13
Barstow R-12
Bartlett Sprs. G-3
Bass Lake L-8
Baxter G-6
Baywood Park Q-5
Bear Valley K-7
Beaumont T-12
Beckwourth F-7
Bel Air . . . . Pg. 114, C-2
Belden E-5
Bell . . . . Pg. 115, E-5
Bell Gardens . . . Pg. 115, E-5
Bella Vista D-4
Bellflower . . . . . Pg. 115, F-6
Bells Station L-5
Belmont . . . . . . Pg. 145, J-3
Belvedere . . . . . Pg. 144, D-1
Ben Lomond L-4
Bend E-4
Benicia . . . . . . Pg. 144, A-4
Benton K-10
Berenda L-7
Berkeley J-4
  Vicinity . . . . Pg. 144, D-3
Berry Creek F-5
Bertsch Terr. A-1
Beverly Hills S-10
  Vicinity . . . . Pg. 114, C-3
Bieber D-6
Big Bar D-3
Big Bear Lake S-13
Big Bend C-5
Big Creek L-8
Big Oak Flat K-7
Big Pine L-10
Big Sur N-4
Biggs G-5
Bishop L-10
Blackwells Corner P-7
Blairsden F-7
Bloomington . . . Pg. 116, B-10
Blue Lake C-2
Blythe U-16
Bodega Bay H-2
Bodfish P-10
Bolinas J-3
Boonville G-2
Boron R-11
Borrego Springs U-13
Boulder Creek L-4
Boulevard V-13
Bowman G-6
Bradley P-6
Brawley V-15
Brea . . . . Pg. 117, G-6
Brentwood J-5
Bridgeport J-9
Bridgeville D-2
Broderick H-5

Browns Valley G-5
Brownsville G-6
Bryn Mawr . . . . Pg. 116, B-12
Buellton R-6
Buena Park . . . . Pg. 117, F-7
Burbank . . . . . . Pg. 114, B-4
Burlingame . . . . Pg. 145, H-2
Burney D-5
Burnt Ranch C-3
Butte City F-4
Butte Meadows E-5
Buttonwillow Q-8
Cabazon T-13
Cahuilla U-13
Calavo Gardens . . Pg. 143, G-6
Calexico V-15
Caliente Q-10
California City Q-11
California Hot Sprs. . . . P-9
Calipatria V-15
Calistoga H-3
Callahan C-4
Calpella G-3
Calpine F-7
Cambria P-5
Cameron Park H-6
Camino H-6
Camp Nelson N-10
Camp Richardson H-8
Campbell . . . . . Pg. 146, E-6
Campo V-13
Camptonville G-6
Canby C-7
Canoga Park . . . Pg. 114, B-1
Cantil Q-10
Canyon Dam E-6
Capay H-4
Capetown D-1
Capitola L-4
Carlotta D-1
Carlsbad U-11
  Vicinity . . . . Pg. 143, E-6
Carmel Valley M-4
Carmichael . . . . Pg. 141, B-5
Carnelian Bay G-8
Carpinteria S-8
Carson . . . . . . Pg. 115, F-4
Carson Hill - Cartago N-11
Caruthers M-7
Casmalia R-6
Caspar F-1
Castaic S-9
Castella C-4
Castroville M-4
Cayucos P-5
Cedar Grove M-10
Cedarville C-8
Century City . . . . Pg. 114, D-3
Ceres K-6
Chalfant L-10
Challenge F-6
Chatsworth . . . . Pg. 114, B-1
Chester E-6
Chico F-5
China Lake P-11
Chino . . . . Pg. 116, D-10
Cholame P-7
Chowchilla L-7
Chula Vista V-12
  Vicinity . . . . Pg. 143, J-5
Cima Q-15
Citrus . . . . Pg. 141, B-6
Claremont . . . . . Pg. 116, C-10
Clarksburg H-5
Clay J-6
Clayton . . . . . . Pg. 144, C-7
Clearlake G-3
Clovis M-8
Clyde . . . . Pg. 144, A-6
Coachella U-14
Coalinga N-6
Coarsegold L-8
Cobb G-3
Colfax G-6
Coloma H-6
Colton . . . . Pg. 116, B-11
Colusa G-4
Commerce . . . . . Pg. 114, D-5
Compton . . . . . Pg. 115, F-4
Concord J-4
  Vicinity . . . . Pg. 144, B-6
Copperopolis J-6
Corcoran N-8
Corning F-4
Corona T-11
Coronado V-12
  Vicinity . . . . Pg. 143, H-2
Costa Mesa . . . . Pg. 117, H-6
Cottonwood D-4
Coulterville K-7
Courtland J-5
Covelo F-3
Covina . . . . Pg. 116, C-8
Crannell C-1
Crescent City B-1
Crescent Mills E-6
Crestmore . . . . . Pg. 116, B-10
Crockett . . . . . . Pg. 144, A-4
Cucamonga . . . . Pg. 116, C-11
Cudahy . . . . . . Pg. 115, E-5
Culver City . . . . . Pg. 114, D-3
Cummings E-2
Cupertino . . . . . Pg. 146, D-4
Cutler N-9
Cutten C-1
Cuyama R-8
Cypress . . . . . . Pg. 115, G-6
Daggett R-12
Dairyville E-4
Dales E-4
Daly City K-3
  Vicinity . . . . Pg. 145, G-1
Dana Point U-10
Danville . . . . . . Pg. 144, D-6
Darwin N-11

Davis H-5
Davis Creek B-8
Death Valley Jct. N-13
Del Mar V-11
  Vicinity . . . . Pg. 143, F-5
Delano P-9
Desert Center T-15
Desert Hot Springs . . . T-13
Desert Shores U-14
Devils Den P-7
Diamond Bar . . . . Pg. 116, C-7
Diamond Sprs. H-6
Dictionary Hill . . . Pg. 143, G-6
Dillon Beach J-2
Dinkey Creek L-9
Dixon H-5
Dobbins G-6
Dominguez . . . . . Pg. 115, F-3
Dorris B-5
Dos Palos L-6
Dos Rios F-2
Douglas City D-3
Downey . . . . . . Pg. 115, E-5
Doyle F-8
Duarte . . . . Pg. 116, C-7
Ducor P-9
Dulzura V-12
Dunsmuir C-4
Durham F-5
Eagle Rock . . . . . Pg. 114, C-5
Eagleville C-8
Earlimart P-9
Earp T-17
East Highlands . . Pg. 116, A-12
East Los Angeles . . Pg. 114, D-5
East Palo Alto . . . Pg. 146, A-2
El Cajon V-12
  Vicinity . . . . Pg. 143, E-6
El Centro V-15
El Cerrito . . . . . . Pg. 144, C-3
El Granada . . . . . Pg. 145, J-1
El Monte . . . . . . Pg. 114, C-6
El Nido L-7
El Portal K-8
El Segundo . . . . . Pg. 115, F-3
Elk Creek F-4
Elk Grove J-5
Elmira J-4
Emeryville . . . . . Pg. 144, D-3
Encinitas V-11
Encino . . . . Pg. 114, C-2
Enterprise D-4
Escalon K-6
Escondido U-11
Esparto H-4
Essex R-15
Etiwanda . . . . . . Pg. 116, C-12
Etna B-4
Eucalyptus Hills . . Pg. 143, C-6
Eureka C-1
Exeter N-9
Fair Oak . . . . . . Pg. 141, A-6
Fairfield J-4
Fall River Mills C-6
Fallbrook U-12
Farmersville N-9
Farmington J-6
Fawnskin S-12
Feather Falls F-6
Fellows Q-8
Fenner R-15
Ferndale D-1
Fields Landing D-1
Fillmore S-9
Firebaugh M-6
Fish Camp L-8
Fish Rock G-2
Five Points N-7
Flintridge . . . . . Pg. 114, B-5
Florence . . . . . . Pg. 115, G-6
  Vicinity . . . . Pg. 141, E-4
Florin H-5
Floriston G-8
Flournoy F-4
Folsom H-6
Fontana . . . . . . Pg. 116, C-12
Foothill Farms . . . Pg. 141, A-5
Forbestown F-6
Ford City Q-8
Forest Glen D-3
Forest Ranch F-5
Foresthill G-6
Forks Of Salmon C-3
Fortuna D-1
Foster City . . . . . Pg. 145, H-4
Fountain Valley . . . Pg. 117, H-7
Fowler M-8
Frazier Park R-9
Fredericksburg H-8
Fremont K-4
  Vicinity . . . . Pg. 145, A-5
Frenbrook . . . . . Pg. 143, B-7
French Gulch D-3
Fresno M-8
  Vicinity . . . . Pg. 141, F-4
Ft. Bidwell B-8
Ft. Bragg F-1
Ft. Dick A-1
Ft. Jones B-4
Fullerton T-11
  Vicinity . . . . Pg. 117, F-7
Furnace Creek Ranch . . N-13
Galt J-5
Garberville E-2
Garden Grove . . . Pg. 117, G-7
Gardena . . . . . . Pg. 115, F-4
Gasquet A-2

CALIFORNIA

Gaviota . . . R-7
Gazelle . . . B-4
Georgetown . . . H-6
Gerber . . . E-4
Geyserville . . . H-3
Giant Forest Village . N-10
Gilroy . . . L-5
Glamis . . . V-16
Glen Avon . . . Pg. 116, D-12
Glen Ellen . . . H-3
Glendale . . . S-10
Vicinity . . . Pg. 114, B-4
Glendora . . . S-11
Vicinity . . . Pg. 116, C-8
Glenn . . . F-4
Glennville . . . P-10
Glenview . . . Pg. 143, E-7
Goffs . . . R-16
Goleta . . . S-7
Gonzales . . . M-5
Gorman . . . R-9
Goshen . . . N-8
Graeagle . . . F-7
Granada Hills Pg. 114, A-1
Grand Terrace
. . . Pg. 116, B-11
Graniteville . . . G-7
Grass Valley . . . G-6
Green Acres . . . Q-9
Greenfield . . . N-5
Greenview . . . B-4
Greenville . . . E-6
Grenada . . . B-4
Gridley . . . G-5
Grimes . . . G-4
Groveland . . . K-7
Grover City . . . Q-6
Guadalupe . . . Q-6
Gualala . . . G-2
Guerneville . . . H-2
Guinda . . . H-4
Gustine . . . L-6
Hacienda Heights
. . . Pg. 116, D-7
Half Moon Bay . . . K-3
Hallelujah Jct. . . . F-8
Hamburg . . . B-3
Hamilton City . . . E-4
Hanford . . . N-8
Happy Camp . . . B-3
Harbor Side . Pg. 143, J-4
Harden Flat . . . K-7
Hawaiian Gardens
. . . Pg. 115, G-3
Hawthorne . . . Pg. 115, F-3
Hayfork . . . D-3
Hayward . . . K-4
Vicinity . . . Pg. 145, G-6
Healdsburg . . . H-3
Heber . . . V-15
Helena . . . D-3
Helendale . . . R-12
Hemet . . . T-12
Hercules . . . Pg. 144, B-3
Herlong . . . E-8
Hermosa Beach
. . . Pg. 115, F-3
Herndon . . . M-7
Hesperia . . . S-12
Highland . . . Pg. 116, A-12
Highland Park
. . . Pg. 114, C-5
Hillsbrough . Pg. 145, H-2
Hilmar . . . L-6
Hilt . . . B-2
Hinkley . . . R-12
Hobart Mills . . . G-7
Hollister . . . M-5
Hollywood . . . Pg. 114, C-3
Holtville . . . V-15
Homewood . . . G-7
Honcut . . . G-5
Honeydew . . . D-1
Hoopa . . . C-2
Hopland . . . G-2
Hornbrook . . . B-4
Hornitos . . . K-7
Hume . . . M-9
Huntington Beach . T-10
Vicinity . . . Pg. 117, H-4
Huntington Park
. . . Pg. 114, E-5
Huron . . . N-7
Idyllwild . . . T-13
Igo . . . D-4
Imperial . . . V-15
Imperial Beach . V-12
Vicinity . . . Pg. 143, K-3
Independence . . . M-10
Indio . . . Pg. 116, D-7
Industry . . . Pg. 116, D-7
Inglewood . . . Pg. 115, E-3
Ingot . . . D-5
Inverness . . . J-3
Inyokern . . . P-11
Ione . . . J-6
Irvine . . . Pg. 117, H-9
Isleton . . . J-5
Ivanpah . . . Q-15
Jackson . . . J-6
Jamacha . . . Pg. 143, F-7
Jamacha Junction
. . . Pg. 143, F-6
Jamestown . . . K-7
Jamul . . . V-12
Janesville . . . E-7
Johannesburg . . . Q-11
Johnsondale . . . N-5
Johnstonville . . . E-7
Johnstown . . . Pg. 143, D-7
Jolon . . . N-5
Joshua Tree . . . S-13
Julian . . . V-13
Junction City . . . D-3
June Lake . . . K-9
Keddie . . . E-6

Keeler . . . N-11
Keene . . . Q-10
Kelseyville . . . G-3
Kelso . . . R-15
Kenwood . . . H-3
Kerman . . . M-7
Kernville . . . P-10
Kettleman City . . . N-7
King City . . . N-5
Kings Beach . . . G-8
Kingsburg . . . N-8
Kirkwood . . . H-8
Kit Carson . . . H-7
Klamath Glen . . . B-2
Klamath River . . . B-4
Kneeland . . . D-2
Knights Ferry . . . K-6
Knights Landing . . . H-5
Kyburz . . . H-7
La Canada . . . Pg. 114, B-5
La Crescenta Pg. 114, B-4
La Grange . . . K-6
La Habra . . . Pg. 117, E-7
La Honda . . . L-3
La Jolla . . . V-11
Vicinity . . . Pg. 143, D-1
La Jolla Mesa
. . . Pg. 143, D-1
La Mesa . . . Pg. 143, F-5
La Mirada . . . Pg. 117, F-7
La Palma . . . Pg. 115, F-6
La Presa . . . Pg. 143, G-5
La Puente . . . Pg. 116, D-7
La Quinta . . . T-13
Lafayette . . . Pg. 144, C-5
Laguna Beach . . . U-10
Lake City . . . B-8
Lake Elsinore . . . T-12
Lake Forest . . . T-11
Lakehead . . . D-4
Lakeport . . . G-3
Lakeside . . . Pg. 143, D-7
Lakewood . . . Pg. 115, F-5
Lamont . . . Q-9
Lancaster . . . R-10
Lawndale . . . Pg. 115, F-3
Laytonville . . . F-2
Lee Vining . . . K-9
Leggett . . . E-2
Lemon Grove Pg. 143, G-5
Lemoore . . . N-7
Lenwood . . . R-12
Leucadia . . . V-11
Likely . . . C-7
Lincoln . . . H-5
Lincoln Acres Pg. 143, H-4
Linda . . . G-5
Linden . . . J-6
Lindsay . . . N-9
Litchfield . . . E-7
Little Lake . . . P-11
Live Oak . . . G-5
Livermore . . . K-4
Livingston . . . L-6
Lockeford . . . J-6
Lockwood . . . N-5
Lodi . . . J-5
Loleta . . . C-1
Loma Linda Pg. 116, B-11
Lomita . . . Pg. 115, G-4
Lompoc . . . R-6
Lone Pine . . . N-10
Long Beach . . . T-10
Vicinity . . . Pg. 115, G-5
Longvale . . . F-2
Lookout . . . C-6
Loomis . . . H-6
Los Alamos . . . R-7
Los Altos . . . Pg. 145, C-3
Los Altos Hills
. . . Pg. 146, C-2
Los Angeles . . . T-9
Vicinity . . . Pg. 114-117
Los Banos . . . L-6
Los Gatos . . . L-4
Vicinity . . . Pg. 146, F-5
Los Molinos . . . E-4
Los Olivos . . . R-7
Lost Hills . . . P-8
Lower Lake . . . G-3
Loyalton . . . F-7
Lucerne . . . G-3
Lucerne Valley . . . S-12
Ludlow . . . R-14
Lynwood . . . Pg. 115, E-5
Lynwood Hills Pg. 143, J-5
Macdoel . . . B-5
Mad River . . . D-2
Madeline . . . D-7
Madera . . . M-8
Malaga . . . M-8
Malibu . . . S-9
Mammoth Lakes . K-9
Manchester . . . G-2
Manhattan Beach
. . . Pg. 115, F-3
Manteca . . . K-5
Manton . . . D-5
Maricopa . . . Q-8
Marina . . . M-4
Markleeville . . . J-8
Martinez . . . Pg. 143, D-1
Marysville . . . G-5
Maxwell . . . G-4
Maywood . . . Pg. 114, D-5
McArthur . . . C-6
McCloud . . . C-5
McFarland . . . P-9
McKinleyville . . . C-1
McKittrick . . . Q-8
Meadow Valley . . . F-6
Meadow Vista . . . H-5
Mecca . . . U-14
Meeks Bay . . . H-8
Mendocino . . . F-2

Mendota . . . M-7
Menlo Park . . . Pg. 146, A-2
Merced . . . L-7
Mercy Hot Springs . M-6
Meridian . . . G-5
Meyers . . . H-8
Mi-wuk Village . . . K-7
Middletown . . . H-3
Midpines . . . K-8
Milford . . . E-7
Millbrae . . . Pg. 145, H-2
Millville . . . D-4
Milpitas . . . K-4
Vicinity . . . Pg. 146, B-6
Mineral . . . E-5
Mira Loma . Pg. 116, E-12
Miramar . . . Pg. 143, C-4
Miranda . . . E-2
Mission Beach
. . . Pg. 143, F-1
Mission Hills Pg. 114, B-2
Mission Viejo . . . T-11
Modesto . . . K-6
Mojave . . . R-10
Mokelumne Hill . . . J-7
Mono Hot Springs . L-9
Mono Lake . . . K-9
Monrovia . . . Pg. 116, C-7
Montague . . . B-4
Montara . . . Pg. 145, H-1
Montclair . . . Pg. 116, D-10
Monte Rio . . . H-2
Monte Serona
. . . Pg. 146, E-4
Montebello . . . Pg. 114, D-6
Montecito . . . S-7
Monterey . . . M-4
Monterey Park
. . . Pg. 114, D-5
Montgomery Creek . C-5
Montrose . . . Pg. 114, B-5
Moorpark . . . S-9
Moraga . . . Pg. 144, C-7
Moreno . . . Pg. 143, C-7
Moreno Valley . . . T-12
Morgan . . . Pg. 146, G-10
Morgan Hill . . . L-4
Mormon Bar . . . L-8
Morongo Valley . . . T-13
Morro Bay . . . Q-5
Moss Beach . Pg. 145, J-1
Moss Landing . . . M-4
Mountain View
. . . Pg. 146, B-3
Mt. Bullion . . . K-7
Mt. Laguna . . . V-13
Mt. Shasta . . . C-4
Mugginsville . . . B-4
Murphys . . . J-7
Murrieta . . . T-12
Napa . . . J-4
National City . Pg. 143, H-4
Navarro . . . G-2
Needles . . . R-16
Nevada City . . . G-6
New Cuyama . . . R-7
New Idria . . . N-6
Newark . . . Pg. 145, A-6
Newberry Springs . R-13
Newell . . . B-6
Newport Beach . . . T-10
Vicinity . . . Pg. 117, J-8
Nice . . . G-3
Niland . . . U-15
Nimbus . . . Pg. 141, B-7
Nipomo . . . Q-6
Nipton . . . Q-15
Norco . . . Pg. 117, E-11
Nord . . . F-5
North Edwards . . . R-11
North Fork . . . L-8
North Highlands
. . . Pg. 141, A-4
North Hollywood
. . . Pg. 114, C-3
Northridge . . . Pg. 114, B-1
Norwalk . . . Pg. 115, F-6
Novato . . . J-3
Noyo . . . F-2
Nubieber . . . C-6
O'Neals . . . L-8
Oakdale . . . K-6
Oakhurst . . . L-8
Oakland . . . K-4
Vicinity . . . Pg. 144, E-4
Oasis . . . L-11
Oceano . . . Q-6
Oceanside . . . U-11
Ocotillo . . . V-14
Ocotillo Wells . . . V-14
Ojai . . . S-8
Olancha . . . N-11
Old Station . . . D-6
Olema . . . J-3
Olinda . . . D-4
Ono . . . D-4
Ontario . . . T-11
Vicinity . . . Pg. 116, D-9
Onyx . . . P-10
Orange . . . Pg. 117, G-8
Orange Cove . . . M-9
Orangevale . . . Pg. 141, A-6
Orcutt . . . R-6
Ordbend . . . F-5
Orick . . . B-1
Orland . . . F-4
Orleans . . . C-2
Oro Grande . . . R-12
Orosi . . . N-9
Oroville . . . F-5
Otay . . . Pg. 143, K-5
Otay Mesa . . . Pg. 143, K-5
Oxnard . . . S-8
Pacific Grove . . . M-4

Pacific Palisades
. . . Pg. 114, D-1
Pacifica . . . K-3
Vicinity . . . Pg. 145, G-1
Paicines . . . M-5
Pala . . . U-12
Palermo . . . G-5
Palm Desert . . . T-13
Palm Springs . . . T-13
Palmdale . . . S-10
Palms . . . Pg. 114, D-3
Palo Alto . . . K-4
Vicinity . . . Pg. 146, B-2
Palo Verde . . . U-16
Palomar Mountain . U-13
Palos Verdes Estates
. . . Pg. 115, G-3
Panamint Sprs. . . . N-12
Panoche . . . M-6
Panorama City
. . . Pg. 114, B-2
Paradise . . . F-5
Paramount . . . Pg. 115, F-5
Parker Dam . . . S-17
Parkfield . . . P-6
Pasadena . . . S-10
Vicinity . . . Pg. 114, C-6
Paskenta . . . E-4
Paso Robles . . . P-6
Patterson . . . L-6
Patton . . . Pg. 116, A-12
Pauma Valley . . . U-12
Pearblossom . . . S-11
Pebble Beach . . . M-4
Pedley . . . Pg. 117, E-12
Penn Valley . . . G-6
Perkins . . . Pg. 141, D-4
Perris . . . T-12
Petaluma . . . J-3
Petrolia . . . D-1
Phelan . . . S-11
Philo . . . G-2
Pico Rivera . Pg. 114, E-6
Piedmont . . . Pg. 144, D-4
Piercy . . . E-2
Pine Grove . . . J-7
Pine Valley . . . V-13
Pinecrest . . . J-8
Pinedale . . . M-8
Pinole . . . Pg. 144, B-3
Pioneer Station . . . J-7
Pismo Beach . . . Q-6
Pittsburg . . . Pg. 144, A-7
Pixley . . . N-9
Placentia . . . Pg. 117, F-8
Placerville . . . H-6
Planada . . . L-7
Pleasant Hill . Pg. 144, B-6
Plymouth . . . H-6
Point Arena . . . G-2
Pollock Pines . . . H-7
Pomona . . . T-11
Vicinity . . . Pg. 116, D-9
Pondosa . . . C-5
Poplar . . . P-9
Port Hueneme . . . S-8
Porterville . . . N-9
Portola . . . F-7
Portola Valley Pg. 146, C-1
Portuguese Bend
. . . Pg. 115, H-3
Potter Valley . . . F-3
Poway . . . U-12
Vicinity . . . Pg. 143, B-5
Pozo . . . Q-6
Princeton . . . G-4
Vicinity . . . Pg. 145, J-1
Project City . . . D-4
Pulga . . . F-6
Pumpkin Center . . . Q-9
Quincy . . . F-6
Raisin . . . M-7
Ramona . . . V-12
Rancho Cordova
. . . Pg. 141, C-6
Rancho Palos Verdes Q-11
Randsburg . . . Q-11
Ravendale . . . D-7
Red Bluff . . . E-4
Red Mountain . . . Q-11
Redcrest . . . D-1
Redding . . . D-4
Redlands . . . Pg. 116, B-12
Vicinity . . . Pg. 115, G-3
Redway . . . E-2
Redondo Beach . . . T-9
Redwood City Pg. 146, J-4
Redwood Valley . . . G-2
Requa . . . B-1
Reseda . . . Pg. 114, B-1
Rialto . . . Pg. 116, A-10
Richmond . . . Pg. 144, C-2
Richvale . . . F-5
Ridgecrest . . . Q-11
Rio Dell . . . D-1
Rio Linda . . . H-5
Vicinity . . . Pg. 141, A-3
Rio Oso . . . G-5
Rio Vista . . . J-5
Ripley . . . U-16
Ripon . . . K-5
River Pines . . . H-6
Riverdale . . . N-7
Riverside . . . T-12
Vicinity . . . Pg. 117, E-12
Riverview . . . Pg. 141, E-1
Robla . . . Pg. 141, A-3
Rock Haven . Pg. 143, A-6
Rocklin . . . H-5
Rockport . . . E-2
Rodeo . . . Pg. 144, A-3
Rohnert Park . . . J-3
Rolling Hills . Pg. 115, G-3
Rolling Hills Estate
. . . Pg. 115, G-3
Romoland . . . T-12

Rosamond . . . R-10
Rosemead . . . Pg. 114, D-6
Rosemont . . . Pg. 141, C-5
Roseville . . . H-5
Rough And Ready . G-6
Round Mountain . . . D-5
Rovana . . . L-10
Rowland Heights
. . . Pg. 116, E-8
Rutherford . . . H-4
Sacramento . . . J-5
Vicinity . . . Pg. 141
Salinas . . . M-5
Salton City . . . U-14
Salyer . . . C-2
San Andreas . . . J-7
San Ardo . . . N-6
San Bernardino . T-12
San Carlos . . . Pg. 145, J-3
San Clemente . . . U-11
San Diego . . . V-12
Vicinity . . . Pg. 143
San Dimas . . . Pg. 116, C-9
San Fernando . . . S-10
Vicinity . . . Pg. 114, A-2
San Francisco . . . K-4
Vicinity . . . Pg. 145
San Gabriel . . . Pg. 114, C-6
San Jacinto . . . T-12
San Joaquin . . . M-7
San Jose . . . L-4
Vicinity . . . Pg. 146, D-8
San Juan Bautista . M-5
San Juan Capistrano U-11
San Leandro Pg. 145, F-5
San Lorenzo Pg. 145, G-5
San Lucas . . . N-5
San Luis Obispo . . . Q-6
San Marcos . . . U-12
San Marino . . Pg. 114, C-6
San Martin . . . L-5
San Mateo . . . K-3
Vicinity . . . Pg. 145, H-3
San Miguel . . . P-6
San Pablo . . . Pg. 144, B-3
San Pedro . . Pg. 115, H-4
San Rafael . . . J-3
Vicinity . . . Pg. 144, B-1
San Simeon . . . P-5
Sanger . . . M-8
Santa Ana . . . T-11
Vicinity . . . Pg. 117, H-8
Santa Barbara . . . S-7
Santa Clara . . . L-4
Vicinity . . . Pg. 146, C-5
Santa Clarita . . . S-9
Santa Cruz . . . L-4
Santa Fe Springs
. . . Pg. 115, E-6
Santa Margarita . Q-6
Santa Maria . . . R-6
Santa Monica . . . T-9
Vicinity . . . Pg. 114, E-2
Santa Nella . . . L-6
Santa Paula . . . S-8
Santa Rosa . . . V-13
Santa Ysabel . . . V-12
Santee . . . Pg. 143, D-6
Vicinity . . . Pg. 143, D-6
Saratoga . . . L-4
Saticoy . . . S-9
Sattley . . . F-7
Sausalito . . . J-3
Sawyers Bar . . . C-3
Scotia . . . D-1
Scotts Valley . . . L-4
Scottys Castle . . . M-12
Seeley . . . V-14
Selma . . . M-8
Shafter . . . Q-8
Shandon . . . P-6
Shasta . . . D-4
Shaver Lake . . . L-9
Sherman Oaks
. . . Pg. 114, C-2
Shingletown . . . D-5
Short Acres . Pg. 144, A-6
Shoshone . . . P-14
Sierra City . . . F-7
Sierra Madre Pg. 114, B-6
Sierraville . . . F-7
Signal Hill . Pg. 115, G-5
Simi Valley . . . S-9
Simmler . . . Q-7
Sisquoc . . . R-7
Sites . . . G-4
Sloat . . . F-7
Smith River . . . A-2
Snelling . . . K-7
Soda Springs . . . G-7
Solana Beach
. . . Pg. 143, A-1
Soledad . . . N-5
Solvang . . . R-7
Somerset . . . H-7
Somes Bar . . . B-3
Sonoma . . . J-3
Sonora . . . K-7
Soquel . . . L-4
Sorrento . . . Pg. 143, C-1
South El Monte
. . . Pg. 114, D-6
South Gate . Pg. 115, E-5
South Lake Tahoe . H-8
South Pasadena
. . . Pg. 114, D-6
South Port . . . Pg. 141, D-1
South San Francisco
. . . Pg. 145, G-2
Spring Valley Pg. 143, G-6
Springville . . . N-9

Squaw Valley . . . G-7
St. Helena . . . H-3
Standish . . . E-7
Stanton . . . Pg. 117, G-7
Stewarts Point . . . H-2
Stirling City . . . F-5
Stockton . . . K-5
Stonyford . . . F-4
Stovepipe Wells . . . N-12
Stratford . . . N-8
Strathmore . . . N-9
Studio City . . Pg. 114, C-3
Suisun City . . . J-4
Summerland . . . S-8
Summit City . . . D-4
Sun City . . . T-12
Sun Valley . . Pg. 114, B-3
Sunland . . . Pg. 114, A-3
Sunnyside . . Pg. 143, H-6
Sunnyvale . . . K-5
Vicinity . . . Pg. 146, C-4
Surf . . . R-6
Susanville . . . E-7
Sutter . . . G-5
Sutter Creek . . . J-6
Taft . . . Q-8
Tahoe City . . . G-7
Talmage . . . G-3
Tarzana . . . Pg. 114, C-1
Taylorsville . . . E-7
Tecopa . . . P-14
Tehachapi . . . Q-10
Temecula . . . U-12
Temple City . Pg. 114, C-6
Templeton . . . P-6
Terminous . . . J-5
Termo . . . D-7
Terra Bella . . . P-8
Thornton . . . J-5
Thousand Oaks . . . S-9
Thousand Palms . T-13
Three Rivers . . . N-10
Tiburon . . . Pg. 144, D-1
Tipton . . . N-8
Tomales . . . J-3
Toms Place . . . L-10
Topanga . . . Pg. 114, D-1
Topanga Beach
. . . Pg. 114, D-1
Topaz . . . H-8
Torrance . . . Pg. 115, F-3
Tracy . . . K-5
Tranquillity . . . M-7
Tres Pinos . . . M-5
Trinidad . . . C-1
Trinity Center . . . C-3
Trona . . . P-12
Truckee . . . G-7
Vicinity . . . Pg. 103, E-7
Tujunga . . . Pg. 114, A-4
Tulelake . . . B-6
Tuolumne . . . K-7
Turlock . . . K-6
Tuttletown . . . K-7
Twain . . . F-6
Twain Harte . . . K-7
Twentynine Palms . S-14
Ukiah . . . G-2
Union City . . Pg. 145, H-6
Universal City Pg. 114, C-3
Upland . . . Pg. 116, C-10
Upper Lake . . . G-3
Vacaville . . . H-4
Vallejo . . . J-4
Valley Springs . . . J-6
Valley View Acres
. . . Pg. 141, A-2
Van Nuys . . Pg. 114, B-2
Venice . . . Pg. 114, E-2
Ventura . . . S-8
Victorville . . . S-12
Vidal . . . T-17
Vina . . . E-4
Vinton . . . F-8
Visalia . . . N-8
Vista . . . U-12
Walker . . . J-8
Walnut . . . Pg. 116, D-8
Walnut Creek . . . K-4
Vicinity . . . Pg. 144, C-6
Walnut Grove . . . J-5
Wasco . . . P-8
Washington . . . G-7
Waterford . . . K-6
Waterloo . . . J-5
Watsonville . . . L-4
Watts . . . Pg. 115, E-4
Wawona . . . K-8
Weaverville . . . D-3
Weed . . . C-4
Weitchpec . . . C-2
Wendel . . . E-8
Weott . . . D-1
West Covina Pg. 116, D-8
West Hollywood
. . . Pg. 114, D-2
West Los Angeles
. . . Pg. 114, D-2
West Point . . . J-7
West Riverside
. . . Pg. 116, D-12
West Sacramento
. . . Pg. 141, C-2
Westley . . . K-6
Westminister Pg. 117, G-7
Westmorland . . . V-14
Westport . . . E-2
Westwood . . . E-6
Wheatland . . . G-5
Whitmore . . . D-5
Whittier . . . Pg. 117, E-7
Williams . . . G-4
Willits . . . F-2
Willow Creek . . . C-2
Willow Ranch . . . B-8

Willow Springs . . . R-10
Willows . . . F-4
Wilmington . Pg. 115, G-4
Winter Gardens
. . . Pg. 143, D-6
Winterhaven . . . V-16
Winters . . . H-4
Winton . . . L-6
Wofford Heights . P-10
Woodfords . . . H-8
Woodlake . . . N-9
Woodland . . . H-4
Woodville . . . N-9
Woody . . . P-9
Wrightwood . . . S-11
Yermo . . . R-12
Yolo . . . H-5
Yorba Linda . Pg. 117, F-9
Yorkville . . . G-2
Yosemite Village . K-8
Yreka . . . B-4
Yuba City . . . G-5
Yucaipa . . . T-12
Yucca Valley . . . S-13

COLORADO
Pages 22-23
Population: 2,889,964
Capital: Denver
Land Area: 103,595 sq. mi.

Abarr . . . C-12
Agate . . . D-10
Aguilar . . . J-9
Akron . . . C-11
Alamosa . . . J-7
Allison . . . J-4
Alma . . . E-7
Almont . . . F-6
Amherst . . . B-12
Antero Jct. . . . F-7
Anton . . . D-11
Antonito . . . J-7
Arapahoe . . . E-12
Arboles . . . J-3
Arlington . . . G-11
Aroya . . . F-11
Arriba . . . E-11
Arriola . . . J-2
Arvada . . . D-8
Vicinity . . . Pg. 103, C-3
Aspen . . . F-6
Atwood . . . B-11
Ault . . . B-9
Aurora . . . D-9
Vicinity . . . Pg. 103, E-7
Austin . . . F-4
Avon . . . D-6
Avondale . . . G-9
Bailey . . . E-7
Barnesville . . . B-9
Bartlett . . . H-12
Basalt . . . E-6
Baxter . . . G-9
Bayfield . . . J-5
Bedrock . . . G-3
Bellvue . . . B-8
Bennett . . . D-9
Berthoud . . . C-8
Beshoar Jct. . . . J-9
Bethune . . . D-12
Beulah . . . G-8
Black Hawk . . . D-8
Blanca . . . H-8
Blue Mountain . . . C-3
Blue River . . . E-7
Bond . . . D-6
Boone . . . G-10
Boulder . . . C-8
Bow Mar . . Pg. 103, H-4
Bowie . . . F-5
Boyero . . . E-11
Brandon . . . F-12
Branson . . . J-10
Breckenridge . . . D-7
Breen . . . J-4
Briggsdale . . . B-9
Brighton . . . C-8
Bristol . . . G-12
Broomfield . . . C-8
Brush . . . C-10
Buckingham . . . B-9
Buena Vista . . . F-7
Buford . . . D-5
Burlington . . . D-12
Byers . . . D-9
Cahone . . . H-3
Calhan . . . E-10
Cameo . . . E-4
Cameron . . . J-12
Canon City . . . F-8
Capulin . . . J-7
Carbondale . . . E-5
Carlton . . . G-12
Castle Rock . . . E-9
Cedaredge . . . F-4
Center . . . H-7
Chama . . . J-8
Cheney Center . . . G-12
Cheraw . . . G-11
Cherry Hill Village
. . . Pg. 103, G-5
Cheyenne Wells . F-12
Chimney Rock . . . J-5
Chipita Park . . . F-9
Chivington . . . F-12
Chromo . . . J-4
Cimarron . . . G-5
Clarkville . . . B-11
Clifton . . . E-4
Climax . . . E-7
Coaldale . . . G-7

Coalmont . . . C-6
Collbran . . . E-4
Colorado City . . . G-8
Colorado Springs . F-9
Columbine Valley
. . . Pg. 103, J-3
Commerce City . . . D-9
Vicinity . . . Pg. 103, D-6
Como . . . E-7
Conejos . . . J-7
Conifer . . . D-8
Cope . . . D-11
Cortez . . . J-3
Cotopaxi . . . G-8
Cowdrey . . . B-6
Craig . . . B-5
Crawford . . . F-5
Creede . . . H-6
Crested Butte . . . F-6
Cripple Creek . . . F-8
Crook . . . B-11
Crowley . . . G-10
Cuchara . . . H-8
Dailey . . . B-11
DeBeque . . . E-4
Deckers . . . E-8
Deer Ridge . . . C-7
Deer Trail . . . D-10
Del Norte . . . H-7
Delhi . . . H-10
Delta . . . F-4
Denver . . . D-9
Vicinity . . . Pg. 103
Dillon . . . D-7
Dinosaur . . . C-3
Divide . . . F-8
Dolores . . . H-4
Dotsero . . . D-5
Dove Creek . . . H-3
Dowd . . . D-6
Doyleville . . . F-6
Drake . . . C-8
Dunton . . . H-4
Dupont . . Pg. 103, C-6
Durango . . . J-5
Eads . . . F-12
Eagle . . . D-6
Eaton . . . B-9
Echo Lake . . . D-7
Eckley . . . C-12
Edgewater . Pg. 103, E-3
Edwards . . . D-6
Egnar . . . H-3
Elbert . . . E-9
Eldorado Springs . D-8
Elizabeth . . . D-9
Elk Springs . . . C-4
Ellicott . . . F-9
Empire . . . D-7
Englewood . . . D-8
Vicinity . . . Pg. 103, G-5
Estes Park . . . C-7
Evans . . . C-9
Fairplay . . . E-7
Falcon . . . E-9
Farisita . . . H-8
Federal Heights
. . . Pg. 103, B-4
Fenders . . . Pg. 103, J-1
Firstview . . . F-12
Flagler . . . E-11
Fleming . . . B-11
Florence . . . G-8
Florissant . . . F-8
Ford . . . G-10
Fort Collins . . . B-8
Fort Garland . . . J-8
Fort Lewis . . . J-4
Fort Lupton . . . C-9
Fort Lyon . . . G-11
Fort Morgan . . . C-10
Fountain . . . F-9
Fowler . . . G-10
Franktown . . . D-9
Fraser . . . D-7
Frederick . . . C-8
Frisco . . . D-7
Fruita . . . E-3
Galatea . . . F-11
Garcia . . . J-8
Gardner . . . H-8
Garfield . . . F-7
Garo Park . . . E-7
Gateway . . . F-3
Genoa . . . E-11
Georgetown . . . D-7
Gilcrest . . . C-9
Gilman . . . D-6
Gladstone . . . H-5
Glendale . . Pg. 103, F-5
Glenwood Springs . D-5
Goodrich . . . C-10
Gould . . . C-6
Granada . . . G-12
Granby . . . C-7
Grand Junction . . . E-3
Grand Lake . . . C-7
Grandview Estates
. . . Pg. 103, J-6
Granite . . . E-7
Grant . . . E-7
Greeley . . . C-9
Greenwood Village
. . . Pg. 103, H-5
Guffey . . . F-8
Gunnison . . . F-6
Gypsum . . . D-6
Hamilton . . . C-5
Hartsel . . . E-7
Hasty . . . G-11
Haswell . . . F-11
Hawley . . . G-10
Haxtun . . . B-11
Hayden . . . C-5

COLORADO

Hermosa J-5
Hesperus J-4
Hiawatha B-3
Hillrose C-10
Hillside G-8
Hoehne J-9
Holly G-12
Holyoke B-12
Homelake H-7
Hooper H-7
Hot Sulphur Springs . C-7
Hotchkiss F-5
Howard F-7
Hudson C-9
Hugo E-11
Idaho Sprs. D-8
Idalia D-12
Idledale . . . . Pg. 103, G-1
Ignacio J-5
Iliff B-11
Indian Hills . Pg. 103, H-1
Jansen J-9
Jaroso J-8
Jefferson E-7
Joes D-12
Johnson Village F-7
Julesburg A-12
Keenesburg C-9
Kersey C-9
Kim J-11
Kiowa D-9
Kit Carson F-12
Kline J-4
Komman G-12
Kremmling C-7
La Jara J-7
La Junta G-11
La Salle C-9
La Veta H-9
Lafayette C-8
Laird C-12
Lake City G-5
Lake George F-8
Lakewood D-8
  Vicinity . . . Pg. 103, F-2
Lamar G-12
Larkspur E-9
Las Animas G-11
Last Chance D-10
Lay C-4
Lazear F-5
Leadville E-7
Lebanon J-4
Lewis J-3
Limon E-10
Lindon D-11
Littleton D-8
  Vicinity . . . Pg. 103, H-4
Lochbule C-9
Log Lane Village . . C-10
Loma E-3
Longmont C-8
Loveland C-8
Lucerne C-9
Lycan H-12
Lyons C-8
Mack E-3
Maher F-5
Malta E-6
Manassa J-7
Mancos J-4
Manitou Springs . . . F-8
Manzanola G-10
Marble E-5
Marvel J-4
Masters C-9
Matheson E-10
Maybell B-4
McClave G-11
McCoy D-6
Meeker C-4
Meeker Park C-8
Merino B-10
Mesa E-4
Mesita J-8
Milliken C-8
Milner B-5
Mineral Hot Springs . G-7
Minturn D-6
Model J-10
Moffat G-7
Molina E-4
Monte Vista H-7
Montrose G-4
Monument E-9
Monument Park . . . J-9
Morrison . . . Pg. 103, G-2
Mosca H-7
Mount Princeton Hot Spr.
  . . . . F-7
Mountain View
  . . . . . . Pg. 103, D-3
Nathrop F-7
Naturita G-3
Nederland D-7
New Castle D-5
Northglenn D-8
Norwood G-4
Nucla G-4
Nunn B-9
Oak Creek C-6
Olathe F-4
Olney Springs . . . G-10
Ophir H-4
Orchard C-9
Orchard City F-4
Ordway G-10
Otis C-11
Ouray G-4
Ovid A-12
Oxford J-4
Pagosa Sprs. J-6
Palisade E-4
Palmer Lake E-8
Paoli B-12

Paonia F-5
Parachute E-4
Paradox F-4
Park F-9
Parkdale F-7
Parker D-9
Parlin F-6
Parshall C-7
Peetz A-11
Penrose F-8
Peyton E-9
Phippsburg C-6
Pierce B-9
Pinewood Springs . . C-8
Placerville G-4
Platoro J-6
Platteville C-9
Pleasant View H-3
Poncha Springs . . . F-7
Poudre Park B-8
Powderhorn G-5
Pritchett H-12
Proctor B-11
Prospect Valley . . . C-9
Pryor H-9
Pueblo G-8
Pueblo West G-9
Punkin Center F-10
Ramah E-9
Rand C-7
Rangely C-3
Raymer B-10
Raymond C-8
Red Mountain H-5
Redcliff E-6
Redmesa J-4
Redstone E-6
Redvale G-4
Rico H-4
Ridgway G-4
Rifle D-4
Rio Blanco D-3
Rockport B-9
Rockwood H-5
Rocky G-10
Roggen C-9
Rollinsville D-7
Romeo J-7
Royal Gorge G-8
Rush F-10
Rustic B-7
Rye H-8
Saguache G-7
Salida F-7
San Acacio J-8
San Francisco J-8
San Luis J-8
San Pablo J-8
Sanford J-7
Sapinero G-5
Sargents F-6
Saw Pit G-4
Security-Widefield . . F-9
Sedalia E-8
Sedgewick A-11
Segundo J-9
Seibert E-11
Shawnee E-8
Sheridan F-12
  Vicinity . . . Pg. 103, G-4
Sheridan Lake F-12
Silt D-5
Silver Cliff G-8
Silverthorne D-7
Silverton H-5
Simla E-10
Skyway E-4
Slick Rock G-3
Snow Mass E-6
Snow Mass Village . E-6
Snyder C-10
Somerset F-5
South Fork H-6
Spar City H-6
Springfield H-12
Starkville J-9
State Bridge D-6
Steamboat Springs . . C-6
Sterling B-11
Stoneham B-10
Stoner H-4
Stonewall J-9
Strasburg D-9
Stratton D-12
Sugar City G-11
Summitville H-6
Sunbeam B-4
Swink G-10
Tabernash D-7
Telluride H-5
Texas Creek G-8
Thatcher H-10
The Forks B-7
Thornton D-8
  Vicinity . . . Pg. 103, B-5
Timpas H-10
Tiny Town . . . Pg. 103, H-1
Tobe J-10
Toonerville H-11
Toponas C-6
Towaoc J-3
Towner F-12
Trinidad J-9
Twin Forks . . . Pg. 103, H-1
Twinlakes E-6
Two Buttes H-12
Tyrone H-10
Uravan G-3
Utleyville J-11
Vail D-7
Valdez J-9
Vancorum G-3
Victor F-8
Vilas H-12

Villa Grove G-7
Vineland G-9
Virginia Dale B-8
Vona E-11
Wagon Wheel Gap . . H-6
Walden B-6
Walsenburg H-8
Walsh H-12
Watkins D-9
Welby . . . . . Pg. 103, C-5
Weldona C-10
Westcliffe G-8
Westcreek E-8
Westminster D-8
  Vicinity . . . Pg. 103, B-3
Weston J-9
Wetmore G-8
Wheat Ridge D-8
  Vicinity . . . Pg. 103, E-3
Whitewater E-4
Wiggins C-10
Wild Horse F-11
Wiley G-12
Windsor B-8
Winter Park D-7
Wolcott D-6
Woodland Park . . . E-8
Woodrow C-10
Woody Creek E-6
Wray C-12
Yampa C-6
Yellow Jacket H-3
Yoder F-9
Yuma C-12

CONNECTICUT
Page 24
Population: 3,107,576
Capital: Hartford
Land Area: 4,872 sq. mi.

Andover F-6
Ansonia H-3
Ashford F-7
Avon F-4
Barkhamsted E-4
Berlin G-4
Bethel H-2
Bethlehem G-3
Bloomfield F-4
Branford J-4
Bridgeport J-2
  Vicinity . . . Pg. 128, A-19
Bristol G-4
Brookfield G-2
Brooklyn F-7
Burlington F-4
Byram . . . . . Pg. 128, F-13
Canaan C-4
Cannondale Pg. 128, B-16
Canterbury F-7
Canton F-4
Chaplin F-7
Cheshire G-4
Chester H-6
Clinton J-5
Colchester G-6
Colebrook E-3
Columbia F-6
Cornwall F-2
Cornwall Bridge . . . F-2
Cos Cob . . . Pg. 128, E-13
Coventry F-6
Cranbury . . . Pg. 128, C-17
Cromwell G-5
Danbury H-1
Darien J-2
  Vicinity . . . Pg. 128, D-15
Dayville F-8
Deep River H-6
Derby H-3
Durham G-5
E. Hartland E-4
East Granby F-4
East Hampton G-5
East Hartford F-5
East Haven J-4
East Lyme H-3
East Norwalk
  . . . . . . Pg. 128, D-16
Eastford F-7
Easton . . . . . Pg. 128, A-18
Ellington E-5
Enfield E-5
Essex H-6
Fairfield J-3
  Vicinity . . . Pg. 128, B-18
Falls Vill. E-2
Farmington F-4
Franklin G-7
Georgetown J-2
Glastonbury F-5
Glen Brook . . . Pg. 128, D-15
Glenville . . . Pg. 128, E-12
Goshen F-3
Granby E-4
Greenfield Hill
  . . . . . . Pg. 128, B-18
Greenwich K-1
  Vicinity . . . Pg. 128, E-12
Groton H-7
Guilford J-5
Haddam H-5
Hamden H-4
Hampton F-7
Hartford F-5
Harwinton F-3
Hebron G-6
Kent F-2
Killingworth H-5
Lebanon G-7
Ledyard Ctr. H-7

Litchfield F-3
Long Ridge . Pg. 128, C-13
Madison H-5
Manchester F-5
Marlborough G-5
Melrose E-5
Meriden G-4
Mianus . . . Pg. 128, E-14
Middlefield G-5
Middletown G-5
Milford J-3
Mill Plain . . Pg. 128, C-18
Monroe H-2
Morris G-3
N. Canton E-4
Naugatuck G-3
New Britain G-4
New Canaan J-1
  Vicinity . . . Pg. 128, C-15
New Fairfield G-2
New Hartford F-3
New Haven H-4
New London H-7
New Milford G-2
Newington F-4
Newtown H-2
No. Stonington . . . H-8
Norfolk E-3
Noroton . . . Pg. 128, E-15
Noroton Heights
  . . . . . . Pg. 128, E-15
North Branford . . . H-4
North Haven H-4
North Stamford
  . . . . . . Pg. 128, C-14
North Wilton Pg. 128, B-15
Norwalk J-2
  Vicinity . . . Pg. 128, D-16
Norwich G-7
Old Saybrook J-6
Plainfield F-7
Plymouth F-3
Pomfret F-7
Prospect H-3
Putnam E-8
Redding H-2
Ridgefield H-1
  Vicintiy . . . Pg. 128, A-15
Riverside . . . Pg. 128, F-14
Rocky Hill G-5
Round Hill . . Pg. 128, D-12
Rowayton . . Pg. 128, D-16
Salem H-6
Salisbury E-2
Scotland F-7
Seymour H-3
Sharon F-2
Shelton H-3
Simsbury F-4
Somers E-6
South Norwalk
  . . . . . . Pg. 128, D-16
South Wilton
  . . . . . . Pg. 128, B-16
South Windsor F-5
Southbury G-2
Southington G-4
Southport . . Pg. 128, C-18
Springdale . Pg. 128, D-14
Stafford E-6
Stamford K-1
  Vicinity . . . Pg. 128, D-14
Sterling F-8
Stratford J-3
Suffield E-5
Thomaston G-3
Thompson E-8
Tolland F-6
Torrington F-3
Trumbull J-2
  Vicinity . . . Pg. 128, A-19
Union E-6
Vernon F-6
Voluntown G-8
Wallingford H-4
Warren F-2
Washington G-2
Waterbury G-3
Waterford H-7
Watertown G-3
West Hartford F-4
West Haven J-4
West Norwalk
  . . . . . . Pg. 128, D-15
Westbrook H-5
Westchester G-6
Weston J-2
  Vicinity . . . Pg. 128, A-17
Westport J-2
  Vicinity . . . Pg. 128, C-17
Wethersfield F-5
Willington F-6
Wilton J-2
  Vicinity . . . Pg. 128, B-16
Windsor F-5
Windsor Locks E-5
Winnipauk . . Pg. 128, C-16
Wolcott G-4
Woodbridge H-3
Woodbury G-2
Woodstock E-7

DELAWARE
Page 43
Population: 594,338
Capital: Dover
Land Area: 1,932 sq. mi.

Angola F-15
Bethany Beach . . . F-15
Blades E-13
Bowers Beach . . . D-14
Bridgeville E-14
Camden D-13
Cheswold C-13
Clayton C-13
Delaware City B-13
Dewey Beach E-15
Dover C-13
Ellendale E-14
Elsmere A-13
Felton D-13
Fenwick Is. F-15
Frankford F-15
Frederica D-14
Georgetown F-14
Greenwood E-13
Gumboro F-14
Harbeson F-15
Hardscrabble F-14
Harrington E-13
Hartly D-13
Houston E-14
Laurel F-14
Leipsic C-14
Lewes E-15
Middletown B-13
Milford D-14
Millsboro F-15
Millville F-15
Milton E-14
Mission F-14
New Castle A-13
Newark A-13
Newport A-13
Odessa B-13
Porter B-13
Seaford F-13
Selbyville F-15
Slaughter Beach . . . E-15
Smyrna C-14
Staytonville E-14
Townsend C-13
Wilmington A-14
Wyoming D-13

DIST. OF COLUMBIA
Page 43
Population: 638,333
Capital: Washington
Land Area: 63 sq. mi.

Washington E-8
Vicinity . . . . . Pg. 150

FLORIDA
Pages 26-27
Population: 9,746,324
Capital: Tallahassee
Land Area: 58,560 sq. mi.

Alachua C-5
Altamonte Springs
  . . . . . . Pg. 133, C-4
Apalachicola Q-6
Apollo Beach H-5
  Vicinity . . . Pg. 148, G-6
Apopka F-7
  Vicinity . . . Pg. 133, B-3
Arcadia J-6
Archer D-5
Atlantic Beach . . . B-7
  Vicinity . . . Pg. 111, G-7
Aventura . . . Pg. 120, D-5
Avon Pk. H-7
Bal Harbor . . Pg. 120, E-6
Baldwin B-6
Bartow G-6
Bay Harbor Island
  . . . . . . Pg. 120, E-5
Bay Pines . . Pg. 148, G-3
Bellair . . . . Pg. 111, H-2
Belle Glade K-9
Belle Isle . . Pg. 133, F-5
Belleair . . . Pg. 148, D-2
Belleair Beach
  . . . . . . Pg. 148, D-2
Belleair Bluffs Pg. 148, E-2
Belleair Shores
  . . . . . . Pg. 148, E-1
Belleview E-6
Biscayne Gardens
  . . . . . . Pg. 120, D-5
Biscayne Park
  . . . . . . Pg. 120, E-5
Blountstown P-6
Bloxham B-1
Boca Grande Pg. 108, A-1
Boca Raton L-10
  Vicinity . . . Pg. 120, G-2
Boca West . . Pg. 120, G-2
Bokeelia . . . Pg. 108, B-3
Bonifay N-5
Bonita Spr. L-6
Boynton Beach . . . K-10
  Vicinity . . . Pg. 120, E-2
Bradenton H-5
Brandon G-5
Branford C-4
Briny Breezes Pg. 120, E-2
Bristol P-6
Brooksville F-5
Buenaventura Lakes
  . . . . . . Pg. 133, J-5
Bunnell D-7
Bushnell F-6
Callahan B-6
Callaway P-5
Campbell City Pg. 133, K-4
Cantonment N-2

Cape Coral K-6
  Vicinity . . . Pg. 108, C-5
Captiva . . . Pg. 108, E-2
Carol City . . Pg. 120, E-5
Carrabelle Q-6
Casselberry F-7
  Vicinity . . . Pg. 133, C-5
Cedar Key E-4
Celebration . . Pg. 133, J-2
Chattahoochee . . . A-1
Chiefland D-4
Chipley N-5
Citrus Park . . Pg. 148, B-5
Citrus Spr. E-5
Clarcona . . . Pg. 133, D-3
Clearwater . . Pg. 148, C-3
Clearwater Beach
  . . . . . . Pg. 148, C-2
Clermont F-6
Clewiston K-8
Cloud Lake . . Pg. 120, D-2
Cocoa Beach F-8
Coconut Creek
  . . . . . . Pg. 120, B-5
Cooper City L-9
  Vicinity . . . Pg. 120, D-4
Coral Gables M-9
  Vicinity . . . Pg. 120, D-4
Coral Springs Pg. 120, B-4
Crawfordville C-2
Crescent City D-7
Crestview N-3
Cross City D-4
Crystal Beach
  . . . . . . Pg. 148, C-3
Crystal River E-5
Cutler Ridge . Pg. 120, F-4
Dade City F-6
Dania . . . . Pg. 120, D-5
Davie . . . . Pg. 120, C-4
Daytona Beach E-8
DeBary E-7
DeFuniak Springs . . N-4
DeLeon Springs . . . D-7
Deerfield Beach
  . . . . . . Pg. 120, A-5
Delray Beach K-10
  Vicinity . . . Pg. 120, F-2
Deltona E-7
Dover G-5
  Vicinity . . . Pg. 148, C-3
Dunedin H-4
Dunnellon E-5
East Palatka D-7
Eastpoint Q-6
Eatonville . . Pg. 133, D-4
Edgewater . . Pg. 133, F-5
Edgewood . . Pg. 120, F-5
El Portal . . . Pg. 120, E-5
Ellenton H-5
Englewood J-5
Ensley N-2
Everglades City . . . M-7
Fellsmere H-9
Fernandina Beach . . B-7
Flagler Beach D-7
Florida City M-9
Fort Basinger H-8
Fort Lauderdale . . . L-9
  Vicinity . . . Pg. 120, C-6
Fort Myers . . Pg. 108, C-5
Fort Myers Beach . . K-6
  Vicinity . . . Pg. 108, F-6
Fort Pierce J-9
Fort Walton Beach . . N-3
Fort White C-5
Freeport N-4
Frost Proof H-7
Gainesville D-5
Gifford H-9
Glen Ridge . Pg. 120, D-2
Golden Beach Pg. 120, E-6
Golden Shores
  . . . . . . Pg. 120, E-6
Golf . . . . . Pg. 120, E-2
Golfview . . . Pg. 120, D-2
Green Cove Spr. . . . C-6
Greenacres City
  . . . . . . Pg. 120, D-2
Greenville B-3
Gretna B-1
Grove City J-5
Gulf Stream . Pg. 120, E-2
Gulfport . . . Pg. 148, H-6
Haines City G-7
Hallandale . . Pg. 120, D-5
Havana B-2
Haverhill . . . Pg. 120, D-2
Hawthorne D-6
Hialeah . . . Pg. 120, E-4
Hialeah Gardens
  . . . . . . Pg. 120, E-3
High Springs C-5
Highland Beach
  . . . . . . Pg. 120, F-3
Hilliard A-6
Hillsboro Beach
  . . . . . . Pg. 120, A-6
Hobe Sound J-10
Hollywood . . Pg. 120, B-5
  Vicinity . . . Pg. 120, D-5
Holmes Beach H-5
Homestead M-9
Homosassa E-5
Hosford B-1
Hudson F-5
Hypoluxo . . Pg. 120, E-2
Indian Creek Pg. 120, E-5
Indian Harbour Beach G-8
Indian Rocks Beach
  . . . . . . Pg. 148, E-2
Indian Shores Pg. 148, F-2

Indiantown J-9
Inglis E-5
Intercession City
  . . . . . . Pg. 133, K-3
Inverness E-5
Islamorada P-9
Jacksonville B-7
Jacksonville Beach . . B-7
  Vicinity . . . Pg. 111, G-7
Jasper B-4
Jay M-1
Juno Beach . . Pg. 120, B-3
Jupiter . . . . Pg. 120, A-2
Jupiter Inlet Colony
  . . . . . . Pg. 120, A-3
Kenneth City Pg. 148, F-4
Key Biscayne Pg. 120, G-5
Key Largo N-9
Key West P-6
Keystone Hts. C-6
Kissimmee F-7
  Vicinity . . . Pg. 133, J-4
Kissimmee View
  . . . . . . Pg. 133, J-3
LaBelle K-7
Lacoochee F-6
Lake Buena Vista . . F-7
  Vicinity . . . Pg. 133, H-2
Lake City C-5
Lake Clarke Shores
  . . . . . . Pg. 120, D-2
Lake Mary . . Pg. 133, A-5
Lake Park K-9
  Vicinity . . . Pg. 120, B-3
Lake Wales G-7
Lake Worth . . Pg. 120, D-4
Lakeland G-6
Lantana K-10
  Vicinity . . . Pg. 120, E-2
Largo . . . . Pg. 148, E-2
  Vicinity . . . Pg. 120, G-4
Lauderdale Lakes
  . . . . . . Pg. 120, B-5
Lauderdale-By-The-Sea
  . . . . . . Pg. 120, B-6
Lauderhill . . Pg. 120, B-5
Leesburg E-6
Lehigh Acres K-7
Lighthouse Pt. L-10
Live Oak B-4
Longboat Key H-5
Longwood . . Pg. 133, B-4
Lutz . . . . . Pg. 148, A-7
Lynn Haven P-5
Macclenny B-6
Madeira Beach
  . . . . . . Pg. 148, G-3
Madison B-3
Magnolia Park
  . . . . . . Pg. 133, D-5
Maitland . . . Pg. 133, D-5
Manalapan . . Pg. 120, E-2
Mangonia Park
  . . . . . . Pg. 120, C-3
Marathon P-8
Marco Is. L-6
Margate . . . Pg. 120, B-5
Marianna N-5
Matlacha . . Pg. 108, C-4
Mayo C-4
Medley . . . Pg. 120, E-4
Melbourne G-9
Merritt Island F-8
Miami M-9
  Vicinity . . . Pg. 120, D-5
Miami Beach M-10
  Vicinity . . . Pg. 120, E-5
Miami Lakes Pg. 120, E-4
Miami Shores Pg. 120, E-5
Miami Springs . . . M-9
  Vicinity . . . Pg. 120, E-4
Mims F-8
Milton N-2
Miramar . . . Pg. 120, D-3
Monticello B-2
Moore Haven K-8
Mount Dora E-6
Naples L-6
Naples Pk. L-6
Narcoossee . Pg. 133, J-7
Neptune Beach . . . B-7
  Vicinity . . . Pg. 111, G-7
New Port Richey . . . G-5
New Smyrna Beach . . E-8
Niceville N-3
North Bay Village
  . . . . . . Pg. 120, E-5
North Fort Myers
  . . . . . . Pg. 108, B-7
North Lauderdale . . L-9
  Vicinity . . . Pg. 120, B-5
North Miami . Pg. 120, E-5
North Miami Beach
  . . . . . . Pg. 120, E-5
  Vicinity . . . Pg. 120, D-5
North Palm Beach . . K-10
  Vicinity . . . Pg. 120, B-3
North Port J-6
North Redington Beach
  . . . . . . Pg. 148, F-2
Oakland . . . Pg. 133, E-4
Oakland Park L-10
  Vicinity . . . Pg. 120, B-5
Ocala E-6
Ocean Ridge Pg. 120, E-3
Ocoee . . . . Pg. 133, D-3
Okeechobee J-8
Oldsmar . . . Pg. 148, C-6
Opa-Locka L-9
  Vicinity . . . Pg. 120, E-4
Orange Pk. C-6
Orlando F-7
  Vicinity . . . Pg. 133
Ormand by the Sea . . D-8
Ormond Beach D-8

FLORIDA

Osprey J-5
Oviedo . . . Pg. 133, C-7
Ozona . . . . Pg. 148, B-3
Pace N-2
Palatka D-6
Palm Bay G-9
Palm Beach Gardens
  . . . . . . Pg. 120, B-2
Palm Harbor Pg. 148, B-3
Palm Springs Pg. 120, D-2
Panama City P-5
Parkland . . Pg. 120, A-5
Pembroke G-6
Pembroke Park
  . . . . . . Pg. 120, D-5
Pembroke Pines . . . G-6
  Vicinity . . . Pg. 120, D-3
Pensacola N-2
Perrine M-9
Perry C-3
Pineland . . . Pg. 108, B-3
Pinellas Park Pg. 148, F-4
Plant City G-6
Plantation . . Pg. 120, C-5
Plymouth . . . Pg. 133, C-2
Pompano Beach . . . L-10
  Vicinity . . . Pg. 120, B-5
Port Charlotte J-6
Port St. Joe P-5
Port St. Lucie H-9
Punta Gorda L-6
Quincy B-1
Reddick D-5
Redington Beach
  . . . . . . Pg. 148, G-2
Redington Shores
  . . . . . . Pg. 148, F-2
Richmond Hts. M-9
Ridge Manor F-5
Riviera Beach K-10
  Vicinity . . . Pg. 120, C-2
Rockledge F-8
Rotonda K-6
Royal Palm Beach
  . . . . . . Pg. 120, C-1
Runnymede . Pg. 133, K-7
Ruskin . . . . Pg. 148, H-7
Safety Harbor Pg. 148, C-4
Sanford E-7
  Vicinity . . . Pg. 133, A-6
Sanibel K-6
  Vicinity . . . Pg. 108, F-4
Sarasota J-5
Satellite Beach . . . G-8
Sea Ranch Lakes
  . . . . . . Pg. 120, B-6
Sebastian H-9
Sebring H-7
Seminole . . Pg. 148, F-2
Semoran . . Pg. 133, C-5
Sneads N-6
Sopchoppy C-1
South Bay K-8
South Miami Pg. 120, G-4
South Palm Beach
  . . . . . . Pg. 120, D-3
South Pasadena
  . . . . . . Pg. 148, G-3
South Venice J-5
Spring Lake H-7
Springfield P-5
St. Augustine C-7
St. Augustine Beach . C-7
St. Cloud G-7
  Vicinity . . . Pg. 133, K-6
St. James City
  . . . . . . Pg. 108, E-4
St. Pete Beach Pg. 148, H-3
St. Petersburg H-5
  Vicinity . . . Pg. 148, G-5
Stuart J-10
Sun City . . . Pg. 148, J-7
Sun City Ctr. H-5
  Vicinity . . . Pg. 148, H-8
Sunny Isles Pg. 120, D-5
Sunrise . . . Pg. 120, B-4
Surfside . . . Pg. 120, E-6
Sweetwater . Pg. 120, F-3
Taft . . . . . Pg. 133, G-5
Tallahassee B-2
Tamarac . . . Pg. 120, B-4
Tampa G-5
  Vicinity . . . Pg. 148, D-7
Tarpon Springs . . . G-5
  Vicinity . . . Pg. 148, A-2
Temple Terrace
  . . . . . . Pg. 148, C-7
Tennille C-3
Thomas City B-2
Tice K-6
Titusville F-8
Treasure Island . . . H-4
  Vicinity . . . Pg. 148, G-3
Trenton D-4
Truckland . Pg. 108, D-6
Tuskawilla . . Pg. 133, C-6
Umitilla E-6
Valparaiso N-3
Venice J-5
Vero Beach H-9
Virginia Gardens
  . . . . . . Pg. 120, F-4
Warrington N-2
Watertown C-5
Wauchula H-6
Wausau N-5
Waverly G-7
West Melbourne . . . G-8
West Miami . Pg. 120, F-4
West Palm Beach
  . . . . . . Pg. 120, C-2
Westwood Lakes . . . M-9
Wewahitchka P-5
White City Q-5
Wildwood E-6

FLORIDA

Williston D-5
Wilma P-6
Wilton Manors . . . . Pg. 120, B-6
Windermere . . . Pg. 133, F-2
Winter Garden F-7
Vicinity . . . . . Pg. 133, D-2
Winter Park F-7
Vicinity . . . . . Pg. 133, C-6
Winter Springs F-7
Vicinity . . . . . Pg. 133, C-6
Woodville B-2
Zellwood . . . . . . Pg. 133, B-1
Zephyrhills G-5
Zolfo Spr. H-6

GEORGIA
Pages 28-29
Population: 6,478,216
Capital: Atlanta
Land Area: 54,153 sq. mi.

Abbeville K-5
Acworth F-3
Adairsville E-2
Adams Park . . Pg. 90, H-3
Adamsville . . Pg. 90, F-2
Adel M-5
Adrian J-7
Alamo K-6
Alapaha L-5
Albany M-4
Aldora H-4
Allentown L-7
Alma L-7
Alpharetta E-4
Alston K-7
Alto E-5
Alvaton H-3
Ambrose L-6
Americus K-4
Amsterdam N-3
Andersonville K-3
Apalachee F-5
Apple Valley . Pg. 90, G-7
Appling G-7
Arabi K-4
Aragon F-2
Arlington L-3
Arnoldsville F-6
Ashburn L-4
Ashford Park . Pg. 90, C-5
Ashley Farms . Pg. 90, H-3
Athens F-5
Atlanta F-4
Vicinity . . . . Pg. 90
Attapulgus N-3
Augusta G-7
Austell F-3
Avalon E-6
Avondale Estates . . . . . . Pg. 90, F-6
Axson M-6
Baconton M-4
Bainbridge N-3
Baldwin E-5
Ball Ground E-4
Barnesville H-4
Barney M-5
Barwick N-5
Baxley L-7
Bellview L-2
Belvedere Gardens . . . . . Pg. 90, F-6
Benevolence K-3
Ben Hill . . . Pg. 90, H-2
Berkeley Lake . Pg. 90, A-7
Berlin M-5
Berryton E-1
Between F-5
Bishop F-5
Blackshear L-8
Blakely L-2
Blue Creek . Pg. 90, H-6
Blue Ridge D-3
Blufton L-2
Bonaire J-5
Boston N-4
Boulder Park . Pg. 90, F-6
Bowden G-2
Bowersville E-6
Bowman E-6
Boykin M-3
Bradley Acres Pg. 90, D-1
Bremen F-2
Briarcliff Woods . . . . . . Pg. 90, D-6
Bridgeboro L-4
Bristol L-7
Bronwood L-3
Brookhaven . Pg. 90, D-5
Brookstone . Pg. 90, J-7
Brook Hollow . Pg. 90, D-7
Brook Glen . Pg. 90, D-7
Broxton L-6
Brunswick M-9
Buchanan F-2
Buckhead . Pg. 90, D-4
Buena Vista J-3
Buford E-4
Butler J-3
Byron J-5
Cadwell J-6
Cairo N-4
Calhoun E-2
Calvary N-3
Camilla M-3
Candler E-6
Canon E-6
Canoochee H-7
Canton E-3

Cardinal Woods . . . . Pg. 90, D-7
Carnegie L-2
Carrollton G-2
Cartersville E-2
Cascade Knolls . . . . Pg. 90, G-1
Cave Spring E-2
Cecil M-5
Cedar Springs M-2
Cedartown F-2
Center F-5
Center Hill . Pg. 90, F-3
Centerville M-2
Chamblee . Pg. 90, C-5
Chatsworth D-2
Chauncey K-5
Cherokee Pines . . . . Pg. 90, C-1
Chester J-6
Chickamauga D-2
Cisco D-3
Clarkesville D-5
Clarkston . Pg. 90, E-7
Claxton K-8
Clayton D-5
Cleveland D-4
Climax N-3
Clyattville N-5
Clyo J-9
Cobbtown J-8
Cochran J-5
Cogdell M-6
Cohutta D-2
Colemans Lake H-7
College Park . Pg. 90, H-3
Collier Heights Pg. 90, F-2
Colquitt M-3
Columbia Valley . . . . . . Pg. 90, G-6
Columbus J-2
Comer E-6
Commerce E-5
Conley . . . . . Pg. 90, J-5
Conyers F-4
Coolidge M-4
Cordele K-4
Cornelia E-5
Cotton M-4
Covena J-7
Covington G-5
Crandall D-3
Crawford F-5
Crawfordville G-6
Creekwood Hills . . . . . . Pg. 90, H-7
Culloden H-4
Cumberland . Pg. 90, C-3
Cumming E-4
Cusseta J-2
Cuthbert L-2
Dacula F-4
Dahlonega D-4
Dallas F-3
Damascus M-3
Danielsville E-6
Darien L-9
Dasher N-6
Davis Woods . Pg. 90, C-4
Davisboro H-7
Dawson L-3
Dawsonville E-4
Decatur . Pg. 90, F-6
Demorest E-5
Dexter M-4
Doerun M-4
Donalsonville M-2
Doraville . Pg. 90, C-6
Douglas L-6
Douglasville F-3
Dublin J-6
Duluth E-4
Dunaire . Pg. 90, E-7
Dunwoody . Pg. 90, B-5
Dupont M-6
East Atlanta . Pg. 90, G-5
East Dublin J-6
East Point F-3
Vicinity . Pg. 90, H-3
Eastglen . Pg. 90, H-7
Eastman K-6
Eatonton G-5
Edgehill H-7
Edgewood . Pg. 90, F-6
Edison L-3
Elberton E-6
Elko J-5
Ellaville K-3
Ellenton L-5
Ellenwood . Pg. 90, J-6
Ellijay D-3
Emerson E-3
Empire J-5
Enigma L-6
Enon Forest . Pg. 90, H-1
Evans F-8
Faceville N-3
Fair Oaks . Pg. 90, B-1
Fairburn . Pg. 90, K-1
Fairmount E-3
Falconhurst . Pg. 90, J-2
Fargo N-7
Fayetteville G-4
Feldwood Pines . . . . Pg. 90, K-2
Fernandina Beach . Pg. 90, J-5
Fernwood . Pg. 90, J-5
Finleyson K-5
Fitzgerald L-5
Flairsville D-4
Flemington K-9
Folkston N-8
Forest Park . Pg. 90, H-4
Vicinity . . . . Pg. 90, J-4

Forsyth H-4
Fort Gaines L-2
Fort Gillem . Pg. 90, J-5
Fort Oglethorpe D-2
Fort Valley J-4
Franklin G-2
Franklin Springs E-6
Gainesville E-4
Garden City K-9
Geneva J-3
Georgetown K-2
Gibson G-7
Gillsville E-5
Girard H-9
Glennville K-8
Glenwood K-7
Gordon H-5
Gracewood G-8
Grantville G-2
Gray H-5
Green Oaks . Pg. 90, H-2
Greenbriar . Pg. 90, H-2
Greensboro F-6
Greenville H-3
Gresham . Pg. 90, E-1
Griffin H-4
Grovania J-5
Grove Park . Pg. 90, F-3
Grove Town G-7
Haddock H-6
Hagan K-8
Hahira M-5
Hamilton H-2
Hampton G-4
Hapeville . Pg. 90, H-3
Haralson H-3
Harlem G-7
Harrison H-6
Hartwell E-6
Hawkinsville K-5
Haynes Manor Pg. 90, E-4
Hazlehurst K-7
Heatherwood . Pg. 90, K-3
Helen D-5
Helena K-6
Hephzibah G-7
Herod L-3
Hiawassee D-5
Hickox M-8
Hilltonia H-9
Hilton M-2
Hinesville K-9
Hoboken M-8
Hogansville G-3
Holly Springs E-3
Hollydale . Pg. 90, K-3
Homeland M-8
Homer E-5
Homerville M-7
Horseshoe Bend . . . . . . Pg. 90, A-6
Ideal J-4
Idlewood . Pg. 90, K-5
Ila E-6
Indian Crossing . . . . Pg. 90, B-7
Irwinton H-5
Irwinville L-5
Ivey H-5
Jackson G-4
Jacksonville K-6
Jasper E-3
Jefferson E-5
Jeffersonville J-5
Jesup L-8
Jonesboro G-3
Juno N-9
Kingsland N-9
Kingston E-2
Kirkwood . Pg. 90, F-5
Kite H-7
Knight Park . Pg. 90, E-3
Knoxville H-4
La Grange H-2
LaFayette D-2
Lake City . Pg. 90, K-5
Lake Park N-6
Lakeland M-6
Lakemont D-5
Lakeshore Estates . . . . . Pg. 90, D-1
Lakewood . Pg. 90, H-4
Lavonia E-6
Lawrenceville F-4
Leary L-3
Leesburg L-4
Leland . . . . . Pg. 90, E-1
Lenox M-5
Lenox Park . Pg. 90, K-4
Leslie K-4
Lexington F-6
Lilburn F-4
Lilly J-5
Lincolndale . Pg. 90, J-6
Lincolnton F-7
Lindmoor . Pg. 90, E-6
Lithonia F-5
Lockheed . Pg. 90, B-1
Locust Grove G-4
Loganville F-5
London Park . Pg. 90, F-7
Louisville H-7
Lovett H-6
Ludowici L-8
Lula E-5
Lumber City K-6
Lumpkin K-3
Luthersville H-3
Lyons J-7
Macon H-5
Madison F-5
Manchester H-3
Mangum Manor Pg. 90, H-4
Manor M-7

Margret D-4
Marietta F-3
Vicinity . . . . Pg. 90, B-1
Marshallville J-4
Maxeys F-6
Maysville E-5
McCaysville D-3
McIntire H-6
McRae K-6
Meadow Lake . Pg. 90, B-5
Meigs M-4
Menlo Park . Pg. 90, K-6
Merrillville M-7
Metcalf N-4
Metter J-8
Middleton F-6
Midtown . Pg. 90, E-4
Midville H-7
Milan K-6
Milledgeville H-6
Millen H-8
Mineral Bluff D-4
Modoc H-7
Molena N-4
Moncrief F-5
Monroe F-5
Montevista . Pg. 90, G-1
Montezuma J-4
Monticello G-5
Morgan L-3
Morganton D-4
Morningside . Pg. 90, E-4
Morris K-2
Morrow . Pg. 90, K-5
Morven M-5
Moultrie M-4
Mountain City D-5
Mountain View Pg. 90, J-4
Mt. Airy D-5
Mt. Vernon K-7
Mt. Zion F-2
Nahunta M-8
Nashville M-6
Naylor N-6
Nelson E-4
Newington J-9
Newnan G-2
Newton M-3
Nicholls L-7
Norcross . Pg. 90, B-7
Norman Park M-4
Norristown J-7
North Atlanta . Pg. 90, C-5
Northlake . Pg. 90, D-6
Northridge . Pg. 90, A-5
Oak Park J-7
Oakfield L-4
Oakland City . Pg. 90, G-3
Oakman D-3
Oakwood E-5
Ochlocknee M-4
Ocilla L-6
Odum L-8
Offerman L-8
Oglethorpe J-4
Ohoopee J-7
Oliver J-9
Omaha K-2
Omega L-5
Orchard Knob . Pg. 90, H-4
Oxford G-3
Palmetto G-3
Panola Woods Pg. 90, J-6
Panthersville . Pg. 90, H-6
Parrott K-3
Patterson L-8
Pavo M-4
Peachtree City G-3
Pearson M-6
Pebblebrook Estates . . . . Pg. 90, E-2
Pelman K-9
Pembroke K-9
Penhurst . Pg. 90, A-3
Percale H-4
Perkerson . Pg. 90, H-4
Perry J-5
Philomath F-6
Piedmont Heights . . . . . . Pg. 90, E-4
Pine Lake . Pg. 90, E-7
Pine Park N-4
Pinehurst K-5
Pineview K-5
Vicinity . Pg. 90, J-2
Pitts K-5
Pittsburg . Pg. 90, C-7
Plains K-3
Ponderosa . Pg. 90, K-2
Pooler K-9
Portal J-8
Poulan L-5
Preston K-3
Pulaski N-5
Quitman N-5
Radium Springs L-4
Raleigh H-3
Ranger D-3
Ray City M-6
Rayle F-6
Red Oak . Pg. 90, J-2
Regency Park Pg. 90, G-1
Reidsville K-8
Resaca D-2
Revecca K-5
Rex . . . . Pg. 90, J-5
Reynolds J-4
Richland K-3
Richmond Hill K-9
Richmond Oaks . . . . Pg. 90, G-4
Rincon J-9
Riverdale . . . . . Pg. 90, K-4
Roberta H-4
Robins J-4

Rochelle K-5
Rockmart F-2
Rocky Ford H-8
Rome E-2
Roopville G-2
Roswell E-3
Round Hill . Pg. 90, C-4
Saffold M-2
Sale City M-4
Sandersville H-6
Sandy Springs Pg. 90, B-4
Sardis H-9
Sasser L-3
Savannah K-10
Scarborough Crossroads . . Pg. 90, J-7
Scottdale . Pg. 90, E-6
Screven L-8
Senoia G-3
Seville K-5
Shady Dale G-5
Shellman L-3
Shiloh H-3
Six Flags . Pg. 90, F-1
Smithville K-4
Smyrna . Pg. 90, C-2
Social Circle F-5
Somerset . Pg. 90, B-3
Soperton J-7
Southwest . Pg. 90, G-2
Spalding Bridge . . . . Pg. 90, A-7
Sparks M-5
Sparta G-6
Springfield J-9
Vicinity . Pg. 90, K-5
St. George N-8
St. Marys N-9
St. Simons Island M-9
Stagecoach Hills . . . . . . Pg. 90, K-7
Statenville N-6
Statesboro J-8
Stillmore J-7
Stockbridge G-4
Stockton M-6
Stone Mountain F-4
Stonewall . Pg. 90, K-1
Strasburg . Pg. 90, H-2
Suches D-4
Sugar Hill E-4
Summertown H-7
Summerville E-1
Sumner L-4
Sun Valley . Pg. 90, J-2
Surrency L-8
Suwanee E-4
Swainsboro J-7
Sycamore L-4
Sylvan Hills . Pg. 90, G-3
Sylvania H-9
Sylvester L-4
Talbotton J-3
Tallulah Falls D-5
Talmo L-7
Tarrytown J-6
Tarver N-6
Tarversville J-5
Tazewell J-3
Tecal . . . . . Pg. 90, H-2
Tenille H-7
Tennga D-3
Thomaston H-4
Thomasville N-4
Thomson G-7
Thornhedge . Pg. 90, K-3
Thunderbolt K-10
Tifton L-5
Tignall F-7
Toccoa D-5
Toco Hills . Pg. 90, E-5
Toombsboro H-6
Towns K-6
Toyston E-6
Trenton D-1
Trion D-2
Tuxedo Park . Pg. 90, D-4
Twin City J-8
Ty Ty L-5
Unadilla J-5
Union City F-3
Vicinity . Pg. 90, K-1
Union Point F-6
Uvalda K-7
Valdosta N-6
Van Wert F-2
Vanna E-6
Vidalia J-7
Vienna K-4
Villa Rica F-2
Vinings . Pg. 90, D-3
Wadley H-7
Waleska E-3
Waresboro M-7
Warlick . Pg. 90, J-2
Warner H-5
Warrenton G-6
Warthen H-6
Warwick K-4
Washington F-6
Watkinsville F-6
Watts Road . Pg. 90, E-2
Waycross M-7
Waynesboro H-8
Wayside . Pg. 90, G-2
Wesley Chapel . . . . Pg. 90, G-7
West End . Pg. 90, G-3
West Point H-2
Whigham N-3
White E-3
Whitesburg G-2
Wildwood . Pg. 90, E-4
Willacoochee L-6

Winder F-5
Winterthur . Pg. 90, B-3
Woodbine M-8
Woodbury H-3
Woodcliff . Pg. 90, A-4
Woodcrest . Pg. 90, J-6
Woodland H-3
Woodmont Landins . . . . . Pg. 90, B-6
Wrens G-7
Wrightsville H-7
Zebulon H-4

HAWAII
Page 30
Population: 964,691
Capital: Honolulu
Land Area: 6,425 sq. mi.

Aiea G-6
Anahola D-3
Apole Pt C-9
Apua Pt G-10
Barbers Pt G-4
Cape Halawa A-6
Cape Hanamanioa C-8
Captain Cook F-9
Eleele F-2
Ewa G-5
Glenwood F-9
Haena D-2
Haena Pt D-2
Haiku A-9
Hakalau F-10
Halawa A-6
Haleiwa F-4
Hana B-10
Hanalei D-2
Hanamalo Pt G-8
Hanamaulu E-3
Hanapepe F-1
Hauula F-6
Hawaii Kai G-6
Hawi E-9
Hekili Pt B-7
Hilo F-10
Honaunau F-8
Honohina E-10
Honokaa E-9
Honokahua A-7
Honolulu G-5
Honuapo F-8
Hookena F-8
Ka Lae G-9
Kaalualu G-9
Kaena Pt G-10
Kahakuloa Pt A-8
Kahaluu F-6
Kahana F-6
Kahlu Pt A-4
Kahuku E-5
Kahuku Pt. E-5
Kahului A-8
Kailua (Hawaii) F-8
Kailua (Oahu) G-7
Kaimu F-10
Kainaliu F-8
Kaka Pt E-7
Kalae A-5
Kalaheo F-2
Kalahu Pt B-10
Kalalau D-2
Kalaoa G-10
Kalapana F-8
Kamalo A-5
Kamiloloa A-5
Kaneohe G-6
Kapaa E-3
Kaumakani F-1
Kauna Pt G-8
Kaunakakai A-5
Kaupo B-9
Kawahae E-8
Keaau F-10
Keahole Pt E-8
Kealia E-3
Keauhou F-8
Kekaha A-3
Keokea B-8
Keomuku D-7
Kepuhi Pt B-8
Kihei B-8
Kikipua Pt A-7
Kilauea D-2
Kipahulu B-10
Koele D-6
Koheo Pt A-7
Koko Head G-7
Kolo A-4
Koloa F-2
Kualapapa A-4
Kualoa Pt A-5
Kukaiau F-10
Kukuihaele F-10
Kurtistown F-10
Laau Pt A-3
Lahaina A-7
Laie E-6
Lamaloa Head A-5
Lanai City D-6
Lawai F-2
Lihue E-3
Lilo Pt A-8
Maalaea B-8
Mahukona E-9
Maili G-4
Makaha G-4
Makaha Pt D-1
Makahuena Pt F-3
Makakilo City G-4

Makanalua Pen A-5
Makapuu Pt G-7
Makawao A-9
Makena B-8
Mana E-1
Mauna Loa A-4
Mililani Town F-5
Miloli G-8
Mokapu Pt. F-7
Moloaa D-3
Mopua B-7
Mountain View F-9
Muolea Pt. B-10
Naalehu G-9
Nakalele Pt. A-7
Nanakuli F-8
Napoopoo F-8
Nawiliwili E-3
Ninini Pt. E-3
Niulii E-9
Nukuele Pt. C-8
Olowalu B-7
Ookala E-9
Opihikao F-10
Pahala F-9
Pahoa F-10
Paia A-8
Papa G-9
Papaaloa E-10
Papaikou F-10
Paukaa F-10
Pauwalu A-6
Pauwela A-8
Pauwela Pt. A-8
Pearl City F-5
Pearl Harbor F-9
Pepeekeo E-10
Pepeekeo Pt. F-10
Pohoiki F-10
Port Allen F-2
Puako E-8
Puhi E-3
Pukaulua Pt. A-10
Pukoo A-5
Puunene A-8
Puuwai B-1
Spreckleisville A-8
Sunset Beach F-5
Ulapue A-5
Ulupalakua B-9
Upola Pt. E-9
Wahiawa F-5
Waiahukini G-9
Waiaka F-10
Waialua (Molokai) A-6
Waialua (Oahu) F-4
Waianae F-4
Waihee Pt. A-8
Waikiki B-8
Wailea B-8
Wailua (Kauai) E-3
Wailua (Maui) A-9
Wailuku A-8
Waimanalo G-7
Waimea (Hawaii) E-8
Waimea (Kauai) E-1
Waiohinu G-9
Waipahu G-5

IDAHO
Page 31
Population: 943,935
Capital: Boise
Land Area: 82,413 sq. mi.

Ahsahka D-2
American Falls J-5
Arco H-5
Arimo J-6
Ashton G-7
Atlanta H-3
Atomic City H-5
Avery C-3
Bellevue H-4
Bigby H-6
Blackfoot H-6
Bliss J-4
Blue Dome G-5
Boise H-3
Bonners Ferry A-2
Bovill D-2
Bruneau J-3
Burley H-5
Butte City H-2
Caldwell H-2
Carey H-4
Cascade G-3
Cataldo C-2
Challis G-4
Chubbuck J-6
Coeur D'Alene C-2
Colburn B-2
Cottonwood D-2
Craigmont D-2
Deary D-2
Declo J-5
Downey J-6
Dubois G-6
Eagle H-2
Eastport A-2
Elba J-5
Elk City E-3
Elk River D-3
Emmett H-2
Fairfield H-4
Fernan Lake C-2
Garden City H-2
Gibbonsville F-4
Golden E-3

Gooding J-4
Grand View J-3
Grangeville E-3
Hagerman J-4
Hailey H-4
Hamer G-6
Harpster E-3
Harvard C-2
Headquarters D-3
Hill City H-3
Holbrook K-6
Hollister J-4
Homedale H-2
Hope B-3
Horseshoe Bend G-2
Howe H-5
Idaho City H-3
Idaho Falls H-6
Jerome J-4
Kamiah D-3
Kellogg C-3
Ketchum H-4
King Hill J-3
Kooskia E-3
Kuna H-2
Lamb Creek A-2
Leadore F-5
Lemhi F-5
Lewiston D-2
Lowell D-3
Lowman G-3
Mackay G-5
Malad City K-6
Malta K-5
May G-4
McCall F-3
Meridian H-2
Middleton H-2
Minidoka J-4
Montpelier J-7
Moreland H-6
Moscow C-2
Mountain Home H-3
Moyie Springs A-3
Mud Lake H-6
Mullan C-3
Murphy H-2
Myrtle D-2
Nampa H-2
Naples A-3
New Meadows F-2
New Plymouth H-2
North Fork E-4
Orofino D-2
Osburn C-3
Patterson G-5
Payette G-2
Pierce D-2
Plummer C-2
Pocatello J-6
Pollock F-2
Porthill A-2
Preston J-7
Rexburg H-6
Ririe H-6
Roberts H-6
Rock Creek J-4
Rockland J-5
Salmon F-4
Samaria J-6
Sandpoint B-2
Shoshone J-4
Silver City J-2
Soda Springs J-7
Spencer G-6
Spirit Lake B-2
Springfield B-2
St. Joe C-3
Sunbeam G-4
Troy D-2
Twin Falls J-4
Victor H-7
Wallace C-3
Weiser G-2
White Bird E-2
Woodland D-3
Worley C-2

ILLINOIS
Page 32-33
Population: 11,426,518
Capital: Springfield
Land Area: 55,645 sq. mi.

Abingdon C-5
Addison . . . . Pg. 98, H-
Albany . . . . D-
Albion H-1
Aledo . . . . C-
Alexis . . . . C-
Algonquin . . . . Pg. 96, A-
Alhambra D-1
Allendale H-1
Allerton . . . . H-
Alma F-1
Alorton . . . . . . Pg. 140, G-
Alpha . . . . C-
Alpine . . . . Pg. 99, L-
Alsip . . . . Pg. 99, K-
Altamont . . . . E-
Alto Pass . . . . D-
Alton . . . . D-
Alvin . . . . E-
Amboy . . . . E
Andover . . . . E-
Anna . . . . D
Annawan . . . . D
Antioch . . . . Pg. 96, A
Aptakisic . . . . . . Pg. 96, E
Arcola . . . . E
Argenta . . . . E

ILLINOIS

Arlington E-3
Arlington Heights ... Pg. 96, F-4
Arthur G-8
Ashland D-8
Ashley F-12
Ashmore H-8
Ashton E-2
Assumption F-9
Astoria C-7
Athens D-7
Atkinson D-3
Atlanta E-7
Atwood G-8
Auburn D-8
Aubury Hills . Pg. 99, M-6
Augusta B-7
Aurora G-3
  Vicinity .... Pg. 98, J-2
Ava E-13
Avon C-6
Baldmond H-1
Bannockburn . Pg. 97, E-5
Barrington .. Pg. 96, E-3
Barrington Hills Pg. 96, F-3
Barry E-8
Bartlett ..... Pg. 96, G-3
Bartonville D-6
Batavia ...... Pg. 98, H-2
Beardstown C-7
Beckemeyer E-11
Bedford Park . Pg. 99, J-6
Beecher City F-9
Belle Rive F-12
Belleville D-11
Bellflower G-6
Bellmont H-11
Bellwood ..... Pg. 99, H-5
Belvidere F-1
Bement G-7
Bensenville . Pg. 96, G-5
Benson E-5
Benton F-12
Berkeley ..... Pg. 99, H-5
Berwyn H-6
  Vicinity .... Pg. 99, H-6
Bethalto D-10
Bethany F-8
Biggsville B-5
Bloomingdale Pg. 96, G-4
Bloomington E-6
Blue Island . Pg. 99, K-7
Blue Mound E-8
Bluffs C-8
Bolingbrook H-2
  Vicinity .... Pg. 98, K-4
Bourbonnais H-4
Bowen B-7
Bradford E-4
Bradley H-4
Braidwood H-4
Bridgeview . Pg. 99, J-6
Brighton C-10
Brimfield D-5
Broadview ... Pg. 99, H-5
Brookfield .. Pg. 99, J-6
Brookport G-15
Brownstown F-10
Buckley H-6
Buffalo Grove Pg. 96, E-4
Bull Valley D-2
Bunker Hill D-10
Burbank ...... Pg. 99, K-6
Burnham ...... Pg. 99, L-8
Burr Ridge .. Pg. 98, J-5
Burtons Bridge Pg. 96, D-3
Bush F-13
Bushnell C-6
Byron E-2
Cabery G-5
Cahokia C-11
  Vicinity ... Pg. 140, G-7
Cairo G-16
Calumet City . Pg. 99, L-8
Calumet Park Pg. 99, H-6
Cambridge C-4
Camden B-7
Camp Point B-7
Campbell Hill E-13
Canton D-6
Capron F-1
Carbondale E-13
Carlinville D-9
Carlyle E-11
Carmi G-12
Carol Stream . Pg. 98, H-3
Carpentersville Pg. 96, F-2
Carriers Mills ... F-13
Carrollton C-9
Carterville F-13
Carthage A-6
Cary .... Pg. 96, E-2
Casey H-9
Caton Farm . Pg. 98, L-3
Cave-In-Rock H-14
Cedarville D-1
Central City F-11
Centralia E-11
Cerro Gordo F-7
Chadwick D-2
Champaign G-7
Chandlerville C-7
Channel Lake B-3
Chapin C-8
Charleston H-9
Chatham D-8
Chatsworth G-5
Chebanse H-5
Chenoa F-5
Cherry Valley F-1
Chester J-2
Chesterfield D-9
  Vicinity .... Pg. 96

Chicago Heights .. J-3
  Vicinity .... Pg. 99, M-7
Chicago Ridge Pg. 99, K-6
Chillicothe E-5
Chrisman H-8
Cicero .... Pg. 99, H-6
Cisco F-7
Cisne G-11
Clarendon Hills Pg. 98, J-5
Clay City G-11
Clayton B-7
Clifton H-5
Clinton F-7
Cloverdale .. Pg. 98, F-2
Coal Village C-4
Cobden E-14
Coffeen E-10
Colchester B-6
Colfax G-6
Collinsville D-11
Columbia C-11
  Vicinity ... Pg. 140, J-5
Compton E-3
Cordova C-3
Cornell G-5
Coulterville E-12
Country Club Hills ... Pg. 99, L-6
Countryside . Pg. 99, J-5
Cowden F-9
Creal Springs F-13
Crest Hill .. Pg. 98, L-3
Crestwood ... Pg. 99, L-6
Crete F-9
  Vicinity .... Pg. 99, M-7
Creve Coeur E-6
Crystal Lake G-1
  Vicinity .... Pg. 96, D-2
Cuba C-5
Cullom G-5
Cutler E-12
Dakota E-1
Dallas City B-6
Damiansville E-11
Danville J-7
Darien .... Pg. 98, J-5
De Kalb F-2
De Soto E-13
Decatur F-8
Deer Grove E-3
Deer Park ... Pg. 96, E-4
Deerfield ... Pg. 97, E-5
Delavan E-6
Des Plaines . Pg. 97, F-5
  Vicinity .... Pg. 96, D-4
Dieterich G-10
Divernon E-9
Dix F-11
Dixmoor ...... Pg. 99, L-7
Dixon E-3
Dolton .... Pg. 99, L-7
Donovan H-5
Downers Grove H-3
  Vicinity .... Pg. 98, J-4
Du Quoin E-12
Dunfermline D-6
Dunlap D-5
Dupo .... Pg. 140, H-5
Dwight F-4
Earlville F-3
East Carondelet ... Pg. 140, H-5
East Chicago Heights ... Pg. 99, K-7
East Dubuque C-1
East Dundee . Pg. 96, F-2
East Hazelcrest ... Pg. 99, L-7
East Peoria E-5
East St. Louis ... D-11
  Vicinity ... Pg. 140, G-7
Easton D-7
Eddyville G-14
Edgewood G-10
Edinburg E-8
Effingham F-10
El Paso F-5
Elburn H-1
Eldorado G-13
Elgin G-2
  Vicinity .... Pg. 96, G-2
Elizabeth C-1
Elizabethtown G-14
Elk Grove Village ... Pg. 96, G-4
Elkhart E-7
Elkville E-13
Elliot G-6
Ellis Grove D-12
Elmhurst H-2
  Vicinity .... Pg. 99, H-5
Elmwood Park Pg. 99, H-6
Enfield G-12
Eola .... Pg. 98, J-3
Equality G-13
Erie D-3
Eureka E-5
Evanston J-2
  Vicinity .... Pg. 97, G-7
Evansville D-12
Evergreen Park ... Pg. 99, K-7
Fairbury G-5
Fairfield G-11
Fairmont .... Pg. 98, L-4
Fairview C-6
Farina F-10
Farmer City F-7
Farmersville E-9
Farmington D-5
Fayetteville D-11
Fieldon C-10
Fisher G-6

Flanagan F-5
Flat Rock H-10
Flora G-11
Flossmoor ... Pg. 99, M-7
Flowerfield . Pg. 98, H-4
Forest Park . Pg. 99, H-6
Forest View . Pg. 99, J-6
Forrest G-5
Forreston E-2
Fox Lake G-1
  Vicinity .... Pg. 96, C-3
Fox Lake Hills Pg. 96, C-3
Fox River Grove ... Pg. 96, E-3
Fox River Valley Gardens ... Pg. 96, D-3
Frankfort ... Pg. 99, M-5
Franklin D-8
Franklin Park . Pg. 99, H-5
Freeburg D-11
Freeport D-1
Fremont Center ... Pg. 96, D-4
Frontenac ... Pg. 98, K-3
Fulton D-2
Gages Lake .. Pg. 96, D-4
Galatia G-13
Galena C-1
Galesburg C-5
Galva D-4
Gardner G-4
Geneseo C-3
Geneva G-2
  Vicinity .... Pg. 98, H-2
Genoa F-2
Georgetown H-7
Germantown E-11
Gibson City G-6
Gilberts .... Pg. 96, F-1
Gillespie D-10
Gilman H-6
Gilmer ...... Pg. 96, D-4
Girard D-9
Gladstone B-5
Glen Ellyn .. Pg. 98, H-4
Glendale Heights ... Pg. 98, H-4
Glenview .... Pg. 97, F-6
Glenwood .... Pg. 99, M-7
Golconda G-14
Golden B-7
Golf F-6
Good Hope B-6
Goodings Grove ... Pg. 98, L-5
Goreville F-14
Gorham E-13
Grafton C-10
Grand Ridge F-4
Grand Tower E-13
Granite City D-11
  Vicinity ... Pg. 140, C-7
Grayslake ... Pg. 96, D-3
Grayville H-11
Green Oaks . Pg. 96, D-5
Greenfield C-9
Greenup H-9
Greenview D-7
Greenville E-10
Greenwood C-1
Gridley F-5
Griggsville B-8
Gurnee ...... Pg. 97, C-5
Hainesville . Pg. 96, D-3
Half Day .... Pg. 97, E-5
Hamel D-10
Hamilton A-6
Hammond G-8
Hampshire G-2
Hanaford F-13
Hanover C-1
Hanover Park Pg. 96, G-4
Hardin B-9
Harrisburg G-13
Harristown F-8
Harvard F-1
Harvey ...... Pg. 99, L-7
Harwood Heights ... Pg. 97, G-6
Hastings .... Pg. 98, K-5
Havana D-6
Hawthorn Woods ... Pg. 96, E-4
Hazel Crest . Pg. 99, L-7
Hebron G-1
Hecker D-12
Hegeler J-7
Hennepin E-4
Henning H-6
Henry E-4
Herrin F-13
Herscher H-5
Heyworth F-6
Hickory Hills Pg. 99, K-6
Highland E-11
Highland Hills Pg. 98, H-4
Highland Park H-1
  Vicinity .... Pg. 97, E-6
Highwood ... Pg. 97, E-6
Hillsboro E-9
Hillside H-5
Hinckley G-3
Hinsdale .... Pg. 98, J-5
Hodgkins .... Pg. 99, J-5
Hoffman Estates ... Pg. 96, F-3
Holiday Hills Pg. 96, D-3
Homer H-7
Hometown .... Pg. 99, K-6
Homewood ... Pg. 99, L-7
Hoopeston J-6
Hoopole D-3

Hopedale E-6
Hoyleton E-11
Hudson F-6
Hull A-8
Humboldt G-9
Huntley E-1
Hurst E-13
Hutsonville H-10
Illiopolis E-8
Imbs Station Pg. 140, H-7
Indian Creek . Pg. 96, E-4
Indian Head Park ... Pg. 99, J-5
Industry B-6
Ingalls Park . Pg. 98, M-4
Inverness ... Pg. 96, F-4
Irvington F-11
Island Lake . Pg. 96, D-3
Itasca ...... Pg. 96, D-4
Ivanhoe ..... Pg. 96, D-4
Jacksonville C-8
Jerseyville C-9
Johnsburg ... Pg. 96, C-2
Joliet H-3
  Vicinity .... Pg. 98, M-4
Jonesboro E-14
Junction City H-13
Justice ..... Pg. 99, J-6
Kampsville B-9
Kankakee H-5
Kansas H-8
Karnak F-14
Kaskaskia D-13
Keeneyville . Pg. 96, G-3
Kenilworth .. Pg. 97, F-7
Kenney E-7
Kewanee D-4
Kilbourne D-7
Kildeer ..... Pg. 96, E-4
Kinderhook B-8
Kingston F-2
Kinmundy F-10
Kirkland F-2
Knollwood ... Pg. 97, D-5
Knoxville C-5
La Fayette D-4
La Fox H-1
La Grange ... Pg. 99, J-6
La Grange Park ... Pg. 99, J-5
La Harpe A-6
La Moille E-3
La Salle F-4
Lacon E-4
Ladd E-4
Lake Barrington ... Pg. 96, E-3
Lake Bluff .. Pg. 97, D-6
Lake Forest H-1
  Vicinity .... Pg. 97, D-6
Lake Villa .. Pg. 96, E-4
Lake Zurich . Pg. 96, E-4
Lake in the Hills ... Pg. 96, E-2
Lakemoor ... Pg. 96, E-2
Lakewood .... Pg. 96, E-1
Lanark D-2
Lansing ..... Pg. 99, L-8
Latham E-8
Lawrenceville J-10
Le Roy F-6
Lee Center E-3
Lemont ...... Pg. 98, K-4
Lena D-1
Lewistown C-6
Lexington F-6
Liberty A-8
Libertyville H-1
  Vicinity .... Pg. 96, D-5
Lilymoor .... Pg. 96, C-3
Lima A-7
Lincoln E-7
Lincoln Estates ... Pg. 99, M-6
Lincolnshire . Pg. 97, E-5
Lincolnwood . Pg. 97, G-6
Lindenhurst . Pg. 96, C-4
Lisle .... Pg. 98, J-4
Litchfield D-9
Little York B-5
Livingston D-10
Lockport .... Pg. 98, L-4
Lombard ..... Pg. 98, H-4
Long Grove .. Pg. 96, E-4
Long Lake ... Pg. 96, C-4
Loon Lake B-4
Loraine A-7
Louisville G-10
Lovington F-8
Ludlow H-6
Lynwood ..... Pg. 99, M-8
Lyons .... Pg. 99, J-6
Machesney Park ... E-1
Mackinaw E-6
Macomb B-6
Madison .... Pg. 140, D-6
Magnolia E-4
Mahomet G-7
Manhattan H-4
  Vicinity .... Pg. 99, M-5
Manlius D-3
Manteno H-4
Maquon C-5
Marengo G-1
Marine D-10
Marion F-13
Marissa D-12
Markham ..... Pg. 99, L-6
Marley ...... Pg. 98, M-5
Maroa F-7
Marseilles G-4
Marshall J-9
Martinsville H-9
Martinton H-5
Marywood ... Pg. 99, J-2

Mascoutah D-11
Mason G-10
Mason City D-7
Matteson ... Pg. 99, M-6
Mattoon G-9
Maywood ..... Pg. 99, H-6
Mazon G-4
McClure E-14
McCook ...... Pg. 99, J-6
McCollum Lake ... Pg. 96, C-2
McHenry G-1
  Vicinity .... Pg. 96, C-2
McHenry Shores ... Pg. 96, B-1
McLean E-6
McLeansboro G-12
McQueens F-1
Medinah ..... Pg. 96, G-4
Medora D-9
Melrose Park Pg. 99, H-5
Melvin G-6
Mendon A-7
Mendota E-3
Meredosia C-8
Merrionette Park ... Pg. 99, K-7
Metamora E-5
Metropolis G-15
Mettawa ..... Pg. 97, D-5
Midlothian . Pg. 99, L-6
Milan B-4
Milford H-5
Mill Shoals G-12
Milledgeville D-2
Milton B-8
Minonk F-5
Minooka ..... Pg. 98, M-2
Mokena ...... Pg. 99, M-5
Moline C-3
Momence J-4
Monmouth B-5
Montgomery . Pg. 98, K-2
Monticello G-7
Montrose G-9
Mooseheart . Pg. 98, J-2
Morris G-4
Morrison D-2
Morrisonville E-9
Morristown E-7
Morton E-6
Morton Grove Pg. 97, F-6
Mound City F-15
Mount Carmel H-11
Mount Carroll D-2
Mount Morris E-2
Mount Olive D-10
Mount Prospect ... Pg. 96, F-5
Mount Pulaski E-7
Mount Sterling ... B-7
Mount Vernon F-12
Mount Zion F-8
Moweaqua F-8
Mundelein G-1
  Vicinity .... Pg. 96, D-4
Murphysboro E-13
Murrayville C-8
Naperville G-3
  Vicinity .... Pg. 98, J-3
Nashville E-12
National City Pg. 140, E-7
Nauvoo A-6
Neoga G-9
New Athens D-12
New Baden E-11
New Boston B-4
New Burnside F-14
New Canton B-8
New Haven H-13
New Holland E-7
New Lenox . Pg. 98, M-5
New Windsor C-4
Newark F-3
Newman H-8
Newton G-10
Niles .... Pg. 97, G-6
Nilwood D-9
Noble G-11
Nokomis E-9
Normal F-6
Normantown . Pg. 98, K-2
Norridge ... Pg. 97, G-6
Norris D-6
Norris City G-12
North Aurora . Pg. 98, J-2
North Barrington ... Pg. 96, E-3
North Chicago Pg. 97, D-6
North Dupo . Pg. 140, H-6
North Riverside ... Pg. 99, H-6
North Wood River ... Pg. 140, A-7
Northbrook .. Pg. 97, E-5
  Vicinity .... Pg. 97, F-6
Northfield . Pg. 97, F-6
Northlake ... Pg. 99, H-5
Oak Brook ... Pg. 98, J-5
Oak Forest .. Pg. 99, L-6
Oak Lawn ... Pg. 99, K-6
Oak Park .... Pg. 99, H-6
Oakbrook Terrace ... Pg. 98, H-5
Oakford D-7
Oakland H-8
Oakwood H-7
Oakwood Hills Pg. 96, D-3
Oblong H-10
Oconee F-9
Odell G-5
Odin F-11
Ogden H-7

Oglesby F-4
Ohio E-3
Okawville D-11
Old Mill Creek Pg. 96, B-4
Olmsted F-15
Olney H-10
Olympia Fields ... Pg. 99, M-7
Omaha G-13
Onarga H-5
Oquawka B-5
Orangeville E-1
Oreana F-7
Oregon E-2
Orion C-4
Orland Hills . Pg. 99, L-6
Orland Park . Pg. 99, L-5
Oswego G-3
  Vicinity .... Pg. 98, K-2
Ottawa F-3
Owaneco E-9
Palatine G-2
  Vicinity .... Pg. 96, F-4
Palestine J-10
Palmyra D-9
Palos Heights Pg. 99, K-6
Palos Hills . Pg. 99, K-6
Palos Park .. Pg. 99, K-6
Pana E-9
Pawnee E-8
Paxton H-6
Payson A-8
Pearl City D-1
Pekin D-5
Peoria D-5
Peotone H-4
Perry B-8
Pesotum G-7
Petersburg D-7
Phoenix ..... Pg. 99, L-7
Pierron E-10
Pinckneyville E-12
Pingree Grove F-1
Piper City G-5
Pittsfield B-8
Plainfield G-3
  Vicinity .... Pg. 98, L-3
Plano G-3
Plato Center G-1
Plattville M-1
Pleasant Hill B-9
Plymouth B-6
Pocahontas E-10
Polo E-2
Pontiac G-5
Port Byron C-3
Posen .... Pg. 99, L-7
Prairie Grove Pg. 96, D-2
Prairie View . Pg. 96, E-5
Prairie du Rocher . F-12
Preston Heights ... Pg. 98, M-4
Prince Crossing ... Pg. 98, H-3
Princeton E-4
Princeville D-5
Prophetstown D-3
Prospect Heights ... Pg. 96, F-5
Pulaski F-15
Quincy A-7
Ramsey F-9
Rankin H-6
Ransom F-4
Rantoul H-6
Rapids City C-3
Raymond E-9
Red Bud D-12
Reynolds C-4
Richton Park Pg. 99, M-6
Richview E-11
Ridge Farm H-7
Ridgefield .. Pg. 96, D-2
Ridgeway G-13
Ridgewood ... Pg. 98, M-4
Ringwood .... Pg. 96, C-2
River Forest . Pg. 99, H-6
River Grove . Pg. 99, H-6
Riverdale ... Pg. 99, L-7
Riverside ... Pg. 99, J-6
Riverwoods . Pg. 97, E-5
Roanoke E-5
Robbins ..... Pg. 99, L-7
Roberts G-6
Robinson H-10
Rochelle E-2
Rochester D-8
Rock Falls D-3
Rock Island C-3
Rockbridge C-9
Rockdale .... Pg. 98, M-3
Rockford D-1
Rockton E-1
Rolling Meadows ... Pg. 96, F-4
Romeoville H-3
  Vicinity .... Pg. 98, K-4
Rondout ..... Pg. 97, D-5
Roodhouse C-9
Roselle ..... Pg. 96, G-4
Rosemont ... Pg. 97, G-5
Roseville C-5
Rosiclare G-14
Rossville H-6
Round Lake . Pg. 96, C-4
Round Lake Beach

Round Lake Heights ... Pg. 96, C-4
Round Lake Park ... Pg. 96, C-4
Royalton E-13
Rushville C-7
Rutland F-5
Sag Bridge .. Pg. 98, K-5
Salem F-11
San Jose E-6
Sandoval E-11
Sandwich F-3
Sauget ..... Pg. 140, F-6
Sauk Village Pg. 99, M-8
Savanna D-2
Savoy G-7
Schaumburg G-2
  Vicinity .... Pg. 96, G-3
Schiller Park Pg. 97, G-5
Schram City E-9
Sesser F-12
Shabbona F-2
Shannon D-2
Shawneetown G-13
Sheffield D-4
Shelbyville F-9
Sheldon J-5
Shorewood G-3
  Vicinity .... Pg. 98, M-3
Shumway F-9
Sibley G-6
Sigel G-9
Silvis C-3
Simpson F-14
Skokie H-2
  Vicinity .... Pg. 97, F-6
Sleepy Hollow Pg. 96, F-2
Smithton D-11
Solon Mills B-2
Somonauk F-3
South Barrington ... Pg. 96, F-3
South Beloit E-1
South Chicago Hts. ... Pg. 99, M-7
South Elgin . Pg. 96, G-2
South Holland Pg. 99, L-7
South Lockport Pg. 98, L-4
Sparland E-4
Sparta D-12
Spencer ..... Pg. 98, M-5
Spring Grove B-2
Spring Valley E-4
Springfield D-8
St. Anne H-4
St. Augustine C-5
St. Charles G-2
  Vicinity .... Pg. 98, H-2
St. Elmo F-10
St. Francisville . H-11
St. Johns E-12
St. Peter F-10
Stanford E-6
Starks F-1
Staunton D-10
Steeleville D-12
Sterling D-3
Stewardson F-9
Stickney .... Pg. 99, J-6
Stillman Valley .. E-2
Stockton D-1
Stolle ..... Pg. 140, H-7
Stone Park . Pg. 99, H-5
Stonefort G-13
Stonington F-8
Strasburg F-9
Streamwood . Pg. 96, G-3
Streator F-4
Stronghurst B-5
Sublette E-3
Sugar Grove G-3
Sugarloaf Hts. Pg. 140, G-8
Sullivan G-8
Summit ...... Pg. 99, J-6
Sumner H-11
Sunnyside ... Pg. 96, A-2
Sunrise Ridge Pg. 96, A-1
Swansea D-11
Sycamore G-2
Table Grove C-6
Tallula D-7
Tamaroa E-12
Tamms F-14
Tampico D-3
Taylor Springs ... E-9
Taylorville F-8
Teutopolis G-9
Thawville G-5
Third Lake . Pg. 96, C-4
Thompsonville G-13
Thomson D-2
Thornton ... Pg. 99, L-7
Tilton J-7
Tinley Park . Pg. 99, L-6
Toledo G-9
Tolono G-7
Toluca E-5
Tonica F-4
Toulon D-4
Tower Hill F-9
Tower Lakes . Pg. 96, E-3
Trenton E-11
Troy D-11
Troy Grove E-3
Tuscola G-8
Udina G-1
Ullin E-14
University Park ... Pg. 99, M-6
Urbana H-7
Valley View . Pg. 96, G-2

Valmeyer C-12
Vandalia F-10
Venetian Village ... Pg. 96, C-4
Venice ..... Pg. 140, D-7
Vernon F-10
Vernon Hills . Pg. 96, D-5
Versailles B-8
Victoria D-4
Vienna F-14
Villa Grove H-8
Villa Park .. Pg. 98, H-5
Viola C-4
Virden D-9
Virginia C-7
Volo .... Pg. 96, C-3
Wadsworth D-8
Waggoner D-9
Walnut E-3
Waltonville F-12
Wapella F-7
Warren D-1
Warrensburg F-7
Warrenville . Pg. 98, J-3
Warsaw A-6
Wasco G-1
Washburn E-5
Washington E-5
Waterloo C-12
Waterman F-3
Watseka H-5
Watson G-10
Wauconda ... Pg. 96, D-3
Waukegan H-1
  Vicinity .... Pg. 96, C-6
Waverly D-8
Wayne .... Pg. 96, G-3
Wayne City G-11
Weldon F-7
Wellington H-6
Wenona F-4
West Chicago Pg. 98, H-3
West City F-12
West Dundee . Pg. 96, F-2
West Frankfort ... F-13
West Miltmore Pg. 96, C-4
Westchester . Pg. 98, H-5
Western Springs ... Pg. 98, J-5
Westfield H-9
Westmont .... Pg. 98, J-5
Westville J-7
Wheaton G-3
  Vicinity .... Pg. 98, H-3
Wheeler G-10
Wheeling .... Pg. 96, F-5
White Hall C-9
Wildwood .... Pg. 96, C-5
Willow Hill H-10
Willow Springs Pg. 98, K-5
Willowbrook . Pg. 98, J-5
Wilmette .... Pg. 97, F-7
Wilmington H-4
Winchester C-8
Winfield .... Pg. 98, H-3
Winnebago E-1
Winnetka .... Pg. 97, F-6
  Vicinity .... Pg. 97, F-6
Winslow D-1
Winthrop Harbor .. H-1
Wolfs .... Pg. 98, K-2
Wonder Lake . Pg. 96, C-2
Wood Dale ... Pg. 96, C-4
Wood River . Pg. 140, B-7
Woodhull C-4
Woodridge ... Pg. 98, K-4
Woodson C-8
Woodstock F-1
Worth .... Pg. 99, K-6
Wyoming D-5
Xenia G-11
Yates City D-5
York Center . Pg. 96, J-4
Yorkville G-3
Zeigler F-13
Zion H-1

INDIANA

Akron D-7
Albany F-9
Albion B-8
Alexandria F-8
Allisonville Pg. 110, B-5
Alton P-6
Alvarado B-10
Ambia F-4
Americus F-4
Anderson F-8
Andersonville J-9
Andrews D-8
Angola A-10
Antrim ...... Pg. 110, F-2
Arcadia G-7
Argos C-6
Atherton J-3
Attica F-3
Auburn B-10
Augusta F-6
Austin M-7
Avilla B-9
Bainbridge H-4
Bargersville J-6
Bass Lake C-5
Batesville K-9
Battletown P-6

INDIANA

Bedford L-5
Beech Grove H-6
 Vicinity . . . . Pg. 110, B-6
Beechwood P-6
Belleview H-6
Belmont K-6
Ben Davis . Pg. 110, E-2
Bennett Switch E-7
Berne E-10
Beverly Shores B-4
Bicknell M-3
Birdseye N-5
Bloomfield L-4
Blooming Grove . . . J-9
Bloomington K-5
Bluffton E-9
Boonville P-3
Boston H-10
Boswell E-3
Bourbon C-6
Bowling Green K-4
Branchville P-5
Brazil J-4
Bremen B-6
Bristol A-7
Brook D-3
Brooklyn J-6
Brookston E-5
Brookville J-10
Brownsburg H-6
Brownstown L-6
Bruceville M-3
Bryant L-8
Bryantsburg L-8
Burlington F-6
Burnettsville E-5
Burns City M-5
Butler B-10
Cadiz G-8
Cambridge City . . H-10
Camby . . . . Pg. 110, F-1
Cannelton Q-5
Carbon J-4
Carbondale F-3
Carefree P-6
Carlisle L-3
Carmel G-6
 Vicinity . . . Pg. 110, A-4
Carp J-5
Castleton G-7
 Vicinity . . . Pg. 110, B-4
Cayuga J-10
Cedar Grove J-10
Cedar Lake B-3
Centerville H-10
Chalmers E-4
Chandler P-3
Charlestown N-8
Chester H-10
Chesterfield G-8
Chesterton B-4
Chrisney P-4
Churubusco C-9
Cicero G-7
Cincinnati L-5
Clarks Hill F-5
Clarksville G-7
 Vicinity . . . Pg. 118, A-2
Clay City K-4
Clayton H-5
Clermont . . Pg. 110, C-1
Clinton H-3
Cloverdale J-5
Coatesville D-4
Collegeville D-4
Columbia City . . . C-8
Columbus K-7
Connersville H-9
Converse E-7
Cory J-3
Corydon P-7
Covington G-3
Crawfordsville . . . G-4
Crothersville M-7
Crown Point B-3
 Vicinity . . . . Pg. 97, E-7
Crows Nest . Pg. 110, C-3
Crystal N-5
Cumberland H-7
Cynthiana P-2
Cypress Q-2
Dale N-4
Dana H-1
Danville H-5
Darmstadt P-2
Dayton F-4
Decatur D-10
Decker N-3
Deep River D-8
Deerfield F-10
Degonia Springs . . P-4
Delphi E-5
Demotte C-4
Denver D-7
Derby P-5
Dillsboro L-9
Dogwood P-7
Dover G-5
Dublin H-9
Dugger L-3
Dunfee C-9
Dunkirk F-9
Dunlap A-7
E. Mt. Carmel N-2
Earl Park E-4
East Gary . . Pg. 97, B-7
Economy G-9
Edinburgh K-7
Effner E-3
Elberfeld P-3
Elizabeth P-7
Elizabethtown . . . K-7
Elkhart A-7
Elletsville K-5

Elwood F-7
Emporia G-8
English N-6
Enos D-3
Evansville P-2
Fairfield J-10
Fairmount F-8
Ferdinand P-5
Fickle F-5
fishers . . . . Pg. 110, A-5
Five Points . Pg. 110, E-5
Flora E-6
Fort Branch P-2
Fort Wayne C-9
Fortville H-7
Foster G-6
Fountain City G-10
Fowler E-4
Francesville D-4
Frankfort F-5
Franklin J-7
Frankton G-7
Freedom K-4
Freetown L-6
Fremont A-10
French Lick M-5
Fulton D-6
Galveston E-6
Garrett B-9
Gary K-5
 Vicinity . . . Pg. 97, C-7
Gas City E-8
Geneva E-10
Gentryville P-4
Glenns Valley Pg. 110, G-3
Goodland E-3
Goshen B-7
Gosport K-5
Grandview N-5
Grass Creek D-6
Grayford M-8
Graysville K-3
Greencastle H-4
Greendale K-10
Greenfield H-7
Greensboro G-8
Greensburg K-8
Greentown E-7
Greenwood J-7
Griffin N-2
Griffith . . . . Pg. 97, D-7
Grovertown B-5
Hagerstown H-9
Hammond H-5
 Vicinity . . . . Pg. 97, L-8
Hanna B-5
Hanover M-8
Hardinsburg M-6
Harlan C-10
Harmony J-4
Harrodsburg L-5
Hartford City F-9
Hartsville K-8
Haysville N-4
Hazelwood D-6
Hazleton N-2
Hebron C-4
Hedrick F-3
Hemlock F-7
Henryville M-8
Heusler H-5
Highland . . . Pg. 97, C-7
Highwood . . Pg. 110, C-3
Hillsboro G-4
Hindustan K-5
Hobart B-3
 Vicinity . . . Pg. 97, D-8
Hobbs F-7
Holland P-4
Homecroft . Pg. 110, F-4
Hope K-7
Howe A-9
Hudson B-9
Hudson Lake A-5
Huntertown C-9
Huntingburg N-4
Huntington D-8
Huron M-5
Indianapolis H-6
 Vicinity . . . . . Pg. 122
Jamestown H-5
Jasonville K-3
Jasper N-4
Jefferson N8
Jeffersonville M-8
 Vicinity . . . Pg. 118, A-2
Johnson N-2
Jonesboro F-8
Jonesville L-7
Kempton F-6
Kendallville B-9
Kentland D-3
Kewanna D-6
Kingman G-4
Kingsbury B-5
Kingsford Hts. . . . B-5
Knightstown H-8
Knox C-5
Kokomo E-6
Kouts C-4
La Crosse C-5
La Fontaine E-8
La Paz B-6
La Porte B-5
Lafayette F-5
Lagrange A-8
Lake Station . Pg. 97, C-8
 Vicinity . . . Pg. 97, C-8
Lake Village B-3
Lakeville B-6
Lawrence H-6
 Vicinity . . . Pg. 110, C-5
Lawrenceburg . . . L-10
Lebanon G-6
Leota M-7
Leroy B-3

Lewistown D-4
Liberty H-10
Libertyville J-3
Ligonier B-8
Linden G-5
Linton L-4
Lizton H-5
Logansport E-6
Loogootee M-4
Lowell C-3
Luther D-8
Lynn G-10
Lynnville P-3
Mace G-5
Madison L-9
Majenica D-8
Malden B-4
Manhattan J-4
Marengo N-6
Marion E-8
Markle D-9
Markleville G-8
Mars Hill . . Pg. 110, H-4
Marshall J-5
Martinsville J-5
Mauckport P-6
Maxwell H-8
Maywood . . Pg. 110, E-3
Mecca H-3
Medaryville C-5
Memphis N-7
Mentone D-7
Meridian Hills Pg. 110, B-3
Merom L-3
Merriam C-8
Merrillville B-4
 Vicinity . . . Pg. 97, D-7
Metamora K-9
Metea D-6
Michiana Shores . A-5
Michigan City . . . A-4
Michigantown . . . F-6
Mickeyville . Pg. 110, E-2
Middlebury A-8
Middlefork F-6
Milan K-9
Millersburg B-8
Milport M-7
Mishawaka B-7
Mitchell M-6
Monon D-4
Monroe F-5
Monroeville D-10
Montezuma H-3
Monticello E-5
Montmorenci . . . F-4
Montpelier E-9
Mooresville J-6
Morgantown K-6
Morocco D-3
Morristown H-7
Morton H-4
Moscow J-8
Mt. Ayr D-4
Mt. Carmel J-10
Mt. Comfort H-7
Mt. Etna D-8
Mt. Meridian J-5
Mt. Pleasant (Cass Cty)
 Vicinity . . . Pg. 97, D-7
Mt. Pleasant (Perry Cty)
 . . . . P-5
Mt. Vernon Q-2
Mt. Zion E-9
Mulberry F-5
Muncie F-8
Munster B-3
 Vicinity . . . Pg. 109, M-8
N. Liberty B-6
N. Manchester . . . D-7
N. Vernon K-9
Napoleon B-7
Nappanee B-6
Nashville K-6
New Albany N-7
 Vicinity . . . Pg. 118, A-1
New Amsterdam . P-6
New Augusta Pg. 110, B-2
New Boston P-7
New Carlisle A-6
New Castle G-9
New Chicago . . . C-8
New Frankfort . . . J-9
New Goshen J-3
New Harmony . . . P-2
New Haven C-10
New Liberty M-7
New Market G-5
New Pekin M-7
New Providence . . M-7
New Richmond . . G-4
New Ross G-5
New Whiteland . . J-6
Newberry L-4
Newburgh Q-3
Newport H-3
Newtown G-4
Nine Mile D-9
Nobelsville G-7
Nora . . . . . Pg. 110, B-4
Norristown K-7
North Crows Nest
 . . . . . . Pg. 110, B-3
North Judson . . . C-5
Oakland City N-3
Oaktown L-3
Odell F-4
Odon L-4
Ogden Dunes . . . B-4
Ogilville K-7
Oolitic L-5
Orestes G-7
Orleans M-5
Osceola A-7
Osgood K-9

Ossian D-9
Otis A-4
Otwell N-4
Owensville P-2
Oxford E-3
Palmyra N-6
Paoli M-6
Paris Crossing . . . L-8
Parr D-4
Patriot L-10
Patronville E-11
Pence G-8
Pendleton G-8
Peoria E-7
Perrysburg D-7
Perrysville G-3
Peru E-7
Petersburg N-3
Pierceton C-8
Pike G-6
Pine Village F-3
Plainfield H-5
Pleasant . . . . . .
Pleasant Mills . . . D-10
Pleasant View . . . H-7
Plymouth B-6
Point Isabel F-7
Portage B-4
Porter B-4
Portland F-10
Poseyville P-2
Prairie City K-3
Prairie Creek K-3
Prairieton K-3
Princeton N-2
Ramsey N-6
Raub E-3
Ravenswood Pg. 110, B-4
Rays Crossing . . . J-8
Reiffsburg E-9
Rensselaer D-4
Reynolds E-5
Richmond H-10
Rising Sun L-10
Riverside H-5
Roachdale H-5
Roann D-7
Rochester C-6
Rockfield E-5
Rockport Q-4
Rockville H-3
Rocky Ripple Pg. 110, C-3
Rogersville G-9
Rome City B-9
Romney F-4
Rosedale J-3
Roseland A-6
Roselawn C-3
Rosston G-6
Rossville F-5
Royal Center D-5
Royalton H-6
Rushville J-8
Russellville H-4
Russiaville E-7
Salem M-6
Sandusky J-8
Santa Claus P-4
Santa Fe E-7
Schererville . . . .
 Vicinity . . . Pg. 97, D-7
Schneider C-3
Scipio J-10
Scott A-8
Scottsburg M-7
Seelyville J-3
Sellersburg N-7
Sexton H-8
Seymour L-7
Shelburn K-3
Shelbyville J-7
Sheridan G-6
Shoals M-5
Shore Acres Pg. 110, B-4
Sidney C-8
Silver Lake C-7
Solitude P-2
South Bend A-6
South Whitley . . . C-8
Southport H-6
 Vicinity . . . Pg. 110, G-4
Speedway H-6
 Vicinity . . . Pg. 110, D-2
Spencer K-5
Spiceland H-8
Spring Hills Pg. 110, C-3
St. Croix P-5
St. Joe C-10
St. John . . . Pg. 99, D-6
St. Leon L-9
St. Paul J-8
Stewartsville P-2
Stilesville H-5
Story K-6
Sullivan K-3
Sulphur Springs . . G-8
Summitville G-8
Sunman K-9
Swayzee E-7
Syracuse B-8
Tell City Q-5
Templeton E-4
Terre Haute J-3
Thorntown G-5
Tipton F-7
Topeka B-8
Traders Point . Pg. 110, B-1
Trafalgar J-6
Tremont . . . Pg. 110, G-2
Troy P-5
Union City G-10
Uniondale D-9
Uniontown Q-2
Upland F-8

Urbana D-7
Valparaiso C-4
Van Buren E-8
Veedersburg G-3
Versailles L-9
Vevay M-9
Vincennes M-3
W. College Corner . J-10
W. Lebanon F-3
W. Terre Haute . . . J-3
Wabash D-7
Waco M-4
Wakarusa B-6
Walkerton B-6
Walton E-6
Wanatah B-4
Warren E-8
Warsaw C-7
Washington M-4
Waterford B-4
Waterloo . . . . . .
Waterloo B-10
Waynetown G-4
Webster H-10
West Lafayette . . . F-4
West Newton Pg. 110, G-2
West Point F-4
Westfield G-7
Westphalia L-3
Westport K-8
Westville B-4
Wheatfield C-4
Whitestown G-6
Whiting H-8
 Vicinity . . . Pg. 99, K-8
Wilkinson H-8
Williams L-5
Williams Creek
 . . . . . . Pg. 110, B-4
Williamsport F-3
Wilmot C-8
Winamac C-5
Winchester G-10
Windfall City F-7
Wingate G-4
Winona Lake C-7
Winslow N-3
Wolcott D-4
Woodburn C-10
Woodstock . Pg. 110, C-3
Worthington K-4
Wynnedale . Pg. 110, C-3
Yorktown G-8
Zionsville G-6
 Vicinity . . . Pg. 110, A-2

IOWA
Page 36
Population: 2,913,808
Capital: Des Moines
Land Area: 55,965 sq. mi.

Abingdon F-7
Ackley C-6
Adair E-4
Adel E-4
Afton E-4
Agency E-6
Ainsworth E-8
Akron C-1
Albia E-6
Alden C-5
Allendorf B-2
Allerton F-4
Allison C-6
Alta C-3
Alta Vista A-7
Alton B-1
Altoona E-5
Amana D-8
Ames D-5
Anamosa D-8
Anderson F-2
Andrew D-10
Anita E-3
Ankeny D-5
Anthon C-2
Aplington C-6
Arcadia D-3
Archer B-2
Aredale C-6
Arispe F-4
Arlington C-7
Armstrong B-4
Arnolds Park A-3
Arthur D-3
Asbury C-9
Ashton B-2
Athelstan G-4
Atkins D-7
Atlantic E-3
Attica E-6
Auburn D-3
Audubon E-3
Aurelia C-2
Aurora C-7
Avery F-7
Avoca E-2
Badger C-4
Bagley E-4
Baldwin D-9
Bancroft B-4
Barnes City E-7
Barnum C-4
Battle Creek D-2
Baxter D-6
Bayard D-4
Beacon E-6
Beaman C-6
Beaver D-4
Bedford G-4
Beech E-6

Belle Plaine D-7
Bellevue D-9
Belmond C-5
Bennett E-9
Bettendorf E-10
Bevington E-5
Blakesburg F-7
Blencoe D-2
Bloomfield F-7
Bonaparte F-8
Boone D-5
Boyden B-2
Bradford C-6
Brayton E-3
Breda D-3
Bridgewater F-4
Brighton E-7
Britt B-5
Brooklyn D-6
Brooks F-3
Brunswick C-1
Bryant D-10
Buffalo Center . . . A-5
Burlington F-8
Burr Oak A-8
Burt B-4
Bussey E-6
Calamus D-9
Calmar B-8
Calumet B-2
Camanche D-9
Cantril F-7
Carbon F-3
Carlisle E-5
Carpenter B-6
Carroll D-3
Carson E-2
Carter Lake E-1
Carter Lake . Pg. 132, D-5
Cascade D-9
Casey E-4
Cedar F-7
Cedar Falls C-7
Cedar Rapids . . . D-8
Center Point D-8
Centerville F-6
Central City D-8
Chapin C-6
Chariton F-6
Charles City B-7
Charlotte D-10
Charter Oak D-2
Chatsworth B-1
Chelsea D-7
Cherokee C-2
Churdan D-4
Cincinnati G-6
Clara . . . . Pg. 132, C-4
Clare C-4
Clarence D-9
Clarinda F-3
Clarion C-5
Clarksville C-7
Clear Lake B-6
Clearfield F-4
Cleghorn C-2
Clinton D-10
Clutier D-7
Coggon D-8
Colesburg C-9
Colfax E-5
Collins D-6
Colo D-5
Columbia F-6
Columbus Jct. . . . E-8
Colwell B-7
Conesville E-8
Conrad D-6
Conroy E-7
Conway F-4
Coon Rapids D-3
Cooper D-4
Coppock E-8
Coralville E-8
Corley E-2
Corning F-3
Correctionville . . . C-2
Corwith C-5
Corydon F-6
Council Bluffs . . . E-2
 Vicinity . . . Pg. 132, E-6
Crescent E-2
 Vicinity . . . Pg. 132, C-5
Cresco B-7
Creston F-4
Curlew C-4
Dakota City C-4
Dana D-4
Danbury D-2
Danville F-8
Davenport E-9
Davis City G-5
Dayton C-4
De Soto E-5
De Witt D-9
Decorah B-8
Dedham D-3
Defiance D-3
Delhi D-8
Delmar D-9
Deloit D-3
Delta E-7
Denison D-3
Denver C-7
Derby F-5
Des Moines E-5
Dexter E-4
Dickens B-3
Dike C-6
Dolliver B-4
Donnellson F-8
Doon B-1
Dorchester A-8
Dow City D-2
Dows C-5
Drakesville F-7

Dubuque C-9
Dumfries . . Pg. 132, G-7
Dumont C-6
Duncombe C-4
Dunkerton C-7
Dunlap D-2
Durant D-9
Dyersville C-9
Dysart D-7
Eagle Grove C-5
Earlham E-4
Earling E-3
Early C-3
Eddyville E-7
Edgewood C-8
Eldon E-7
Eldora C-6
Eldridge E-10
Elgin B-8
Elk Horn E-3
Elkader C-8
Elkhart D-5
Elliott F-3
Ellsworth D-5
Emerson F-2
Emmetsburg B-4
Epworth C-9
Essex F-3
Estherville B-4
Evansdale C-7
Everly B-2
Exira E-3
Fairbank C-7
Fairfield F-8
Farley C-8
Farnhamville D-4
Farragut F-2
Fayette B-8
Fenton B-4
Floyd B-6
Fonda C-3
Fontanelle E-3
Forest City B-5
Fort Dodge C-4
Fort Madison . . . F-9
Fostoria B-3
Frankville B-8
Fraser D-5
Fredericksburg . . . B-7
Fremont E-7
Froelich B-8
Frytown E-8
Fulton D-9
Garden City D-6
Garnavillo C-9
Garner C-5
Garwin D-6
George B-2
Gibson E-7
Gilbert D-5
Gilman D-6
Gilmore City C-4
Gladbrook D-6
Glenwood F-2
Glidden D-4
Goldfield C-5
Goodell C-5
Gowrie C-4
Graettinger B-4
Grafton B-5
Grand Jct. D-4
Grand River G-5
Grandview E-9
Grant F-3
Green Mountain . . D-6
Greene C-6
Greenfield E-4
Grimes D-5
Grinnell E-6
Griswold E-3
Grundy Center . . . D-6
Guernsey E-7
Gunder B-8
Guthrie Center . . . E-4
Guttenberg C-9
Hamburg G-2
Hamilton E-6
Hamlin E-3
Hampton C-6
Hancock E-2
Hanlontown B-6
Harcourt C-4
Harlan E-3
Harper's Ferry . . . B-9
Hartley B-3
Hartwick E-7
Harvey E-6
Havelock C-4
Haven D-7
Hawarden B-1
Hawkeye B-8
Hazleton C-8
Hedrick E-7
Henderson F-2
Hepburn F-3
Hesper A-8
Hiawatha D-7
Hillsboro F-8
Hinton C-1
Holmes C-5
Holstein C-2
Honey Creek Pg. 132, A-5
Hopeville F-5
Hopkinton D-8
Hospers B-2
Hubbard C-5
Hudson C-7
Hull B-1
Humboldt C-4
Humeston F-5
Huxley D-5
Ida Grove D-2

Imogene F-3
Independence . . . C-8
Indianola E-5
Inwood B-1
Iowa Center D-5
Iowa City E-8
Iowa Falls C-6
Ireton B-1
Irwin E-3
Jackson Jct. B-7
Jamaica D-4
Janesville C-7
Jefferson D-4
Jerico B-7
Jesup C-7
Jewell D-5
Joice B-5
Kalona E-8
Kamrar C-5
Kanawha C-5
Kellogg E-6
Kendallville B-8
Kent F-4
Keokuk G-8
Keosauqua F-7
Keota E-7
Keswick E-7
Keystone D-7
Killduff E-6
Kingsley C-2
Kirkman E-3
Kiron D-3
Klemme B-5
Knoxville E-6
La Porte City D-7
Lake City C-3
Lake Mills B-5
Lake Park B-3
Lake View D-3
Lamoni G-4
Lamont C-8
Lansing B-8
Larchwood A-1
Larrabee C-2
Laurel D-6
Laurens C-3
Le Claire D-9
Le Mars C-1
Ledyard B-4
Lehigh C-4
Leighton E-7
Lenox F-4
Leon F-5
Lester B-1
Lewis E-3
Liberty Center . . . F-6
Lime Springs B-7
Linderwood E-2
Lineville G-5
Lisbon D-8
Little Rock B-2
Little Sioux D-2
Livermore C-4
Logan E-2
Lohrville C-3
Long Grove D-9
Long Tree F-5
Lorimor F-5
Lost Nation D-9
Lovilia F-6
Lowden D-9
Lucas F-5
Luther D-5
Luxemburg C-9
Lyman F-3
Lytton C-3
Macedonia F-2
Macksburg E-4
Madrid D-5
Malcom E-7
Mallard B-4
Malvern F-2
Manchester C-8
Manilla D-3
Manly B-6
Manning D-3
Manson C-4
Mapleton D-2
Maquoketa D-10
Marathon C-3
Marcus C-2
Marengo E-7
Marion D-8
Marne E-3
Marquette B-9
Marshalltown . . . D-6
Mason City B-6
Massena E-4
Matlock B-2
Maxwell D-5
May City B-3
Maynard C-8
McGregor B-9
McIntire B-7
Mechanicsville . . . D-9
Mediapolis F-9
Melbourne D-6
Melcher E-5
Melvin B-2
Meriden C-2
Merrill C-1
Meservey B-6
Milford B-3
Millerton F-5
Millville C-9
Milo E-5
Milton G-7
Minburn E-4
Minden E-2
Mingo E-5
Missouri Valley . . E-2
Mitchellville E-5
Modale E-2
Mondamin E-2
Moneta B-2
Monona B-9

IOWA

Monroe E-6
Montezuma E-7
Monticello D-8
Montrose G-8
Moorhead D-2
Moravia F-6
Morning Sun F-9
Morse E-8
Moulton G-7
Mount Ayr F-4
Mount Etna F-4
Mount Sterling G-8
Mount Union F-8
Moville C-1
Mt. Pleasant F-8
Mt. Vernon D-8
Murray F-4
Muscatine E-9
Nashua B-7
Neola E-2
Nevada D-5
Nevinville F-4
New Albin A-8
New Hampton B-7
New Haven B-7
New London F-9
New Market F-3
New Providence . . . D-6
New Sharon E-7
New Virginia F-5
Newburg D-7
Newkirk B-2
Newton E-6
Nichols E-9
Nora Springs B-6
North English E-7
Northboro G-3
Northwood B-6
Norwalk E-5
Norway D-7
Oakland E-3
Ocheyedan A-2
Odebolt D-3
Oelwein C-8
Ogden D-4
Olin D-9
Onawa D-2
Onslow D-9
Orange City B-2
Orient F-4
Osage B-6
Osceola F-5
Oskaloosa E-7
Otho D-5
Oto D-2
Ottumwa F-7
Oxford E-8
Oyens C-2
Pacific City . . . Pg. 132, J-6
Pacific Junction
. . . . Pg. 132, K-6
Panama E-3
Panora E-4
Park View E-10
Parkersburg C-7
Parnell E-7
Paullina B-2
Pella E-6
Percival F-2
Perkins B-1
Perry D-5
Persia E-2
Pierson C-2
Pilot Mound D-5
Pisgah D-2
Plain View E-9
Plainfield C-7
Plano F-6
Pleasant Plain F-7
Pleasantville E-5
Pocahontas C-4
Polk City E-5
Pomeroy C-4
Popejoy C-6
Portsmouth E-3
Postville B-8
Prairie City E-6
Preston D-10
Primghar B-2
Prole E-5
Pulaski F-7
Quasqueton C-8
Quimby C-2
Rathbun F-6
Reasnor E-6
Red Oak F-3
Redding G-4
Redfield E-4
Reinbeck D-7
Rembrandt C-3
Remsen C-2
Renwick C-5
Rhodes D-6
Riceville B-6
Richland E-7
Rickardsville C-9
Ridgeway B-8
Ringsted A-3
Rippey D-4
Rochester E-9
Rock Rapids B-2
Rock Valley B-1
Rockford B-6
Rockwell B-6
Rockwell City C-4
Roland C-5
Rolfe C-4
Roselle D-3
Rossie B-3
Rossville B-8
Royal B-3
Russell F-6
Ruthven B-3
Ryan C-8

Sabula C-10
Sac City C-3
Sanborn B-2
Saratoga B-7
Schaller C-3
Schleswig D-2
Schley B-7
Scranton D-4
Searsboro E-7
Selma F-7
Sergeant Bluff C-2
Seymour F-5
Shambaugh G-3
Sharpsburg F-3
Sheffield B-6
Sheldon B-2
Shell Rock B-6
Shellsburg D-8
Shenandoah F-3
Sibley A-2
Sidney F-2
Sigourney E-7
Sioux Center B-1
Sioux City C-1
Sioux Rapids B-3
Sloan D-1
Smithland D-2
Soldier D-2
Solon D-8
Somers C-4
Spencer B-3
Spirit Lake A-3
Springville D-8
St. Ansgar B-6
St. Charles E-5
St. Joseph B-4
St. Marys D-3
Stacyville A-6
Stanton E-2
Stanwood D-8
State Center D-6
Steamboat Rock . . . C-6
Storm Lake C-3
Story City D-5
Stout C-7
Strawberry Point . . . C-8
Stuart E-4
Sully D-6
Sulphur Springs . . . C-3
Sumner C-7
Superior B-3
Sutherland B-2
Swea City B-4
Tabor F-2
Tama D-7
Templeton D-3
Terril B-3
Thompson B-5
Thornton C-6
Thurman F-2
Tiffin E-8
Tipton D-9
Titonka B-4
Toledo D-6
Traer D-7
Trenton F-8
Tripoli C-7
Truesdale C-3
Truro F-5
Turin D-2
Ulmer E-2
Underwood E-2
Union D-7
Urbana D-7
Urbandale E-5
Ute D-2
Vail D-3
Valeria E-6
Van Horne D-7
Van Wert F-5
Varina C-4
Ventura B-5
Victor E-7
Villisca F-3
Vining D-7
Vinton D-7
W. Burlington F-8
Walford D-8
Walker D-8
Wall Lake C-3
Wallingford B-4
Washington E-8
Washta C-2
Waterloo C-7
Waukee E-5
Waukon B-8
Waverly C-7
Webster E-7
Webster City C-5
Weldon F-5
Wellman E-8
Wellsburg C-6
Welton D-10
Wesley B-5
West Bend B-4
West Des Moines . . E-5
West Grove F-7
West Liberty E-9
West Point F-9
West Union C-8
Westfield C-1
Weston . . . . Pg. 132, C-7
Wheatland D-9
Whiting D-2
Whittemore B-4
Wick E-5
Willey E-4
Williams C-5
Williamsburg E-7
Williamson B-5
Wilton D-9
Winfield F-8
Winterset E-4
Wiota E-3

Woodbine E-2
Woodburn F-5
Woodward D-4
Woolstock C-5
Wyoming D-9
Yale E-4
Zwingle C-9

KANSAS
Page 37
Population: 2,363,679
Capital: Topeka
Land Area: 81,781 sq. mi.

Abbeyville E-5
Abilene D-7
Admire D-8
Agenda C-7
Agra C-4
Alden E-5
Alexander D-4
Allen D-8
Alma D-8
Almena B-4
Alta Vista D-8
Altamont F-9
Alton C-5
Altoona F-8
Americus E-8
Andale E-6
Andover F-7
Anthony F-6
Arcadia F-9
Arkansas City F-7
Arlington E-5
Ashland F-4
Atchison C-9
Athol C-5
Atlanta F-7
Attica F-5
Atwood B-2
Augusta F-7
Axtell C-8
Baldwin City D-9
Barnard D-6
Barnes C-7
Bartlett F-9
Basehor D-9
Bassett E-8
Baxter Springs F-9
Bazine D-4
Beattie C-8
Belle Plaine F-7
Belleville C-7
Beloit D-6
Belpre E-4
Belvue D-8
Benedict E-8
Bennington D-6
Bentley E-6
Benton E-7
Bern C-8
Beverly D-6
Bird City B-2
Bison D-4
Blue Mound E-9
Blue Rapids C-7
Bluff City F-6
Bogue C-4
Brewster D-2
Bronson E-9
Brookville D-6
Brownell D-4
Bucklin F-4
Buffalo E-9
Buhler E-6
Bunker Hill D-5
Burden F-7
Burdett E-4
Burlingame D-8
Burlington D-8
Burns E-7
Burr Oak C-5
Burrton E-6
Bushong D-8
Bushton D-5
Byers F-5
Caldwell F-6
Cambridge F-7
Caney F-8
Canton E-6
Carbondale D-9
Carlton D-7
Cassoday E-7
Cawker City C-5
Cedar C-5
Cedar Point E-7
Cedar Vale F-8
Centralia C-8
Chanute E-9
Chapman D-7
Chase E-5
Chautauqua F-8
Cheney E-6
Cherokee F-9
Cherryvale F-9
Chetopa F-9
Cimarron E-3
Circleville C-8
Claflin D-5
Clay Center C-7
Clayton C-3
Clearwater F-6
Clifton C-7
Climax F-7
Clyde C-7
Coats F-5
Coffeyville F-9
Colby C-2
Coldwater F-4

Collyer C-3
Colony E-9
Columbus F-9
Concordia C-6
Conway Springs . . . F-6
Coolidge E-1
Copeland F-3
Cottonwood Falls . . E-7
Council Grove D-8
Countryside . Pg. 112, H-2
Courtland C-6
Cuba C-6
Cullison F-5
Culver D-6
Cunningham F-5
Damar C-4
De Soto D-9
Dearing F-8
Deerfield E-2
Delphos C-6
Denison C-9
Denton C-9
Derby F-7
Dexter F-7
Dighton D-3
Dodge City E-3
Douglass F-7
Downs C-5
Dresden C-3
Dunlap D-8
Dwight D-7
Earlton F-9
Easton C-9
Edgerton D-9
Edmond C-4
Edna F-9
Effingham C-9
El Dorado F-7
Elbing E-7
Elgin F-8
Elk City F-8
Elk Falls F-8
Elkhart F-1
Ellinwood E-5
Ellis D-4
Ellsworth D-5
Elmdale E-7
Emmett C-8
Emporia D-8
Englewood F-3
Ensign E-3
Enterprise D-7
Erie E-9
Esbon C-5
Eskridge D-8
Eudora D-9
Eureka E-8
Fairview C-9
Florence E-7
Fontana E-9
Ford E-4
Formoso C-6
Fort Scott E-9
Fowler F-3
Frankfort C-8
Fredonia E-8
Freeport F-6
Frontenac F-9
Fulton E-9
Galatia D-4
Galena F-9
Galesburg F-9
Galva E-6
Garden City E-2
Garden Plain F-6
Gardner D-9
Garfield E-4
Garnett E-9
Gaylord C-5
Gem C-2
Geneseo D-5
Girard F-9
Glade D-4
Glasco C-6
Glen Elder C-5
Goessel E-6
Goodland C-1
Gorham D-5
Gove D-3
Grainfield D-4
Grandview Plaza . . . D-7
Great Bend D-5
Greenleaf C-7
Greensburg F-4
Gridley D-8
Grinnell C-2
Halstead E-6
Hamilton E-8
Hamlin C-8
Hanover C-7
Hanston E-4
Hardtner F-5
Harper F-6
Hartford D-8
Harveyville D-8
Havana F-8
Haven E-6
Havensville C-8
Haviland F-4
Hays D-4
Haysville F-6
Hazelton F-5
Healy D-3
Herington D-7
Herndon B-2
Hesston E-6
Hiawatha C-9
Highland C-9
Hill City C-3
Hillsboro D-7
Hoisington D-5
Holcomb E-2
Hollenberg C-7

Holton C-8
Holyrood D-5
Hope D-7
Horton C-9
Howard F-8
Hoxie C-3
Hoyt C-8
Hudson E-5
Hugoton F-2
Humboldt F-9
Hunter C-5
Huron C-9
Hutchinson E-6
Independence F-8
Ingalls E-3
Inman E-6
Iola E-9
Isabel F-5
Jamestown C-6
Jennings C-3
Jetmore E-3
Jewell C-6
Johnson City E-1
Junction City D-7
Kanapolis D-6
Kansas City D-9
    Vicinity . . . Pg. 112, E-1
Kensington C-4
Kincaid E-9
Kingman F-5
Kinsley E-4
Kiowa F-5
Kirwin C-4
Kismet F-2
La Crosse D-4
La Cygne E-9
La Harpe E-9
Lakin E-2
Lane E-9
Langdon E-5
Larned E-4
Latham F-7
Latimer D-7
Lawrence D-9
Le Roy E-8
Leavenworth C-9
Leawood . . . Pg. 112, K-3
Lebanon C-5
Lebo D-8
Lecompton D-9
Lehigh E-7
Lenexa . . . . Pg. 112, J-1
Lenora C-4
Leon E-7
Leona C-9
Leonardville C-7
Leoti D-2
Lewis E-4
Liberal F-2
Lincoln D-6
Lincolnville E-7
Lindsborg D-6
Linn C-7
Linwood D-9
Little River E-6
Logan C-4
Lone Elm E-9
Long Island B-4
Longford D-7
Longton F-8
Lorraine D-5
Lost Springs D-7
Louisburg E-9
Louisville D-8
Lucas D-5
Luka F-5
Luray D-5
Lyndon D-8
Lyons E-6
Macksville E-4
Madison E-8
Maize E-6
Manchester D-7
Manhattan D-8
Mankato C-5
Manter E-1
Maple Hill D-8
Mapleton E-9
Marion E-7
Marquette D-6
Marysville C-7
Matfield Green E-7
Mayetta C-8
Mayfield F-6
McCracken D-4
McCune F-9
McDonald B-2
McFarland D-8
McPherson E-6
Meade F-3
Medicine Lodge . . . F-5
Melvern D-8
Meriden C-9
Merriam . . . Pg. 112, H-2
Milan F-6
Mildred E-9
Milford D-7
Miltonvale C-6
Minneapolis D-6
Minneola F-3
Mission . . . . Pg. 112, H-2
Mission Hills Pg. 112, G-3
Moline F-8
Montezuma E-3
Moran E-9
Morganville C-7
Morland C-3
Morrill C-8
Morrowville C-7
Moscow F-2
Mound City E-9
Mound Valley F-9
Moundridge E-6
Mount Hope E-6

Mullinville F-5
Mulvane F-7
Munden C-6
Muscotah C-9
Narka C-6
Nashville F-5
Natoma C-4
Neodesha E-9
Neosho Falls E-9
Ness City D-3
Netawaka C-8
New Cambria D-6
New Strawn D-8
Newton E-6
Nickerson E-6
Norcatur C-3
Norton C-4
Nortonville C-9
Norwich F-6
Oak Hill C-7
Oakley C-2
Oberlin C-3
Offerle E-4
Ogden D-7
Oketo C-7
Olmitz D-5
Olpe D-8
Olsburg C-7
Onaga C-8
Osage City D-8
Osawatomie E-9
Osborne C-5
Oskaloosa D-9
Oswego F-9
Otis D-4
Ottawa D-9
Overbrook D-9
Overland Park
    . . . . Pg. 112, J-2
Oxford F-7
Palco C-4
Palmer C-7
Paola E-9
Paradise D-5
Park C-3
Park City E-7
Parker E-9
Parsons F-9
Pawnee Rock E-4
Paxico D-8
Peabody E-7
Perry D-9
Peru F-8
Phillipsburg C-4
Pittsburg F-10
Plains F-3
Plainville C-4
Pleasanton E-9
Plevna E-5
Pomona D-9
Portis C-5
Potwin E-7
Powhattan C-8
Prairie View C-4
Prairie Village Pg. 112, H-3
Pratt F-5
Prescott E-9
Preston F-5
Pretty Prairie E-6
Princeton E-9
Protection F-4
Quenemo D-8
Quinter C-3
Ramona D-7
Randall C-6
Randolph C-7
Ransom D-3
Rantoul E-9
Raymond E-5
Reading D-8
Redfield E-9
Republic C-6
Rexford C-3
Richfield F-1
Richmond D-9
Riley C-7
Robinson C-9
Roeland Park
    Vicinity . . . Pg. 112, G-3
Rolla F-1
Rose Hill F-7
Rossville D-8
Rozel E-4
Rush Center D-4
Russell D-5
Russell Springs . . . D-2
Sabetha C-8
Salina D-6
Satanta F-2
Sawyer F-5
Scandia C-6
Schoenchen D-4
Scott City D-3
Scottsville C-6
Sedan F-8
Sedgwick E-6
Selden C-3
Seneca C-8
Severy E-8
Seward E-5
Sharon F-5
Sharon Springs D-1
Shawnee . . . Pg. 112, H-1
Silver Lake D-8
Simpson C-6
Smith Center C-5
Smolan D-6
Solomon D-7
South Haven F-6
Spearville E-4
Spivey F-6
Spring Hill D-9
St. Francis B-1
St. John E-5

St. Marys D-8
St. Paul F-9
Stafford E-5
Stark F-9
Sterling E-6
Strong City E-8
Sublette F-2
Summerfield C-8
Sun City F-5
Sylvan Grove C-5
Sylvia E-5
Syracuse E-1
Tampa E-7
Tescott D-6
Thayer F-9
Timken D-4
Tipton C-5
Tonganoxie D-9
Topeka D-8
Toronto E-8
Towanda E-7
Tribune D-1
Troy C-9
Turon F-5
Tyro F-8
Udall F-7
Ulysses E-2
Uniontown F-9
Utica D-3
Valley Center E-6
Valley Falls C-9
Vermillion C-8
Victoria D-4
Vining C-7
Virgil E-8
WaKeeney D-4
Wakefield D-7
Waldo D-5
Waldron F-5
Wallace D-2
Walnut F-9
Walton E-7
Wamego D-8
Washington C-6
Waterville C-7
Wathena C-9
Waverly E-9
Webber C-6
Weir Scammon F-9
Wellington F-6
Westmoreland C-8
Westphalia E-9
Wetmore C-8
Wheaton C-8
White City D-7
Whitewater E-7
Whiting C-9
Wichita F-6
Williamsburg E-9
Willowbrook E-6
Wilmore F-4
Wilsey D-7
Wilson D-5
Winchester C-9
Windom E-6
Winfield F-7
Winona C-2
Woodbine D-7
Woodston C-4
Yates Center E-8
Zenda F-5
Zurich C-4

KENTUCKY
Pages 38-39
Population: 3,660,777
Capital: Frankfort
Land Area: 39,669 sq. mi.

Adairville F-6
Albany F-9
Alexandria B-10
Allen D-12
Allensville F-6
Arlington F-3
Ashland C-12
Auburn F-6
Audubon Park
    . . . . Pg. 118, D-3
Augusta B-10
Barbourville F-11
Bardstown D-8
Bardwell F-3
Barlow E-3
Beattyville D-11
Beaver Dam E-6
Bedford B-8
Beech Grove D-6
Bellefonte C-12
Bellevue . . . Pg. 100, E-4
Benham E-12
Benton F-4
Berea D-10
Berry C-10
Bloomfield D-9
Bonnieville E-7
Boone D-10
Boonesboro D-10
Booneville E-11
Bowling Green E-6
Bradfordsville D-9
Brandenburg D-7
Breckinridge C-10
Bremen E-5
Broadfields . Pg. 118, C-5
Brodhead D-10
Bromley A-10
    Vicinity . . . Pg. 100, F-3
Brooksville B-10
Brownsville E-7
Buckhorn E-11

Buffalo E-8
Burgin D-9
Burkesville F-8
Burnside F-10
Burton E-12
Butler B-10
Cadiz F-5
Calhoun D-6
Callaway F-11
Calvert City E-4
Campbellsburg B-8
Campbellsville D-11
Campton D-11
Caneyville E-7
Carlisle C-10
Carrollton B-9
Carrsville E-4
Carter C-11
Caseyville D-4
Catlettsburg C-12
Cave City E-6
Centertown E-6
Central City E-6
Cerulean F-5
Clairfield F-10
Clay E-5
Clay City D-10
Clearfield C-11
Clinton F-3
Cloverport D-7
Cold Spring . Pg. 100, G-5
Columbia E-8
Columbus F-3
Concord B-11
Constance . . Pg. 100, F-1
Corbin F-10
Corydon D-5
Covington B-9
    Vicinity . . . Pg. 100, F-3
Crab Orchard E-9
Crescent Springs
    . . . . Pg. 100, F-2
Crestview Hills
    . . . . Pg. 100, G-2
Crestwood C-8
Crittenden B-10
Crofton E-5
Cynthiana C-10
Danville D-9
Dawson Springs . . . E-5
Dayton . . . . Pg. 100, E-4
Dexter F-4
Dixon D-5
Dover B-11
Drakesboro E-6
Druid Hills . . Pg. 118, B-5
Dry Ridge B-10
Dunmor E-6
Dycusburg E-4
Earlington E-5
Eddyville E-4
Edmonton E-8
Ekron D-7
Elizabethtown D-7
Elkhorn City E-13
Elkton F-5
Elsmere B-10
    Vicinity . . . Pg. 100, G-2
Eminence C-9
Erlanger . . . Pg. 100, G-2
Eubank E-9
Evarts F-12
Fairdale C-8
Fairfield D-9
Fairview F-6
Falmouth B-10
Ferguson E-10
Flatwoods C-12
Fleming-Neon E-12
Flemingsburg C-11
Florence B-10
Fordsville D-7
Fountain Run F-8
Frankfort C-9
Franklin F-6
Fredonia E-5
Freeburn D-13
Frenchburg D-11
Frogue F-9
Ft. Mitchell . Pg. 100, G-3
Ft. Thomas . Pg. 100, F-5
Ft. Wright . . Pg. 100, F-3
Fulton F-3
Gamaliel F-8
Georgetown C-10
Ghent B-9
Glasgow E-7
Golden Pond F-5
Goshen C-8
Grand Rivers E-4
Gratz C-9
Grayson C-12
Greensburg E-8
Greenup B-12
Greenville E-6
Guthrie F-6
Hanson E-5
Hardin F-4
Hardinsburg D-7
Harlan F-11
Harned D-7
Harrodsburg D-9
Hartford D-6
Hawesville D-6
Hazard E-12
Hazel F-4
Hazel Green D-11
Hellier E-12
Henderson D-5
Hickman F-3
Highland Hts. Pg. 100, G-5
Hodgenville D-8
Hopkinsville F-6

KENTUCKY

KENTUCKY

Horse Cave ... E-8
Hustonville ... E-9
Hyden ... E-11
Independence ... B-10
Inez ... D-12
Irvine ... D-10
Irvington ... D-7
Island ... E-6
Jackson ... D-11
Jamestown ... E-9
Jeffersontown ... C-8
Jenkins ... E-12
Junction City ... D-9
Kenton Vale ... Pg. 100, G-3
Kirkmansville ... E-6
Knob Creek ... D-8
Kuttawa ... E-4
La Fayette ... F-5
La Grange ... C-8
LaCenter ... E-3
Lackey ... E-12
Lakeside Park ... Pg. 100, G-3
Lakeview ... Pg. 100, G-4
Lancaster ... D-10
Lawrenceburg ... C-9
Leatherwood ... E-11
Lebanon ... D-9
Lebanon Jct. ... D-8
Lee City ... D-11
Leitchfield ... D-7
Lewisburg ... C-11
Lewisport ... D-6
Lexington ... E-9
Liberty ... E-9
Livermore ... D-6
Livingston ... E-10
Lockport ... C-9
London ... E-10
Loretto ... D-8
Lothair ... E-11
Louisa ... C-12
Louisville ... C-8
  Vicinity ... Pg. 118
Loyall ... F-11
Lucas ... F-8
Ludlow ... Pg. 100, F-3
Lynch ... F-12
Lynnview ... Pg. 118, E-4
Madisonville ... E-5
Manchester ... E-10
Marion ... E-5
Martin ... D-12
Mason ... B-10
Mayfield ... F-4
Maysville ... B-11
McCreary ... D-10
McHenry ... E-6
McKee ... E-10
McRoberts ... E-12
Middlesboro ... F-10
Middletown ... C-8
Midway ... C-9
Midway ... F-4
Millersburg ... C-10
Milton ... B-8
Mockingbird Valley ... Pg. 118, B-5
Monkeys Eyebrow ... E-3
Monroe ... E-8
Monterey ... C-9
Monticello ... E-9
Morehead ... C-11
Moreland ... D-9
Morgan ... B-10
Morganfield ... D-5
Morgantown ... E-7
Mortons Gap ... E-5
Mount Olivet ... C-11
Mount Sterling ... C-11
Mount Vernon ... E-10
Mount Washington ... C-8
Muldraugh ... D-8
Munfordville ... E-8
Murray ... F-4
Nebo ... E-5
New Castle ... C-9
New Haven ... D-8
Newport ... A-10
  Vicinity ... Pg. 100, F-4
Nicholasville ... D-9
North Middletown ... C-10
Nortonville ... E-6
Oak Grove ... F-5
Oakland ... E-7
Olive Hill ... C-11
Owensboro ... D-6
Owenton ... C-9
Owingsville ... C-10
Paducah ... E-4
Paintsville ... D-12
Paris ... C-10
Park City ... E-8
Park Hills ... Pg. 100, F-3
Parkers Lake ... F-10
Parkway Village ... Pg. 118, D-3
Pembroke ... F-5
Perryville ... D-9
Phelps ... D-13
Pikeville ... E-13
Pine Knot ... F-10
Pineville ... F-11
Pleasureville ... C-9
Prestonsburg ... D-12
Prestonville ... B-8
Princeton ... E-5
Prospect ... C-8
Providence ... E-5
Raceland ... B-12
Radcliff ... D-7
Ravenna ... D-11
Reidland ... E-4
Renfro Valley ... E-10

Richmond ... D-10
Rockcastle ... F-5
Rockport ... E-6
Rolling Fields ... Pg. 118, B-5
Russell ... B-12
Russell Springs ... E-9
Russellville ... E-6
Sadieville ... C-10
Salt Lick ... C-11
Salyersville ... D-12
Sanders ... B-9
Sandy Hook ... C-12
Sardis ... C-11
Science Hill ... E-9
Scottsville ... F-7
Sebree ... D-5
Seco ... E-12
Sedalia ... F-4
Sharpsburg ... C-11
Shelby City ... D-9
Shelbyville ... C-9
Shepherdsville ... C-8
  Vicinity ... Pg. 118, D-1
Silver Grove ... Pg. 100, G-6
Simpsonville ... C-8
Slaughters ... D-5
Smithland ... E-4
Smiths Grove ... E-7
Somerset ... E-10
Sonora ... D-7
South Shore ... B-12
South Williamson ... D-13
Springfield ... D-9
Stamping Ground ... C-9
Stanford ... D-10
Stanton ... D-11
Stearns ... F-9
Sturgis ... D-5
Taylorsville ... D-9
Tompkinsville ... F-8
Trenton ... F-6
Trimble ... D-9
Tyner ... E-11
Union ... B-9
Uniontown ... D-5
Upton ... E-8
Valley Station ... C-8
Van Lear ... D-12
Vanceburg ... B-11
Vancleve ... D-11
Versailles ... C-9
Villa Hills ... Pg. 100, F-2
Vine Grove ... D-7
Wallins Creek ... F-11
Walton ... B-10
Warfield ... D-13
Warsaw ... B-9
Washington ... B-11
Water Valley ... F-4
Waverly ... D-5
Wayland ... E-12
Webster ... D-7
West Beauchel ... Pg. 118, D-5
West Liberty ... D-11
West Point ... D-8
Wheatley ... B-9
Wheelwright ... E-12
Whitesburg ... E-12
Whitesville ... D-6
Whitley City ... F-10
Wickliffe ... E-3
Wilder ... Pg. 100, F-3
Willard ... C-12
Williamsburg ... F-10
Williamstown ... B-10
Wilmore ... D-9
Winchester ... D-10
Wingo ... F-4
Woodburn ... F-7

LOUISIANA
Page 40
Population: 4,205,9000
Capital: Baton Rouge
Land Area: 44,521 sq. mi.

Abbeville ... F-5
Abington ... B-2
Abita Springs ... E-8
Acme ... D-5
Acy ... E-7
Ada ... B-3
Addis ... E-6
Adeline ... F-6
Afton ... B-6
Aimwell ... C-5
Airline Park ... Pg. 125, C-4
Ajax ... C-3
Albany ... E-7
Alco ... D-3
Alden Bridge ... A-2
Alexandria ... D-4
Alsaita ... A-6
Alto ... B-5
Ama ... Pg. 125, C-2
Amelia ... G-7
Amite ... D-8
Anacoco ... D-3
Angie ... D-9
Angola ... B-6
Ansley ... B-4
Antioch ... A-4
Arabi ... F-9
  Vicinity ... Pg. 125, C-8
Archibald ... B-5
Archie ... C-5
Arcola ... D-8
Armistead ... B-3
Arnaudville ... E-5

Ashland ... B-3
Athens ... A-3
Atlanta ... C-4
Augusta ... Pg. 125, F-7
Avery Island ... F-5
Avondale ... Pg. 125, D-4
Aycock ... A-3
Bains ... D-6
Baker ... E-6
Baldwin ... F-6
Ball ... C-4
Bancroft ... E-2
Barataria ... F-8
Basile ... E-4
Baskin ... B-5
Bastrop ... A-5
Batchelor ... D-6
Baton Rouge ... E-7
Bayou Cane ... G-7
Bayou Chicot ... D-5
Bayou Sorrel ... F-6
Bayou Vista ... F-6
Baywood ... E-7
Beaver ... E-4
Beekman ... A-5
Beggs ... E-5
Bell City ... F-3
Belle Chasse ... F-8
  Vicinity ... Pg. 125, E-8
Belle Rose ... F-7
Bellwood ... C-3
Belmont ... C-2
Benson ... C-2
Bentley ... C-4
Benton ... A-2
Bernice ... A-4
Bertrandville ... F-9
  Vicinity ... Pg. 125, G-7
Berwick ... F-6
Bienville ... B-3
Blackburn ... A-3
Blanchard ... A-2
Bogalusa ... D-9
Bohemia ... G-9
Bolinger ... B-4
Bonita ... A-5
Book ... E-4
Boothville ... G-10
Bordelonville ... D-5
Bosco ... B-5
Bossier City ... A-3
Bourg ... G-8
Boyce ... C-4
Braithwaite ... Pg. 125, D-4
Branch ... E-5
Breaux Bridge ... E-5
Bridge City ... Pg. 125, D-4
Broussard ... E-5
Brusly ... E-6
Bryceland ... B-3
Bunkie ... D-5
Buras ... G-9
Burnside ... F-7
Burr Ferry ... D-2
Bush ... E-8
Cade ... F-5
Caernarvon ... Pg. 125, E-9
Calhoun ... B-4
Calvin ... B-3
Cameron ... F-3
Campti ... C-3
Caney ... D-2
Carencro ... E-5
Carlisle ... F-9
Carville ... E-7
Caspiana ... B-2
Castor ... B-3
Cedar Grove ... Pg. 125, F-7
Center Point ... D-5
Centerville ... F-6
Chacahoula ... F-7
Chackbay ... F-7
Chalmette ... F-8
  Vicinity ... Pg. 125, D-8
Chase ... B-5
Chataignier ... E-4
Chatham ... B-4
Chauvin ... G-8
Cheneyville ... D-5
Chestnut ... B-3
Chipola ... D-7
Chopin ... C-4
Choudrant ... B-4
Church Point ... E-5
Clarence ... C-3
Clarks ... B-5
Clay ... B-4
Clayton ... C-6
Clifton ... D-7
Clinton ... D-7
Cloutierville ... C-4
Cocodrie ... G-7
Colfax ... C-4
Collinston ... A-5
Columbia ... B-4
Concession ... Pg. 125, F-8
Convent ... F-7
Converse ... C-2
Cotton Valley ... A-3
Cottonport ... D-5
Coushatta ... B-3
Covington ... E-8
Cravens ... D-3
Creole ... F-3
Creston ... B-3
Crowley ... E-4
Crown Point ... Pg. 125, G-6
Crowville ... B-5
Cullen ... A-3
Cut Off ... G-8
Cypress ... C-3
Dalcour ... Pg. 125, F-8

Darlington ... D-7
Darnell ... F-9
Davant ... G-9
De Quincy ... E-3
De Ridder ... C-6
Deer Park ... C-6
Delacroix ... F-8
Delcambre ... F-5
Delhi ... A-6
Derry ... C-3
Des Allemands ... F-8
Destrehan ... Pg. 125, D-1
Deville ... D-5
Diamond ... G-9
Dixie Inn ... A-2
Dodson ... B-4
Donaldsonville ... F-7
Downsville ... A-4
Dry Creek ... E-3
Dry Prong ... C-4
Dubach ... A-4
Dubberly ... B-2
Dubuisson ... E-5
Dulac ... G-7
Dupont ... D-5
Duson ... F-5
Duty ... C-5
Easlyville ... D-7
Eastwood ... B-2
Echo ... C-4
Edgerly ... F-2
Effie ... D-5
Elizabeth ... D-4
Elm Grove ... B-2
Elton ... E-4
Empire ... G-9
Englishturn ... Pg. 125, E-8
Enon ... D-8
Enterprise ... C-5
Erath ... F-5
Eros ... B-4
Estelle ... Pg. 125, E-6
Estherwood ... E-4
Esto ... D-2
Ethel ... E-6
Eunice ... E-4
Eva ... C-5
Evangeline ... E-4
Evans ... D-3
Evelyn ... B-2
Evergreen ... D-5
Farmerville ... A-4
Felps ... D-7
Fenton ... E-3
Ferriday ... C-6
Fields ... E-2
Fillmore ... A-2
Fisher ... C-3
Flatwoods ... D-4
Flora ... C-3
Florien ... D-2
Folsom ... E-8
Fondale ... B-5
Fordoche ... E-5
Forest ... A-6
Forest Hill ... D-4
Fort Jesup ... C-3
Fort Necessity ... B-5
Foules ... C-6
Franklin ... F-6
Franklinton ... D-8
French Settlement ... E-7
Frenier ... F-8
Frogmore ... C-5
Frost ... E-7
Galbraith ... C-4
Galion ... A-5
Galliano ... G-8
Gandy ... D-2
Gardner ... D-4
Georgetown ... C-4
Gheens ... F-8
Gibsland ... B-3
Gibson ... G-7
Gilbert ... C-5
Gillis ... E-3
Glade ... C-5
Glenmora ... D-4
Gloster ... B-2
Golden Meadow ... G-8
Goldonna ... B-4
Gonzales ... E-7
Gordon ... A-3
Gorum ... C-3
Goudeau ... D-5
Grambling ... B-4
Grand Bayou ... B-3
Grand Cane ... B-2
Grand Chenier ... F-4
Grand Coteau ... E-5
Grand Isle ... G-9
Grand Lake ... F-3
Grangeville ... D-7
Grayson ... B-5
Greensburg ... D-7
Gretna ... F-8
  Vicinity ... Pg. 125, D-7
Grosse Tete ... E-6
Gueydan ... F-4
Hackberry ... F-3
Haile ... A-5
Hall Summit ... B-3
Hamburg ... D-6
Hammond ... E-8
Hanna ... C-3
Harahan ... F-8
  Vicinity ... Pg. 125, D-4
Harrisonburg ... C-5
Harvey ... Pg. 125, D-6
Hathaway ... E-4
Hayes ... F-3
Haynesville ... A-4
Hebert ... B-5
Henderson ... E-6
Hermitage ... Pg. 125, F-8

Hessmer ... D-5
Hickory ... E-9
Hicks ... D-3
Hico ... A-4
Highland ... A-6
Hodge ... B-4
Holloway ... D-5
Holly Beach ... F-2
Holmwood ... F-3
Holton ... E-8
Holum ... A-3
Homer ... A-3
Hornbeck ... D-3
Hosston ... A-2
Hot Wells ... D-4
Houma ... G-7
Humphreys ... G-7
Hutton ... D-3
Ida ... A-2
Independence ... E-8
Indian Mound ... E-7
Indian Village ... F-6
Iota ... F-4
Iowa ... F-3
Ivan ... A-2
Jackson ... D-6
Jamestown ... B-3
Jean Lafitte ... F-8
  Vicinity ... Pg. 125, G-5
Jeanerette ... F-5
Jefferson Hts. ... Pg. 125, C-4
Jena ... C-5
Jennings ... F-4
Jesuit Bend ... Pg. 125, E-9
Jigger ... B-5
Johnsons Bayou ... F-2
Jones ... A-5
Jonesboro ... B-4
Jonesville ... C-5
Kaplan ... F-4
Keatchie ... B-2
Keithville ... B-2
Kenner ... F-8
  Vicinity ... Pg. 125, B-3
Kentwood ... D-8
Kilbourne ... A-6
Killian ... E-8
Kinder ... E-3
Kingston ... B-2
Kisatchie ... D-3
Krotz Springs ... D-5
Kurthwood ... D-3
La Place ... F-7
Labadieville ... F-7
Labarre ... E-6
Lacamp ... D-3
Lacassine ... E-4
Lacombe ... E-8
Lafayette ... F-5
Lafitte ... F-8
Lafourche ... F-7
Lake Arthur ... F-3
Lake Charles ... E-3
Lake End ... C-3
Lake Providence ... A-6
Lakeland ... E-6
Larose ... F-8
Larto ... C-5
Latanier ... D-4
Lawtell ... E-5
Le Blanc ... E-3
LeMoyen ... D-4
Leander ... D-4
Lebeau ... D-5
Lecompte ... D-4
Leesville ... D-3
Leeville ... G-8
Leonville ... E-5
Libuse ... D-4
Lillie ... A-4
Linville ... A-5
Lisbon ... A-3
Lismore ... C-5
Live Oak ... Pg. 125, G-7
Live Oak Manor ... Pg. 125, C-3
Livingston ... E-7
Livonia ... E-6
Lockport ... F-8
Logansport ... C-2
Lone Star ... Pg. 125, D-1
Longstreet ... B-2
Longville ... E-3
Lottie ... E-6
Louisa ... F-6
Lucas ... B-2
Lucky ... B-3
Luling ... Pg. 125, D-1
Luna ... B-5
Lutcher ... F-7
Madisonville ... E-8
Mamou ... E-4
Manchac ... E-8
Mandeville ... E-8
Mangham ... B-5
Manifest ... C-5
Mansfield ... C-2
Many ... C-3
Maringouin ... E-6
Marion ... A-5
Marksville ... D-5
Marrero ... Pg. 125, D-6
Marsalis ... A-3
Martin ... B-3
Mathews ... F-8
Maurepas ... E-7
Maxie ... E-4
Mayna ... A-5
McDade ... B-2
McNary ... D-4
Melder ... D-4
Melrose ... C-4
Melville ... D-5
Mer Rouge ... A-5

Meraux ... Pg. 125, D-9
Mermentau ... F-4
Merryville ... E-2
Metairie ... F-8
  Vicinity ... Pg. 125, C-5
Midland ... F-4
Midway ... A-2
Mill ... B-4
Minden ... A-3
Mira ... A-2
Mitchel ... E-4
Mittie ... E-4
Mix ... E-6
Monroe ... G-8
Montegut ... G-8
Monterey ... C-6
Montgomery ... C-3
Montpelier ... E-7
Mooringsport ... A-2
Moreauville ... D-5
Morgan City ... F-7
Morganza ... E-6
Morrow ... D-5
Mount Carmel ... C-3
Myrtle Grove ... G-8
Nairn ... G-9
Naomi ... F-8
Napoleonville ... F-7
Natchez ... C-3
Natchitoches ... C-3
Negreet ... C-2
New Era ... D-5
New Iberia ... F-6
New Llano ... D-3
New Orleans ... F-8
  Vicinity ... Pg. 125, A-7
New Roads ... E-6
Newellton ... B-6
Newlight ... B-6
Noble ... C-2
North Hodge ... B-4
Norwood ... D-6
Oak Grove
  (Cameron Cty) ... F-3
Oak Grove
  West Carroll Cty) ... A-6
Oak Ridge ... A-5
Oakdale ... E-4
Oakland ... A-4
Oakville ... Pg. 125, G-7
Oberlin ... D-3
Oil City ... A-2
Olivier ... F-6
Olla ... C-4
Opelousas ... E-5
Oscar ... E-6
Oxford ... C-4
Packton ... C-4
Paincourtville ... F-7
Parks ... F-5
Patterson ... F-6
Pearl River ... E-9
Pecan Island ... G-4
Perryville ... A-5
Phoenix ... F-9
Pickering ... D-3
Pierre Part ... F-6
Pigeon ... F-6
Pilot Town ... G-10
Pine ... D-8
Pine Grove ... E-7
Pine Prairie ... E-4
Pineville ... D-4
Pitkin ... D-3
Plain Dealing ... A-2
Plaquemine ... E-6
Pleasant Hill ... C-2
Pointe a La Hache ... G-9
Pollock ... C-4
Ponchatoula ... E-8
Port Allen ... E-6
Port Barre ... E-5
Port Sulphur ... G-9
Port Vincent ... E-7
Powhatan ... C-3
Poydras ... Pg. 125, E-10
Provencal ... C-3
Quitman ... B-4
Raceland ... F-7
Ragley ... E-3
Ramah ... E-6
Rayne ... E-5
Rayville ... B-5
Readhimer ... B-3
Reddell ... E-4
Reeves ... E-3
Reggio ... F-8
Reserve ... F-7
Richmond ... B-5
Richwood ... B-5
Ridgecrest ... C-6
Ringgold ... B-3
Riverton ... B-5
Robeline ... C-3
Robert ... E-8
Rocky Mountain ... A-2
Rodessa ... A-1
Rosedale ... E-6
Rosefield ... C-5
Rosepine ... D-3
Ruddock ... F-8
Ruston ... B-4
Sailes ... B-3
Saint Bernard ...
  Pg. 125, E-10
Saint Clair ... Pg. 125, E-8
Saint Francisville ... D-6
Saint Gabriel ... E-7
Saint Joseph ... B-6
Saint Martinville ... F-5
Saint Rose ... Pg. 125, D-1
Saline ... C-3
Sarepta ... A-3
Scarsdale ... Pg. 125, E-9

Scott ... F-5
Shaw ... D-6
Sheridan ... D-9
Shongaloo ... A-3
Shreveport ... B-2
Sibley ... A-3
Sicily Island ... C-5
Sieper ... D-4
Sikes ... B-4
Simmesport ... D-5
Simpson ... D-3
Singer ... E-3
Slagle ... D-3
Slaughter ... E-6
Slidell ... E-9
Slocum ... D-6
Somerset ... B-6
Sondheimer ... A-6
Sorrento ... F-7
Spearsville ... A-4
Spencer ... A-5
Spokane ... C-6
Spring Ridge ... B-2
Springfield ... E-7
Springhill ... A-2
Stanley ... C-2
Starks ... F-2
Start ... B-5
State Line ... A-5
Stella ... Pg. 125, F-8
Sterlington ... A-5
Stonewall ... B-2
Sugartown ... E-3
Sulphur ... F-3
Summerfield ... A-4
Sun ... E-9
Sunset ... E-5
Supreme ... F-7
Talisheek ... E-9
Tallulah ... B-6
Tangipahoa ... D-8
Tannehill ... B-4
Taylortown ... B-2
Terry ... A-6
Tete ... E-6
Thibodaux ... F-7
Tidewater ... G-9
Tioga ... D-4
Toomey ... F-2
Toro ... D-2
Transylvania ... A-6
Triumph ... G-10
Truxno ... A-4
Tullos ... C-5
Turkey Creek ... F-7
Union ... F-7
Union Hill ... C-4
Urania ... C-4
Vacherie ... F-7
Varnado ... D-9
Venice ... G-10
Verda ... C-4
Vidalia ... C-6
Vienna ... A-4
Ville Platte ... E-5
Vinton ... F-2
Violet ... Pg. 125, D-9
Vivian ... A-2
Vixen ... B-5
Waggaman ... Pg. 125, D-3
Wakefield ... D-6
Waldheim ... E-8
Walters ... C-4
Warnerton ... D-8
Washington ... E-5
Waterproof ... B-6
Watson ... E-7
Weeks ... F-6
Welsh ... F-4
West End ... Pg. 125, B-5
Weston ... B-4
Westwego ... B-4
  Vicinity ... Pg. 125, E-4
Weyanoke ... D-6
White Castle ... F-7
Whitehall ... C-5
Williana ... C-4
Wills Point ... Pg. 125, G-8
Willswood ... Pg. 125, D-3
Wilmer ... D-8
Wilson ... D-6
Winfield ... C-4
Winnsboro ... B-5
Woodworth ... D-4
Worden ... D-6
Wye ... F-5
Youngsville ... F-5
Yscloskey ... F-9
Zenoria ... C-4
Zwolle ... C-2

MAINE
Page 41
Population: 1,124,660
Capital: Augusta
Land Area: 30,995 sq. mi.

Acton ... J-2
Addison ... F-6
Albion ... G-3
Alexander ... E-6
Allagash ... B-4
Andover ... G-2
Anson ... F-3
Appleton ... G-4
Ashland ... B-5
Athens ... F-3
Auburn ... H-3
Augusta ... G-3
Avon ... F-2

Bailey Island ... H-3
Balleyville ... E-6
Bangor ... F-4
Bar Harbor ... G-5
Baring ... E-6
Bath ... H-3
Beddington ... F-5
Belfast ... G-4
Belgrade ... G-3
Benton ... G-3
Berwick ... J-2
Bethel ... G-2
Biddeford ... J-3
Bigelow ... F-2
Bingham ... F-3
Blaine ... C-5
Blanchard ... F-3
Blue Hill ... G-4
Boothbay Harbor ... H-4
Bradford ... F-4
Bradley ... F-5
Brewer ... F-4
Bridgewater ... C-5
Bridgton ... H-2
Brighton ... F-3
Bristol ... H-4
Brooks ... G-4
Brownfield ... H-2
Brownville ... E-4
Brownville Jct. ... E-4
Brunswick ... H-3
Buckfield ... G-3
Bucks Harbor ... F-6
Bucksport ... G-5
Burlington ... F-4
Burnham ... F-4
Buxton ... J-2
Byron ... G-2
Calais ... E-6
Cambridge ... F-3
Camden ... G-4
Canton ... G-2
Cape Elizabeth ... J-3
Cape Porpoise ... J-2
Caratunk ... F-3
Caribou ... B-5
Carmel ... F-4
Carrabassett ... F-3
Carroll ... E-5
Cary ... D-5
Casco ... H-2
Castine ... G-4
Charleston ... F-4
Cherryfield ... G-6
Chester ... E-5
Chisolm ... G-2
Clayton Lake ... C-3
Clinton ... G-4
Coburn Gore ... E-2
Colby ... E-6
Columbia ... F-6
Conner ... B-5
Cooper ... G-6
Corea ... G-6
Corinna ... F-4
Cornish ... H-1
Costigan ... F-4
Crawford ... F-6
Crouseville ... B-5
Cumberland Center ... H-2
Cutler ... F-7
Daigle ... B-4
Dallas ... F-2
Damariscotta ... H-4
Danforth ... D-5
Deblois ... F-5
Dedham ... F-4
Deer Isle ... G-5
Dennistown ... E-2
Dennysville ... F-6
Dickey ... B-4
Dixfield ... G-2
Dixmont ... F-4
Dover Foxcroft ... F-4
Durham ... H-3
Eagle Lake ... B-4
East Hampden ... F-4
East Machias ... F-6
East Millinocket ... E-4
East Sumner ... G-2
East Wilton ... G-3
Eastbrook ... F-5
Easton ... C-5
Eastport ... F-7
Eaton ... E-6
Eddington ... F-4
Ellsworth ... G-5
Estcourt Sta. ... A-4
Eustis ... F-2
Fairfield ... G-3
Farmingdale ... G-3
Farmington ... G-3
Fort Fairfield ... B-5
Fort Kent ... A-4
Franklin ... G-5
Freeport ... H-3
Frenchville ... A-5
Friendship ... H-4
Frye ... G-2
Fryeburg ... H-1
Gardiner ... G-3
Gilead ... G-1
Glenburn Center ... F-4
Gorham ... J-2
Gouldsboro ... G-5
Grand Isle ... A-5
Grand Lake Stream ... E-5
Gray ... H-2
Greenville ... E-3
Grove ... F-5
Guerette ... A-5
Guilford ... F-3
Hallowell ... G-3

MAINE

Hamlin B-5
Hampden F-4
Hancock G-5
Hanover G-2
Harrington F-5
Harrison H-2
Hartford Center G-2
Hartland F-3
Haven G-5
Haynesville D-5
Hersey D-5
Hinckley G-3
Hiram H-2
Hogdon C-5
Houghton F-2
Houlton D-5
Howland E-4
Island Falls D-5
Jackman E-2
Jay G-3
Jefferson H-4
Jemtland B-5
Jonesboro F-6
Jonesport G-6
Keegan B-5
Kenduskeag F-4
Kennebago Lake F-2
Kennebunk J-2
Kennebunkport J-3
Kingfield F-2
Kingman E-5
Kingsbury F-3
Kittery K-2
Kittery Point K-2
Knowles Corner C-4
Kokadjo E-3
Lagrange F-4
Lake Parlin E-2
Lambert Lake E-6
Larone G-3
Lee E-5
Lewiston H-2
Liberty G-4
Lille F-2
Lily Bay E-3
Limerick J-2
Limestone B-5
Limington J-2
Lincoln D-5
Lincolnville H-4
Linneus D-5
Lisbon H-3
Lisbon Falls H-2
Littleton C-5
Livermore Falls G-3
Long Pond E-3
Lovell H-2
Lubec F-7
Ludlow D-5
Lynchville G-2
Machias F-6
Macwahoc D-5
Madawaska A-4
Madison F-3
Madrid F-2
Manchester G-3
Mapleton F-6
Marion F-6
Mars Hill C-5
Masardis C-4
Mattawamkeag E-5
Mayfield F-3
Medford F-3
Medway E-4
Mexico G-2
Milbridge G-5
Milford F-5
Millinocket D-4
Milo E-4
Molunkus E-5
Monarda D-5
Monroe G-3
Monson E-3
Monticello C-5
Moose River E-2
Morrill G-4
Moscow F-3
Naples H-2
Newcastle H-3
New Gloucester H-2
Newfield J-2
Newport F-4
Newry G-2
Nobleboro G-3
Norcross E-4
Norridgewock G-3
North Amity D-6
North Anson F-2
North Berwick J-2
North Lovell H-2
North Lyndon B-5
Northeast Carry D-3
Northeast Harbor G-5
Northfield F-6
Norway H-2
Oakland G-3
Ogunquit J-2
Old Orchard Beach J-2
Old Town F-5
Oquossoc F-2
Orient D-5
Orland G-4
Orono F-5
Orrington F-4
Ouellette B-4
Oxbow C-4
Oxford G-2
Palmyra F-3
Paris G-2
Parkman F-3
Patten D-4
Pittston H-3
Poland H-2
Portage B-4

Portland J-3
Presque Isle B-5
Princeton E-6
Quimby B-4
Randolph G-3
Rangeley F-2
Raymond H-2
Readfield G-3
Red Beach E-7
Reed D-5
Richmond H-3
Ripley F-3
Ripogenus Dam D-4
Robbinston E-7
Robinsons C-5
Rockland H-4
Rockport H-4
Rockwood E-3
Rome G-3
Roxbury G-2
Rumford G-2
Sabattus H-3
Saco H-2
Saint Albans F-3
Saint David A-5
Saint Francis B-4
Saint George G-4
Saint John B-4
Salem F-2
Sanford J-2
Sangerville F-4
Saponac E-5
Scarborough J-2
Seal Harbor G-5
Searsmont G-4
Searsport G-4
Sebago H-2
Sebec Lake E-4
Seboeis E-4
Seboomook D-3
Sedgewick G-4
Selden D-5
Sheridan B-4
Sherman D-4
Sherman Mills D-5
Sherman Sta. D-4
Shin Pond D-4
Shirley Mills E-3
Sidney G-3
Skowhegan F-3
Smyrna Mills C-5
Soldier Pond B-4
Solon F-3
South Arm F-2
South Bancroft D-5
South China G-4
South Hope G-4
South Paris H-2
South Portland J-3
Southwest Harbor G-5
Springfield E-5
Springvale J-2
Squa Pan C-4
Stacyville D-4
Standish J-2
Starboard F-6
Stetson F-4
Steuben G-6
Stockton Springs G-4
Stonington G-5
Stow H-2
Stratton F-2
Strong F-2
Sweden H-2
The Forks E-3
Thomaston H-4
Topsfield E-6
Topsham H-3
Tremont G-5
Turner H-2
Union G-4
Unity G-4
Upton G-2
Van Buren B-5
Vanceboro E-6
Vienna G-3
Vinalhaven G-4
Waite E-6
Waldoboro H-4
Waltham F-5
Warren H-4
Washburn B-5
Washington G-4
Waterboro J-2
Waterford H-2
Waterville G-3
Wells J-2
Wesley F-6
West Enfield E-5
West Forks E-3
West Newfield J-2
West Paris G-2
Westbrook J-2
Weston D-5
Whiting F-6
Williamantic E-3
Wilsons Mills F-1
Wilton G-2
Winn E-5
Winslow G-3
Winter Harbor G-5
Winterport G-4
Winterville B-4
Winthrop G-3
Wiscasset H-3
Woodland B-4
Woolwich H-3
Wytopitlock D-5
Yarmouth H-3
York Beach K-2
York Village K-2

MARYLAND
Pages 42-43
Population: 4,216,975
Capital: Annapolis
Land Area: 9,837 sq. mi.

Aberdeen B-12
Accident B-1
Accokeek F-12
Airy F-12
Altamont B-1
Altoona Beach Pg. 91, H-5
Andersontown E-13
Andrews G-12
Annapolis D-11
Annapolis Junction Pg. 91, J-1
Arbutus Pg. 91, F-3
Arnold D-10
Aspen Hill D-9
Avenue G-10
Baltimore C-10
Vicinity Pg. 91, F-3
Barclay D-13
Barnesville C-7
Bay Ridge E-11
Bayard E-10
Bayview F-2
Belair Edison Pg. 91, D-5
Bel Air B-11
Belltown Pg. 91, B-1
Benfield Pg. 91, J-4
Berlin G-15
Berwyn Heights Pg. 150, B-8
Bethesda D-8
Vicinity Pg. 150, C-5
Betterton C-12
Bladensburg Pg. 150, C-9
Blenheim Pg. 91, A-5
Bloomsbury Pg. 91, F-2
Bonaparte Estates Pg. 91, A-7
Boonsboro B-7
Bowie D-10
Braddock Hts. C-7
Brandywine F-9
Brentwood Pg. 150, C-9
Bristol E-11
Broadwater Beach Pg. 91, K-6
Brooklyn Pg. 91, F-4
Brookview F-13
Broomes Island G-10
Brunswick C-7
Bryans Road F-8
Buckeystown C-7
Bucktown G-12
Burkittsville C-7
Butler B-10
California G-11
Cambridge F-12
Cape St. Claire D-11
Capitol Heights Pg. 150, E-8
Carney Pg. 91, D-4
Cascade A-7
Catonsville C-10
Vicinity Pg. 91, F-2
Caves Park Pg. 91, B-2
Cavetown B-7
Cayots B-13
Cecilton C-12
Centreville D-12
Chaptico G-9
Charlestown B-12
Charlotte Hall F-9
Chesapeake B-13
Chesapeake Beach F-10
Chestertown C-12
Cheverly Pg. 150, D-8
Chevy Chase Pg. 150, C-5
Church Creek F-12
Church Hill D-12
Clear Spring B-6
Cliffs City D-12
Clinton Pg. 150, G-8
Cobb Island G-9
Cockeysville B-10
Vicinity Pg. 91, A-4
Colesville Pg. 150, A-6
College Park Pg. 91, A-7
Vicinity Pg. 150, B-8
Colmar Manor Pg. 150, D-7
Columbia C-9
Columbia Hills Pg. 91, F-1
Cooksville C-9
Corriganville A-3
Cottage City Pg. 150, D-7
Cove Point G-11
Cresaptown B-3
Crisfield J-13
Crofton D-10
Cronhardt Pg. 91, B-3
Cub Hills Pg. 91, B-6
Cumberland B-3
Damascus C-8
Dares Beach F-11
Deale E-10
Delight Pg. 91, B-1
Delmar G-13
Denton E-13
District Heights Pg. 150, E-9
Doncaster F-8
Dorsey Pg. 91, F-2
Drawbridge G-13
Drummond Pg.150, G-12
Drum Point G-11
Dublin A-11

Dunbrook Pg. 91, J-6
Dundalk C-10
Vicinity Pg. 91, F-6
Dunkirk F-10
Eagle Harbor F-10
East Point Pg. 91, E-6
Easton E-12
Edgemere C-11
Vicinity Pg. 91, F-7
Edgewood C-11
Edmonston Pg. 150, C-8
Eldersburg C-9
Eldorado F-13
Elkridge Pg. 91, G-2
Elkton B-13
Ellicott City C-9
Vicinity Pg. 91, F-1
Elliott G-12
Elmhurst Pg. 91, H-3
Emmitsburg A-8
Essex Pg. 91, E-6
Fair Hill A-12
Fairmont Heights Pg. 150, D-8
Fallston B-11
Federalsburg E-13
Ferndale Pg. 91, G-4
Fishtown Pg. 91, C-2
Font Hill Pg. 91, G-1
Foremans Corner Pg. 91, G-5
Forest Heights Pg. 150, F-7
Fork Pg. 91, A-7
Fort Howard Pg. 91, F-7
Fountain Head A-7
Foxridge Pg. 91, C-1
Frederick C-8
Friendship Heights Pg. 150, C-5
Friendsville A-1
Frostburg B-3
Fruitland G-14
Fullerton Pg. 91, C-6
Furnace Branch Pg. 150, C-9
Gaithersburg D-8
Galena C-12
Gambrills Pg. 91, K-5
Garrett Park Pg. 150, A-5
Germantown C-8
Vicinity Pg. 91, B-7
Gittings Pg. 91, A-6
Glen Burnie D-10
Vicinity Pg. 91, H-4
Glen Echo Pg. 150, C-4
Glen Morris Pg. 91, A-1
Glenarden Pg. 150, D-9
Glenarm Pg. 91, A-6
Glenmar (Baltimore Cty) Pg. 91, D-7
Glenmar (Howard Cty) Pg. 91, F-1
Glyndon Pg. 91, A-1
Golden Beach F-10
Goldsboro D-13
Grantsville A-2
Grasonville E-12
Green Haven Pg. 91, H-5
Green Hill G-13
Green Valley C-8
Green Valley North Pg. 91, A-3
Greenbelt D-9
Vicinity Pg. 150, B-9
Greengate Pg. 91, C-3
Greensboro D-13
Guilford Pg. 91, H-1
Hagerstown B-7
Halethorpe Pg. 91, F-3
Halfway B-6
Hampstead B-9
Hampton Pg. 91, B-5
Hancock A-5
Hanover Pg. 91, H-3
Hanover Woods Pg. 91, J-7
Harkins A-11
Harmans Pg. 91, H-3
Harmony E-13
Harrisonville Pg. 91, C-1
Harundale Pg. 91, H-4
Hebbville Pg. 91, D-2
Hebron G-13
Hereford B-10
Hillsboro E-12
Hollifield Pg. 91, E-1
Honga G-13
Hoyes A-1
Hurlock F-13
Hyattsville Pg. 150, C-7
Hyde Park Pg. 91, E-7
Hydes Pg. 91, A-6
Ilchester Landing Pg. 91, F-2
Jacobsville Pg. 91, J-6
Jarrettsville B-11
Jenkins Pg. 91, A-7
Jessup Pg. 91, H-2
Joppatowne C-11
Josenhans Corner Pg. 91, D-7
Kennedyville C-12
Kensington Pg. 150, B-6
Kenwood Pg. 91, D-6
Kingsville Pg. 91, B-7
Kitzmiller C-2
Kraft Corner Pg. 91, D-1
LaPlata F-9
LaVale B-3
Lake Shore Pg. 91, J-6
Landover Hills Pg.150, D-8
Lansdowne Pg. 91, F-3

Largo E-10
Laytonsville C-8
Leonardtown G-10
Lexington Pk. G-11
Liberty Manor Pg. 91, D-1
Linthicum Pg. 91, G-3
Lipins Corner Pg. 91, J-5
Lochearn Pg. 91, E-3
Lonaconing B-2
Long Beach G-11
Long Green Pg. 91, A-6
Longridge G-14
Longwoods E-12
Luke B-2
Lutherville B-10
Vicinity Pg. 91, B-4
Lynch C-13
Maceys Corner Pg. 91, K-6
Manchester B-9
Manor Woods Pg. 91, A-6
Marbury F-8
Marion H-13
Marston B-8
Maryland City Pg. 91, K-1
Mays Chapel Pg. 91, A-4
Mayo E-11
McHenry B-1
Meadowcliff Pg. 91, A-6
Melrose A-9
Middle River Pg. 91, D-7
Middleborough Pg. 91, E-7
Middletown B-7
Midland B-3
Milford Pg. 91, D-2
Millington C-13
Millstone A-5
Morganza G-10
Morningside Pg. 150, F-8
Mt. Airy C-8
Mt. Pleasant B-9
Mt. Rainier Pg. 150, C-7
Mtn. Lake Park C-1
Myersville B-7
New Carrollton Pg. 150, C-9
New Market C-8
Newburg G-9
Newport G-9
Newtown C-11
Nordeau Pg. 91, H-1
North Beach E-10
North Brentwood Pg. 150, C-7
North Chevy Chase Pg. 150, B-5
North East B-12
Oakland (Garrett Cty) C-1
Oakland (Carroll Cty) C-9
Ocean City G-15
Odenton Pg. 91, K-3
Olde Mill Pg. 91, H-4
Olney C-8
Orchard Beach Pg. 91, H-6
Oriole H-13
Overlea Pg. 91, D-6
Owings Mills C-10
Vicinity Pg. 91, B-2
Oxford F-12
Oxon Hill E-9
Vicinity Pg. 150, G-7
Park Hill H-11
Parkton B-10
Parkville C-10
Vicinity Pg. 91, C-5
Pasadena Pg. 91, J-5
Pasadena Beach Pg. 91, H-7
Patapsco B-9
Perry Hall B-11
Vicinity Pg. 91, C-6
Perryville C-12
Pheiffer Corner Pg. 91, C-7
Pikesville C-10
Vicinity Pg. 91, C-2
Pine Ridge Pg. 91, H-3
Pinehurst on the Bay Pg. 91, J-7
Piney Grove A-4
Piney Point H-11
Pittsville G-14
Pleasant Hills B-11
Plum Point F-11
Pocomoke City H-13
Point Lookout H-11
Poolesville D-7
Port Deposit B-12
Pot Spring Pg. 91, B-4
Potomac Park B-3
Powellville G-14
Pratt A-4
Preston E-12
Price F-12
Prince Frederick F-10
Princess Anne A-11
Providence Pg. 91, B-5
Queen Anne E-12
Queenstown D-12
Randallstown B-9
Vicinity Pg. 91, C-1
Redhouse C-11
Reisterstown B-9
Vicinity Pg. 91, A-1
Relay Pg. 91, F-3
Ridge H-11
Ridgely D-12
Ridgeway Pg. 91, J-3
Rising Sun A-11
Riva E-10
Riverdale Pg. 150, C-8
Riverside G-8
Riviera Beach Pg. 91, H-6
Vicinity Pg. 91, H-6
Rock Hall D-11
Rockdale Pg. 91, D-2

Rockville D-8
Vicinity Pg. 150, A-4
Rodgers Forge Pg. 91, C-4
Roe D-12
Rolling Ridge Pg. 91, E-1
Rosedale Pg. 91, D-6
Rosemont C-7
Vicinity Pg. 91, E-3
Rush B-4
Ruthsburg D-12
Ruxton Pg. 91, C-4
Salisbury G-13
Sandy Bottom C-11
Savage Pg. 91, H-1
Seat Pleasant E-9
Vicinity Pg. 150, D-9
Secretary F-12
Seven Oaks Pg. 91, J-2
Severn D-10
Vicinity Pg. 91, J-3
Severna Park D-10
Vicinity Pg. 91, J-5
Shady Side E-11
Sharonville Pg. 91, J-6
Sharpsburg C-6
Sharptown F-13
Silver Spring D-9
Vicinity Pg. 150, B-6
Snow Hill H-14
Solley Pg. 91, H-5
Somerset Pg. 150, C-5
Southgate D-10
Sparrows Point Pg. 91, G-6
Springbrook Pg. 91, C-1
St. Charles F-9
St. Michaels F-9
Stevenson Pg. 91, B-3
Stockton H-14
Stonecrest Hills Pg. 91, F-1
Suburbia Pg. 91, A-1
Sudlersville C-13
Sunrise Beach Pg. 91, K-4
Swanton B-1
Sykesville C-9
Takoma Park Pg. 150, C-7
Taneytown B-8
Taylors Island F-11
Taylorsville B-8
Templeville D-13
Texas Pg. 91, A-4
The Oaks Pg. 91, E-1
The Provinces Pg. 91, J-2
Thurmont B-8
Timonium Pg. 91, B-4
Towson C-10
Vicinity Pg. 91, C-4
Turner G-10
Union Bridge B-8
University Park Pg. 150, C-7
Upper Marlboro E-10
Valleywood Pg. 91, B-4
Venice on the Bay Pg. 91, H-7
Ventnor Pg. 91, J-7
Vienna F-13
Waldorf F-9
Walkersville B-8
Warren Pg. 91, A-4
Waterloo Pg. 91, H-1
Waterview G-13
Wenona H-12
Wesley G-14
Westerlee Pg. 91, E-2
Westernport B-2
Westminster B-9
Westover A-11
White Marsh Pg. 91, C-7
White Oak Pg. 150, A-7
White Plains F-9
Whiteford A-11
Widgeon G-13
Willards G-15
Windemere Pg. 91, A-5
Woodlawn Pg. 91, D-2
Woodmoor Pg. 91, D-2

MASSACHUSETTS
Pages 24-25
Population: 5,737,037
Capital: Boston
Land Area: 7,824 sq. mi.

Abington D-11
Acton B-9
Acushnet F-11
Adams B-3
Agawam E-5
Amesbury A-11
Amherst C-5
Andover A-11
Arlington Pg. 93, D-3
Ashburnham B-8
Ashfield B-4
Athol B-7
Attleboro E-10
Auburn D-8
Avon D-11
Ayer B-9
Baldwinville B-7
Barnstable F-13
Barre C-7
Becket C-3
Bedford B-10
Vicinity Pg. 93, B-1
Belchertown C-6
Bellingham E-9
Belmont Pg. 93, D-3
Berkley F-11

MASSACHUSETTS

Bernardston B-5
Beverly B-12
Billerica B-10
Vicinity Pg. 93, A-1
Blackstone E-9
Blanford D-4
Bolton C-9
Boston C-11
Vicinity Pg. 93
Bourne F-13
Boxborough C-9
Boxford B-11
Boylston C-8
Braintree D-11
Vicinity Pg. 93, J-6
Brewster F-14
Bridgewater E-11
Brimfield D-7
Brockton E-11
Brookfield D-7
Brookline Pg. 93, F-3
Buckland B-4
Burlington Pg. 93, B-2
Buzzards Bay F-12
Cambridge Pg. 93, E-4
Canton D-11
Vicinity Pg. 93, K-3
Carlisle B-10
Carver E-12
Centerville G-13
Charlemont B-4
Charlton D-7
Chatham F-15
Chelmsford B-10
Vicinity Pg. 93, H-4
Chelsea C-11
Vicinity Pg. 93, E-5
Cheshire B-3
Chesterfield C-4
Chicopee D-5
Chilmark H-12
Clarksburg A-3
Cliftondale Pg. 93, C-6
Clinton C-9
Cochituate C-9
Colrain A-4
Concord C-10
Conway B-5
Cummington B-4
Dalton B-3
Danvers B-11
Dartmouth G-11
Dedham Pg. 93, H-3
Deerfield B-5
Dennis F-14
Dennis Port G-14
Dighton E-11
Dover Pg. 93, J-1
Dracut B-10
Dudley E-7
Duxbury E-12
East Bridgewater E-11
East Falmouth G-13
East Longmeadow E-6
Eastham F-15
Easthampton C-4
Easton E-11
Edgartown H-13
Essex B-12
Everett Pg. 93, D-5
Fairhaven G-12
Fall River F-10
Falmouth G-12
Fitchburg B-8
Framingham D-9
Freetown F-11
Gardner B-7
Gay Head H-12
Georgetown A-11
Gilbertville C-6
Gill B-5
Gloucester B-13
Grafton D-9
Granby D-5
Granville E-4
Great Barrington D-2
Greenfield B-5
Groton B-9
Groveland A-11
Hadley C-5
Halifax E-11
Hamilton B-12
Hampden E-6
Hanover D-12
Hardwick C-6
Harvard B-9
Harwich F-15
Hatfield C-5
Haverhill A-11
Hawley B-4
Heath A-4
Hingham D-11
Vicinity Pg. 93, J-7
Holbrook D-11
Holden C-8
Holland E-7
Holyoke D-5
Hopedale D-9
Hopkinton D-9
Hudson C-9
Hull C-11
Huntington C-4
Hyannis G-14
Ipswich B-11
Kingston E-12
Lee C-3
Leicester D-8
Lenox C-3
Leominster B-8
Leverett B-5
Lexington C-10
Vicinity Pg. 93, C-2
Leyden A-5
Lincoln C-10
Vicinity Pg. 93, D-1

Littleton B-9
Longmeadow D-5
Lowell B-10
Lunenburg B-8
Lynn C-11
Vicinity Pg. 93, B-6
Lynnfield B-11
Vicinity Pg. 93, A-5
Malden Pg. 93, D-4
Manchester B-12
Mansfield E-10
Marblehead B-12
Marion F-12
Marlborough C-9
Marshfield D-12
Mattapoisett G-12
Maynard C-9
Medfield D-9
Vicinity Pg. 93, K-1
Medford Pg. 93, D-4
Medway D-9
Melrose Pg. 93, C-5
Mendon D-9
Merrimac A-11
Methuen A-10
Middleborough F-11
Middlefield C-3
Middleton B-11
Milford D-9
Millbury D-8
Millers Falls B-6
Millis D-10
Milton Pg. 93, H-4
Vicinity Pg. 93, H-4
Monson D-6
Montague B-5
Monterey D-3
N. Attleborough E-10
Nahant C-11
Vicinity Pg. 93, D-7
Nantucket H-14
Natick D-10
Needham Pg. 93, G-2
New Bedford G-11
New Braintree C-7
New Marlborough D-3
Newbury A-12
Newton D-10
Vicinity Pg. 93, F-2
Norfolk D-10
North Adams A-3
North Brookfield C-7
North Reading B-11
Northampton C-4
Northborough C-8
Northbridge D-9
Northfield A-6
Norton E-10
Norwood D-10
Vicinity Pg. 93, K-2
Oak Bluffs H-13
Oakham C-7
Orange B-6
Orleans F-15
Osterville G-13
Otis D-3
Oxford D-6
Palmer D-6
Paxton C-8
Peabody B-11
Vicinity Pg. 93, A-7
Pepperell B-9
Peru C-3
Petersham B-7
Pinehurst Pg. 93, A-2
Pittsfield B-2
Plainfield B-4
Plymouth E-12
Plympton E-12
Princeton C-8
Provincetown E-14
Quincy D-11
Vicinity Pg. 93, J-6
Randolph D-11
Vicinity Pg. 93, K-5
Raynham E-11
Reading B-11
Vicinity Pg. 93, A-4
Rehoboth F-10
Revere C-11
Vicinity Pg. 93, D-5
Richmond C-2
Rochester F-12
Rockland D-11
Rockport B-13
Rowley A-12
Royalston A-7
Rutland C-7
Sagamore F-13
Salem B-12
Vicinity Pg. 93, B-7
Salisbury A-12
Sandisfield D-3
Sandwich F-13
Saugus C-11
Vicinity Pg. 93, C-6
Savoy B-4
Scituate D-12
Seekonk F-10
Sharon D-10
Sheffield D-2
Shelburne B-5
Shirley B-9
Shrewsbury C-9
So. Yarmouth G-14
Somerset Pg. 93, E-4
Somerville Pg. 93, E-4
South Hadley D-5
Southbridge E-7
Spencer D-7
Sterling C-8
Stockbridge C-2
Stoneham Pg. 93, B-4
Stoughton D-11

MASSACHUSETTS

MICHIGAN

Stow C-9
Sturbridge D-7
Sunderland C-5
Sutton D-8
Swampscott C-12
  Vicinity ...... Pg. 93, B-7
Swansea F-10
Taunton E-10
Templeton B-7
Tewksbury B-10
Three Rivers D-6
Tisbury H-12
Topsfield B-11
Townsend B-9
Truro E-15
Tyngsborough A-10
Upton D-9
Uxbridge E-9
Vineyard Haven H-13
Wakefield H-7
  Vicinity ...... Pg. 93, B-5
Wales D-6
Walpole D-10
  Vicinity ...... Pg. 93, K-1
Waltham D-6
Ware D-6
Wareham F-12
Warren D-7
Warwick A-6
Washington C-3
Watertown ...... Pg. 93, E-3
Wayland C-10
Webster E-7
Wellesley C-10
  Vicinity ...... Pg. 93, G-1
Wellfleet E-14
Wendell B-6
Wenham B-11
West Boylston C-8
West Brookfield D-7
West Dennis G-14
West Newbury A-11
West Springfield D-5
West Stockbridge C-2
West Tisbury H-12
Westborough D-8
Westfield D-4
Westford B-9
Westhampton C-4
Westminster B-7
Weston .... Pg. 93, E-1
Westport G-11
Westwood D-10
  Vicinity ...... Pg. 93, J-2
Weymouth D-11
  Vicinity ...... Pg. 93, J-7
Whately C-5
Whitinsville D-8
Whitman E-11
Wilbraham D-6
Williamstown C-3
Wilmington B-10
  Vicinity ...... Pg. 93, A-3
Winchendon A-7
Winchester ...... Pg. 93, C-3
Windsor B-3
Winthrop C-11
  Vicinity ...... Pg. 93, E-6
Woburn C-10
  Vicinity ...... Pg. 93, B-1
Worcester C-7
Worthington C-4
Wrentham D-10
Yarmouth F-14

MICHIGAN
Pages 44-45
Population: 9,262,078
Capital: Lansing
Land Area: 56,954 sq. mi.

Acme F-6
Adamsville L-4
Adrian L-8
Afton E-7
Agnew J-4
Ahmeek A-2
Akron H-8
Alabaster G-8
Alanson E-7
Alaska J-5
Alba F-6
Alberta B-2
Albion L-6
Alcona F-9
Alger G-8
Algonac K-10
Allegan K-5
Allen L-6
Allen Park ...... Pg. 107, J-8
Allendale J-5
Allenville D-7
Allouez A-2
Alma J-7
Almena L-5
Almont K-9
Aloha E-7
Alpena F-9
Alpha D-2
Alston B-2
Alto K-6
Alverno J-10
Amador J-10
Amasa C-2
Amble H-6
Anchorville K-10
Ann Arbor L-8
  Vicinity ...... Pg. 106, H-1
Antrim F-6
Applegate J-10
Arbutus Beach F-7

Arcadia G-4
Argentine K-7
Argyle H-9
Arnheim B-2
Arnold D-3
Arthur J-8
Ashley J-7
Ashton H-6
Assinins B-2
Athens L-6
Atlanta F-8
Atlantic Mine B-2
Attica H-6
Atwood E-6
Au Gres G-8
Au Sable G-9
Au Train C-4
Auburn H-7
Austin C-3
Averill H-7
Bad Axe H-9
Bailey J-5
Baldwin H-5
Banat D-3
Bancroft K-8
Banfield K-6
Bangor K-4
Baraga B-2
Bark River D-3
Barker Creek F-6
Barryton H-6
Barton City F-8
Batavia L-6
Bates F-6
Bath K-7
Battle Creek K-6
Bay City H-8
Bay Mills C-7
Bay Park H-8
Bay Port H-8
Bay View E-7
Beacon C-2
Bear Lake G-5
Beaverton H-7
Beechwood C-2
Belding J-6
Belleville ...... Pg. 106, K-6
Bellevue K-6
Bendon F-5
Bennington J-7
Benton Harbor L-4
Benzonia F-5
Bergland A-10
Berkley .... Pg. 107, D-8
Berrien Sprgs. L-4
Bessemer B-9
Bethel F-5
Beulah F-5
Beverly Hills ...... Pg. 106, C-7
Big Bay B-3
Big Rapids H-6
Birch Creek E-3
Birch Run J-8
Birmingham ...... Pg. 107, C-8
Bitely H-5
Black River F-9
Blanchard H-6
Blaney Park D-5
Blissfield L-8
Bloomfield Hills ...... Pg. 106, B-7
Boyne City E-6
Boyne Falls E-7
Bradley K-5
Brampton D-3
Branch H-5
Bravo K-5
Breckenridge J-7
Brethren G-5
Brevort D-6
Bridgeport J-8
Bridgeton J-5
Bridgman L-4
Brighton K-8
Brimley C-7
Britton L-8
Brockway J-9
Brohman H-5
Bronson L-7
Brooklyn L-7
Brown City J-9
Bruce Crossing C-1
Brunswick E-7
Brutus E-7
Buchanan L-4
Buckley F-6
Burlington L-6
Burnside J-9
Burt J-8
Burton J-8
Byron Center K-5
Cadillac G-6
Cadmus L-7
Caledonia K-6
California A-2
Calumet A-2
Camden L-6
Capac J-9
Carbondale E-8
Carleton L-8
Carney E-3
Caro J-9
Carp Lake E-7
Carsonville J-10
Caseville H-9
Casnovia J-5
Cass City J-9
Cassopolis L-4
Cathro F-8
Cedar E-5
Cedar River E-3
Cedar Springs J-6
Cedarville D-8
Center Line ...... Pg. 107, D-11

Centreville L-5
Ceresco L-6
Channing C-2
Charlevoix E-6
Charlotte K-6
Chase H-6
Chatham C-4
Cheboygan E-7
Chelsea L-7
Chesaning J-7
Christmas C-4
Cilo J-8
Clare H-6
Clarendon L-6
Clarion E-7
Clarksville K-6
Clawson .... Pg. 107, C-9
Clayton L-7
Cliff A-2
Climax L-5
Clinton L-8
Cloverdale L-6
Coldwater L-6
Coleman H-7
Coloma L-4
Colon L-5
Comins F-8
Concord L-7
Constantine L-5
Conway E-7
Coopersville J-5
Copemish G-5
Copper Harbor A-3
Cornell D-3
Corunna J-8
Covert K-4
Covington C-2
Cross Village E-7
Croswell J-10
Croton H-5
Crump H-7
Crystal Falls C-2
Cunard D-3
Curran F-8
Curtis D-6
Custer H-4
Dafter C-7
Daggett E-3
Dansville K-7
Darragh F-6
Davison K-8
Dayton L-4
DeTour Village D-8
Dearborn L-9
Dearborn Heights ...... Pg. 106, G-7
Decatur L-5
Deer Park C-6
Deerton C-4
Deford J-9
Delano K-5
Delton K-5
Denton L-8
Detroit L-9
  Vicinity ...... Pg. 107, F-8
Devereaux K-7
Dewitt K-7
Dexter L-8
Dighton G-6
Disco K-9
Dixboro L-8
Donaldson C-8
Donken B-1
Dorr K-5
Douglas K-4
Dowagiac L-4
Dowling K-6
Drayton Plains D-8
Drummond D-8
Dublin G-5
Dundee L-8
Dunningville K-5
Durand K-8
Eagle Habor A-3
Eagle River A-3
East Detroit ...... Pg. 107, E-12
East Gilead L-6
East Grand Rapids J-5
East Jordan E-6
East Lake G-5
East Leroy L-6
East Tawas G-8
Eastport E-6
Eaton Rapids K-7
Eckerman C-7
Ecorse .... Pg. 107, J-9
Edenville H-7
Edmore J-6
Edwardsburg L-5
Elba J-8
Elberta F-5
Elk Rapids F-6
Elkton H-9
Elmer J-9
Elmira F-7
Elwell J-7
Emmett K-9
Empire F-5
Engadine D-6
Ensign D-4
Epoufette D-6
Erie M-8
Escanaba D-4
Essexville H-8
Estey J-7
Estral Beach L-9
Evans J-6
Evart H-6
Ewen C-1
Fair Haven K-9
Fairfield L-7
Fairgrove J-8
Fairview F-8
Farmington ...... Pg. 106, D-5

Farmington Hills ...... Pg. 106, D-5
Farwell H-6
Fawn River L-6
Fayette D-3
Felch D-3
Felch Mountain D-3
Fennville K-5
Fenton K-8
Ferndale .... Pg. 107, E-9
Ferry H-5
Ferrysburg J-4
Fibre D-7
Fife Lake G-6
Filer City G-4
Filion H-9
Filmore K-5
Flat Rock L-8
Flint J-8
Flushing J-8
Ford River D-4
Forest Hill J-7
Forest Lake C-4
Forester H-10
Forestville H-10
Foster City D-3
Fouch F-5
Fountain G-5
Fowler J-7
Fowlerville K-8
Frankenmuth J-8
Frankfort F-5
Franklin .... Pg. 106, C-7
Fraser .... Pg. 107, C-12
Frederick F-7
Freeland H-7
Freesoil G-5
Fremont H-5
Frontier L-7
Fruitport J-5
Galesburg K-5
Galien L-4
Ganges K-4
Garden D-4
Garden City ...... Pg. 106, G-6
Garden Corners D-5
Gardendale J-10
Garfield J-7
Garnet D-6
Gaylord F-7
Gera J-8
Germfask C-5
Gibraltar L-9
Girard L-6
Gladstone D-4
Gladwin H-7
Glen Arbor F-5
Glen Haven F-5
Glenn K-4
Glennie F-8
Glenwood L-5
Gobles K-5
Goetzville D-8
Good Hart E-6
Goodrich K-8
Gould City D-5
Gourley D-3
Grand Beach L-4
Grand Blanc K-8
Grand Haven J-4
Grand Ledge K-6
Grand Marais C-5
Grand Rapids J-5
Grange L-5
Granite Bluff D-2
Grant J-5
Grawn F-6
Grayling F-7
Greenbush G-9
Greenland B-1
Greenville J-6
Gregory K-7
Grindstone City H-9
Gros Cap D-7
Grosse Pointe ...... Pg. 107, F-13
Grosse Pointe Farms ...... Pg. 107, F-13
Grosse Pointe Park ...... Pg. 107, G-12
Grosse Pointe Shores ...... Pg. 107, F-13
  Vicinity ...... Pg. 107, E-13
Grosse Pointe Woods ...... Pg. 107, E-13
Gulliver D-5
Gwinn C-3
Hale G-8
Hamburg K-8
Hamilton K-5
Hamlin Lake G-4
Hamtramck ...... Pg. 107, B-2
Hancock B-2
Harbert L-4
Harbor Beach H-10
Harbor Springs E-6
Hardwood D-3
Harper Woods ...... Pg. 107, E-12
Harris D-3
Harrison H-7
Harrisville F-9
Hart H-4
Hartford L-4
Hartland K-8
Harvey C-3
Hastings K-6
Hawks E-8
Hazel Park ...... Pg. 107, E-10
Helmer C-5
Hemans J-9
Henderson J-7
Hermansville D-3
Herron F-8
Hesperia H-5

Hessel D-7
Higgins Lake G-7
Highland Park ...... Pg. 107, F-9
Hilliards K-5
Hillman F-8
Hillsdale L-7
Hockaday G-7
Hodunk L-6
Holland K-4
Holly K-8
Holt K-7
Holton H-5
Homer L-6
Honor F-5
Horton L-7
Houghton B-1
Houghton Heights G-7
Houghton Lake G-7
Howard City J-5
Howell K-8
Hubbard Lake F-8
Hubbell B-2
Hudson L-7
Hudsonville J-5
Huntington Woods ...... Pg. 107, D-8
Huron Beach E-8
Huron City H-9
Hyde D-4
Idlewild H-5
Imlay City J-9
Ingalls E-3
Inkster .... Pg. 106, H-6
Interlochen F-5
Ionia J-6
Iron Mountain D-2
Iron River C-1
Irons G-5
Ironwood B-9
Isabella D-4
Ishpeming C-3
Ithaca J-7
Jackson L-7
Jamestown J-5
Jasper M-8
Jeddo J-10
Johannesburg F-7
Jones L-5
Jonesville L-6
Joppa L-6
Kalamazoo K-5
Kaleva G-5
Kalkaska F-6
Karlin F-5
Kawkawlin H-8
Kearsarge A-2
Kendall K-5
Kent City J-5
Kenton C-1
Kentwood J-5
Kewadin E-6
Keweenaw Bay B-2
Kibbie K-4
Kinde H-9
Kinderhook L-6
Kingsford D-2
Kingston J-9
Kinross C-7
Kiva B-2
L'Anse B-2
La Salle M-8
LaBranche D-3
Lachine F-8
Lacota K-4
Laingsburg K-7
Lake City G-6
Lake George H-6
Lake Leelanau E-5
Lake Linden A-2
Lake Odessa K-6
Lake Orion K-9
Lake Roland B-1
Lakeland K-8
Lakeport J-10
Lakeview J-6
Lambertville M-8
Langston J-6
Lansing K-7
Lapeer J-9
Laporte C-4
Lathrop K-4
Lathrup Village ...... Pg. 107, D-8
Laurium A-2
Lawton L-5
Le Roy G-6
Leland E-5
Leoni L-7
Leonidas L-5
Leslie K-7
Levering E-7
Lexington J-10
Liberty L-7
Lilley H-5
Lincoln F-9
Lincoln Park ...... Pg. 107, J-8
Linden K-8
Linwood H-8
Litchfield L-7
Little Lake C-4
Livonia K-8
  Vicinity ...... Pg. 106, G-6
Long Lake G-8
Long Rapids F-8
Longrie E-3
Loomis H-7
Loretto D-3
Lowell J-6
Lucas G-6
Ludington G-4
Luna Pier M-8
Lupton G-7
Luzerne G-7

Madison Heights ...... Pg. 107, D-9
Mancelona F-6
Mandan A-3
Manistee G-4
Manistique D-5
Manton G-6
Maple Rapids J-7
Marcellus L-5
Marenisco B-10
Marine City K-10
Marion J-6
Marlette J-9
Marne J-5
Marquette C-4
Marshall L-6
Martin K-5
Marysville K-10
Mashek D-3
Mason K-7
Masonville D-4
Mass City B-1
Matchwood B-10
Matherton J-7
Mattawan L-5
Mayville J-9
McBain G-6
McFarland C-3
McMillan C-5
Meade K-9
Mears H-4
Mecosta H-6
Melstrand C-5
Melvin J-9
Memphis K-9
Mendon L-5
Menominee E-3
Meredith H-7
Merriman D-2
Merritt G-6
Merriweather A-10
Mesick G-6
Metz E-8
Michigamme C-3
Michigan Center L-7
Middleville K-6
Midland H-7
Mikado G-8
Milburg L-4
Milford .... Pg. 106, B-2
  Vicinity
Millbrook H-6
Millersburg E-8
Millington J-8
Mineral Hills C-2
Mio F-8
Mohawk A-2
Moline K-5
Monroe L-8
Monroe Center F-6
Montague H-4
Montrose J-8
Moorestown G-6
Moran D-7
Morley H-6
Morneci M-7
Morrice K-7
Moscow L-7
Mottville L-5
Mt. Clemens ...... Pg. 107, B-13
Mt. Forest H-8
Mt. Morris J-8
Mt. Pleasant H-6
Muir J-6
Mullett Lake E-7
Munger H-8
Munising C-5
Muskegon J-4
Muskegon Heights J-4
Muttonville K-9
Napoleon L-7
Nashville K-6
Nathan D-3
Naubinway D-6
Negaunee C-3
New Baltimore K-9
New Buffalo L-4
New Era H-4
New Greenleaf H-9
New Haven K-9
Newaygo J-5
Newberry C-6
Newport L-9
Niles L-4
Nirvana H-5
Nisula B-1
North Branch J-9
North Ironwood A-9
North Muskegon J-4
Northland D-3
Northport E-5
Northville ...... Pg. 106, E-6
Norton Shores J-4
Norwalk G-5
Norway D-3
Novi K-8
  Vicinity ...... Pg. 106, D-4
O'Neil F-7
Oak Grove K-8
Oak Park .... Pg. 107, E-8
Oakley K-7
Oakwood K-9
Occqueoc E-8
Ogden Center M-8
Oil City H-7
Okemos K-7
Olivet K-6
Omena E-5
Onaway E-8
Onekama G-4
Onondaga K-7
Ontonagon B-1
Orchard Lake ...... Pg. 106, B-5

Orleans J-6
Ortonville K-8
Oscoda G-9
Oskar A-2
Osseo L-7
Ossineke F-9
Otisville J-8
Otsego K-5
Otsego Lake F-7
Ottawa Lake M-8
Ovid J-7
Owosso J-8
Oxbow H-5
Oxford K-9
Ozark D-7
Painesdale B-2
Palmer C-3
Palmyra L-8
Palo J-6
Paradise C-7
Parchment K-5
Paris H-6
Parisville H-9
Parkdale G-4
Parkville L-5
Paulding C-1
Paw Paw L-5
Peck J-9
Pellston E-7
Pentwater H-4
Perkins D-4
Perrinton J-6
Perronville D-3
Perry K-7
Petersburg L-8
Petoskey E-7
Pewamo J-6
Phoenix A-2
Pickford D-7
Piconning H-8
Pierport G-4
Pierson J-6
Pigeon H-9
Pine River G-6
Pittsford L-7
Plainfield K-8
Plainwell K-5
Pleasant Ridge ...... Pg. 107, D-9
Plymouth .... Pg. 106, F-4
Pointe Aux Barques H-9
Polaski K-8
Pontiac K-8
  Vicinity ...... Pg. 106, A-4
Port Hope H-10
Port Huron K-10
Port Sanilac J-10
Portage K-5
Portland J-6
Posen E-8
Poseyville H-7
Potterville K-6
Powers D-3
Prescott G-8
Princeton D-3
Prudenville G-7
Pullman K-4
Quanicassee H-8
Quimby H-8
Quincy L-6
Quinnesec D-2
Raber D-8
Ralph D-3
Ramsay B-9
Randville D-3
Ransom M-7
Rattle Run L-6
Ray L-6
Reading L-7
Redford .... Pg. 106, F-7
Reed City H-6
Reese J-8
Remus H-6
Republic C-2
Rexton D-6
Rhodes H-7
Richland K-5
Richmond K-9
Richmondville H-10
Richville J-8
Ridgeway L-8
River Rouge ...... Pg. 107, J-9
Riverdale J-6
Rives Junction K-7
Roberts Landing K-10
Rochester K-9
Rock D-4
Rockford J-6
Rockland B-1
Rockwood L-9
Rodney H-6
Rogers City E-8
Rome Center L-7
Romeo K-9
Romulus .... Pg. 106, J-5
Roosevelt Park J-5
Roscommon G-7
Rose City G-7
Roseburg J-9
Rosebush H-6
Roseville .... Pg. 107, D-12
Rothbury H-4
Royal Oak .... Pg. 107, C-9
Rudyard C-7
Rumely C-4
Ruth H-9
Saginaw J-7
Sagola D-3
Saline L-8
Samaria M-8
Sands C-3
Sandusky J-9
Sanford H-7
Sans Souci K-10

Saranac J-6
Saugatuck K-4
Sault Ste. Marie C-8
Sawyer L-4
Schaffer D-3
Schoolcraft L-5
Scottdale L-3
Scottville H-4
Sears H-6
Sebewaing H-9
Seney C-5
Sharon G-6
Shelby H-4
Shelbyville K-5
Shepherd H-7
Sherman G-5
Shingleton C-5
Shore E-6
Sidnaw C-2
Sigma F-6
Silver City A-10
Sister Lakes L-4
Six Lakes J-6
Skandia C-3
Skidway Lake G-8
Smithville G-6
Smyrna J-6
Snover J-9
Somerset L-7
Soo Junction C-6
South Boardman F-6
South Branch G-8
South Haven K-4
South Range B-1
Southfield .... Pg. 106, E-7
Southgate .... Pg. 107, K-8
Spratt F-8
Spring Lake J-5
Springport K-7
Spruce F-9
St. Clair K-10
  Vicinity ...... Pg. 107, D-13
St. Clair Shores K-9
St. Ignace D-7
St. James D-6
St. Johns J-7
St. Louis J-7
Stager D-2
Stalwart D-7
Standish H-8
Stanton J-6
Stanwood H-6
Stephenson E-3
Sterling H-8
Sterling Hts. ...... Pg. 107, B-10
Steuben C-4
Stevensville L-4
Stockbridge K-7
Stronach G-5
Strongs C-7
Sturgis L-5
Stutsmanville E-6
Sundell C-4
Sunfield K-6
Suttons Bay E-5
Swanson E-3
Swartz Creek J-8
Sylvester H-6
Tawas City G-8
Taylor .... Pg. 106, J-7
Tecumseh L-8
Tekonsha L-6
Theodore D-1
Thompson D-5
Thornville J-9
Three Lakes C-2
Three Oaks L-4
Three Rivers L-5
Tiovola B-1
Tipton L-7
Tower E-7
Traunik C-4
Traverse City F-5
Trenary C-4
Trenton L-9
Triangle Ranch C-2
Trout Creek C-1
Trout Lake D-7
Troy K-9
  Vicinity ...... Pg. 107, B-9
Turner G-8
Tustin G-6
Twin Lake J-4
Twin Lakes B-2
Twining G-8
Ubly H-9
Union L-5
Union City L-6
Union Pier L-4
Unionville H-9
Utica K-9
  Vicinity ...... Pg. 107, A-11
Vandalia L-5
Vanderbilt F-7
Vassar J-8
Vernon K-7
Verona H-9
Vicksburg L-5
Vienna G-7
Vogel Center G-6
Vriesland J-5
Vulcan D-3
Wacousta K-7
Wadhams J-10
Wakefield B-9
Waldron L-7
Walhalla H-5
Walkerville H-5
Wallace E-3
Walled Lake ...... Pg. 106, C-4
Walton G-6
Warren K-9
  Vicinity ...... Pg. 107, D-1
Washington K-9

MICHIGAN

Waterford .... Pg. 106, A-6
Waterloo K-7
Waters F-7
Watersmeet C-1
Watertown J-9
Watervliet L-4
Watson (Marquette Cty)
.... D-3
Watson (Allegan Cty) K-5
Watton C-2
Waucedah D-3
Wayland J-5
Wayne .... Pg. 106, J-5
Webberville K-7
Wells D-4
Wellston G-5
West Branch G-7
West Olive J-5
Westland ... Pg. 106, G-5
Weston M-7
Wetmore C-4
White L-5
White Cloud H-5
White Pine A-10
White Rock H-10
Whitehall J-4
Whitney D-3
Whittemore G-8
Williamston K-7
Willis L-8
Windsor (Canada)
.... Pg. 107, J-11
Winegars H-7
Winona B-2
Wisner H-8
Wixom .... Pg. 106, C-3
Wolf Lake G-5
Wolverine E-7
Wolverine Lake
.... Pg. 106, B-4
Woodbury K-6
Woodhaven L-9
Woodland J-5
Wyandotte Pg. 107, K-8
Wyoming J-9
Yale J-9
Yalmer J-8
Ypsilanti L-8
Vicinity ... Pg. 106, J-2
Yuma G-5
Zeeland J-5
Zilwaukee J-8

MINNESOTA
Pages 46-47
Population: 4,075,970
Capital: St. Paul
Land Area: 79,548 sq. mi.

Ada D-2
Adams L-6
Adrian L-2
Ah-gwah-ching ... E-4
Aitkin F-5
Akeley E-4
Albany G-4
Albert Lea L-5
Alberta G-2
Alden L-5
Alexandria G-3
Alvarado C-1
Alwood D-5
Amboy L-4
Andover H-6
Angle Inlet A-3
Angora C-7
Annandale H-5
Anoka H-6
Appleton H-2
Arden Hills . Pg. 122, A-4
Argyle C-1
Arlington J-4
Ashby G-2
Askov F-7
Atwater H-4
Audubon E-2
Aurora D-7
Austin L-6
Avoca K-2
Avon G-4
Babbitt D-8
Backus E-4
Badger B-2
Bagley D-3
Ball Club D-5
Barnesville F-1
Barnum F-7
Barrett G-2
Barry G-1
Battle Lake F-3
Baudette B-4
Baxter F-4
Beardsley G-1
Beaver Bay D-9
Beaver Creek L-1
Becker H-5
Bejou D-2
Belgrade H-3
Belle Plaine J-5
Bellingham H-1
Beltrami D-1
Bena D-4
Benedict E-4
Benson H-3
Bertha G-3
Big Falls C-5
Big Fork D-5
Big Lake H-5

Bigelow L-2
Birchdale B-5
Birchwood . Pg. 123, A-9
Bird Island J-4
Biwabik D-7
Blackduck D-4
Blomkest J-3
Blooming Prairie . K-6
Bloomington Pg. 122, E-3
Blue Earth L-5
Bluffton F-3
Bock G-5
Borup D-2
Bovey D-5
Bowstring D-5
Boy River E-5
Boyd J-2
Braham G-6
Brainerd F-4
Branch H-6
Brandon G-3
Breckenridge F-1
Brewster L-2
Britt D-7
Brook Park G-6
Brooklyn Center
.... Pg. 122, A-4
Brooklyn Park Pg. 122, A-2
Brooks C-2
Brookston E-7
Brooten H-3
Browerville F-4
Browns Valley ... G-1
Brownsdale L-6
Brownsville L-8
Brownton J-4
Bruno F-7
Buffalo H-5
Buffalo Lake J-4
Buhl D-6
Burnsville J-6
Vicinity .. Pg. 122, G-4
Burtrum G-4
Butterfield K-4
Buyck C-7
Byron K-7
Caledonia L-8
Callaway E-2
Cambridge H-6
Campbell F-2
Canby J-1
Cannon Falls J-6
Canyon E-7
Carlos G-3
Carlton E-7
Cass Lake D-4
Cedar Mills J-4
Centerville K-8
Ceylon L-4
Chandler K-2
Chaska J-5
Chatfield L-7
Chickamaw Beach .. E-4
Chisholm D-6
Clara City H-3
Claremont K-6
Clarissa F-3
Clarkfield J-2
Clarks Grove L-6
Clear Lake H-5
Clearbrook D-3
Clearwater H-5
Clementson B-4
Climax D-1
Clinton H-1
Clitherall F-3
Clontarf H-3
Cloquet E-7
Cokato H-5
Cold Spring H-4
Coleraine D-6
Cologne J-5
Columbia Heights
.... Pg. 122, A-4
Comfrey K-4
Comstock E-1
Cook C-7
Coon Rapids H-6
Correll H-2
Cosmos J-4
Cottage Grove ... J-6
Cotton E-7
Cottonwood J-2
Croftville D-10
Cromwell E-7
Crookston C-2
Crosby F-5
Crystal ... Pg. 122, A-3
Currie K-2
Cushing F-4
Cuyuna F-5
Cyrus G-2
Dakota K-8
Dalton F-2
Danube J-3
Danvers H-2
Darfur K-4
Dassel H-4
Dawson J-2
De Graff H-3
Deer River D-5
Deerwood F-5
Delano H-5
Dent F-3
Detroit Lakes ... E-2
Dilworth E-1
Dodge Center K-6
Donaldson B-1
Donnelly G-2
Doran F-2
Dovray K-3
Duluth E-8
Dumont G-2
Dunnell L-4

Duquette F-7
Eagle Bend F-3
Eagle Lake K-5
East Bethel H-6
East Grand Forks . C-1
East Gull Lake .. F-4
Easton L-5
Echo J-3
Eden Prairie Pg. 122, E-1
Eden Valley H-4
Edgerton K-2
Edina ..... Pg. 122, E-3
Effie C-5
Elbow Lake G-2
Eldred D-1
Elgin K-7
Elizabeth F-2
Elk River H-6
Ellendale K-6
Ellsworth L-2
Elmer E-6
Elmore L-5
Elrosa G-3
Ely C-8
Emily F-5
Erhard F-2
Ericsburg B-6
Erskine D-2
Evansville G-3
Eveleth D-7
Eyota K-7
Fairfax J-4
Fairbault K-6
Fairmont L-4
Falcon Heights
.... Pg. 122, C-6
Farmington J-6
Farwell G-3
Felton E-2
Fergus Falls F-2
Fertile D-2
Finland D-8
Finlayson F-6
Fisher C-1
Flom E-2
Floodwood E-6
Florence K-2
Foley G-5
Forbes D-7
Forest Lake H-6
Fort Ripley F-4
Fosston D-3
Fountain L-7
Fox Home F-2
Franklin J-3
Frazee E-3
Freeport G-4
Fridley ... Pg. 122, A-4
Frost L-5
Fulda K-2
Funkley C-4
Garfield G-3
Garrison F-5
Garvin K-2
Gary E-2
Gatzke B-3
Gaylord J-4
Gem Lake . Pg. 123, A-8
Geneva L-6
Georgetown E-1
Gheen C-7
Gibbon J-4
Gilbert D-7
Gilman G-5
Glencoe J-5
Glenville L-6
Glenwood G-3
Gluek H-3
Glyndon E-1
Golden Valley Pg. 122, B-4
Gonvick D-3
Good Thunder K-5
Goodhue K-7
Goodland E-6
Goodridge C-3
Goodview K-8
Graceton B-4
Graceville G-2
Granada L-5
Grand Falls C-5
Grand Marais D-9
Grand Meadow L-7
Grand Portage ... C-10
Grand Rapids D-5
Granite Falls ... J-2
Grasston G-6
Greenbush B-2
Greenfield H-5
Grey Eagle G-4
Grove City H-4
Grygla C-3
Gully D-3
Guthrie D-4
Hackensack E-4
Hallock B-1
Halma B-2
Halstad D-1
Ham Lake H-6
Hancock H-2
Hanley Falls J-3
Hanska K-4
Harding F-5
Hardwick L-1
Harmony L-7
Harris H-6
Hastings J-6
Hawley E-2
Hayfield K-6
Hayward L-6
Hazel Run J-2
Hector J-4
Heidelberg J-5
Henderson J-5
Hendricks J-1

Hendrum D-1
Henning F-3
Herman G-2
Hermantown E-7
Heron Lake L-3
Hewitt F-3
Hibbing D-6
Hill City E-5
Hills L-1
Hilltop ... Pg. 122, A-4
Hinckley G-6
Hines D-4
Hitterdal E-2
Hoffman G-2
Hokah L-8
Holland K-2
Holloway H-2
Holt C-2
Holyoke F-7
Hope K-6
Hopkins ... Pg. 122, D-2
Houston L-8
Hovland C-10
Howard Lake H-5
Hoyt Lakes D-7
Humboldt B-1
Hutchinson J-4
Ihlen K-1
Independence H-5
Indus B-5
International Falls B-5
Inver Grove Hts.
.... Pg. 123, F-8
Iona K-2
Ironton F-5
Isabella D-8
Isanti H-6
Isle F-5
Ivanhoe J-2
Jackson L-4
Jacobson E-6
Janesville K-5
Jasper K-1
Jeffers K-3
Jenkins E-4
Johnson G-2
Jordan J-5
Karlstad B-2
Kasota K-5
Kasson K-7
Keewatin D-6
Kelliher C-4
Kellogg K-7
Kelsey E-7
Kennedy B-1
Kensington G-2
Kent F-1
Kenyon K-6
Kerkhoven H-3
Kerrick F-7
Kettle River F-6
Kiester L-5
Kimball H-5
Kingston H-4
Knife River E-8
La Crescent L-8
La Prairie E-6
Lafayette J-4
Lake Benton K-2
Lake Bronson B-1
Lake City J-7
Lake Crystal K-5
Lake Elmo . Pg. 123, B-10
Lake George D-3
Lake Henry H-4
Lake Lillian J-4
Lake Park E-2
Lake Shore F-4
Lake Wilson K-2
Lakefield L-3
Lakeville J-6
Lamberton K-3
Lancaster A-1
Lanesboro L-8
Laporte E-4
Larsmont E-8
Lastrup G-5
Lauderdale . Pg. 122, B-5
Le Center K-5
LeRoy L-7
LeSueur J-5
Lengby D-3
Leonard D-3
Lester Prairie .. J-5
Lewiston K-8
Lilydale .. Pg. 123, D-6
Linden Grove C-6
Lindford B-5
Lindstrom H-6
Lismore L-2
Litchfield H-4
Little Canada Pg. 123, B-7
Little Falls G-4
Little Fork C-5
Little Rock G-5
Lockhart D-1
Loman B-5
Long Prairie G-4
Longville E-5
Lonsdale J-5
Lowry G-3
Lucan K-3
Lutsen D-9
Lyle L-6
Lynd K-2
Mable L-8
Madelia K-4
Madison H-2
Madison Lake K-5
Magnolia L-2
Mahnomen D-3
Mahtomedi . Pg. 123, A-9
Mahtowa F-6

Malmo F-6
Manchester L-5
Mankato K-4
Mantorville K-7
Maple Lake H-5
Mapleton K-5
Mapleview L-6
Maplewood . Pg. 123, B-8
Marcell D-5
Margie C-5
Marietta H-1
Markham D-7
Marshall J-2
McGrath F-6
McGregor F-6
McIntosh D-2
Meadowlands E-7
Medford K-6
Meire Grove G-3
Melrose G-4
Menagha E-3
Mendota ... Pg. 122, E-6
Mendota Heights
.... Pg. 123, E-7
Mentor D-2
Middle River B-2
Milaca G-5
Milan H-2
Millroy K-2
Miltona G-3
Minneapolis J-5
Vicinity ...... Pg. 122
Minneota J-2
Minnesota Lake .. L-5
Minnetonka Pg. 122, D-1
Mizpah C-5
Montevideo H-3
Montgomery J-5
Monticello H-5
Moorhead E-1
Moose Lake F-6
Mora G-6
Morgan J-3
Morris H-2
Morton J-4
Motley F-4
Mountain Iron ... D-7
Mountain Lake ... K-3
Murdock H-3
Myrtle L-6
Nashua K-2
Nashwauk D-6
Nassau H-1
Nay-Tah-Waush ... C-3
Nevis E-4
New Brighton Pg. 122, A-5
New Hope .. Pg. 122, B-2
New London H-4
New Prague J-5
New Richland K-5
New Ulm K-4
New York Mills .. F-3
Newfolden B-2
Nicollet K-4
Nielsville D-1
Nimrod E-3
Nisswa F-4
Norcross G-2
North Branch H-6
North Mankato ... K-4
North St. Paul Pg. 123, B-9
Northfield J-6
Northome C-5
Northrop L-4
Norwood J-5
Noyes A-1
Oak Island A-4
Oakdale ... Pg. 123, C-9
Odessa H-1
Ogema E-2
Ogilvie G-5
Oklee C-2
Olivia J-3
Onamia G-5
Orleans A-1
Ormsby K-4
Oronoco K-7
Orr C-6
Ortonville H-2
Osage E-3
Osakis G-3
Oslo C-1
Ottertail F-3
Outing E-5
Owatonna K-6
Palisade E-6
Park Rapids E-3
Parkers Prairie . F-3
Paynesville H-4
Pelican Rapids .. F-2
Pencer B-3
Pennock H-3
Perley E-1
Pierz G-5
Pine City G-6
Pine Island K-7
Pine River E-4
Pine Springs Pg. 123, A-9
Pinewood D-4
Pipestone K-1
Pitt B-4
Plainview K-8
Plummer C-2
Plymouth .. Pg. 122, A-1
Ponemah C-4
Ponsford E-3
Porter J-2
Preston L-7
Princeton H-6
Prinsburg J-3
Prior Lake J-5
Proctor E-7
Quamba G-6
Randall F-4

Randolph J-6
Raudette B-4
Ray B-6
Raymond H-3
Red Lake C-3
Red Lake Falls .. C-2
Red Wing J-7
Redby C-4
Redwood Falls ... J-3
Regal H-4
Remer E-5
Renville J-3
Rice G-4
Richfield . Pg. 122, E-4
Richmond H-4
Richville F-2
Robbinsdale Pg. 122, B-3
Rochester K-7
Rock Creek G-6
Roosevelt B-4
Rose Creek L-6
Roseau B-3
Roseville . Pg. 122, B-5
Ross B-2
Rothsay F-1
Round Lake L-3
Round Prairie ... G-4
Royalton G-4
Rush City G-6
Rushford L-8
Russell K-2
Ruthton K-2
Sabin E-1
Sacred Heart J-3
Saint Anthony Pg. 122, B-5
Saint Charles ... K-7
Saint Clair K-5
Saint Cloud H-5
Saint Francis ... H-6
Saint Hilaire ... C-2
Saint James K-4
Saint Joseph H-4
Saint Louis Park
.... Pg. 122, D-2
Saint Michael ... H-5
Saint Paul H-6
Vicinity ...... Pg. 123
Saint Paul Park
.... Pg. 123, F-9
Saint Peter K-5
Saint Vincent ... A-1
Salol B-3
Sanborn K-3
Sandstone G-7
Sartell G-7
Sauk Centre G-4
Sauk Rapids G-4
Saum C-4
Sawyer F-6
Scanlon E-7
Schroeder D-9
Sebeka E-3
Sedan G-3
Shakopee J-5
Shelly D-1
Sherburn L-4
Shevlin D-3
Shoreview . Pg. 123, A-6
Silver Bay D-9
Silver Lake J-4
Slayton K-2
Sleepy Eye K-4
Solway D-3
South International B-6
South St. Paul
.... Pg. 123, E-8
Spicer H-4
Spring Grove L-8
Spring Lake D-5
Spring Valley ... L-7
Springfield K-4
Squaw Lake D-4
Staples F-4
Starbuck G-3
Stephen B-1
Stewartville K-7
Storden K-3
Strandquist B-2
Strathcona B-2
Sturgeon Lake ... F-6
Sunberg H-3
Sunfish Lake Pg. 123, E-7
Swan River E-5
Swanville G-4
Swatara E-5
Swift B-3
Taconite D-6
Taconite Harbor . D-9
Talmoon D-5
Tamarack F-6
Taunton J-2
Taylors Falls ... H-7
Tenney G-2
Tenstrike D-4
Terrace H-3
Thief River Falls C-2
Togo D-5
Tommald F-5
Toopi L-7
Tower D-7
Tracy K-3
Trail C-3
Trimont L-4
Trosky K-1
Truman L-4
Turtle River D-4
Twig E-7
Twin Lakes L-6
Twin Valley D-2
Two Harbors E-8
Tyler K-2
Ulen E-2
Underwood F-2

Vadnais Hts. Pg. 123, A-7
Verdi K-1
Vergas E-2
Verndale F-4
Vesta J-3
Viking C-2
Villard G-3
Vining F-3
Viola K-7
Virginia D-7
Wabasha K-7
Wabasso J-3
Waconia J-5
Wadena F-3
Wahkon F-5
Waite Park H-4
Walker E-4
Walnut Grove K-3
Waltham L-6
Wanamingo K-6
Warba E-6
Warraska B-3
Warren C-1
Warroad B-3
Waseca K-5
Waskish C-4
Watertown J-5
Waterville K-5
Watkins H-4
Watson H-2
Waubun E-2
Wawina E-6
Welcome L-4
Wells L-5
West Concord K-6
West St. Paul Pg. 123, E-7
Westbrook K-3
Wheaton G-1
Whipholt E-4
White Bear Lake
.... Pg. 123, A-9
White Earth D-2
Wilder L-3
Willernie . Pg. 123, A-9
Williams B-4
Willmar H-3
Willow River F-6
Wilton D-4
Windom K-3
Winger D-2
Winnebago L-5
Winona K-8
Winthrop J-4
Winton C-8
Wirt D-5
Wolf Lake E-3
Wolverton F-1
Woodbury J-6
Vicinity .. Pg. 123, D-10
Woodland E-6
Worthington L-3
Wrenshall H-7
Wyoming H-6
Zemple D-5
Zim D-7
Zimmerman H-6
Zumbro Falls K-7
Zumbrota K-7

MISSISSIPPI
Page 50
Population: 2,520,638
Capital: Jackson
Land Area: 47,233 sq. mi.

Abbeville B-5
Aberdeen C-6
Ackerman D-5
Alcorn G-2
Algoma B-5
Alligator C-3
Amory C-6
Anguilla E-3
Arcola D-3
Arkabutla A-4
Artesia D-6
Ashland A-5
Askew B-3
Avalon D-2
Avon D-2
Bailey F-6
Baird D-3
Baldwyn B-6
Banner B-5
Bassfield H-4
Batesville B-4
Baxterville H-5
Bay Saint Louis . K-5
Bay Springs G-5
Beaumont H-6
Beauregard G-3
Becker C-6
Belden B-6
Belen B-3
Bellefontaine ... C-5
Belmont B-6
Belzoni D-3
Benoit D-2
Benton E-4
Bentonia E-3
Beulah C-2
Big Creek C-5
Bigbee Valley ... D-6
Biloxi K-6
Blue Mountain ... A-5
Bogue Chitto H-3
Bolton F-3
Booneville A-6
Boyle C-3
Braxton G-4

MISSISSIPPI

Brookhaven H-3
Brooklyn H-5
Brooksville D-6
Bruce C-5
Buckatunna G-6
Bude H-3
Burnsville A-6
Byhalia A-4
Caledonia C-6
Calhoun City C-5
Call Town J-6
Camden E-4
Canton E-4
Carlisle G-3
Carpenter G-3
Carriere J-5
Carrollton D-4
Carson H-4
Carthage E-4
Cary E-3
Cascilla C-4
Cedarbluff C-5
Centreville J-3
Charleston C-4
Chatawa J-4
Chatham E-2
Chunky F-6
Church Hill G-2
Clara G-6
Clarksdale B-3
Cleveland C-3
Clifftonville ... D-6
Clinton F-3
Coahoma B-3
Coffeeville C-4
Coila D-4
Coldwater A-4
Collins G-5
Collinsville E-6
Columbia H-4
Columbus C-6
Como B-4
Conehatta F-5
Corinth A-6
Courtland B-4
Crawford D-6
Crenshaw B-3
Crosby H-2
Cross Roads A-6
Crowder B-3
Crystal Springs . G-3
D'Lo G-4
Daleville E-6
Darling B-3
Darlove D-3
Darlove D-3
DeKalb E-6
Decatur F-5
Dennis A-6
Derma C-5
Doddsville C-3
Dorsey B-6
Drew C-3
Dublin C-3
Duck Hill C-4
Dumas A-5
Duncan C-3
Dundee B-3
Durant D-4
Eastabuchie H-5
Ebenezer E-4
Ecru B-5
Eden E-3
Edinburg E-5
Edwards F-3
Electric Mills .. E-6
Elizabeth D-3
Ellisville G-5
Enid B-4
Enterprise F-6
Ethel D-5
Etta B-5
Eupora D-5
Falcon B-3
Falkner A-5
Fannin F-4
Fayette G-2
Fitler F-2
Flora F-3
Florence F-4
Forest F-4
Forkville F-4
Fort Adams H-2
Foxworth H-4
French Camp D-5
Friar's Point ... B-3
Fruitland Park .. J-5
Fulton B-6
Futheyville C-4
Gallman G-3
Gattman C-6
Gautier K-6
Georgetown G-4
Gillsburg J-3
Glen A-6
Glen Allan E-2
Glendora C-3
Golden B-6
Goodman E-4
Gore Springs C-4
Grace E-2
Grand Gulf G-2
Greenville D-2
Greenwood D-4
Grenada C-4
Gulfport K-6
Gunnison C-2
Guntown B-6
Hamilton C-6
Harperville F-5
Harriston G-2
Harrisville G-4
Hatley B-6
Hattiesburg H-5

MISSISSIPPI

MISSOURI

Hazlehurst G-3
Heidelberg G-6
Helena B-3
Hermanville G-3
Hernando A-4
Hickory F-5
Hickory Flat A-5
Hilhouse C-2
Hillsboro F-5
Hiwannee G-6
Holcomb C-4
Hollandale D-3
Holly Bluff E-3
Holly Springs A-5
Homewood F-5
Horn A-3
Houston C-5
Hurley J-6
Independence A-4
Indianola D-3
Inverness D-3
Isola D-3
Itta Bena D-3
Iuka A-6
Jackson F-4
Jayess H-4
Johnstons Station H-4
Jonestown B-3
Kewanee F-6
Kilmichael C-4
Kiln K-5
Kokomo E-5
Kosciusko C-4
Lafayette Springs B-5
Lake E-5
Lake View .... Pg. 119, G-2
Lakeshore K-5
Lambert B-3
Lauderdale E-6
Laurel G-5
Lawrence F-5
LeFlore C-4
Leaf H-6
Leakesville H-6
Leland D-3
Lena E-4
Lessley G-5
Lexington D-4
Liberty H-3
Little Rock F-5
Long Beach K-5
Lorman G-2
Louin F-5
Louise E-3
Louisville D-5
Lucedale J-6
Lucien H-3
Ludlow D-4
Lula B-3
Lumberton J-5
Lyman K-5
Lyon B-3
Maben D-5
Macon E-5
Madden E-5
Madison F-4
Magee G-4
Magnolia H-3
Mantachie B-6
Mantee C-5
Marietta B-6
Marion F-6
Marks B-3
Martinsville G-3
Mathiston D-5
McAdams E-4
McCall Creek H-3
McCarley D-4
McComb H-3
McCondy C-5
McCool D-5
McHenry J-5
McLain H-6
McNeill J-5
Meadville H-3
Mendenhall G-4
Meridian F-6
Merigold C-3
Metcalfe D-2
Michigan City A-5
Mineral Wells A-4
Vicinity .... Pg. 119, G-7
Minter City C-3
Mize G-5
Money C-3
Monticello H-4
Montpelier C-5
Montrose F-5
Mooreville B-6
Moorhead D-3
Morgan City D-3
Morgantown H-4
Morton F-4
Moselle H-5
Moss G-5
Moss Point K-6
Mound Bayou C-3
Mount Olive G-5
Myrtle A-5
Natchez H-2
Necaise J-5
Nesbit A-3
Neshoba E-5
Nettleton B-6
New Albany B-5
New Augusta H-5
New Hebron G-4
New Houlka C-5
New Site A-6
Newton F-5
Nicholson K-5
Nitta Yuma D-3
North Carrollton D-4
Noxapater E-5

Oak Vale H-4
Oakland C-4
Ocean Springs K-6
Ofahoma E-4
Okolona B-6
Olive Branch A-4
Oma G-4
Onward E-3
Osyka H-3
Oxford B-4
Pace C-2
Pachuta F-6
Paden A-6
Panther Burn D-3
Parchman C-3
Paris B-4
Pascagoula K-7
Pass Christian K-5
Paulding F-5
Paulette D-6
Pearl F-4
Pearlington K-5
Pelahatchie F-4
Perkinston J-5
Petal H-5
Pheba C-5
Philadelphia E-5
Philipp C-3
Picayune K-5
Pickens E-4
Pinkneyville J-2
Pinola G-4
Plantersville B-6
Plum Point .... Pg. 119, G-3
Pocahontas F-3
Pond J-2
Pontotoc B-5
Pope B-4
Poplarville J-5
Port Gibson G-2
Porterville E-6
Potts Camp A-5
Prairie C-6
Prairie Point D-6
Prentiss G-4
Preston E-6
Puckett F-4
Pulaski F-5
Purvis H-5
Quentin H-3
Quitman G-5
Raleigh G-4
Randolph B-5
Raymond F-3
Red Banks A-4
Redwood F-3
Reform D-5
Rena Lara B-2
Richland F-4
Richton H-6
Ridgecrest H-2
Ridgeland F-4
Rienzi A-6
Ripley A-5
Robinsonville A-3
Rolling Fork D-2
Rome C-3
Rosedale C-2
Roxie H-2
Ruleville C-3
Runnelstown H-6
Ruth H-3
Sallis E-4
Saltillo B-6
Sandersville G-6
Sandhill F-4
Sandy Hook H-5
Sanford H-5
Sarah B-3
Sardis B-4
Sarepta B-5
Satartia E-3
Saucier J-5
Savage A-3
Schlater D-3
Scobey C-4
Scooba E-6
Scott D-2
Sebastopol F-5
Seminary G-5
Senatobia A-4
Sessums D-6
Seypal Lake A-3
Shannon B-6
Sharon E-4
Shaw D-2
Shelby C-3
Sherard B-3
Sherman B-6
Shivers G-4
Shubuta G-6
Shuqualak E-6
Sibley H-2
Sidon D-3
Silver City E-3
Silver Creek G-4
Skene C-3
Slate Springs C-5
Slayden A-4
Sledge B-3
Smithdale H-3
Smithville B-6
Sontag G-4
Soso G-5
Southaven A-3
Star F-4
Starkville D-5
State Line H-6
Steens D-6
Stewart D-5
Stoneville D-2
Stonewall F-6
Stovall B-3
Stringer G-5

Sturgis D-5
Summit H-3
Sumner C-3
Sumrall H-5
Sunflower D-3
Suqualena F-5
Swan Lake C-3
Swiftown D-3
Sylvarena G-5
Taylor B-4
Taylorsville G-5
Tchula D-4
Terry G-3
Thaxton B-5
Thomastown E-4
Thorn C-5
Thornton D-3
Thyatira A-4
Tie Plant C-4
Tillatoba C-4
Tinsley E-3
Tippo C-4
Tiplersville A-5
Tishomingo A-6
Toccopola B-5
Tomnolen D-5
Toomsuba F-6
Trebloc C-5
Tremont B-6
Tula B-4
Tunica A-3
Tupelo B-6
Tutwiler C-3
Tylertown H-4
Union E-5
Union Church G-3
University B-4
Utica G-3
Vaiden D-4
Valley Park E-3
Van Vleet C-5
Vance C-3
Vancleave K-6
Vardaman C-5
Vaughan E-4
Verona B-5
Vicksburg F-2
Victoria A-4
Vossburg G-5
Wade J-6
Walls A-3
Walnut A-5
Walnut Grove E-5
Walthall E-5
Washington H-2
Water Valley B-4
Waterford B-4
Waveland K-5
Waynesboro G-6
Wayside D-2
Weathersby G-4
Webb C-3
Weir D-5
Wenasoga A-6
Wesson G-3
West Gulfport J-5
West Point C-6
Wheeler A-6
Whitfield F-4
Wiggins J-5
Winona D-4
Winstonville C-3
Woodland C-5
Woodville J-2
Yazoo City E-3

MISSOURI
Pages 48-49
Population: 4,916,686
Capital: Jefferson City
Land Area: 68,945 sq. mi.

Adair D-5
Adrian H-2
Advance K-9
Agency F-2
Albany D-2
Alexandria D-7
Allendale D-3
Alma G-4
Altamont E-3
Alton L-7
Amoret H-2
Anderson L-2
Annapolis K-8
Anniston K-10
Appleton City H-3
Arab K-9
Arbela D-6
Arbyrd M-9
Arcadia J-8
Archie H-3
Arcola J-3
Arkoe E-2
Arnold K-8
Vicinity .... Pg. 140, K-3
Arroll K-6
Arrow Rock G-4
Asbury K-2
Ash Grove K-3
Ashland G-6
Ashley F-7
Athens D-6
Atlanta E-5
Aullville G-3
Aurora K-3
Auxvasse G-6
Ava K-5
Avalon F-4
Avondale .... Pg. 112, K-6
Bado K-6

Bakersfield L-6
Ballard H-3
Bardley L-7
Baring E-1
Barnard E-2
Battlefield K-4
Bay H-7
Beaufort H-7
Bel Nor .... Pg. 140, C-4
Bel Ridge .... Pg. 140, C-3
Bell City K-9
Bella Villa .... Pg. 140, H-4
Bellair G-5
Belle H-6
Bellefontaine Neighbors
    .... Pg. 140, B-5
Bellerive .... Pg. 140, C-4
Belton G-2
Bem H-7
Bendavis K-5
Bennett Springs J-5
Benton K-10
Berkeley .... Pg. 140, B-3
Bernie L-9
Bertrand K-10
Bethany D-3
Bethel E-6
Beulah J-6
Beverly Hills .... Pg. 140, D-4
Bevier E-5
Bible Grove D-6
Bigelow E-1
Bigspring G-7
Birch Tree K-6
Birmingham .... Pg. 112, E-5
Bismarck J-8
Bixby J-7
Black Jack .... Pg. 140, A-5
Blackburn G-4
Blodgett K-10
Bloomfield K-9
Blue Eye L-4
Blue Springs G-3
Blythedale D-3
Bogard F-3
Bolckow E-2
Bolivar J-4
Bonne Terre J-8
Boonesboro G-5
Boonville G-4
Bosworth F-4
Bourbon H-7
Bowling Green F-7
Boynton D-4
Bradleyville L-4
Branson L-4
Braymer F-3
Brazeau J-10
Breckenridge E-3
Breckenridge Hills
    .... Pg. 140, F-3
Brentwood .... Pg. 140, F-3
Briar L-8
Bridgeton .... Pg. 140, B-2
Brighton K-4
Brimson E-3
Brinktown H-6
Bronaugh J-2
Brookfield E-4
Broseley L-9
Brownbranch L-5
Browning E-4
Brumley H-5
Bruner K-5
Brunswick F-4
Buckhorn K-9
Bucklin E-5
Buckner G-3
Buffalo J-4
Bunker J-7
Burlington Jct. D-1
Butler H-2
Cabool K-6
Cainsville E-3
Cairo F-5
California G-5
Callao E-5
Calverton Park
    .... Pg. 140, B-4
Calwood G-6
Camdenton H-5
Cameron E-3
Campbell L-9
Canton E-7
Cape Girardeau J-10
Caplinger Mills J-3
Cardwell M-9
Carrington G-6
Carrollton F-3
Carsonville .... Pg. 140, C-4
Carthage K-2
Caruthersville M-10
Cascade K-9
Cassville L-3
Catherine Place J-9
Caulfield L-6
Center E-7
Centerville J-8
Centralia F-6
Chadwick K-4
Chaffee K-10
Chain-O-Lakes L-3
Chamois H-6
Champ .... Pg. 140, B-1
Charlack .... Pg. 140, C-3
Charleston K-10
Cherryville J-7
Chilhowee G-3
Chillicothe E-4
Chula E-4
Clarence E-5
Clarksdale E-2
Clarkson F-7
Clarkton L-9
Fordland K-4

Claycomo .... Pg. 112, D-5
Clayton .... Pg. 140, E-3
Clearmont D-1
Clever K-4
Clifton City G-4
Climax Springs H-4
Clinton H-3
Clyde D-2
Coal H-3
Coatsville D-5
Coldwater K-8
Cole Camp H-4
Collins J-3
Coloma F-4
Columbia G-6
Concordia G-3
Connelsville D-5
Conway J-5
Cook Station H-4
Cool Valley .... Pg. 140, C-4
Corning D-1
Corridon K-7
Couch L-7
Country Club Hills
    .... Pg. 140, C-5
County Life Acres
    .... Pg. 140, E-1
Craig E-1
Crane K-4
Crestwood .... Pg. 140, G-2
Creve Coeur .... Pg. 140, E-1
Crocker J-6
Cross Timbers H-4
Crystal Lake Park
    .... Pg. 140, E-1
Cuba H-7
Curryville F-7
Cyrene F-7
Dadeville J-3
De Soto H-8
Dearborn F-2
Deerfield J-2
Defiance G-8
Dellwood .... Pg. 140, B-4
Denver D-3
Des Arc K-8
Des Peres .... Pg. 140, F-1
Desloge J-8
Dexter K-9
Diamond K-2
Dixon H-6
Doe Run J-8
Dongola L-8
Doniphan L-8
Doolittle J-6
Dorena L-10
Downing D-5
Drexel H-2
Drury K-5
Duenweg K-2
Duncans Bridge F-5
Dunlap E-4
Dunnegan J-4
Durham E-6
Dutchtown K-9
Eagleville D-3
East Prairie L-10
Edgar Springs J-6
Edgerton F-2
Edina E-6
Edinburg E-3
Edmundson .... Pg. 140, B-3
El Dorado Springs J-3
Eldon H-4
Eldridge J-5
Elkland K-4
Ellington K-7
Ellsinore K-8
Elmira F-3
Elmo D-1
Elsberry F-8
Elwood E-2
Emden E-6
Eminence K-7
Eolia F-7
Essex L-9
Ethel E-5
Eudora J-4
Eunice K-6
Eureka H-8
Everton K-3
Ewing E-6
Excello F-5
Excelsior Springs F-2
Exeter L-3
Fagus L-9
Fair Grove K-4
Fair Play J-4
Fairdealing L-8
Fairfax D-1
Fairmont D-6
Fairview K-6
Farber F-6
Farley F-2
Farmersville E-4
Farmington J-8
Faucett F-2
Fayette F-5
Fayetteville J-3
Fenton .... Pg. 140, H-1
Ferguson .... Pg. 140, C-4
Ferrelview .... Pg. 112, A-2
Festus H-8
Filley J-3
Fillmore E-2
Fisk L-9
Flordell Hills .... Pg. 140, C-4
Florence G-4
Florida F-6
Florissant .... Pg. 140, A-4
Foley F-8
Forbes E-1

Forest City E-1
Forest Green F-5
Foristell G-8
Forsyth L-5
Fortescue E-1
Fortuna H-5
Fountain Grove F-4
Frankford F-7
Fredericktown J-9
Freeburg H-6
Fremont K-7
French Village J-9
Frontenac .... Pg. 140, E-2
Fulton G-6
Gainesville L-5
Galena L-3
Gallatin E-3
Galt E-4
Garden City H-3
Garwood L-7
Gatewood L-7
Gentry D-2
Gerald H-7
Gilliam F-4
Gladden J-7
Gladstone .... Pg. 112, C-4
Glasgow F-5
Glen Echo Park
    .... Pg. 140, C-4
Glenaire .... Pg. 112, C-5
Glendale .... Pg. 140, F-2
Glenwood D-5
Glover J-8
Golden City K-3
Goodman L-2
Gower F-2
Graham D-1
Grain Valley G-3
Granby K-3
Grand Pass F-4
Grandin L-8
Granger D-6
Grant City D-2
Grantwood Village
    .... Pg. 140, G-3
Granville F-6
Grassy K-9
Gray Summit H-8
Graysville D-4
Green City D-4
Green Ridge H-4
Greencastle D-5
Greendale .... Pg. 140, D-4
Greenfield K-3
Greensburg D-6
Greentop D-5
Greenville K-8
Greer L-7
Grovespring K-5
Halfway J-4
Hallsville F-6
Halltown K-3
Hamilton E-3
Hanley Hills .... Pg. 140, D-4
Hannibal E-7
Hardin F-3
Harris D-4
Harrisburg G-5
Harrisonville G-3
Hartford D-5
Hartsburg K-5
Hartville H-3
Hartwell H-3
Harwood H-3
Hatfield D-2
Hawk Point G-7
Hayti M-9
Hayti Heights M-10
Hazelwood .... Pg. 140, A-3
Helena E-2
Hermann G-7
Hermitage J-4
Higbee F-5
Higginsville G-3
High Point H-5
Hillsboro H-8
Hillsdale .... Pg. 140, D-4
Hinton G-5
Hitt D-6
Holcomb L-9
Holden G-3
Hollister L-4
Holt F-2
Holts Summit G-6
Hopkins D-2
Hornersville M-9
House Springs H-8
Houston K-6
Houston Lake
    .... Pg. 112, D-2
Houstonia G-4
Humansville J-4
Humphreys E-4
Hunter K-8
Huntleigh .... Pg. 140, F-2
Huntsdale G-5
Huntsville F-5
Hurdland E-6
Hurricane Deck H-5
Iberia H-6
Idlewild K-9
Independence G-2
Vicinity .... Pg. 112, C-6
Ironton J-8
Jackson J-10
Jacksonville F-5
Jameson E-3
Jamesport E-3
Jamestown G-5
Jane L-2
Jasper K-2
Jefferson City H-5
Jenkins L-3
Jennings ....
Vicinity .... Pg. 140, C-4

Jerico Springs J-3
Joplin K-2
Kahoka D-6
Kansas City G-2
Vicinity .... Pg. 124-125
Kearney F-2
Kendricktown K-3
Kennett L-10
Kewanee L-10
Keytesville F-5
Kidder E-3
Kimberling City L-4
King City E-2
Kingston E-3
Kinloch .... Pg. 140, B-3
Kirksville E-5
Kirkwood .... Pg. 140, F-2
Kliever G-5
Knob Noster G-3
Knox City E-6
Knoxville F-3
Koshkonong L-6
La Grange E-7
La Plata E-5
La Tour G-3
LaBelle E-6
LaMonte G-4
Laddonia F-6
Ladue .... Pg. 140, E-2
Lake Lotawana G-2
Lake Saint Louis G-8
Lake Spring J-7
Lake Waukomis
    .... Pg. 112, C-2
Lakenan F-6
Lakeshire .... Pg. 140, H-3
Lamar K-3
Lancaster D-5
Lanton L-6
Lathrop F-2
Latty J-8
Lawson F-3
Leadwood J-8
Leasburg H-7
Lebanon J-5
Lee's Summit .... Pg. 112, K-6
Leeper K-8
Leeton H-3
Lemons D-4
Lentner E-5
Leonard E-5
Lewistown E-6
Lexington G-3
Liberal J-2
Liberty F-2
Vicinity .... Pg. 112, C-6
Licking J-6
Lilbourn L-10
Lincoln H-4
Linn H-6
Linneus E-4
Lockwood K-3
Lone Jack G-3
Long Lane J-5
Longrun L-5
Longwood G-4
Louisiana F-7
Lowry City H-3
Ludlow E-4
Luray D-6
Macks Creek J-5
Macon F-5
Madison F-6
Malden L-9
Manchester .... Pg. 140, F-1
Vicinity .... Pg. 140, G-1
Manes K-5
Mansfield K-5
Maplewood .... Pg. 140, F-3
Marble Hill K-9
Marceline E-4
March J-4
Marionville K-4
Marlborough .... Pg. 140, G-3
Marshall F-4
Marshfield K-5
Marthasville G-7
Martinsburg F-6
Maryland Heights
    .... Pg. 140, C-1
Maryville D-1
Matthews L-10
Maysville E-2
McBaine G-5
McFall E-2
Melbourne E-3
Memphis D-5
Mercer D-4
Mexico F-6
Miami F-4
Miami Station F-4
Middle Grove F-6
Midway G-5
Milan E-4
Milford J-3
Mill Grove D-4
Millard E-5
Miller K-3
Millersburg G-6
Milo J-2
Mineola G-7
Mineral Point J-8
Mirabile F-3
Moberly F-5
Mokane G-6
Moline Acres .... Pg. 140, B-5
Monett K-3
Monroe City F-6
Montevallo J-3
Montgomery City G-7
Monticello E-6
Montreal J-5
Montrose H-3
Moody L-6

Morley K-10
Morrisville J-4
Mound City E-1
Moundville J-2
Mount Moriah D-3
Mount Vernon K-3
Mount Zion K-5
Mountain Grove K-5
Mountain View K-7
Myrtle L-7
Mystic E-4
Nashville K-2
Naylor L-8
Nebo J-5
Neelyville L-8
Neosho L-2
Nevada J-2
New Bloomfield G-6
New Boston E-4
New Florence G-7
New Franklin G-5
New Hartford F-7
New Haven H-7
New Hope F-8
New London F-7
New Madrid L-10
New Market F-2
New Melle G-7
New Point E-1
Newburg J-6
Niangua K-5
Nixa K-4
Noel L-2
Norborne F-3
Normandy .... Pg. 140, C-4
Northmoor .... Pg. 112, D-3
Northview K-4
Northwoods .... Pg. 140, C-4
Norwood Court
    .... Pg. 140, C-4
Noser Mill H-7
Novelty E-5
Novinger E-5
O'Fallon G-8
Oak Grove G-3
Oak Hill H-6
Oakland .... Pg. 140, G-2
Oaks .... Pg. 112, D-4
Oakview .... Pg. 112, D-4
Oakville .... Pg. 140, K-4
Oakwood .... Pg. 112, D-4
Oakwood Park
    .... Pg. 112, D-4
Ocie L-5
Odessa G-3
Oermann H-8
Olivette .... Pg. 140, D-3
Olympian Village H-8
Oran K-10
Orchard Farm G-8
Oregon E-1
Orrick F-3
Osage Beach H-5
Osceola H-3
Osgood E-4
Oskaloosa J-2
Otto H-8
Overland .... Pg. 140, D-3
Owensville H-6
Ozark K-4
Pacific H-8
Pagedale .... Pg. 140, D-4
Palmyra E-7
Paris F-6
Parkville .... Pg. 112, D-3
Parma L-9
Pasadena Hills
    .... Pg. 140, C-4
Pasadena Park
    .... Pg. 140, C-4
Passaio H-2
Patton J-9
Pattonsburg E-2
Peace Valley L-6
Peach Orchard L-9
Peculiar G-2
Pennsboro K-3
Perrin E-2
Perry F-6
Perryville J-9
Pevely H-8
Phelps K-3
Philadelphia E-6
Phillipsburg J-5
Piedmont K-8
Pierce City K-3
Pilot Grove G-4
Pilot Knob J-8
Pine Lawn .... Pg. 140, D-5
Pineville L-2
Plad J-5
Plato J-6
Platte Woods .... Pg. 112, C-2
Plattsburg F-2
Pleasant Green G-4
Pleasant Valley
    .... Pg. 112, C-
Plevna .... E-
Pocahontas .... J-
Polk .... J-
Pollock .... D-
Polo .... F-
Pomona .... L-
Poplar Bluff .... L-
Portageville L-1
Potosi .... J-
Prairie Hill .... F-
Prairie Home .... G-
Preston .... J-
Princeton .... D-
Protem .... L-
Purdin .... E-
Purdy .... L-
Puxico .... K-

MISSOURI

Queen City D-5
Quincy H-4
Qulin L-9
Racine K-2
Randolph .. Pg. 112, E-5
Ravanna D-4
Ravenwood D-2
Raymondville K-6
Raymore G-2
Raytown ... Pg. 112, H-5
Rea E-2
Redford K-8
Reeds Spring L-4
Regal F-3
Reger E-4
Renick F-5
Rensselaer F-7
Republic K-4
Reynolds K-8
Rhineland G-7
Rich Hill H-2
Richland J-5
Richmond F-3
Richmond Heights
.... Pg. 140, E-3
Ridgedale L-4
Ridgeway D-3
Risco L-9
Riverside ... Pg. 112, D-2
Riverton L-7
Riverview .. Pg. 140, B-6
Rock Hill .. Pg. 140, F-2
Rock Port D-1
Rockville H-3
Rocky Comfort L-3
Rogersville K-4
Rolla J-6
Romance L-5
Rombauer K-8
Rosati H-7
Rosebud H-7
Rosendale E-2
Rothville F-4
Round Spring K-7
Rover L-7
Rushville F-1
Saint Ann . Pg. 140, D-4
Saint Charles G-8
  Vicinity .... Pg. 140, A-1
Saint Clair H-8
Saint Clement F-7
Saint George Pg. 140, H-4
Saint James H-6
Saint John .. Pg. 140, C-3
Saint Joseph E-2
Saint Louis G-8
  Vicinity .... Pg. 140
Saint Marys J-9
Saint Patrick E-7
Saint Robert J-6
Sainte Genevieve H-8
Salem J-7
Saline D-3
Salisbury F-5
Sandy Hook G-5
Santa Fe F-6
Sarcoxie K-3
Savannah E-2
Scott City K-10
Sedalia G-4
Sedgewickville J-9
Seligman L-3
Senath M-9
Seneca L-2
Seymour K-5
Shannondale F-5
Shelbina E-6
Shelbyville E-6
Sheldon J-3
Sheridan D-2
Shirley J-7
Shrewsbury . Pg. 140, F-3
Sikeston K-10
Silva K-8
Silver Lake J-9
Simmons K-6
Skidmore D-1
Slater F-4
Sleeper J-5
Sligo J-7
Smithton G-4
Smithville F-2
South Fork L-6
South Gifford E-5
South Lineville D-4
Southwest City L-2
Sparta K-4
Spickard E-4
Spokane K-4
Springfield K-4
Squires L-5
Stanberry E-2
State Line M-9
Steele M-9
Steelville J-7
Stockton J-3
Stoutsville F-6
Stover H-4
Strafford K-4
Strasburg G-3
Sturgeon F-6
Sugar Creek Pg. 112, F-5
Sullivan H-7
Summersville K-7
Sumner F-4
Sunset Hills . Pg. 140, H-2
Sweet Springs G-4
Sycamore L-6
Sycamore Hills
.... Pg. 140, C-3
Tarkio D-1
Tebbetts G-6
Thayer L-7
Theodosia L-5

Thomas Hill F-5
Thomasville L-6
Thompson F-6
Thornfield L-5
Tiffin J-3
Tina F-5
Tindall E-4
Tipton G-5
Town & Country
.... Pg. 140, F-1
Townley L-9
Trenton E-4
Troy G-8
Truesdale G-7
Truxton G-7
Tunas J-4
Turney F-2
Tuscumbia H-5
Tyrone K-6
Union H-7
Union Star E-2
Unionville D-4
Unity Village Pg. 112, J-6
University City
.... Pg. 140, D-3
Uplands Park Pg. 140, D-4
Urich H-3
Utica E-3
Van Buren K-8
Vandalia F-7
Vanzant K-6
Velda City .. Pg. 140, D-4
Velda Village Hills
.... Pg. 140, D-4
Versailles H-5
Viburnum J-7
Vichy H-6
Vienna H-6
Vinita Park .. Pg. 140, D-3
Vinita Terrace Pg. 140, D-3
Vulcan K-8
Wainwright G-6
Walnut Grove K-4
Wardsville H-6
Warren K-7
Warrensburg G-3
Warrenton G-7
Warsaw H-4
Warson Woods
.... Pg. 140, F-2
Washington G-7
Wasola L-5
Waverly F-4
Wayland D-7
Waynesville J-6
Weatherby Lake
.... Pg. 112, C-2
Weaubleau J-4
Webb City K-2
Weber Hill H-8
Webster Groves
.... Pg. 140, F-3
Wellston .. Pg. 140, D-4
Wellsville G-7
Wentworth K-3
West Plains L-6
Westboro D-1
Weston F-2
Westphalia H-6
White Oak L-9
Wilbur Park . Pg. 140, G-4
Wilcox D-2
Willard K-4
Williamsburg G-6
Williamsville K-8
Willow Springs K-6
Wilson City K-10
Windsor H-4
Winfield G-8
Winigan E-4
Winona K-7
Winston E-3
Winthrop F-1
Woodlawn F-5
Woods Heights F-3
Woodson Terrace
.... Pg. 140, C-3
Wooldridge G-5
Worth D-2
Wyaconda D-7
Yarrow E-5
Yount J-7
Yukon K-6
Zalma K-9

MONTANA
Page 51
Population: 786,690
Capital: Helena
Land Area: 145,398 sq.mi.

Absarokee E-6
Acton E-7
Alberton D-2
Alder E-4
Alzada D-10
Anaconda E-3
Angela D-8
Antelope B-10
Arlee D-2
Ashland E-8
Augusta C-4
Avon D-3
Babb B-3
Bainville B-10
Baker E-10
Basin E-4
Bearcreek F-6
Belfry F-6
Belgrade E-4
Belt C-5

Biddle E-9
Big Fork C-2
Big Sandy C-5
Big Sky E-4
Big Timber E-6
Bighorn E-7
Billings E-7
Birney E-8
Black Eagle C-5
Blackfoot B-3
Bloomfield C-9
Bonner D-2
Boulder E-4
Box Elder C-5
Bozeman E-5
Brady C-4
Bridger F-6
Broadus E-9
Broadview E-6
Brockton C-9
Brockway C-9
Browning B-3
Busby E-8
Butte E-3
Bynum C-4
Cameron F-4
Canyon Creek D-4
Capitol D-10
Carter C-5
Cartersville D-8
Cascade C-4
Checkerboard D-5
Chester C-4
Chico Hot Springs F-5
Chinook B-6
Choteau C-4
Christina C-6
Churchill E-4
Circle C-9
Cleveland C-6
Clinton D-2
Clyde Park E-5
Coffee Creek C-5
Cohagen D-8
Colstrip E-8
Columbia Falls B-2
Columbus E-6
Conner E-2
Conrad C-4
Cooke City F-6
Corvallis D-2
Craig D-4
Crane C-10
Crow Agency E-7
Culbertson B-9
Custer E-7
Cut Bank B-4
Darby E-2
DeBorgia C-1
Dean E-6
Decker F-8
Deer Lodge D-3
Dell F-3
Denton C-5
Dillon F-3
Dixon C-2
Dodson B-7
Drummond D-3
Dupuyer C-4
Dutton C-4
East Glacier Park ... B-3
East Helena D-4
Edgar E-6
Ekalaka D-10
Elliston D-3
Elmo C-2
Emigrant E-5
Ennis E-4
Ethridge B-4
Eureka B-2
Fairfield C-4
Fairview C-10
Fallon D-9
Flatwillow D-7
Flaxville B-9
Florence D-2
Ford E-9
Forestgrove D-6
Forsyth E-8
Fort Belknap Agency . C-6
Fort Benton C-5
Fort Peck C-8
Fort Shaw C-4
Fortine B-2
Frenchtown D-2
Froid C-9
Fromberg E-6
Galen D-3
Gallatin Gateway E-4
Gardiner F-5
Garneill D-6
Garryowen E-7
Geraldine C-5
Geyser C-5
Glasgow C-8
Glen E-3
Glendive D-10
Grant F-3
Grantsdale D-2
Grassrange D-6
Great Falls C-4
Hall D-3
Hamilton D-2
Hammond D-10
Happy's Inn C-1
Hardin E-7
Harlem B-6
Harlowton D-6
Harrison E-4
Hathaway D-9
Havre B-6
Helena D-4

Helmville D-3
Heron C-1
Hilger D-6
Hingham F-4
Hinsdale B-8
Hobson D-5
Homestead B-9
Hot Springs C-2
Hungry Horse B-2
Huntley E-7
Huson D-2
Hysham D-8
Ingomar D-8
Jackson E-3
Jefferson City D-4
Joliet E-6
Joplin E-4
Jordan C-8
Judith Gap D-6
Kalispell B-2
Kiowa B-3
Klein D-6
Kremlin F-4
Lakeside C-2
Lambert C-9
Lame Deer E-8
Laurel E-6
Laurin E-4
Lavina D-6
Lewistown D-6
Libby B-1
Lima F-3
Lincoln D-3
Lindsay C-9
Livingston E-5
Lloyd B-6
Lodge Grass E-7
Lohman D-2
Lolo D-2
Lolo Hot Springs D-2
Loma C-5
Loring B-7
Lothair B-4
Malta B-7
Manhattan E-4
Marion C-2
Martin City B-2
McLeod E-5
Medicine Lake B-9
Melrose E-3
Melstone D-7
Melville D-6
Miles City D-9
Missoula D-2
Moccasin D-5
Monarch C-5
Montague C-4
Montana City D-4
Moore D-6
Musselshell D-7
Nashua C-8
Neihart C-5
Niarada C-2
Norris E-4
Noxon C-1
Nye E-6
Olney B-2
Opheim B-8
Oswego C-8
Ovando D-3
Pablo C-2
Paradise C-2
Pendroy C-4
Philipsburg D-3
Plains C-1
Plentywood B-9
Plevna D-10
Polebridge B-2
Polson C-2
Pompeys Pillar E-7
Poplar C-8
Port of Del Bonita ... B-3
Port of Morgan B-7
Port of Opheim B-8
Port of Raymond B-9
Potomac D-2
Powderville E-9
Power C-4
Pray E-5
Rapelje E-5
Raymond B-9
Raynesford C-5
Red Lodge F-6
Redstone B-9
Reedpoint E-6
Rexford B-1
Richey C-9
Richland B-9
Ringling E-5
Roberts F-6
Rock Springs D-8
Rollins C-2
Ronan C-2
Rosebud D-8
Roundup D-6
Roy D-6
Rudyard F-4
Ryegate D-6
Saco B-8
Saint Ignatius C-2
Saint Mary B-3
Saint Regis C-1
Santa Rita B-4
Savage C-10
Scobey B-9
Seeley Lake D-3
Shawmut D-6
Shelby B-4
Sheridan E-4
Sidney C-10
Silesia E-6
Silver Star E-4
Simms C-4

Somers C-2
Springdale E-5
Stanford D-5
Stevensville D-2
Stryker B-2
Suffolk C-6
Sumatra D-7
Sun River C-4
Sunburst B-4
Superior C-2
Swan Lake C-2
Sweetgrass B-4
Tarkio D-2
Teigen D-7
Terry D-9
Thompson Falls C-2
Three Forks E-4
Toston E-4
Townsend E-4
Trego B-2
Trout Creek C-1
Troy B-1
Turner B-7
Twin Bridges E-4
Twodot D-5
Valier B-4
Vaughn C-5
Victor D-2
Vida C-9
Virginia City E-4
Volborg E-9
Walkerville E-3
Warmsprings D-3
Waterloo E-4
West Glacier B-3
West Yellowstone F-4
Westby B-10
White Hall E-4
White Sulphur Springs B-5
Whitefish B-2
Whitetail B-9
Whitewater B-8
Wibaux D-10
Willow Creek E-4
Wilsall E-5
Winifred C-6
Winnett D-7
Winston E-4
Wisdom E-3
Wise River E-3
Wolf Creek D-4
Wolf Point C-9
Worden E-7
Wyola F-8
Yaak B-1
Zurich B-6

NEBRASKA
Pages 52-53
Population: 1,569,825
Capital: Lincoln
Land Area: 76,664 sq. mi.

Abie F-11
Adams H-12
Ainsworth D-7
Albion E-10
Alda G-9
Alexandria H-11
Allen D-11
Alliance D-3
Alma H-8
Almeria E-8
Amelia D-9
Ames F-12
Amherst G-8
Angora D-3
Anoka C-9
Anselmo E-7
Ansley F-8
Antioch D-4
Arapahoe H-7
Arcadia F-8
Archer F-10
Arlington F-12
Arnold F-7
Arthur E-5
Ashby D-4
Ashland G-12
Ashton F-9
Atkinson D-9
Atlanta H-8
Auburn H-12
Aurora G-10
Axtell H-8
Ayr H-9
Bancroft E-12
Barneston J-12
Bartlett E-9
Bartley H-6
Bassett D-8
Battle Creek E-10
Bayard E-3
Bazile Mills D-10
Beatrice H-11
Beaver City H-7
Beaver Crossing G-11
Beemer E-11
Belden D-11
Belgrade F-10
Bellevue G-12
  Vicinity .... Pg. 132, G-5
Belvidere H-10
Benedict G-10
Benkelman H-5
Bennet G-12
Bertrand H-7
Berwyn F-8
Big Springs F-4
Bingham D-4
Bladen H-9
Blair F-12

Bloomfield D-10
Blue Hill H-9
Blue Springs H-11
Boelus G-9
Boone F-10
Boys Town F-12
  Vicinity .... Pg. 132, E-5
Bradshaw G-10
Brady F-6
Brandon G-4
Brewster E-7
Bridgeport E-3
Bristow C-9
Broadwater E-3
Brock H-12
Broken Bow F-7
Brownlee D-6
Brule F-4
Bruning H-10
Bruno F-11
Brunswick D-10
Burchard H-12
Burr H-12
Burton C-8
Burwell E-8
Bushnell F-2
Butte C-9
Cairo G-9
Callaway F-7
Cambridge H-6
Campbell H-9
Capehart ..... Pg. 132, H-4
Carleton H-10
Carroll D-11
Carter lake .. Pg. 132, D-4
Cedar Bluffs F-12
Cedar Creek . Pg. 132, K-1
Cedar Rapids F-10
Center D-10
Central City G-9
Ceresco G-12
Chadron C-3
Chalco ..... Pg. 132, F-1
Chambers E-9
Champion G-5
Chapman G-9
Chappell F-4
Chester J-10
Clarks F-10
Clarkson E-11
Clatonia H-11
Clay Center H-10
Clearwater D-10
Clinton C-4
Cody C-6
Coleridge D-11
Columbus F-11
Comstock F-8
Concord D-11
Cook H-12
Cornlea F-10
Cortland H-11
Cotesfield F-9
Cowles H-9
Cozad G-7
Crab Orchard H-12
Craig E-12
Crawford C-3
Creighton D-10
Creston E-11
Crete H-11
Crofton C-10
Crookston C-6
Culbertson H-6
Cullom ..... Pg. 132, K-2
Curtis G-6
Dakota City D-12
Dalton E-3
Danbury H-6
Dannebrog F-9
Davenport H-10
David City F-11
Dawson J-13
Daykin H-11
Debolt ..... Pg. 132, C-3
Decatur E-12
Denton G-11
Deshler H-10
Dewitt H-11
Dickens G-6
Diller H-11
Dix F-2
Dodge E-11
Doniphan G-9
Dorchester G-11
Douglas H-12
DuBois J-12
Dunbar G-12
Duncan F-10
Dunning E-7
Dwight G-11
Eddyville G-7
Edgar H-10
Edison H-7
Elba F-9
Elgin E-9
Eli C-5
Elk Creek H-12
Elkhorn F-12
Elm Creek G-8
Elmwood G-12
Elsie G-5
Elsmere D-7
Elwood G-7
Elyria E-8
Emerson D-11
Emmet D-9
Enders H-5
Endicott J-11
Ericson E-9
Eustis G-7
Exeter G-10
Fairbury H-11

Fairfield H-10
Fairmont H-10
Falls City J-13
Farnam G-7
Farwell F-9
Filley H-11
Firth H-11
Fordyce D-11
Foster D-10
Franklin H-8
Fremont F-12
Friend G-10
Fullerton F-10
Funk H-8
Gandy F-6
Garland G-11
Garrison F-11
Geneva H-10
Genoa F-10
Gering E-2
Gilmore ..... Pg. 132, H-4
Giltner G-9
Glenvil H-9
Goehner G-11
Gordon C-4
Gothenburg G-7
Grafton G-10
Grainton G-5
Grand Island G-9
Grant G-5
Greeley F-9
Greenwood G-12
Gresham G-11
Gretna F-12
Guide Rock J-9
Gurley F-3
Hadar E-11
Haigler H-4
Hallam H-11
Halsey E-7
Hamlet H-5
Hampton G-10
Harrisburg E-2
Harrison C-2
Hartington D-11
Harvard H-9
Hastings H-9
Hay Springs C-4
Hayes Center H-5
Hazard F-8
Hebron H-10
Hemingford D-3
Henderson G-10
Herman E-12
Hershey F-6
Hildreth H-8
Holdrege H-7
Holstein H-9
Hooper F-11
Hoskins E-11
Howells E-11
Humboldt J-12
Humphrey E-10
Huntley H-8
Hyannis D-5
Imperial G-5
Inavale H-9
Indianola H-6
Inman D-9
Ithaca F-11
Johnson H-12
Johnstown D-7
Juniata G-9
Kearney G-8
Kenesaw H-9
Kennard F-12
Keystone F-5
Kilgore C-6
Kimball F-2
La Vista ..... Pg. 132, F-3
Lakeside D-4
Laurel D-11
Lawrence H-9
Lebanon H-7
Leigh E-11
Lemoyne F-5
Lewellen F-4
Lewiston H-12
Lexington G-7
Liberty J-12
Lincoln G-12
Linwood F-11
Lisco E-4
Litchfield F-8
Lodgepole F-4
Long Pine D-7
Loomis H-7
Louisville G-12
Loup City F-8
Lyman D-2
Lynch C-9
Lyons E-12
Madison E-11
Madrid G-5
Magnet D-10
Malmo F-11
Marquette G-10
Martell H-11
Martinsburg D-11
Mason City F-8
Max H-5
Maxwell F-6
May ..... Pg. 132, G-3
Maywood G-6
McCook H-6
McCool Jct. G-10
McGrew E-2
Mead F-12
Meadow ... Pg. 132, K-1
Melbeta E-2
Memphis G-12
Merna F-7
Merriman C-5
Milford G-11

Millard ..... Pg. 132, F-1
Miller G-8
Milligan H-10
Mills C-8
Minden H-8
Minatare E-2
Mitchell D-2
Monowi C-9
Moorefield G-6
Morrill D-2
Mullen D-6
Murray G-12
Naper C-8
Naponee J-8
Nashville ... Pg. 132, B-3
Nebraska City H-12
Neligh E-10
Nelson H-10
Nenzel C-6
Newman Grove E-10
Newport D-8
Nickerson F-12
Niobrara C-10
Norden C-7
Norfolk E-10
North Bend F-11
North Loup F-9
North Platte F-6
O'Neill D-9
Oak H-10
Oakdale E-10
Oakland E-12
Obert D-11
Oconto F-7
Octavia F-11
Odell J-11
Odessa G-8
Ogallala F-5
Ohiowa H-10
Omaha F-12
  Vicinity .... Pg. 132
Ong H-9
Ord E-8
Oreapolis ..... Pg. 132, J-5
Orleans H-8
Osceola F-10
Oshkosh E-4
Osmond D-10
Overton G-8
Oxford H-7
Page D-9
Palisade H-5
Palmer F-9
Palmyra G-12
Panama H-12
Papillion G-12
  Vicinity .... Pg. 132, G-3
Parks H-4
Pawnee City J-12
Paxton F-5
Pender E-12
Petersburg E-10
Phillips G-9
Pickrell H-11
Pierce D-10
Pilger E-11
Plainview D-10
Platte Center F-10
Plattsmouth G-12
  Vicinity .... Pg. 132, K-5
Pleasanton G-8
Plymouth H-11
Polk G-10
Poole G-8
Potter F-3
Prague F-11
Primrose E-9
Prosser G-9
Purdum D-7
Raeville E-10
Ragan H-8
Ralston ..... Pg. 132, F-2
Randolph D-11
Ravenna G-9
Raymond G-11
Red Cloud H-9
Republican City H-8
Reynolds J-11
Richfield ..... Pg. 132, H-2
Richland F-11
Riverdale G-8
Rising City F-11
Riverton H-9
Roca G-11
Rockville F-9
Rogers F-11
Rosalie E-12
Rose D-8
Roseland H-9
Rushville C-4
Ruskin H-9
Saint Edward F-10
Saint Helena C-11
Saint Libory G-9
Saint Mary H-12
Saint Paul F-9
Santee C-10
Sargent E-8
Saronville H-9
Schuyler F-11
Scotia F-9
Scottsbluff D-2
Scribner F-11
Seneca D-6
Seward G-11
Shelby F-10
Shelton G-8
Shickley H-10
Sholes D-11
Shubert H-12
Sidney F-3
Silver Creek F-10
Smithfield G-7
Snyder E-11

South Bend G-12
South Souix City . . . D-12
Spalding E-9
Sparks C-7
Spencer C-9
Springfield G-12
  Vicinity . . . Pg. 132, J-1
Springview C-8
Stamford H-7
Stanton E-11
Staplehurst G-11
Stapleton J-1
Steele City J-11
Steinauer H-12
Stockville G-6
Strang H-10
Stratton H-5
Stromsburg F-10
Stuart D-8
Summerfield J-12
Sumner G-8
Superior J-10
Surprise G-10
Sutherland F-6
Sutton H-10
Syracuse H-12
Table Rock H-12
Tarnov F-10
Taylor E-8
Tecumseh H-12
Tekamah E-12
Terrytown D-2
Thayer G-10
Thedford E-6
Thurston E-12
Tilden E-10
Tobias H-11
Trenton H-6
Trumbull G-9
Tryon E-6
Uehling E-12
Ulysses G-11
Unadilla G-12
Upland H-8
Valentine C-7
Valley F-12
Valparaiso G-11
Venango C-10
Verdel D-10
Verdigre D-10
Verdon J-13
Waco G-10
Wahoo F-12
Wakefield D-11
Wallace G-5
Walthill E-12
Wauneta H-5
Wausa D-10
Waverly G-12
Wayne D-11
Weeping Water . . . G-12
Weissert F-8
Wellfleet G-6
West Point E-11
Western H-11
Westerville F-8
Whitman D-5
Whitney C-3
Wilber H-11
Wilcox H-8
Willow Island G-7
Wilsonville H-7
Winnebago D-12
Winnetoon D-9
Winside E-11
Winslow F-12
Wisner E-11
Wolbach F-9
Wood Lake C-7
Wood River G-9
Wymore J-12
Wynot C-11
York G-10

NEVADA
Page 54
Population: 800,493
Capital: Carson City
Land Area: 109,893 sq. mi.

Adaven F-5
Alamo G-5
Arden . . . . . Pg. 113, G-1
Ash Springs G-5
Austin D-4
Babbitt E-2
Baker D-6
Battle Mountain . . . C-4
Beatty G-4
Beowawe C-4
Blue Diamond J-5
Boulder City J-6
Bracken . . Pg. 113, E-3
Bunkerville H-6
Cactus Springs . . . H-5
Cal Nev Ari J-6
Caliente G-6
Carlin C-5
Carp G-6
Carson City E-1
Carver's E-3
Caselton F-6
Cherry Creek D-6
Coaldale F-3
Cold Spring D-3
Contact A-6
Crescent Valley . . . C-4
Currant E-5
Currie C-6
Deeth B-5
Duckwater E-5

Dyer F-3
Eagle Picher Mine . . C-2
East Ely E-6
East Las Vegas
  . . . . Pg. 113, E-6
Elko C-5
Ely E-6
Empire C-2
Eureka D-5
Fallon D-2
Fernley D-2
Frenchman E-3
Gabbs E-3
Gerlach C-2
Glendale H-6
Golconda B-3
Gold Point G-3
Goldfield G-3
Goodsprings J-5
Halleck B-5
Hawthorne E-2
Henderson J-6
  Vicinity . . . Pg. 113, G-6
Hiko G-5
Imlay C-3
Indian Springs H-5
Ione E-3
Jack Creek B-5
Jackpot A-6
Jarbridge A-5
Jean J-5
Jiggs C-5
Kimberly D-6
Lage's D-6
Lamoille C-5
Las Vegas J-5
  Vicinity . . . . . Pg. 113
Las Vegas Beach
  . . . . Pg. 113, J-6
Laughlin K-6
Lee C-5
Lida G-3
Lovelock C-2
Lund E-6
Luning F-3
Major's Place E-6
McDermitt A-3
McGill D-6
Mercury H-5
Mesquite H-6
Midas B-4
Middle Gate E-3
Mill City C-3
Mina F-3
Moapa H-6
Montello B-6
Mountain City A-5
Nelson J-6
Nixon D-2
North Las Vegas . . . J-6
  Vicinity . . . Pg. 113, B-3
Nyala F-5
Oasis B-6
Oreana C-3
Orovada B-3
Overton H-6
Owyhee A-5
Panaca G-6
Paradise Valley B-3
Pioche F-6
Preston E-6
Rachel G-5
Reno D-1
Round Mt. E-4
Ruby Valley C-5
Ruth E-5
Sandy J-5
Schurz E-2
Scotty's Jct. G-4
Searchlight K-6
Shantytown C-5
Silver City D-2
Silver Peak F-3
Silver Springs D-2
Sloan J-5
Sparks D-2
Sulphur B-2
Sutcliffe D-1
Thousand Springs . . B-6
Tonopah F-3
Tuscarora B-4
Unionville C-3
Ursine F-6
Valmy C-4
Virginia City D-2
Wadsworth D-2
Warm Springs F-4
Weed Heights E-2
Wellington E-2
Wells B-6
Winnemucca B-3
Yerington E-2

Barnstead H-6
Bartlett E-6
Bath E-4
Bayside J-7
Bedford J-5
Belmont G-5
Bennington J-4
Berlin D-6
Bethlehem D-5
Boscawen H-5
Bow Center H-5
Bradford H-4
Brentwood J-6
Bretton Woods E-5
Bridgewater G-5
Bristol G-5
Brookfield G-6
Brookline K-5
Canaan G-4
Canaan Center F-4
Candia J-6
Carroll D-5
Cascade D-6
Center Conway E-6
Center Ossipee F-6
Charlestown H-3
Cheever F-4
Chester J-6
Chesterfield J-3
Chichester H-5
Chocorua F-6
Cilleyville G-4
Claremont G-4
Coburn H-3
Cold River H-3
Colebrook B-5
Columbia B-5
Concord H-5
Contoocook H-5
Conway E-6
Coos Junction D-5
Cornish City G-3
Cornish Flat G-3
Crystal C-6
Danbury G-4
Davisville H-5
Derry J-6
Derry Village J-6
Dixville B-6
Dorchester F-4
Dover H-7
Drewsville H-3
Dublin J-4
Dummer H-7
Durham J-7
East Alton G-6
East Barrington . . . H-6
East Grafton G-4
East Hebron F-5
East Kingston J-6
East Lempster H-3
East Madison E-6
Easton E-5
Eaton Center F-6
Effingham Falls F-6
Elkins G-4
Epping J-6
Epsom H-5
Epsom Four Corners H-6
Errol B-6
Exeter J-7
Fabyan D-6
Farmington G-7
Fish Market J-4
Francestown J-4
Franconia D-5
Franklin G-5
Freedom F-6
Fremont J-6
Gerrish H-5
Gilford G-6
Gilmans Corner F-4
Gilmanton G-6
Gilsum J-4
Glen E-6
Glen House D-6
Glendale G-6
Goffs Falls J-5
Goffstown J-5
Gorham D-6
Goshen H-4
Gossville H-6
Grafton G-4
Grantham G-4
Greenfield J-4
Greenville K-4
Groton C-5
Groveton C-5
Guild G-4
Guildhall C-5
Hampton J-7
Hampton Beach . . . J-7
Hancock J-4
Hanover F-4
Hanover Center F-4
Harts Location E-6
Haverhill E-4
Hebron F-4
Henniker H-4
Hillsborough H-4
Hinsdale J-3
Hooksett H-5
Hopkinton H-5
Hoyts Corner H-4
Hudson K-6
Jackson D-6
Jaffrey J-4
James City H-6
Jefferson D-5
Jefferson Highlands . D-5

NEW HAMPSHIRE
Page 55
Population: 920,610
Capital: Concord
Land Area: 8,993 sq. mi.

Albany E-6
Allenstown H-6
Alstead H-3
Alton G-6
Alton Bay G-6
Amherst J-5
Andover G-5
Antrim J-4
Ashland F-5
Ashuelot K-3
Atkinson J-6
Auburn J-6

Laconia G-5
Lancaster D-5
Laskey Corner G-7
Leavitts Hill H-6
Lebanon G-4
Lincoln E-5
Lisbon D-5
Little Boars Head . . . J-7
Littleton D-5
Loudon H-5
Lower Shaker Village G-4
Lower Village H-4
Lyme F-4
Lyme Center F-4
Madbury H-7
Madison F-6
Manchester J-5
Marlborough J-4
Marlow H-4
Martin K-5
Mason K-5
Meadows D-5
Meredith G-5
Meriden G-3
Merrimack K-5
Milan C-6
Milford J-5
Milton G-7
Mirror Lake F-6
Monroe D-4
Mont Vernon J-5
Moultonborough . . . F-6
Moultonville F-6
Mount Sunapee . . . H-4
Munsonville J-4
Nashua K-5
New Durham G-6
New Hampton G-5
New Ipswich K-4
New London G-4
New Rye J-7
Newbury H-4
Newfields J-7
Newington H-7
Newmarket J-7
Newport H-4
Newton J-7
North Chatham D-6
North Conway E-6
North Grantham . . . G-4
North Groton F-5
North Haverhill E-4
North Rochester . . . H-6
North Sandwich . . . F-6
North Stratford C-5
North Sutton H-4
North Wakefield . . . G-6
North Woodstock . . . E-5
Northfield G-5
Northumberland . . . C-5
Northwood H-6
Orford F-4
Orfordville F-4
Ossipee F-6
Otterville G-4
Pages Corner J-5
Parker J-5
Pearls Corner H-5
Pelham K-6
Pembroke H-5
Penacook H-5
Peterborough J-4
Pinardville J-5
Pittsburg B-6
Pittsfield H-6
Plainfield G-3
Plaistow J-6
Plymouth F-5
Portsmouth H-7
Potter Place G-4
Province Lake F-7
Randolph D-6
Raymond J-6
Redstone E-6
Richmond K-3
Rindge K-4
Riverton D-5
Rochester H-6
Rollinsford H-7
Rumney F-5
Rye J-7
Rye Beach J-7
Salem J-6
Salisbury H-5
Sanbornton G-5
Sanbornville G-7
Sandwich F-6
Seabrook Beach . . . J-7
Sharon J-4
Shelburne D-6
Somersworth H-7
South Acworth H-4
South Cornish G-3
South Danbury G-5
South Stoddard J-4
South Weare J-4
Spofford J-3
Springfield G-4
Squantum J-4
Stark C-6
Stewartstown B-6
Stoddard H-4
Stratford C-5
Stratham J-7
Sunapee H-4
Surry J-3
Sutton H-4
Swiftwater E-4
Tamworth F-6
Temple J-4
Thornton F-5
Tilton G-5
Trapshire H-4
Troy J-4

Tuftonboro F-6
Twin Mountain D-5
Union G-6
Wakefield G-7
Wallis Sands J-7
Walpole J-3
Warner H-5
Warren F-4
Washington H-4
Weare J-5
Wendell H-4
Wentworth F-4
Wentworths Location B-6
West Campton F-5
West Lebanon G-3
West Milan C-6
West Ossipee F-6
West Rindge K-4
West Rumney F-5
West Stewartstown . . B-5
West Swanzey J-3
Westmoreland J-3
Westville J-6
Willey House E-5
Wilton J-5
Winchester J-3
Windsor H-4
Winnisquam G-5
Wolfeboro G-6
Wonalancet F-6
Woodman F-7
Woodsville E-4

NEW JERSEY
Pages 56-57
Population: 7,364,823
Capital: Trenton
Land Area: 7,468 sq. mi.

Absecon M-6
Adelphia H-7
Allamuchy C-4
Allendale . . Pg. 126, D-4
Allentown H-6
Alloway M-2
Alpha E-3
Alpine B-6
  Vicinity . . . Pg. 126, F-7
Andover C-5
Asbury Park G-8
Atlantic City N-7
Atlantic Highlands . . F-8
Atsion K-5
Audubon J-4
Audubon Park Pg. 134, F-7
Avalon P-5
Avenel . . . . Pg. 127, P-1
Baptistown F-4
Barnegat K-8
Barnegat Light K-8
Barrington . . Pg. 134, G-7
Bay Head H-8
Bay Point N-3
Bayonne F-8
  Vicinity . . . Pg. 127, M-4
Beach Haven M-7
Beachwood J-7
Bedminster E-5
Beesley Pt. N-5
Belleplain N-4
Belleville D-7
  Vicinity . . . Pg. 127, J-3
Bellmawr K-3
  Vicinity . . . Pg. 134, G-6
Belmar H-8
Belvidere D-3
Bergenfield C-8
  Vicinity . . . Pg. 126, F-6
Berlin K-4
Bernardsville E-5
Beverly H-4
  Vicinity . . . Pg. 134, C-9
Blairstown C-4
Blawenburg F-5
Bloomfield D-7
  Vicinity . . . Pg. 127, J-3
Bloomingdale C-7
  Vicinity . . . Pg. 126, D-1
Bloomsbury E-3
Bogata . . . . Pg. 126, G-6
Boonton D-6
Bordentown H-5
Bound Brook F-6
Bradley Beach H-8
Branchville B-5
Bridgeboro . . Pg. 134, D-9
Bridgeport K-2
Bridgeton M-2
Brielle H-8
Brigantine N-6
Broadway D-3
Brooklawn . . Pg. 134, G-6
Browns Mills J-6
Budd Lake C-5
Buena M-4
Burlington H-5
Butler C-6
Buttzville D-4
Caldwell . . . Pg. 127, H-1
Califon E-5
Camden J-4
  Vicinity . . . Pg. 134, E-6
Cape May Q-4
Cape May Court House
  . . . . Q-4
Carls Corner M-3
Carlstadt . . . Pg. 127, H-5
Carneys Pt. L-1
Carteret E-6
  . . . . Pg. 127, P-2
Cassville H-7

Cedar Bridge K-7
Cedar Grove D-7
  Vicinity . . . Pg. 134, F-8
Cedarville N-3
Centerton M-3
Chatham D-6
Chatsworth K-6
Cherry Hill J-4
  Vicinity . . . Pg. 134, F-7
Chesilhurst K-4
Chester D-5
Cinnaminson H-4
  . . . . Pg. 126, E-6
Clark . . . . . . Pg. 127, N-1
Clarksburg H-6
Clarksville L-1
Clayton L-3
Clementon K-4
Clermont P-5
Cliffside Park Pg. 127, J-6
Clifton D-8
  Vicinity . . . Pg. 126, H-3
Clinton E-4
  Vicinity . . . Pg. 127, F-3
Closter . . . . Pg. 126, E-7
Coffins Corner
  . . . . Pg. 134, G-9
Colesville A-5
Collingswood J-4
  Vicinity . . . Pg. 134, F-7
Colonia . . . . Pg. 127, P-1
Colts Neck G-8
Columbus H-5
Colwick . . . . Pg. 134, E-8
Corbin City N-5
Coxs Corner Pg. 134, F-10
Cranbury G-6
Cranford . . . Pg. 127, M-1
Cresskill B-6
  Vicinity . . . Pg. 126, F-7
Crestwood Village . . J-7
Croton F-5
Cumberland L-2
Deacons J-5
Deerfield M-3
Delaware C-3
Demarest . . Pg. 126, F-7
Denville C-6
Dividing Creek N-3
Dover C-6
Dumont . . . Pg. 126, F-7
Dunellen F-6
East Newark Pg. 127, K-4
East Orange D-7
  Vicinity . . . Pg. 127, J-3
East Rutherford
  . . . . Pg. 127, H-4
East Vineland M-4
Eatontown G-8
Edgewater Park . . . J-4
Edinburg G-5
Edison F-7
Egg Harbor M-6
Elizabeth E-7
  Vicinity . . . Pg. 127, M-3
Elmer L-3
Elmwood Park
  . . . . Pg. 126, G-4
Elwood M-5
Emerson . . . Pg. 126, E-6
Englewood C-8
  Vicinity . . . Pg. 127, G-6
Englewood Cliffs . . . C-8
  . . . . Pg. 126, B-1
Englishtown G-7
Erskine . . . . Pg. 126, B-2
Estell Manor N-5
Everittstown E-4
Ewingville G-5
Fair Haven G-8
  Vicinity . . . Pg. 127, J-1
Fair Lawn C-8
  Vicinity . . . Pg. 126, G-4
Fairfield . . . Pg. 126, G-1
Fairmount D-5
Fairton N-3
Farmingdale H-7
Flemington F-4
Florham Park D-7
  Vicinity . . . Pg. 134, G-8
Folsom M-5
Fords . . . . . Pg. 127, P-1
Forked River K-8
Fort Dix J-6
Fort Lee D-9
  Vicinity . . . Pg. 126, H-6
Four Mile F-6
Franklin B-6
Franklin Lakes
  . . . . Pg. 126, G-5
Franklinville L-3
Fredon C-5
Freehold G-7
Freewood Acres . . . H-7
Frenchtown F-4
Garfield C-8
  Vicinity . . . Pg. 126, G-5
Garwood . . . Pg. 127, M-1
Gibbsboro K-4
Gilford Park J-8
Glassboro L-3
Glen Gardner E-4
Glen Ridge . . Pg. 127, H-3
Glen Rock . . Pg. 126, G-4
Glendale . . . Pg. 134, G-8
Glenwood A-6
Gloucester City K-3
  Vicinity . . . Pg. 134, G-6
Gouldtown M-3
Great Meadows . . . D-4
Green Bank K-6
Guttenberg . . Pg. 127, J-5
Hackensack C-8
  Vicinity . . . Pg. 126, G-5
Hackettstown D-4
Haddon Heights
  . . . . Pg. 134, G-7

Haddonfield K-4
Hainesburg C-4
Haledon . . . Pg. 126, F-3
Hamburg B-6
Hamilton Sq. G-6
Hammonton L-5
Hampton E-4
Hanover D-6
Harmony D-3
Harrington Park
  . . . . Pg. 126, E-6
Harrison . . . Pg. 127, K-4
Harrisonville L-1
Harvey Cedars L-8
Hasbrouck Hts.
  . . . . Pg. 126, G-5
Haworth . . . Pg. 126, E-6
Hawthorne C-8
  Vicinity . . . Pg. 126, F-3
Helmetta G-7
Hewitt A-6
  Vicinity . . . Pg. 126, B-1
High Bridge E-4
Highland Park F-7
Highlands F-9
Hightstown G-6
Hillsdale B-6
Ho-Ho-Kus . Pg. 126, F-4
Hoboken D-7
  Vicinity . . . Pg. 127, K-5
Holmdel G-7
Hopatcong C-5
Hopewell F-5
Hurdtown C-6
Irvington D-7
  Vicinity . . . Pg. 127, L-2
Iselin . . . . . Pg. 127, P-1
Island Heights J-8
Jamesburg G-6
Jersey City D-8
  Vicinity . . . Pg. 127, L-5
Johnsonburg C-4
Keansburg F-8
Kearny . . . . Pg. 127, K-4
Kenilworth E-7
Kenvil . . . . . Pg. 127, M-1
Keyport F-8
Kinnelon C-6
Lafayette B-5
Lakehurst J-7
Lakeside B-7
Lakewood J-7
Lambertville G-4
Larisons Cor. F-4
Laurence Harbor . . . F-7
Lavallette J-8
Lawnside . . Pg. 134, G-8
Lawrence G-5
Lebanon E-5
Lenola . . . . Pg. 134, E-4
  Vicinity . . . Pg. 134, E-9
Liberty Cor. E-5
Lincoln Park C-7
  Vicinity . . . Pg. 126, F-1
Linden E-7
  Vicinity . . . Pg. 127, N-2
Lindenwold K-4
Linwood N-6
Little Egg Harbor . . . M-7
Little Falls . . Pg. 126, G-2
Little Ferry . . Pg. 126, H-5
Livingston . . Pg. 127, J-1
Lodi . . . . . . Pg. 126, G-4
Long Branch G-9
Long Valley D-4
Longport N-6
Lumberton J-5
Lyndhurst . . Pg. 127, J-4
Madison D-6
  Vicinity . . . Pg. 134, G-8
Magnolia . . Pg. 134, G-8
Mahwah A-6
  Vicinity . . . Pg. 126, C-4
Manahawkin L-8
Manalapan G-6
Manasquan H-8
Mantoloking J-8
Manville F-6
Maple Shade J-3
Maplewood . Pg. 127, K-2
Marcella C-6
Margate City N-6
Marlboro G-7
Marlton . . . . Pg. 134, G-9
Marshallville N-5
Matawan F-7
Maurice River N-4
Mays Landing M-5
Maywood . . Pg. 126, G-5
McAfee B-6
Medford K-5
Medford Lakes K-5
Mendham D-6
Merchantville Pg. 134, E-7
Metuchen F-7
Mickleton K-3
Midland Park Pg. 126, F-4
Milburn . . . . Pg. 127, K-1
Milford E-3
Millside Heights
  . . . . Pg. 134, D-9
Millstone F-6
Milltown G-6
Millville N-3
Monmouth Jct. G-6
Monroe G-6
Montague A-4
Montclair . . Pg. 127, H-3
Montvale . . . Pg. 126, D-5

Montville C-7
Moorestown J-4
  Vicinity . . . Pg. 134, E-8
Morris . . . . . Pg. 134, E-7
Morris Plains D-6
Morristown D-6
Morrisville E-3
Mt. Arlington C-6
Mt. Ephraim Pg. 134, G-6
Mt. Holly J-5
Mt. Laurel . . Pg. 134, F-10
Mullica Hill L-3
National Park K-3
  Vicinity . . . Pg. 134, G-5
Neptune F-8
Neshanic F-5
Netcong C-5
New Brunswick F-6
New Egypt J-6
New Gretna L-7
New Milford . Pg. 126, F-6
New Providence . . . E-6
New Rochelle Pg. 126, G-5
Newark D-8
  Vicinity . . . Pg. 127, K-3
Newfield M-4
Newfoundland B-6
Newton B-5
North Arlington
  . . . . Pg. 127, J-4
North Bergen Pg. 127, J-6
North Caldwell
  . . . . Pg. 126, G-2
North Cape May . . . Q-4
North Dennis P-4
North Haledon C-7
  Vicinity . . . Pg. 126, F-3
North Wildwood . . . Q-5
Northfield N-6
Northvale . . Pg. 126, D-7
Norwood C-9
  Vicinity . . . Pg. 127, E-7
Nutley D-8
  Vicinity . . . Pg. 127, H-3
Oakland . . . Pg. 126, D-2
Oaklyn . . . . Pg. 134, F-7
Ocean City N-6
Ocean Gate J-8
Oceanport G-8
Ogdensburg B-5
Old Bridge F-7
Old Tappan C-8
  Vicinity . . . Pg. 126, D-6
Oldwick E-5
Oradell . . . . Pg. 126, F-6
Orange D-7
  Vicinity . . . Pg. 127, K-2
Oxford D-4
Palisades Park
  . . . . Pg. 126, H-6
Palmyra . . . Pg. 134, D-7
Paramus C-8
  Vicinity . . . Pg. 126, F-5
Park Ridge . . Pg. 126, D-5
Parry . . . . . Pg. 134, D-8
Parsippany-Troy Hill . D-6
Passaic C-8
  Vicinity . . . Pg. 126, H-4
Patterson . . . Pg. 126, F-3
Paulsboro K-2
Peapack E-5
Pemberton J-5
Pennington G-5
Penns Grove L-2
Pennsauken E-3
  Vicinity . . . Pg. 134, E-7
Pennsville L-1
Penny Pot M-5
Pequannock Pg. 126, F-1
Perth Amboy F-7
  Vicinity . . . Pg. 127, Q-2
Phillipsburg E-3
Pine Beach . . Pg. 126, H-1
Pine Grove . . Pg. 134, G-10
Pine Hill K-4
Pitman L-3
Pittstown E-4
Plainfield E-6
Plainsboro G-6
Pleasantville N-6
Pole Tavern L-3
Pomona M-6
Pompton Lakes . . . C-7
  Vicinity . . . Pg. 126, D-1
Pompton Plains . . . B-6
  Vicinity . . . Pg. 126, E-1
Port Elizabeth N-4
Port Norris P-4
Port Reading Pg. 127, P-2
Port Republic M-6
Princeton G-5
Princeton Jct. G-6
Prospect Park C-8
Pt. Pleasant H-8
Pt. Pleasant Beach . H-8
Quinton M-2
Rahway E-7
  Vicinity . . . Pg. 127, N-2
Ramsey . . . Pg. 126, C-4
Raritan E-5
Readington E-5
Reaville F-5
Red Bank G-8
  Vicinity . . . Pg. 134, G-5
Red Lion K-5
Ridgefield . . Pg. 127, H-6
Ridgefield Park
  . . . . Pg. 126, G-6
Ridgewood C-8
  Vicinity . . . Pg. 126, E-4
Ringwood B-7
  Vicinity . . . Pg. 126, B-2
Rio Grande Q-4

NEW JERSEY

River Edge . . . Pg. 126, F-5
River Vale B-6
  Vicinity . . . Pg. 126, E-6
Riverdale C-7
Riverside J-4
Riverton J-4
  Vicinity . . . Pg. 134, D-8
Robertsville E-7
Rochelle Park Pg. 126, F-5
Rockaway C-6
Rockleigh . . Pg. 126, E-7
Rocky Hill F-5
Roosevelt H-6
Roseland . . . Pg. 127, H-1
Roselle C-7
  Vicinity . . . Pg. 127, M-2
Roselle Park . . . C-7
  Vicinity . . . Pg. 127, M-2
Ross Corners . . . B-5
Rumson G-8
Runnemede K-3
  Vicinity . . . Pg. 134, G-7
Rutherford . . Pg. 127, H-4
Saddle Brook Pg. 126, G-5
Saddle River . . . C-6
  Vicinity . . . Pg. 126, D-4
Salem M-1
Sayreville F-7
Sea Isle City . . . P-5
Seabrook M-3
Seaside Heights . . J-8
Seaside Park . . . J-8
Seaville P-5
Secaucus . . . Pg. 127, J-5
Sewaren . . . Pg. 127, P-2
Sharptown L-2
Shiloh M-2
Ship Bottom L-8
Shrewsbury G-8
Silverton J-8
Smithburg H-7
Smithville M-6
Somerdale F-4
Somers Pt. N-6
Somerville F-5
South Amboy . . . F-7
South Brunswick . G-6
South Dennis . . . P-5
South Hackensack . . Pg. 126, G-5
South Orange . . . Pg. 127, K-2
South Plainfield . . E-6
South River F-7
South Toms River . J-7
Sparta C-5
Speedwell K-6
Spotswood F-6
Spring Lakes Heights H-8
Spring Mills E-3
Springdale F-4
  Vicinity . . . Pg. 134, G-8
Springfield . . Pg. 127, L-1
Stanhope C-5
Stockholm B-6
Stockton F-4
Stone Harbor . . . Q-5
Stratford K-4
Summit D-7
Surf City L-8
Sussex A-5
Swedesboro . . . K-2
Tabernacle K-5
Tavistock . . Pg. 134, G-8
Teaneck . . . Pg. 126, G-6
Tenafly C-9
  Vicinity . . . Pg. 126, F-7
Teterboro . . Pg. 126, H-5
Tinton Falls J-7
Toms River J-7
Totowa C-7
  Vicinity . . . Pg. 126, G-3
Trenton G-5
Tuckerton L-7
Tuttles Cor. F-8
Union Beach . . . F-8
  Vicinity . . . Pg. 127, L-2
Union City C-8
  Vicinity . . . Pg. 127, K-5
Upper Saddle River . . Pg. 126, C-4
Ventnor City . . . N-6
Vernon B-5
Verona . . . . Pg. 127, H-2
Villas Q-4
Vineland M-4
Waldwick C-6
  Vicinity . . . Pg. 126, D-4
Wallington . . Pg. 126, H-4
Wanaque B-7
  Vicinity . . . Pg. 126, D-3
Waretown K-8
Warren E-6
Warren Grove . . . K-7
Washington D-4
Washington Crossing G-4
Watchung C-8
Wayne C-6
  Vicinity . . . Pg. 126, F-2
Weehawken Pg. 127, K-6
Welchville L-2
Wells Mills K-7
Wenonah K-3
West Caldwell . . . Pg. 126, H-1
West Cape May . . Q-5
West Long Branch . G-8
West Milford . . . B-6
West New York . . D-8
  Vicinity . . . Pg. 127, J-6
West Orange . . . D-7
  Vicinity . . . Pg. 127, J-2
West Patterson . . C-7
  Vicinity . . Pg. 126, G-3
West Portal E-4

Westfield E-7
Westville K-3
  Vicinity . . . Pg. 134, G-6
Westwood C-8
  Vicinity . . . Pg. 126, E-6
Weymouth M-6
Wharton C-6
White Horse H-5
Whitehouse E-5
Whitesboro Q-4
Whitesville H-7
Wildwood Q-5
Wildwood Crest . . Q-5
Williamstown . . . L-4
Winslow L-4
Wood Ridge Pg. 126, H-5
Woodbine P-4
Woodbridge F-6
  Vicinity . . . Pg. 127, P-2
Woodbury K-3
Woodbury Heights . K-3
Woodcliff Lake . . . Pg. 126, D-5
Woodlynne . . Pg. 134, F-6
Woods Tavern . . . L-4
Woodstown L-2
Woodsville G-4
Wrightstown H-5
Yardville H-5

NEW MEXICO
Page 62
Population: 1,302,894
Capital: Santa Fe
Land Area: 121,335 sq. mi.

Abbott C-5
Abeytas E-3
Abiquiu C-3
Abo E-4
Alameda D-3
Alamo E-2
Alamogordo F-4
Albuquerque D-3
Alcalde C-3
Algodones D-3
Alma G-1
Alto F-4
Amalia B-4
Ambrosia Lake . . . D-2
Amistad C-7
Anapra J-3
Ancho F-4
Angus G-4
Animas J-1
Antelope Wells . . J-1
Apache Creek . . . F-1
Aqua Fria D-4
Arabela E-6
Aragon F-1
Arch E-7
Archuleta B-2
Armijo D-3
Arrey H-2
Arroyo Hondo . . . B-4
Arroyo Seco B-4
Artesia G-6
Atoka G-6
Aztec B-2
Bayard H-2
Beklabito B-1
Belen E-3
Bellview D-7
Bent G-4
Berino J-3
Bernal D-5
Bernalillo D-3
Bernardo E-3
Bingham F-4
Black Lake C-5
Black River Village . H-6
Black Rock D-2
Blanco B-2
Blanco Trading Post . C-2
Bloomfield B-2
Bluewater D-2
Bosque Farms . . . E-3
Brazos B-3
Broadview B-7
Buckhorn G-1
Bueyeros C-6
Caballo G-3
Canjilon B-3
Canon C-3
Canon Plaza B-4
Capitan F-4
Caprock F-7
Capulin B-6
Carlsbad H-6
Carlsbad Caverns . H-6
Carrizozo F-4
Causey F-7
Cebolla B-3
Cebolleta D-2
Cebolletita D-2
Cedar Crest D-4
Cedar Hill B-2
Cedarvale E-4
Central H-2
Cerro B-4
Chacon C-5
Chama B-3
Chamberino J-3
Chamizal F-3
Chaparral J-4
Chilili E-4
Chimayo C-4
Cimarron B-5
Clapham C-6
Claunch F-4
Clayton B-7

Cleveland C-4
Cliff G-1
Clines Corners . . . D-4
Cloudcroft G-4
Clovis E-7
Cochiti Lake C-3
Columbus J-2
Conchas D-6
Coolidge D-1
Corona E-4
Costilla B-4
Cotton City J-1
Counselors C-2
Coyote C-3
Coyote Canyon . . C-1
Crossroads F-7
Crownpoint D-1
Cruzville F-1
Crystal C-1
Cuba C-3
Cuchillo G-3
Cuervo D-6
Cundiyo C-4
Datil F-2
Deming H-2
Derry H-3
Des Moines B-6
Dexter G-6
Dilia D-5
Domingo D-3
Dona Ana H-3
Dora E-7
Dulce B-3
Dunken G-5
Duran E-5
Dwyer H-2
Eagle Nest B-5
Edgewood D-4
El Morro D-2
El Paso Gap J-5
El Porvenir C-4
El Rito C-4
El Vado B-3
Elephant Butte . . G-3
Elida E-6
Elk G-5
Elk Silver G-4
Elkins E-6
Embudo C-4
Encino E-5
Endee D-7
Engle G-3
Ensenada B-3
Escobosa E-3
Escondida F-3
Espanola C-4
Estancia E-4
Eunice H-7
Fairacres H-3
Farley B-6
Farmington B-1
Fence Lake E-1
Flora Vista B-1
Floyd E-7
Folsom B-6
Forrest E-5
Fort Stanton G-4
Fort Sumner E-5
Fort Wingate . . . D-1
Frijoles C-4
Gage H-2
Galisteo D-4
Gallina C-3
Gallinas E-4
Gallup D-1
Gamerco D-1
Garfield H-3
Gila H-1
Gladstone B-6
Glenrio D-7
Glenwood G-1
Golden D-4
Grady D-6
Gran Quivira E-4
Grants D-2
Greenfield G-6
Grenville B-6
Guadalupita C-5
Hachita J-2
Hagerman G-6
Hanover H-2
Hatch H-3
Hayden C-7
Hernandez C-4
High Rolls G-4
Hilburn City G-7
Hillsboro H-3
Hobbs G-7
Holman C-5
Hondo G-5
Hope G-5
House E-6
Humble City G-7
Hurley H-2
Jal H-7
Jarales E-3
Jemez Springs . . C-3
Jicarilla F-4
Kenna E-6
Kingston H-2
Kirtland B-1
Knowles G-7
La Cienega C-4
La Cueva C-5
La Jara C-3
La Joya E-3
La Luz G-4
La Madera C-4
La Mesa J-3
La Mesilla H-3
La Plata B-1
La Puente B-3
La Union J-3

Laborcita F-3
Laguna E-3
Lake Arthur G-6
Lake Valley C-2
Lamy D-4
Las Cruces H-3
Las Nutrias E-3
Las Palomas . . . G-3
Las Vegas C-5
Ledoux C-5
Lemitar F-3
Lincoln G-5
Lindrith C-2
Lingo F-7
Loco Hills G-6
Logan D-7
Lordsburg H-1
Los Alamos C-4
Los Cerrillos . . . D-4
Los Chavez E-3
Los Lunas E-3
Los Ojos B-3
Los Padillas D-3
Loving H-6
Lovington G-7
Luis Lopez F-3
Lumberton B-3
Luna F-1
Madrid D-4
Magdalena F-3
Malaga H-6
Maljamar G-7
Manuelito D-1
Manzano E-4
Maxwell B-5
Mayhill G-5
McAlister E-6
McCartys D-2
McDonald F-7
Melrose E-6
Mentmore D-1
Mesa E-6
Mescalero G-4
Mesita D-3
Mesquite H-3
Mexican Springs . C-1
Miami C-5
Miera D-4
Milan D-2
Mills C-6
Milnesand F-7
Mimbres H-2
Mineral Hill D-4
Mogollon G-1
Monero B-3
Montezuma C-5
Monticello G-2
Montoya D-6
Monument H-7
Mora C-4
Moriarty D-4
Mosquero C-6
Mountainair E-4
Mt. Dora B-6
Mule Creek G-1
Nadine H-7
Nageezi C-2
Nara Visa C-7
Naschitti C-1
Navajo C-1
Navajo C-1
Newcomb C-1
Newkirk D-6
Ocate C-5
Oil Center H-7
Ojo Caliente C-4
Ojo Feliz C-5
Old Horse Springs . F-2
Omega E-2
Organ H-3
Orogrande H-4
Oscuro F-4
Paguate D-2
Paraje D-2
Pastura E-5
Pecos D-4
Pena Blanca D-3
Penasco C-4
Pep F-7
Peralta E-3
Pescado D-1
Picacho G-5
Pie Town E-2
Pinon H-5
Pine Lodge F-6
Pinon H-5
Pinos Altos H-1
Placita C-4
Placitas D-4
Pleasant Hill E-7
Pleasanton G-1
Pojoaque C-4
Portales E-7
Prewitt D-1
Pueblo D-4
Pueblo Bonito . . . C-2
Puerto De Luna . . E-5
Punta E-4
Quay D-6
Quemado E-1
Questa B-4
Radium Springs . . H-3
Ragland E-6
Rainsville C-5
Ramah D-1
Ramon E-5
Ranchos De Taos . B-4
Ranchvale E-7
Raton B-6
Rayado B-5
Red Hill F-1
Red River B-4
Red Rock H-1
Regina C-3
Reserve F-1

Rincon H-3
Rinconada C-4
Rio Rancho D-3
Riverside G-6
Rociada C-4
Rodeo J-1
Rogers F-7
Romeroville D-5
Roswell E-6
Rowe D-4
Roy C-6
Ruidoso G-4
Ruidoso Downs . . G-4
Rutheron B-3
Sabinal E-3
Sacramento H-4
Saint Vrain E-7
Salem H-3
Salt Lake E-1
San Acacia E-3
San Antonio F-3
San Antonito . . . D-4
San Fidel D-2
San Ignacio C-4
San Jon D-7
San Juan H-2
San Lorenzo H-2
San Mateo D-2
San Miguel G-4
San Patricio G-4
San Rafael D-2
Santa Cruz C-4
Santa Fe C-4
Santa Rita H-2
Santa Rosa D-5
Sapello C-5
Sedan C-7
Sena D-5
Seneca B-6
Separ H-1
Seven Rivers . . . H-6
Shadybrook C-4
Sheep Springs . . C-1
Shiprock B-1
Silver City H-2
Socorro F-3
Solano C-6
Springer B-5
Standing Rock . . . C-1
Stanley D-4
Sunset D-5
Sunshine J-2
Sunspot H-4
Taiban E-6
Tajique E-3
Talpa B-4
Taos B-4
Tatum G-7
Terrero C-4
Tesuque C-4
Thoreau D-1
Three Rivers . . . G-4
Tierra Amarilla . . . B-3
Tierra Monte . . . C-5
Tijeras D-3
Tinnie G-5
Tohatchi C-1
Tolar E-6
Tome E-3
Torreon C-3
Torreon D-4
Tres Piedras B-4
Tres Ritos C-4
Truchas C-4
Trujillo D-5
Truth or Consequences . . . G-3
Tucumcari D-6
Tularosa G-4
Turley B-2
Turn F-4
Tyrone H-1
Ute Park B-5
Vado J-3
Valencia E-3
Vallecitos C-3
Valmora C-5
Variadero D-5
Vaughn E-5
Veguita E-3
Velarde C-4
Villanueva D-5
Virden H-1
Wagon Mound . . C-5
Watrous C-5
Weed G-5
Wheatland D-7
White Horse C-2
White Oaks F-4
White Rock C-4
White Sands Missile Range H-4
Whites City H-6
Whitewater D-1
Willard E-4
Williamsburg . . . G-3
Winston G-2
Yeso E-5
Youngsville C-3

NEW YORK
Pages 58-61
Population: 17,558,072
Capital: Albany
Land Area: 47,377 sq. mi.

Adams F-12
Addison N-8
Afton M-13
Airmont . . Pg. 126, B-4
Akron J-5

NEW YORK

Albany K-18
Albion H-6
Alden K-5
Alexander K-5
Alexandria Bay . . D-12
Alfred M-7
Allegany N-5
Almond M-7
Altamont K-18
Altmar G-12
Amagansett C-9
Amenia O-19
Ames K-16
Amherst . . Pg. 94, C-5
Amityville . Pg. 129, N-16
Amsterdam J-18
Andes M-16
Andover N-7
Angelica M-6
Angola L-3
Angola-on-the-Lake . L-3
  Vicinity . . . Pg. 94, K-1
Antwerp D-13
Apalachin N-12
Arcade L-5
Archville . . Pg. 126, B-8
Ardsley . . . Pg. 126, D-9
Argyle H-20
Arkport M-7
Arlington N-19
Armonk . . Pg. 128, C-11
Armor . . . Pg. 94, H-5
Asharoken . Pg. 128, G-17
Astoria . . . Pg. 127, J-8
Athens M-19
Athol Springs Pg. 94, H-4
Atlantic Beach . . . N-8
  Vicinity . . Pg. 129, Q-11
Attica K-5
Atwell G-15
Auburn K-10
Aurora K-10
Avoca M-8
Avon K-7
Babylon N-8
  Vicinity . . Pg. 129, M-18
Bainbridge M-13
Baldwin E-4
  Vicinity . . Pg. 129, P-13
Baldwinsville J-11
Ballston Spa J-18
Balmville A-3
Bardonia . . Pg. 126, B-6
Barker H-5
Barneveld H-14
Barnum Island . . . Pg. 129, Q-13
Batavia J-6
Bath M-8
Bay Park . . Pg. 129, P-12
Bay Ridge . . Pg. 127, M-6
Bay Shore N-8
  Vicinity . . Pg. 129, M-19
Bay View . . Pg. 94, H-4
Bayberry J-11
Bayside . . . Pg. 127, K-10
Bayville D-5
  Vicinity . . Pg. 129, H-14
Beach Ridge Pg. 94, A-4
Beacon A-3
Bedford B-4
  Vicinity . . Pg. 128, B-13
Bedford Hills Pg. 128, A-11
Bellevue . . Pg. 94, E-6
Bellmore . . Pg. 129, N-14
Belmont N-6
Bemus Pt. N-3
Benson Hurst Pg. 127, N-7
Bergen J-6
Berkholtz . . Pg. 94, A-3
Bethpage N-8
  Vicinity . . Pg. 129, L-15
Big Flats N-9
Big Tree . . . Pg. 94, H-5
Binghamton N-12
Black River E-13
Blasdell L-4
  Vicinity . . Pg. 94, G-4
Blauvelt . . Pg. 126, C-7
Bloomingburgh . . . A-2
Bloomingdale . . . C-18
Bloomington N-18
Blossom . . Pg. 94, F-7
Bolivar N-6
Boonville G-14
Bovsen Bay N-4
Bowmansville Pg. 94, D-7
Brasher Falls B-16
Brentwood D-6
  Vicinity . . Pg. 129, L-19
Brewerton J-11
Brewster B-4
Briarcliff Manor . . C-4
Bridgehampton . . C-9
Bridgewater K-14
Brighton . . Pg. 138, K-4
Brightwaters Pg. 129, M-19
Broadalbin J-18
Brockport L-5
Brocton M-2
Bronx . . . Pg. 126, D-8
Brooklyn . . Pg. 127, L-7
Brookville . Pg. 129, K-14
Brownsville E-12
Brushton B-17
Buchanan B-3
Buffalo K-4
  Vicinity . . Pg. 94
Burdett M-10
Burke B-17
Cairo M-18
Caledonia K-7
Calverton D-7
Cambridge J-20

Camden H-13
Camillus J-11
Canajoharie K-16
Canandaigua K-8
Canaseraga M-7
Canastota J-13
Candor M-11
Canisteo M-8
Canton C-14
Cape Vincent . . . D-11
Carnegie . . Pg. 94, H-4
Carthage E-13
Cassadaga M-2
Castile L-6
Castleton Corners . . Pg. 127, N-4
Castleton-on-Hudson L-18
Castorland F-13
Cato J-10
Catskill M-19
Cattaraugus M-4
Cayuga K-10
Cayuga Heights . . L-11
Cazenovia K-13
Cedarhurst Pg. 129, P-11
Celoron N-2
Center Moriches . . D-7
Center Port Pg. 129, H-17
Centereach D-6
Central Islip Pg. 129, K-20
Central Nyack . . . Pg. 126, C-7
Central Square . . . H-12
Central Valley . . . B-3
Champlain A-19
Chappaqua Pg. 126, A-9
Chateaugay A-17
Chatham K-19
Chaumont E-12
Cheektowaga Pg. 94, F-6
Chelsea . . Pg. 127, N-3
Cherry Creek M-3
Cherry Valley . . . K-16
Chester A-3
Chili Center . Pg. 138, K-2
Chippawa (Canada) . . . Pg. 94, B-1
Chittenango J-13
Churchville J-7
Clarence Center . . K-5
Clarkstown Pg. 126, B-6
Claverack M-19
Clayton D-12
Clayville J-14
Cleveland H-13
Clifton Heights Pg. 94, H-3
Clifton Knolls . . . K-18
Clifton Springs . . K-9
Clinton J-14
Clintondale O-18
Clyde J-10
Cobleskill K-17
Cohocton L-8
Cohoes K-19
Cold Brook H-15
Cold Springs J-11
Coldspring Harbor . . . Pg. 129, J-16
College Point Pg. 127, J-9
Colonie K-18
Commack K-18
Coney Island Pg. 127, P-7
Constableville . . . G-14
Constantia H-12
Cooperstown . . . K-15
Copenhagen F-13
Copiague . . Pg. 129, N-17
Coram D-6
Corfu K-5
Corinth H-18
Corning N-9
Cornwall-on-Hudson . A-3
Cortland L-11
County Knolls . . . J-18
Cove Neck . Pg. 129, J-15
Coxsackie M-19
Crescent Beach . . . Pg. 138, F-3
Crescent Park (Canada) . . . Pg. 94, E-2
Crittenden . Pg. 138, E-5
Croghan F-14
Croton-on-Hudson . B-3
Crystal Beach (Canada) . . . Pg. 94, F-1
Cuba N-5
Cutchogue C-8
Dannemora B-18
Dansville L-7
DeRuyter K-13
DeWitt J-11
Deer Park D-5
  Vicinity . . Pg. 129, L-18
Deferiet E-13
Delanson K-17
Delavan L-5
Delhi M-15
Delmar L-18
Depew K-5
  Vicinity . . Pg. 94, E-6
Deposit N-13
Derby . . . Pg. 94, K-2
Dexter E-12
Dobbs Ferry C-3
  Vicinity . . Pg. 126, D-8
Dolgeville J-16
Dongan Hills Pg. 127, N-4
Dover Plains O-19
Dresden L-9
Dryden L-11
Duells Corners Pg. 94, H-6
Dundee L-9

Dunkirk M-2
Earlville K-13
East Amherst . Pg. 94, B-6
East Aurora K-4
East Bloomfield . . K-8
East Eden . . Pg. 94, K-5
East Glenville . . . J-18
East Hamburg Pg. 94, H-6
East Hampton . . . C-9
East Hills . . Pg. 129, K-13
East Marion C-9
East Meadow . . . D-6
  Vicinity . . Pg. 129, M-14
East New York . . . Pg. 127, M-8
East Northport . . . D-5
  Vicinity . . Pg. 129, J-17
East Penfield Pg. 138, J-7
East Quoque D-8
East Randolph . . . N-3
East Rochester . . . J-8
  Vicinity . . Pg. 138, J-6
East Rockaway . . . Pg. 129, P-12
East Seneca Pg. 94, F-6
East View . . Pg. 126, C-9
Eastchester Pg. 126, E-9
Eatons Neck C-7
Eatons Neck . . . Pg. 128, H-17
Ebenezer . . Pg. 94, F-6
Echota . . . Pg. 94, A-2
Eden L-4
Eden Valley Pg. 94, K-4
Edgemere . Pg. 129, Q-11
Edgewater . Pg. 94, B-3
Edwards D-14
Eggertsville Pg. 94, C-5
Elba J-6
Elbridge J-11
Ellenville O-17
Ellicott . . . Pg. 94, H-6
Ellicott Heights Pg. 94, H-7
Ellicottville M-4
Ellisburg F-12
Elma K-4
  Vicinity . . Pg. 94, F-7
Elma Center Pg. 94, F-7
Elmira N-10
Elmira Hts. N-10
Elmont . . . Pg. 129, N-12
Elmsford . . Pg. 126, C-9
Elsers Corners Pg. 94, A-7
Elwood . . . Pg. 129, J-17
Endicott N-12
Endwell N-12
Erie Beach (Canada) . . . Pg. 94, E-3
Esperance K-17
Evans . . . Pg. 94, K-2
Evans Mills E-12
Fabius K-12
Fair Haven H-10
Fairport J-8
  Vicinity . . Pg. 138, K-6
Falconer N-3
Farmingdale Pg. 129, M-16
Farnham L-3
Fayetteville J-12
Fernwood H-19
Ferry Village . Pg. 94, C-3
Fillmore M-6
Firthcliffe A-3
Fishkill A-3
Flatbush . . Pg. 127, M-7
Fleischmanns . . . N-17
Floral Park Pg. 129, M-11
Florida A-3
Flower Hill Pg. 129, K-12
Flushing . . Pg. 127, K-9
Fonda J-17
Forest Hills . Pg. 127, L-9
Forest Lawn Pg. 138, F-5
Forestville M-3
Fort Ann G-19
Fort Edward H-19
Fort Erie (Canada) . . . Pg. 94, E-3
Fort Erie North (Canada) . . . Pg. 94, D-3
Fort Johnson J-17
Fort Plain K-16
Fort Salonga . . . Pg. 128, H-18
Frankfort J-15
Franklin M-15
Franklinville M-5
Freeport E-4
  Vicinity . . Pg. 129, P-14
Frewsburg N-3
Friendship N-6
Fulton H-11
Fultonville K-17
Gainesville L-6
Galway J-18
Gang Mills N-9
Garden City Pg. 129, M-12
Gardenville . Pg. 94, F-6
Gate . . . . . Pg. 138, J-2
Geneseo K-7
Geneva K-9
Getzville . . Pg. 94, B-6
Gilbertsville L-14
Glasco N-18
Glen Cove D-4
  Vicinity . . Pg. 129, J-12
Glen Head . Pg. 129, K-13
Glen Park E-12
Glenham A-3
Glens Falls H-19
Gloversville J-17
Goldens Bridge . . B-4
Gouverneur D-14
Gowanda M-3

NEW YORK

Grand View Heights . . . Pg. 138, F-3
Grandview-on-Hudson . . . Pg. 126, C-8
Grandyle Village . . . Pg. 94, C-2
Granville G-20
Great Kills . . . Pg. 127, P-4
Great Neck D-4
  Vicinity . . . Pg. 129, K-11
Greece J-7
  Vicinity . . . Pg. 138, G-2
Green Island K-19
Green Lawn . . Pg. 129, J-17
Green Point . . Pg. 127, K-7
Greenburgh . . Pg. 126, D-9
Greene M-13
Greenport D-19
Greenwich J-20
Greenwood Lake B-2
Griffins Mills . . Pg. 94, J-7
Groton L-11
Hadley H-19
Hagaman J-18
Halesite . . . Pg. 129, H-16
Hamburg L-4
  Vicinity . . . . Pg. 94, J-5
Hamilton K-14
Hammond C-13
Hammondsport M-8
Hampton Bays D-8
Hancock O-15
Hannibal H-10
Harriman B-2
Harris Hill . . . Pg. 94, C-7
Harrison C-4
  Vicinity . . . Pg. 128, F-11
Harrisville E-14
Hastings-On-Hudson . . . Pg. 126, E-8
Hauppage . . Pg. 129, K-19
Haverstraw B-3
Haviland O-19
Hawthorne . . Pg. 126, B-10
Hempstead E-4
  Vicinity . . . Pg. 129, N-13
Herkimer J-15
Hermon C-14
Herrings E-13
Heuvelton C-14
Hewlett Bay Park . . . . Pg. 129, P-12
Hewlett Harbor . . . Pg. 129, P-12
Hicksville D-5
  Vicinity . . . Pg. 129, L-15
Highland O-18
Highland Falls B-3
Highland Mills B-3
Highland-on-the-Lake . . Pg. 94, J-2
Hillburn C-2
Hillcrest . . . Pg. 126, A-6
Hillside Lake P-19
Hilton H-7
  Vicinity . . . Pg. 138, F-1
Hobart M-18
Hoffman . . . . Pg. 94, A-5
Holbrook D-6
Holcomb K-8
Holland L-5
Holland Patent H-14
Holley J-6
Homer L-11
Honeoye Falls K-7
Hoosick Falls J-20
Hornell M-7
Horseheads N-10
Houghton M-6
Hudson M-19
Hudson Falls H-19
Hugenot Park Pg. 127, Q-3
Huguenot . . . Pg. 127, Q-2
Hunter M-17
Huntington D-5
  Vicinity . . . Pg. 129, J-16
Huntington Sta. D-5
Hurley O-18
Hyde Park O-18
Ilion J-15
Interlaken L-10
Inwood . . . . Pg. 129, P-11
Irondequoit . . Pg. 138, H-4
Irvington . . . Pg. 126, D-8
Island Park Pg. 129, Q-12
Islip D-6
Ithaca M-11
Jamaica . . . Pg. 129, N-11
Jamesport C-8
Jamestown N-3
Jefferson Hts M-18
Jefferson Valley B-4
Jeffersonville O-15
Jericho D-5
  Vicinity . . . Pg. 129, L-14
Jerusalem Corners . . . . Pg. 94, K-1
Jewittville . . . Pg. 94, J-6
Johnson City N-12
Johnstown J-17
Jones Island . . . Pg. 129, Q-14
Jordan J-11
Keeseville C-19
Kenmore K-3
  Vicinity . . Pg. 94, C-2
Kensington . . Pg. 129, L-12
Kerhonkson O-17
Keuka Park L-9
Kinderhook M-19
Kings Park . . Pg. 129, J-19
Kings Point D-4
Kingston N-18
Kiryas Joel B-2

La Salle . . . . . Pg. 94, A-3
Lackawanna K-4
  Vicinity . . . Pg. 94, G-4
Lacona G-12
Ladentown . . Pg. 126, A-5
Lake Carmel A-4
Lake Erie Beach L-3
Lake George G-19
Lake Luzerne H-18
Lake Placid D-18
Lake Ronkonkoma D-6
Lakeview . . . . Pg. 94, J-3
Lakewood N-2
Lancaster K-4
  Vicinity . . . Pg. 94, E-7
Lansing L-11
Larchmont . . Pg. 126, F-10
Latham K-19
Lattington . . Pg. 129, H-13
Laurel Hollow . . . Pg. 129, J-15
Laurens . . . . Pg. 129, Q-11
Lawrence . . . Pg. 129, Q-11
LeRoy K-6
Leicester K-6
Levittown E-5
  Vicinity . . . Pg. 129, N-15
Lewiston J-3
Liberty O-16
Lido Beach Pg. 129, Q-13
Lima K-7
Lime Lake M-5
Limestone N-4
Lincoln Park N-18
Lindenhurst C-6
  Vicinity . . . Pg. 129, N-17
Lisle M-12
Little Falls J-16
Little Valley M-4
Liverpool J-11
Livingston Manor O-16
Livonia K-7
Lloyd Harbor D-5
  Vicinity . . . Pg. 129, H-15
Lloyd Neck Pg. 128, H-16
Lockport J-4
Locksley Park Pg. 94, H-3
Locust Grove . . . . . . Pg. 129, K-15
Locust Valley Pg. 129, J-13
Lodi L-10
Long Beach E-4
  Vicinity . . . Pg. 129, Q-12
Long Island City . . . . Pg. 127, K-7
Lorenz Pk M-19
Lowville F-14
Lynbrook . . . Pg. 129, P-12
Lyndonville H-5
Lyons J-9
Lyons Falls G-14
Macedon J-8
Machias M-5
Madison K-14
Mahopac B-4
Malone B-17
Malverne . . Pg. 129, N-12
Mamaroneck C-4
  Vicinity . . Pg. 126, E-10
Manchester J-8
Manhasset Pg. 129, K-12
Manhattan . . Pg. 127, J-7
  Vicinity . . . Pg. 94, B-4
Manlius J-12
Mannsville F-12
Manorhaven Pg. 129, K-11
Marathon M-12
Marcellus J-11
Margaretville N-16
Marlboro P-18
Martinsville . . Pg. 94, B-5
Massapequa E-5
  Vicinity . . . Pg. 129, N-15
Massapequa Park . . . Pg. 129, N-16
Massena B-15
Mastic D-7
Mastic Beach D-7
Matinecock Pg. 129, J-14
Mattituck C-8
Mattydale J-11
Maybrook A-2
Mayfield M-2
Mayville M-2
McGraw L-12
Meadow Island . . . Pg. 129, Q-14
Mechanicville K-19
Medford D-6
Medina J-5
Melville . . . Pg. 129, L-16
Menands K-19
Meridian J-11
Merrick . . . . Pg. 129, P-14
Merriewold Lake B-2
Mexico H-11
Middle Hope P-18
Middleburgh L-17
Middleport J-5
Middletown A-2
Middleville J-15
Milford M-16
Mill Neck . . Pg. 129, H-14
Millbrook O-19
Millersport . . Pg. 94, A-7
Millerton N-19
Millport M-10
Milton O-18
Mineola . . . . Pg. 129, M-13
Minetto H-11
Mineville C-19
Minoa J-12
Mohawk J-15
Monroe B-2
Monsey C-3
  Vicinity . . . Pg. 126, B-5

Montauk C-10
Montgomery A-2
Monticello P-16
Montour Falls M-10
Mooers A-19
Moravia L-11
Morris L-15
Morristown C-13
Morrisville K-13
Mount Ivy . . Pg. 126, A-6
Mount Kisco B-4
Mount Morris L-7
Mount Pleasant . . . Pg. 126, C-9
Mount Vernon D-4
  Vicinity . . Pg. 126, F-9
Mt. Vernon . . Pg. 94, H-3
Munnsville J-13
Muttontown Pg. 129, K-14
Nanuet C-3
Napanoch O-17
Naples L-8
Nashville . . . Pg. 94, A-4
Nassau L-19
Nelliston J-16
Nelson K-13
New Berlin L-14
New Brighton . . . Pg. 127, M-5
New Cassel Pg. 129, M-14
New Dorp . . Pg. 127, P-4
New Dorp Beach . . . Pg. 127, P-4
New Hartford J-14
New Hempstead . . . Pg. 126, A-5
New Hyde Park . . . Pg. 129, M-12
New Paltz O-18
New Rochelle D-4
  Vicinity . . Pg. 126, F-10
New Suffolk C-8
New York City E-3
  Vicinity . . . Pg. 126-129
New York Mills J-14
Newark J-9
Newark Valley M-12
Newburgh A-3,P-18
Newfane H-4
Newport H-15
Niagara Falls J-3
Niagara Falls (Canada) . . . Pg. 94, A-1
Nichols N-11
Norfolk B-15
North Bailey . . Pg. 94, C-4
North Boston . . Pg. 94, K-6
North Chili . . Pg. 138, J-1
North Collins L-3
North Evans . . Pg. 94, J-3
North Greece Pg. 138, G-2
North Haven C-9
North Hills . . Pg. 129, L-12
North Hornell M-7
North New Hyde Park . . . Pg. 129, M-12
North Sea C-9
North Syracuse J-12
North Tarrytown . . . Pg. 126, B-8
North Tonawanda . . . J-4
  Vicinity . . . Pg. 94, B-4
Northville H-17
Norwich (Chenango Cty) . . . L-13
Norwich (Nassau Cty) . . . Pg. 129, J-14
Norwood B-15
Noyack C-9
Nunda L-6
Nyack C-3
  Vicinity . . . Pg. 126, B-6
Oak Beach Pg. 129, P-19
Oakfield J-5
Ocean Beach E-6
Oceanside . . Pg. 129, P-13
Odessa M-10
Ogden Center . . . Pg. 138, H-1
Ogdensburg B-13
Olcott H-4
Old Bethpage . . . Pg. 129, L-16
Old Brookville . . . Pg. 129, K-13
Old Forge G-14
Old Westbury . . . Pg. 129, K-13
Olean N-4
Oneida J-13
Oneida Castle J-13
Oneonta M-15
Orange Lake A-3
Orangeburg . Pg. 126, D-7
Orangetown . Pg. 126, C-6
Orchard Park K-4
  Vicinity . . . Pg. 94, H-6
Orient C-9
Oriskany J-14
Oriskany Falls J-13
Ossining B-3
Oswego H-10
Otego M-14
Otisville A-1
Ovid L-10
Owego M-11
Oxford M-13
Oyster Bay Pg. 129, J-15
Oyster Bay Cove . . . Pg. 129, J-15
Ozone Park Pg. 127, L-9
Painted Post N-9
Palatine Bridge K-16

Palisades . . Pg. 126, D-8
Palmyra J-9
Panama N-2
Parish H-12
Parma Center Pg. 138, F-1
Parma Corners . . . Pg. 138, G-1
Patchin . . . . Pg. 94, K-6
Patchoque D-6
Pawling A-4
Peach Haven . . Pg. 94, A-3
Pearl River C-3
  Vicinity . . Pg. 126, C-6
Peconic C-9
Peekskill B-3
Pelham . . . . Pg. 126, F-9
Pelham Manor . . . Pg. 126, G-9
Pendleton . . . Pg. 94, A-6
Penfield . . . Pg. 138, J-6
Penfield Center . . . Pg. 138, H-7
Penn Yan L-9
Perry L-6
Perrysburg M-3
Peru C-19
Phelps K-9
Philadelphia E-13
Philmont M-19
Phoenix H-11
Piermont . . . Pg. 126, C-8
Pike L-6
Pine Bush N-17
Pine Hill N-17
Pine Plains N-19
Pinehurst . . . Pg. 94, J-3
Pittsford J-7
  Vicinity . . Pg. 138, K-5
Plainview D-5
  Vicinity . . . Pg. 129, L-16
Plandome Manor . . . Pg. 129, K-11
Plattsburgh B-19
Pleasantville C-4
Pocantico Hill Pg. 126, B-9
Poestenkill K-20
Point Abino (Canada) . . . Pg. 94, E-1
Poland H-15
Pomona B-3
Port Byron J-10
Port Chester Pg. 128, F-12
Port Dickinson N-13
Port Ewen N-18
Port Henry E-19
Port Jefferson C-6
Port Jervis B-1
Port Leyden G-14
Port Richmond . . . Pg. 127, M-3
Port Washington . . . Pg. 129, K-12
Port Washington North . . . Pg. 129, K-12
Portville N-5
Potsdam B-15
Poughkeepsie O-19
Pound Ridge B-4
Prospect H-14
Pulaski G-12
Queens . . . . Pg. 127, K-9
Queens Village . . . Pg. 129, M-11
Quogue D-8
Ramapo . . . . Pg. 126, A-3
Randolph N-3
Ransomville J-4
Rapids . . . . . Pg. 94, A-7
Ravena L-18
Red Creek H-10
Red Hook N-19
Red Oaks Mill O-19
Remsen H-15
Rensselaer L-19
Rensselaer Falls C-14
Rhinebeck N-19
Richburg N-6
Richfield Springs K-15
Richmond Hill Pg. 127, L-9
Richmondville L-17
Richville C-14
Ridge D-7
Ridgeway (Canada) . . . Pg. 94, E-1
Rigney Bluff . Pg. 138, F-3
Riverdale . . . Pg. 126, H-7
Riverhead D-8
Riverside N-9
Rochester J-7
  Vicinity . . . Pg. 138
Rockville Center . . . Pg. 129, N-13
Rocky Pt. C-7
Roessleville K-18
Rome J-13
Roosevelt . . Pg. 129, N-14
Rosendale O-18
Roslyn . . . . Pg. 129, K-12
Roslyn Harbor . . . Pg. 129, J-15
Roslyn Hts. Pg. 129, L-13
Rossville . . . Pg. 127, P-3
Round Lake J-19
Rouses Point A-19
Ruby N-18
Rushville K-9
Rye C-4
  Vicinity . . . Pg. 128, G-3
Rye Brook C-4
Sackets Harbor F-12
Sag Harbor C-9
Saint Johnsville J-16

Saint Lawrence Park . . . D-12
Salamanca N-4
Salem H-20
Saltaire . . . Pg. 129, P-20
San Remo . . . Pg. 129, J-19
Sand Ridge J-11
Sands Point Pg. 129, J-11
Sandy Beach . . Pg. 94, B-2
Sandy Creek G-12
Saranac Lake D-18
Saratoga Springs J-18
Saugerties N-18
Savona M-9
Sawyer . . . . . Pg. 94, A-4
Sayville D-6
Scarsdale C-4
  Vicinity . . Pg. 126, E-10
Schaghticoke K-19
Schenectady K-18
Schenevus L-15
Schoharie L-17
Schuylerville J-19
Scotch Town A-2
Scotia K-18
Scottsville J-7
Scranton . . . . Pg. 94, H-4
Sea Cliff . . . Pg. 129, J-12
Seaford . . . . Pg. 129, P-15
Searington . . Pg. 129, L-12
Selden D-6
Seneca Falls K-10
Sharon Springs K-16
Shelter Island C-9
Sherburne L-14
Sherman N-1
Sherrill J-13
Shirley D-7
Shortsville K-8
Sidney M-14
Silver Creek L-3
Silver Springs L-6
Sinclairville M-2
Skaneateles J-11
Sloan . . . . . Pg. 94, E-5
Sloatsburg C-2
  Vicinity . . Pg. 126, A-3
Smithtown D-6
Smyrna L-13
Snyder . . . . Pg. 94, D-5
Snyder (Canada) . . . Pg. 94, D-1
Sodus H-9
Sodus Point H-9
Solvay J-11
Sound Beach C-6
South Corning N-9
South Fallsburg O-16
South Farmingdale . . . Pg. 129, M-16
South Glens Falls H-18
South Greece . . . Pg. 138, H-2
South Nyack . Pg. 126, C-8
Southampton D-9
Southold C-8
Southport N-10
Sparkill . . . Pg. 126, D-7
Speculator G-17
Spencer N-11
Spencerport J-7
  Vicinity . . . Pg. 138, H-1
Spring Valley B-3
  Vicinity . . Pg. 126, B-6
Springbrook . . Pg. 94, G-7
Springfield Gdns. . . . Pg. 127, M-10
Springs C-9
Springville L-4
St. Johnsburg Pg. 94, A-3
Stamford M-16
Stannards N-6
Star Lake D-15
Staten Island Pg. 127, N-5
Stevensville (Canada) . . . Pg. 94, D-1
Stillwater J-19
Stony Brook D-6
  Vicinity . . . Pg. 128, H-20
Stony Pt. B-3
Stottville M-19
Success . . . . Pg. 129, L-12
Suffern C-2
  Vicinity . . Pg. 126, B-4
Swormville . . . Pg. 94, B-7
Sylvan Beach J-13
Syosset . . . . Pg. 129, K-15
Syracuse K-12
Tall Man . . . Pg. 126, B-4
Tannersville M-18
Tarrytown C-3
  Vicinity . . Pg. 126, C-8
Theresa D-13
Thornwood Pg. 126, B-10
Thunder Bay (Canada) . . . Pg. 94, F-2
Ticonderoga F-19
Tillson O-18
Tivoli N-18
Tonawanda J-4
  Vicinity . . . Pg. 94, C-3
Town Line K-5
Tribes Hill J-17
Troy K-19
Trumansburg L-10
Tuckahoe D-8
Tully K-12
Tupper Lake D-17
Turin F-14
Tuxedo Park C-2
  Vicinity . . Pg. 126, A-3
Unadilla M-14
Union Hill . . Pg. 138, G-7
Union Springs K-10
Uniondale . . Pg. 129, M-13
Unionville B-15

University Gardens . . . Pg. 129, L-11
Upper Brookville . . . Pg. 129, J-14
Upper Nyack Pg. 126, B-7
Utica J-15
Valatie M-19
Valhalla . . . Pg. 128, E-11
Valley Cottage . . . Pg. 126, B-7
Valley Falls J-20
Valley Stream E-4
  Vicinity . . . Pg. 129, N-11
Van Etten N-11
Vernon J-14
Verona J-12
Victor K-8
Victory J-10
Village of the Branch . . . Pg. 129, J-20
Viola . . . . . Pg. 126, A-5
Voorheesville L-18
Waddington B-14
Wading River C-7
Walden A-2
Wallkill A-2
Walton N-15
Walton Park B-2
Wampsville J-13
Wanakah . . . . Pg. 94, H-3
Wantagh . . . Pg. 129, N-15
Wappinger Falls A-3
Warrensburg G-19
Warsaw K-6
Warwick B-2
Washingtonville A-2
Water Valley . . Pg. 94, J-4
Waterford K-19
Waterloo K-9
Watertown E-13
Waterville K-14
Watervliet K-19
Watkins Glen M-10
Waverly N-11
Wayland L-7
Wayneport . . Pg. 138, K-7
Webster J-7
  Vicinity . . . Pg. 138, G-7
Webster Corners . . . Pg. 94, H-6
Weedsport J-10
Wellsburg N-10
Wellsville N-6
Wendelville . . Pg. 94, A-5
Wesley Hills Pg. 126, A-5
West Carthage F-13
West Chili . . Pg. 138, K-1
West End L-15
West Falls . . . Pg. 94, J-6
West Greece Pg. 138, G-2
West Plattsburgh B-19
West Point B-3
West Sand Lake L-19
West Seneca . . Pg. 94, F-5
West Walworth . . . Pg. 138, J-7
West Webster . . . Pg. 138, G-5
West Winfield K-15
Westbury . . . Pg. 129, M-13
Westfield M-2
Westhampton D-8
Westmere K-17
Westons Mills N-5
Westport D-19
White Plains C-4
  Vicinity . . . Pg. 126, D-10
Whitehall G-20
Whitesboro J-14
Whitney Point M-12
Willard L-10
Williamsville K-4
  Vicinity . . . Pg. 94, D-6
Williston Park . . . Pg. 129, L-13
Willow Brook Pg. 127, N-4
Wilson H-4
  Vicinity . . . Pg. 94, G-5
Windom . . . . Pg. 94, G-5
Windsor N-13
Winthrop B-16
Witherbee C-19
Wolcott H-10
Woodbury . . Pg. 129, K-15
Woodhull N-8
Woodlawn . . . Pg. 94, G-4
Woodmere . . Pg. 129, P-11
Woodridge O-17
Woodsburg Pg. 129, Q-12
Woodstock N-18
Wurlitzer Park Pg. 94, A-4
Wyadanch Pg. 129, L-17
Wyoming K-6
Yaphank D-7
Yonkers D-3
  Vicinity . . Pg. 126, E-8
Yorkshire L-5
Yorktown Hts B-3
Yorkville J-13
Youngstown H-3
Zena N-18

NORTH CAROLINA

Alexis . . . . Pg. 95, A-1
Allen D-7
Allenton E-9
Andrews D-2
Apex . . . . . Pg. 138, D-2
Arapahoe D-12
Archdale C-7
Arcola B-10
Arlington B-6
Asheboro C-8
Asheville C-4
Ashland B-12
Askin D-12
Auburn . . . Pg. 138, E-6
Aurora D-12
Avent Ferry Pg. 138, D-4
Avery Creek D-4
Avon C-14
Ayden C-11
Badin C-10
Bagley C-10
Bald Creek C-4
Baldwin B-5
Bandana B-4
Banner Elk B-5
Barclay Downs . . . Pg. 138, C-6
Barco A-13
Bat Cave D-4
Battleboro B-11
Bayleaf . . . Pg. 138, A-5
Bear Creek C-9
Beaufort D-13
Belgrade D-11
Belhaven C-12
Belmont D-6
  Vicinity . . Pg. 95, A-2
Benson D-10
Bertha A-13
Bessemer City D-6
Bethel B-11
Bethel Hill A-9
Beulaville D-11
Biscoe D-8
Black Mtn. C-4
Bladenboro E-9
Blowing Rock B-5
Bolton E-10
Boone B-5
Bottom A-6
Bowdens D-10
Brandon Station . . . Pg. 138, A-4
Brasstown D-2
Brentwood . . Pg. 138, C-5
Brevard D-4
Bridgeton D-12
Bridgewater C-5
Brookford C-6
Brooks Cross Roads . . . B-6
Brooksdale B-9
Browns Summit B-8
Brunswick F-10
Bryson City D-2
Bulade B-4
Bullock A-9
Bunn B-10
Burch B-6
Burgaw E-10
Burlington B-8
Burnsville B-4
Buxton C-14
Calypso D-10
Camden A-13
Cameron D-9
Candor D-8
Canto C-3
Canton D-3
Carolina Beach F-11
Carr B-8
Carrboro B-9
Cary C-9
  Vicinity . . Pg. 138, D-3
Casville B-8
Cedar Creek D-10
Celo C-4
Centerville B-10
Chadbourn F-10
Chapel Hill C-9
Charlotte D-7
  Vicinity . . . Pg. 95
Cherokee D-2
Cherryville D-5
China Grove C-7
Chinquapin D-11
Chocowinity C-12
Churchland C-7
Cid C-7
Clemmons C-6
Clinton D-10
Cloverdale . Pg. 138, E-5
Coinjock A-13
Colerain B-12
College B-8
Columbia B-13
Columbus D-4
Comfort D-11
Concord D-7
Conover C-6
Conway A-12
Corapeake A-12
Cornelius D-6
Council E-10
Cove Creek C-3
Cramerton . . Pg. 95, E-1
Creedmoor B-9
Creswell B-13
Culberson D-1
Currie E-10
Dalton B-7
Darden C-11
Davidson C-6
Deep Gap B-5
Del Mar Beach E-12

Delway E-10
Derita . . . . Pg. 95, C-7
Diane . . . . Pg. 138, B-4
Dillsboro D-3
Dixie . . . . . Pg. 95, C-8
Dobson B-7
Dortches B-10
Dudley D-10
Dunn D-9
Durham B-9
  Vicinity . . Pg. 138, A-14
East Lake B-13
East Laport D-3
Eastwood D-8
Eden A-8
Edenhouse B-12
Edenton B-12
Edneyville D-4
Edward C-12
Ela D-3
Eldorado C-7
Elizabeth City A-13
Elizabethtown E-10
Elk Park B-4
Elkin B-6
Emerald Village . . . Pg. 138, E-6
Emery D-8
Enfield B-11
Englehard C-13
Erwin D-9
Essex B-10
Ether C-8
Evergreen E-9
Fair Bluff F-9
Fairfield . . Pg. 138, B-1
Fairmont E-9
Faison D-10
Falls . . . . Pg. 138, A-6
Farmville C-11
Fayetteville D-9
Flat Rock D-4
Fletcher D-4
Folkston E-11
Fontana Village D-2
Forest City D-5
Fountain C-11
Franklin D-2
Freeman E-8
Fremont C-10
Friendship . . Pg. 138, E-1
Frisco C-14
Fuquay-Varina C-9
Garner . . . . Pg. 138, E-5
Garysburg A-11
Gastonia D-6
  Vicinity . . . Pg. 95, D-1
Gates A-12
Genlee . . . Pg. 138, B-1
Gilkey D-5
Glade Valley B-6
Glenridge . . Pg. 138, E-3
Glenview B-10
Glenwood C-5
Gneiss D-3
Godwin D-9
Gold Rock B-11
Goldsboro C-10
Goldston C-8
Gordonton B-9
Graingers C-11
Grandy A-13
Granite Falls C-5
Granite Quarry C-7
Grantham D-10
Green Level . . Pg. 138, D-1
Greenbrier Estates . . . Pg. 138, E-5
Greensboro B-8
Greenville C-11
Grifton C-11
Grissettown F-10
Guilford B-8
Halifax A-11
Hamlet D-8
Hampstead E-11
Harbinger B-14
Harmony B-6
Harrells E-10
Harrisburg D-7
Harrisburg D-7
  Vicinity . . Pg. 95, C-8
Hatteras C-14
Hazelwood D-3
Heartsease B-11
Hedingham . Pg. 138, C-6
Henderson B-10
Hendersonville D-4
Henrietta D-5
Hertford B-12
Hester B-9
Hickory C-6
Hickory Grove Pg. 95, E-8
High Hampton D-3
High Point B-7
Hightowers B-8
Hill Crest D-8
Hillsborough B-9
Hiwassee D-2
Hoffman D-8
Holly Ridge E-11
Hollyville (Cash Corner) . . . D-12
House C-11
Hope Mills D-9
Hubert D-11
Hudson C-5
Huntersville . . . Pg. 95, A-6
Ingleside B-10
Jackson A-11
Jacksonville D-11
Jamesville B-12
Jarvisburg A-13
Jason C-11
Johns E-9

NORTH CAROLINA
Pages 64-65
Population: 5,881,766
Capital: Raleigh
Land Area: 48,843 sq. mi.

Abbotsburg E-10
Aberdeen D-8
Acre C-12
Ahoskie A-12
Albemarle D-7

Jonas Ridge ... C-5
Jonesville ... B-6
Julian ... B-8
Justice ... B-10
Kannapolis ... C-7
Keener ... D-10
Kelley ... E-10
Kenansville ... D-11
Kenly ... C-10
Kernersville ... B-7
Kilkenny ... B-13
King ... B-7
Kings Mountain ... D-5
Kinston ... D-11
Kittrell ... B-10
Knightdale ... Pg. 138, D-7
Kuhns ... D-12
Kure Beach ... F-11
La Grange ... D-11
Lake Landing ... C-13
Lakeview ... D-9
Landis ... C-7
Lauada ... D-3
Laurinburg ... E-9
Lawrence ... B-11
Leasburg ... A-9
Leechville ... C-13
Leesville ... Pg. 138, A-4
Lemon Springs ... C-8
Lenoir ... C-5
Level Cross ... B-8
Lewis ... A-9
Lexington ... C-7
Liberia ... B-10
Liberty ... B-8
Lilesville ... D-8
Lillington ... C-9
Lincolnton ... D-5
Linwood ... C-7
Lizzie ... C-11
Logan ... D-5
Long Beach ... F-10
Longview ... C-5
Louisburg ... B-9
Lowell ... Pg. 95, D-1
Lowesville ... Pg. 95, A-3
Lucama ... C-11
Lucia ... Pg. 95, B-3
Luck ... A-9
Lumber Bridge ... D-9
Lumberton ... E-9
Lynn Crossroads ... Pg. 138, A-3
Macedonia ... Pg. 138, D-4
Macgregor Downs ... Pg. 138, D-4
Maco ... E-10
Madison ... B-7
Magnolia ... D-10
Maiden ... C-6
Mamie ... B-13
Manns Harbor ... B-13
Manteo ... B-14
Maple Hill ... E-11
Marble ... D-2
Marion ... C-5
Mars Hill ... C-4
Marshall ... C-3
Marshville ... D-7
Marston ... D-8
Matthews ... D-7
Vicinity ... Pg. 95, G-8
Maxton ... E-9
Mayodan ... B-8
Maysville ... D-12
Mesic ... C-12
Micro ... C-10
Middleburg ... A-10
Midway ... B-12
Midway Park ... E-11
Milburnie ... Pg. 138, C-6
Mint Hill ... D-7
Vicinity ... Pg. 95, F-9
Mocksville ... C-7
Moncure ... C-9
Monroe ... D-7
Monticello ... B-8
Mooresville ... C-6
Morehead City ... D-12
Morgans Corner ... A-13
Morganton ... C-5
Morrisville ... Pg. 138, C-7
Mount Airy ... A-7
Mount Gilead ... D-7
Mount Holly ... D-6
Vicinity ... Pg. 95, D-3
Mount Mourne ... C-6
Mount Olive ... D-11
Mountain Home ... D-4
Mulberry ... B-6
Murfreesboro ... A-11
Nags Head ... B-14
Nakina ... F-10
Nantahala ... D-2
Nashville ... B-10
Nelson ... Pg. 138, B-2
Neuse ... Pg. 138, B-6
New Bern ... D-12
New Holland ... C-13
New Hope ... Pg. 138, C-6
New Salem ... D-7
Newell ... Pg. 95, D-7
Newport ... D-12
Newton ... C-6
Newton Grove ... D-10
Norlina ... A-10
Norman ... D-7
North Wilkesboro ... B-6
Northside ... B-9
Oak Grove ... B-9
Oakboro ... D-7
Ocracoke ... D-14
Old Dock ... F-10

Old Ford ... C-12
Old Fort ... C-4
Olivia ... D-9
Osceola ... B-8
Oswalt ... C-6
Oteen ... C-4
Otto ... D-3
Oxford ... B-9
Pantego ... C-12
Parkwood ... Pg. 138, A-1
Patterson ... B-5
Peachtree ... D-2
Pembroke ... E-9
Penderlea ... E-10
Picks ... B-9
Pilot Mountain ... B-7
Pine Ridge ... A-6
Pinebluff ... D-8
Pineola ... B-5
Pinetops ... B-11
Pineville ... D-6
Pinnacle ... B-7
Pireway ... F-10
Pittsboro ... C-9
Pleasant Hill ... A-11
Plymouth ... B-12
Point Harbor ... B-13
Polkton ... D-7
Pollocksville ... D-11
Portsmouth ... D-13
Postell ... D-1
Powells Point ... B-14
Preston ... Pg. 138, C-2
Raeford ... D-9
Rainbow Springs ... D-2
Raleigh ... B-10
Vicinity ... Pg. 138, B-5
Randleman ... C-8
Ranger ... D-1
Ransomville ... C-12
Rapids ... A-11
Red Hill ... B-4
Red Springs ... E-9
Reidsville ... B-8
Rheasville ... A-11
Rich Square ... A-11
Roanoke Rapids ... A-11
Robbinsville ... D-2
Robersonville ... B-11
Rockingham ... D-8
Rocky Mount ... B-11
Rodanthe ... B-14
Roduco ... A-12
Roper ... C-13
Rose Hill ... D-10
Roseboro ... D-9
Roseneath ... B-11
Rougemont ... B-9
Rowan ... E-10
Rowland ... E-9
Roxboro ... A-9
Ruth ... D-5
Rutherfordton ... D-4
Saint Pauls ... E-9
Salemburg ... D-10
Salisbury ... C-7
Salvo ... B-14
Sanford ... C-9
Schley ... B-9
Scotland Neck ... B-11
Scott's Hill ... E-11
Scranton ... C-13
Seabreeze ... F-11
Seagrove ... C-8
Selma ... C-10
Shallotte ... F-10
Sharpsburg ... B-11
Shelby ... D-5
Shopton ... Pg. 95, F-8
Siler City ... C-8
Sioux ... B-5
Six Forks ... Pg. 138, A-5
Six Forks Crossroads ... Pg. 138, B-7
Skyland ... C-4
Smith ... F-10
Smithfield ... C-10
Snow Hill ... C-11
Southern Pines ... D-9
Southport ... F-10
Sparta ... A-6
Spencer ... C-7
Spivey's Corner ... D-10
Spout Springs ... D-9
Spring Hill ... B-11
Spring Lake ... D-9
Spruce Pine ... B-5
Stanhope ... B-10
Stanley ... Pg. 95, B-1
Stanleyville ... B-7
State Road ... B-6
Statesville ... C-6
Steeds ... C-8
Stocksville ... C-4
Stokes ... C-12
Stonebridge ... Pg. 138, A-1
Stony Point ... C-6
Stovall ... A-10
Stratford ... A-6
Sunbury ... A-12
Supply ... F-10
Surf City ... E-11
Surl ... B-9
Swann ... C-9
Swannanoa ... C-4
Swansboro ... E-12
Swiss ... C-4
Sylva ... D-3
Tabor City ... F-9
Tapoco ... D-2
Tarboro ... B-11
Taylorsville ... C-6

Teachey ... D-10
Terp ... Pg. 138, D-4
The Woods of Chatham ... Pg. 138, C-1
Thomasville ... C-7
Tillery ... B-11
Tin City ... E-10
Tobaccoville ... B-7
Toluca ... C-5
Topsail Beach ... E-11
Topton ... D-2
Tramway ... C-9
Trent Woods ... D-12
Trenton ... D-11
Trust ... C-3
Tryon ... D-4
Turnersburg ... C-6
Tuxedo ... D-4
Twin Oaks ... A-6
Ulah ... C-8
Unaka ... D-2
Upchurch ... Pg. 138, C-2
Uwharrie ... C-8
Valdese ... C-5
Vanceboro ... C-11
Vander ... D-9
Violet ... D-1
Wadesboro ... E-7
Wadeville ... D-7
Wagram ... D-9
Wake Crossroads ... Pg. 138, B-7
Wake Forest ... B-10
Vicinity ... Pg. 138, A-7
Walkers Crossroads ... Pg. 138, A-7
Wallace ... E-11
Walnut ... C-4
Walnut Creek ... C-11
Wanchese ... B-14
Wards Corner ... E-10
Warsaw ... D-10
Waves ... B-14
Waynesville ... D-3
Weldon ... A-11
Wendell ... C-10
Wesser ... D-2
West Concord ... Pg. 95, A-10
West Onslow Beach ... E-12
Westminster ... C-4
Westover ... Pg. 138, C-4
Whalebone ... B-14
White Lake ... E-10
White Oak ... E-10
Whiteville ... F-10
Wilbar ... B-6
Wilkesboro ... B-6
Willard ... E-10
Williamsburg ... B-8
Williamston ... B-12
Wilmar ... C-12
Wilmington ... F-10
Wilmington Beach ... F-11
Wilson ... C-11
Windsor ... B-12
Wingate ... D-7
Winnabow ... F-10
Winston-Salem ... B-7
Winterville ... C-11
Winton ... A-12
Wise ... A-10
Wise Fork ... D-11
Woodland ... B-11
Woodley ... B-13
Wrightsville Beach ... F-11
Yadkinville ... B-7
Yancyville ... A-8
Yeatesville ... C-12
Youngsville ... B-10
Zebulon ... B-10

NORTH DAKOTA
Page 63
Population: 652,717
Capital: Bismarck
Land Area: 69,300 sq. mi.

Abercrombie ... F-9
Adams ... B-8
Alamo ... B-2
Alexander ... C-2
Alice ... E-9
Almont ... E-4
Alsen ... B-7
Ambrose ... A-2
Amenia ... E-9
Amidon ... E-2
Anamoose ... D-6
Aneta ... D-8
Antler ... A-5
Ardoch ... C-9
Arena ... D-6
Argusville ... E-10
Arnegard ... C-2
Arthur ... E-9
Ashley ... F-6
Ayr ... E-9
Balfour ... D-6
Balta ... C-6
Bantry ... B-5
Barney ... F-9
Barton ... B-6
Battleview ... B-3
Beach ... D-1
Belcourt ... A-7
Belfield ... D-2
Benedict ... C-5
Berlin ... F-8
Berthold ... B-4

Berwick ... C-6
Beulah ... D-4
Binford ... D-8
Bisbee ... B-7
Bismarck ... E-5
Bottineau ... B-6
Bowbells ... B-3
Bowden ... D-6
Bowman ... E-2
Braddock ... E-6
Breien ... E-5
Bremen ... D-7
Brinsmade ... C-7
Brocket ... C-8
Bucyrus ... F-2
Buffalo ... E-9
Burlington ... B-4
Butte ... C-5
Buxton ... D-9
Calio ... B-7
Calvin ... B-7
Cando ... C-7
Carbury ... B-6
Carpio ... B-4
Carrington ... D-7
Carson ... E-4
Casselton ... E-9
Cathay ... D-7
Cavalier ... B-9
Cayuga ... F-9
Center ... D-4
Charlson ... C-3
Churchs Ferry ... C-7
Cleveland ... E-7
Clifford ... D-9
Colehabor ... D-5
Colfax ... F-9
Columbus ... A-3
Conway ... C-9
Cooperstown ... D-8
Courtenay ... D-8
Crary ... C-8
Crosby ... A-2
Crystal ... B-9
Davenport ... E-9
Dawson ... E-6
Dazey ... D-8
Deering ... B-5
Des Lacs ... B-4
Devils Lake ... C-7
Dickey ... E-7
Dickinson ... D-3
Dodge ... D-3
Donnybrook ... B-4
Douglas ... C-4
Drake ... C-6
Drayton ... B-9
Driscoll ... E-6
Dunn Center ... D-3
Dunseith ... B-7
Dwight ... F-10
Edgeley ... F-7
Edinburg ... B-8
Edmore ... C-8
Elgin ... E-4
Ellendale ... F-8
Elliott ... F-8
Emerado ... C-9
Enderlin ... E-8
Epping ... B-2
Esmond ... C-6
Fairdale ... B-8
Fairfield ... D-2
Fargo ... E-10
Fairmont ... F-10
Fessenden ... D-6
Fingal ... E-8
Finley ... D-8
Flasher ... E-4
Flaxton ... A-3
Fordville ... C-8
Forest River ... C-9
Forman ... F-8
Fort Ransom ... E-8
Fort Yates ... F-5
Fortuna ... A-2
Freda ... E-4
Fredonia ... F-7
Fullerton ... F-8
Gackle ... E-7
Galesburg ... D-9
Garrison ... C-4
Gascoyne ... F-2
Gilby ... C-9
Gladstone ... D-3
Glen Ullin ... E-4
Glenfield ... D-8
Golden Valley ... D-3
Golva ... D-1
Goodrich ... D-6
Grafton ... C-9
Grand Forks ... C-9
Grandin ... D-9
Grano ... B-4
Grassy Butte ... D-2
Great Bend ... F-10
Grenora ... B-1
Gwinner ... F-8
Hague ... F-6
Haley ... F-2
Halliday ... D-3
Hamberg ... C-7
Hampden ... B-8
Hankinson ... F-9
Hanks ... B-2
Hannaford ... D-8
Hannah ... B-8
Harlow ... C-7
Harvey ... C-6
Harwood ... E-10
Hatton ... D-9
Havana ... F-8

Haynes ... F-3
Hazelton ... E-5
Hazen ... D-4
Hebron ... D-4
Heimdal ... D-6
Hensel ... B-9
Hettinger ... F-2
Hillsboro ... D-9
Hoopie ... B-9
Hope ... D-8
Hunter ... D-9
Hurdsfield ... D-6
Inkster ... C-9
Jamestown ... E-7
Jud ... E-7
Karlsruhe ... C-6
Kathryn ... E-8
Kenmare ... B-4
Kensal ... D-7
Killdeer ... D-3
Kindred ... E-9
Kramer ... B-6
Kulm ... F-7
La Moure ... F-8
Lakota ... C-8
Landa ... B-5
Langdon ... B-8
Larimore ... C-8
Larson ... A-3
Lawton ... C-8
Leal ... D-7
Leeds ... C-7
Lehr ... F-6
Leith ... E-4
Leonard ... E-8
Lidgerwood ... F-9
Lignite ... A-3
Lincoln ... E-5
Linton ... F-5
Lisbon ... F-9
Litchville ... E-8
Loma ... B-8
Ludden ... F-8
Maddock ... C-7
Makoti ... C-4
Mandan ... E-5
Manfred ... C-6
Manning ... D-3
Mantador ... F-9
Manvel ... C-9
Marion ... E-8
Marmarth ... E-1
Marshall ... D-3
Martin ... C-6
Max ... C-4
Maxbass ... B-5
Mayville ... D-9
Maza ... C-7
McClusky ... D-5
McHenry ... D-7
McVille ... D-8
Medina ... E-6
Medora ... D-2
Mercer ... D-5
Merricourt ... F-7
Michigan ... C-8
Milnor ... F-9
Milton ... B-8
Minnewaukan ... C-7
Minot ... C-4
Minto ... C-9
Mohall ... B-4
Monango ... F-7
Montpelier ... E-7
Mooreton ... F-9
Mott ... E-3
Mountain ... B-9
Munich ... B-7
Mylo ... B-6
Napoleon ... E-6
Neche ... A-9
Nekoma ... B-8
New England ... E-2
New Leipzig ... E-3
New Rockford ... D-7
New Salem ... E-4
New Town ... C-3
Newburg ... B-5
Nome ... E-8
Noonan ... A-3
Northwood ... D-9
Oakes ... F-8
Oberon ... C-7
Oriska ... E-8
Osnabrock ... B-8
Page ... E-9
Palermo ... B-3
Park River ... C-9
Parshall ... C-4
Pekin ... D-8
Pembina ... B-9
Perth ... B-7
Petersburg ... C-8
Pettibone ... D-7
Pick City ... D-4
Pillsbury ... D-9
Pingree ... D-7
Pisek ... C-9
Plaza ... C-4
Portal ... A-3
Powers Lake ... B-3
Prairie Rose ... E-9
Rawson ... C-2
Ray ... B-2
Reeder ... F-2
Regan ... D-5
Regent ... E-3
Rhame ... E-1
Richardton ... D-3
Riverdale ... D-4
Riverside ... D-4
Robinson ... D-6
Rock Lake ... B-7

Rogers ... E-8
Rolette ... B-6
Rolla ... B-6
Ross ... B-3
Rugby ... C-6
Ruso ... C-5
Rutland ... F-9
Ryder ... C-4
Saint Thomas ... B-9
Sanborn ... E-8
Sarles ... B-7
Sawyer ... C-5
Scranton ... E-2
Selfridge ... F-4
Sentinel Butte ... D-1
Sharon ... D-8
Sheilds ... F-4
Sheldon ... E-8
Sherwood ... A-4
Sheyenne ... C-7
Sibley ... D-8
Solen ... E-5
Souris ... B-5
South Heart ... D-2
Spring Brook ... B-2
Stanley ... B-3
Stanton ... D-4
Starkweather ... B-7
Steele ... E-6
Strasburg ... F-6
Streeter ... E-7
Surrey ... C-5
Sydney ... E-7
Sykeston ... D-7
Tappen ... E-6
Thompson ... D-9
Tioga ... B-2
Tolley ... B-4
Tolna ... C-8
Tower City ... E-8
Towner ... B-5
Turtle Lake ... D-5
Tuttle ... D-6
Underwood ... D-5
Upham ... B-5
Valley City ... E-8
Velva ... C-5
Venturia ... F-6
Verendrye ... C-5
Verona ... F-8
Voltaire ... C-5
Wahpeton ... F-10
Walcott ... E-9
Wales ... B-8
Walhalla ... A-8
Walseth ... B-5
Warwick ... C-7
Washburn ... D-5
Watford City ... C-2
West Fargo ... E-9
Westfeild ... F-5
Westhope ... B-5
Wheelock ... B-3
White Earth ... B-3
Wildrose ... B-2
Williston ... B-2
Willow City ... B-6
Wilton ... D-5
Wimbledon ... D-7
Wing ... D-6
Wishek ... F-6
Wolford ... B-6
Woodworth ... D-7
Wyndmere ... F-9
York ... C-6
Ypsilanti ... E-7
Zap ... D-4

OHIO
Pages 66-67
Population: 10,797,630
Capital: Columbus
Land Area: 41,004 sq. mi.

Abbeville ... Pg. 101, J-1
Aberdeen ... N-3
Ada ... G-3
Addyston ... M-1
Adena ... J-9
Akron ... G-8
Albany ... M-7
Alexandria ... J-5
Alger ... H-3
Alliance ... G-9
Amanda ... K-5
Amberley ... Pg. 100, C-5
Amelia ... M-2
Vicinity ... Pg. 100, D-2
Amesville ... L-7
Amherst ... F-6
Amsterdam ... J-9
Andover ... E-10
Anna ... J-2
Ansonia ... J-1
Antwerp ... F-1
Apple Creek ... H-7
Arcadia ... G-4
Arcanum ... K-1
Archbold ... E-2
Arlington ... G-3
Ashland ... G-6
Ashley ... H-5
Ashtabula ... D-9
Ashville ... K-5
Athalia ... N-7
Athens ... M-7
Attica ... G-5
Aurora ... F-8
Avon Lake ... E-7
Bainbridge ... M-4
Baltic ... H-8
Baltimore ... K-6

Barberton ... G-8
Barnesville ... K-9
Barnsburg ... Pg. 100, B-2
Batavia ... M-2
Bath ... Pg. 101, K-4
Bath Center ... Pg. 101, K-4
Bay View ... E-5
Beach City ... H-8
Beallsville ... K-9
Beavercreek ... K-3
Beaverdam ... G-3
Bedford ... Pg. 101, E-6
Bedford Heights
Vicinity ... Pg. 101, K-7
Beechwood ... Pg. 101, E-6
Beliot ... G-9
Bellaire ... K-10
Bellbrook ... L-2
Belle Center ... H-3
Belle Valley ... K-8
Bellefontaine ... H-3
Bellevue ... F-5
Bellville ... H-6
Belmont ... J-9
Belpre ... M-8
Belvis ... Pg. 100, A-2
Bennetts Corner ... Pg. 101, H-2
Berea ... Pg. 101, F-7
Vicinity ... Pg. 101, F-7
Bergholz ... H-9
Berlin Heights ... F-6
Bethel ... N-2
Bethesda ... J-9
Bettsville ... F-4
Beverly ... L-8
Bexley ... J-5
Blanchester ... M-3
Bloomdale ... F-4
Bloomingburg ... L-4
Bloomville ... G-5
Blue Ash ... Pg. 101, B-6
Bluffton ... G-3
Boston Heights ... Pg. 101, H-6
Botkins ... H-2
Botzum ... Pg. 101, K-5
Bowersville ... L-3
Bowling Green ... F-3
Bradford ... J-2
Bradner ... F-3
Brathenal ... Pg. 101, B-5
Brecksville ... Pg. 101, F-6
Vicinity ... Pg. 101, F-6
Bremen ... K-6
Brewster ... H-8
Bridgetown ... Pg. 100, D-1
Brilliant ... J-10
Broadview Heights
Vicinity ... Pg. 101, G-4
Brook Park ... Pg. 101, E-5
Brooklyn ... Pg. 101, D-3
Brooklyn Heights ... Pg. 101, D-4
Brunswick ... Pg. 101, F-7
Vicinity ... Pg. 101, J-2
Bryan ... E-2
Buchtel ... L-7
Bucyrus ... G-5
Burton ... E-9
Butler ... H-6
Byesville ... K-8
Cadiz ... J-9
Cairo ... G-2
Caldwell ... K-8
Caledonia ... H-5
Cambridge ... J-8
Camden ... L-1
Campbell ... F-10
Canal Fulton ... G-8
Canal Winchester ... K-5
Vicinity ... Pg. 102, J-7
Canfield ... G-9
Canton ... G-8
Cardington ... H-5
Carey ... G-4
Carroll ... K-5
Carrollton ... H-9
Castalia ... F-5
Cedarville ... K-3
Celina ... H-1
Center Village ... Pg. 102, B-7
Centerburg ... J-5
Centerville ... L-2
Chardon ... E-9
Chauncey ... L-7
Chesapeake ... O-6
Chesterhill ... L-7
Cheviot ... M-1
Vicinity ... Pg. 100, D-2
Chillicothe ... L-5
Christianburg ... J-3
Cincinnati ... M-2
Vicinity ... Pg. 100, H-2
Circleville ... L-5
Clarington ... K-9
Clarksville ... L-3
Cleveland ... E-7
Vicinity ... Pg. 101, C-6
Cleveland Heights ... E-8
Vicinity ... Pg. 101, C-6
Cleves ... L-1
Clyde ... F-5
Coal Grove ... O-6
Coalton ... M-6
Coldwater ... H-1
Columbiana ... G-10
Columbus ... J-5
Vicinity ... Pg. 102, E-4
Columbus Grove ... G-2
Commercial Point ... Pg. 102, K-3
Conneaut ... D-10
Continental ... F-2

Convoy ... G-1
Coolville ... M-7
Corning ... L-7
Cortland ... F-10
Coshocton ... J-7
Covington ... J-2
Craig Beach ... G-9
Crestline ... G-5
Cridersville ... H-2
Crooksville ... K-7
Crown City ... O-6
Cuyahoga Falls ... F-8
Vicinity ... Pg. 101, K-7
Cuyahoga Heights ... Pg. 101, D-5
Cygnet ... F-3
Dalton ... G-8
Danville ... H-6
Darbydale ... K-4
Vicinity ... Pg. 102, J-1
Dayton ... K-2
De Graff ... J-3
Delaware ... J-4
Delphos ... G-2
Delta ... E-3
Dennison ... H-9
Derby ... Pg. 102, K-1
Deshler ... F-3
Dover ... H-8
Dresden ... J-7
Dublin ... J-4
Vicinity ... Pg. 102, C-2
Dunkirk ... G-3
Dunlap ... Pg. 100, A-1
Duvall ... Pg. 102, K-5
East Canton ... G-9
East Cleveland ... E-7
Vicinity ... Pg. 101, B-5
East Liverpool ... H-10
East Palestine ... G-10
East Sparta ... H-8
Eastlake ... E-8
Eaton ... K-1
Edgerton ... E-1
Edgewater Park ... Pg. 102, G-6
Edison ... H-5
Edon ... E-1
Eldorado ... K-1
Elmore ... E-4
Elmwood Place ... Pg. 100, C-4
Elyria ... F-7
Emery ... Pg. 101, D-6
Englewood ... K-2
Enon ... K-3
Euclid ... E-8
Vicinity ... Pg. 101, B-6
Evendale ... Pg. 100, B-5
Everett ... Pg. 101, J-5
Fairfax ... Pg. 100, D-6
Fairfield ... L-1
Fairlawn ... Pg. 101, J-2
Fairport Harbor ... D-9
Fairview Park ... Pg. 101, D-1
Fayette ... E-2
Felicity ... N-2
Findlay ... G-3
Flint ... Pg. 102, G-9
Flushing ... J-9
Forest ... G-4
Forest Park ... M-1
Vicinity ... Pg. 100, A-3
Fostoria ... F-4
Frankfort ... L-4
Franklin ... L-2
Frazeysburg ... J-7
Fredericksburg ... H-7
Fredericktown ... H-6
Freeport ... J-8
Fremont ... F-5
Ft. Jennings ... G-2
Ft. Loramie ... J-2
Ft. Recovery ... H-1
Ft. Shawnee ... H-2
Gahanna ... J-5
Vicinity ... Pg. 102, E-6
Galena ... Pg. 102, A-6
Galion ... H-5
Gallipolis ... N-7
Galloway ... Pg. 102, G-2
Gambier ... J-6
Garfield Heights ... F-8
Vicinity ... Pg. 101, D-5
Garrettsville ... F-9
Geneva ... D-9
Geneva-on-the-Lake ... D-9
Genoa ... E-4
Georgetown ... N-3
Georgeville ... Pg. 102, H-1
Germantown ... L-2
Gettysburg ... J-1
Ghent ... Pg. 101, K-4
Gibsonburg ... F-4
Girard ... F-10
Glandorf ... G-2
Glendale ... Pg. 100, A-4
Glenwillow ... Pg. 101, G-7
Glouster ... L-7
Gnadenhutten ... J-8
Golf Manor ... Pg. 100, C-5
Gould Park ... Pg. 102, D-6
Grafton ... F-7
Grand Rapids ... F-3
Grandview Heights ... Pg. 102, F-4
Granger ... Pg. 101, K-3
Granville ... J-6
Gratis ... L-1
Green Springs ... F-5
Greenfield ... L-4
Greenhills ... Pg. 100, A-3
Greenville ... J-1
Greenwich ... G-6

OHIO

OKLAHOMA

Grove City K-4
Vicinity . . . Pg. 102, H-3
Groveport K-5
Vicinity . . . Pg. 102, J-6
Hamden M-6
Hamersville N-3
Hamilton L-1
Hamler F-3
Hanover J-6
Hanoverton G-9
Harlem . . . . . Pg. 102, B-6
Harrisburg . . . Pg. 102, K-1
Harrison M-1
Harrod H-3
Hartville G-9
Hayden . . . . . Pg. 102, D-1
Hayesville G-7
Heath K-6
Hebron K-6
Hicksville F-1
Higginsport N-3
Highland Heights
. . . . Pg. 101, B-7
Hilliard K-4
Vicinity . . . Pg. 102, E-1
Hillsboro M-3
Hinckley . . . . Pg. 101, H-2
Hiram F-9
Holgate F-2
Holland E-3
Hopedale J-9
Hubbard F-10
Huber Heights K-2
Huber Ridge Pg. 102, C-6
Hudson . . . . Pg. 101, H-7
Huron F-6
Hyatts . . . . . Pg. 102, A-3
Independence
. . . . Pg. 101, F-7
Ironton O-6
Jackson M-5
Jackson Center H-3
Jacksonville L-7
Jamestown L-3
Jefferson E-9
Jeffersonville L-4
Jerome . . . . . Pg. 102, B-1
Jeromesville G-7
Jewett J-9
Johnstown J-6
Junction City K-6
Kalida G-2
Kellys Island E-6
Kent F-8
Kenton H-3
Kettering K-2
Kileville . . . . Pg. 102, C-1
Killbuck H-7
Kingston L-5
Kirkersville K-6
Kirtland Hills E-9
Lagrange F-7
Lakemore G-8
Lakeview H-3
Lakewood E-7
Vicinity . . . Pg. 101, C-6
Lancaster K-6
Laurelville L-5
Lebanon L-2
Leesburg L-4
Leetonia G-10
Leipsic G-3
Lewis Center Pg. 102, A-4
Lewisburg K-1
Lexington H-6
Liberty Center E-2
Lima H-3
Lincoln Heights
. . . . Pg. 100, B-4
Lindsey F-5
Linworth . . . . Pg. 102, C-3
Lisbon G-10
Lithopolis . . . Pg. 102, K-7
Lockburn . . . . Pg. 102, K-4
Lockland . . . . Pg. 100, B-4
Lodi G-7
Logan L-6
London K-4
Lorain E-6
Lordstown F-9
Loudonville H-6
Louisville G-9
Loveland M-2
Lowell L-8
Lowellville G-10
Luckey F-4
Lynchburg M-3
Lyndhurst . . . Pg. 101, B-7
Lyons E-2
Macedonia F-8
Vicinity . . . Pg. 101, G-6
Madei . . . . . Pg. 100, C-6
Madeira M-2
Madison H-8
Magnolia K-7
Malta K-7
Malvern H-9
Manchester N-3
Mansfield H-6
Maple Heights
. . . . Pg. 101, E-5
Marble Cliff . . Pg. 102, F-3
Marblehead E-5
Marietta L-8
Marimet . . . . Pg. 100, D-6
Marion H-4
Martins Ferry J-10
Martinsville L-3
Marysville J-4
Mason L-2
Massillon G-8
Maumee E-3
Mayfield Heights
. . . . Pg. 101, B-7

McArthur M-6
McClure F-3
McConnelsville L-7
McGuffey H-3
Mechanicsburg J-4
Medina F-7
Vicinity . . . Pg. 101, K-1
Mentor E-8
Mentor-on-the-Lake E-8
Metamora E-3
Miamisburg L-2
Middle Point G-2
Middleburg Hts
. . . . Pg. 101, F-2
Middleport M-7
Middletown L-1
Midvale H-8
Midway K-4
Milan F-6
Milford M-2
Milford Center J-4
Millersburg H-7
Millersport K-6
Millville L-1
Mineral City . . . . H—8
Minerva G-9
Minerva Park J-5
Vicinity . . . Pg. 102, D-4
Mingo Junction J-10
Minster H-2
Monroe L-2
Monroeville F-6
Montpelier E-1
Moraine K-2
Moreland Hills
. . . . Pg. 101, D-7
Morrow L-2
Mt. Air . . . . . Pg. 102, B-3
Mt. Blanchard G-4
Mt. Gilead H-5
Mt. Healthy . . Pg. 100, B-3
Mt. Orab M-3
Mt. Sterling K-4
Mt. Vernon H-6
Mt. Victory H-4
Mudsock . . . . Pg. 102, E-1
Murray City L-7
Napoleon F-2
Navarre H-8
Nelsonville L-6
Nevada G-5
New Albany . . Pg. 102, C-7
New Boston N-5
New Bremen H-2
New Carlisle K-3
New Concord K-7
New Holland L-4
New Knoxville H-3
New Lebanon K-1
New Lexington L-6
New London G-6
New Madison K-1
New Matamoras L-9
New Miami L-1
New Middletown G-10
New Paris K-1
New Philadelphia H-8
New Richmond N-2
New Rome . . . Pg. 102, F-2
New Straitsville L-7
New Vienna L-3
New Washington G-5
New Waterford G-10
Newark J-6
Newburgh Heights
. . . . Pg. 101, D-4
Newcomerstown J-8
Newton M-2
Newton Falls F-9
Niles F-10
North Baltimore G-4
North Bend M-1
North Canton G-8
North College Hill
. . . . Pg. 100, C-3
North Fairfield F-6
North Kingsville D-10
North Lewisburg J-4
North Olmsted F-7
North Randall
. . . . Pg. 101, D-6
North Ridgeville F-7
North Royalton
. . . . Pg. 101, F-3
Northfield . . . Pg. 101, G-6
Northwood E-4
Norton G-8
Norwalk F-6
Norwood . . . . Pg. 100, D-4
Oak Harbor E-5
Oak Hill N-6
Oakwood
(Paulding Cty) F-2
Oakwood
(Montgomery Cty) . . . K-2
Vicinity . . . Pg. 101, F-6
Oberlin F-6
Obetz K-5
Vicinity . . . Pg. 102, H-5
Ohio City G-1
Ontario H-6
Orange . . . . . Pg. 101, D-7
Orangeville F-10
Oregon E-4
Orient . . . . . Pg. 102, K-2
Orrville G-7
Orwell E-9
Ottawa G-3
Ottawa Hills E-3
Ottoville G-2
Otway N-4
Owensville M-2
Oxford L-1

Pandora G-3
Parma F-8
Vicinity . . . Pg. 101, E-3
Parma Heights
. . . . Pg. 101, E-2
Pataskala K-6
Paulding F-1
Payne G-1
Pemberville F-4
Peninsula . . . Pg. 101, J-5
Pepper Pike . Pg. 101, C-7
Perry E-9
Perrysburg E-4
Perrysville H-6
Philo K-7
Pickerington K-5
Piketon M-5
Pioneer E-2
Piqua J-2
Plain City J-4
Pleasant Corners
. . . . Pg. 102, J-2
Pleasant Hill J-2
Pleasantville K-6
Plymouth G-6
Poland G-10
Pomeroy M-7
Port Clinton E-5
Port Washington J-8
Portsmouth N-5
Powell . . . . . Pg. 102, B-3
Powhatan Point K-9
Proctorville O-6
Prospect H-4
Put-in-Bay E-5
Quaker City K-8
Quincy J-3
Racine M-7
Rathbone . . . Pg. 102, A-2
Ravenna F-9
Reading M-2
Vicinity . . . Pg. 100, B-5
Reese . . . . . Pg. 102, H-5
Remsen Corners
. . . . Pg. 101, K-3
Republic F-5
Reynoldsburg K-6
Vicinity . . . Pg. 102, F-7
Richfield . . . . Pg. 101, H-5
Richmond H-9
Richmond Heights
. . . . Pg. 101, A-6
Rio Grande N-6
Ripley N-3
Rising Sun F-4
Rittman G-7
Riverlea . . . . Pg. 102, D-4
Roaming Shores E-10
Rock Creek E-9
Rockford H-2
Rocky River . Pg. 101, C-1
Rome N-4
Roseville K-7
Rossford E-4
Rushsylvania H-3
Russells Point H-3
Rutland M-7
Sabina L-3
Sagamore Hills
. . . . Pg. 101, G-5
Saint Bernard Pg. 100, D-4
Saint Clairsville J-9
Saint Henry H-1
Saint Marys H-2
Saint Paris J-3
Salem G-9
Salineville H-9
San Margherita
. . . . Pg. 102, F-2
Sandusky E-6
Sarahsville K-8
Sardinia N-3
Scio H-9
Seaman N-4
Sebring G-9
Senecaville K-8
Seven Hills . . Pg. 101, E-4
Seven Mile L-1
Seville G-7
Shadeville . . . Pg. 102, J-4
Shadyside J-10
Shaker Heights F-8
Vicinity . . . Pg. 101, C-6
Sharonville . . Pg. 100, A-5
Shawnee L-7
Shawnee Hills
. . . . Pg. 102, B-1
Sheffield Lake E-6
Shelby G-6
Sherwood F-1
Shiloh H-7
Shreve H-7
Sidney J-2
Silverton . . . . Pg. 100, C-5
Sinking Spring N-4
Smithfield J-10
Solon . . . . . . Pg. 101, E-7
Somerset K-6
South Bloomfield K-5
South Charleston K-3
South Euclid Pg. 101, B-6
South Lebanon L-2
South Point O-6
South Russell F-9
South Webster N-6
South Zanesville K-7
Spencer F-7
Spencerville H-2
Spring Valley L-3
Springboro L-2
Springdale . . Pg. 100, A-4
Springfield K-3
Stockport L-7
Stoutsville L-5

Stow F-8
Vicinity . . . Pg. 101, K-7
Strasburg H-8
Streetsboro F-9
Strongsville F-7
Vicinity . . . Pg. 101, G-1
Struthers G-10
Stryker E-2
Stuebenville H-10
Sugar Grove L-6
Sugarcreek H-8
Sunbury J-5
Swanton E-3
Sycamore G-4
Sylvania E-3
Syracruse M-7
Tallmadge G-8
Terrace Park M-2
Thornville K-6
Tiffin G-5
Tiltonsville J-10
Tipp City K-2
Toledo E-4
Toronto H-10
Trenton L-1
Trimble L-7
Trotwood K-2
Troy J-3
Tuscarawas H-8
Twinsburg . . Pg. 101, G-7
Uhrichsville H-8
Union K-2
Union City J-1
University Heights
. . . . Pg. 101, C-6
Upper Arlington K-4
Vicinity . . . Pg. 102, E-3
Upper Sandusky G-4
Urbana J-4
Urbancrest K-4
Vicinity . . . Pg. 102, H-3
Utica J-6
Valley View . . Pg. 101, E-5
Valleyview . . . Pg. 102, F-2
Van Wert G-1
Vandalia K-2
Vermilion F-6
Versailles J-2
Vinton M-6
Wadsworth G-7
Wakeman F-6
Walbridge E-4
Walton Hills . Pg. 101, F-6
Wapokoneta H-2
Warren F-10
Warrensville Heights
. . . . Pg. 101, D-6
Warsaw J-7
Washington C.H. L-4
Washingtonville G-10
Waterloo . . . . Pg. 102, J-7
Waterville E-3
Wauseon E-2
Waverly M-5
Wayne F-4
Waynesburg H-9
Waynesfield H-3
Waynesville L-3
Wellington F-6
Wellston M-6
Wellsville H-10
West Alexandria K-1
West Carrollton K-2
West Farmington F-9
West Jefferson K-4
West Lafayette J-8
West Liberty J-3
West Mansfield H-4
West Milton K-2
West Richfield
. . . . Pg. 101, H-4
West Salem G-7
West Union N-4
West Unity E-2
Westerville J-5
Vicinity . . . Pg. 102, C-5
Westfield Center G-7
Weston F-3
Whitehall K-5
Vicinity . . . Pg. 102, F-6
Whitehouse E-3
Wickliffe . . . . Pg. 101, A-7
Wilkesville M-6
Willard G-5
Williamsburg M-2
Williamsport L-4
Willoughby E-8
Willoughby Hills E-8
Willowby Hills Pg. 101, A-7
Willowick E-8
Willshire H-1
Wilmington L-3
Winchester N-3
Windham F-9
Wintersville H-10
Woodlawn . . Pg. 100, B-4
Woodmere . . Pg. 101, D-7
Woodsfield K-9
Woodville F-4
Wooster G-7
Worthington J-5
Vicinity . . . Pg. 100, B-4
Wyoming . . . . Pg. 100, B-4
Xenia L-3
Yellow Springs K-3
Yorkville J-10
Youngstown F-9
Zanesville K-7

OKLAHOMA
Pages 68-69
Population: 3,025,487
Capital: Oklahoma City
Land Area: 68,655 sq. mi.

Achille J-11
Acme G-8
Ada G-10
Adair C-13
Addington H-9
Afton C-13
Agawam G-8
Agra E-10
Ahloso G-10
Albany H-11
Albert F-8
Albion G-13
Alcorn C-9
Alderson F-12
Aledo E-7
Alex F-9
Alfalfa F-8
Aline C-8
Allen G-11
Alpers G-9
Altus G-6
Alva C-7
Amber F-9
Ames D-8
Amorita B-8
Angora E-6
Antioch G-9
Apache G-8
Apperson C-10
Apple H-12
Aqua Park E-13
Arapaho E-7
Arcadia E-9
Vicinity . . . Pg. 131, A-7
Ardmore H-10
Arnett D-6
Arpelar F-12
Asher G-10
Ashland G-11
Atoka H-11
Atwood F-11
Avant C-11
Avard C-7
Avery E-10
Aydelotte E-10
Babbs G-7
Bache F-12
Bado D-7
Balko C-5
Bald Hill E-12
Balko C-5
Barnesdall C-11
Barr D-8
Bartlesville C-11
Battiest G-13
Baum H-11
Bearden F-11
Beggs E-11
Bellvue E-11
Belva C-7
Bengal G-13
Bennington H-11
Bernice C-13
Bessie E-7
Bethany . . . . Pg. 131, D-2
Bethel H-13
Bethel Acres F-10
Big Cabin D-13
Big Cedar G-13
Bigheart C-11
Billings C-9
Binger F-8
Bison D-9
Bixby D-12
Blackburn D-11
Blackwell C-10
Blair G-6
Blanchard F-9
Blocker F-12
Blue H-11
Boise City C-2
Boley E-11
Bomar J-10
Boswell H-11
Bowlegs F-11
Box E-13
Boyd C-4
Boynton E-12
Brace C-7
Braggs E-12
Braman C-9
Bray G-9
Briartown F-13
Bridgeport E-8
Brinkman F-6
Bristow E-11
Broken Arrow D-11
Broken Bow H-13
Bromide H-11
Brooksville F-10
Brown H-11
Brushy E-13
Bryan's Corner C-4
Bryant F-11
Buffalo C-6
Bugtussle F-12
Bunch E-13
Burbank C-10
Burlington C-8
Burmah G-9
Burns Flat E-7
Butler E-7
Byars G-10
Byng G-10
Byron C-8
Cabiniss F-11

Cache G-8
Caddo H-11
Calvin F-11
Camargo D-7
Canadian F-12
Canadian Club City F-9
Caney H-11
Canton D-8
Capron C-8
Carleton D-8
Carmen C-8
Carnegie F-8
Carney E-10
Carrier C-8
Carter F-6
Cartwright J-10
Cashion E-9
Castle E-11
Caston E-13
Catesby C-6
Catoosa D-12
Cedar Springs F-8
Cement G-8
Centrahoma G-11
Centralia C-12
Ceres D-10
Cestos D-7
Chandler E-10
Chattanooga G-7
Checotah E-12
Chelsea C-12
Cherokee C-8
Chester D-7
Cheyenne E-6
Chickasha F-8
Childers C-12
Chilocco B-10
Chisney F-10
Chloeta C-13
Chockie G-11
Choctaw . . . . Pg. 131, E-7
Choska E-12
Chouteau D-12
Cimmarron City E-9
Claremore D-12
Clayton G-12
Clemscott H-9
Cleo Springs D-8
Cleveland D-11
Clinton E-7
Cloud Chief F-7
Coalgate G-11
Cogar F-8
Colbert J-11
Cole G-9
Coleman H-11
Collinsville D-12
Colony F-8
Comanche H-9
Commerce B-13
Connerville G-11
Cookietown H-8
Cookson E-13
Cooperton G-7
Cora C-7
Cordell F-7
Corinne H-13
Corn F-7
Cornish H-9
Corum H-9
Council Hill E-12
Courtney J-9
Covington D-9
Cowden F-11
Coweta D-12
Cowlington F-13
Coyle D-10
Crawford E-6
Crekola F-12
Crescent D-9
Creta F-6
Criner F-9
Cromwell F-11
Crowder F-12
Curtis C-7
Cushing D-10
Custer City E-7
Cyril G-8
Dacoma C-8
Daisy G-12
Dale F-10
Darwin H-12
Davenport E-10
Davidson H-7
Davis G-10
Deer Creek C-9
Del City . . . . . Pg. 131, F-5
Delaware C-12
Dempsey E-6
Denman E-11
Denver F-13
Depew E-11
Devol H-7
Dewey C-12
Dibble F-9
Dickson H-10
Dill City F-7
Dillworth B-10
Dougherty G-10
Douglas D-9
Dover D-9
Doxey F-6
Drake H-10
Driftwood C-8
Drummond D-8
Drumright D-11
Duke G-6
Dunbar G-12
Duncan G-9
Durant H-11
Durham E-6
Durwood H-10
Dustin F-11
Eagle City D-8
Eakly F-8

Earlsboro F-10
Eason F-10
Eddy C-9
Edith C-7
Edmond . . . . Pg. 131, A-5
El Reno E-8
Eldon D-13
Eldorado G-6
Elgin G-8
Elk City E-6
Elmer G-6
Elmore City G-9
Elmwood C-5
Emet H-10
Empire City G-9
Enid D-9
Enterprise F-12
Erick F-6
Eubanks G-12
Eufaula F-12
Eva C-3
Fair Oaks D-12
Fairfax C-10
Fairland C-13
Fairmont D-9
Fairview D-8
Fallis E-10
Fallon F-12
Fanshawe F-13
Fargo D-6
Farris H-12
Faxon G-8
Fay E-7
Featherston F-12
Felt C-2
Fewell G-13
Fillmore H-11
Finley H-12
Fireworks City
. . . . Pg. 131, G-2
Fittstown G-10
Fitzhugh G-10
Fleetwood H-9
Fletcher G-8
Floris B-5
Folsom H-11
Foraker C-11
Forest Park . . Pg. 131, D-5
Forgan B-5
Fort Arbuckle G-9
Fort Cobb F-8
Fort Gibson E-13
Fort Supply C-6
Fort Towson H-13
Forty One F-7
Foss E-7
Fowler E-10
Fox H-9
Foyil C-12
Francis G-10
Frederick G-7
Freedom C-7
Gage D-6
Gans F-13
Gansel D-9
Garber D-9
Garvin H-13
Gate C-5
Gay H-12
Geary E-8
Gene Autry H-10
Gerty G-11
Gibbon B-8
Gideon D-13
Glencoe D-10
Glenpool D-11
Glover H-13
Goldsby F-9
Goltry C-8
Goodland H-12
Goodwell C-3
Goodwin D-6
Gore E-13
Gotebo F-7
Gould G-6
Gowen G-12
Gracemont F-8
Grady H-9
Grainola B-11
Grandfield H-7
Granite F-6
Grant H-12
Gray C-4
Grayson E-12
Green D-13
Greenfield E-8
Griggs C-3
Grove C-13
Guthrie E-9
Guymon C-3
Haileyville G-12
Hall Park F-9
Hammon E-6
Harden City G-11
Hardesty C-4
Hardy B-10
Harmon D-6
Harrah E-10
Hartshorne G-12
Haskell E-12
Hastings H-8
Hayward D-9
Haywood G-11
Hayworth J-13
Headrick G-7
Healdton H-9
Heavener G-13
Hectorville E-12
Helena C-8
Hennepin G-9
Hennessy D-9
Henryetta E-11
Hickory G-10

Higgins G-12
Hillsdale C-8
Hinton E-8
Hitchcock D-8
Hobart F-7
Hodgen G-13
Holdenville F-11
Hollis G-6
Hollister H-7
Hollow C-12
Homestead D-8
Hominy D-11
Honobia G-13
Hooker B-4
Hoot Owl D-13
Hopeton C-7
Hough B-3
Howe F-13
Hucmac D-7
Hugo H-12
Hulah B-11
Hulbert D-13
Hulen G-8
Humphreys G-7
Hunter C-9
Huskey H-12
Hydro E-8
Idabel H-13
Indiahoma G-7
Indianola F-12
Ingersoll C-8
Inola D-12
Isabella D-8
Jay C-13
Jefferson C-9
Jenks D-11
Jennings D-11
Jesse G-11
Jet C-8
Jones . . . . . . Pg. 131, C-7
Joy G-10
Kansas D-13
Karma J-11
Karns E-8
Kellyville E-11
Kendrick E-10
Kent H-12
Kenton B-2
Keota F-13
Keyes C-3
Kiamichi G-12
Kildare C-10
Kingfisher E-9
Kingston H-10
Kinta F-13
Kiowa G-11
Knowles C-5
Konawa F-10
Kosoma H-12
Kremlin C-9
Kusa E-12
Lacey D-8
Lahoma D-8
Lake Aluma . . Pg. 131, C-5
Lake Valley G-9
Lamar F-11
Lambert C-8
Lamont C-9
Lane H-11
Langston E-10
Latta G-10
Laverne C-6
Lawton G-8
Leach D-13
Lebanon H-10
Leedey E-7
Lehigh G-11
Lela D-10
Lenapah C-12
Leon H-9
Leonard E-11
Lequire F-13
Letitia G-8
Lewisville F-12
Lexington F-10
Lima F-10
Lincoln G-6
Lindsay F-9
Little Axe F-10
Little City H-10
Loco H-9
Locust Grove D-12
Lone Grove H-9
Lone Wolf F-7
Longdale D-8
Lookeba F-8
Lookout B-7
Lovedale C-6
Loveland H-7
Lovell D-9
Loyal D-8
Lucien D-9
Lugert F-7
Lula G-11
Luther E-10
Lyman G-8
Lyons E-13
Macomb F-10
Madill H-10
Manchester B-9
Mangum F-6
Manitou G-7
Mannsville H-10
Maramac D-10
Marietta H-10
Marland C-10
Marlow G-9
Marshall D-9
Martha F-6
Mason E-11
Maud F-10
May C-6
Mayfield F-6
Maysville G-9

OKLAHOMA

Mazie D-12
McAlester F-12
McBride H-11
McCurtain F-13
McLoud E-10
McQueen G-6
McWillie C-8
Mead H-10
Medford C-9
Meeker E-10
Meers G-8
Meno D-8
Meridian E-10
Messer H-12
Miami C-13
Middleberg F-9
Midwest City Pg. 131, E-6
Milburn H-11
Milfay E-11
Mill Creek G-10
Millerton H-13
Milo H-9
Milton F-13
Minco F-9
Mocane B-5
Moore ..... Pg. 131, H-5
Mooreland C-7
Morris E-12
Morrison D-10
Mounds E-11
Mountain View .. H-12
Moyers H-12
Mulhall D-9
Muskogee E-12
Mustang F-9
Mutual D-7
Narcissa C-13
Nardin C-9
Nash C-8
Nashoba G-13
Navina E-9
Nebo H-10
New Alluwe C-12
New Eucha D-13
New Prue D-11
New Ringold H-13
New Tulsa D-12
New Woodville .. H-10
Newcastle F-9
  Vicinity .. Pg. 131, J-2
Newkirk C-9
Nichols Hills Pg. 131, C-4
Nicoma Park Pg. 131, D-7
Nida H-11
Ninnekah F-9
Noble F-9
Norge F-8
Norman F-9
  Vicinity .. Pg. 131, K-5
North Miami B-13
Nowata C-12
Numa C-9
Oakland H-10
Oaks C-13
Oakwood D-7
Ochelata C-12
Octavia G-13
Oilton D-11
Okeene D-8
Okemah F-11
Okesa C-11
Okfuskee E-11
Oklahoma City ..
  Vicinity ...... Pg. 131
Okmulgee E-11
Oleta H-12
Olney G-11
Olustee G-6
Omega E-8
Onapa F-12
Oneta D-12
Oologah D-12
Optima C-4
Ord H-12
Orienta D-7
Orion D-7
Orlando D-9
Osage D-11
Ottawa C-13
Overbrook H-10
Owasso D-12
Owen B-11
Ozark G-7
Paden E-11
Panama F-13
Panola F-12
Paoli G-10
Patton C-13
Pauls Valley ... G-10
Pawhuska C-11
Pawnee D-10
Payne C-9
Pearson F-10
Pearsonia C-11
Peggs D-13
Peoria B-13
Perkins D-10
Perry D-10
Pershing C-11
Petersburg H-9
Pharoah F-11
Phillips G-11
Picher B-13
Pierce F-12
Pink F-10
Pittsburg G-12
Plainview C-7
Platter H-11
Poccasset F-9
Ponca City C-10
Pond Creek C-9
Pontotoc G-11
Pooleville G-9
Porter E-12

Porum F-13
Poteau F-13
Prague E-10
Preston E-11
Proctor D-13
Pryor D-12
Pumpkin Center . G-8
Purcell F-9
Purdy G-9
Putnam D-8
Pyramid Corners C-12
Quapaw B-13
Quay D-10
Quinlan C-7
Quinton F-12
Ralston C-10
Ramona C-11
Randlett H-8
Rankin E-6
Ratliff City ... G-9
Rattan H-12
Ravia H-10
Reagan H-10
Red Bird E-12
Red Oak F-13
Red Rock D-10
Redden G-12
Reed F-6
Remus C-7
Renfrow B-9
Retrop F-7
Reydon E-6
Rhea E-7
Richards Spur .. G-8
Ringling H-9
Ringold H-12
Ringwood D-8
Roberta H-11
Rocky F-7
Roff G-10
Roll E-6
Roosevelt G-7
Rose D-13
Rosedale G-10
Rosston C-6
Rubottom H-9
Rush Springs ... G-9
Ryan H-9
Saddle Mountain G-7
Saint Louis F-10
Salem F-12
Salina D-13
Sallisaw E-13
Salt Fork C-9
Sand Springs ... D-11
Sapulpa D-11
Sasakwa F-10
Sayre F-6
Scraper D-13
Scullin G-10
Seiling D-7
Selman C-6
Seminole F-11
Sentinel F-7
Shamrock E-11
Sharon D-6
Shattuck D-6
Shawnee F-10
Shidler C-11
Skedee D-10
Skiatook D-11
Slapout C-6
Slaughterville . F-9
Slick E-11
Smithville G-13
Smith Village Pg. 131, E-5
Snow G-12
Snyder G-7
Soper H-12
South Coffeyville C-12
Southard D-8
Sparks E-10
Spear H-11
Spencer .. Pg. 131, D-6
Sperry D-11
Spiro F-13
Springer H-10
Stanley G-12
Steadman G-11
Stecker F-8
Sterling G-8
Stidham F-12
Stigler F-13
Stillwater D-10
Stilwell E-13
Stonewall G-11
Stratford G-10
Stringtown G-11
Strong City E-6
Stroud E-11
Stuart G-11
Sturgis B-3
Sugden H-9
Sulphur G-10
Summerfield G-13
Summit E-12
Sumner D-10
Sumpter C-10
Surrey Hills ... B-3
Sweetwater E-6
Sylvian F-11
Tabler F-9
Taft E-12
Tahlequah D-13
Talala C-12
Talihina G-13
Tallant C-11
Taloga D-7
Tangier C-6
Tatums G-9
Taylor H-8
Tecumseh F-10
Tegarden C-7
Temple H-8

Terlton D-11
Terral H-9
Texola E-6
The Village . Pg. 131, C-3
Thomas E-7
Three Sands C-10
Tiawah D-12
Tipton G-7
Tonkawa C-10
Trail D-7
Tribbey F-10
Trousdale F-10
Troy H-10
Tryon E-10
Tullahassee E-12
Tulsa D-11
Tupelo G-11
Turpin C-4
Tushka H-11
Tuskahoma G-13
Tuttle F-9
Tyrone B-4
Unger H-12
Union City F-8
Utica H-11
Valley Brook Pg. 131, F-5
Valliant H-13
Vanoss G-10
Velma G-9
Vera C-12
Verdigris D-12
Vernon F-11
Vian E-13
Vici D-7
Vinita C-12
Vinson F-6
Wade H-11
Wadena H-12
Wagoner D-12
Wakita C-9
Wanette F-10
Wapanucka H-11
Warner E-12
Warr Acres . Pg. 131, C-4
Warren G-7
Warwick E-10
Waters H-8
Watonga E-8
Watova C-12
Watson G-13
Waukomis D-8
Waurika H-8
Wayne F-10
Waynoka C-7
Weatherford E-7
Webb City C-10
Webbers Falls .. E-12
Welch C-13
Weleetka F-11
Wellston E-10
Welty E-11
Westport D-11
Wetumka F-11
Wewoka F-11
Wheeless C-2
White Bead G-9
White Oak C-12
Whitefield F-12
Whitesboro G-13
Wilburton F-12
Willis J-10
Willow F-6
Wilson H-9
Wolco C-11
Woodford H-10
Woodlawn Park ..
  .... Pg. 131, D-2
Woodward D-7
Wyandotte C-13
Wynnewood G-10
Wynona C-11
Yale D-10
Yeager F-11
Yewed C-8
Yost D-10
Yuba J-11
Yukon E-9
Zeb E-13
Zena C-13

OREGON
Pages 70-71
Population: 2,633,105
Capital: Salem
Land Area: 98,184 sq. mi.

Adair Village .. D-3
Adams C-9
Adel J-7
Adrian G-11
Agness H-1
Albany D-3
Algoma J-5
Alicel C-10
Allegany F-2
Alpine E-3
Alsea E-3
Amity D-3
Andrews J-9
Antelope D-6
Applegate J-2
Arlington C-7
Arock H-10
Ashland J-3
Ashwood D-6
Astoria A-3
Athena C-9
Aurora D-4
Azalea H-3
Baker E-10

Bandon G-1
Banks B-3
Barlow C-4
Barview C-4
Bay City C-2
Beatty J-5
Beaver C-2
Beaverton . Pg. 137, E-4
Belknap Springs E-4
Bend F-5
Biggs C-6
Birkenfeld B-3
Blalock C-7
Blodgett D-2
Blue River E-4
Bly J-5
Boardman B-8
Bonanza J-5
Bonneville C-5
Boring C-5
Breitenbush Springs . D-5
Bridge G-2
Bridgeport E-10
Brightwood C-5
Broadbent G-2
Brogan F-10
Brookings J-1
Brooks C-3
Brothers F-6
Brownsville E-4
Burns G-8
Burns Jct. J-9
Butte Falls H-4
Buxton B-3
Camas Valley ... G-2
Camp Sherman .. E-5
Canby C-4
Cannon Beach ... B-2
Canyon City E-9
Canyonville H-2
Carlton C-3
Cascade Locks .. C-5
Cascadia E-4
Cave Junction .. J-2
Cecil C-7
Central Point .. J-3
Charleston G-1
Chemult G-5
Cheshire E-3
Chiloquin H-5
Christmas Valley . H-6
Clackamas . Pg. 137, G-6
Clatskanie A-3
Cloverdale C-2
Coburg E-3
Colton C-4
Columbia City .. B-3
Condon D-7
Coos Bay F-1
Coquille G-2
Corvallis D-2
Cottage Grove .. F-3
Council Crest Pg. 137, E-4
Cove C-10
Crabtree D-4
Crane G-9
Crawfordsville . E-4
Crescent G-5
Crescent Lake .. G-4
Creswell F-3
Culp Creek F-3
Culver E-5
Curtin F-3
Cushman E-2
Dairy J-5
Dallas D-3
Days Creek H-3
Dayton C-3
Dayville E-8
Dee B-5
Deer Island B-3
Denmark G-1
Depoe Bay D-2
Detroit D-4
Dexter F-3
Diamond H-9
Diamond Lake ... G-4
Dillard G-2
Disston F-4
Donald C-4
Dorena F-4
Drain F-3
Drew H-3
Drewsey F-9
Dufur C-6
Dunes City F-2
Durkee E-10
Eagle Creek C-4
Eagle Point J-3
Eastside G-2
Echo C-8
Eddyville D-3
Elgin C-10
Elk City E-2
Elkton F-2
Elmira E-3
Enterprise C-11
Estacada C-5
Eugene E-3
Falls City D-3
Falls Creek F-4
Fields J-9
Flora B-11
Florence E-2
Forest Grove ... C-3
Fort Klamath ... H-4
Fort Rock G-6
Fossil D-7
Fox E-8
Frenchglen H-8
Friend C-6
Gales Creek B-3
Gardiner F-2
Garibaldi B-2
Gaston C-3

Gates D-4
Gaylord H-2
Gearhart A-2
Gervais C-4
Gibbon C-9
Gilchrist G-5
Gladstone . Pg. 137, G-6
Glenada E-2
Glendale H-2
Gleneden Beach . D-2
Glenwood B-3
Glide G-3
Goble B-4
Gold Beach H-1
Gold Hill H-3
Goshen E-3
Government Camp C-5
Grand Ronde C-3
Grangeville B-12
Granite D-9
Grants Pass H-2
Grass Valley ... C-6
Graveford G-2
Greenhorn E-9
Gresham C-4
Haines D-10
Halfway D-11
Halsey E-3
Hamilton D-8
Hammond A-2
Hampton G-6
Harbor J-1
Hardman D-7
Harlan D-2
Harper F-10
Harrisburg E-3
Hebo C-2
Heceta Beach ... E-2
Helix B-9
Heppner C-8
Hereford E-10
Hermiston B-8
Hillsboro C-3
Hillsdale . Pg. 137, E-4
Hines G-8
Holley E-4
Homestead D-11
Hood River B-5
Horton Blachly . E-3
Hoskins D-3
Hubbard C-4
Huntington E-10
Idanha D-5
Ideyld Park G-3
Imbler C-10
Imnaha C-11
Independence ... D-3
Ione C-8
Ironside E-10
Irrigon B-8
Island City C-10
Jacksonville ... J-3
Jamieson F-10
Jasper E-4
Jefferson D-4
Jewell B-3
John Day E-9
Jordan Valley .. H-10
Joseph C-11
Junction City .. E-3
Juntura G-9
Kamela C-9
Keizer D-3
Keno J-4
Kent C-7
Kerby J-2
Kernville D-2
Kimberly D-7
King City . Pg. 137, G-2
Kings Valley ... D-2
Kinzua D-8
Klamatch Agency H-4
Klamath Falls .. J-4
La Grande C-10
La Pine G-5
Lacomb D-4
Lafayette C-3
Lake Grove . Pg. 137, G-3
Lakecreek J-3
Lakeside F-1
Lakeview J-7
Langlois G-1
Lawen G-9
Leaburg E-4
Lebanon D-4
Lexington C-7
Lincoln Beach .. D-2
Lincoln City ... D-2
Lonerock D-7
Long Creek E-8
Lorane F-3
Lostine C-11
Lowell F-3
Lyons D-4
Mabel E-4
Madras E-6
Malin K-5
Manning B-4
Manzanita B-2
Mapleton E-2
Marcola E-4
Marion D-4
Maupin C-6
Mayville D-7
McCredie Springs F-4
McKenzie Bridge E-5
McMinnville C-3
McNary B-8
Meacham C-9
Medford J-3
Medical Springs D-10
Merlin H-2
Merrill K-5
Metolius E-6

Metzger ... Pg. 137, F-2
Midland J-5
Mikkalo C-7
Mill City D-4
Millersburg D-3
Millican F-6
Milo H-3
Milton Freewater B-10
Milwaukie . Pg. 137, F-5
Minam C-10
Mission C-9
Mist B-3
Mitchell E-7
Mohawk E-4
Mohler B-2
Molalla C-4
Monmouth D-3
Monroe E-3
Monument D-8
Moro C-6
Mosier C-6
Mount Hood C-5
Mount Vernon ... E-8
Mt. Angel C-4
Mulino C-4
Multnomah . Pg. 137, E-3
Murphy J-2
Myrtle Creek ... G-3
Myrtle Point ... G-1
Nehalem B-3
Neskowin C-2
Netarts C-2
New Bridge E-11
New Princeton .. G-9
Newberg C-3
Newport D-2
North Bend F-2
North Plains ... B-4
North Powder ... D-10
Norway G-1
Noti E-3
Nyssa F-11
O'Brien J-2
Oak Grove . Pg. 137, G-5
Oakland G-3
Oakridge F-4
Oceanside C-2
Odell C-5
Olene J-5
Ontario F-11
Ophir H-1
Oregon City C-4
Otis D-2
Otter Rock D-2
Owyhee F-11
Pacific City ... C-2
Paisley H-6
Parkdale C-5
Paulina F-7
Pendleton C-8
Philomath D-3
Phoenix J-3
Pilot Rock C-9
Pinehurst J-4
Pistol River ... J-1
Pleasant Hill .. F-3
Pleasant Valley E-10
Plush J-7
Port Orford H-1
Portland ....
  Vicinity ...... Pg. 137
Post E-7
Powell Butte ... E-6
Powers H-2
Prairie City ... E-9
Prescott B-4
Prineville E-6
Prospect H-4
Rainier B-4
Raleigh Hills Pg. 137, E-3
Redmond E-5
Reedsport F-2
Remote G-2
Rhododendron ... C-5
Richland E-11
Riddle G-2
Riley G-8
Ritter D-8
Riverton G-1
Rockaway B-2
Rogue River H-3
Rome H-10
Roseburg G-3
Rufus C-7
Saginaw F-3
Saint Helens ... B-4
Saint Paul C-4
Salem D-3
Sandy C-4
Scappoose B-3
Scio D-4
Scottsburg F-2
Seal Rock D-2
Seaside A-2
Selma J-2
Seneca F-8
Shady Cove H-3
Shaniko D-6
Sheaville H-11
Shedd D-4
Sheridan C-3
Sherwood C-3
Siletz D-2
Siltcoos F-2
Silver Lake G-6
Silverton D-4
Sisters E-5
Sitkum G-2
Sixes H-1
Skipanon A-2
Sodaville E-4
South Beach D-2
Sprague River .. J-5
Spray D-7

Springfield E-3
Stanfield B-8
Stayton D-4
Sublimity D-4
Summer Lake H-6
Summerville C-10
Sumner G-2
Sumpter E-9
Sunriver F-5
Sutherlin G-2
Sweethome E-4
Swisshome E-2
Talent J-3
Tangent D-3
Telocaset D-10
Tenmile G-2
Terrebonne E-5
The Dalles C-6
Tidewater E-2
Tiernan E-2
Tigard C-4
Tillamook C-3
Tiller H-3
Timber B-3
Toledo D-2
Trail ....
  Vicinity .. Pg. 136, G-2
Troutdale C-5
Troy B-10
Tualatin C-4
Turner D-3
Tygh Valley C-6
Ukiah D-8
Umapine B-9
Umatilla B-8
Umpqua G-2
Union D-10
Union Creek H-3
Unity E-10
Vale F-10
Valley Falls ... J-6
Valsetz D-2
Veneta E-3
Vernonia B-3
Vida E-4
Waldport E-2
Walker F-3
Wallowa C-10
Walterville E-4
Walton E-2
Wamic C-6
Warm Springs ... D-5
Warren B-4
Warrenton A-2
Wasco C-7
Waterloo E-4
Wedderburn H-1
Wemme C-5
West Fir F-4
West Linn C-4
West Slope . Pg. 137, D-2
West Stayton ... D-3
Westfall F-10
Weston B-9
Westport A-3
Wheeler B-2
White City J-3
Whitney E-9
Wilbur G-3
Wilderville J-2
Willamina C-3
Williams J-3
Willow Creek ... F-10
Wilsonville C-4
Winchester G-3
Winchester Bay . F-1
Winston G-3
Wolfcreek H-2
Wonder H-2
Woodburn C-3
Yachats E-2
Yamhill C-3
Yoncalla F-3
Zigzag C-5

PENNSYLVANIA
Pages 72-73
Population: 11,863,895
Capital: Harrisburg
Land Area: 44,888 sq. mi.

Abington ... Pg. 134, B-6
Academy Gardens
  .... Pg. 134, C-8
Adamstown H-11
Addison K-4
Akron H-11
Alba C-9
Alba ....
  Vicinity .. Pg. 134, F-4
Alburtis G-12
Aldan ..... Pg. 134, F-3
Aliquippa H-2
Allentown G-13
Altoona F-7
Ambler H-13
Ambridge H-2
Andorra ... Pg. 134, A-4
Archbald D-12
Arendtsville ... J-8
Armagh G-4
Aronimink . Pg. 134, E-3
Ashley E-11
Ashville F-6
Athens C-10
Austin D-7
Avalon .... Pg. 136, B-1
Avis D-8
Avonmore G-3
Baden H-2
Bala-Cynwyd Pg. 134, D-4

Baldwin ... Pg. 136, F-5
Bally H-12
Bangor F-13
Barnesboro G-5
Bartram Village
  .... Pg. 134, F-4
Bath G-13
Beaver G-1
Beaver Falls ... F-1
Beavertown F-9
Bedford J-6
Beech Creek E-8
Belle Vernon ... J-2
Bellefonte F-7
Bellevue ....
  Vicinity .. Pg. 136, B-2
Bellwood G-6
Ben Avon .. Pg. 136, A-1
Bendersville ... J-8
Benson H-5
Benton E-10
Berlin J-4
Berrysburg G-9
Berwick F-11
Bessemer F-1
Bethel Park ....
  Vicinity .. Pg. 136, F-4
Bethlehem G-13
Big Beaver F-1
Big Run F-5
Birdsboro G-12
Black Horse Pg. 134, F-1
Blain H-7
Blairsville G-4
Blakely D-12
Blooming Valley C-2
Bloomsburg F-10
Blossburg C-9
Blue Bell . Pg. 134, A-3
Bolivar H-4
Boswell H-4
Bowmanstown F-12
Boyertown H-12
Brackenridge ... G-3
Bradford C-6
Brentwood . Pg. 136, F-4
Briar Creek F-11
Bridgeport . Pg. 134, B-2
Bridgeville H-2
Bristol J-14
Broad Axe . Pg. 134, A-4
Broad Top City . H-6
Brockway E-5
Brookhaven J-13
Brookville .....
  Vicinity .. Pg. 136, G-1
Brookville E-4
Broomall .. Pg. 134, D-2
Brownstown H-5
Brownsville J-2
Bruin E-3
Bryn Athyn . Pg. 134, A-7
Bryn Mawr . Pg. 134, D-2
Burgettstown ... H-1
Burlington C-10
Burnham G-8
Bustleton . Pg. 134, B-7
Butler G-3
Calico Corner Pg. 134, B-9
California J-2
Callensburg E-3
Callery G-2
Cambridge Springs C-2
Canonsburg H-2
Canton D-9
Carbondale D-12
Carlisle H-9
Carmichaels J-2
Carnegie G-2
Carroll Park Pg. 134, D-4
Carroll Valley . K-8
Carrolltown G-5
Cassandra H-5
Castle Shannon
  .... Pg. 136, F-3
Catasauqua G-12
Catawissa F-10
Cedarbrook Pg. 134, B-5
Center Square ..
  .... Pg. 134, A-3
Centerville
  (Washington Cty) . J-2
Centerville
  (Crawford Cty) . C-3
Central City ... J-5
Centre Hall F-7
Chalfont H-13
Chambersburg ... H-7
Charleroi H-2
Cherry Tree G-5
Chester J-13
  Vicinity .. Pg. 134, F-4
Chester Heights J-12
Chester Hill ... F-6
Chestnut Hill Pg. 134, C-4
Chicora F-3
Clairton H-2
Clarendon C-4
Clarion E-4
Clarks Summit .. D-12
Clearfield F-6
Cleona H-10
Clifton Heights
  .... Pg. 134, F-3
Clintonville ... E-3
Clymer G-5
Coalport G-5
Coatesville H-12
Cobbs Creek Pg. 134, D-4
Cochranton D-2
Cokeburg H-2
Collegeville ... H-13
Colling Dale Pg. 134, F-3
Columbia J-10
Colwyn .... Pg. 134, F-4

PENNSYLVANIA

PENNSYLVANIA

Conneautville C-1
Connellsville J-3
Connoquenessing .. F-2
Conshohocken J-13
  Vicinity ... Pg. 134, B-8
Conway G-2
Conyngham F-11
Coopersburg G-13
Cooperstown D-3
Coraopolis G-2
Cornwall H-10
Corry C-3
Corsica E-4
Coudersport C-7
Crafton ..... Pg. 136, D-2
Cranesville C-2
Creekside G-4
Cresson G-5
Cressona G-11
Croydon ..... Pg. 134, B-10
Curwensville F-6
Dallastown J-10
Dalton D-12
Danville F-10
Darby J-13
  Vicinity ... Pg. 134, F-3
Dauphin H-9
Dayton F-3
Deepdale .... Pg. 134, C-1
Delaware Water Gap F-13
Delta K-11
Denver H-11
Derry G-4
Dickson City D-12
Dillsburg J-9
Donegal J-4
Donora H-2
Dormont H-2
  Vicinity ... Pg. 136, D-2
Dover J-9
Downingtown J-12
Doylestown H-13
Dresher ..... Pg. 134, A-8
Driftwood E-6
DuBois E-5
Duboistown E-9
Dudley H-6
Dunbar J-3
Duncannon H-8
Duncansville H-6
Dunmore D-12
Dushore D-10
Eagles Mere D-10
Eagleville .. Pg. 134, A-9
East Berlin J-9
East Brady F-3
East Butler F-3
East Falls .. Pg. 134, D-5
East Greenville . H-12
East Lansdowne
      Pg. 134, D-3
East Mt. Airy Pg. 134, C-5
East Oak Lane
      Pg. 134, C-5
East Stroudsburg . F-13
East Washington .. H-2
Easton G-13
Eastwick .... Pg. 134, F-4
Eau Claire F-3
Ebensburg G-5
Economy G-2
Eddington Park
      Pg. 134, B-9
Eddystone .. Pg. 134, G-2
Edinboro C-2
Edwardsville E-11
Eldred C-6
Elizabethtown ... H-10
Elizabethville .. G-10
Elkland C-8
Ellport F-2
Ellwood City F-2
Elmwood .... Pg. 134, F-4
Elwyn ...... Pg. 134, F-1
Emlenton E-3
Emmaus G-12
Emporium D-6
Ephrata H-11
Erie B-2
Etna .... Pg. 136, B-5
Evans City F-2
Everett J-6
Everson J-3
Factoryville D-12
Fairchance J-3
Fairfield K-8
Fairview B-2
Fairview Village
      Pg. 134, A-1
Falls Creek E-5
Farrell E-1
Fawn Grove K-10
Fentonville . Pg. 134, D-6
Fern Rock .. Pg. 134, C-6
Fitzwatertown Pg. 134, A-5
Fleetwood G-12
Flemington E-8
Flourtown .. Pg. 134, B-4
Folcroft ... Pg. 134, G-3
Ford City F-3
Ford Cliff F-3
Forest City D-12
Forksville D-10
Fort Washington
      Pg. 134, A-4
Forty Fort E-12
Fountain Hill ... G-13
Foxcroft ... Pg. 134, D-2
Frackville F-11
Frankford .. Pg. 134, D-7
Franklin D-3
Franklin Park ... G-2
Freeburg G-9
Freeland F-12

Freemansburg G-13
Freeport G-3
Galeton C-8
Gallitzin G-5
Garrett J-4
Geistown H-5
Germantown . Pg. 134, D-5
Gettysburg K-9
Girard B-2
Gladwyne ... Pg. 134, C-3
Glen Campbell ... F-5
Glen Hope F-6
Glen Rock K-10
Glenolden .. Pg. 134, F-3
Glenside ... Pg. 134, B-6
Gordon G-11
Grampian F-5
Gratz G-10
Great Bend C-12
Greencastle K-7
Greensboro K-2
Greensburg H-3
Greentree .. Pg. 136, E-2
Greenville D-1
Grove City F-2
Halifax G-9
Hallstead C-12
Hamburg G-11
Hanover K-9
Harmonville Pg. 134, B-3
Harmony F-2
Harrisburg H-9
Harrisville F-3
Harveys Lake D-11
Hastings G-5
Hatboro H-13
Havertown .. Pg. 134, D-3
Hawley D-13
Hawthorn E-4
Hazleton F-11
Heidelberg . Pg. 136, E-1
Herndon G-9
Hershey H-10
Hollidaysburg ... H-6
Holmesburg . Pg. 134, C-7
Homer City G-4
Homestead .. Pg. 136, E-6
Honesdale D-13
Honey Brook J-12
Hooversville H-5
Hop Bottom C-12
Hopewell H-6
Houston H-2
Houtzdale F-6
  Vicinity .. Pg. 147, A-10
Hughesville E-10
Hulmeville . Pg. 134, A-9
Hummelstown H-10
Huntingdon G-7
Huntingdon Valley
      Pg. 134, B-7
Hydetown C-3
Hyndman K-5
Indian Lake J-5
Indiana G-4
Industry G-1
Ingram ..... Pg. 136, D-1
Irvona F-5
Ithan ...... Pg. 134, C-1
Jackson Center .. E-2
Jacobus J-10
Jamestown D-1
Jeanette H-3
Jeddo F-12
Jefferson F-12
Jeffersonville Pg. 134, A-2
Jenkintown . Pg. 134, B-6
Jennerstown H-4
Jermyn D-12
Jersey Shore E-9
Jim Thorpe F-12
Johnsonburg D-5
Johnstown H-5
Juniata .... Pg. 134, D-6
Kane C-5
Karns City F-3
Kennett Square .. J-12
Kensington . Pg. 134, E-6
King of Prussia
      Pg. 134, B-1
Kingston E-12
Kistler H-7
Kittanning F-3
Knox E-3
Knoxville C-8
Kulpmont F-10
Kutztown G-12
Lake City B-2
Lancaster J-11
Landisburg H-8
Lanesboro C-12
Langhorne H-14
Langhorne Manor
      Pg. 134, A-9
Lansdale H-13
Lansdowne .. Pg. 134, E-3
Lansford F-12
Laporte D-10
Larchmont Meadows
      Pg. 134, E-1
Latrobe H-4
Laureldale G-12
Lawn Crest . Pg. 134, C-7
Lawrence Park
      Pg. 134, D-2
Le Raysville F-13
Lebanon H-10
Leesport G-11
Lehighton F-12
Lemoyne H-9
Levittown H-14
Lewisberry H-9
Lewisburg F-9
Lewistown G-8

Lexington Park
      Pg. 134, C-7
Liberty D-9
Ligonier H-4
Lilly H-5
Lincoln H-11
Linesville C-1
Lititz J-11
Little Meadows .. C-11
Littlestown K-9
Liverpool G-9
Lock Haven E-8
Logan ...... Pg. 134, D-6
Loganton E-8
Loretto G-5
Lower Burrell ... G-3
Lumar Park . Pg. 134, B-8
Lumber City F-5
Lykens G-10
Macungie G-12
Mahanoy City F-11
Manayunk ... Pg. 134, D-4
Manchester J-10
Manheim J-11
Manns Choice J-5
Mansfield C-9
Marble Hall Pg. 134, B-4
Marcus Hook K-13
  Vicinity .. Pg. 134, F-3
Marianna J-2
Marietta J-10
Marion Center ... F-4
Marklesburg H-6
Mars G-2
Martinsburg H-6
Marysville H-9
Masontown J-2
Matamoras D-14
Mayfair .... Pg. 134, C-7
McKean B-2
McKeesport H-2
McSherrytown K-9
McVeytown G-7
Mckee's Rocks
      Pg. 136, C-2
Meadville D-2
Mechanicsburg ... H-9
Media ...... Pg. 134, F-1
Mercer E-2
Mercersburg K-7
Meshoppen D-11
Meyersdale K-4
Middleburg G-9
Middletown H-10
  Vicinity .. Pg. 134, C-9
Midland G-1
Mifflinburg F-9
Mifflintown G-8
Milesburg F-7
Milford E-14
Mill Creek H-7
Mill Hall E-8
Mill Village C-2
Millbourne . Pg. 134, D-3
Millerbrook Pg. 134, C-8
Millersburg G-9
Millerstown G-9
Millersville J-10
Millheim F-8
Millridge .. Pg. 134, D-2
Milton F-9
Minersville G-11
Mohnton H-11
Monaca G-2
Monessen H-2
Monroe C-10
Monroeville H-3
Mont Alto J-8
Montoursville ... E-9
Montrose C-12
Moosic D-12
Morrisville H-14
Morton ..... Pg. 134, C-5
Moscow E-12
Mountville J-10
Mt. Carmel F-10
Mt. Holly Springs J-9
Mt. Jewett C-5
Mt. Joy J-10
Mt. Pleasant H-3
Mt. Pocono E-13
Mt. Union H-7
Mt. Wolf J-10
Murrysville H-3
Myerstown H-11
Nanticoke E-12
Nanty-Glo G-5
Narberth ... Pg. 134, D-3
  Vicinity .. Pg. 134, D-3
Nazareth G-13
Nescopeck F-11
New Albany D-10
New Alexandra ... H-3
New Beaver F-1
New Berlin F-9
New Bethlehem ... F-4
New Brighton F-2
New Buffalo G-9
New Castle F-2
New Centerville . J-4
New Cumberland .. H-9
New Eagle H-2
New Florence H-4
New Freedom K-10
New Holland J-11
New Kensington .. G-3
New Lebanon D-2
New Milford C-12
New Oxford J-9
New Paris J-5
New Philadelphia F-11
New Salem J-2
New Stanton H-3
New Wilmington .. E-1

Newburg F-5
Newburg J-8
Newport G-9
Newry H-6
Newtown Heights
      Pg. 134, E-1
Newtown Square
      Pg. 134, D-1
Newville
Nicetown-Tioga
      Pg. 134, D-5
Nicholson D-12
Normandy ... Pg. 134, B-8
Norristown J-13
  Vicinity .. Pg. 134, A-2
Norritonville Pg. 134, A-2
North Apollo G-3
North Belle Vernon H-2
North East B-3
North Hills . Pg. 134, B-5
North Wales H-13
North York J-10
Northampton G-12
Northumberland .. F-10
Norwood .... Pg. 134, F-3
Nuangola E-11
Oakland C-12
Oakmont G-3, D-4
Ohiopyle J-3
Oil City D-3
Old Forge D-12
Olyphant D-12
Orangeville E-10
Orbisonia H-7
Orrstown J-8
Orwigsburg G-11
Osceola Mills ... F-6
Oswayo C-7
Overbrook .. Pg. 134, D-4
Oxford K-11
Palmerton F-12
Palmyra H-10
Parker E-3
Parkesburg J-11
Parkside ... Pg. 134, G-2
Patton G-5
Paxton G-9
Pen Argyl F-13
Penfield E-5
Penn Square Pg. 134, A-2
Pennsburg H-13
Perkasie H-13
Petersburg G-7
Petrolia F-3
Philadelphia .... Pg. 134
Philipsburg F-6
Phoenixville H-12
Picture Rocks ... E-10
Pillow G-9
Pine Grove G-10
Pittsburgh G-2
  Vicinity ...... Pg. 136
Pittston E-12
Platea B-2
Pleasantville
  (Venango Cty) .. D-3
Pleasantville
  (Bedford Cty) .. H-5
Plum G-3
Plumville F-4
Plymouth Valley
      Pg. 134, B-3
Point Marion K-2
Polk D-2
Port Allegany ... C-6
Port Carbon G-11
Port Matilda F-7
Port Royal G-8
Portage H-5
Portersville F-2
Portland F-13
Pottstown H-12
Pottsville G-11
Prospect Park
      Pg. 134, G-2
Punxsutawney F-4
Pymble ..... Pg. 134, F-1
Quakertown G-13
Quarryville J-11
Radnor ..... Pg. 134, C-2
Rainsburg J-5
Ramey F-6
Reading H-12
Red Hill H-13
Red Lion J-10
Renovo E-7
Reynoldsville ... E-5
Rices Landing ... J-2
Richland H-11
Richlandtown H-13
Richmond ... Pg. 134, D-6
Ridgway D-5
Ridley Park Pg. 134, G-2
Rimersburg E-3
Ringtown F-11
Riverside F-10
Roaring Spring .. H-6
Robesonia H-11
Rockledge .. Pg. 134, B-6
Rockwood J-4
Rome C-11
Rose Valley Pg. 134, F-1
Rosemont ... Pg. 134, D-2
Roseto F-13
Roseville C-9
Roslyn ..... Pg. 134, B-6
Rosslyn Farms
      Pg. 136, D-1
Rouseville D-3
Roxborough . Pg. 134, C-4
Royersford H-12
Rural Valley F-4
Rutledge ... Pg. 134, G-2
Saegertown C-2

Saint Clair G-11
Saint Marys D-5
Saint Petersburg E-3
Salisbury K-4
Saladasburg G-3
Saltillo H-7
Saltsburg G-3
Sandy Lake D-2
Sankertown G-5
Saxonburg F-3
Saxton H-6
Sayre C-10
Scalp Level H-5
Schuylkill Haven G-11
Scottdale H-3
Scranton D-12
Selinsgrove F-9
Sellersville H-13
Seward H-4
Shade Gap H-7
Shamokin F-10
Shamokin Dam F-9
Sharon E-1
Sharon Hill Pg. 134, F-3
Sharpsburg . Pg. 136, B-5
Shenandoah F-11
Shickshinny E-11
Shillington H-11
Shinglehouse C-6
Shippensburg J-8
Shippenville E-3
Shirleysburg H-7
Shoemakersville . G-11
Shrewsbury K-10
Sligo E-3
Slippery Rock ... E-2
Smethport C-6
Smithfield K-3
Snow Shoe F-7
Society Hill Pg. 134, D-5
Somerset J-4
Somerton ... Pg. 134, B-8
Souderton H-13
South Bethlehem . F-4
South Coatesville J-12
South Connellsville J-3
South Fork H-5
South Philadelphia
      Pg. 134, F-5
South Renovo E-7
South Waverly ... B-10
South Williamsport E-9
Spangler G-5
Spartansburg C-3
Spring City H-12
Spring Grove J-9
Spring Mill Pg. 134, C-3
Springboro C-1
Springfield Pg. 134, F-2
Stanwood ... Pg. 134, B-9
State College ... F-7
Stillwater E-10
Stoneboro D-2
Stoystown J-4
Strasburg J-11
Strattanville ... E-4
Strausstown G-11
Stroudsburg F-13
Sugar Grove B-4
Sugarcreek D-3
Summerhill H-5
Summerville E-4
Summit Hill F-12
Sunbury F-10
Suscon ..... Pg. 134, E-4
Susquehanna C-12
Swarthmore . Pg. 134, F-2
Sykesville B-9
Sylvania B-9
Tamaqua F-12
Tatamy G-13
Taylor D-12
Telford H-12
Temple H-11
Terre Hill H-11
Thompsontown ... G-8
Thornburg .. Pg. 136, D-1
Three Springs ... H-7
Tidioute C-4
Timberlake . Pg. 134, E-1
Tioga B-9
Titusville D-3
Topton G-12
Towanda C-10
Tower City G-10
Townville C-3
Trainer J-13
Trappe H-12
Tremont G-10
Trooper .... Pg. 134, A-1
Troutville F-5
Troy C-10
Tullytown H-14
Tunkhannock D-11
Tyrone G-6
Union City C-3
Union Dale C-11
Uniontown J-3
Upland ..... Pg. 134, G-2
Upper Fairview
      Pg. 134, A-1
Upper Roxborough
      Pg. 134, C-4
Ursina K-4
Vandergrift G-3
Venango C-2
Villanova .. Pg. 134, D-2
Walnutport G-12
Wampum F-1
Warren C-4
Washington H-2
Waterford C-2
Waterloo Mills Pg. 134, D-1

Watsontown E-9
Wattsburg B-3
Waymart D-13
Wayne ...... Pg. 134, C-1
Waynesboro K-8
Waynesburg J-2
Weatherly F-12
Wellersburg K-5
Wellsboro C-8
Wellsville J-9
Wesleyville B-2
West Brownsville J-2
West Chester J-12
West Conshohocken
      Pg. 134, C-3
West Easton G-13
West Gate Hills
      Pg. 134, D-3
West Grove K-12
West Hazleton ... F-11
West Homestead
      Pg. 136, E-5
West Kensington
      Pg. 134, D-6
West Kittanning . F-3
West Liberty F-3
West Middlesex .. E-1
West Mifflin H-3
  Vicinity .. Pg. 136, G-5
West Newton H-3
West Oak Lane
      Pg. 134, C-5
West Philadelphia
      Pg. 134, D-4
West Pittston ... E-12
West Reading H-11
West View .. Pg. 136, A-2
West York J-10
Westfield C-8
Westmont H-5
Westover F-5
Wheatland E-1
White Haven E-12
White Marsh Pg. 134, A-6
White Oak G-12
Whitehall G-12
  Vicinity .. Pg. 136, G-5
Wilkes-Barre E-12
Wilkinsburg G-3
Williamsburg G-6
Williamsport E-9
Williamstown G-10
Willow Grove Pg. 134, A-6
Wilson G-13
Wind Gap F-13
Windber H-5
Winterstown H-10
Womelsdorf H-11
Woodbury H-6
Worthington F-3
Wrightsville J-10
Wyalusing D-11
Wyola ...... Pg. 134, D-1
Wyomissing H-11
Yardley H-14
Yeadon J-13
  Vicinity .. Pg. 134, F-4
York J-10
York Springs J-9
Youngsville C-4
Youngwood H-3
Zelienople F-2

SOUTH CAROLINA
Pages 64-65
Population: 3,121,820
Capital: Columbia
Land Area: 30,203 sq. mi.

RHODE ISLAND
Page 25
Population: 947,154
Capital: Providence
Land Area: 1055 sq. mi.

Ashton E-8
Auburn F-9
Barrington F-10
Berkeley F-10
Bristol G-10
Carolina H-9
Charlestown H-9
Chepachet F-8
Clayville F-9
Cranston F-9
East Greenwich .. G-9
East Providence . F-10
Esmond F-9
Exeter G-9
Fiskeville G-9
Foster Center ... F-8
Glocester F-8
Greene G-8
Harmony F-9
Harrisville F-8
Homestead G-10
Hope G-9
Hope Valley G-8
Jamestown G-9
Lippitt F-9
Little Compton .. G-11
Mapleville F-9
Middletown G-10
Millville F-9
Narragansett Pier H-9
Nasonville F-8
Newport G-10
Nooseneck G-9
North Foster F-8
North Scituate .. F-9
North Tiverton .. G-10

Pascoag E-8
Pawtucket F-10
Portsmouth G-10
Providence F-10
Slatersville E-9
Usquepaug G-9
Vernon F-9
Wakefield H-9
Warren F-10
Warwick G-10
Washington F-9
West Greenwich .. G-8
Westerly H-8
Wickford G-9
Wood River Jct. . H-8
Woodville H-8
Woonsocket E-9

SOUTH CAROLINA
Pages 64-65
Population: 3,121,820
Capital: Columbia
Land Area: 30,203 sq. mi.

Abbeville F-4
Adams Run J-7
Aiken G-5
Allendale H-6
Almeda J-6
Anderson F-4
Andrews G-9
Antreville F-4
Appleton H-6
Awendaw H-8
Aynor F-9
Ballentine F-6
Bamberg H-6
Barnwell H-6
Batesburg G-6
Bayboro F-9
Belton E-4
Bennettsville ... E-8
Bethany F-5
Bethune F-7
Bishopville F-7
Blacksburg D-5
Blackville H-6
Blenheim E-8
Bonneau H-8
Bowman H-7
Boykin F-7
Bradley F-4
Branchville H-6
Brownsville E-8
Buffalo E-5
Bullock Creek ... E-5
Cades G-8
Cainhoy H-8
Calhoun Falls ... F-4
Camden F-7
Canadys H-7
Carlisle E-6
Cassatt F-7
Cayce G-6
Centenary F-9
Central E-3
Chappells F-5
Charleston J-8
Chelsea K-7
Cheraw E-8
Chesnee D-5
Chester E-6
Chesterfield E-8
Clarkshill G-5
Clemson E-3
Cleveland D-4
Clinton F-5
Clio E-8
Clover E-6
Columbia F-6
Conway F-9
Cool Spring F-9
Cresent Beach ... G-10
Cross H-7
Cross Hill F-5
Cross Keys E-5
Dalzell F-7
Darlington F-7
De Kalb F-7
Debidue Beach ... H-6
Denmark H-6
Dillon E-8
Dovesville E-8
Due West F-4
Edgefield G-5
Edgemoor E-6
Edisto Beach J-8
Edisto Island ... J-7
Effingham F-8
Ehrhardt H-6
Elgin F-6
Enoree E-5
Estill H-6
Eureka G-5
Evergreen F-5
Fair Bluff F-9
Fairfax H-6
Filbert D-6
Florence F-8
Floydale F-9
Folly Beach J-8
Forest Beach K-7
Foreston G-7
Fork J-8
Fork Shoals E-4
Fort Mill D-6
Fountain Inn E-5
Furman J-6
Gaffney D-5
Galivants Ferry . F-9
Garden City G-9

Gardens Corner .. J-7
Garnett J-6
Georgetown G-9
Givhans H-7
Goose Creek H-8
Gourdin G-8
Gownesville D-4
Grays J-6
Great Falls E-6
Greeleyville G-8
Green Pond J-7
Green Sea F-9
Greenville E-4
Greenwood F-4
Greer E-4
Hampton J-6
Hanahan H-8
Hannah G-8
Hardeeville K-6
Hartsville F-7
Hickory Grove ... F-9
Hickory Grove ... D-5
Hilda H-6
Hilton Head Island K-7
Holly Hill H-7
Honea Path E-4
Indiantown G-8
Inman D-4
Islandton H-7
Isle of Palms ... J-8
Iva F-4
Jackson H-5
Jacksonboro J-7
James Island J-8
Jamestown H-8
Jefferson E-7
Jenkinsville F-6
Joanna F-5
Johnston G-5
Jonesville E-5
Kershaw E-7
Kingsburg F-9
Kingstree G-8
Kitchings Mill .. G-5
Kline H-6
Lake City G-8
Lamar F-7
Lancaster E-6
Landrum D-4
Lane F-8
Latta F-8
Laurens E-5
Leeds E-5
Lena J-6
Lesslie E-6
Lewis E-6
Lexington F-6
Liberty E-4
Litchfield Beach G-9
Little River F-10
Lockhart E-5
Lodge H-6
Loris F-9
Manning G-7
Manville F-7
Marietta D-4
Marion F-9
Martin H-5
Mauldin E-4
Mayesville F-7
McBee E-7
McColl E-8
McConnells E-6
McCormick G-4
Moncks Corner ... H-8
Mount Pleasant .. J-8
Mountville F-5
Mt. Carmel F-4
Mullins F-9
Myrtle Beach G-10
New Ellenton H-5
New Prospect D-5
Newberry F-5
Nichols F-9
Nine Times E-3
Ninety Six F-5
Nixonville F-9
North G-6
North Augusta ... G-5
North Charleston J-8
Oatland G-9
Oats F-8
Olanta F-8
Olar H-6
Orangeburg G-6
Outland G-9
Owdoms G-5
Pacolet E-5
Pageland E-7
Pamplico F-8
Parksville G-5
Patrick E-7
Pauline E-5
Pawleys Island .. G-9
Pelion G-6
Pendleton E-3
Pickens E-4
Pineland J-6
Pineville G-7
Pinewood G-7
Plum Branch G-4
Pontiac F-6
Prosperity F-5
Pumpkintown E-4
Rantowles J-8
Rhems G-8
Richburg E-6
Ridgeland J-6
Ridgeville H-7
Ridgeway F-6
Rock Hill E-6
Rockton F-6
Rockville J-8
Rocky Bottom E-3

Ruby . . . E-7
Salters . . . G-8
Saluda . . . F-5
Sampit . . . H-9
Sandy Run . . . G-6
Santee . . . G-7
Sardinia . . . G-8
Sardis . . . F-8
Scranton . . . F-8
Seneca . . . E-3
Sharon . . . E-6
Simpson . . . F-6
Simpsonville . . . E-4
Smallwood . . . F-6
Smoaks . . . H-7
Society Hill . . . E-8
Spartanburg . . . E-5
Springfield . . . G-6
St. George . . . H-7
St. Matthews . . . G-7
St. Stephen . . . G-8
Starr . . . F-4
Stateburg . . . F-7
Steedman . . . G-6
Stoney Hill . . . F-5
Stuckey . . . G-9
Sullivans Island . . . J-8
Summerton . . . G-7
Summerville . . . H-7
Sumter . . . G-7
Surfside Beach . . . G-9
Switzerland . . . K-6
Sycamore . . . H-6
Tamassee . . . E-3
Tatum . . . E-8
Taylor . . . E-4
Tillman . . . J-6
Timmonsville . . . F-8
Tradesville . . . E-7
Travelers Rest . . . E-4
Trenton . . . G-5
Ulmer . . . H-6
Union . . . E-5
Varnville . . . J-6
Wagener . . . G-6
Walhalla . . . E-3
Walterboro . . . J-7
Ward . . . G-5
Ware Shoals . . . F-4
Wateree . . . G-7
Wells . . . H-7
Westminster . . . E-3
Westville . . . E-7
Whitehall . . . J-8
Whitmire . . . E-5
Willington . . . F-4
Williston . . . H-5
Winnsboro . . . F-6
Woodruff . . . E-5
Yauhannah . . . G-9
Yemassee . . . J-7
Yonges Island . . . J-8
York . . . D-6

SOUTH DAKOTA
Page 74
Population: 690,768
Capital: Pierre
Land Area: 75,952 sq. mi.

Aberdeen . . . C-8
Agar . . . C-6
Akaska . . . C-6
Albee . . . F-10
Alcester . . . E-8
Alexandria . . . D-10
Alpena . . . C-9
Altamont . . . C-9
Andover . . . D-10
Arlington . . . D-10
Armour . . . E-8
Artas . . . B-6
Artesian . . . E-8
Ashton . . . D-10
Astoria . . . D-10
Aurora . . . D-10
Badger . . . D-9
Bancroft . . . D-9
Batesland . . . F-4
Belle Fourche . . . C-2
Belvidere . . . E-5
Beresford . . . F-10
Bison . . . B-3
Blunt . . . D-6
Bonesteel . . . F-7
Bowdle . . . C-9
Bradley . . . C-9
Brandon . . . E-10
Brandt . . . D-10
Brentford . . . C-8
Bristol . . . C-9
Britton . . . D-8
Broadland . . . D-8
Brookings . . . D-10
Bruce . . . D-10
Bryant . . . D-9
Buffalo . . . B-2
Buffalo Gap . . . E-2
Burke . . . E-6
Bushnell . . . D-10
Butler . . . C-9
Camp Crook . . . B-2
Canova . . . E-9
Canton . . . F-10
Carthage . . . D-9
Castle Rock . . . C-2
Cavour . . . D-9
Centerville . . . F-9
Central City . . . D-2
Chamberlain . . . E-7
Chelsea . . . C-8

Claire City . . . B-9
Clark . . . C-9
Clear Lake . . . D-10
Colman . . . E-10
Colton . . . E-9
Columbia . . . B-8
Conde . . . C-8
Corona . . . C-10
Corsica . . . E-8
Cottonwood . . . E-4
Cresbard . . . C-7
Crooks . . . E-10
Custer . . . E-2
Dallas . . . F-6
Dante . . . F-8
Deadwood . . . D-2
Dell Rapids . . . E-10
Delmont . . . E-8
Dimock . . . E-8
Doland . . . D-8
Dolton . . . E-9
Draper . . . E-5
Dupree . . . C-4
Eagle Butte . . . C-5
Eden . . . B-9
Edgemont . . . E-2
Elk Point . . . G-10
Elm Springs . . . D-3
Emery . . . E-9
Enning . . . D-3
Erwin . . . D-9
Estelline . . . D-9
Ethan . . . E-8
Eureka . . . B-7
Fairburn . . . E-2
Fairfax . . . F-7
Fairpoint . . . C-3
Fairview . . . F-10
Faith . . . C-4
Farmer . . . E-8
Farmingdale . . . D-3
Faulkton . . . C-7
Flandreau . . . E-10
Florence . . . D-9
Fort Pierre . . . D-6
Fort Thompson . . . D-7
Frankfort . . . C-8
Frederick . . . B-8
Freeman . . . F-9
Fruitdale . . . C-2
Fulton . . . E-8
Gann Valley . . . D-7
Garden City . . . C-9
Garretson . . . E-10
Gary . . . D-10
Gayville . . . F-9
Geddes . . . F-8
Gettysburg . . . C-6
Glad Valley . . . B-4
Glenham . . . B-6
Goodwin . . . C-10
Greenwood . . . F-8
Gregory . . . F-7
Grenville . . . C-9
Groton . . . C-8
Hammer . . . B-9
Harrisburg . . . F-10
Harrold . . . D-6
Hayti . . . D-9
Hecla . . . B-8
Hermosa . . . E-2
Herreid . . . B-6
Herrick . . . F-7
Highmore . . . D-7
Hill City . . . D-2
Hillsview . . . B-7
Hitchcock . . . D-8
Hosmer . . . B-7
Hot Springs . . . E-2
Houghton . . . B-8
Hoven . . . C-6
Howard . . . E-9
Howes . . . D-4
Huron . . . D-8
Interior . . . E-4
Ipswich . . . C-7
Irene . . . F-9
Iroquois . . . D-9
Isabel . . . B-5
Java . . . B-6
Jefferson . . . G-10
Kadoka . . . E-4
Kennebec . . . E-6
Keystone . . . D-2
Kimball . . . E-7
Kranzburg . . . C-10
Kyle . . . E-4
La Bolt . . . C-10
La Plant . . . C-6
Lake Andes . . . F-8
Lake City . . . B-9
Lake Preston . . . D-9
Lane . . . E-8
Langford . . . B-9
Lead . . . D-2
Lebanon . . . C-6
Lee's Corner . . . E-7
Lemmon . . . B-4
Lennox . . . F-10
Leola . . . B-7
Letcher . . . E-8
Lily . . . C-9
Little Eagle . . . B-5
Lodgepole . . . B-3
Long Lake . . . B-7
Long Valley . . . E-4
Lowry . . . C-6
Loyalton . . . B-7
Ludlow . . . B-3
Lyman . . . E-6
Madison . . . E-9
Marion . . . F-9
Martin . . . F-4

Marty . . . F-8
Marvin . . . C-10
Maurine . . . C-3
McIntosh . . . B-5
McLaughlin . . . B-5
Meadow . . . B-4
Mellette . . . C-8
Menno . . . F-9
Midland . . . D-5
Milbank . . . C-10
Miller . . . D-7
Mission . . . F-5
Mitchell . . . E-8
Mobridge . . . B-6
Monroe . . . E-9
Montrose . . . E-9
Morristown . . . B-4
Mound City . . . B-6
Mount Vernon . . . E-8
Mud Butte . . . C-3
Murdo . . . E-5
Naples . . . D-9
New Effington . . . B-10
Newell . . . C-2
Nisland . . . C-2
North Sioux City . . . G-10
Northville . . . C-8
Nunda . . . E-9
Oacoma . . . E-6
Oelrichs . . . E-2
Oglala . . . F-3
Okreek . . . E-5
Oldham . . . D-9
Olivet . . . F-9
Onaka . . . C-7
Onida . . . D-6
Opal . . . C-3
Orient . . . C-7
Ortley . . . C-9
Parker . . . F-9
Parkston . . . F-8
Parmelee . . . E-5
Philip . . . D-4
Pierpont . . . C-9
Pierre . . . D-6
Pine Ridge . . . F-3
Plainview . . . D-3
Plankinton . . . E-8
Platte . . . F-7
Pollock . . . B-6
Prairie City . . . B-3
Presho . . . E-6
Pringle . . . E-2
Provo . . . E-1
Pukwana . . . E-7
Quinn . . . D-4
Ramona . . . E-9
Rapid City . . . D-3
Ravinia . . . F-8
Raymond . . . C-9
Red Owl . . . C-3
Red Shirt . . . E-3
Redfield . . . C-8
Redig . . . B-2
Ree Heights . . . D-7
Reliance . . . E-7
Revillo . . . C-10
Ridgeview . . . C-5
Rockerville . . . D-2
Rockham . . . C-7
Roscoe . . . C-7
Rosebud . . . F-5
Roslyn . . . C-9
Roswell . . . E-9
Saint Charles . . . F-7
Saint Francis . . . E-5
Saint Lawrence . . . D-7
Salem . . . E-9
Scenic . . . E-3
Scotland . . . F-9
Selby . . . B-6
Seneca . . . C-7
Shadehill . . . B-4
Sharp Corner . . . E-3
Sherman . . . E-10
Sioux Falls . . . E-9
Sisseton . . . B-10
South Shore . . . C-10
Spearfish . . . D-2
Springfield . . . F-8
Stephan . . . D-7
Stickney . . . E-8
Stockholm . . . C-10
Stoneville . . . C-3
Stratford . . . D-8
Sturgis . . . D-2
Summit . . . C-10
Tabor . . . F-8
Tea . . . F-10
Timber Lake . . . C-5
Tolstoy . . . C-7
Toronto . . . D-10
Trail City . . . B-5
Trent . . . E-10
Tripp . . . F-8
Tulare . . . D-8
Turton . . . C-8
Tyndall . . . F-9
Union Center . . . C-3
Veblen . . . B-9
Verdon . . . C-8
Vermillion . . . F-10
Viborg . . . F-9
Vienna . . . D-9
Vilas . . . E-9
Vivian . . . E-6
Wagner . . . F-8
Wakonda . . . F-9
Wall . . . D-4
Wallace . . . C-9
Ward . . . E-10
Wasta . . . D-3
Watertown . . . D-9

Waubay . . . C-9
Webster . . . C-9
Wessington . . . D-7
Wessington Springs . . . E-8
Westport . . . B-8
Wetonka . . . B-8
Wewala . . . F-7
White . . . D-10
White Butte . . . B-4
White Lake . . . E-8
White River . . . E-5
Whitewood . . . D-2
Willow Lake . . . D-9
Wilmot . . . C-10
Winner . . . E-6
Wood . . . E-5
Woonsocket . . . E-8
Worthing . . . F-10
Yale . . . D-9
Yankton . . . F-9
Zeona . . . C-3

TENNESSEE
Pages 38-39
Population: 4,591,120
Capital: Nashville
Land Area: 41,155 sq. mi.

Adams . . . F-6
Adamsville . . . J-4
Aetna . . . H-5
Alamo . . . H-3
Alcoa . . . H-11
Alexandria . . . G-8
Algood . . . G-8
Allardt . . . G-9
Allens . . . E-5
Allisona . . . H-7
Allred . . . G-9
Alpine . . . G-9
Altamont . . . J-8
Alto . . . J-8
Antioch . . . Pg. 124, F-7
Arlington . . . J-2
  Vicinity . . . Pg. 119, A-10
Arrington . . . H-7
Arthur . . . F-11
Ashland City . . . G-6
Ashport . . . H-2
Athens . . . H-10
Atoka . . . H-2
Atwood . . . G-4
Avondale . . . Pg. 124, A-9
Bailey . . . Pg. 119, F-9
Banner Hill . . . G-13
Bartlett . . . J-2
  Vicinity . . . Pg. 119, C-7
Beacon . . . Pg. 124, G-6
Bean Station . . . G-12
Beardstown . . . H-5
Beersheba Springs . . . H-8
Belfast . . . J-7
Bell Buckle . . . H-7
Belle Meade . . . G-6
  Vicinity . . . Pg. 124, E-4
Bellevue . . . Pg. 124, F-2
Bells . . . H-3
Belvidere . . . J-7
Benjestown . . . Pg. 119, B-3
Benton . . . J-10
Berry Hill . . . Pg. 124, E-6
Bethel . . . J-6
Bethel Springs . . . J-4
Big Sandy . . . G-4
Big Springs . . . J-9
Birchwood . . . J-9
Blaine . . . G-11
Bluff City . . . F-13
Bogota . . . G-3
Bolivar . . . J-3
Bolton . . . Pg. 119, A-9
Bon Air . . . H-8
Braden . . . H-2
Bradford . . . G-4
Brentwood . . . G-6
  Vicinity . . . Pg. 124, G-5
Briceville . . . G-10
Brighton . . . H-2
Bristol . . . F-13
Brooklin . . . Pg. 124, G-8
Brownsville . . . H-3
Bruceton . . . G-4
Brunswick . . . Pg. 119, B-8
Bulls Gap . . . G-12
Bumpus Mills . . . F-5
Burlison . . . H-2
Burns . . . G-6
Byrdstown . . . F-9
Calhoun . . . J-10
Camden . . . G-5
Camelot . . . F-12
Capleville . . . J-2
  Vicinity . . . Pg. 119, G-6
Carlisle . . . J-3
Carthage . . . G-8
Caryville . . . G-10
Cash Point . . . J-6
Cedar Hill . . . F-6
Celina . . . F-9
Center Point . . . J-6
Centertown . . . H-7
Centerville . . . H-5
Central . . . G-3
Charleston . . . J-9
Charlotte . . . G-5
Chattanooga . . . J-9
Church Hill . . . F-12
Clarksburg . . . H-4
Clarksville . . . F-5
Cleveland . . . J-9
Clifton . . . J-5

Clinton . . . G-10
Coalmont . . . J-8
Collegedale . . . J-9
Collierville . . . J-2
  Vicinity . . . Pg. 119, F-6
Collinwood . . . J-5
Columbia . . . H-6
Cookeville . . . G-8
Copperhill . . . J-10
Cordova . . . Pg. 119, D-8
Cornersville . . . J-6
Cosby . . . H-11
Covington . . . H-2
Crab Orchard . . . H-9
Cross Plains . . . F-6
Crossville . . . H-9
Culleoka . . . H-6
Cumberland City . . . G-5
Cumberland Furnace . . . G-5
Cumberland Gap . . . F-11
Dancyville . . . H-3
Dandridge . . . G-11
Darden . . . H-4
Dayton . . . H-9
Decatur . . . H-9
Decaturville . . . H-5
Decherd . . . J-8
Dibrell . . . H-8
Dickson . . . G-5
Dixon Springs . . . G-8
Donelson . . . G-7
  Vicinity . . . Pg. 124, D-7
Dover . . . F-5
Dowelltown . . . G-8
Doyle . . . H-8
Dresden . . . G-4
Ducktown . . . J-10
Dunlap . . . J-9
Dyer . . . G-3
Dyersburg . . . G-3
Eads . . . Pg. 119, C-10
Eagan . . . F-10
East Ridge . . . J-9
Eastview . . . J-4
Egypt . . . Pg. 119, B-6
Elizabethton . . . G-13
Elkton . . . J-6
Ellandale . . . Pg. 119, B-7
Elmore Park . . . Pg. 119, C-7
Elora . . . J-7
Elza . . . G-10
Englewood . . . J-10
Erin . . . G-5
Erwin . . . G-13
Estill Springs . . . J-7
Ethridge . . . J-6
Etowah . . . J-10
Evensville . . . H-9
Fairview . . . H-6
Farmington . . . J-6
Fayetteville . . . J-6
Finley . . . G-3
Fisherville . . . Pg. 119, D-10
Flat Woods . . . H-5
Flatcreek . . . J-7
Forbus . . . F-9
Forest Hill . . . Pg. 119, F-8
Forest Hills . . . Pg. 124, F-4
Foster Corners . . . Pg. 124, F-8
Franklin . . . H-6
Friendship . . . G-3
Fruitvale . . . H-3
Gadsden . . . H-3
Gainesboro . . . G-8
Gallatin . . . G-7
Gates . . . H-3
Gatlinburg . . . H-11
Germantown . . . Pg. 124, B-8
Germantown . . . J-2
  Vicinity . . . Pg. 119, E-8
Gibson . . . G-3
Gildfield . . . Pg. 119, A-8
Gilt Edge . . . H-2
Gleason . . . G-4
Goodlettsville . . . G-7
  Vicinity . . . Pg. 124, A-6
Goodspring . . . J-6
Gordonsville . . . G-8
Gower . . . Pg. 124, E-3
Grand Junction . . . J-3
Grandview . . . H-9
Gray . . . G-13
Graysville . . . H-9
Green Hill . . . Pg. 124, C-9
Greenback . . . H-10
Greenbrier . . . F-6
Greeneville . . . G-12
Greenfield . . . G-4
Grimsley . . . G-9
Habersham . . . F-10
Haletown . . . J-8
Halls . . . G-3
Halls Crossroads . . . G-11
Hampshire . . . H-5
Hampton . . . G-13
Hanging Limb . . . G-9
Harriman . . . H-10
Harrogate . . . F-11
Hartsville . . . G-7
Henderson . . . H-4
Hendersonville . . . G-7
  Vicinity . . . Pg. 124, A-8
Henning . . . H-2
Henry . . . G-4
Hermitage Hills . . . Pg. 124, C-8
Hickory Valley . . . J-3
Highland . . . G-9
Hohenwald . . . H-5
Hopewell . . . Pg. 124, J-3
Hornsby . . . J-3
Humboldt . . . H-3
Hunter . . . G-13

Huntingdon . . . G-4
Huntland . . . J-7
Huntsville . . . G-10
India . . . G-4
Inglewood . . . G-7
  Vicinity . . . Pg. 124, C-6
Iron City . . . J-5
Isham . . . F-10
Ivydell . . . G-10
Jacksboro . . . G-10
Jackson . . . H-3
Jamestown . . . G-9
Jasper . . . J-8
Jefferson City . . . G-11
Jellico . . . F-10
Joelton . . . G-6
  Vicinity . . . Pg. 124, A-4
Johnson City . . . G-13
Jonesboro . . . G-12
Keeling . . . H-2
Kelso . . . J-7
Kenton . . . G-3
Kimbro . . . Pg. 124, G-5
Kingsport . . . F-13
Kingston . . . H-10
Kirkland . . . H-7
Knoxville . . . H-10
Kodak . . . H-11
Kyles Ford . . . F-12
La Vergne . . . G-7
  Vicinity . . . Pg. 124, G-9
LaFollette . . . G-10
Laager . . . J-8
Lafayette . . . F-8
Lake City . . . G-10
Lake Mont . . . H-10
Lakesite . . . J-9
Lancing . . . G-9
Lascassas . . . H-7
Latham . . . G-4
Lawrenceburg . . . J-5
Leach . . . G-4
Lebanon . . . G-7
Leipers Fork . . . H-6
Lenoir City . . . H-10
Lenow . . . Pg. 119, C-9
Lewisburg . . . H-6
Lexington . . . H-4
Liberty . . . G-8
Lickton . . . Pg. 124, A-5
Little Creek . . . Pg. 124, B-5
Livingston . . . G-8
Lobelville . . . H-5
Locke . . . J-2
Loretto . . . J-5
Loudon . . . H-10
Lucy . . . Pg. 119, A-6
Luttrell . . . G-11
Lutts . . . J-5
Lyles . . . H-6
Lynchburg . . . J-7
Lynnville . . . J-6
Madisonville . . . H-10
Malesus . . . H-3
Manchester . . . H-7
Marrowbone . . . Pg. 124, C-1
Martin . . . G-4
Maryville . . . H-10
Mason . . . H-2
Maury City . . . H-3
Mayland . . . J-8
Maynardville . . . G-10
McBurg . . . J-6
McEwen . . . G-5
McKenzie . . . G-4
McMinnville . . . H-8
Medina . . . H-3
Medon . . . H-3
Memphis . . . J-1
  Vicinity . . . Pg. 119
Mercer . . . H-3
Michie . . . J-4
Middleton . . . J-3
Midtown . . . H-10
Milan . . . H-4
Milledgeville . . . J-4
Milligan College . . . G-13
Millington . . . J-2
Minor Hill . . . J-6
Miston . . . G-2
Monteagle . . . J-8
Monterey . . . G-9
Morganton . . . H-9
Morris Chapel . . . J-4
Morrison . . . H-7
Morristown . . . G-11
Moscow . . . J-3
Mosheim . . . G-12
Moss . . . F-9
Mound City . . . Pg. 119, C-2
Mount Carmel . . . F-12
Mount Crest . . . H-9
Mount Juliet . . . G-7
  Vicinity . . . Pg. 124, C-10
Mount Olive . . . H-11
Mount Pleasant . . . H-6
Mount Vernon . . . J-10
Mount Zion . . . Pg. 124, A-2
Mountain City . . . F-14
Munford . . . H-2
Murfreesboro . . . H-7
Nashville . . . G-7
  Vicinity . . . Pg. 124
New Hope . . . K-8
New Johnsonville . . . G-5
New Market . . . G-11
New River . . . G-10
New Tazwell . . . G-11
Newbern . . . G-3
Newport . . . H-11
Niota . . . H-10
Nixon . . . J-4
Nobles . . . G-4

Norris . . . G-10
Nunnelly . . . H-5
Oak Hill . . . Pg. 124, F-6
Oak Ridge . . . G-10
Oakdale . . . G-9
Oakland . . . J-2
  Vicinity . . . Pg. 119, F-5
Oakwood . . . F-5
Obion . . . G-3
Ocoee . . . J-9
Oglesby . . . Pg. 124, G-6
Old Hickory . . . Pg. 124, B-8
Olivehill . . . J-4
Oliver Springs . . . G-10
Oneida . . . F-10
Palmer . . . J-8
Palmyra . . . F-5
Parago Mill . . . Pg. 124, F-7
Paris . . . G-4
Parrottsville . . . G-12
Parsons . . . H-4
Pasquo . . . Pg. 124, F-3
Peakland . . . H-9
Pegram . . . G-6
Pelham . . . J-8
Petersburg . . . J-6
Philadelphia . . . H-10
Pigeon Forge . . . H-11
Pikeville . . . H-9
Pinewood . . . H-5
Pinson . . . H-4
Pisgah . . . G-11
Pleasant Hill . . . G-8
Pleasant View . . . G-6
Portland . . . F-7
Providence . . . G-7
  Vicinity . . . Pg. 124, F-7
Pulaski . . . J-6
Puncheon Camp . . . G-11
Puryear . . . F-4
Quebeck . . . H-8
Raleigh . . . J-2
  Vicinity . . . Pg. 119, B-6
Ramer . . . J-4
Ramsey . . . Pg. 124, F-6
Raus . . . J-7
Rayon City . . . Pg. 124, B-7
Red Bank . . . J-9
Red Boiling Springs . . . F-8
Riceville . . . J-10
Richland . . . Pg. 124, D-3
Rickman . . . G-8
Ridgely . . . G-2
Ridgetop . . . G-6
Ripley . . . H-2
Rives . . . G-3
Roan Mountain . . . G-13
Robbins . . . G-9
Rockwood . . . H-9
Rocky Fork . . . J-2
Rogersville . . . G-12
Rossville . . . J-2
Rural Hill . . . Pg. 124, F-8
Russellville . . . G-12
Rutherford . . . G-3
Rutledge . . . G-11
Sadlersville . . . F-6
Saint Bethlehem . . . F-5
Saint Joseph . . . J-5
Sale Creek . . . J-9
Saltillo . . . J-4
Sardis . . . H-4
Saundersville . . . Pg. 124, A-9
Savannah . . . J-4
Scotts Hill . . . H-4
Selmer . . . J-4
Seven Points . . . Pg. 124, E-9
Sevierville . . . H-11
Sewanee . . . J-8
Shacklett . . . G-6
Shady Valley . . . F-13
Sharon . . . G-3
Shelby Farms . . . Pg. 119, D-7
Shelbyville . . . H-7
Shooks Gap . . . H-11
Shop Springs . . . G-7
Signal Mtn. . . . J-8
Silver Point . . . G-8
Skiem . . . J-6
Smartt . . . H-8
Smith Springs . . . Pg. 124, F-8
Smithville . . . G-8
Smyrna . . . G-7
Sneedville . . . F-11
Soddy-Daisy . . . J-9
Somerville . . . J-2
South Carthage . . . G-8
South Dyersburg . . . G-3
South Fulton . . . F-3
South Pittsburg . . . J-8
Sparta . . . H-8
Spencer . . . H-8
Spring City . . . H-9
Spring Creek . . . H-4
Spring Hill . . . H-6
Spring Lake . . . Pg. 119, B-7
Springfield . . . F-6
Stanton . . . H-2
Sullivan Gdn. . . . F-12
Summertown . . . J-5
Sunbright . . . G-10
Surgoinsville . . . F-12
Sweetwater . . . H-10
Sycamore . . . Pg. 124, A-1
Taft . . . J-6
Tarpley . . . J-6
Tazewell . . . F-11
Tellico Plains . . . J-10
Tennessee Ridge . . . G-5
Timberlake . . . H-4
Tiptonville . . . F-3
Toone . . . J-3
Tracy City . . . J-8
Trenton . . . G-3

Trezevant . . . G-4
Triune . . . H-7
Troy . . . G-3
Tullahoma . . . J-7
Tusculum . . . G-13
  Vicinity . . . Pg. 124, F-6
Una . . . Pg. 124, F-7
Unicoi . . . G-13
Union City . . . G-3
Union Grove . . . J-9
Union Hill . . . Pg. 124, A-5
Vaughlans Gap . . . Pg. 124, F-4
Victoria . . . J-8
Viola . . . H-8
Violet . . . J-10
Vonore . . . H-10
Waco . . . J-6
Walden . . . J-9
Walkertown . . . J-4
Walling . . . H-8
Wartburg . . . G-10
Wartrace . . . H-7
Watertown . . . G-8
Waverly . . . G-5
Waynesboro . . . J-5
Webber City . . . J-5
West Meade . . . Pg. 124, E-4
West Shiloh . . . J-4
Westmoreland . . . F-7
White Bluff . . . G-6
White House . . . F-7
White Pine . . . G-12
Whites Creek . . . Pg. 124, B-4
Whitesburg . . . G-12
Whiteville . . . J-3
Whitwell . . . J-8
Wilder . . . G-9
Williston . . . J-3
Winchester . . . J-7
Winfield . . . F-10
Woodbury . . . H-8
Woodland Mills . . . F-3
Woodstock . . . Pg. 119, B-5
Wrencoe . . . Pg. 124, G-7
Wyanoke . . . Pg. 119, E-1
Wynnburg . . . G-3

TEXAS
Pages 75-79
Population: 14,229,191
Capital: Austin
Land Area: 262,017 sq. mi.

Abernathy . . . E-7
Abilene . . . G-10
Acala . . . J-2
Ackerly . . . G-7
Acme . . . D-10
Adamsville . . . J-12
  Vicinity . . . Pg. 109, D-1
Addicks . . . L-15
Addison . . . Pg. 105, A-8
Adrian . . . C-7
Agua Dulce . . . P-12
Aiken . . . E-8
Alamo . . . Pg. 142, D-5
Alanreed . . . C-9
Alba . . . F-15
Albany . . . G-10
Aldine . . . L-15
Aledo . . . F-12
Alexander . . . H-12
Alfred . . . P-12
Algoa . . . M-16
Alice . . . P-12
Alief . . . Pg. 109, E-2
Allamoore . . . J-3
Allen . . . F-14
Alleyton . . . L-14
Allison . . . B-10
Allred . . . F-6
Almeda . . . Pg. 109, G-4
Alpine . . . K-5
Altair . . . M-14
Alto . . . H-16
Alvarado . . . G-13
Alvin . . . M-16
Alvord . . . E-12
Amarillo . . . C-7
Ambrose . . . E-14
Ames . . . L-16
Amherst . . . E-7
Anderson . . . K-15
Andice . . . K-12
Andrews . . . G-5
Angleton . . . M-16
Anna . . . E-14
Annona . . . E-16
Anson . . . G-10
Antelope . . . F-12
Anthony . . . H-2
Anton . . . E-7
Apple Springs . . . J-16
Aquilla . . . H-13
Aransas Pass . . . P-13
Archer City . . . F-12
Argyle . . . F-13
Arlington . . . F-13
  Vicinity . . . Pg. 104, E-5
Arp . . . G-15
Artesia Wells . . . P-10
Arthur City . . . D-14
Asherton . . . N-10
Ashtola . . . C-8
Aspermont . . . F-9
Athens . . . G-15
Atlanta . . . F-17
Aubrey . . . E-13
Austin . . . L-13

TEXAS

Austonio J-15
Austwell N-14
Avery F-16
Avinger F-17
Avoca G-10
Azle G-13
Bacliff M-16
Bagwell E-16
Baird G-10
Bakersfield K-7
Balch Springs G-14
  Vicinity . . Pg. 105, E-11
Balcones Heights
  . . . . Pg. 142, D-3
Ballinger H-10
Balmorhea J-5
Bammel . . . . Pg. 109, A-4
Bandera L-11
Bangs H-11
Barclay J-13
Bardwell H-14
Barksdale L-10
Barnhart J-8
Barrett L-16
  Vicinity . . Pg. 109, C-10
Barry H-14
Barstow J-5
Bartlett K-13
Bassett F-16
Bastrop L-13
Batesville N-10
Batson L-16
Bay City M-15
Baytown L-16
  Vicinity . . Pg. 109, E-10
Beasley M-15
Beaumont L-17
  Vicinity . . Pg. 109, C-7
Beckville G-17
Bedias K-15
Bee Cave L-12
Beeville N-12
Belfalls J-13
Bellaire . . . . Pg. 109, E-3
Bellevue E-12
Bellmead H-13
Bells E-14
Bellville L-14
Belmont M-13
Belton J-13
Ben G-15
Ben Arnold J-14
Ben Bolt P-12
Benavides Q-11
Benbrook G-13
Benchley K-14
Benjamin F-10
Bertram K-12
Bettie G-16
Big Lake J-7
Big Sandy G-16
Big Spring H-8
Big Wells N-10
Bigfoot M-11
Birthright F-15
Bishop Q-12
Bivins F-17
Black D-7
Blackwell H-9
Blanco L-11
Blanket H-11
Bleakwood K-18
Bledsoe E-6
Blessing N-15
Blewett M-9
Blooming Grove H-14
Bloomington N-15
Blossom E-15
Blue Mound . . Pg. 104, C-3
Blue Ridge F-14
Bluegrove E-12
Bluff Dale G-12
Bluffton K-11
Boca Chica S-13
Boerne L-11
Bogata F-15
Boling M-14
Bomarton F-10
Bon Wier K-18
Bonham E-14
Booker A-9
Boonsville F-12
Borger B-8
Boston F-17
Bovina D-6
Bowie E-12
Boxelder F-16
Boyd F-13
Boys Ranch Tacosa . . B-7
Brackettville M-9
Bradshaw H-10
Brady J-11
Brandon H-14
Brashear F-15
Brazoria M-15
Breckenridge G-11
Bremond J-14
Brenham L-14
Brice D-9
Bridge City L-18
Bridgeport F-12
Briggs K-12
Briscoe B-9
Broaddus J-17
Bronco F-6
Bronson J-17
Bronte H-9
Brookeland J-17
Brookesmith J-11
Brookshire L-15
Brookside Village
  . . . . Pg. 109, G-6
Brownfield F-7
Brownsboro G-15

Brownsville S-13
Brownwood H-11
Brundage N-10
Bruni Q-11
Bryan K-14
Bryson F-12
Buchanan Dam K-12
Buckholts K-13
Buda L-12
Buena Vista . . Pg. 142, H-5
Buffalo J-14
Buffalo Gap G-10
Bula E-6
Bulcher E-13
Bullard G-16
Buna K-17
Bunavista B-8
Bunker Hill . . Pg. 109, E-3
Burke J-16
Burkett H-10
Burkeville J-18
Burleson G-13
  Vicinity . . Pg. 104, G-3
Burlington J-14
Burnet K-12
Burton L-14
Bushland C-7
Bustamanete R-11
Butler K-13
Byers E-12
Bynum H-14
Cactus A-7
Caddo G-11
Caddo Mills F-15
Caldwell K-14
Calf Creek J-10
Calliham N-12
Calvert K-14
Camden K-16
Cameron K-14
Camilla K-16
Camp Verde L-11
Camp Wood L-10
Campbell F-15
Campbellton N-12
Canadian B-9
Canton G-15
Canutillo H-1
Canyon C-7
Caps G-10
Carbon H-11
Carlos K-15
Carlsbad H-9
Carlton H-12
Carmine L-14
Carmona J-16
Carrizo Springs N-10
Carrollton F-13
  Vicinity . . Pg. 105, A-8
Carta Valley L-9
Carthage H-17
Cash F-14
Cassin . . . . . Pg. 142, H-4
Castle Hills M-11
  Vicinity . . Pg. 142, C-4
Castroville M-11
Catarina N-10
Cayuga H-15
Cedar Creek L-13
Cedar Hill . . . Pg. 105, F-7
Cedar Park K-12
Celeste F-14
Celina F-14
Center H-17
Centerville J-15
Champions . . Pg. 109, A-3
Chandler G-15
Channelview L-16
  Vicinity . . Pg. 109, D-8
Channing B-7
Chapman H-16
Chapman Ranch P-13
Chappell Hill L-15
Charco N-13
Charlotte N-11
Cherokee J-11
Cherry Spring K-11
Chester J-17
Chico F-12
Childress D-9
Chillicothe D-10
Chilton J-13
China L-17
China Grove . . Pg. 142, F-7
Chireno J-17
Chisos Basin M-5
Chriesman K-14
Christine N-11
Christoval J-9
Circle Back E-6
Cisco G-11
Cistern L-13
Clairemont F-9
Clairette H-12
Clarendon C-9
Clarksville E-16
Claude C-8
Clayton H-17
Cleburne G-13
Cleveland K-16
Clifton H-13
Clint H-1
Cloverleaf . . . Pg. 109, D-8
Clute M-15
Clyde G-10
Coady . . . . . Pg. 109, D-10
Coahoma G-8
Cockrell Hill . . Pg. 105, D-6
Coffey City H-15
Coldspring K-16
Coleman H-10

College Station K-14
Colleyville . . . Pg. 104, B-5
Collinsville F-13
Colmesneil K-17
Colorado City G-9
Columbus L-14
Comanche H-11
Combes R-12
Comfort L-11
Commerce F-15
Como F-15
Comstock L-8
Concan M-10
Concepcion Q-12
Concord H-16
Conroe K-16
Converse L-11
Conway C-8
Cooks Point K-14
Cookville F-16
Coolidge H-14
Cooper F-15
Coppell . . . . Pg. 105, A-7
Copperas Cove J-12
Cornudas H-3
Corpus Christi P-13
Corrigan J-16
Corsicana H-14
Coryell City J-13
Cost M-13
Cotton Center E-7
Cottonwood K-15
Cottonwood H-11
Cotulla N-10
Country Campus K-16
Coy City N-12
Coyanosa J-5
Crabbs Prairie K-15
Crandall G-14
Crane J-6
Cranvills Gap H-13
Crawford J-13
Cresson G-13
Crews H-10
Crockett J-15
Crosby L-15
  Vicinity . . Pg. 109, B-9
Crosbyton E-8
Cross K-15
Cross Cut H-11
Cross Plains H-11
Cross Roads H-15
Crow G-16
Crowell E-10
Crowley G-13
  Vicinity . . Pg. 104, F-3
Crystal City N-10
Cuero M-13
Cumby F-14
Cushing H-16
Cut & Shoot K-15
Cypress L-15
Cypress Mill K-12
D'Hanis M-10
Dabney M-9
Dacosta N-14
Daingerfield F-16
Daisetta K-16
Dalhart B-7
Dallas G-14
  Vicinity . . . . . . Pg. 105
Dalworthington Gardens
  . . . . Pg. 104, E-5
Damon M-15
Danbury M-15
Danevang M-15
Darrouzett A-9
Dawn C-7
Dawson H-14
Dayton L-16
De Berry G-17
De Kalb E-16
De Leon H-11
De Wees M-12
DeSoto . . . . . Pg. 105, F-8
Deanville K-14
Decatur F-13
Deer Park L-16
  Vicinity . . Pg. 109, F-9
Del Rio M-8
Del Valle L-12
Dell City H-3
Denison E-14
Denton F-13
Denver City F-6
Deport E-15
Derby N-11
Desdemona H-12
Devers L-17
Devine M-11
Dew H-15
Deweyville K-18
Diana G-16
Diboll J-16
Dickens E-9
Dickinson M-16
Dilley N-11
Dime Box K-14
Dimmitt D-7
Dinero P-12
Divot N-11
Dobbin K-15
Dodd City E-15
Donie J-14
Donna S-12
Doole J-10
Doucette K-17
Dougherty E-8
Douglass H-16
Douglassville F-17
Dozier C-9
Draw F-8
Dripping Springs L-12

Driscoll P-12
Dryden L-7
Dublin H-12
Dumas B-7
Dumont E-9
Duncanville . . Pg. 105, F-7
Dundee E-11
Dunlay M-11
Dunn H-9
Dyersdale . . . Pg. 109, B-7
Eagle Lake M-14
Eagle Pass N-9
Early H-11
Earth D-7
East Columbia M-15
Easterly J-14
Eastland G-11
Easton G-16
Edcouch R-12
Eddy J-13
Eden J-10
Edgecliff . . . Pg. 104, E-3
Edinburg R-12
Edmonson D-7
Edna M-14
Edom G-15
Edroy P-13
Egypt M-14
El Campo . . . Pg. 109, M-14
El Lago . . . . Pg. 109, G-8
El Paso H-2
El Sauz R-10
Elbert F-11
Eldorado K-9
Electra E-11
Elgin L-13
Elkhart H-15
Ellinger L-14
Elmendorf M-12
  Vicinity . . Pg. 142, J-7
Elmo G-15
Elsa R-12
Elysian Fields G-17
Emory F-14
Encinal P-10
Encino Q-12
Energy H-12
Enloe F-15
Ennis G-14
Enochs E-6
Escobas R-11
Estelline D-9
Etoile J-17
Etter B-7
Euless . . . . . Pg. 104, C-6
Eureka H-14
Eustace G-15
Evadale K-17
Evant J-12
Evergreen K-16
Everman . . . . Pg. 104, F-3
Fabens H-1
Fairbanks . . . Pg. 108, C-2
Fairfield H-15
Fairlie F-15
Fairview F-14
Fairview G-8
Fairy H-12
Falcon R-11
Falfurrias Q-12
Falls City N-12
Fannett L-17
Fannin N-13
Farmers Branch
  . . . . Pg. 105, B-8
Farmersville F-14
Farrar J-14
Farwell D-6
Fayetteville L-14
Fedor K-13
Fentress L-13
Ferris G-14
  Vicinity . . Pg. 105, G-10
Fieldton E-7
Fink E-14
Finney E-9
Flatonia M-13
Flomot D-8
Florence J-12
Floresville M-12
Flower Mound
  . . . . Pg. 104, A-6
Floydada E-8
Fluvanna F-8
Follett A-10
Forest J-16
Forest Hill . . Pg. 104, E-4
Forestburg F-13
Forney G-14
Forreston G-14
Fort Clark Springs . . . M-9
Fort Davis K-5
Fort Gates J-12
Fort Griffin G-10
Fort Hancock J-2
Fort McKavett K-10
Fort Stockton J-6
Fort Worth G-13
  Vicinity . . . . . . Pg. 104
Fostoria K-16
Four Corners
  . . . . Pg. 109, D-10
Fowlerton N-11
Frame Switch K-13
Francitas N-14
Frankel City G-6
Franklin J-14
Frankston H-15
Fransworth A-9
Fred K-17
Fredericksburg L-11
Fredonia K-11
Freeport N-16
Freer P-11
Friday J-16

Frio Town M-10
Friona D-6
Frisco F-13
Fritch B-8
Frost H-14
Fruitland F-12
Fruitvale G-15
Fullbright F-16
Fulton P-13
Funston G-10
Gail G-8
Gainesville F-13
Galena Park . . Pg. 109, E-7
Galveston M-16
Ganado M-14
Garden City H-8
Garden Valley G-15
Gardendale H-7
  Vicinity . . Pg. 142, E-7
Garland F-14
  Vicinity . . Pg. 105, B-10
Garrison H-17
Garwood M-14
Gary H-17
Gatesville J-12
Gause K-14
Geneva J-17
George West N-12
Georgetown K-13
Geronimo L-12
Giddings L-13
Gilchrist M-17
Gillett M-12
Gilliland E-10
Gilmer G-16
Girard F-9
Girvin J-7
Gladewater G-16
Glazier B-9
Glen Cove H-10
Glen Flora M-15
Glen Rose H-13
Glenn H-8
Glenn Heights
  . . . . Pg. 105, G-8
Glenrio C-6
Glenwood G-16
Glidden L-14
Gober F-15
Godley G-13
Goldsboro H-10
Goldthwaite J-11
Goliad N-13
Gonzales M-13
Goodland E-6
Goodlett D-10
Goodnight C-8
Goodrich K-16
Gordon G-12
Gordonville E-13
Goree F-10
Gorman H-11
Gouldbusk J-10
Graford F-12
Graham F-11
Granbury G-12
Grand Prairie G-13
  Vicinity . . Pg. 105, D-6
Grand Saline G-15
Grandfalls J-6
Granger K-13
Grapeland J-15
Grapevine . . . Pg. 104, B-6
Grassland F-8
Grayback E-11
Greenville F-15
Grey Forest . . Pg. 142, A-1
Grit K-10
Groesbeck J-14
Groom C-8
Groves L-17
Groveton J-16
Gruver A-8
Gun Barrel City G-14
Gustine H-12
Guthrie E-9
Guy M-14
Hagansport F-15
Hale Center E-7
Halletsville M-14
Hallsville G-16
Haltom City . . Pg. 104, C-3
Hamilton H-12
Hamlin G-9
Hamshire L-17
Happy C-7
Hardin L-17
Hargill R-12
Harker Heights J-13
Harleton G-16
Harlingen S-13
Harper L-10
Harrold E-11
Hart D-6
Hartley B-7
Harwood L-13
Haskell F-10
Haslet . . . . . Pg. 104, A-3
Hatchel H-10
Hawkins G-16
Hawley G-10
Hearne J-14
Hebbronville Q-11
Hebron . . . . Pg. 105, A-8
Hedley C-9
Helena N-13
Helotes . . . . Pg. 142, B-1
Hemleigh G-9
Hemphill J-18
Hempstead L-14
Henderson G-16
Henrietta E-12
Hereford C-6

Hext K-10
Hico H-12
Hidalgo S-12
Higgins B-10
Highbank J-14
Highland Park
  . . . . Pg. 105, C-9
Highlands L-16
  Vicinity . . Pg. 109, D-9
Hill Country Village
  . . . . Pg. 142, A-5
Hillister K-17
Hillsboro H-13
Hillshire Village
  . . . . Pg. 109, D-3
Hilltop Lakes J-14
Hindes N-11
Hitchcock M-16
Hobson N-12
Hochheim M-13
Hockley L-15
Holland K-13
Holliday E-11
Hollywood Park
  . . . . Pg. 142, A-5
Hondo M-11
Honey Grove E-15
Horizon City H-1
Houmont Park
  . . . . Pg. 109, C-7
Houston L-15
  Vicinity . . . . . . Pg. 109
Howe F-14
Howellville . . Pg. 109, E-1
Hubbard H-14
Huckabay G-12
Hudson J-16
Hughes Springs F-16
Hull K-16
Humble L-16
  Vicinity . . Pg. 109, A-7
Hunt L-10
Hunters Creek
  . . . . Pg. 109, D-3
Huntington J-17
Huntsville K-15
Hurlwood E-7
Hurst . . . . . . Pg. 104, C-5
Hutchins G-14
  Vicinity . . Pg. 105, E-10
Hutto K-13
Hye L-11
Idalou E-7
Imperial J-6
Inadale G-9
Independence L-14
Indian Gap J-12
Industry L-14
Inez N-14
Ingleside P-13
Ingram L-11
Iola K-15
Iowa Park E-11
Ira G-8
Iraan K-7
Iredell H-12
Ireland J-12
Irving G-13
  Vicinity . . Pg. 105, C-7
Itasca H-13
Jacinto City . . Pg. 109, D-7
Jacksboro F-12
Jacksonville H-15
Jamestown J-18
Jarrell K-13
Jasper J-17
Jayton F-9
Jean F-11
Jefferson G-17
Jermyn F-12
Jersey Village Pg. 109, C-2
Jewett J-14
Joaquin H-17
Johnson City L-11
Johntown F-16
Jolly E-12
Jollyville . . . Pg. 109, D-5
Jones Creek M-15
Jonesboro H-12
Jonestown K-12
Joshua G-13
Jourdanton N-11
Joy E-12
Junction K-10
Juno L-8
Justiceburg F-8
Justin F-13
Kalgary F-8
Kamay E-11
Kanawha E-16
Karnack G-17
Karnes City N-12
Katemcy K-10
Katy L-15
Kaufman G-14
Keene G-13
Keller . . . . . Pg. 104, B-4
Kellerville C-9
Kemp G-14
Kempner J-12
Kendleton M-15
Kenedy N-12
Kennard J-16
Kennedale . . . Pg. 104, E-4
Kenney L-14
Kent J-4
Kenwood . . . . Pg. 109, B-6
Kerens H-14
Kermit H-5
Kerrville L-11
Kildare G-17
Kilgore G-16
Killeen J-13
Kings Mill C-8

Kingsland K-11
Kingsville Q-12
Kirby . . . . . . Pg. 142, D-6
Kirbyville K-17
Kirkland D-9
Kirvin H-14
Kleburg . . . . Pg. 105, E-11
Knickerbocker J-9
Knippa M-10
Knott G-7
Knox City F-10
Kopperl H-13
Kosse J-14
Kountze K-17
Kress D-7
Krum F-13
Kyle L-12
La Gloria R-11
La Grange L-13
La Grulla R-11
La Joya R-11
La Marque M-16
La Paloma S-13
La Porte . . . Pg. 109, F-10
La Pryor N-10
La Reforma R-12
La Vernia M-12
La Villa R-12
La Ward N-14
Ladonia F-15
Lago Vista K-12
Laguna Park H-13
Lake Hills M-11
Lake Jackson M-15
Lake Worth . . Pg. 104, C-2
Lakeport G-16
Lakeside . . . . Pg. 104, C-1
Lakeside Village H-13
Lakeview D-9
Lamesa G-7
Lamkin H-12
Lampasas J-12
Lancaster G-14
  Vicinity . . Pg. 105, F-9
Lane City M-15
Langtry L-7
Laredo Q-10
Lariat D-6
Lark C-8
Larue H-15
Lasara R-12
Latexo J-15
Lavon F-14
Lawn H-10
LeFors C-9
League City L-15
Leakey L-10
Leander K-12
Leesburg F-16
Leesville M-13
Leggett K-16
Lehman E-6
Leigh G-17
Lela C-9
Lelia Lake C-9
Leming M-12
Lenorah G-7
Leon Springs L-11
Leon Valley L-11
  Vicinity . . Pg. 142, C-2
Leona J-15
Leonard F-14
Levelland E-6
Lewisville F-13
  Vicinity . . Pg. 105, A-6
Lexington K-13
Liberty L-16
Liberty Hill K-12
Libscomb A-9
Lincoln L-13
Lincoln City . . Pg. 108, C-5
Linden F-17
Lindsay F-13
Lingleville H-12
Linus . . . . . Pg. 109, D-10
Littlefield E-7
Live Oak . . . Pg. 142, B-7
Liverpool M-16
Livingston K-16
Llano K-11
Lobo J-3
Lockett E-10
Lockhart L-13
Lockney E-8
Lodi F-17
Loma Alta L-8
Lomax H-8
Lometa J-12
London K-10
Lone Star F-16
Long Branch H-16
Long Mott N-14
Longview G-16
Longworth G-9
Loop F-7
Lopeno R-11
Loraine G-9
Lorena J-13
Lorenzo E-8
Los Angeles N-11
Los Fresnos S-12
Losoya . . . . Pg. 142, J-5
Lott J-13
Louise M-14
Lovelady J-15
Loving F-11
Loyal Valley K-11
Lubbock F-8
Luckenbach L-11
Lueders G-10
Lufkin J-16
Luling L-13
Lumberton K-17

Lutie C-9
Lydia F-16
Lyford R-13
Lynchburg . . Pg. 109, E-9
Lyons K-14
Lytle M-11
Mabank G-15
Macdona . . . Pg. 142, G-1
Madisonville J-15
Magnolia M-15
Malakoff H-15
Malta F-16
Mangus Corner
  . . . . Pg. 142, H-2
Mankins E-11
Mansfield G-13
  Vicinity . . Pg. 104, F-5
Maple E-6
Marathon K-5
Marble Falls K-12
Marfa K-4
Marietta F-17
Marion M-12
Markham M-15
Marlin J-14
Marquez J-15
Marshall G-16
Mart J-14
Martindale L-13
Martinsville H-17
Maryneal G-9
Mason K-11
Masterson B-7
Matador E-8
Matagorda N-15
Mathis P-12
Maud F-17
Mauriceville L-17
Maxwell L-12
May H-11
Maydelle H-16
Maypearl G-13
McAdoo E-8
McAllen S-12
McCamey J-7
McCaulley G-9
McDade L-13
McFaddin N-13
McGregor J-13
McKinney F-14
McLean C-9
McLeod F-17
McMahan L-13
McNair . . . . Pg. 109, D-10
McNary J-2
McQueeney L-12
Meadow F-7
Medicine Mound D-10
Medina L-11
Megargel F-11
Melissa F-14
Melrose H-17
Melvin J-10
Memphis D-9
Menard K-10
Mendoza L-13
Mentone H-5
Mercedes S-12
Meridian H-13
Merkel G-9
Mertzon J-8
Mesquite G-14
  Vicinity . . Pg. 105, C-11
Mexia H-14
Miami B-9
Mico M-11
Midland H-7
Midlothian G-13
Midway K-15
Milam J-18
Milano K-14
Miles H-9
Milford G-13
Millersview J-10
Millett N-11
Millican K-14
Mineola G-15
Mineral N-12
Mineral Wells G-12
Mingus G-12
Mirando City Q-11
Mission S-12
Missouri City . Pg. 109, G-3
Mobeetie C-9
Moline J-12
Monahans H-6
Monkstown E-15
Monroe L-17
Mont Belvieu L-16
Montague E-12
Montalba H-15
Monte Alto R-12
Montgomery K-15
Monthalia M-13
Moody J-13
Moore M-11
Mooring J-14
Moran G-11
Morgan H-13
Morgan Mill G-12
Morgans Point
  . . . . Pg. 109, F-10
Morse B-8
Morton E-6
Morton Valley G-11
Moscow J-16
Moss Hill K-16
Moulton M-13
Mount Calm H-13
Mount Enterprise H-16
Mount Houston
  . . . . Pg. 109, C-6

TEXAS

Mount Pleasant F-16
Mount Sylvan G-15
Mount Vernon F-16
Mountain Home L-10
Muenster E-13
Muldoon L-14
Muleshoe D-6
Mullin J-11
Mumford K-14
Munday F-10
Murchison G-15
Murphy .. Pg. 105, A-11
Myrtle Springs G-15
N. Richland Hills
..... Pg. 104, C-4
Nacogdoches H-16
Nada M-14
Naples F-16
Nash F-17
Natalia M-11
Navasota K-15
Nazareth D-7
Neches H-15
Nederland K-17
Needmore E-6
Needville M-15
Nelsonville L-14
New Baden J-14
New Boston F-17
New Braunfels L-12
New Caney L-15
New Deal E-7
New Gulf M-15
New Home F-7
New London G-16
New Summerfield .. H-16
New Ulm L-14
New Waverly K-15
Newark .... Pg. 104, A-1
Newcastle F-11
Newlin D-9
Newman H-2
Newsome F-16
Newton K-18
Nixon M-13
Nocona G-12
Nolan G-9
Nolanville J-13
Nome K-16
Noodle G-10
Nordheim N-13
Normandy N-9
Normangee J-15
Normanna N-13
North Houston
..... Pg. 109, B-3
North Zulch K-14
Northcrest H-13
Northfield D-9
Norton H-9
Notrees H-6
Novice H-10
Nuevo Laredo P-10
Nursery N-13
O'Brien F-10
O'Donnell F-7
Oak Hill L-12
Oakalla J-12
Oakland M-14
Oakwood H-15
Odem P-13
Odessa H-7
Oglesby J-13
Oilton Q-11
Oklaunion E-11
Old Boston F-17
Old Center H-17
Old Glory F-9
Old Ocean M-15
Olden G-11
Oldenburg L-14
Olivia N-14
Olmito S-13
Olmos Park .. Pg. 142, D-4
Olney F-11
Olton E-7
Omaha F-16
Oplin H-10
Orange L-18
Orange Grove P-12
Ore City F-16
Orla H-5
Osceola H-13
Ottine M-13
Ovalo H-10
Overton .. Pg. 105, G-8
Ovilla .. Pg. 104, G-4
Ozona K-8
Paducah E-9
Paige L-13
Paint Rock J-10
Painview D-7
Palacios N-14
Palestine H-15
Palmer G-14
Palo Pinto G-12
Pampa B-8
Pandora M-13
Panhandle C-8
Panna Maria M-12
Panola G-17
Paradise F-13
Paris E-15
Parnell D-9
Pasadena L-16
Vicinity ... Pg. 109, F-8
Patricia G-7
Patroon H-17
Pattonville E-16
Pawnee N-12
Pearland .. Pg. 109, G-6
Pearsall N-11
Pecos J-5
Peggy N-12

Penwell H-6
Perrin F-12
Perry J-13
Perryton A-9
Petersburg E-8
Petrolia E-12
Pettus N-12
Petty E-15
Pflugerville K-13
Phalba G-15
Pharr S-12
Phillips B-7
Pilot Point F-13
Pine Mills G-16
Pinehurst K-17
Pineland J-17
Piney Pt. .. Pg. 109, E-3
Pioneer H-11
Pipecreek L-11
Pittsburg F-16
Placedo N-14
Plains F-6
Plano F-14
Vicinity ... Pg. 105, A-10
Plantersville K-15
Plata L-4
Pleasanton N-12
Point Comfort N-14
Pollok J-16
Ponder F-13
Ponta H-16
Pontotoc K-11
Poolville F-12
Port Aransas P-13
Port Arthur L-17
Port Bolivar L-16
Port Isabel S-13
Port Lavaca N-14
Port Mansfield R-13
Port Neches L-17
Port O'Connor N-14
Porter L-16
Portland P-13
Posey F-8
Post F-8
Poteet N-11
Poth M-12
Pottsboro E-14
Pottsville H-12
Powderly E-15
Powell H-14
Poynor H-15
Prairie Dell K-13
Prairie Hill H-14
Prairie Lea L-15
Prairie View L-15
Premont Q-12
Presidio L-4
Priddy H-11
Princeton F-14
Pritchett G-16
Proctor H-12
Prosper F-14
Purmela J-12
Putnam G-11
Pyote H-5
Quail C-9
Quanah D-10
Queen City F-17
Quemado N-9
Quinlan G-14
Quitaque D-8
Quitman G-15
Rachal R-12
Ralls E-8
Ramirez Q-12
Randado Q-11
Randlett Charlie .. E-12
Randolph F-14
Ranger G-11
Rankin J-7
Ratcliff J-16
Ravenna E-14
Rayland D-9
Raymondville R-12
Raywood K-16
Reagan J-14
Realitos Q-11
Red Bluff .. Pg. 109, G-10
Red Oak G-13
Vicinity ... Pg. 105, G-4
Red Springs E-10
Redford M-4
Reese Vill. E-7
Refugio P-13
Reklaw H-16
Reno E-15
Retta .... Pg. 104, G-4
Rhome F-13
Ricardo Q-12
Rice H-14
Richardson F-13
Vicinity ... Pg. 105, A-9
Richland G-14
Richland Hills Pg. 104, C-4
Richland Springs .. J-11
Richmond L-15
Richwood M-16
Ridge J-14
Riesel J-13
Ringgold E-12
Rio Grande City .. R-11
Rio Vista G-13
Riomedina M-11
Rios Q-12
Rising Star G-11
River Oaks .. Pg. 104, D-2
Riverside K-15
Riviera Q-12
Roans Prairie K-15
Robbins J-15
Robert Lee H-9
Robinson H-13
Robstown P-13
Roby G-9

Rochelle J-11
Rochester F-10
Rock Island M-14
Rockdale K-14
Rockland J-17
Rockport P-13
Rocksprings L-9
Rockwood J-10
Roganville K-17
Rogers K-13
Roma R-10
Romayor K-16
Roosevelt K-9
Ropesville F-7
Rosanky L-13
Roscoe G-9
Rosebud J-14
Rosenberg M-15
Rosevine J-17
Rosser G-14
Rotan G-9
Round Mountain .. K-12
Round Rock K-13
Round Top L-14
Rowena H-9
Roxton E-15
Royalty J-6
Rule F-10
Runge M-12
Rusk H-16
Rye K-16
Sabinal M-10
Sacul H-16
Sadler E-14
Sagerton F-10
Saginaw .. Pg. 104, C-2
Vicinity ... Pg. 104, C-2
Saint Hedwig M-12
Saint Jo E-13
Salado J-13
Salt Falt H-3
Samnorwood C-9
San Angelo J-9
San Antonio M-12
Vicinity ..... Pg. 142
San Augustine H-17
San Benito S-13
San Diego P-12
San Elizario H-1
San Felipe L-14
San Gabriel K-13
San Isidro R-11
San Juan R-12
San Marcos L-12
San Patricio P-12
San Perlita R-13
San Saba J-11
San Ygnacio Q-10
Sanderson L-6
Sandia P-12
Sanford B-8
Sanger F-13
Sansom Park Pg. 104, C-2
Santa Anna H-11
Santa Elena R-12
Santa Fe L-15
Santa Maria S-12
Santa Rosa S-12
Saragosa J-5
Saratoga K-17
Sarita Q-12
Satsuma .. Pg. 109, B-1
Savoy E-14
Schertz M-12
Schulenburg L-14
Scotland E-11
Scottsville G-17
Scranton G-11
Seabrook L-16
Vicinity ... Pg. 109, G-6
Seadrift N-14
Seagraves F-6
Sealy L-14
Sebastian R-13
Sebastopol K-16
Segovia K-10
Seguin M-12
Seminole G-6
Seven Points G-14
Seymour E-11
Shafter L-4
Shallowater E-7
Shamrock C-9
Shannon F-12
Shavano Park Pg. 142, A-4
Sheffield K-7
Shelbyville H-17
Sheldon L-16
Vicinity ... Pg. 109, C-9
Sheridan M-14
Sherman E-14
Sherwood J-9
Shiner M-13
Shiro K-15
Shoreacres Pg. 109, G-10
Sidney H-11
Sierra Blanca J-3
Silsbee K-17
Silver H-9
Silverton D-8
Simms F-16
Singleton K-15
Sinton P-13
Sisterdale L-11
Sivells Bend E-13
Skellytown B-8
Skidmore P-12
Slaton F-8
Slidell F-13
Slocum H-15
Smiley M-13
Smyer E-7
Snook K-14
Snyder G-8
Socorro H-1

Somerset M-11
Vicinity .. Pg. 142, A-1
Somerville K-14
Sonora K-9
Sour Lake L-17
South Bend F-11
South Houston
..... Pg. 109, F-7
South Padre Island . S-13
South Plains D-8
Southlake .. Pg. 104, B-5
Southland D-7
Southton .. Pg. 142, H-6
Spade E-7
Spanish Fort E-12
Speaks M-14
Spearman B-8
Spicewood K-12
Splendora L-16
Spofford M-9
Spring L-15
Spring Branch L-11
Spring Valley Pg. 109, D-3
Springlake D-7
Springtown F-12
Spur F-9
Spurger K-17
Stafford M-15
Vicinity ... Pg. 109, G-2
Stamford F-10
Stanton H-7
Star J-12
Stephenville H-12
Sterling City H-8
Stinnett B-8
Stockdale M-12
Stoneburg E-12
Stoneham K-15
Stonewall L-11
Stowell L-16
Stratford A-7
Strawn G-11
Streetman H-14
Study Butte M-5
Sudan E-7
Sugar Land L-15
Vicinity ... Pg. 109, G-1
Sullivan City S-11
Sulphur Sprs. F-15
Summerfield D-6
Sumner E-15
Sundown F-6
Sunray B-8
Sunset F-13
Sutherland Springs . M-12
Sweeny M-15
Sweetwater G-9
Swenson F-9
Taft P-13
Tahoka F-7
Talco F-16
Talpa H-10
Tankersley J-9
Tarpley M-10
Tarzan G-7
Tatum G-17
Taylor K-13
Taylor Lake Village
..... Pg. 109, G-9
Teague H-14
Telegraph K-9
Telephone E-14
Telferner N-14
Tell D-9
Temple J-13
Tenaha H-17
Tennesee Colony .. H-15
Tennyson H-9
Terlingua M-5
Terrell G-14
Terrell Hills Pg. 142, D-5
Texarkana F-17
Texas City M-16
Texhoma A-8
Texico D-6
Texline A-6
Thackerville E-13
Thalia E-10
The Grove J-13
The Woodlands L-15
Thelma .... Pg. 142, K-5
Thomaston M-13
Thorndale K-13
Thornton J-14
Thorp Spring G-12
Thrall K-13
Three Rivers N-12
Throckmorton F-11
Tilden N-11
Timpson H-17
Tioga F-13
Tira F-15
Tivoli N-14
Toco E-15
Tolar G-12
Tomball L-15
Tool H-14
Topsey J-12
Tornillo H-1
Toyah J-5
Trent G-10
Trenton F-14
Trickham H-11
Trinidad H-14
Trinity J-15
Troup H-16
Troy J-13
Tucker H-15
Tuleta N-12
Tulia D-7
Turkey D-8
Turnertown H-16
Tuscola H-10
Twin Sisters L-12
Twitty C-9

Tye G-10
Tyler G-16
Tynan P-12
Umbarger C-7
Unity E-15
Universal City M-12
University Park
..... Pg. 105, C-9
Utopia M-10
Uvalde M-10
Valentine K-4
Valera H-10
Valley Mills H-13
Valley Spring K-11
Valley View F-13
Van G-15
Van Alstyne F-14
Van Horn J-3
Van Vleck M-15
Vancourt J-9
Vanderbilt N-14
Vanderpool L-10
Vashti E-12
Vealmoor G-8
Vega C-7
Venus G-13
Vera E-10
Vernon E-11
Victoria N-13
Vidor L-17
Village Mills K-17
Vincent G-8
Voca J-11
Von Ormy .. Pg. 142, H-2
Voss H-10
Votaw K-16
Waco H-13
Wadsworth N-15
Waelder L-13
Waka A-9
Wake Village E-17
Wall J-9
Waller L-15
Wallis L-14
Walnut Sprs. H-13
Warda L-13
Warren K-17
Washington K-15
Waskom G-17
Water Valley H-9
Watson K-12
Watsonville . Pg. 104, F-5
Waxahachie G-14
Wayside D-8
Weatherford G-12
Weaver F-15
Webster M-16
Weches N-13
Weesatche N-13
Weimar L-14
Weinort F-10
Welch F-7
Wellington D-9
Wellman F-7
Wells J-16
Weslaco S-12
West H-13
West Columbia .. M-15
West Orange K-17
West Point L-13
Westbrook G-8
Westfield L-15
Vicinity ... Pg. 109, A-4
Westhoff M-13
Westlake .. Pg. 104, A-4
Westover F-11
Westworth Village
..... Pg. 104, D-2
Wharton M-15
Wheeler C-9
Wheeler B-9
Wheelock K-14
White Deer C-8
Whiteface E-6
Whiteflat E-9
Whitehouse G-15
Whitesboro E-13
Whitewright F-14
Whitharral E-7
Whitney H-13
Whittsett N-12
Wichita Falls E-12
Wickett H-5
Wiergate J-18
Wildorado C-7
Wildwood K-17
Wilkinson F-16
Willow City K-11
Wills Point G-15
Wilmer .. Pg. 105, F-10
Wilson F-8
Wimberly L-12
Winchell J-11
Windcrest .. Pg. 142, C-7
Windom F-15
Windthorst E-12
Winfield F-16
Wingate H-9
Wink H-5
Winnsboro F-15
Winona G-16
Winters H-9
Wolfe City F-15
Wolfforth F-7
Woodlake J-16
Woodlawn G-16
Woodsboro P-13
Woodson F-11
Woodville K-17
Woodward N-10
Wortham H-14
Yoakum M-13
Yorktown M-13

Zavalla J-17
Zephyr H-11
Zorn L-12

UTAH

UTAH
Pages 80-81
Population: 1,461,037
Capital: Salt Lake City
Land Area: 82,073 sq. mi.

Abraham H-4
Adamsville K-4
Alpine F-5
Alta F-6
Altamont F-8
Alton L-4
American Fork F-5
Aneth M-9
Angle K-5
Annabella J-5
Antimony K-5
Arcadia F-8
Aurora J-5
Austin J-5
Axtell J-5
Bacchus .. Pg. 141, K-2
Bear River City .. D-5
Beaver K-4
Benjamin F-5
Beryl K-2
Bicknell K-5
Birdseye G-6
Black Rock J-4
Blanding L-9
Blue Cr. C-4
Bluebell F-8
Bluff L-9
Bluffdale F-5
Bonanza G-9
Boneta F-7
Boulder K-6
Bountiful E-5
Vicinity ... Pg. 141, F-6
Brian Head L-4
Bridgeland F-8
Brigham City D-5
Bryce Canyon L-4
Burmester E-4
Burrville J-5
Cannonville L-4
Carbonville G-7
Castle Dale H-7
Castle Rock E-6
Cave C-5
Cedar City L-3
Cedar Creek C-3
Cedar Fort F-5
Cedar Springs D-4
Cedarview F-8
Center Creek F-6
Centerfield H-5
Centerville E-5
Vicinity ... Pg. 141, F-6
Central J-5
Central L-2
Charleston F-6
Chester H-5
Circleville K-4
Cisco J-9
Clarkston C-5
Clawson H-6
Clear Creek C-3
Clearcreek G-6
Clearfield E-5
Cleveland H-7
Clinton D-5
Clover F-4
Coalville E-6
Colton G-6
Corinne D-5
Cornish C-5
Cove Fort J-4
Crescent Jct. J-8
Croydon E-6
Delle E-4
Delta H-4
Deseret H-4
Desert Mound L-3
Dividend G-5
Draper F-5
Duchesne F-8
Dugway H-4
East Carbon City .. H-8
East Mill Creek
..... Pg. 141, J-7
Eastland L-9
Echo E-6
Elberta G-5
Elmo H-7
Elsinore J-5
Emery J-6
Enoch L-3
Enterprise L-2
Ephraim H-6
Escalante L-5
Etna D-2
Eureka G-5
Fairfield F-5
Fairview H-6
Farmington E-5
Faust F-4
Fayette H-5
Ferron H-6
Fillmore H-5
Fish Springs H-3
Flowell H-4
Fort Duchesne F-8
Fountain Green H-5
Francis F-6
Freedom H-5
Fremont J-6
Fremont Jct. J-6

Fruit Heights E-5
Fruitland F-7
Fry Canyon K-8
Gandy G-2
Garden City C-6
Garrison H-2
Geneva F-5
Genola G-5
Glendale L-4
Glenwood J-5
Goshen G-5
Grantsville E-4
Green Lake E-9
Green River H-8
Greenville K-4
Greenwich J-5
Greenwood J-5
Grouse Creek C-2
Gunlock L-2
Gunnison H-5
Gusher F-8
Hamilton Fort L-3
Hanksville K-7
Hanna F-7
Harrisville D-5
Hatch L-4
Hatton J-4
Heber City F-6
Henefer E-6
Henrieville L-5
Hiawatha H-6
Hinckley H-4
Holden H-5
Holladay E-5
Vicinity ... Pg. 141, K-7
Honeyville D-4
Hot Springs D-5
Howell D-4
Hoytsville E-6
Huntington H-7
Huntsville D-6
Hurricane M-3
Hyde Park C-5
Hyrum D-5
Indianola G-6
Ioka F-8
Iron Springs L-3
Ivins M-2
Jensen F-9
Jericho G-5
Joseph J-5
Junction K-4
Kamas F-6
Kanab M-4
Kanarraville L-3
Kanosh J-4
Kaysville E-5
Kelton D-4
Kenilworth G-7
Kimball Jct. E-6
Kingston K-4
Knolls E-3
Koosharem J-5
La Sal K-9
La Sal Jct. K-9
La Verkin L-3
Lake Pt. Jct. E-4
Lake Shore F-5
Lake View F-5
Laketown C-6
Lapoint F-8
Leamington H-5
Leeds L-3
Leeton L-3
Lehi F-5
Leota F-9
Levan G-5
Lewiston C-5
Loa J-6
Logan D-5
Long Valley Jct. .. L-4
Low E-3
Lucin D-2
Lund K-3
Lyman J-6
Lynndyl G-4
Maeser F-9
Magna E-5
Vicinity ... Pg. 141, K-2
Manderfield J-4
Manila E-9
Manti H-6
Mantua D-5
Mapleton F-6
Marion F-6
Marysvale J-4
Mayfield H-6
Meadow J-4
Meadowville C-6
Mendon D-5
Mexican Hat M-8
Midvale E-5
Midway F-6
Milburn G-6
Milford J-3
Mills G-5
Minersville K-3
Moab J-9
Modena K-2
Molen H-6
Mona G-5
Monarch F-8
Monroe J-5
Montezuma Creek . M-9
Monticello L-9
Moore H-6
Morgan E-5
Moroni H-5
Mountain Home .. F-7
Mt. Carmel L-4
Mt. Carmel Jct. .. L-4
Mt. Emmons F-7
Mt. Pleasant G-6

Murray E-5
Myton F-8
N. Logan C-6
N. Salt Lake F-5
Vicinity ... Pg. 141, F-5
Naples F-9
Neola F-8
Nephi G-5
New Harmony L-3
Newcastle L-2
Newton C-5
Oak City H-5
Oakley E-6
Oasis H-4
Ogden D-5
Orangeville H-6
Orderville L-4
Orem F-6
Ouray F-9
Panguitch K-4
Paradise D-5
Paragonah K-4
Park City E-6
Park Valley C-3
Parowan K-4
Payson G-5
Peoa E-6
Perry Willard D-5
Pigeon Hollow Jct. . H-6
Pine Valley L-2
Pintura L-3
Plain City D-5
Pleasant Grove .. F-6
Pleasant View D-5
Plymouth C-5
Portage C-5
Porterville E-6
Price G-7
Providence D-5
Provo F-6
Randolph D-6
Redmond H-5
Richfield J-5
Richmond C-5
Riverdale D-5
Riverton F-5
Rockville M-3
Roosevelt F-8
Rosette C-3
Rowley Jct. E-4
Roy E-5
Ruby's Inn L-4
Saint George M-3
Saint John Sta. .. F-4
Salem G-5
Salina H-5
Salt Lake City .. F-4
Vicinity ..... Pg. 141
Sandy F-5
Santa Clara M-2
Santaquin G-5
Scipio H-5
Scofield G-6
Sevier J-4
Shivwits M-2
Sigurd J-5
Silver City G-5
Smithfield C-5
Smyths J-3
Snowville C-4
Soldier Summit .. G-7
South Jordan F-5
South Ogden D-5
South Salt Lake .. E-5
Vicinity ... Pg. 141, J-5
Spanish Fork F-6
Spring City H-6
Spring Lake G-5
Springdale M-3
Springville F-6
Sterling H-6
Stockton F-4
Summit K-3
Summit Pt. K-9
Sunnyside G-8
Sunset E-5
Sutherland H-4
Syracuse E-5
Tabiona F-7
Talmage F-8
Teasdale K-6
Terrace D-6
Thistle G-6
Thompson H-9
Tooele F-4
Toquerville L-3
Torrey K-6
Tremonton D-5
Tropic L-5
Trout Cr. G-2
Tucker G-6
Upalco F-8
Uvada L-2
Venice J-5
Vernal F-9
Vernon F-4
Veyo M-2
Virgin M-3
W. Valley City .. D-5
Wahsatch D-6
Wales H-5
Wanship E-6
Washington M-3
Washington Terrace . D-5
Wellington G-7
Wellsville D-5
Wendover E-1
West Jordan F-5
West Point D-5
West Valley City .. E-5
Vicinity ... Pg. 141, J-4
Whiterocks F-8
Widtsoe Jct. K-5
Woodruff D-6

UTAH

WEST VIRGINIA

Woods Cross E-5
  Vicinity . . . Pg. 141, F-5
Woodside H-8
Zane K-2

VERMONT
Page 55
Population: 511,456
Capital: Montpelier
Land Area: 9,273 sq. mi.

Addison E-1
Albany C-3
Alburg B-1
Arlington J-1
Ascutney G-3
Averill B-5
Bakersfield B-2
Barnard F-3
Barnet D-4
Barre E-3
Barton C-4
Bellows Falls H-3
Bennington J-1
Bethel F-3
Bloomfield C-5
Bomoseen G-1
Bondville H-2
Bradford E-4
Brandon F-2
Brattleboro J-3
Bridgewater Cors. . . . G-3
Bridport E-1
Bristol E-1
Broadford Cen. E-3
Brunswick Sprs. C-5
Burlington D-1
Cambridge J-1
Cambridgeport H-3
Canaan B-5
Castleton G-1
Charlotte D-1
Chelsea E-3
Chester H-3
Chester Depot H-3
Chimney Cor. C-2
Concord D-4
Cornwall E-1
Danby G-2
Dorset H-1
E. Barnet D-4
E. Berkshire C-2
E. Braintree E-3
E. Brookfield E-3
E. Burke C-4
E. Calais D-3
E. Dorset H-2
E. Fairfield C-2
E. Granville E-2
E. Hardwick D-3
E. Haven C-4
Eden C-3
Eden Mills C-3
Enosburg Falls B-2
Essex Jct. D-2
Fair Haven G-1
Fairfax C-2
Ferrisburg E-1
Franklin B-2
Gassetts H-3
Gaysville F-3
Glover C-4
Grafton H-3
Grand Isle C-1
Granville E-2
Groton E-4
Guilford J-3
Hancock F-2
Hardwick D-3
Heartwellville J-2
Hinesburg D-2
Holland B-4
Hubbardton F-1
Hyde Park C-3
Irasburg B-3
Irasville E-2
Island Pond C-4
Jacksonville J-2
Jamaica H-2
Jay B-3
Jeffersonville C-2
Johnson C-3
Lake Elmore C-3
Leicester F-2
Londonderry H-2
Lowell B-3
Ludlow G-2
Lunenberg D-5
Lyndon C-4
Lyndonville C-4
Maidstone C-5
Manchester H-2
Manchester Cen. H-2
Marlboro J-2
Marshfield D-3
Middlebury E-1
Middletown Sprs. G-1
Mill Village E-3
Montgomery Cen. . . . B-3
Montpelier D-3
Morgan Cen. B-4
Morrisville C-3
New Haven E-1
New Haven Jct. E-1
Newbury E-4
Newfane J-2
Newport B-4
North Concord D-4
North Dorset H-2
North Hero C-1
North Hyde Park C-3

North Rupert H-1
Northfield E-2
Norton B-4
Norwich F-3
Orleans B-4
Orwell F-1
Passumpsic D-4
Pawlet H-1
Pittsfield F-2
Pittsford F-2
Pittsford Mills F-2
Plainfield D-3
Plymouth C-2
Plymouth Union G-2
Pompanoosuc F-3
Post Mills F-3
Poultney G-1
Pownal J-1
Pownal Cen. J-1
Putney J-3
Quechee G-3
Randolph E-2
Richford B-2
Richmond D-2
Ripton E-2
Robinson E-2
Rochester F-2
Roxbury E-2
Royalton F-2
Rutland G-2
Saint Albans B-2
Saint George D-2
Saint Johnsbury D-4
Searsburg J-1
Shaftsbury J-1
Shaftsbury Cen. J-2
Shelburne D-1
Sherburne Cen. F-2
Shoreham F-1
Simonsville H-2
South Burlington D-1
South Dorset G-2
South Hinesburg D-2
South Royalton F-3
South Ryegate E-4
South Shaftsbury J-2
South Starksboro E-2
South Walden D-3
South Wallingford . . . G-2
Springfield H-3
Starksboro E-2
Stockbridge F-2
Sudbury F-1
Sunderland J-2
Swanton B-1
Ticonderoga F-1
Townshend J-2
Troy B-3
Tunbridge F-3
Tyson G-2
Underhill Flats D-2
Union Village F-3
Vergennes E-1
Vershire E-3
Waits River E-3
Waitsfield E-2
Wallingford G-2
Waltham E-1
Wardsboro J-2
Warren E-2
Washington E-3
Waterbury D-2
Waterbury Ctr. D-3
Websterville E-3
Wells G-1
West Addison E-1
West Braintree E-2
West Bridgewater . . . G-2
West Burke C-4
West Danville D-3
West Dover J-2
West Fairlee F-3
West Groton E-3
West Hartford F-3
West Rutland G-2
West Topsham E-3
West Wardsboro J-2
Westfield B-3
White River Jct. G-3
Whiting F-1
Wilmington J-2
Windsor G-3
Wolcott C-3
Woodbury D-3
Woodford J-1
Woodstock G-3
Worcester D-3

VIRGINIA
Pages 82-83
Population: 5,346,818
Capital: Richmond
Land Area: 39,703 sq. mi.

Abingdon K-3
Achilles H-12
Alexandria E-12
  Vicinity . . . Pg. 150, F-4
Altavista J-8
Amber Wood Pg. 139, J-1
Amelia H-10
Amherst H-8
Annandale . . Pg. 150, F-3
Appalachia K-1
Appomattox J-8
Arlington D-12
  Vicinity . . . Pg. 150, E-3
Ashcake . . . . Pg. 139, A-5
Ashland G-10
Bailey's Crossroads
  . . . . Pg. 150, E-4

Ballston . . . . Pg. 150, E-6
Bassett J-7
Bastian J-5
Bavon H-13
Beach . . . . . Pg. 139, J-2
Bedford J-7
Belle Haven G-13
Bensley . . . . Pg. 139, G-5
Bermuda Hundred
  . . . . Pg. 139, J-7
Berryville D-10
Big Island H-8
Big Stone Gap J-2
Blacksburg H-6
Blackstone J-11
Bluefield H-4
Bon Air . . . . . Pg. 139, H-11
  Vicinity . . . Pg. 139, E-3
Boones Mill H-7
Bowling Green F-11
Boydton K-9
Brandermill . Pg. 139, G-1
Brandy Creek Estates
  . . . . Pg. 139, C-6
Bridgewater F-8
Bristol K-3
Broadway E-8
Brodnax J-10
Brookneal J-8
Buchanan H-7
Buckingham G-9
  Vicinity . . . Pg. 139, D-2
Buena Vista G-8
Burgess G-12
Burke . . . . . Pg. 150, G-2
Burkeville H-9
Cape Charles H-13
Carmel Church G-10
Castlewood J-3
Cedarbluff J-4
Central Garage G-11
Centralia . . . . Pg. 139, H-4
Chamberlayne Heights
  . . . . Pg. 139, C-5
Charlottesville F-9
Charlottesville F-9
Chase City J-9
Chatham J-8
Cheriton H-13
Chesapeake J-13
  Vicinity . . . Pg. 130, A-4
Chester H-11
  Vicinity . . . Pg. 139, J-5
Chesterfield . Pg. 139, H-4
Chilhowie K-4
Chincoteague F-14
Christiansburg J-6
Churchville F-8
Clarksville K-9
Claudville K-6
Clifton Forge G-7
Clinchco J-3
Clintwood J-3
Coeburn J-3
Colonial Beach F-11
Colonial Hts. H-11
Courtland J-11
Covington G-6
Craigsville F-8
Crestview . . . Pg. 139, C-3
Crewe H-10
Crittenden . . . Pg. 130, L-1
Crozet G-9
Culpeper E-10
Cumberland H-9
Dale City E-11
Damascus K-4
Dante J-3
Danville K-7
Dayton F-8
Deltaville G-13
Dillwyn H-9
Drakes Branch J-9
Drewrys Bluff Pg. 139, G-4
Dublin J-5
Dugspur J-6
Dumbarton . . Pg. 139, C-4
Eagle Rock G-7
Eastville H-13
Edinburg E-10
Elkton F-9
Elmont . . . . . Pg. 139, A-4
Emporia K-11
Enon . . . . Pg. 139, J-7
Ewing K-1
Exmore G-13
Fairfax D-11
  Vicinity . . . Pg. 150, E-1
Falling Creek Pg. 139, G-2
Falls Church . Pg. 150, E-3
Falmouth E-11
Farmville H-9
Fieldale K-7
Five Forks . . . Pg. 139, H-3
Floyd J-6
Franconia . . . Pg. 150, G-4
Franklin K-11
Fredericksburg E-11
Fries K-5
Front Royal D-9
Galax K-5
Gate City K-2
Glade Spring K-4
Gladys H-8
Glasgow G-8
Glen Allen . . Pg. 139, B-4
Gloucester H-12
Gloucester Pt. H-12
Gordonsville F-9
Goshen G-8
Gretna J-8
Grottoes F-8
Groveton . . . Pg. 150, G-5
Grundy H-3

Gum Springs G-10
Gwynn H-13
Halifax J-8
Hampden-Sydney . . . H-9
Hampton J-13
  Vicinity . . . Pg. 130, A-2
Hanover G-11
Harrisonburg E-8
Herndon D-10
Hillsville J-6
Hollins H-7
Honaker J-3
Hopewell H-11
  Vicinity . . . Pg. 139, K-7
Hughes Corner
  . . . . Pg. 139, B-7
Hurt J-8
Hylas . . . . . . Pg. 139, A-1
Independence K-5
Innsbrook . . . Pg. 139, B-2
Iron Gate G-7
Irvington G-12
Jarratt J-11
Jonesville K-1
Keene Mill Heights
  . . . . Pg. 150, G-2
Kenbridge J-10
Keysville J-9
Kilmarnock G-12
King & Queen C.H. . . . G-12
Kingsland Acres
  . . . . Pg. 139, G-5
Kiptopeke K-10
La Crosse K-10
Lancaster G-12
Langley . . . . Pg. 150, C-4
Laurel . . . . . Pg. 139, B-3
Lawrenceville J-10
Lebanon J-3
Leesburg D-10
Lees Village . Pg. 139, H-6
Lexington G-7
Lottsburg F-12
Lovingston G-8
Luray E-9
Lynchburg H-8
Madison F-9
Madison Hts. H-8
Manassas E-10
Mappsville G-13
Marion J-4
Marshall E-10
Martinsville K-7
Mathews H-13
McKenney J-10
McLean . . . . Pg. 150, D-3
Meadowville Pg. 139, H-7
Mechanicsville G-11
  Vicinity . . . Pg. 139, C-6
Middleburg D-10
Middletown D-9
Midlothian . . Pg. 139, F-1
Monterey F-8
Montross F-12
Mt. Jackson E-9
Narrows J-5
Nassawadox H-13
New Castle H-7
New Market E-9
Newmans . . . Pg. 139, C-7
Newport News J-13
  Vicinity . . . Pg. 130, A-1
Norfolk J-13
  Vicinity . . . . . . Pg. 130
Norton J-2
Oak Forest . . Pg. 139, B-6
Oak Grove F-12
Onancock G-13
Onley G-14
Orange F-9
Otterdale . . . Pg. 139, F-1
Palmyra G-9
Pamplin City H-8
Parksley G-13
Patrick Springs K-7
Pearisburg J-5
Pearsons Corner
  . . . . Pg. 139, A-6
Pembroke H-6
Pennington Gap J-2
Petersburg H-10
Pickadat Corner
  . . . . Pg. 139, K-5
Pimmit Hills . Pg. 150, D-3
Poindexters . Pg. 139, A-5
Pole Green . . Pg. 139, B-6
Poquoson H-12
  Vicinity . . . Pg. 130, A-3
Port Royal F-11
Portsmouth J-12
  Vicinity . . . Pg. 130, F-3
Pound J-2
Powhatan H-10
Prospect Hill Pg. 150, C-2
Pulaski J-5
Purcellville D-10
Quantico E-11
Radford J-4
Raven J-4
Ravensworth Pg. 150, F-2
Red Ash J-3
Remington E-10
Richlands E-4
Richmond H-10
  Vicinity . . . Pg. 139, E-4
Ripplemead H-6
Roanoke H-7
Robious . . . . Pg. 139, F-2
Rockville . . . Pg. 139, A-1
Rocky Mount J-7
Ruckersville F-9
Rural Point . . Pg. 139, B-6
Rural Retreat J-4
Rustburg H-8

Salem H-7
Saltville J-4
Sandston H-11
Saxis G-13
Seaford H-12
Shady Oak . . Pg. 150, B-1
Shenandoah E-9
Shipman G-8
Short Pump . Pg. 139, B-2
Simpkins Corner
  . . . . Pg. 139, C-7
Smithfield J-12
South Boston K-8
Sperryville E-9
Spring Grove H-11
Springfield . . Pg. 150, G-3
St. Paul J-3
Stafford F-11
Stanley E-9
Stanleytown J-7
Staunton F-8
Stephens City D-9
Strasburg D-9
Stuart K-6
Stuarts Draft F-8
Studley . . . . . Pg. 139, A-7
Suffolk J-12
  Vicinity . . . Pg. 130, H-1
Sugar Grove J-4
Surry H-12
Sussex J-11
Swan Hill . . . Pg. 139, G-2
Sydnorsville J-7
Tangier G-13
Tappahannock G-11
Tazewell J-4
Timberville E-8
Triangle E-11
Tysons Corner
  . . . . Pg. 150, D-2
Urbanna G-12
Vanderpool F-7
Vansant H-3
Verona F-8
Victoria J-9
Victoria Hills Pg. 139, J-5
Vienna D-11
  Vicinity . . . Pg. 150, E-2
Vinton H-7
Virginia Beach J-13
  Vicinity . . . Pg. 130, A-4
Volens J-8
Wakefield J-12
Walthall . . . . Pg. 139, K-5
Warm Springs F-7
Warrenton E-10
Warsaw G-11
Waverly J-11
Waynesboro F-8
Weber City K-3
West Point H-12
Williamsburg H-11
Winchester D-9
Windsor J-12
Wise J-2
Woodbridge E-11
Woodlawn K-5
Woodstock E-9
Wylliesburg J-9
Wytheville J-5
Zion G-9

WASHINGTON
Pages 84-85
Population: 4,132,156
Capital: Olympia
Land Area: 66,511 sq. mi.

Aberdeen F-3
Acme B-6
Addy B-13
Airway Heights D-14
Albion F-14
Alderwood Maner
  . . . . Pg. 147, A-4
Algona . . . . . Pg. 147, A-4
Almira D-11
Altoona H-3
Anacortes B-5
Anatone F-14
Appleyard E-9
Arlington B-6
Asotin G-14
Auburn C-6
  Vicinity . . . Pg. 147, C-4
Battle Ground J-5
Bellevue C-6
  Vicinity . . . Pg. 147, E-6
Bellingham A-5
Benton City H-10
Bickleton H-9
Bingen J-7
Black Diamond C-6
Blaine A-5
Bonney Lake C-6
Bossburg B-13
Bothell D-6
  Vicinity . . . Pg. 147, B-5
Boundary A-13
Bremerton D-5
Brewster C-10
Bridgeport C-10
Brier . . . . . . Pg. 147, A-5
Bryn Mawr . . Pg. 147, H-5
Buckley E-6
Bucoda F-5
Burien . . . . . Pg. 147, G-4
Burlington B-6
Camas J-5
Carbonado E-6
Carnation D-6

Cashmere E-9
Castle Rock H-4
Cathlamet G-4
Centralia G-5
Chehalis G-5
Chelan D-9
Cheney E-14
Chewelah C-13
Clarkston G-14
Clayton C-13
Cle Elum E-8
Coalfield . . . Pg. 147, H-6
Coles Corner D-8
Colfax F-14
College Place H-12
Colton G-14
Colville B-13
Conconully B-10
Concrete B-7
Connell G-12
Copalis Beach F-3
Cosmopolis F-3
Coulee City D-11
Coulee Dam C-11
Coupeville C-5
Crescent Bar E-9
Creston D-12
Cusick C-14
Darrington C-7
Davenport D-13
Dayton H-13
Deer Park C-14
Deming A-6
Des Moines C-6
  Vicinity . . . Pg. 147, K-3
Disautel C-11
Discovery Bay C-5
Dodge G-13
Duluth J-5
Dusty F-13
Duvall D-6
East Wenatchee E-9
Eastgate . . . Pg. 147, F-6
Eatonville F-6
Edmonds D-5
  Vicinity . . . Pg. 147, A-2
Edwall F-6
Elbe F-6
Eldon D-4
Electric City D-11
Ellensburg F-9
Elma F-4
Elmer City C-11
Endicott F-13
Entiat D-9
Enumclaw E-6
Ephrata E-10
Eureka H-12
Everett C-6
Everson A-6
Fairfield E-14
Fairholm C-3
Farmington F-15
Ferndale A-5
Fircrest E-5
Forks C-2
Friday Harbor B-5
Garfield F-14
George F-10
Gifford C-13
Gig Harbor E-5
Glenoma G-6
Gold Bar D-7
Goldendale J-8
Grand Coulee D-11
Grandview H-9
Granger G-9
Granite Falls C-6
Greenwater F-7
Hamilton B-6
Harrah G-9
Harrington E-12
Hartline D-11
Hatton G-11
Hoodsport E-4
Hoquiam F-3
Humptulips E-3
Husum J-7
Hyak E-7
Ilwaco G-3
Index D-7
Ione B-14
Issaquah E-6
Joyce C-3
Juanita . . . . . Pg. 147, C-4
Kahlotus G-12
Kalama H-5
Keller C-12
Kelso H-5
Kenmoore . . . Pg. 147, B-5
Kennewick H-11
Kent C-6
  Vicinity . . . Pg. 147, J-4
Kettle Falls B-13
Kingston . . . Pg. 147, A-1
Kirkland C-6
  Vicinity . . . Pg. 147, D-5
Kittitas F-9
Klaus G-5
Klickitat J-7
Krupp E-11
La Center J-5
La Conner B-5
La Crosse F-13
La Push C-2
Lacey E-5
Lake Stevens C-6
Lamont E-13
Langley C-5
Latah E-14
Leavenworth D-9
Lebam G-3
Lind F-12

Littlerock F-4
Long Beach G-3
Longview H-4
Lyman B-6
Lynden A-5
Lynnwood D-5
  Vicinity . . . Pg. 147, A-3
Mabton H-9
Malone F-4
Maltby . . . . . Pg. 147, A-6
Mansfield D-10
Manson D-9
Maplewood . . Pg. 147, H-5
Marcus B-13
Marysville C-6
Mattawa G-10
McCleary F-4
Medical Lake E-13
Megler H-3
Menlo G-3
Mercer Island D-5
  Vicinity . . . Pg. 147, F-4
Mesa G-11
Metaline A-14
Metaline Falls A-14
Methow C-9
Millwood D-14
Monroe D-6
Montesano F-3
Morton G-6
Moses Lake F-11
Mossyrock G-5
Mount Baker A-7
Mount Vernon B-5
Mountlake Terrace . . . D-5
  Vicinity . . . Pg. 147, A-3
Moxee City G-9
Mukilteo D-6
Naches F-8
Napavine G-4
Naselle G-3
Neah Bay B-2
Neilton E-3
Newcastle . . Pg. 147, G-5
Newport C-14
Normandy Park Pg. 147, J-2
North Bend E-7
North Bonneville J-6
North Cove F-2
Northport A-13
Oak Harbor C-5
Oakesdale F-14
Oakville F-4
Ocean Park G-3
Ocean Shores F-2
Odessa E-12
Okanogan C-10
Olympia F-5
Omak B-10
Orchards J-5
Orient A-13
Oroville A-10
Orting F-6
Othello F-11
Ozette C-2
Pacific E-6
Pacific Beach E-2
Packwood G-6
Palouse F-14
Pasco H-11
Pateros C-10
Pe Ell G-4
Pomeroy G-14
Port Angeles C-4
Port Gamble D-5
Port Orchard D-5
Port Townsend C-5
Poulsbo D-5
Prescott H-12
Prosser H-10
Pullman G-14
Puyallup E-6
Queets E-2
Quincy E-10
Rainier F-5
Randle G-6
Raymond G-3
Reardan D-13
Redmond D-6
Renton C-6
  Vicinity . . . Pg. 147, H-4
Republic B-12
Richland H-11
Richland Highlands
  . . . . Pg. 147, B-3
Richmond Beach
  . . . . Pg. 147, B-3
Ridgefield J-5
Rimrock A-5
Ritzville F-12
Riverside B-10
Rochester F-4
Rock Island E-9
Rockford E-14
Rockport B-7
Rollingbay . . Pg. 147, D-1
Roosevelt J-9
Rosalia E-14
Rosburg G-3
Roslyn E-8
Roy F-5
Royal City F-10
Ryderwood G-4
Salmon La Sac E-8
Sappho C-2
Seattle D-5
  Vicinity . . . . . . Pg. 147
Sedro Woolley B-6
Selah G-9
Sequim C-4
Shelton E-4
Silver Creek G-5
Skykomish D-7

Snohomish D-6
Snoqualmie E-7
Soap Lake E-10
South Bend G-3
South Cle Elum F-8
South Prairie F-6
Spangle E-14
Spokane D-14
Sprague E-13
Springdale C-13
St. John F-14
Stanwood C-6
Starbuck G-13
Steilacoom E-5
Stella H-4
Steptoe J-6
Stevenson J-6
Sultan D-7
Sumas A-6
Sumner E-6
Sunnyside H-10
Tacoma E-5
Taholah E-2
Tekoa E-14
Telma D-8
Tenino F-5
Tieton G-8
Toledo G-5
Tonasket B-10
Toppenish H-9
Trout Lake H-7
Tukwila E-6
Tumwater F-4
Twisp C-9
Union E-4
Union Gap G-9
Uniontown G-14
Vader G-4
Vancouver J-4
  Vicinity . . . Pg. 137, A-5
Vantage F-9
Vashon Heights
  . . . . Pg. 147, G-1
Vashon Island
  . . . . Pg. 147, K-1
Waitsburg H-13
Walla Walla H-12
Wallula H-11
Wapato G-9
Warden F-11
Washougal J-5
Washtucna G-12
Waterville D-9
Wauconda B-11
Waverly E-14
Wenatchee E-9
Wenatchee Heights . . E-9
West Richland H-11
Westport F-2
White Salmon J-7
White Swan H-8
Wickersham B-6
Wilbur D-12
Wilkeson F-6
Wilson Creek E-11
Winlock G-4
Winslow D-5
Winthrop B-9
Wishram Heights J-8
Withrow D-10
Woodinville . . Pg. 147, B-6
Woodland J-5
Yacolt J-5
Yakima G-9
Yelm F-5
Zillah G-9

WEST VIRGINIA
Pages 82-83
Population: 1,949,644
Capital: Charleston
Land Area: 24,119 sq. mi.

Alderson G-6
Arnoldsburg E-5
Ashton H-5
Athens H-5
Augusta D-8
Baileysville G-4
Baker D-9
Barbourville F-3
Barrackville C-7
Beckley G-5
Belington D-7
Belmont D-5
Bethlehem B-6
Beverly E-7
Big Chimney F-4
Big Otter F-5
Birch River E-6
Blacksville C-6
Bluefield H-5
Bradley G-4
Bramwell H-4
Bridgeport D-7
Buckhannon D-6
Buffalo F-3
Burnsville E-6
Cairo D-5
Camden-on-Gauley . . E-6
Cameron C-6
Cedar Grove F-4
Center Pt. C-6
Chapmanville G-3
Charles Town D-10
Charleston F-4
Chesapeake F-4
Chester A-6
Clarksburg D-6
Clay E-5
Clendenin E-5

WEST VIRGINIA

WYOMING

West Virginia

Coxs Mills ... D-6
Craigsville ... F-6
Danville ... F-4
Davis ... E-7
Delbarton ... G-3
Dunbar ... F-4
Dunmore ... F-7
Durbin ... E-7
East Bank ... F-4
Eleanor ... E-4
Elk Garden ... C-8
Elkins ... D-7
Ellenboro ... D-5
Fairmont ... C-7
Fairview ... C-6
Farmington ... C-6
Fayetteville ... G-5
Flatwoods ... E-6
Follansbee ... A-6
Forest Hill ... H-5
Franklin ... F-7
Friendly ... C-5
Ft. Ashby ... C-8
Ft. Gay ... F-3
Gandeeville ... E-4
Gap Mills ... H-6
Gary ... H-4
Gassaway ... E-6
Gauley Bridge ... G-5
Gerrardstown ... C-9
Gilbert ... H-4
Gilmer ... E-6
Glen Dale ... B-6
Glenville ... D-6
Grantsville ... D-6
Hambleton ... D-7
Hamlin ... F-4
Harman ... E-8
Harrisville ... D-5
Hedgesville ... C-9
Henderson ... E-3
Hillsboro ... G-6
Hinton ... G-5
Hundred ... B-6
Huntington ... F-3
Hurricane ... F-3
Huttonsville ... E-7
Iaeger ... H-4
Ingleside ... H-5
Inwood ... C-10
Jane Lew ... D-6
Jolo ... H-4
Junction ... C-8
Junior ... E-7
Kenna ... E-4
Kenova ... F-3
Kermit ... G-3
Keyser ... C-9
Keystone ... H-4
Kimball ... H-4
Kingwood ... C-7
Leon ... E-4
Lester ... G-5
Lewisburg ... G-6
Liberty ... E-4
Linn ... D-6
Logan ... G-4
Lost City ... D-8
Lost Cr. ... D-7
Lumberport ... D-6
Mabscott ... G-5
Madison ... G-4
Man ... H-4
Mannington ... C-7
Marlinton ... F-6
Marmet ... F-4
Martinsburg ... C-9
Mason ... D-4
Masontown ... C-7
Matewan ... G-3
Matoaka ... H-5
Meadow Bridge ... G-5
Middlebourne ... C-5
Midkiff ... F-3
Mill Creek ... E-7
Milton ... F-3
Monongah ... C-6
Montgomery ... G-5
Montrose ... D-8
Moorefield ... D-9
Morgantown ... C-7
Mossy ... G-4
Moundsville ... B-6
Mt. Hope ... G-5
Mt. Storm ... D-8
Muddlety ... F-5
Mullens ... H-5
Naoma ... G-4
Neola ... G-7
Nettie ... F-5
New Cumberland ... A-6
New Haven ... D-4
New Martinsville ... C-6
Newton ... E-5
Nitro ... F-4
Nutter Fort ... D-6
Oak Flat ... E-8
Oak Hill ... G-5
Oceana ... H-4
Omar ... G-3
Paden City ... C-5
Parkersburg ... D-5
Parsons ... D-7
Paw Paw ... C-9
Pennsboro ... D-5
Petersburg ... D-8
Peterstown ... H-5
Philippi ... D-7
Pine Grove ... C-6
Pineville ... H-4
Poca ... E-4
Pocatalico ... E-4
Prichard ... F-3
Princeton ... H-5
Pt. Pleasant ... E-3
Racine ... F-4
Rainelle ... G-5
Rand ... F-4
Ranson ... D-10
Ravenswood ... D-4
Reedy ... E-5
Renick ... G-6
Rhodell ... H-5
Richwood ... F-6
Ridgeley ... C-9
Ripley ... E-4
Roanoke ... E-6
Rock Cave ... E-6
Romney ... D-9
Ronceverte ... G-6
Rowlesburg ... D-7
Rupert ... G-6
Salem ... D-6
Scherr ... D-8
Seneca Rocks ... E-8
Shepherdstown ... C-10
Shinnston ... C-6
Slatyfork ... F-6
Smithers ... F-5
Smithfield ... C-6
Sophia ... G-5
Spencer ... E-5
South Charleston ... F-4
St. Albans ... F-4
St. Mary's ... C-5
Star City ... C-7
Stonewood ... D-7
Summersville ... F-5
Sylvester ... G-4
Terra Alta ... C-8
Thomas ... D-7
Thornwood ... E-7
Triadelphia ... B-6
Tunnelton ... D-7
Union ... H-6
Valley Head ... E-7
Van ... G-4
Vienna ... D-4
War ... H-4
Wardensville ... D-8
Wayne ... F-3
Webster Spr. ... E-6
Weirton ... A-6
Welch ... H-4
Wellsburg ... A-6
West Hamlin ... F-3
West Logan ... G-4
West Union ... D-5
Weston ... D-6
Westover ... C-7
Wheeling ... B-6
White Sulphur Spr. ... G-6
Whitesville ... G-4
Williamson ... G-3
Williamstown ... D-4
Yawkey ... F-4

Wisconsin

WISCONSIN
Pages 86-87
Population: 4,705,767
Capital: Madison
Land Area: 54,426 sq. mi.

Abbotsford ... F-5
Adams ... H-5
Adell ... J-8
Algoma ... G-8
Alma ... G-2
Alma Center ... G-4
Almena ... F-2
Altoona ... G-3
Amery ... F-2
Aniwa ... F-6
Antigo ... F-6
Appleton ... G-7
Arcadia ... H-3
Argyle ... J-6
Arlington ... J-6
Ashland ... D-4
Ashwaubenon ... G-7
Athens ... F-5
Auburndale ... G-5
Augusta ... G-4
Avoca ... K-5
Baldwin ... F-2
Balsam Lake ... F-1
Bangor ... H-4
Baraboo ... J-6
Barneveld ... K-5
Barron ... F-2
Bay City ... G-2
Bayfield ... C-4
Bayside
Vicinity ... Pg. 121, A-6
Beadstown ... J-6
Beaver Dam ... J-7
Belgium ... J-8
Belleville ... K-6
Belmont ... K-5
Beloit ... L-6
Benton ... L-5
Berlin ... H-7
Big Bend ... Pg. 121, H-1
Birchwood ... E-3
Birnamwood ... F-6
Black Creek ... G-7
Black Earth ... K-5
Black River Falls ... G-4
Blair ... H-3
Blanchardville ... K-5
Bloomer ... F-3
Bloomington ... K-5
Bonduel ... G-7
Boscobel ... K-4
Boyceville ... F-2
Boyd ... G-3
Brandon ... J-7
Brillion ... H-8
Brodhead ... L-6
Brokaw ... F-6
Brookfield ... Pg. 121, D-3
Brown Deer ... Pg. 121, A-5
Browntown ... L-6
Bruce ... F-3
Buena Park ... Pg. 121, K-1
Buffalo ... H-2
Burlington ... L-7
Butler ... Pg. 121, C-3
Butternut ... D-5
Cable ... D-3
Caddy Vista ... Pg. 121, J-6
Cadott ... F-3
Caledonia ... Pg. 121, K-6
Cambra ... J-6
Cambridge ... K-7
Cameron ... F-3
Camp Douglas ... H-5
Campbellsport ... J-8
Cascade ... J-8
Casco ... G-8
Cashton ... J-4
Cassville ... K-4
Catawba ... E-4
Cazenovia ... J-5
Cecil ... G-7
Centuria ... E-1
Chetek ... F-3
Chilton ... H-8
Chippewa Falls ... F-3
Clayton ... F-2
Clear Lake ... F-2
Cleveland ... H-8
Clinton ... L-7
Clintonville ... G-7
Cochrane ... H-3
Colby ... F-5
Coleman ... G-7
Colfax ... F-3
Colgate ... Pg. 121, A-1
Coloma ... H-6
Columbus ... J-7
Coon Valley ... J-4
Cornell ... F-3
Couderay ... E-3
Crandon ... E-6
Crivitz ... F-8
Cross Plains ... K-6
Cuba City ... L-4
Cudahy ... Pg. 121, F-6
Cumberland ... E-2
Dane ... J-6
Darien ... L-7
Darlington ... K-5
De Pere ... G-8
De Soto ... J-4
DeForest ... J-6
Deerfield ... K-6
Delavan ... K-7
Denmark ... G-8
Dickeyville ... L-4
Dodgeville ... K-5
Dorchester ... F-5
Dousman ... K-7
Dresser ... F-1
Duplainville ... Pg. 121, D-2
Durand ... G-2
Eagle ... K-7
Eagle River ... E-6
East Troy ... K-7
Eastman ... K-4
Eau Claire ... G-3
Eden ... J-7
Edgar ... F-5
Edgerton ... K-6
Egg Harbor ... F-9
Elano ... F-6
Eleva ... G-3
Elk Mound ... G-3
Elkhart Lake ... H-8
Elkhorn ... K-7
Ellsworth ... G-2
Elm Grove ... Pg. 121, D-3
Elmwood ... G-2
Elroy ... J-5
Embarrass ... G-7
Ephraim ... F-9
Ettrick ... H-3
Evansville ... K-6
Exeland ... E-3
Fairchild ... G-4
Fall Creek ... G-4
Fall River ... J-7
Fennimore ... K-4
Ferryville ... K-4
Fifield ... E-5
Florence ... E-7
Fond Du Lac ... H-7
Fontana ... L-7
Footville ... L-6
Forestville ... G-8
Fort Atkinson ... K-7
Fountain City ... H-3
Fox Lake ... J-7
Fox Point ... Pg. 121, B-6
Francis Creek ... H-8
Franklin ... K-8
Vicinity ... Pg. 121, H-4
Frederic ... E-2
Fremont ... H-7
Friendship ... H-6
Galesville ... H-3
Gays Mills ... J-4
Genoa ... J-3
Genoa City ... L-8
Germantown ... J-8
Vicinity ... Pg. 121, A-3
Gillett ... F-7
Gilman ... F-4
Glen Flora ... E-4
Glenbeulah ... J-8
Glendale ... Pg. 121, B-6
Glenwood City ... F-2
Grafton ... J-8
Granton ... G-5
Grantsburg ... E-1
Gratiot ... L-5
Green Bay ... G-8
Green Lake ... H-6
Greendale ... Pg. 121, G-4
Greenfield ... Pg. 121, F-5
Greenwood ... G-4
Gresham ... G-7
Hales Corners ... Pg. 121, G-4
Hammond ... F-2
Hancock ... H-6
Hartford ... J-7
Hartland ... K-8
Haugen ... E-2
Hawkins ... E-4
Hawthorne ... D-3
Hayward ... E-3
Hazel Green ... L-4
Heafford Jct. ... E-5
Highland ... K-5
Hilbert ... H-8
Hillsboro ... J-4
Hillsdale ... F-3
Holmen ... H-3
Horicon ... J-7
Hortonville ... G-7
Howard ... G-8
Howards Grove ... H-8
Hudson ... F-1
Hurley ... D-5
Husher ... Pg. 121, J-6
Independence ... G-3
Ingram ... E-4
Iola ... G-6
Iron River ... C-3
Jackson ... J-8
Janesville ... K-6
Jefferson ... K-7
Johnson Creek ... K-7
Junction City ... G-5
Juneau ... J-7
Kaukauna ... H-8
Kendall ... H-5
Kennan ... E-4
Kenosha ... L-8
Keshena ... F-7
Kewaskum ... J-8
Kewaunee ... G-9
Kiel ... H-8
Kimberly ... H-8
Kingston ... J-6
Kneeland ... Pg. 121, J-5
La Crosse ... H-3
La Farge ... J-4
Lac Du Flambeau ... D-5
Ladysmith ... E-3
Lake Delton ... J-5
Lake Geneva ... L-7
Lake Nebagamon ... D-3
Lancaster ... K-4
Lannon ... Pg. 121, B-2
Lena ... F-8
Linden ... K-5
Little Chute ... H-8
Livingston ... K-5
Lodi ... J-6
Loganville ... J-5
Lomira ... J-7
Lone Rock ... K-5
Loyal ... G-4
Lublin ... F-4
Luck ... E-2
Luxemburg ... G-8
Madison ... K-6
Manawa ... G-7
Manitowish ... D-5
Manitowoc ... H-9
Marathon City ... F-5
Marinette ... F-8
Marion ... G-7
Markesan ... J-6
Marshall ... K-7
Marshfield ... G-5
Mason ... D-4
Mauston ... H-5
Mayville ... J-7
Mazomanie ... J-6
Medford ... F-5
Mellen ... D-4
Melrose ... H-4
Melvina ... H-4
Menasha ... H-7
Menomonee Falls ... J-7
Vicinity ... Pg. 121, A-2
Menomonie ... G-2
Mequon ... Pg. 121, A-5
Merrill ... F-5
Merrillan ... G-4
Middleton ... K-6
Milltown ... E-2
Milton ... K-7
Milwaukee ... K-8
Vicinity ... Pg. 121
Mineral Point ... K-5
Minong ... D-3
Mishicot ... H-8
Mondovi ... G-3
Monico ... E-6
Monona ... K-6
Monroe ... L-5
Montello ... H-6
Montfort ... K-5
Monticello ... K-6
Montreal ... D-4
Mosinee ... F-6
Mount Horeb ... K-6
Mount Sterling ... J-4
Mukwonago ... K-7
Muscoda ... K-5
Muskego ... K-8
Vicinity ... Pg. 121, G-2
Necedah ... H-5
Neenah ... H-7
Neillsville ... G-4
Nekoosa ... G-5
Nelson ... G-2
Nelsonville ... G-6
Neshkoro ... H-6
New Berlin ... K-8
Vicinity ... Pg. 121, E-2
New Glarus ... K-6
New Holstein ... H-8
New Lisbon ... H-5
New London ... G-7
New Richmond ... F-1
Niagara ... E-8
North Cape ... Pg. 121, K-4
North Fond du Lac ... H-7
North Hudson ... F-1
Norwalk ... J-4
Oak Creek ... K-8
Vicinity ... Pg. 121, H-5
Oconomowoc ... K-7
Oconto ... F-8
Oconto Falls ... F-7
Omro ... H-7
Onalaska ... H-3
Ontario ... J-4
Oostburg ... J-8
Orfordville ... K-6
Osceola ... F-1
Oshkosh ... H-7
Osseo ... G-4
Owen ... F-4
Oxford ... H-6
Paddock Lake ... L-7
Palmyra ... K-7
Pardeeville ... J-6
Park Falls ... E-4
Park Ridge ... G-6
Patch Grove ... K-4
Pembine ... E-8
Pepin ... G-2
Peshtigo ... F-8
Pewaukee ... Pg. 121, C-1
Phelps ... D-6
Phillips ... E-5
Pigeon Falls ... G-3
Pittsville ... G-5
Plain ... J-5
Plainfield ... H-6
Platteville ... K-4
Plover ... G-6
Plum City ... G-2
Plymouth ... J-8
Poplar ... C-3
Port Edwards ... G-5
Port Washington ... J-8
Portage ... J-6
Potosi ... K-4
Pound ... F-8
Prairie du Chien ... K-4
Prairie du Sac ... J-5
Prentice ... E-5
Prescott ... G-1
Princeton ... H-6
Pulaski ... G-7
Racine ... K-8
Radisson ... E-3
Randolph ... J-7
Raymond ... Pg. 121, K-4
Redgranite ... H-6
Reedsburg ... J-5
Reedsville ... H-8
Rhinelander ... E-6
Rib Lake ... E-5
Rice Lake ... E-3
Richland Center ... J-5
Ridgeland ... F-2
Ridgeway ... K-5
Rio ... J-6
River Falls ... G-1
River Hills ... Pg. 121, A-5
Riverside ... D-2
Roberts ... F-2
Rosendale ... H-7
Rosholt ... G-6
Rothschild ... F-6
Saint Croix Falls ... E-2
Saint Francis ... K-8
Vicinity ... Pg. 121, F-7
Sauk City ... J-5
Saukville ... J-8
Schofield ... F-6
Seymour ... G-7
Sharon ... L-7
Shawano ... G-7
Sheboygan ... H-9
Sheboygan Falls ... H-8
Sheldon ... F-4
Shell Lake ... E-2
Shiocton ... G-7
Shorewood ... Pg. 121, C-7
Shullsburg ... L-5
Siren ... E-2
Sister Bay ... F-9
Soldiers Grove ... J-4
Solon Springs ... D-3
Somerset ... F-1
South Milwaukee ... K-8
Vicinity ... Pg. 121, G-7
Sparta ... H-4
Spencer ... G-4
Spooner ... E-3
Spring Green ... J-5
Spring Valley ... G-2
Stanley ... F-4
Stevens Point ... G-5
Stockbridge ... H-7
Stockholm ... G-2
Stoddard ... J-4
Stoughton ... K-6
Stratford ... G-5
Strum ... G-3
Sturgeon Bay ... F-8
Sturtevant ... K-7
Sun Prairie ... K-7
Superior ... C-2
Suring ... F-7
Sussex ... Pg. 121, B-1
Tabor ... Pg. 121, J-7
Taylors Falls ... E-1
Tennyson ... K-4
Theresa ... J-7
Thompsonville ... Pg. 121, K-5
Thorp ... F-4
Tichigan ... Pg. 121, J-1
Tigerton ... G-7
Tomah ... H-4
Tomahawk ... E-6
Tony ... E-4
Trego ... E-3
Trempealeau ... H-3
Turtle Lake ... F-2
Two Rivers ... H-9
Union Center ... J-5
Union Church ... Pg. 121, J-4
Union Grove ... K-8
Unity ... G-5
Valders ... H-8
Vernon ... Pg. 121, G-1
Verona ... K-6
Vesper ... G-5
Village of Superior ... C-2
Viroqua ... J-4
Walworth ... L-7
Washburn ... C-3
Waterford ... K-7
Waterloo ... K-7
Watertown ... J-7
Waukesha ... K-7
Vicinity ... Pg. 121, E-1
Waunakee ... K-6
Waupaca ... G-7
Waupun ... J-7
Wausau ... F-6
Wausaukee ... F-8
Wautoma ... H-6
Wauwatosa ... K-8
Vicinity ... Pg. 121, D-4
Webster ... E-2
West Allis ... Pg. 121, E-4
West Bend ... J-8
West Milwaukee ... Pg. 121, E-5
Westby ... J-4
Westfield ... H-6
Weyauwega ... H-6
White Lake ... F-7
Whitefish Bay ... K-8
Vicinity ... Pg. 121, C-6
Whitehall ... G-3
Whitelaw ... H-8
Whitewater ... K-7
Whiting ... G-6
Wild Rose ... H-6
Wind Pt. ... K-8
Winneconne ... H-7
Winter ... E-4
Wisconsin Dells ... J-6
Wisconsin Rapids ... G-5
Withee ... F-4
Wittenberg ... G-6
Wonewoc ... J-5
Woodruff ... E-6
Wrightstown ... H-8
Wyeville ... H-5
Wyocena ... J-6
Yuba ... J-4

Wyoming

WYOMING
Pages 88-89
Population: 469,559
Capital: Cheyenne
Land Area: 96,989 sq. mi.

Acme ... B-8
Afton ... F-3
Aladdin ... B-12
Albany ... J-9
Albin ... H-12
Alcova ... E-9
Alpine Jct. ... E-3
Alva ... B-11
Arapahoe ... E-7
Arlington ... H-9
Arminto ... E-8
Arvada ... B-9
Atlantic City ... G-6
Auburn ... F-3
Baggs ... J-7
Bairoil ... G-8
Banner ... B-8
Bar Nunn ... F-9
Barnum ... D-8
Basin ... C-7
Beckton ... B-8
Bedford ... F-3
Beulah ... B-12
Big Horn ... B-8
Big Piney ... G-4
Big Sandy ... G-5
Big Trails ... D-8
Bill ... E-10
Bitter Creek ... H-6
Bondurant ... E-4
Border ... G-3
Bosler ... H-10
Boulder ... F-5
Boxelder ... F-10
Buffalo ... C-8
Burgess Jct. ... B-7
Burlington ... C-7
Burns ... J-12
Burntfork ... J-4
Burris ... E-5
Byron ... B-7
Calpet ... G-4
Canyon Jct. ... B-5
Carpenter ... J-12
Carter ... H-3
Casper ... F-9
Centennial ... H-10
Cheyenne ... J-11
Chugwater ... H-11
Clareton ... D-11
Clark ... B-5
Clearmont ... B-8
Cody ... C-5
Cokeville ... G-3
Colony ... B-12
Cora ... F-4
Cowley ... B-6
Creston Jct. ... H-8
Crowheart ... E-5
Daniel ... F-4
Dayton ... B-8
Devil's Tower Jct. ... B-11
Diamondville ... H-3
Dixon ... J-7
Douglas ... F-10
Dubois ... D-6
East Thermopolis ... D-7
Eden ... G-5
Edgerton ... E-9
Egbert ... J-12
Elk Basin ... B-6
Elk Mountain ... H-9
Elkol ... H-4
Elmo ... H-9
Emblem ... C-6
Encampment ... J-9
Ethete ... F-6
Etna ... E-3
Evanston ... J-3
Evansville ... F-9
Fairview ... F-3
Farson ... G-5
Federal ... J-11
Fort Bridger ... J-4
Fort Laramie ... G-11
Fort Washakie ... F-6
Four Corners ... C-12
Frannie ... B-6
Freedom ... F-3
Frontier ... H-4
Garland ... C-6
Gillette ... C-10
Glendo ... F-11
Glenrock ... F-10
Granger ... H-4
Grass Creek ... D-6
Green River ... H-5
Greybull ... C-7
Grover ... F-3
Guernsey ... G-11
Hamilton Dome ... D-6
Hampshire ... D-11
Hanna ... H-9
Hartville ... G-11
Hawk Springs ... H-12
Hiland ... E-8
Hillsdale ... J-12
Hobock Jct. ... E-3
Horse Creek ... J-11
Hudson ... E-7
Hulett ... B-11
Huntley ... H-12
Hyattville ... C-8
Iron Mountain ... H-11
Jackson ... E-3
Jay Em ... G-12
Jeffrey City ... F-7
Jenny Lake ... D-3
Kaycee ... D-9
Keeline ... F-11
Kelly ... E-4
Kemmerer ... H-3
Kinnear ... E-6
Kirby ... D-7
La Barge ... G-3
La Grange ... H-12
Lake Jct. ... B-4
Lamont ... G-8
Lance Creek ... E-11
Lander ... F-6
Laramie ... J-10
Lightning Flat ... B-11
Linch ... D-9
Lingle ... G-12
Little America ... J-4
Lonetree ... J-4
Lost Cabin ... E-8
Lost Springs ... F-11
Lovell ... B-6
Lucerne ... D-7
Lusk ... F-12
Lyman ... J-4
Lysite ... E-7
Madison Jct. ... B-5
Mammoth Springs Jct. ... B-3
Manderson ... C-7
Manville ... F-11
Marbleton ... F-4
Mayoworth ... D-8
McFadden ... H-10
McKinnon ... K-4
Medicine Bow ... H-9
Meeteetse ... C-6
Merna ... F-4
Midwest ... E-9
Millburne ... J-4
Mills ... F-9
Moneta ... E-7
Moorcroft ... C-11
Moose ... D-3
Moran Jct. ... D-3
Morrisey ... D-11
Morton ... E-6
Mountain Home ... J-10
Mountain View ... J-4
Mule Cr. Jct. ... E-12
Natrona ... E-9
New Haven ... B-11
Newcastle ... D-12
Node ... F-12
Norris Jct. ... B-3
Old Faithful ... C-3
Opal ... H-4
Orin ... F-11
Orpha ... F-10
Osage ... D-11
Oshoto ... B-11
Otto ... C-7
Parkman ... B-8
Pavillion ... E-6
Piedmont ... J-4
Pine Bluffs ... J-12
Pine Tree Jct. ... D-10
Pinedale ... F-5
Pitchfork ... D-5
Point of Rocks ... H-6
Powder River ... F-8
Powell ... B-6
Quealy ... J-5
Ralston ... B-6
Ranchester ... B-8
Rawlins ... H-8
Recluse ... B-10
Red Desert ... H-7
Redbird ... E-12
Reliance ... H-6
Reno Jct. ... D-10
Riverside ... J-9
Riverton ... F-7
Robertson ... J-4
Rochelle ... D-10
Rock River ... H-10
Rock Springs ... H-6
Rocky Point ... B-11
Rozet ... C-10
Sage ... H-3
Saint Stephens ... F-6
Saratoga ... J-9
Savageton ... D-10
Savery ... J-8
Shawnee ... F-11
Shell ... C-7
Sheridan ... B-8
Shirley Basin ... G-9
Shoshoni ... E-7
Sinclair ... H-8
Slater ... H-11
Smoot ... F-3
South Pass City ... G-6
Spotted Horse ... B-10
Story ... C-8
Sundance ... C-12
Sunrise ... G-11
Superior ... H-6
Sussex ... D-8
Table Rock ... H-7
Ten Sleep ... D-8
Teton Village ... D-3
Thayne ... F-3
Thermopolis ... D-6
Tie Siding ... J-10
Torrington ... G-12
Tower Jct. ... B-4
Turnerville ... F-3
Ucross ... C-9
Upton ... C-11
Urie ... J-4
Valley ... C-5
Van Tassell ... F-12
Veteran ... G-12
Walcott ... H-9
Waltman ... E-8
Wamsutter ... H-7
West Thumb Jct. ... C-3
Weston ... B-10
Wheatland ... G-11
Wilson ... E-3
Woods Landing ... J-10
Worland ... D-7
Wright ... D-10
Yoder ... H-12